CW00537821

Tewkesbury Abbey

Tewkesbury Abbey
History, Art & Architecture

Edited by
Richard K. Morris & Ron Shoesmith

Logaston Press

LOGASTON PRESS
Little Logaston, Logaston,
Woonton, Almeley, Herefordshire HR3 6QH

First published by Logaston Press 2003

ISBN
1 904396 03 8 (Paperback)

1 904396 02 X (Hardback)

Hardback Copy No: / (of 300 copies)

Set in Times by Logaston Press
and printed in Great Britain by
Bell & Bain Ltd. Glasgow

Cover illustrations:
Front: Tewkesbury Abbey from the meadow (photo, 2003, R.K. Morris)
Rear: Tewkesbury Abbey, interior looking east (photo, c.*1997, L. Pitt)*

To
the memory of
E.F. (Ted) Potter
(1907-1986)

Contents

Pen Portraits of the Authors

David Aldred recently retired as the Head of History at Cleeve School in Bishop's Cleeve. He is well-known as a lecturer and writer on the history of North Gloucestershire. Before becoming a teacher he worked in the Tewkesbury Archaeological Unit and contributed to the report on the Holm Hill excavations (Hannan 1997).

Joseph Bettey was formerly Reader in Local History at the University of Bristol, and is President of the British Association for Local History. He is the author of numerous books and articles on the economic, religious and social history of the Bristol region. His books include *Wessex from AD1000* (Longman, 1986), and *Suppression of the Monasteries in the West Country* (Alan Sutton, 1989). He has also researched and written extensively on the history of the Augustinian monastery at Bristol, now Bristol Cathedral.

Jane Birdsall has recently completed an MSc thesis on the subject of the monuments in Tewkesbury Abbey. She has been working as a sculpture conservator for the past six years and lives and works in London.

Neil Birdsall has been in practice as an architect for 30 years. By far the largest proportion of the work undertaken by him and his partners concerns the repair and conservation of churches and their contents. He has been the abbey's architect for 25 years.

Sarah Brown is chairman of the British *Corpus Vitrearum Medii Aevi* and head of research for places of worship at English Heritage. Her most recent publication is *York Minster. An Architectural History* c.*1200-1500* (English Heritage, 2003).

Michael Donmall is Senior Research Fellow at the University of Manchester Medical School. He received his doctorate from the University of London in 1984 for research on the anthropology of the population of the Shetlands. In the 1980s he worked with Martin Biddle, Birthe Kjølby-Biddle and Richard Morris at St. Albans Abbey, where he was responsible for the osteological analysis of the bones of the abbots and other monastic remains.

John Eisel has been a ringer since 1995 and is deeply interested in the history of bells and change ringing. He specializes in the development of bell frames. Formerly a lecturer, in recent years he has worked in archaeology. He is a Fellow of the Society of Antiquaries.

Carolyn Heighway is a former head of Gloucester Museum Archaeology Unit, and is now an independent archaeological consultant. She is at present Archaeological Consultant to Gloucester Cathedral. She has published *Anglo-Saxon Gloucestershire* (Gloucester 1987), *The Golden Minster* (with Richard Bryant: a report on excavations at St. Oswald's Priory, Gloucester), and numerous articles on the early medieval archaeology of Gloucester and Gloucestershire.

Michael Hicks is Professor of Medieval History at King Alfred's College, Winchester. He is biographer of successive patrons of Tewkesbury Abbey, notably *Warwick the Kingmaker* (Blackwell), *False Fleeting Perjur'd Clarence* (Headstart), and *Richard III* (Tempus). His most recent books are *English Political Culture in the Fifteenth Century* (Routledge) and *Edward V* (Tempus).

Anthea Jones read Modern History at St. Hugh's College, Oxford and obtained a doctorate at the University of Kent at Canterbury. She has been a lecturer in higher education, and for 15 years was head of history and latterly also director of studies at Cheltenham Ladies' College. *Tewkesbury* was published in 1987, *The Cotswolds* in 1994, and *A thousand years of the English Parish* in 2000.

Kenneth Jones was educated in Dublin and obtained his degrees in Arts and in Engineering from Trinity College, Dublin. After practising as an engineer in West Africa from 1957 to 1964 he decided to become an organ builder—a long held wish—and trained in the practical aspects of the discipline (mostly in Holland). He and his team have designed and built well over a hundred new organs, and carried out many important restorations.

Phillip Lindley is a Reader in the History of Art at the University of Leicester. He has published widely on English medieval art and architecture, and has a particular interest in late medieval sculpture. He was co-curator, with Richard Deacon, of the acclaimed exhibition *Image and Idol* at Tate Britain in 2001-2.

Julian M. Luxford is currently a Research Fellow at Clare College Cambridge. From January 2004, he will be a lecturer in the Department of History of Art at St. Andrews University. He has a keen interest in Tewkesbury Abbey, having written his Ph.D. dissertation on the patronage of Benedictine art and architecture in the West of England during the later Middle Ages.

Richard K. Morris is an architectural historian specializing in the medieval and Tudor periods. He was until recently a Reader in the History of Art Department, University of Warwick, and throughout his career he has endeavoured to communicate his enthusiasm for old buildings—their beauty and significance—through lectures, visits and publications. His research on Tewkesbury Abbey goes back to 1967, and he is the abbey's Archaeological Consultant.

Michael Peterson was assistant organist at Wells Cathedral from 1946, then organist at St. Peter's church, Bournemouth, from 1953 and at Tewkebury Abbey between 1966 and 1985. He was also director of music at the Abbey School from 1973 to 1985, and organs advisor to the Gloucester Diocesan Advisory Committee from 1983 to 2000.

Michael Tavinor studied for the priesthood at Ripon College, Cuddlesdon, was ordained in 1982 and served his title at St. Peter's, Ealing. He spent five years as Precentor and Sacrist of Ely Cathedral and became Vicar of Tewkesbury in 1990. In 2002 he moved from Tewkesbury to become Dean of Hereford. He is author of the Canterbury Press Pilgrim Guides to Tewkesbury Abbey and to Hereford Cathedral.

Malcolm Thurlby was born in London and educated at the University of East Anglia where he completed his Ph.D. in 1976. He moved to Canada in that year and is now Professor of Visual Arts at York University, Toronto. He has published widely on aspects of medieval architecture and sculpture, and 19th-century architecture in Canada. His passion for buildings extends to fine food and wine, rock music and football.

Alan Vince has been studying the medieval ceramic industries of the Severn Valley for over 25 years. He has published widely on medieval pottery and tiles as well as co-authoring *Medieval Towns* with John Schofield (Continuum, 2003). He is currently running an archaeological consultancy in Lincoln, specialising in post-excavation analysis.

Preface

There has not been a major monograph on Tewkesbury Abbey since the publication of H.J.L. Massé's *Tewkesbury Abbey and Deerhurst Priory* (1st edition, 1900) in the Bell's 'Cathedral' Guide series, which has long since been out of print. The British Archaeological Association's series of Conference Transaction volumes, commenced in 1978, had been envisaged in some respects as successors to the Bell's guides, but the 1981 conference of the Association was as much about Gloucester Cathedral as Tewkesbury Abbey. The subsequent publication—*Medieval Art and Architecture at Gloucester and Tewkesbury*, edited by Sandy Heslop and Veronica Sekules (Leeds, 1985)—was restricted in its coverage of the abbey to medieval architecture, especially the Norman church.

The present book has had a long and rather convoluted gestation, though I imagine that anyone who has been involved with producing a 'history of a great church' will not be surprised at this saga. In a letter of September 1982 to the then vicar, Michael Moxon, I had noted the relative imminence of the 900th anniversary of the foundation of the abbey in 1987, and floated the idea of a new book to celebrate the occasion. Amongst possible authors for such an enterprise, who had new unpublished research to offer, I mentioned three scholars who ultimately have contributed chapters to this book—Malcolm Thurlby, Alan Vince and Michael Donmall. Nothing came of the idea, perhaps in part because of the appearance of the British Archaeological Association volume in the interim; but probably mainly because of the problem which dogs all similar projects—finding someone with enough time to see it through to publication.

Then, in 1993, Charles Whitney, lay reader, expressed an interest to the new vicar, Michael Tavinor, in producing a major history of the abbey. My involvement was requested, and at a meeting of the three of us held in March 1994, the starting point for the present book was established. It was to be a 'History of Tewkesbury Abbey', joint-edited by Charles Whitney and myself, and a list of 11 chapters with potential authors was established. Publication was anticipated 'before the end of the decade'. Clearly we had taken on board the time it takes to get such a multi-authored publication to press, but even so, we were over-optimistic! Lack of spare time on the part of the editors meant that little progress was made for several years, even though Malcolm Thurlby kindly offered his services as editor in 1996.

In 1998 Michael Tavinor breathed new life into the project by proposing that the book should be retitled 'Tewkesbury Abbey 1102-2002', and that its publication should form part of the abbey's celebrations in 2002 of the 900th anniversary of the formal arrival of the Benedictine monks from Cranborne. Letters of invitation to write chapters for it were accepted by almost all those whose names appear in the present book. By 1999, I was back as 'joint-editor', though I cannot recall now with certainty the person with whom I was sharing that dubious honour; I assume that it must have been Malcolm Thurlby.

However, the project lacked one essential component, and one not easy to find for a book of this sort—a publisher! By the end of 2000, Michael Tavinor had secured the services of Logaston Press, and I had a new partner as joint-editor—Ron Shoesmith, who had edited a number of previous volumes by this publisher, including a comparable volume on Dore Abbey. We (that is to say, the contributing authors and myself) have been very fortunate for the way in which Andy Johnson of Logaston Press has taken on so wholeheartedly the coordinating of this project, especially after the departure of Michael Tavinor in 2002 to become Dean of Hereford. For my part, had I not taken the decision to make an early departure from my post at the University of Warwick in 2001, it is most unlikely that I could have fulfilled my commitments as editor and contributor in the time available.

The fact that the present book has 22 chapters, twice the number envisaged almost ten years ago, demonstrates how much the project has expanded and how much new and interesting material the authors have produced on their topics. Even so, as the texts of the chapters arrived, we became conscious of subjects which could receive only superficial coverage, and inevitably of conflicting interpretations between different authors. Life would be dull without such an exchange of ideas, and the editors have endeavoured to do no more than cross-reference different viewpoints on contested issues, such as whether the early medieval parish used the nave of the Norman abbey as their church. Likewise, we are now aware that much more could have been included on subjects such as medieval painted stonework, medieval sculpture and roof bosses, the early medieval tombs, and the Victorian fittings and stained glass; and that some topics remain uncovered, such as the seals of the abbey, and vestments and plate. To explain these omissions I must plead partly some weaknesses in my original plan for the publication, but mainly a combination of lack of space in the book, combined with the fact that for some of these topics the modern research has still to be done. Much as we might have liked to flatter ourselves originally that the wide-ranging nature of this book would make it definitive, in reality it should be viewed as much a stimulant for further research as an end in itself.

The accessible style and content of this book is aimed to appeal to the public at large, but in co-editing it and writing my contributions, I have been mindful of several potential special constituencies of readership. First, there are the numerous professional friends and acquaintances of mine who have shown a particular interest in Tewkesbury's medieval art and architecture in the last 40 years or so, such that the abbey has become almost a 'cult' building for art historians. It gives me pleasure to think that the contributors to this book have produced information and ideas new even to such a specialized group. Second—quite selfishly—is myself! As the abbey's archaeological consultant, the book will be of enormous assistance to my work by providing a well-ordered dossier for reference and a foundation on which to develop further research initiatives. Third—and most important—are all the people connected with the many facets of looking after the abbey. I hope, for example, that the welcomers and guides will find this a useful handbook of historical information to aid their presentations to visitors. For this reason the book has been dedicated to the late Ted Potter and his boundless enthusiasm for discovering more about the abbey's past and putting the information in accessible form. Through the 1970s and 1980s, until his death in 1986, he organised the guides, supplied them with learned notes, and encouraged visiting scholars in their various avenues of research on the abbey. I like to think that this publication has resulted particularly from his initiative. In his 'Guide Lines for Abbey Guides', Ted stated, 'Every guided tour should be a journey of exploration'. I trust that this holds true for the book as well.

Richard K. Morris
Kenilworth (September 2003)

Editorial Notes

The editors and the publisher would like to thank all the authors for their kindness and understanding in meeting tight deadlines, in being prepared to enter into discussion about the first drafts of their papers and in some cases to accept substantial changes to avoid unnecessary duplication between chapters. Some authors have also generously supplied photographs, and have responded selflessly to requests for additional illustrations or for changes to drawings. We are particularly indebted to Lionel Pitt for searching out images from his splendid collection—more than we have been able to use in the book; and to Charles Whitney who has so generously volunteered to compile the index. At the abbey we are also grateful for the help and advice of Brian Wardrobe, Christine Aplin and David Lees, with regard to the launch of the book and the logistics of its local distribution.

For the purposes of bringing uniformity to the various names and terms used by different authors, it has been necessary to establish standardized forms of reference, albeit somewhat arbitrary in some instances.

1. Documentary Sources: The three main documentary sources for the medieval history of the abbey are cited in the book as follows—'the Annals', 'the Founders' Book' and 'the chronicle'. The first refers to the 13th-century annals and cartulary of the abbey, *Annales de Theokesberia*, which cover the period 1066-1263, and are best known through the 1864 transcription edited by H.R. Luard. The second is an early 16th-century manuscript in the Bodleian Library, Oxford, MS Top.Glouc.d.2, providing an illustrated chronicle of the abbey's history and its patrons, compiled by the monks between the 12th and 15th centuries. There is no published edition of this manuscript. The third—'the chronicle'—generally refers to the mid-16th-century unillustrated copy of the Founders' Book, in British Library manuscript Cotton Cleopatra C.III. This is best known to scholars through the version printed in Sir William Dugdale's *Monasticon Anglicanum*, volume II (1661). It should not be confused with other brief abbey chronicles, such as that which records Lancastrian burials after the Battle of Tewkesbury, and which are specifically cited in the text. Further details on the Annals appear in Chapter 5, and on the Founders' Book and the chronicle in Chapter 6.

2. Medieval Personal Names: For the spellings of the names of the abbots of Tewkesbury, we have retained the forms given in the list in the *Victoria County History: Gloucestershire*, II (1907), p.65. For the names of secular persons connected with the abbey in the Anglo-Saxon period, we have adopted the spellings of current orthodoxy in this field, whereas for names from 1066 onward we have steered a middle course closer to established conventions. Numbers have been allocated to lords of the same name, to facilitate easy identification. Thus, amongst the de Clare family, we have Richard I (d.1217), Gilbert I (d.1230), Richard II (d.1262), Gilbert II (the Red Earl, d.1295) and Gilbert III (d.1314); amongst the Despensers, Hugh I (the Elder, d.1326), Hugh II (the Younger, also d.1326) and Hugh III (d.1349). For further information, see the family trees in Chapters 2 and 3.

3. Nomenclature of the eastern parts of the Abbey Church: The precise description of this area in any historic church is always problematic because some terms are used architecturally and others are used

liturgically. At Tewkesbury, the matter is complicated by its change of use from an abbey to a parish church, and by the fact that the choir-stalls are placed in the crossing under the central tower. In this volume, the term 'the monks' church' denotes the whole area of the medieval abbey church east of the former rood screen in the second bay of the nave. The term 'choir' is used architecturally, when referring to the medieval abbey church, to denote the whole of the main vessel east of the crossing, i.e. excluding the crossing (for example, the 14th-century stained glass is in 'the choir clerestory windows'). The term 'chancel' is used architecturally, when referring to the post-medieval parish church, to denote the whole of the main vessel including the crossing. The term 'sanctuary' is used more specifically to refer to the area in the direct vicinity of the high altar, and is preferred here to 'presbytery'. Where other liturgical spaces are being described, such as the liturgical 'choir', the context should be clear in the text.

4. Chapel names in the Abbey Church: In the text we have endeavoured to standardize references to chapels by the names or dedications in use today. In some cases, these update the information on the Masterplan of 1894. The main changes in the chevet chapels are that the chapel of 'St. Edmund the Martyr' is now the double chapel of St. Edmund the Martyr (the more northerly altar) and St. Dunstan; and the chapel between St. Faith's and the vestry is now SS. John the Baptist and Catherine, usually abbreviated in the text to the chapel of St. John the Baptist. The apsidal chapel off the south transept has been the Lady Chapel since 1939, and the westernmost bay of the nave south aisle is known as the Holy Cross Chapel. The original dedications of the former chapels to the east and north-east of the north transept are more controversial, as explained in Chapter 10. They are no longer used as chapels today: that identified as of St. Nicholas in the Masterplan is the abbey song school (*Camera Cantorum*), and that of St. James is the abbey shop.

5. Numbering the bays in the Nave: The nave has eight bays, which are referred to by numbers running from east to west; thus the bay next to the crossing is 'bay 1', the bay with the font is 'bay 7', etc. The north and south arcades of the nave each have seven piers, which are referred to by a separate sequence of numbers also running east to west; thus 'north pier 1' (by the pulpit), 'north pier 7' (the last pier on the north side), etc. The nave aisles each have an additional bay beyond bay 8, called 'the westernmost bay'.

6. Reference to Post-Medieval Cathedrals: A number of great churches were elevated to cathedral status after the Reformation, but were monastery churches in the Middle Ages. We have adopted the convention that where the reference is to the building fabric, especially to a feature surviving in such a church, the modern cathedral name is used; but where the reference is historical, to the monastic institution, the dedication of the medieval abbey church is used. The main examples in the text are: Bristol Cathedral (St. Augustine's, Bristol), Chester Cathedral (St. Werburgh's, Chester), Gloucester Cathedral (St. Peter's, Gloucester) and Oxford Cathedral (St. Frideswide's, Oxford).

7. County Names: The names of places in the United Kingdom, which are unlikely to be well known, are given a location in one of the pre-1974 counties, usually an abbreviation of the county name. This convention has not been applied to places in Gloucestershire.

Acknowledgments

Richard Morris has inevitably accumulated debts of gratitude to many individuals during his long association with the abbey for the purposes of scholarly research, to all of whom he sends his sincerest thanks, though there is space here to name only a few. He owes an outstanding debt to Professor Peter Kidson, who introduced him to the medieval architecture of the abbey. His work there has benefitted greatly from the encouragement of successive vicars—Canon Cosmo Pouncey, Canon Michael Moxon and Canon Michael Tavinor—and of two stewards since deceased, Ted Potter and Dick Chorley. It has been facilitated by the friendly unlocking of doors by Ernest Leach, Ray Mulcuck, Don Freeman, and all the sacristans and vergers over the past 35 years; and by their wide knowledge of the church most generously shared with him, especially by Pat Webley. He is also grateful to Carolyn Methven, Gus Strawford, Bernard Beecher and Martin Dyke for assistance of various kinds, and, amongst other contributors to this book, he has gained particularly from discussions with Neil Birdsall, Anthea Jones, Phillip Lindley and Julian Luxford. Since 1974, he has received invaluable assistance from Loveday Gee, Maureen Bourne and Alan Watson in the History of Art Slide and Photograph Library at the University of Warwick. He also has happy memories of Liz Chapple, Jocelyn Morris, Rex Adams, Donald Smith and the many other University of Warwick students and University of Birmingham extramural students who have assisted him in sorting and cataloguing the artefacts of the abbey.

Away from the abbey, he is indebted to Logaston Press (Andy Johnson and his co-editor, Ron Shoesmith) for seeing this book through to publication. In particular, he is enormously grateful to Andy Johnson for the many hours spent on all aspects of its production, receiving constant amendments and last-minute corrections almost always with customary good humour. Andy's dedication to producing interesting books at reasonable prices is second to none.

In addition the authors wish to add their own acknowledgements as follows:

David Aldred would wish to thank the staffs at the County and Diocesan Record Office and Central Library in Gloucester, who have been extremely helpful. Dr. Steven Blake at Cheltenham Art Gallery and Museum made available the collection of prints held there. David Lees, the abbey steward, gave his time generously. Dr. Richard Morris discussed many points of interpretation with him. His wife, Margaret, painstakingly checked drafts for errors and inconsistencies. Permission to publish is acknowledged in the List of Illustrations.

Michael Donmall and Richard K. Morris are grateful particularly to the following for assistance and advice during their research for chapter 4: Michael Hicks, Julian Litten, Canon Michael Moxon, Ray Mulcuck, the late Ted Potter, Pamela Lady Wedgwood and William White.

John Eisel would like to thank Malcolm Taylor, ringing master, for arranging access to the belfry and going over it with him.

Carolyn Heighway wishes to thank particularly Michael Hare, John Rhodes, Julian Luxford, and Robin Whitaker for their help with the text; also Gemma Bryant who redrew Fig.1.1, and Rob Read and Tewkesbury Borough Council for permission to use and redraw Figs.1.1 and 1.3.

Anthea Jones wishes to gratefully acknowledge the help in studying Tewkesbury offered by the staff of Gloucester Record Office, and permission to reproduce the drawings of the vicarage house in the Gloucester Diocesan Records which are held there.

Phillip Lindley would like to thank Mr. Bernard Beecher, Dr. Matthew Craske, Dr. Miriam Gill, Dr. Julian Luxford, Ms. Laura Martin, Dr. Sophie Oosterwijk, Dr. Christopher Wilson and, above all, Dr. Richard Morris for their useful comments and help of various kinds.

Julian M. Luxford wishes to thank Dr. Richard Morris and Andy Johnson for their time and helpfulness, and also Mr. John A. Goodall and Dr. Colin Tite for discussing matters relating to the Founders' Book with him.

Michael Tavinor would like to thank the following who have helped at various stages of the preparation of the book: the Revd. David Harding, Mr. Charles Whitney and Mr. Gus Strawford. In addition Carolyn Methven has helped him in the preparation of my chapter, and Miss Joan Williams, Librarian, Hereford Cathedral; Mr. Tim Bridges and the Revd. Hubert Pitts in its proof-reading.

Malcolm Thurlby is deeply indebted to many friends who have helped in various ways with the preparation of his chapter, in particular Eric Fernie, Duncan Givans, Richard Halsey, Hugh McCague, John McNeill, Richard K. Morris and Richard Plant. The late R.A. (Dick) Chorley was of great help in facilitating access to all parts of the church in the 1990s, and David Lees has similarly assisted with recent visits.

Alan Vince offers particular thanks to Richard K. Morris who has provided constant support in his study of the abbey floor tiles over a period now to be counted in decades, and his students provided the labour to record the loose floor tiles. He is also grateful to Jon Hoyle of Gloucestershire County Council for permission to study the 1992 abbey meadow tiles.

List of Illustrations

All subjects are Tewkesbury Abbey, unless indicated otherwise. Old photographs are indicated, as well as the approximate date or decade of more recent photographs (where known). Photographs by R.K. Morris are marked 'RKM'.

Figures in the text

List of Colour Plates

Masterplan

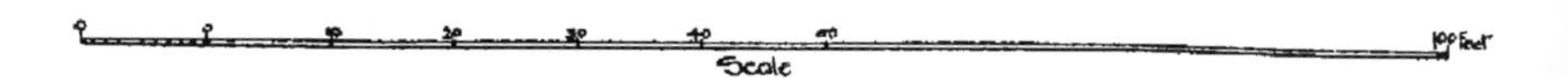

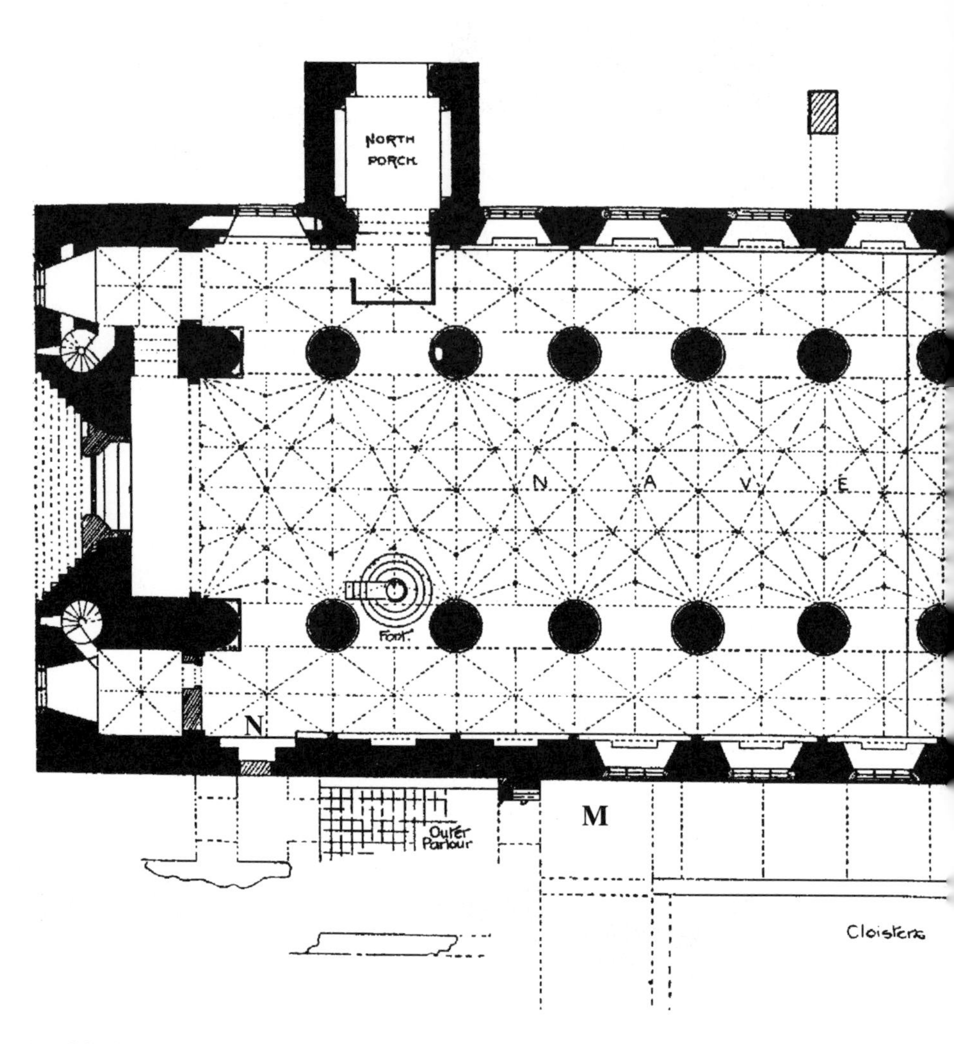

Drawn by Roland Paul (1894) and published in The Builder *(1 December, 1894), this plan of the abbey church has never been bettered and therefore is published here without amendment, even though it differs in some details and terminology from current research presented in this book. Specifically, the Chapel of St. Nicholas should be sited with that of St. James; the diagonal flying buttress at an angle to 'St. Nicholas' Chapel is 14th century; and the monuments named as of 'Lord Wenlock' and 'Duke of Somerset' were not erected for these individuals. Letters (A,B.C, etc.) have been added to identify parts of the church referred to in the text*

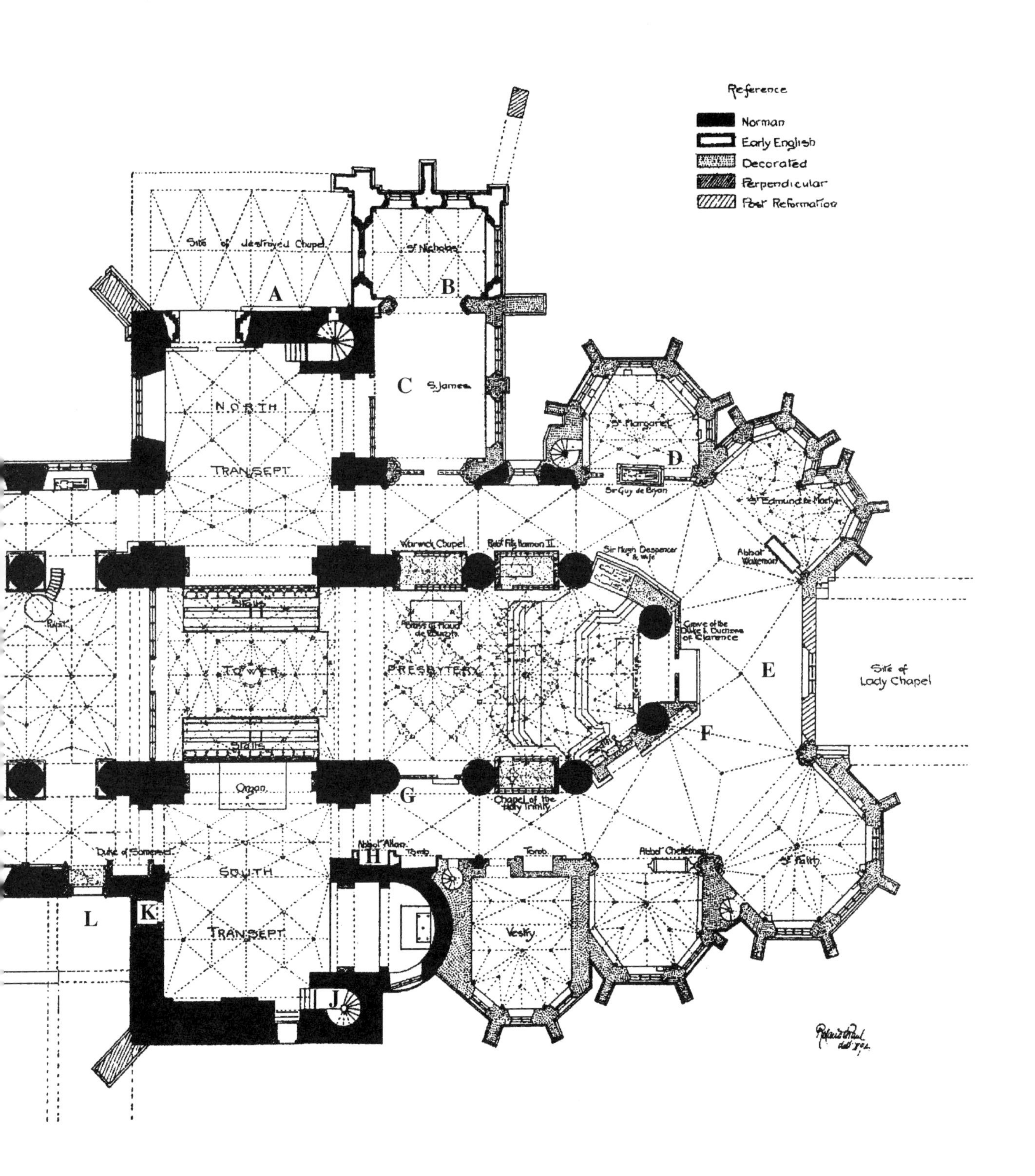
Reference
Norman
Early English
Decorated
Perpendicular
Post Reformation
Site of destroyed Chapel
St Nicholas
A
B
C
S. James
NORTH
TRANSEPT
St Margaret
D
Sir Guy de Bryan
St Edmund the Martyr
Abbot Wakeman
Warwick Chapel
Robt Fitz Hamon II
Sir Hugh Despencer & wife
Grave of the Duke & Duchess of Clarence
E
Site of Lady Chapel
Pulpit
Stalls
TOWER
Brass of Maud de Burgh
PRESBYTERY
Stalls
F
Organ
G
Chapel of the Holy Trinity
Duke of Somerset
Abbot Alan
H
Tomb
Tomb
Abbot Cheltenham
St Faith
SOUTH
TRANSEPT
L
K
Vestry
J

CHAPTER 1

Tewkesbury before the Normans

by Carolyn Heighway

The town of Tewkesbury is located at the confluence of the Avon and Severn, major rivers of the west midlands which in the Roman and Anglo-Saxon periods were navigable down to the sea as well as further inland. This major river crossing was at the centre of an agriculturally rich area, and the settlement was well-sited for both military purposes and trade.[1]

The terrain of the town is based on a ridge of Keuper Marl, cut through by the Avon and Swilgate rivers. Part of the town is on a more elevated deposit of gravel, well above the flood level: this area, known as the Oldbury, was a focal point of intermittent settlement from the Neolithic period onwards. A trackway, probably prehistoric in origin, led past Oldbury both north and south alongside the river Avon.

The development of the town (Fig.1.1) was influenced strongly by the rivers and their confluence. It may have been in the Roman period that the Avon was bridged, providing an important road link north-west towards Worcester. The Severn, however, was not bridged until 1826; there were ferries at Upper and Lower Lode in the medieval period and probably long before.[2] The 'Mill Avon', which defines the west side of the town, is held to be an artificial leet.[3] Its course is of some importance to the topographical development of the town. The Mill Avon today is a considerable watercourse some 20 metres wide. In medieval times it may have been used for wharfage, and was certainly useful for the tanning industry, as well as driving mills. The construction of this watercourse must have been a major undertaking, probably carried out around the time of the building of the abbey:[4] Abbey Mill, on the Mill Avon, was the abbey mill recorded in 1291 and was almost certainly one of the two mills granted to the abbey at its foundation.[5] The cut, when made, may have been a much narrower stream, subsequently enlarged in the later Middle Ages. There is also a possibility that the cut was created in the Anglo-Saxon period.[6]

The Roman Period

Tewkesbury in the Romano-British period could be described as a large rural settlement, perhaps with some administrative functions for the surrounding region. In the Oldbury area, excavations have shown complexes of timber buildings of the late 1st to 2nd century, followed by stone (or stone-cill) buildings of the late 2nd or early 3rd century. There was evidence of industrial activity—a common feature of Roman agricultural settlements. Two late-Roman burials were found in wooden coffins with iron fittings;[7] burials are not uncommon on late Roman settlement sites, usually taking place when the focus of occupation had moved elsewhere.

There was another Roman settlement, so far unexcavated, further south (Fig.1.1). Most ground disturbances in the area of the present abbey produce Roman coins or pottery[8] and not far away was a Roman cemetery which included

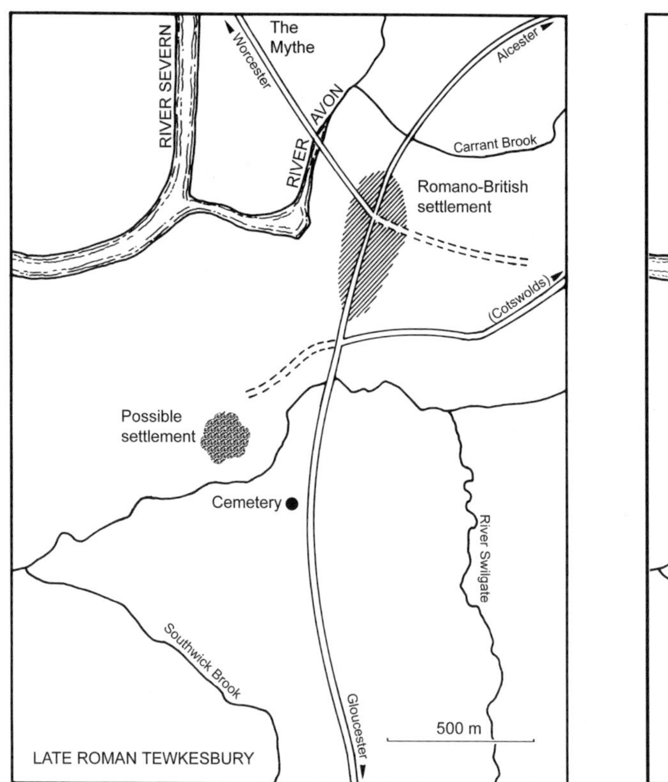

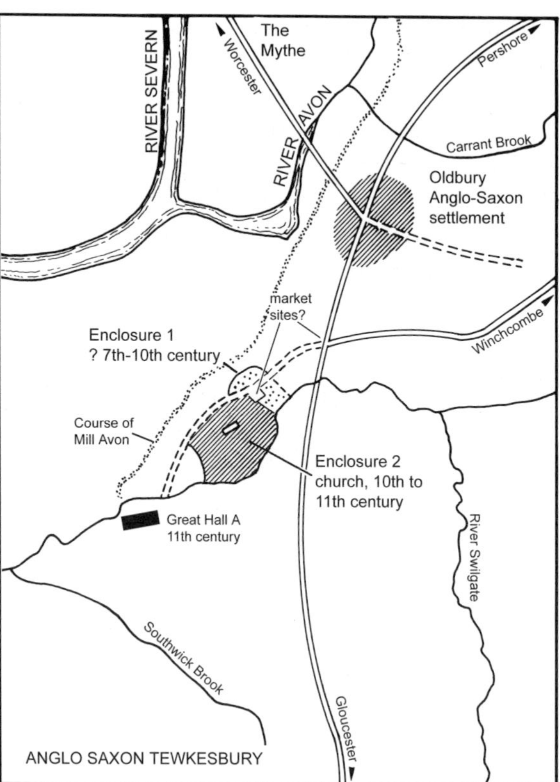

Fig.1.1 An interpretation of the topography of the Roman and Anglo-Saxon development of the town of Tewkesbury

burials in stone coffins.[9] The two settlements may have been contemporary for a time, and may have been of different kinds: for instance one an élite group, and the other an agricultural community.

The Anglo-Saxon Period

As is often the case, the archaeological evidence fails us beyond the end of the Roman period. It is likely that the Severn valley remained for some time under the control of native British princes who operated their control from the decayed Roman towns. By the late 7th century, the area known today as Gloucestershire was in the territory of the Hwicce, a sub-kingdom of Mercia. By the early 10th century the power of Mercia had declined. Its eastern regions had been settled by the Danes, and its western area, including the territory of the Hwicce, subjected to the southern kingdom of Wessex. By 1016 the county of Gloucestershire was created, comprising roughly the southern half of what had been Hwiccian territory. Tewkesbury and its hundred lay on the northern boundary of the new shire.[10]

There is no reliable written evidence for Tewkesbury, either for the abbey or the town, earlier than the Domesday entry. That entry, however, indicates a place of considerable wealth and importance. It was a nascent town, and had a wealthy church, a great hall and a market. These were at the administrative centre of a great estate which was assessed in Domesday at 95 hides, of which 20 hides belonged to Tewkesbury church. The estate included land in 16 vills besides Tewkesbury itself. The whole was worth £100 in 1066 and Beorhtric (Brictric), then lord of Tewkesbury, was 'perhaps the very richest thegn below the rank of earl in pre-Conquest England'.[11]

The physical evidence of landscape and town plan, as well as archaeological discoveries, provide some clues about the development of such a significant place. The Roman settlement at Oldbury may have been succeeded by an Anglo-

Saxon settlement. Its name is Old English, meaning 'old fortified place'.[12] This could refer either to Roman or Saxon defences, but earthworks, whatever their date, were presumably still evident when the place was given its name. Excavations in the area have produced evidence of a post-Roman ditch about 2m. wide which could be an Anglo-Saxon boundary ditch.[13]

Studies of Anglo-Saxon settlement patterns suggest that early settlements were often polyfocal. So it would not be surprising if there was another centre of population as well as the site at Oldbury. The town plan analysis by Keith Lilley suggests that there had been, beside the present precinct, a sub-circular or D-shaped enclosure marked by St. Mary's Lane (Fig.1.1, enclosure

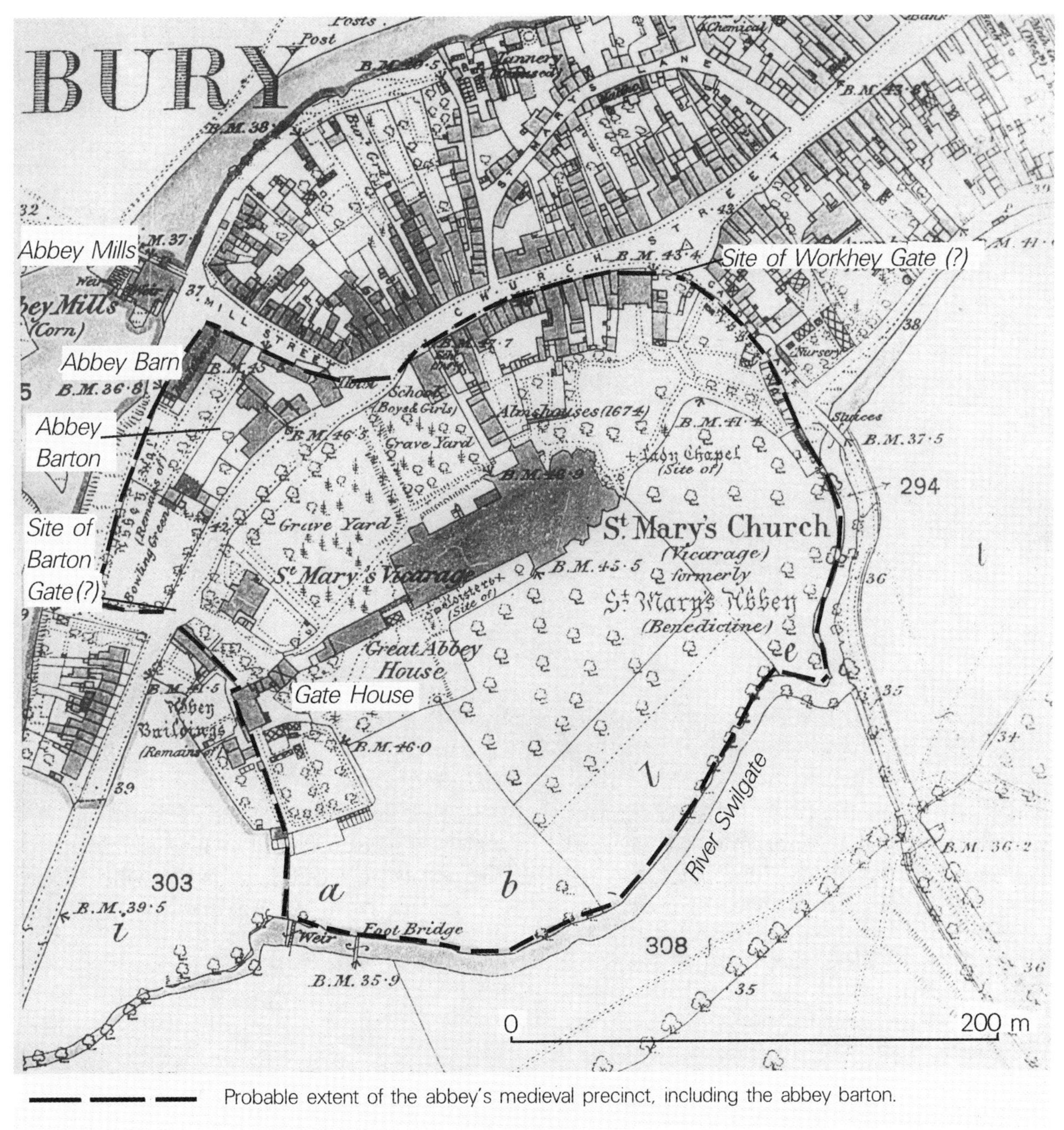

Fig.1.2 Tewkesbury from the OS 1st edition map of 1880, with annotations

1) as an early element of the town plan.[14] The enclosure was close to the River Swilgate and on ground raised above flood level, given that this is higher today than formerly. Lilley, in his plan analysis, sees three enclosures in all, superimposed or combined, the last being the precinct of 1102. This would imply a sequence of some antiquity. However, the 1880 Ordnance Survey map displays a slightly less curved outline than those plotted by Lilley—only the 'circular' phase, in my view, can be seen as possibly representing an early enclosure. The medieval abbey precinct[15] represents another enclosure (Fig.1.1, enclosure 2), extending from Church Street on the north to the River Swilgate on the south.

It is impossible to interpret these various features with much confidence. The circular enclosure could belong to an early church or chapel, possibly of the 8th to 10th century. The precinct enclosure could have been that of the 10th- to 11th-century church, subsequently taken over by the Norman abbey. On the other hand, it is not clear that the circular enclosure predates the other one: it could have been an addition to it.

The market at Tewkesbury is supposed to have been established by Queen Matilda, wife of William the Conqueror, between 1076 and her death in 1083.[16] However, the importance of Tewkesbury as an estate centre strongly suggests that there would have been a market well before this. The plan analysis indicates the early importance of The Cross, east of the abbey precinct, and this is one candidate for the site of the pre-conquest market.[17] Another is the circular enclosure, which Hannan suggested might have been the late Saxon market area, later colonised.[18] My favoured site for the market would be the enlarged space at the centre of the circular enclosure, which still survives in the street pattern (Fig.1.2). This site might place it outside the gate of the abbey precinct (the Workhey Gate), where one would expect it to be as the earliest markets were often established by the minster churches.[19]

At the time of Domesday, Tewkesbury was already starting to acquire the characteristics of an urban settlement. The town had 13 burgesses in 1086, as well as holding eight burgage plots in Gloucester, suggesting it could obtain access to other markets as well as maintaining its own.[20]

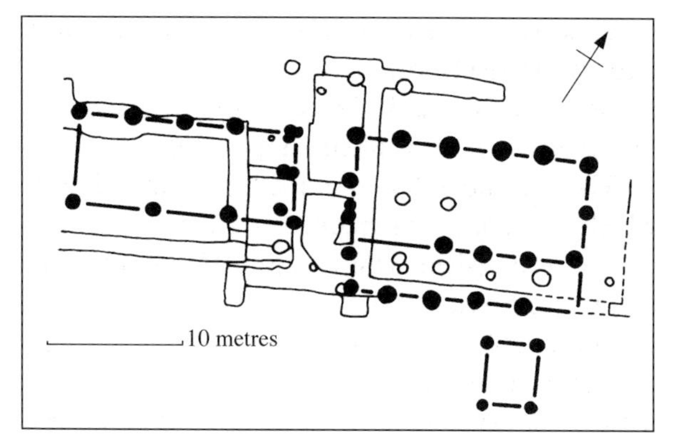

Fig.1.3 The late Anglo-Saxon hall at Holm Hill, Tewkesbury, a reconstruction of the plan. Outlined features are late phases

As the head of a large and prosperous agricultural estate, Tewkesbury would have had a great hall, where the lord feasted, presided over courts, and from which he hunted. Excavations at Holm Hill in 1974, on the site of what is now the Borough Council offices, uncovered stone manor houses of the 11th and the 14th centuries. Beneath these was a series of massive post-pits representing the timber supports of a mid-11th-century building up to 40 metres long—almost certainly the hall mentioned in the Domesday Survey around which lived 16 smallholders (Fig.1.3).[21]

The abbey and its predecessors

The present abbey was founded by Robert Fitzhamon, a follower of the Conqueror, who received the manor of Tewkesbury from King William I in 1087. The new abbey was staffed by monks from Cranborne in Dorset.[22] The lord of this manor in King Edward the Confessor's time had been Beorhtric, son of Ælfgar (Algar), and a great thegn under the king. Beorhtric held altogether 350 hides of land in the south-western shires, half of which lay in Gloucestershire. Tewkesbury was the centre of his wealth,[23] and the manor was one of the largest in England, privileged by being exempt from geld (army tax) and royal service. The church of Tewkesbury, which already existed before the Conquest, owned a fifth of the manor's wealth. There is no indication that this church was dependent on any other.[24]

There is no reliable evidence of the church which the abbey supplanted—not even its site can be established with certainty. However it is likely that the early church was close to the site of the present abbey. The discovery of a wall under the south transept of the abbey in the 1970s at least hints at the existence of a pre-Norman building.[25]

This independence and wealth suggest that Tewkesbury's church must once have been a minster, or mother church. The Domesday Book entry certainly shows that the church fulfilled many of the criteria by which a minster church may be judged: it had independence, a generous endowment, possessions valued separately, and a large number of places dependent on it.[26] Many, but not all, minsters were founded in the late 7th to 8th centuries—Tewkesbury might be among these. C.S. Taylor, for example, thought that, 'there can be little doubt that Tewkesbury, like Berkeley, had been the estate of a great minster which may not have been secularized until the 11th century'.[27] Sims-Williams commented that the paucity of evidence might itself indicate that Tewkesbury was an early independent minster.[28]

The idea of an early origin for Tewkesbury church is not new. Indeed it was fostered with enthusiasm by an early 16th-century monk of the abbey, who compiled a chronicle of his house—the Founders' Book. A version of this chronicle, printed by Dugdale in *Monasticon Anglicanum* (1655)[29] and translated by Atkyns (1712),[30] may have thus acquired more credence than it really deserved. Atkyns' translation runs:[31]

> In the times of the most illustrious princes and kings of Mercia, Ethelred, Kenred and Ethelbald, there flourished in Mercia under those kings, two great men truly noble, to wit, Oddo and Doddo, persons of very honourable parentage, and eminent in themselves for their great virtue ... pious men and honoured God ... they granted many estates to divers monasteries built by themselves or their ancestors, for the sake of religion, and for promoting divine service.
>
> These two noblemen ... founded in the year 715 a monastery to the glory of God and the honour of the Virgin Mary, on their own estate, near the Severn, 7 miles distant from Gloster, in the place where a certain hermit called Theocus had made his abode, and therefore called Tewkesbury. They granted the manor called Stanway with its members and other smaller possessions, towards the maintenance of the monks, who were few in number, not exceeding four or five, fighting the good fight of Christ under the obedience of a prior, according to the rules of our father St. Benedict. The bodies of these noblemen ... lie buried in the church of Pershore, which they had enriched with many possessions. These aforesaid noblemen had a certain brother named Almaric, whose body was buried at Deerhurst, in a little chapel over against the gate of the priory. This chapel was formerly part of a royal palace and his sepulchre is shown at this day, with an inscription on the wall over the gate,[32] that duke Doddo caused this royal palace to be consecrated into a church, to the honour of the Virgin Mary, for the love which he bore to his brother Almaric.

This account is an intriguing melange of contemporary observation and pious fiction. It has most recently been discussed and unravelled by Steve Bassett.[33] The foundation date and the eponymous hermit are probably inventions—as Samuel Rudder delightfully put it, 'I am not without suspicion that the story of the hermit is fabulous'.[34] Nevertheless, Odda was a real person. He was born in the late 900s, a kinsman of Edward the Confessor. In 1051 at the exile of earl Godwin of Wessex, Odda was made earl of the western shires; the following year he was joint commander of the royal fleet. In 1052, when Godwin was restored, Odda retained an earldom in the west midlands. In 1056 he died at Deerhurst, and was buried at Pershore Abbey. He was a benefactor of Pershore and also built the church of Holy Trinity at Deerhurst, now known as Odda's Chapel. Odda died without heirs and his estates passed to the king.[35]

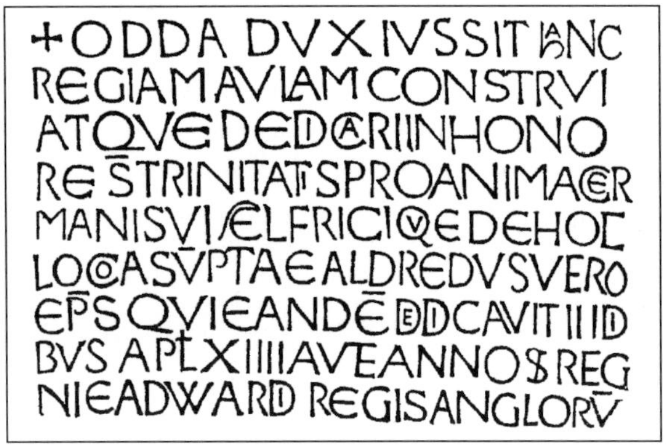

+ODDA DVX IVSSIT HANC
REGIAM AVLAM CONSTRVI
ATQVE DEDICARI IN HONO
RE S TRINITATIS PRO ANIMA GER
MANI SVI ÆLFRICI QVE DE HOC
LOCO ASVPTA EALDREDVS VERO
EPS QVI EANDE DEDICAVIT II ID
BVS APL XIIII AVTE ANNO S REG
NI EADWARD REGIS ANGLORV

Fig.1.4 The inscription tablet at Odda's Chapel, Deerhurst

It is clear that the Tewkesbury chronicle is concerned with the 11th-century Odda and that, striving for respectable antiquity, it simply placed him in the early 8th century—the era of the Church's great hero, the Venerable Bede.[36] An inscription in Odda's chapel at Deerhurst, which can be seen today, established the chapel's date of foundation (1056), records a 'royal hall',[37] and honours Odda's brother Ælfric who was buried at Pershore (Fig.1.4). The inscription was in position over the chapel door in the early 16th century, and may have contributed to the story told in the chronicle.[38]

Another claim of the Tewkesbury chronicle was that King Beorhtric of Wessex (786-802) was buried at Tewkesbury. This cannot be true for it is known that King Beorhtric was buried at Wareham, Dorset. But Beorhtric of Tewkesbury, who held the great manor in 1066, could well have been buried in Tewkesbury church, indeed he was probably an important benefactor. This transposed event is another attempt by the chronicler to promote Tewkesbury's antiquity.[39]

Bassett proposes that the endowment and power of Tewkesbury church might have originated in the 11th century, when an existing chapel was enhanced. The founder, Bassett suggests, could even have been Odda of Deerhurst, though the ancestors of Beorhtric of Tewkesbury would also be strong candidates.

Bassett envisages the church being refounded in the early 11th century as a 'secular college', staffed by a community of clerks, not monks, well-endowed with land, and with a pastoral role in the territory.[40] It is still possible, however, that Tewkesbury had prior existence as a lesser church or chapel. The Tewkesbury chronicle has a tradition that the grandfather of Beorhtric, Æthelweard (Haylward), known as 'Snow', founded a monastery at Cranborne, in Dorset, about 980 and subjected Tewkesbury to it. Beorhtric of Tewkesbury probably did have a grandfather called Æthelweard, nicknamed 'Mæw' ('Seagull') who founded Cranborne.[41] In 1102 the abbot of Cranborne set up the new house at Tewkesbury and from then on Cranborne was a cell of Tewkesbury. It seems unlikely, however, that Tewkesbury had been a cell of Cranborne until then, as the chronicle relates. The Domesday book entry makes it clear that the church of Tewkesbury was not then dependent on any other; such a dependency would have been noted.

However, a dependency on another church before a refoundation in the early 11th century is a possibility. Bassett suggests that originally Tewkesbury may have been dependent on the old minster at Deerhurst. St. Mary's Deerhurst now stands at the northern edge of its parish, as if it had lost the northern half of its parish to Tewkesbury. According to Bassett, Tewkesbury church with its parish was detached from Deerhurst in the early 11th century and refounded as a minster. Before that, it was perhaps either a parochial chapel founded from Deerhurst, or a domestic chapel serving the lord's residence at Tewkesbury.[42]

There have been other interpretations of Tewkesbury's early ecclesiastical history. One relates to a minster being founded before about 740 at *Tweonaeum*.[43] The name means 'between the rivers' and is usually taken to be Twyning,[44] although Bassett prefers to identify *Tweonaeum* with Ripple (Worcs.).[45] Anthea Jones, however, has proposed that *Tweonaeum* was Tewkesbury.[46] She suggests that the name 'Tewkesbury' could mean 'Twixt Rivers' and that the early minster was not on today's site but on the confluence between the rivers, in the area called the Mythe. She cites evidence that a chapel on the Mythe was being used by the parishioners as late as the 14th century (see below). There are fortifications on the Mythe, probably Iron Age, which she suggests were also used in the 9th century and were then deliberately acquired for strategic purposes.[47] There is at the Mythe an ancient building, originally a possession of the abbot of Tewkesbury, which the monks used as a retreat, known as 'King John's Castle'.[48] This ancient building includes a tower, which Jones suggests might be part of a church (Fig.1.5).

None of these scenarios is inherently unlikely, but different interpretations have been proposed by others. The English Place Name Society cites the meaning of the name 'Tewkesbury' as 'burh of Teodec'.[49] Even if 'Tewkesbury' means 'between the rivers', this could be a reference to its position between the Severn and the River Swilgate; it does not prove that Tewkesbury is *Tweonaeum*. The Mythe was an abbey possession and part of Tewkesbury manor;[50] it is still part of Tewkesbury parish. The evidence that it was an early Anglo-Saxon possession selected specially for defensive purposes is no more than suggestive. An evaluation of the fabric of King John's Castle has failed to demonstrate that it has an ecclesiastical origin, and it appears to be only a domestic building.[51] The chapel that was still extant on The Mythe in 1540[52] may be interpreted as a private chapel of the hall, part of the usual accoutrements of a great house. The human bones and stone coffin found at The Mythe in the 19th century[53] might be expected at a chapel site; there is no evidence that these are other than late medieval in date.

In the 16th century it was said that the parishioners of Tewkesbury had nowhere for their parish church other than the nave of the abbey church; and the *Victoria County History* judges that it is likely that this had been the case since the Norman abbey's foundation.[54] James Bennett encountered some difficulty with this topic in his *History of Tewkesbury* (1830), since there was

Fig.1.5 King John's Castle, The Mythe: exterior from the south

apparently a local antiquarian view at the time that the ancient Saxon parish church had been on St. Mary's Lane. Bennett clearly did not believe this; he took the view that the nave had always been the parishioners' church, as implied by statements from the Court of Augmentations and in the grant of the abbey church to the parishioners, both cited by him.[55] However, he had to pay some lip-service to local traditions at the time: '*it has been conjectured* [my italics] that the townspeople purchased the privilege [of using the nave] ... when their original parish church (which is supposed to have been at the end of St. Mary's Lane ...) became so ruinous as no longer suitable ...'.[56] Who made this conjecture is not made clear, but the rumour of a church in St. Mary's Lane was still rife in 1902, when the Bristol and Gloucestershire Archaeological Society visited Tewkesbury.[57] The Mayor of Tewkesbury, Mr. W. Moore, gave an address in which he described the historical interest of the town. 'At the corner of St. Mary's Lane, in Church Street, stands a small house, in the basement of which is to be seen to the present day what they [i.e. the townspeople] believed to be a relic of Saxon architecture. It had been thought that this was the only relic extant of what was probably the crypt of St. Mary's Church, which would have been at least 200 years older than the abbey.'[58] The comments of the visitors are not recorded, but more recent research has established that this masonry is part of a 14th-century cellar.[59] This seems to be an example of a cherished local conviction, accepted out of politeness and passing into secondary literature, whence it becomes difficult to dislodge.

One piece of evidence cited by Jones, however, could suggest the existence in 1367 of a separate parish church.[60] This is a record of a dispute between abbey and town:

> Whereas, on account of a certain payment of procuration which William, bishop of Worcester, requires of the parishioners of Tewkesbury for the reconciliation of their church, which is appropriated to the abbot and convent of Tewkesbury, lately defiled by the shedding of blood, touching which payment a suit is pending before the official of the Canterbury Court of Arches, London, on appeal by the said parishioners, the parishioners rashly withdraw tithes and oblations due to the said Church, go about with armed force, lie in ambush day and night to wound and ill-treat the abbot and monks and their servants and threaten them in life and limb *so that they dare not go outside the abbey gates to serve the said church* [ecclesia] *or do other business* [my italics]; the king has taken the abbey, the church, the abbot and convent and their monks and servants, their men lands rents and possessions, into his special protection for one year.[61]

To Jones, the entry implies that to serve the church the monks had to leave by the abbey gate, which would hardly be the case if the parish church had been in the nave of the abbey church. However, this passage is potentially ambivalent in proving the existence of a separate parish church, because it could be argued that 'serving the church' included ministering to the parishioners in the town.

Further information derives from an entry in the Register of Bishop Giffard for 1301. This records a complaint from the abbot and convent of St. Mary at Tewkesbury against the bishop. The bishop had announced his intention to establish a perpetual vicarage in the church of St. Mary. The abbot and convent claimed that it was their right to serve the church themselves, that nobody could obtain vicarages or institute vicars against the wishes of the abbot and convent, and that they and their predecessors had always held the church for their own use.[62] This entry suggests that in 1301 all took the view that the parish church was given to the abbey and became St. Mary's Abbey church.[63]

There is yet another candidate for the site of Tewkesbury minster. The first entry under 'lands of Tewkesbury church' in the Domesday survey reads: *Stanway: ibi monaster[ium].*[64] Ann Williams assumes this was the Domesday church of Tewkesbury, abandoned when the new abbey was established in 1102.[65] Stanway was always the jewel in the list of Tewkesbury Abbey's possessions. Throughout the Middle Ages it was a grange of the abbey. The spectacular group of buildings at Stanway includes a church of at least 12th-century origin, a gatehouse, and a 14th-century tithe barn[66] (see also Chapter 7 and Fig.7.1). But though the Stanway entry is at the head of the list of Tewkesbury church possessions, marked with an extra big red cross, the entry is very far from implying that the 'church of Tewkesbury' and Stanway are the same place. Stanway is ten miles from the core of Tewkesbury manor, being part of its separated manors in the Cotswolds. It was perhaps in origin simply a small independent monastery which was taken over by Tewkesbury church. Or perhaps the word *monasterium* might here just mean an ordinary church, as C.S. Taylor once suggested.[67]

Thus it is still not possible to take the Anglo-Saxon history of Tewkesbury very far. An interpretation of the topographical development is attempted in Figure 1.1. It is suggested that an early Anglo-Saxon settlement at Oldbury could have been accompanied in the 7th-8th centuries by a church or chapel, sited in a circular enclosure further south. Perhaps the chapel was subject to Deerhurst, or perhaps it was a private chapel to a great hall, which might have been nearby. If we adopt Bassett's suggestion that a minster was founded in the early 11th century, it might be at this time that a rebuilt church was sited in an enlarged precinct. This could also have been the occasion of the re-siting of the great hall on the scarp slope at Holm Hill.

This scenario is mostly speculation. The documents are not going to yield much more of the story, in spite of the work of scholars such as Ann Williams and Steve Bassett who have extracted so much from unpromising material.[68] It remains for archaeologists to take up the challenge, and following Alan Hannan's pioneering work, to amplify the physical history of the important Anglo-Saxon centre of Tewkesbury.

Appendix
The Medieval Precinct of Tewkesbury Abbey

The medieval precinct proper was confined to the area south of Church Street. To the east, the OS map of 1880 marks the abbey wall along Gander Lane; there was once a gate in this wall called Workhey Gate.[69] The north precinct wall originally ran along the line of Church Street; the row of properties along its south side represents development by the abbey in the Middle Ages (see Fig.5.6). The surviving gatehouse (see

Fig.1.6 The abbey barn by the mill

Fig.12.10) is set back from the road and was an inner gate to the inner court—there was probably an outer gate on the road frontage. The western boundary of the precinct was just west of the gatehouse and extended down to the River Swilgate.[70]

Although the abbey owned extensive property (mill, barn, tannery) north of Church Street, this area may not have been part of the actual precinct. This was presumably mostly abbey property in the 12th century, and must owe its commercial development to the building of the Mill Avon. These areas, as well as the bulge of property to the south-west on the west side of Church Street, might all constitute pre-12th century plan formations.[71]

The abbey barn (Fig.1.6), near the mill, has running west from it a length of medieval wall marked on the 1880 OS map as 'Abbey Wall' (Fig.1.2). If this formed part of a precinct wall, then the precinct must have angled north from Church Street, and one would have expected the main road to have been diverted round this block. There is no real evidence of this.[72] I assume that this block was abbey land and so walled, but not an integral part of the ecclesiastical precinct.

CHAPTER 2

The Early Lords: Robert Fitzhamon to the de Clares *by* Michael Hicks

The patrons of Tewkesbury Abbey were the lords of Tewkesbury which was part of the honour of Gloucester from *c*.1108-1314, the period covered in this chapter. The later lords after 1314, when the honour was divided, are discussed in the following chapter. The lords as patrons built, endowed, and repeatedly enriched the abbey, which was obliged to pray for their souls and to receive their bodies for burial. Tewkesbury Abbey was the mausoleum of the earls of Gloucester and their heirs. Many of their tombs are still visible today. This reciprocal relationship emerges from the interest displayed by the abbey's successive chroniclers in their patrons. These patrons, however, were also great national figures, who have attracted the attention of historians ever since their own day, and have left their imprint on the public records. Their own residence at Holm Hill and their own Tewkesbury estate are documented in the extents (surveys) after their deaths (inquisitions post mortem), in their own estate accounts, and in the archaeological record.

Robert Fitzhamon

Queen Matilda, consort of King William I (1066-87), held Tewkesbury until her death in 1083. Their son William II (1087-1100) granted it and much else in 1088 to Robert Fitzhamon (d.1107, Pl.23) in reward for good service against the Conqueror's rebellious half-brother Odo, bishop of Bayeux. Fitzhamon's ancestors had been settled in Normandy for more than a century; his grandfather Hamo Dentatus, lord of Torigny-sur-Vire, had been killed in rebellion in 1047 but his father, also Hamo (d.*c*.1100), was sheriff of Kent. Robert, landless and possibly a younger son, was extraordinarily favoured by William Rufus. Ever present with the king, eighth most frequent lay witness to his charters and the only one to hold no household office, he was exceptionally close to Rufus and may indeed have been his lover. He was with the king when he was killed and was supposedly forewarned by reports of a prophetic dream. William Rufus gave him in marriage Sibyl, daughter of Roger Montgomery, earl of Shrewsbury. William and King Henry I (1100-35) gave Robert the great estate that later became known as the honour of Gloucester, which included the patronage of both the Benedictine monastery at Cranborne and the church at Tewkesbury. Robert duly decided to transfer the abbey, Abbot Gerald and his monks, to Tewkesbury, reducing Cranborne to the status of a dependent cell.

Robert was one of the most successful of those Normans who carried the conquest beyond England into the domains of the Celts. After capturing Newport, he conquered the coastal strip where he built the first Cardiff Castle. As a result of those conquests Robert was able to endow the refounded abbey extremely generously, including, for example, with the mother church of Cardiff. It was his successors who conquered the Welsh kingdom of Morganwg and established instead Glamorgan, the greatest of all the Welsh marcher lordships. Glamorgan was the most valuable part of the inheritance that Robert was to pass to his Fitzroy, de Clare, Despenser, Beauchamp, and Neville descendants. It was whilst campaigning for Henry I against his brother Robert Curthose, duke of Normandy, that Robert suffered the head wound that robbed him of his reason, his liberty, and eventually his life.[1]

The First Earls of Gloucester

Robert's death in 1107 was the first of three occasions that his great estate was threatened with division amongst coheiresses. Two of his daughters were placed in nunneries, where they rose to become abbesses, and were thus excluded from inheritance. The third, Mabel, was married to Robert (Fitzroy) of Caen, a bastard son of King Henry I born to an English lady before his accession. Robert and Mabel acquired all Fitzhamon's possessions. Robert, who was created the first earl of Gloucester in 1122, constructed the original castle at Bristol and made it the *caput* of his honour (centre of his fief) of Gloucester, which contained the extraordinary number of 260 knights' fees. He founded the priory of St. James outside Bristol, where he himself was to be buried, as a cell of Tewkesbury. The abbey chronicler's statement that Earl Robert had the abbot and 12 monks to dine each Sunday can only rarely have applied. He was also the founder of the abbeys at Neath and Margam. Contemporary chroniclers admired Earl Robert because he was exceptionally cultured, literate, militarily adept, and politically astute. He was both an informant of the distinguished chronicler, William of Malmesbury, and the dedicatee of his *Deeds of the Kings*. Robert's political career commenced as early as 1113, when he first witnessed his father's charters, and developed following the death of Henry's sole legitimate son on the *White Ship*. He was second only to Stephen, the king's nephew, in Henry's last years and was even entrusted with the custody of Robert Curthose at Cardiff. He was with Henry I at his death and at first accepted Stephen (1135-54) as king. Subsequently, however, the two men quarrelled and Robert sided instead with his half-sister, the Empress Matilda, becoming her principal partisan.[2] So important were his services that in 1141 he was exchanged as a prisoner for Stephen himself. He served her both in Normandy and in England, holding the west against Stephen up until his death in 1147, by which time Matilda's cause was already lost.

Earl Robert was succeeded by his son, Earl William (Fitzcount), who was a witness to the

Fig.2.1 Robert Fitzroy. The base of a 15th-century statuette, with the inscription 'Rob[ertus] Consull filius Regis'

Fig.2.2 William Fitzcount. The base of a 15th-century statuette, with the inscription 'Willelm[us] comes glouc[estriam]

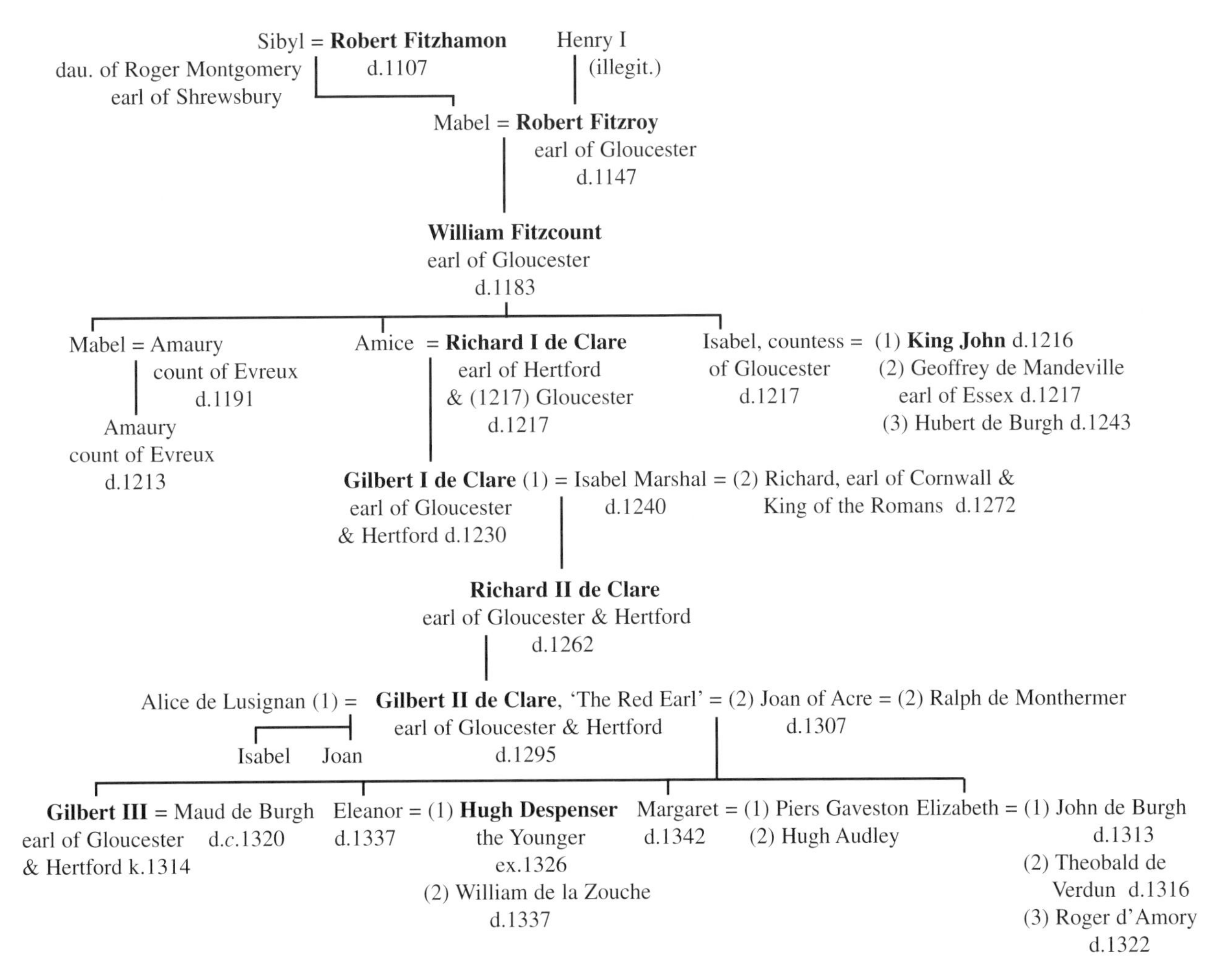

Fig.2.3 Selective family tree of Robert Fitzhamon and the de Clares, with the lords of Tewkesbury in bold

treaty of 1153 between Stephen and his successor, Matilda's son King Henry II (1154-89). It was Henry, however, who deprived Earl William of Bristol—by then the third city in the kingdom—in 1164-5. Although this loss was not at first accepted, it proved permanent and may have raised Tewkesbury from a significant estate and occasional residence to something much more important.

Earl William died in 1183 and, like Robert Fitzhamon, left three daughters but no son. Once again the estate was too important for the normal processes of inheritance, and, as before, was coveted by a king for his son. Two daughters, presumably the two oldest, Mabel and Amice, were already married respectively to Amaury, count of Evreux, and Richard de Clare, earl of Hertford (d.1217). The third daughter, Isabel, was betrothed by King Henry II to his youngest son, John Lackland, count of Mortain, and they were married shortly after Henry II's death in 1189. Isabel became countess of Gloucester and John acquired all her estates, mere fragments being reserved to her sisters and their husbands. John dated several charters at Tewkesbury and may have resided there, at Holm Castle, quite frequently.[3] He developed its recreational facilities and is credited both with building the bridge over the Avon and with endowing it with some of the tolls of Tewkesbury market.[4] He continued to reside there occasionally after his accession in 1199: he was there in 1201-2, for Christmas in 1204, with his queen in 1205, and again in 1209. Similarly his son, King Henry III (1216-72), resided there during the lord of the estate's minority in 1232; in 1233 for the feasts of the Assumption (15 August) and Nativity of the Blessed Virgin (8 September), when his clerks sang the anthem *Christus Vincit* (Christ has Conquered); in 1236, when a truce was concluded with the Welsh prince Llewellyn the Great, and in 1237-8. It was also at Tewkesbury in 1278 that King Alexander III of Scotland did homage to Edward I.[5] Tewkesbury was a convenient crossing of the Severn when journeying to and from Glamorgan and was suitable also for operations against the Welsh.

The Manor of Tewkesbury

The Tewkesbury estate was particularly large and valuable, being worth £169 in 1262.[6] The Anglo-Saxon hundred of Tewkesbury contained a number of properties in Gloucestershire, south Worcestershire and south Warwickshire once held by the thane Beorhtric and his tenants, including the monastery at Tewkesbury.[7] Those later called the southern division of Tewkesbury Hundred consisted of the manor of Tewkesbury itself, which included not merely the medieval borough and modern town, but also their environs (Fig.2.4). The estate recorded in Domesday Book in 1086 and later described in short-hand as the manor of Tewkesbury comprised not merely the borough, manor and parish of Tewkesbury (with Northway and Mythe), but also the modern parishes of Ashchurch, Tredington, and Forthampton (including Fiddington), to the west and south. The total area comprised 10,376 acres, of which the demesne amounted to 1,167 acres in 1296.[8] Late in the Middle Ages these were often administered as separate (sub-) manors, with their own manorial courts and ministers, Tewkesbury itself remaining the administrative centre and site of the superior court of frankpledge, which had law-keeping and police powers. The 13th-century earls of Gloucester had also claimed return of writs within their property. However, the town of Tewkesbury was exempt, for elements of self-government had been included among the rights and privileges bestowed by earls Robert and William on the burgesses of their towns of Tewkesbury and Cardiff. The lands of the abbey itself, including its part of the town, were also outside the lords' jurisdiction.[9]

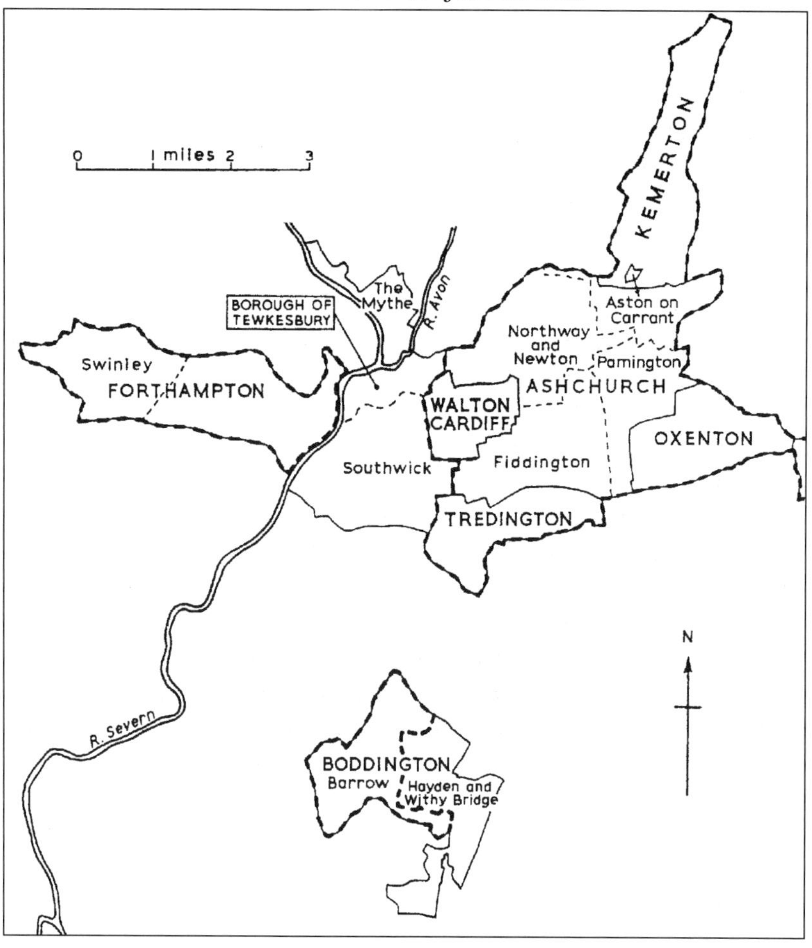

Fig.2.4 The Hundred of Tewkesbury (Lower Division) showing the lands that belonged to the abbey in the vicinity of Tewkesbury

Such overlapping and contradictory courts may have confused contemporaries as much as later historians. It is fortunate, perhaps, that the lords were generous patrons to the abbey and that the abbey was anxious to accommodate its founders whenever it could. Complexity also poses other problems to the historian. The manor of Tewkesbury recorded in an extent of 1296 evidently included all the component members, which helps explain why the totals of demesne arable (740 acres), mowable meadow (176 acres), and park (200 acres) so greatly exceeded the acreages, respectively 460, 85 and 80 acres, recorded later: the balance lay in the sub-manors.[10] Similarly the manor of Ashchurch accounted for from 1488, which included Holm Hill and Barton, was the same as Tewkesbury itself.[11] When the lord's residence and park and the town are excluded, most of the manor may well have lain to the east, in the direction of the modern parish of Ashchurch. In the town, the 13 burgages created by Queen Matilda (d.1083) had grown into 114 burgages by 1328 arranged around three principal streets.[12]

The 'capital messuage' at Tewkesbury of the last earl of Gloucester in the 1314 inquisition, that adjoined a garden, vineyard, dovecote and vivary, was clearly in the same location as the close of the earls of Gloucester called the upper garden with a dovecot in it that was called the Holm in 1488-9.[13] Holm Hill lies south-west of the abbey near the confluence of the rivers Avon and Swilgate. Regrettably, the low walls still recognizable there in 1540 had been so thoroughly robbed out that the partial rescue excavation of 1975 is rather uncertain in its conclusions.[14] It is safe, however, to identify the large timber aisled structure, described as being of uncertain date, with the *aula* (hall) recorded in Domesday Book (Fig.1.2). This first hall was replaced by a somewhat smaller and shoddily constructed single-storeyed aisled hall and western solar block, apparently destroyed by fire—which may, therefore, be the *magnificum domum* (magnificent house) of Earl Robert destroyed by Waleran, count of Meulan in his campaign on behalf of King Stephen in 1140.

A third block, apparently including a first-floor hall, was built of stone to much higher specifications in the mid- to late 12th century. Not only were the foundations better, but fragments of high-quality stone decoration, notably hood-moulds, were recovered during the excavation. Such structures were parts of larger complexes, indicated by a large area of paving and other foundations to the south including a circular structure which was possibly the dovecote. Whether this new hall antedated the tenure of Count John, as the datable features suggest, or whether he actually constructed it, a palace up to royal standards was evidently standing at his accession which he continued to use as king and his son after him. King John's pipe rolls record regular small scale expenditure there—on chimneys and windows in 1201, on repairs to the king's houses in 1203-6, and on the roofing of a new kitchen, dovecote, granary, larder, and chamber in 1211—but nothing substantial. Probably the greater chapel and the lesser chapel in the chamber that Henry III upgraded with glass windows in 1241 had been there in King John's day. There are few masonry fragments datable as late as the 13th century and none thereafter.

Tewkesbury already possessed some of the facilities that great lords expected and they were further developed by John, first as count and then as king. Proximity to the river made the supply of tuns of wine from Bristol relatively simple: Tewkesbury was a staging post also for royal wine destined for the king at Worcester and Woodstock.[15] Perhaps the supplies were supplemented from Tewkesbury's own working vineyard, first mentioned with its vintner in 1183-4. It was of considerable size, since in 1307 labour services totalling 291 days were owed for digging there and another 54 days for gathering grapes. There are no references to it after 1314,[16] probably because climate change made it unviable; it may have been recategorized as a garden.

A park was being enclosed from 1185-7—probably the Tewkesbury Park south of Holm Hill which was later described as being of 80 acres. It was kept in the king's hands in 1204 when all else was leased out, the hunting being reserved to himself, and was cared for by its own parker, Jordan, in 1214. The king's huntsmen and dogs were there in 1203, 1205, and 1209-12. It was restocked in 1238 and in 1240 ten bucks were taken for the king's use. Despite its modest size, it was kept stocked with wild beasts and as late as 1540 contained the unexpectedly large number of 300 deer. Red, fallow and roe deer were consumed at Holm Hill.[17] Fish were available both from the River Severn and from the vivary—maybe the fishponds still discernible to the south of the abbey. Twenty bream were despatched to Marlborough in 1204 and salmon and lampreys were supplied in 1205.[18] The lord's stables—the ruined Great Stable of 1528-9—were located at a distance, near the granaries in Barton Street, which was described variously as the manor or grange of Barton. Probably this was the lord's stud—certainly King John and Henry III kept horses there; the Countess Anne kept her horses there both in 1460-1 and in 1488-9, the stables having being leased in the interim.[19] Enough fragments of horse furniture were excavated at Holm Hill to indicate that both riding and hunting horses were kept there, as one would expect.

King John and the de Clares

King John's continued occupation of Tewkesbury, and indeed the whole inheritance after his accession, is a striking instance of his arbitrary pursuit of his own interests at the expense of the rights of his subjects. He had taken possession originally as consort of the Countess Isabel who, however, failed to provide him with the heir he required. On his accession, he set her aside, divorcing her on grounds of consanguinity, and married instead Isabel of Angoulême, who was to bear him the future Henry III. Initially the Countess Isabel was imprisoned to prevent her marrying again.

In 1200 her nephew, Count Amaury, was created earl of Gloucester, but received few of the lands. Following Amaury's childless death in 1213, the Countess Isabel was reluctantly allowed to marry first Geoffrey de Mandeville, earl of Essex—who was charged the huge fine of 20,000 marks (£13,333) for the match—and then Hubert de Burgh, the justiciar, but died in 1217 still without offspring. At this point, at last, Richard I de Clare, Isabel's other brother-in-law, was allowed to inherit. Dying almost at once, the whole estate passed to his son, Gilbert I, who died in Brittany in 1230. His widow, Isabel Marshal (d.1240), remarried to Henry III's brother Richard, earl of Cornwall, king of the Romans (and founder of nearby Hailes Abbey) to whom she bore four children. Her heart was interred at Tewkesbury, where she had hoped to lie, but her body was buried at Earl Richard's command at King John's abbey of Beaulieu.[20]

With 456 knights' fees, the de Clares were the greatest noble family of 13th-century England. The honour of Gloucester combined with their Welsh marcher lordships dwarfed their original inheritance, the East Anglian honour of Clare. They saw themselves first and foremost as lords of the march, where they held all the regalian rights of the crown and could even wage war against their neighbours. This special status was severely restricted in 1292, when Edward I (1272-1307) intervened in the private warring of Earl Gilbert II, lord of Glamorgan, and the earl of Hereford as lord of Brecon, and imposed peace on them. This was all the more humiliating since both men were the king's sons-in-law.[21] It was as marcher lords, however, that the de Clares played the prominent role in national politics commensurate with their wealth and power.

Earl Richard II was a leader in the baronial reform movement against Henry III, most concerned perhaps by Henry's ineffectiveness against the Welsh. Having bound himself early in 1258 to Simon de Montfort, earl of Leicester (k.1265) by oaths of mutual assistance, he was one of the council nominated under the Provisions of Oxford to run the kingdom. He rejoined the king in 1260—he had become hostile to Earl Simon himself—but had reverted to opposition before his sudden death in 1262. 'His apparent inconsistency', concludes his biographer, was not because he was vague about constitutional principles, but because his stance in politics was shaped by his 'own personal power, influence, and interests. Earl Richard is perhaps the prime example of such a man'.[22]

Although under age, Gilbert II—the Red Earl—joined Simon de Montfort in 1263, forcing Henry III to observe the Provisions of Oxford. Following the Mise of Amiens, whereby King Louis IX of France (1223-72) as arbiter annulled the Provisions, Gilbert II participated in the battle of Lewes in 1264 in which Henry III was defeated. He was one of the committee of three whose advice the king was obliged to take. Problems in the marches and the autocracy of Earl Simon caused him to join Prince Edward and contributed to de Montfort's defeat and death at Evesham in 1265. Gilbert exploited the situation to his own advantage—'Gilbert's actions were often quite arbitrary'[23]—but he also eventually forced the king to restore their property to those disinherited after Evesham. He proved a moderating influence on the extremes of either side.

Gilbert II also feared that he would be the last of his line. His first wife, Alice de Lusignan, kinsman of the king, bore him only two daughters. Gilbert and Alice were separated by 1271. From at least 1283 he considered setting her aside and marrying Edward I's daughter Joan of Acre, but the divorce and remarriage were not concluded until 1290. The whole de Clare inheritance was resettled on Gilbert and Joan jointly and their heirs, with reversion if there were none to the king. This last clause proved unnecessary, for Joan bore him four children before Gilbert's death in 1295: the desired son, Gilbert III, and three daughters, Eleanor, Margaret and Elizabeth.[24] Their royal blood and their prospects should their brother die were well understood at the time. Hence the second daughter's marriage to Piers Gaveston (ex.1312), the first favourite of King Edward II (1307-27). The widowed Countess Joan, still young, remarried to the obscure Ralph de Monthermer in a classic instance of the *mésalliances* that the greatest noblewomen were inclined to contract when finding themselves unsupervised by fathers, brothers and husbands. At first Edward I was furious but he subsequently came round. Monthermer was allowed to take the title of earl of Gloucester during Joan's lifetime—she died in 1307—and both he and his son were treated thereafter as barons.

Gilbert III, the intended fruit of the resettlement of 1290, was a grandson of Edward I and nephew of Edward II. He was also the only magnate wealthy enough to rival his cousin Thomas, earl of Lancaster. Though scarcely of age, Gilbert's chance to demonstrate his worth came in 1314, at the Battle of Bannockburn. A splendid English army led by Edward II was confronted by a formidable Scottish force commanded by Robert Bruce himself. Gilbert sided with those veterans who counselled caution, prudently advising postponement of the battle for a day, which his cousin Edward II foolishly attributed to treason and deceit. Such insults had to be borne from a king, however unworthy, and Gilbert determined to prove Edward wrong. "'Today," said the earl, "it will be clear that I am neither a traitor nor a liar"'.[25] He and his marcher rival Hereford disputed who should lead the English van.

> The Earl of Hereford said that this should be lawfully his, because he was constable of England. Gloucester replied that his forebears had always led the van, and therefore this pertained to him by custom. While they disputed in this fashion, and the Scottish forces were approaching rapidly, the Earl of Gloucester dashed forward in disorder, seeking the glory of the first encounter; but see! The earl is met by onrushing Scots and his horse immediately killed; because when thrown from his horse there was no one to defend him, he was pierced by many wounds and shamefully killed. Alas! Twenty armed knights could have saved the earl, but among some five hundred not one was found to help! Accursed be the chivalry whose courage fails in the hour of greatest need![26]

Whilst doubtless Gilbert's inexperience and rashness contributed to his death and the English defeat, he had added yet more lustre to his family's renown even as he brought to an end both the de Clare dynasty and the earldom of Gloucester. Gilbert had no son. The infant John (b.1312) had predeceased him and the posthumous son that Gilbert III's countess, Maud, hoped for did not materialise. His possessions were divided amongst his three sisters, never to be re-united. Following the death of the countess by 1320, Tewkesbury fell with Glamorgan to the eldest daughter Eleanor, wife of Hugh II Despenser (d.1326). Hugh Audley (d.1347), the second husband of her sister, Margaret, was briefly earl of Gloucester from 1337 before their share passed to the Staffords—earls of Stafford and dukes of Buckingham. The third sister, Elizabeth, the Lady of Clare, was the mother-in-law of Edward III's son Lionel, duke of Clarence (d.1368) and ancestress through him of the Mortimers and of the Yorkist kings of England. Neither Margaret nor Elizabeth or any of their descendants ever held Tewkesbury.

CHAPTER 3

The Later Lords: The Despensers and their Heirs *by* Michael Hicks

This chapter takes up the story after the death of the last de Clare earl of Gloucester in 1314, after which Tewkesbury was allocated to the eldest coheiress, Eleanor, and her husband, Hugh II Despenser, as part of her third share. For a century, until 1414, it descended in the male line of the Despensers and then amongst their Beauchamp, Neville and Plantagenet heirs, who brought national politics to Tewkesbury in 1471, when the battle of Tewkesbury was fought nearby and the vanquished Lancastrian commanders were buried in the abbey. The line of lords ended in 1492, when the hundred, lordship, manor and patronage of the abbey passed to the crown. Long before then, it appears, the lords had ceased to use Tewkesbury as their residence.

The Despensers

The Despenser who married Eleanor de Clare was Hugh II, the Younger, later to become the notorious favourite of Edward II. His father and namesake, Hugh the Elder, was a distinguished soldier and devoted royal servant who was rewarded with the earldom of Winchester. From 1318 they dominated Edward II and his government.

> No baron could approach the King without their consent, and then a bribe was usually necessary; they answered petitions as they wished; they removed household officials without consulting the baronage; and any who displeased them or whose lands they coveted they threw into prison. The King would take advice from none but them.[1]

A third share of the de Clare inheritance transformed the family fortunes, but did not satisfy the younger Despenser, who sought to extend his share of the Welsh properties to embrace them all and also those of adjoining lords. He thereby provoked the Despenser war in Wales in 1321, forcing Edward II to exile him. Returning in 1322, when his critics were destroyed at the Battle of Boroughbridge, the Despensers then did as they chose and established their own tyranny. Hugh the Younger was ruthless, violent, corrupt, acquisitive, and untouchable. It took a revolution to overthrow him in 1326, when both he and his father were executed. 'Shockingly, treacherously and cruelly, without judgement or the chance to defend himself', so the Tewkesbury chronicler writes, Hugh the Younger 'was hanged, drawn, and quartered' at Hereford. Later he was buried at Tewkesbury Abbey (Fig.13.2).[2] Their master, Edward II, lost his throne, then his life, and rests in Gloucester Cathedral.

Eleanor de Clare survived until 1337. Her inheritance escaped forfeiture and passed to her son, Hugh (d.1349) (Fig.3.1), who also recovered the Despensers' own property, and thence to her grandson Edward (d.1375) (Pl.14). Eleanor's share of the de Clare inheritance consisted mainly of Glamorgan, Tewkesbury and other

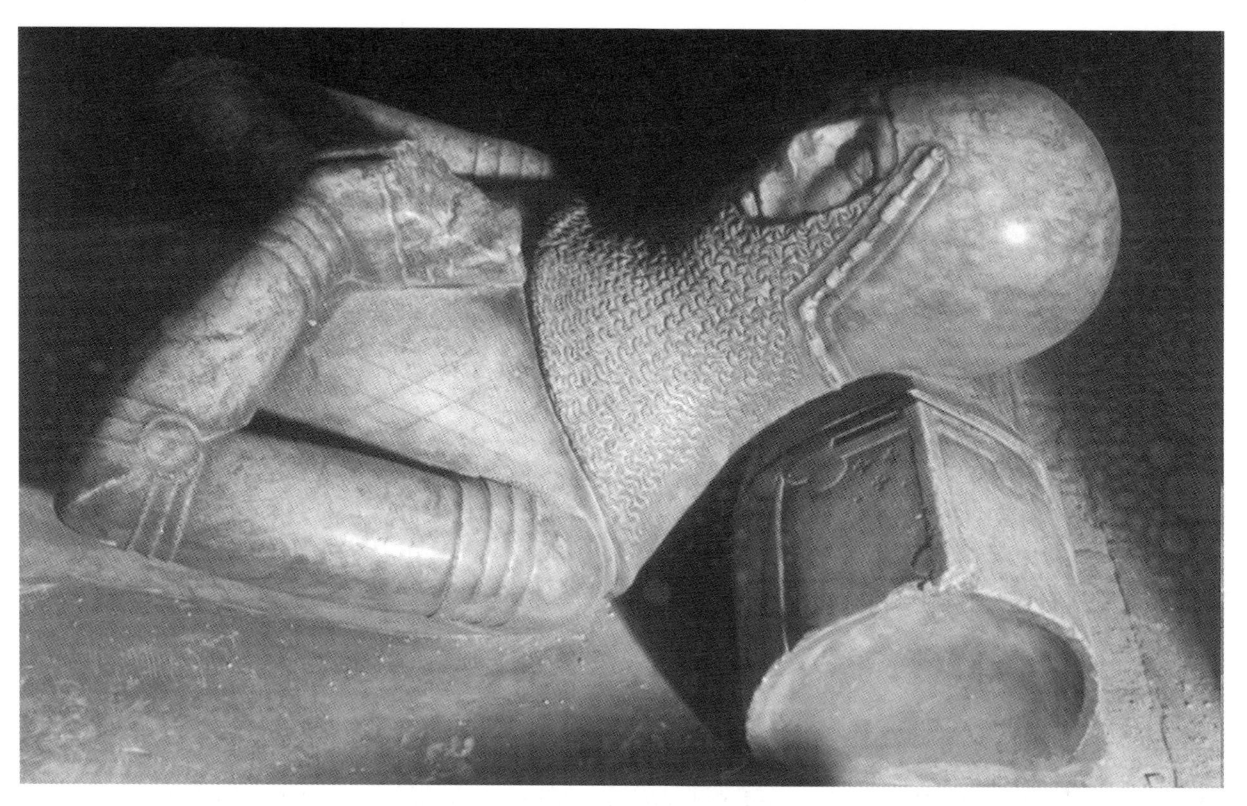

Fig.3.1 The effigy of Hugh III Despenser

Gloucestershire lands; Thornbury passed to her sister Margaret and the Staffords. Eleanor retained the honour of Gloucester itself and lordship over its knights' fees; the honorial court (Earl's Court) continued to meet at the manor of Barton by Bristol as long as her line endured. She was also assigned within her share the patronage of Tewkesbury Abbey and its dependent priories. Cardiff Castle was the Despensers' principal seat, where they were most commonly recorded, yet they maintained their estate and house at Tewkesbury and it was Tewkesbury Abbey that they made their mausoleum, following the practice of the de Clare earls since 1217. It was in their time that the Norman choir and ambulatory was recast with Decorated vaulting and windows, and the existing circle of tombs and chapels began to be inserted between the piers.[3] Tewkesbury contains the tombs of all four Despenser lords, their spouses, and several second husbands of Despenser dowagers, such as William de la Zouche (d.1337) and Sir Guy de Bryan KG (d.1390) (Fig.3.2).

Edward married Elizabeth Burghersh and following his death she held Tewkesbury in dower until her own death in 1409. After a long minority her son, Thomas, Lord Despenser, became one of the courtiers of King Richard II (1377-99). In 1397 he was one of the Lords Appellant who charged the king's uncle, Thomas of Woodstock, duke of Gloucester, and the earls of Arundel and Warwick with treason. When six senior Appellants were created dukes and nicknamed the *duketti* (little dukes), Thomas was created (at last) earl of Gloucester. Two years later, however, Richard II was deposed, Henry IV (1399-1413) became king, the *duketti* lost their dukedoms, and Thomas reverted to his barony. Richard had abdicated unwillingly and for many years was rumoured still to be alive, Thomas being amongst the late king's committed supporters who rose in rebellion in 1400 and was lynched by a mob at Bristol.[4] Another long minority loomed.

Although Thomas died a traitor and his notoriously immoral spouse Constance dabbled in

Fig.3.2 The effigy of Guy de Bryan

treason, their young children were allowed to inherit the family estates (Fig.3.3). Their son, Richard, had already married Eleanor Neville in one of the famous Neville child marriages before his death in 1414: although the match was childless, Eleanor (now countess of Northumberland) enjoyed her Despenser dower until her death in 1474. The eldest of Richard's sisters, Elizabeth, died young, leaving Isabel, born in 1400 only seven months after her father's death, as sole heiress. In 1411 she was married in Tewkesbury Abbey to Richard Beauchamp of Abergavenny. He was created earl of Worcester in 1421 but was killed by a ballister bolt at the siege of Meaux in France in 1422. Isabel constructed a splendid chantry for him and herself to the south of the abbey's choir.[5] Early in 1423, in her brief interlude as *femme sole*, she appointed William Parker as parker and hayward of Tredington.[6] Later that year she remarried to her first husband's cousin, another Richard Beauchamp, the great earl of Warwick, a chivalric hero, distinguished both for military prowess and courtesy (Fig.3.4).[7] Initially Tewkesbury revenues repaid his debts; supposedly he planned clearing the mills on the Avon to make it navigable from Tewkesbury to Warwick, but nothing came of the scheme.[8] During their lifetimes their son Henry bore the courtesy title Lord Despenser. It was as lieutenant of France that Earl Richard died at Rouen in 1439—he was buried in his splendid Beauchamp Chapel at St. Mary's, Warwick—and it was at the Grey Friars in London that the already ailing Isabel died soon after. She was buried in Tewkesbury Abbey.

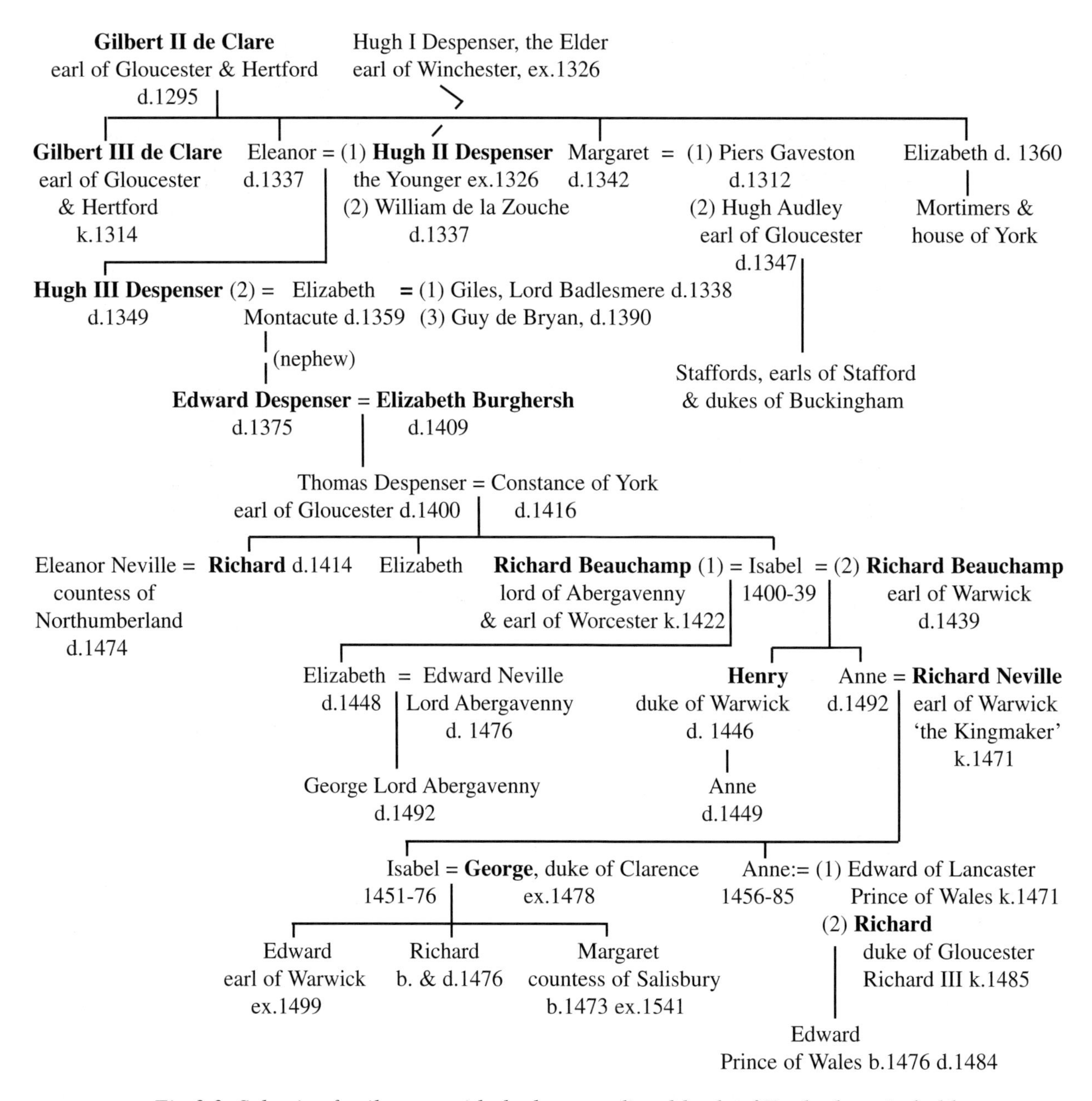

Fig.3.3 Selective family tree, with the later medieval lords of Tewkesbury in bold

Warwick had been tutor of the young Henry VI (1422-61), and perhaps it was personal contacts developed then that explain the king's approval of Isabel's will and his subsequent promotion of her son Henry (Fig.3.5) first as premier earl, with an entitlement to wear a coronet, and then as duke of Warwick. Isabel was allowed to settle most of her lands including Tewkesbury in trust; it was sometime after 1457 that the trustees finally handed over their lands to her heirs, though they had done as they were told by the heirs before then.[9] Duke Henry died in 1446, however, leaving as heiress only an infant daughter Anne, who died in 1449. The inheritance was again disputed.

Isabel had borne three children: Duke Henry and two daughters, Elizabeth, her daughter by her first husband, and Anne, daughter by her second husband. Which one was the heir? If the issue was which was heir to Isabel, the two daughters

Fig.3.4 Richard Beauchamp, earl of Warwick, d.1439, from the Rous Roll

Fig.3.5 Henry Beauchamp, duke of Warwick, d.1446, from the Rous Roll

were equally related to her and both should have inherited equally. If, however, the issue was who was heir to Henry and his infant daughter Anne—as surely it had to be—his sister Anne was sole heiress, since she was Henry's sister of the whole blood, sister by both parents; her half-sister Elizabeth was merely his step-sister (Fig.3.3). Elizabeth was in fact already dead by 1449, but her husband Edward Neville (d.1476), who assumed the title of Lord Abergavenny, asserted her claims vigorously and repeatedly on behalf of himself and their young son, George. Some juries appear to have agreed and so briefly did the abbey chronicler. In 1450, 1470, and 1484 first Edward and then George secured formal royal recognition of their claims to half the Despenser inheritance. However, they were never able to make them effective. The victor was Anne and her husband Richard Neville, earl of Warwick, better known as Warwick the Kingmaker, who maintained possession throughout and whom Tewkesbury Abbey had accepted as rightful patron by 1451. Warwick confirmed the charters of his predecessors Fitzhamon, de Clare, and Despenser, and was commemorated in return in the abbey chronicle.[10]

The Kingmaker (Fig.3.6) was the eldest son of Richard Neville (d.1460) and Alice Montacute, earl and countess of Salisbury, who were great landowners in the North and in central southern

Fig.3.6 Richard Neville, 'the Kingmaker', k.1471, from the Rous Roll

Fig.3.7 George, duke of Clarence, ex.1478, from the Rous Roll

England. Following their deaths in the 1460s he was to become the greatest English landholder. In 1449, however, he was only 20 years of age. The acquisition of the Despenser estates and the Beauchamp earldom of Warwick, which Anne had inherited from her father, transformed him unexpectedly into the leading nobleman in the west midlands and Wales at a time of great political upheaval and enabled him to play an outstanding role that befitted his extraordinary administrative abilities and energy. If, during the Wars of the Roses, anyone deserved the description 'overmighty subject', it was Warwick. He could have (and perhaps should have) allowed Glamorgan to be divided, but chose instead to resist, rebutting his rivals by force, and was thus drawn into support of King Henry's Yorkist critics. He helped replace the Lancastrian Henry VI with the Yorkist Edward IV (1461-83) and from 1461-7 was the dominant figure in the new regime.

King Edward had succeeded at the age of 19. As he grew up, he increasingly assumed personal control, pursuing a foreign policy directly opposed to Warwick's. Warwick accordingly allied himself to the king's brother George, duke of Clarence (d.1478) (Fig.3.7), to whom he married his daughter Isabel (d.1476). He attempted to seize the government in 1469, when Edward IV would have become a puppet, and in 1470, when Clarence would have succeeded. When both failed, earl and duke were driven into exile. They allied themselves with exiled Lancastrians, invaded England, and briefly restored Henry VI to his throne. For six months in 1470-71, Henry VI reigned again—it was called his Readeption—and Warwick was supreme. Edward IV returned, however, allied himself anew with Clarence, captured London and Henry VI, and on 14 April (Easter Sunday) 1471 defeated Warwick in a great battle at Barnet, where Warwick himself was killed. On hearing the news the Countess Anne, who had recently disembarked at Portsmouth, took sanctuary in Beaulieu Abbey in the New Forest.[11]

The Battle of Tewkesbury, 1471[12]

The Readeption was founded on an alliance (the Treaty of Angers) between Warwick and the Lancastrians forged by the marriage in 1470 of Warwick's younger daughter Anne and Henry VI's 17-year-old son, Edward of Lancaster, Prince of Wales. The Lancastrians had not worked well with Warwick, who after all had defeated and ruined them before, and some at least rejoiced at his death. 'Their party was never the feebler, but rather stronger'. Most of the principal Lancastrians were not at Barnet but in the south-west, where they met up with Henry VI's queen, Margaret of Anjou, their son, Prince Edward, and his new princess, when at length they crossed from France. Long-delayed by contrary winds, they had landed at Weymouth on 14 April, the same day as the Battle of Barnet. At Cerne Abbey (Dorset) Margaret was joined by Edmund Beaufort, duke of Somerset, and John Courtenay, earl of Devon, the main West Country magnates, who were reputed 'old inheritors of that country'. Starting first with local adherents in Somerset, Dorset and Wiltshire, they moved to Exeter, where they 'arrayed the whole might of Cornwall and Devonshire', and thence to Bath and Bristol, recruiting all the way. Their next objective was not to seek out King Edward but rather to join up with Henry VI's half-brother, Jasper Tudor, earl of Pembroke, who had been recruiting in Wales. Edward IV, in contrast, was anxious to force a battle before the Lancastrians could bring all their supporters together.

Replacing the casualties of Barnet with fit men and assembling an artillery train, he marched across from London to confront them; he was at Cirencester on 29 April and hoped, wrongly, to intercept the Lancastrians at Sodbury. The official Yorkist chronicle *The Arrival of King Edward IV*, written by Nicholas Harpsfield, tells a tale of feint and counter-feint as the Lancastrians sought to avoid Edward, whilst Edward tried to bring them to battle. The key issue was whether the Lancastrians could cross the Severn and thus join with Jasper Tudor. A crucial day of forced marches on 3 May in appallingly hot and dusty conditions saw both armies race to the Severn crossings. Starting from Berkeley, the Lancastrians reached Gloucester first but, finding it held against them, were obliged to continue to Tewkesbury, covering 24 miles in one day. Here they found an unopposed crossing and if they had forded the Severn at once, they might perhaps have avoided a battle; although *The Arrival*, admittedly biased, suggests that Edward would have caught them anyway. Edward had taken the better road along the Cotswold scarp from where he could hold the Lancastrians in sight, and was never more than five or six miles away. Having reached Cheltenham after marching 36 miles in the day, he apparently deployed in battle formation with a view to fighting that evening, bivouacing three miles from Tewkesbury. His arrival and determination to fight, before the Lancastrians could secure Welsh support, made inescapable a battle next day.

The Lancastrian army had first choice of terrain. The battlefield lies to the south of town and abbey, in an area that included the Gastons field identified by Leland: too large an area all to have been utilised by what historians agree were armies of modest size, perhaps 20,000 altogether. On the evening before, *The Arrival* declares, the Lancastrians took up position 'in a close even at the town's end; the town and the abbey at their backs; before them, and upon every hand of them, evil lanes, and deep dikes, so many hedges, trees and bushes, that [made it] right hard to approach them near and come to hands' and which apparently allowed for troop movements invisible to the enemy. Apart from the indication that their backs were to the abbey,[13] none of these features are visible now. It is not possible to safely restrict the Gastons to a particular section of the site. Later, so most historians seem to presume, the Lancastrians moved southwards, taking up a defensive line east-west between a brook and the road to Tredington, whence Edward IV advanced in order of battle.

The course of the battle, in contrast, seems clear enough (Pl.1). Both sides failed to secure their flanks to the west, in the Lancastrian case a wood in which Edward secretly placed 200 spearmen, and in the Yorkist case a small knoll in an enclosed field. Unwilling to attack such a strong position, Edward apparently embattled his own position at a distance from the Lancastrian line, and exploited his superiority in ordnance and archery, to which the Lancastrians could not effectively respond. 'Sore annoyed' by 'a right sharp shower' of gunshot and arrows, whether unable to put up with it or determined on a bolder course, Somerset gave up his defensive position, somehow manoeuvred unseen in front of his own line through paths past the Yorkist vanguard, and fell from the knoll onto the flank of the main Yorkist battle commanded by King Edward himself. Surprise proved not to be enough against the most successful commander in the Wars of the Roses.

> The king, full manly, set forth upon them, entered and won the ditch and hedge against them into the close, and with great violence pushed them up towards the hill, and so also, the king's vanguard, being in the rule of [his brother Richard] the Duke of Gloucester.

Attacked from behind by the hidden spearmen, Somerset's forces were scattered, and the Yorkists enveloped the main Lancastrian battle and dispersed it too. Lancastrians fled westwards into the park, southwards to the millstream—where many were drowned—across what came to be called the Bloody Meadow—where many were killed—and into the town and the abbey.

King Edward proceeded to the abbey (Pl.3)

> To give unto Almighty God laud and thanks for the victory that, of his mercy, he had that day [been] granted and given unto him. Where he was received with procession, and so conveyed throughout the church and the quire to the high altar, with great devotion praising God and rendering unto him convenient laud.

The security risk posed by unreconciled Lancastrians in the abbey would surely have rendered this service impossible. Similarly removing them by force would have desecrated the church and prevented the thanksgiving service. Sanctuary in churches was at that time a well-established means for criminals, traitors, and others threatened by the law or the king to escape punishment. It was the sacrilegious

Fig.3.8 Lancastrian forces seeking shelter in the abbey

murder of St. Thomas à Becket in Canterbury Cathedral that had brought King Henry II to his knees. Edward IV's own queen, chancellor, and other adherents had taken sanctuary at Westminster Abbey and St. Martin's-le-Grand in London during the Readeption. Defeated Lancastrians now hoped for similar immunity (Fig.3.8). Times were changing, however. In 1405 King Henry IV had executed Archbishop Scrope of York for treason. In 1486 Henry VII was to remove traitors from sanctuary at Culham (Berks) and execute them—the sanctuary's charter did not explicitly cover treason. This new doctrine was anticipated in 1471, when *The Arrival* reports that Tewkesbury Abbey lacked any such privilege. It was therefore to Edward's great credit, in Harpsfield's eyes at least, that he freely pardoned them and thus enabled them to leave the church. Harpsfield found nothing strange or to be condemned in the subsequent execution of Somerset and others removed from sanctuary. Execution of defeated noblemen not in sanctuary after battles had become commonplace since that of Edward IV's own father at Wakefield in 1460. Of course, none of them had received written pardons.

It is a strange illogical story because Harpsfield, with his intended audience in mind, has modified it to present what happened in the best possible light. Quite what did happen is less certain. A brief abbey chronicle, presumably written by an eyewitness, tells an incompatible story of how town and abbey were furiously sacked and of killings in both the churchyard and the close.[14] *Warkworth's Chronicle*, though written a decade later, can be squared with both. It reports how Edward, on entering the church, sword in hand, was confronted by a priest bearing the sacrament, who forced him to pardon all those taking refuge. Some of those pardoned nevertheless distrusted the promise, remained and were still in the abbey church the following Monday, when they were removed by force.[15] Whatever the actual details, some violence must have polluted the church since it was out of use for a month until reconsecrated by the suffragan of the bishop of Worcester.

Lords Devon, Dorset, and Wenlock were killed in the battle. Prince Edward of Lancaster may have been slain in the field also,[16] perhaps calling out to his brother-in-law Clarence, or he may have been despatched in cold blood after the battle as a near-contemporary illumination reveals.[17] Somerset, the Prior of St John and others found in the abbey or elsewhere in the town were summarily tried for treason by the constable and marshal of England, respectively the dukes of Gloucester and Norfolk, and condemned to death. A special scaffold was set up in the town for their executions (Pl.2). Each was merely beheaded, Harpsfield records; they were spared quartering—the exhibition of head and quarters on town gateways. They and all those slain in the field, including Prince Edward, were allowed to be buried in the abbey or wherever else their relatives chose. An abbey chronicle records some of their resting places.

Tewkesbury was a decisive victory and once again Edward IV was secure on his throne. His queen emerged from sanctuary with their son, the future Edward V, who acceded 12 years later on his father's natural death. Prince Edward of Lancaster, in contrast, was the last of the direct male line of the house of Lancaster. Somerset and Dorset were the last male Beauforts. With their deaths, there was no longer any advantage to Edward in keeping Henry VI alive—he died soon after the Yorkists returned to London, ostensibly naturally, but most probably violently. With Henry dead and many irreconcilable Lancastrians slain or executed, and Queen Margaret of Anjou in custody, there was no longer any cause for those who remained. Richard III's usurpation was necessary to breathe reality into Tudor resistance.

The Last Lords

Richard Neville, the earl of Warwick, had no son to inherit his estates, only two daughters: Isabel (b.1451) and Anne (b.1456); moreover a nephew was heir to the Neville lands in the North. Following Neville's death, his wife, Anne, should have resumed possession of her own inheritance including Tewkesbury; she was also entitled to jointure and, perhaps, dower. She claimed repeatedly to have petitioned first the king and then parliament for her rights, but to no avail. Instead on 16 April 1471,[18] two days after Barnet, the king had recognized Clarence as sole heir in right of his wife Isabel. Clarence, like his predecessors, was anxious to deny his widowed sister-in-law, Anne, a share of the inheritance. Reportedly he kept her concealed as a kitchen maid in London, whence she was removed (rescued?) by his younger brother Richard, duke of Gloucester. Whilst Richard had been Warwick's ward and therefore knew Anne, his prime motive was to secure her estate. In time Edward IV changed his mind and chose to support Richard, who removed his mother-in-law, the Countess Anne, from sanctuary to put pressure on Clarence. After two years of disagreement which threatened domestic peace, a partition was imposed in 1474 and confirmed by parliament. Gloucester secured the lands in Wales and the North, Clarence those in the west midlands and the rest of England, including Tewkesbury. Tewkesbury and Glamorgan were separated at last. 'This left little or nothing', writes the Crowland Continuator, 'at the disposal of the Countess, the true heiress and lady of Warwick to whom, during her lifetime, the noble inheritance of Warwick and Despenser belonged'. Political expediency prevailed.[19]

Anne, duchess of Gloucester, became Queen Anne in 1483 on the accession of her husband Richard III (1483-5). Both died in 1485, Anne probably naturally (though allegedly by poison) and Richard in battle at Bosworth. Their only known child, Edward, Prince of Wales, died in 1484. On their deaths, their share of the Warwick, Despenser and Salisbury inheritances should have reverted under the 1474 Act to the issue of Anne's sister, Duchess Isabel (Fig.3.3). But she had died at Warwick in 1476, probably from the after-effects of childbirth but allegedly from poison. Her husband, Clarence, had been arrested in 1477, tried on trumped-up charges of treason in parliament, and executed on 18 February 1478. Both were buried at Tewkesbury Abbey in a crypt behind the high altar. They had four children, two of whom predeceased them, leaving Edward, earl of Warwick, born in 1475, and Margaret, born in 1473. Edward was recognized as heir to his mother's and aunt's estates, but he was too close to the crown to be allowed to inherit or marry. Humphrey Stafford's Warwickshire uprising in 1486 was intended to make Edward king but resulted only in Stafford's execution.[20]

Following Richard III's death, Neville's countess Anne, who had presumably spent the last decade in Richard's custody, again petitioned parliament for her rights, unsuccessfully. Late in 1486 Henry VII granted her 500 marks (£333) a year, later redefined as specific properties including Tewkesbury, in return for her resignation of all her hereditary rights to the king. The 1474 Act was reversed. Anne thus provided for her last years at the price of disinheriting her grandchildren. She died in 1492. Her grandson Edward, still styled earl of Warwick, was imprisoned until 1499, when he was executed for treason, and her granddaughter Margaret, countess of Salisbury, was not allowed the Despenser lands. She was executed, supposedly for further treason, in 1541.[21]

The Tewkesbury Estate and Residence

Only two carucates of arable remained in demesne by 1375, and by 1488 everything had been farmed out.[22] There are no intervening accounts for the main manor, although the sub-manors were already leased by 1423. Tewkesbury had become an administrative centre of the Despenser lands in England—it was there that estate officers (ministers) went to have their accounts audited in 1423. Subsequent union with the larger Beauchamp estates led to reorganisation. In 1434 ministers' accounts were audited at Caversham near Reading (Berks.) and from 1439 at Warwick.[23] Indeed, the last lords had relatively little to do with Tewkesbury. If Holm Hill was the lord's chief residence, there is no archaeological evidence that the predominantly 12th-century structure was updated other than cosmetically to late medieval expectations or whether it went wholly out of use and was demolished. Some surviving heraldic Droitwich-style tiles are of mid- to late 14th-century date—it may be significant that the lords held salt pans at Droitwich and that some Tewkesbury tenants owed the service of carrying the salt.[24] There are relatively few 15th-century finds. Much later the Tudor antiquary John Leland suggested that the lodge in the park was an alternative residence, from which Hannan postulated abandonment of the house at Holm Hill in the late 14th century.[25] Since the house itself brought in no income, surviving inquisitions post mortem reveal neither its state of repair nor even its continued existence. The Despensers and their successors seem to have visited Tewkesbury seldom and briefly. Ministers' accounts for Tewkesbury's sub-manors (but not the manor of Tewkesbury itself) contain no convincing evidence that the lords or ladies were in residence in any of the eight random years between 1423 and 1461 for which accounts survive.[26]

Cardiff and Warwick Castles were much more popular residences: so too was nearby Hanley Castle in south Worcestershire, where Elizabeth and Henry Beauchamp were born and Henry died, and where Richard Neville was in residence twice in 1455. Amongst his new Despenser estates, it was not Tewkesbury, but Hanley, that was selected by that great builder Richard Beauchamp, earl of Warwick, to be new built.[27] Earl Richard Neville never resided at Tewkesbury for long, but visited it en route between Wales and Warwick—it was a convenient Severn crossing—both in 1452 and 1453. He was among the Yorkist rebels retreating via Tewkesbury to the bloodless rout at Ludford near Ludlow (Shrops.) in 1459.[28] Other concerns, in Calais and the Channel in the late 1450s and in the North in the 1460s, diverted Neville from Wales and hence from Tewkesbury, but in 1470 it was again on his route southwards as he fled from the North to Exeter and hence into exile. The next lord, Clarence, was at the battle in 1471. He appears both late in 1471 and 1476 at Tewkesbury;[29] it was a convenient stopping off point between his seats at Cardiff (before 1473) and Tiverton (Devon) and those at Warwick and Tutbury (Staffs.). He must surely have attended his wife's funeral at Tewkesbury on 4 January 1477. Richard III's first progress in 1483 brought him to Tewkesbury.[30] Whilst Warwick, Clarence, and Richard could have stayed as guests of the abbey, the abbey chronicle seldom mentions such visits. It did, however, mention that it was in the new chamber of the abbey infirmary that the Duchess Isabel gave birth to her fourth child, Richard, in 1476.[31] It is more likely, therefore, that lords normally overnighted at their own house, in which case it was still habitable if perhaps unsuitable for a longer stay. It may be this residence which by 1487 the Countess Anne had exonerated the lessees from keeping in repair.[32] The lodge was also much too small to accommodate the several-hundred-strong households of Neville and Clarence.

The manor and house should be distinguished from the abbey, which by the 15th century was the grandest or one of the grandest monasteries still with a lay patron. No duke had another to compare. A complement of about 30 monks, and revenues assessed at £1,598 in the 16th century, fully justify the abbot's subsequent elevation to the House of Lords. After 1492 it was deemed of royal patronage. Isabel Despenser, her son Henry, her granddaughter the Duchess Isabel, and Clarence himself all chose to be buried there, rejecting—for instance—the counter claims of St. Mary's, Warwick, and the Neville mausoleum at Bisham Priory (Berks.). Apart from Isabel Despenser's own chantry, to which she added further bequests in 1439, her second husband and son desired chantries there. Richard Beauchamp's endowment was Kinver and Stourton (both in Staffs.), and Duke Henry's was the church of Sherston (Wilts.).[33] Plate and vestments were commonly bequeathed to the abbey. Successive abbots officiated at the christenings, confirmations, marriages and funerals of their lords. Abbot Strensham was godfather to Clarence's son, Edward, and it was he who conducted the particularly grand service of burial for the duchess.

This was the last great event entered in the Founders' Book. Isabel, duchess of Clarence, died at Warwick on 22 December 1476. Her body was removed to Tewkesbury on 4 January, where it was received by Abbot Strensham and other abbots in pontifical robes and the whole convent and was taken in procession to the choir. There, two suffragan bishops conducted a service of nine lessons with the assistance of the abbots, monks, and the dean and chaplains of the duke's own household chapel. Next day three further masses were conducted: a mass of the Virgin in the Lady Chapel, of the Trinity at the high altar, and of Requiem in the choir. A sermon was preached. The body lay in state on its hearse in the choir until 25 January, when her new vault was finished and she could be interred in it.[34] Clarence commissioned a splendid new tomb, for which £373 was due to the abbey on his death.[35] Whatever was achieved has since disappeared. Since the de Clare monuments are also lost, it is not safe to presume that it was never completed. Regrettably we know nothing about the 'worshipful funeral' on 25 February 1478 that King Edward ordered for his unfortunate brother, George. No subsequent lord or lady was to be buried there. The new royal patrons preferred Windsor and Westminster.

CHAPTER 4

The Bones in the Clarence Vault

by Michael Donmall *and* Richard K. Morris

Behind the high altar in Tewkesbury Abbey, beneath an iron grill in the east bay of the ambulatory, steps lead down to the 'Clarence Vault' which is reputed to contain the remains of George, duke of Clarence, his wife Isabel Neville and their infant son, Richard.

George was the third surviving son of Richard Plantagenet, duke of York, born on 21 October 1449. As described in the previous chapter, on 11 July 1469 he married Isabel, the daughter of Richard Neville the Kingmaker, and on the latter's death at the Battle of Barnet in 1471, Clarence took the titles of earl of Warwick and Salisbury. 'False, fleeting, perjur'd Clarence', lord of Tewkesbury, was accused of conspiring against his brother King Edward IV and executed in the Tower of London on 18 February 1478.

His wife Isabel, born on 15 September 1451, pre-deceased her husband by just over a year, dying at Warwick on 22 December 1476, following the birth of their son, Richard. Her body was received at Tewkesbury Abbey on 4 January 1477 and lay in state in the choir until 25 January, after which it was placed in a vault in the ambulatory. It is very probable, though not specifically documented, that the duke was also buried in the same vault in 1478.[1] With regard to the possibility that the infant son, Richard, was buried at Tewkesbury with his mother, there is no certainty. For example, the account of John Rous, the 15th-century Warwick historian, lacks precision but should probably be read as indicating burial at Warwick.[2]

The Bones: Evidence from Life

The likely circumstances of death for both the duke and the duchess are obviously potentially significant for this investigation. For the duke, both Michael Hicks and Pamela Tudor-Craig have found it hard to dismiss out-of-hand the tradition that he was drowned in a butt of Malmsey wine,[3] and Hicks pointed out that a more violent death might well have left some trace on the surviving remains. The duchess is most likely to have died from the after-effects of childbirth; the story that she was poisoned, with the infant Richard, lacks credibility.[4]

However, if Clarence was drowned in a butt of Malmsey, or possibly was stabbed to death, no positively identifiable skeletal trace would be found even if the remains were complete. Skeletal evidence of beheading or of other violence such as a blow to the head sometimes exists, but only where remains are complete. No skeletal evidence would be expected of death following childbirth; neither would any skeletal evidence be expected of an infant child because ossification of the skeleton would be only very partial. Thus the most probable causes of death for the duke and duchess are unlikely to be detectable in an examination of fragmentary remains.

Unfortunately, too, there seems to be no firm evidence for either of them with regard to any distinctive physical characteristics, such as height or any deformity, which might aid the identity of the remains. The impression is gained, however, from Clarence's military reputation that he may have been a large man for his time, like his brother Edward IV.[5] Nonetheless, the most significant fact relevant to the skeletal record is the known age of the individuals concerned. Both were relatively young at death—Clarence was only 28 years old, while his wife Isabel was just 25.

Fig.4.1 The bones and other remains in the glass case (as in 1982)

Examination of the Remains

At the time of examination the bones were preserved in a sealed glass case fixed to the south wall of the 'Clarence vault' (Figs.4.1, 4.4). This was opened on 13 June 1982 in the presence of the vicar, the Revd. Michael Moxon and the glass case removed to a room above the sacristy for examination by Michael Donmall. Subsequent to this examination the entire remains were returned to their cleaned glass case and placed again in the vault.[6]

A mixed assemblage of variably preserved human bones was revealed: parts of two skulls, an assortment of long bones, pelvic and shoulder girdle fragments, parts of the spinal column and some foot bones. There were no remains of teeth or hand bones. From the first it was clear that the remains of at least two individuals were very incomplete. The fragments had been arranged for display, with the two crania resting on the largest long bones (Fig.4.1). Six iron coffin handles, a fragment of flat metal and a nail were also found amongst the bones.

After cleaning, necessary reconstruction of the skeletons was attempted using a water-soluble adhesive. The bones were formally assessed (i.e. morphologically) in order to assign where possible sex, the number of individuals, their pathology, and an estimate of age at death and stature. No scientific tests were undertaken.

In terms of preservation and morphology, the assemblage of bones is consistent with being the skeletal remains of two individuals: a female and a male skull alongside female and male post-cranial (i.e. neck-down) fragments. The likelihood of there being two individuals represented is concluded because no complete or fragmentary bone is duplicated and because of morphological associations between several skeletal elements. However, in spite of this and the fact that the male skull articulates with an atlas neck bone, it was not possible from this examination to determine whether the skull and post-cranial material belong to the same individuals. All that can be said of the remaining bones assigned to each sex is that they may be associated. Evidence in support of this was sometimes suggested by similarities in size, robusticity or preservation. It remains possible therefore that more than two individuals are represented here. Figure 4.2 summarizes diagrammatically the skeletal remains and areas of morphological association.

Estimated Age at Death

Determination of the age at death of persons preserved in the archaeological record has been the subject of much discussion over the years. Up to the age of maturity, estimates can be made with a fair degree of accuracy, based mainly on epiphyseal (growing surface) closure and dental eruption, although even here it is important to recognise that there are differential trends in speed and onset of maturity between population groups. Beyond adulthood most of the changes occurring to the human skeleton are degenerative in nature, such as age-related arthritic changes and dental wear. At best, estimation of age at death from skeletal remains is subject to a wide margin of error, estimates being more accurate if based on several criteria.

Changes to the pubic symphysis[7] are useful, as are degrees of age-related arthritic change occurring to the spine. Cranial suture closure is prob-

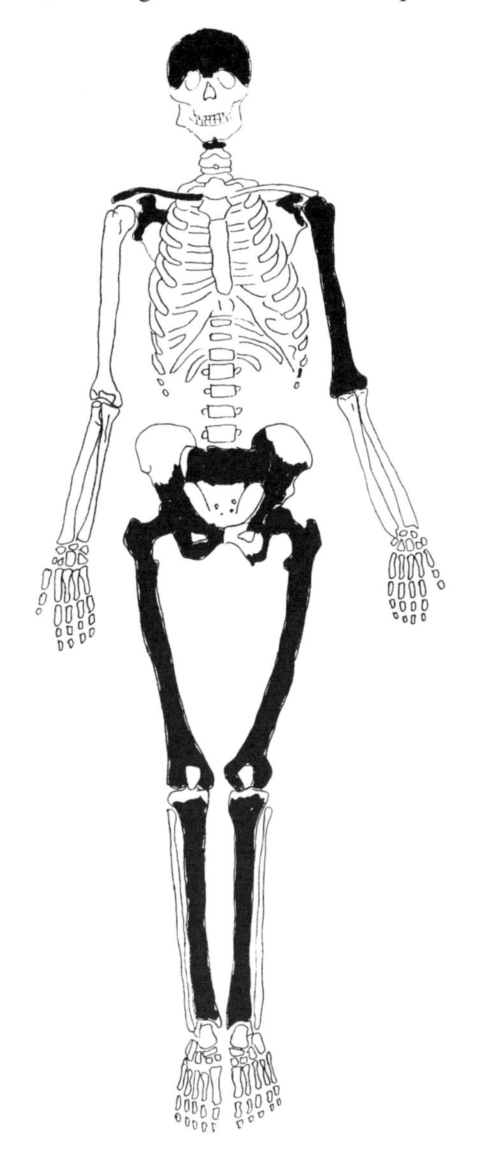

Fig.4.2A Diagramatic representation of the male remains

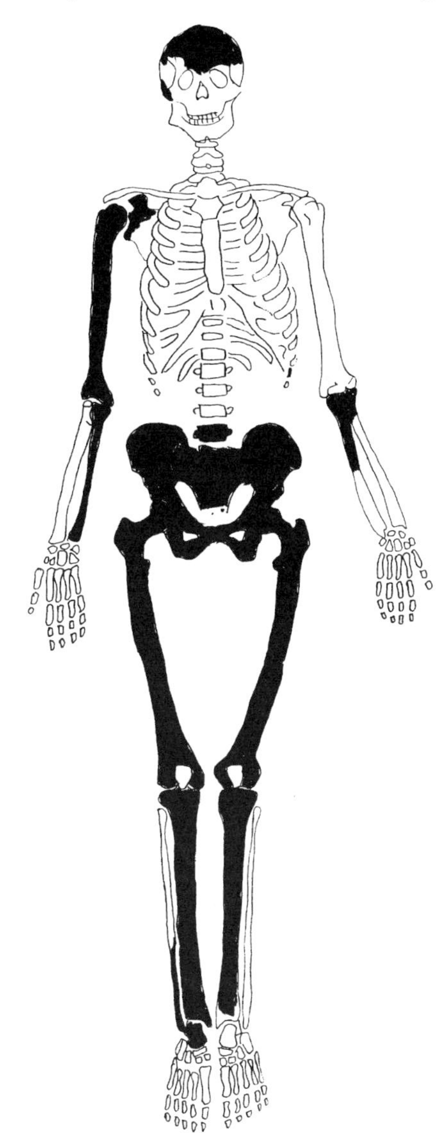

Fig.4.2B Diagramatic representation of the female remains

ably not such a reliable indicator of maturity as was once thought, although it may give an indication of immaturity, maturity and old age, useful in the absence of other more reliable methods. In the case of British pre-medieval material, a system of ageing based on dental attrition, taking account of diet, has been described by Brothwell,[8] and this is useful where appropriate. Other methods include examination of the cortical (outer) layer of bone in skeletal remains, which depends upon morphological changes to the cortical bone which occur as an individual gets older and which can be seen microscopically in thin section.

For the Tewkesbury remains, the absence of any teeth was a major disadvantage, since established methods of ageing by dental attrition would have been broadly applicable. Instead rather gross estimates have been based on a combination of age-related arthritic changes, on the morphology of the pubic symphysis and on the extent of cranial suture closure. These estimates should be considered provisional until more accurate methods of ageing skeletal remains become available.

The remains of the male were clearly those of an adult. Mild, broad-based arthritic changes, as well as the presence of a complete rim to the pubic symphysis with the beginnings of breakdown to the upper ventral surface, and the degree of cranial suture closure, are consistent with at least late middle age, perhaps 40-60+ years.

Likewise, the female remains were clearly of an adult. The presence of advanced, if localised, osteo-arthritic change, coupled with the degree of suture obliteration, suggests an individual of late middle to old age, perhaps 50-70+ years.

Estimations of Stature

These are calculated from regression equations given by Trotter in the absence of more suitable equations.[9] Only bones whose entire length was preserved without reconstruction, have been utilised in these estimates. Thus female stature is based on the length of the female right femur. Male stature is based on the average length of both male femora since these were of slightly different sizes. An age correction has been included in the estimates.

The estimated stature of the male, allowing for his age of 40-60+, is 160.113cm. ± 3.27 cm. (5ft $1\frac{3}{4}$ins – 5ft $4\frac{1}{3}$ins), whilst that of the female, aged 50-70+, is 163.503cm. ± 3.72 cm. (5ft 3ins – 5ft $5\frac{3}{4}$ins). Thus their average estimated heights are about 5ft 3ins and 5ft $4\frac{1}{2}$ins respectively.

Arthritic Change

Despite poor preservation, several examples of osteo-arthritic change were observed. The male skeleton shows minor age-related osteo-arthritic change, most marked in the lower spine. This region of the body, which carries most of the upright weight, is usually the first to become affected by osteo-arthritis and is frequently the worst affected part of the body. The female skeleton shows moderate to severe arthritic change at the elbow and knee joints including 'ivory polishing' at the right elbow, and mild to moderate changes elsewhere, although incomplete preservation of much of the skeleton prevents a complete picture. In the unassigned category of remains, the foot bones alone show mild signs of arthritic change.

Inflammation of the Bone

The pathology of the distal half of the right female tibia and fibula indicates an area of osteitis in the lower right leg. The tibia shows inflammation distally and the formation of an area of periosteal new bone, especially with two plaques laterally. The adjacent area of the fibula is similarly affected and the extent of new bone formation is such that the surface anatomy of this bone is completely altered. On X-ray these inflammatory changes were confirmed as affecting only the periosteum.

The condition can therefore be described as a chronic periostitis ossificans, an infection probably resulting from trauma such as a heavy blow (although no fracture was observed on X-ray), or associated with soft-tissue damage such as ulcer-

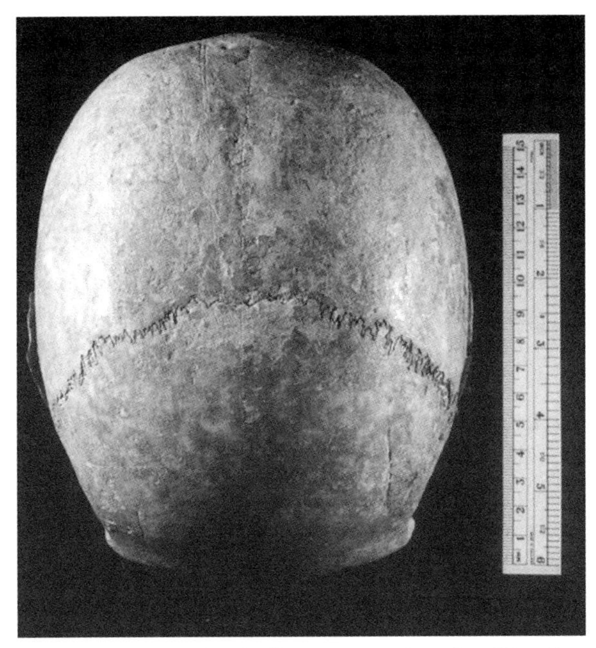

Fig.4.3A Male skull, top view (scale: 15cm)

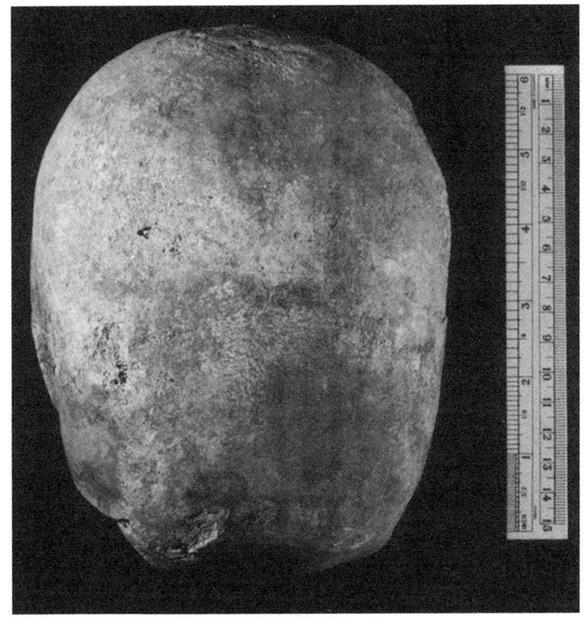

Fig.4.3B Female skull, top view (scale: 15cm)

ation and varicose veins. Similar areas of osteitis are sometimes produced in the treponemal diseases such as yaws and syphilis, as well as in leprosy. However, extensive pathology elsewhere in the skeleton would be required to suggest these conditions as the most likely cause, over and above injury or ulceration.

A further possible example of osteitis is found on the right male femur. A small process on the mesial side of the distal femur, about 4cm. above the medial epicondyle, may indicate an underlying lesion, but it is so small and localised that this seems unlikely.

Hyperostosis frontalis interna

On the internal surface of the female frontal skull bone is a small patch of new bone formation (Fig.4.3B). This condition, known as *hyperostosis frontalis interna*, is sometimes said to occur predominately in females of post-menopausal or advanced years. However it probably results from the natural process of ageing in both sexes and also occurs in between 4-8% of normal young people, probably as a result of auto-immune disorders.

Green Colouration

The pale green staining noted in a rough band across the frontal bones of the female skull suggests that this part of the skull has lain in contact with a metal containing copper traces. This may relate to a head garment worn at burial or could result from processes at a later stage in the obscure history of these remains.

Cranial Markings

The presence of cranial striations deserves some comment. On the male skull they stretch both along the sagittal axis and coronal axes, while on the female skull they pass mainly along the coronal axis (Fig.4.3). It is difficult to suppose that these might have been caused by anything other than some process of post-mortem cleaning such as scraping or brushing. There is a strong suggestion from the historical record that the vault was flooded in 1852 and it may be that the bones at that time became covered by silt or similar material, later to be cleaned before display; probably in 1876 (see below).

Breakages

The mid-shaft breakages (female left femur, right tibia and male left humerus) are recent in origin, the broken surfaces being uneroded and bright, even before this examination. It seems that the femur and tibia had previously been crudely 'mended' by the insertion of sections of wooden doweling into the medullary cavities for purposes of display, the skulls being placed on top of the main long bones in 'classic' pose, with the tibia to the front of the glass case in which the bones had been placed (Fig.4.1). The presence of recent post-mortem breakages to some of the long bones suggests that the breakages may have occurred subsequent to the flooding of 1852 when the waterlogged bones would probably have been somewhat soft and friable. It seems probable that the bones were broken not long before display.

Summary

We can be sure that the bones constitute the remains of a minimum of two individuals, and it seems likely that two adults, a male and a female, are represented here. Both skeletons are incomplete and the bones in a somewhat poor condition. On the basis of the extant remains and with the reservations already described, it has been possible to suggest an age at death of 40-60+ years for the male and 50-70+ years for the female. Physically the male was rather short, being approximately 5 feet 3 inches tall, and the bones showed mild age-related arthritic changes. The female was only a little taller at about 5 feet $4\frac{1}{2}$ inches and showed evidence of more advanced arthritic change, especially to the elbow and knee joints, as well as a severe trauma to the lower right leg resulting in a chronic inflammatory condition in this region.

The paucity of hand, foot and spinal bones has been noted, as has the total absence of teeth and lack of facial bones.[10] The picture is built up of a collection of mainly large bones (limbs, pelvis and cranium) such as might result from a 'rescue' of bones gathered together without due care for individual small bones such as hand, foot, spine and teeth, rather than a systematic collection of remains from distinct coffins.

The Vault and the history of its bones

There can be little doubt that the so-called 'Clarence vault' is the one in which the remains of the duchess were interred in 1477, and probably also of her husband in the next year (Fig.4.4). A frequently cited passage in the abbey chronicle describes the site of the vault in which she was buried as 'behind the high altar, before the door of the Virgin Mary's chapel [i.e. former eastern Lady Chapel], and opposite the door of St. Edmund the Martyr's chapel' (Fig.10.9).[11] The vault is constructed of ashlar, and there seems no reason to question that the existing access to it is the medieval arrangement, by a short flight of steps down from the north. A comparable burial vault, with barrel vaulted roof, survives at St. Albans beneath the monument and chantry of Humphrey, duke of Gloucester (d.1447).[12]

It must be virtually certain that the Clarence vault was also intended to have an elaborate monument over it, but whether anything was ever erected is unknown. Michael Hicks considers that this may have been the purpose of substantial payments by Clarence before his own death, and later by his brothers Edward IV and Richard III.[13] However, Mark Duffy is of the opinion that the tomb was never built.[14] An intention to match the fine series of de Clare and Despenser monuments is a reasonable assumption, by finding new space in the ambulatory in the general manner of King Henry V's chantry chapel at Westminster Abbey (1422-48). Nevertheless, had anything been built, it is surprising that no trace has been identified of its form or appearance in the fabric at Tewkesbury.[15] It was reported in 1826 that the entrance to the vault was covered by 'a large flat blue slab, bearing evident marks of once having been inlaid with brass',[16] but whether this was the original medieval slab intended for monumental brasses, or the result of a reflooring before 1826, is unknown. The 18th-century antiquarians, Atkyns and Rudder, were mistaken in illustrating the tomb of Hugh III Despenser (d.1349) and his wife as that of Clarence and Isabel (Fig.13.5);[17] and it was Samuel Lysons who corrected the error in 1803.[18]

Fig.4.4 The Clarence vault, looking south from the entrance steps (in 2003)

The vault was appropriated in 1709 for the burial of Samuel Hawling, a Tewkesbury alderman; and reopened again in 1729 and 1753 respectively for the interments of his wife, Mary, and son, John.[19] All three were of considerable age at death, according to Bigland's notes: Samuel was 72, Mary 96, and John 86.[20] The next opening of the vault occurred in 1826, attested by a report in the *Gentleman's Magazine* in that year, and by a graffito incised on the east wall by the entrance steps—'[?Henry] Witherington Jun[e] 1826'. The report describes how the Hawlings' burials were quite separate from other bones found in the vault:

> In the north-west corner [i.e. nearest to the entrance] were found two skulls, and other bones, of a man and a woman; but there was nothing by which these relics could be identified as belonging to the unfortunate Duke and Duchess of Clarence, though there is much greater probability in that idea ... The vault was probably ransacked soon after the dissolution of the monastery ... and the bones probably thrown into a corner of the sepulchre, only because they could not be converted into money. This receptacle for royal dust was destined again to be disturbed ... to admit the bodies of Samuel Hawling, his wife and son: the two former lie inclosed by a brick-wall at the south end of the vault [i.e. furthest from the entrance], and that of John Hawling is placed to the northward of his parents, and cased in another brick-wall.[21]

The vault was sealed up again, and it was not until 1829 that the remains of the Hawling family were removed to a new grave to the south of the vault;[22] and presumably the 18th-century brick sub-divisions were removed then as well. At the same time, the male and female bones noted there in 1826, thought to be those of the duke and duchess, were deposited in an 'ancient stone coffin' brought into the vault from elsewhere, and a large stone was placed on top of the coffin to secure its new contents.[23] The three pieces of reused stone, still present on the floor at the south end of the pavement today, were presumably placed there in 1829 to raise the coffin off the floor (Fig.4.4).

On 26 April 1876, the vault was opened again, for a purpose not stated, and a surprising discovery was made:

> Although the vault was perfectly dry, the coffin ... was full of very clear water. A tolerable perfect skull of a small size lay at the head and near it the occiput of another. Many bones lay in the lower part of the coffin. In 1852 there was a great flood in Tewkesbury which reached the Abbey. It is thought that this may have penetrated the crypt, risen above the coffin so as to fill it ... [the water in the coffin] has remained without evaporation for 24 years. This singular immersion for so long in water of the bones of one said to have been drowned in wine seems like a freak of the 'irony of fate'.[24]

This date appears to be when the bones were cleaned by scraping and repaired, as described above. It is also likely that the 'blue stone slab' noted in 1876 was removed, because by 1878 the present iron grills were installed at floor level, which provide access and ventilation.[25] It is not recorded when the coffin was removed and the bones transferred to a glass case, but it is said that the existing metal-framed case was made in Canon Gough's incumbency (1930-42), replacing an earlier wooden-framed case.[26] A glass case was definitely in the vault by the later 1930s, when the bones were inspected by Sir Gavin de Beer.[27] So it would appear that most likely that the move from coffin to case took place in 1876. There is no trace of the coffin today, though there is the bottom half of a medieval coffin lid in the vault, propped up on reused stones against the west wall, rather like an altar; perhaps intended as a shelf for candles. It seems unlikely that this lid is part of the 'large stone' placed over the coffin in 1829, and its introduction into the vault is probably relatively recent.[28]

Of other features present in the vault today, the tiled floor incorporates 15th-century heraldic tiles forming a large cross-pattern on an east/west axis (Fig.4.4). The arms of the cross are created by single rows of tiles, some of which were designed to be used in 4- or 9-tile designs.[29] There is a reasonable possibility that this constitutes the original medieval arrangement. The cross pattern was noted as in existence when the vault was opened in 1876,[30] and previously in 1826. The report in the *Gentleman's Magazine* for that year noted that 'the floor was paved with hard thin square bricks, a considerable number of which were decorated with various devices ...',[31] and Bennett's account asserts that 'in the centre [of the floor] was the representation of a cross'.[32] Moreover, the left (south) arm of the cross is missing its last four tiles, which must have been lost either when the Hawlings vault was inserted in this area in 1709, or when it was removed in 1829. The stone coffin of a child on the west side of the pavement (Fig.4.4, right) was probably introduced into the vault after the 1876 opening, to embellish the story of Clarence's infant son, Richard, being buried at Tewkesbury.[33] There is no mention of a child's coffin when the vault was opened in 1826.

The six coffin handles, the nail and the thin iron plate (which was part of the grip-plate for one of the handles) could all derive from a late medieval burial, though a post-medieval date is also possible.[34] From this evidence, and on the basis of other high-status burials of the period, Julian Litten suggested that each body would have been wrapped in cere-cloth (a waxed linen), then sealed in a mummy-like inner coffin made of lead. This would then be placed in an outer coffin of wooden plank construction, and the metal items—if they derive from the Clarence burials—could be survivals of this coffin furniture. The most relevant information available for a high-status burial at Tewkesbury is Blunt's first-hand account of the discovery of the body of Isabel Despenser (d.1439) under the sanctuary pavement on 5 March 1875. According to this, her body was wrapped in linen and lay in a wooden coffin lined with damask silk, but there was no trace of a lead inner coffin.[35]

Conclusion

The question remains as to whether it is possible to identify these bones as belonging to the 15th century Duke and Duchess of Clarence. It must be emphasised that the positive identification of historical persons from skeletal remains is, in most cases, fraught with difficulty. Indeed, identification with any confidence can only be achieved in one of the following circumstances: where the grave itself is preserved and there is proof of undisturbed burial location; where the incumbent was known to have had particular physical characteristics or pathology, or where DNA or dental evidence can be matched with known records.

On the basis of the morphological examination of the bones, we must conclude that the estimated age of the persons makes it unlikely that these are primarily the remains of George, duke of Clarence, and Isabel his duchess. Considerably older persons are implied by the examination, and it is tempting to think that some bones from the Hawling family members may have found their way into the surviving assemblage. Nor does the estimated height of the male suggest the physical stature of Clarence. However, it remains possible that we have here a mixed assemblage containing the fragmentary remains of more than two individuals, and possibly including some skeletal material from the burials of 1477-78.

In contrast, the historical analysis of the vault's contents has proved slightly more promising. It has been shown that the metal furniture could belong to a 15th-century burial; and that at the first opening of the vault for which we have any descriptive account, in 1826, the bones of a male and a female were noted. These bones were discrete from those of the Hawling family,[36] and in 1829 they were placed in a coffin which was next inspected in 1876. That account suggests that the coffin contained the sort of assemblage noted in 1826 and still in the glass case today—including two skulls. However, this implied continuity is probably deceptive, because the description of one of these skulls as 'perfect' and 'of a small size', if correct, would not seem to fit either of the crania now in the case. So we are left to ponder whether—or to what degree—the final form of the skeletal collection post-dates the opening of 1876.

To try to resolve these issues, further investigations of these skeletal remains are possible, given appropriate permissions and modest resources. For example, radiocarbon dating required too large a sample when we wrote our report, but nowadays it presents one acceptable scientific method which could establish the age of the remains to within about 50 years. This would ascertain whether they include bones from the 15th century. We have also considered the cortical bone ageing method for confirming the estimated age of each individual.[37] However, the most promising technique for identifying Clarence's bones specifically, which has been developed in recent years, is DNA testing. At St. George's Chapel, Windsor—the burial place of Clarence's brother, Edward IV—there exists a lock of hair taken from Edward's remains when his tomb was opened in 1789.[38] This suggests itself as the ideal specimen to compare with samples from the male bones at Tewkesbury, to see if any particular genetic similarities can be established.[39] The quest for the bones of 'false, fleeting, perjur'd Clarence' is far from over.

CHAPTER 5

The Benedictine Foundation and Monastic Life *by* Joseph Bettey

The foundation and rapid development of Tewkesbury as a major Benedictine abbey was due to the wealth and influence of its founder, Robert Fitzhamon, who was one of the greatest and most powerful Norman noblemen during the reigns of William Rufus and Henry I. As a royal kinsman he dominated much of the Severn valley and the Welsh border, controlling both Bristol and the honour of Gloucester. Like many Norman lords in England, Fitzhamon was notable for acts of piety as well as for formidable prowess on the battlefield.

The honour of Gloucester included the patronage of the Benedictine abbey of Cranborne in Dorset, of which the existing priory of Tewkesbury was a subsidiary establishment.[1] The abbot of Cranborne, Gerald, was a well-connected Norman who had been a monk at St. Mary's, Winchester, before being elected abbot of Cranborne in 1086. Soon after the accession of William Rufus in 1087, Robert Fitzhamon, possibly influenced by his wife, Sibilla, and with the co-operation of Gerald, began the building of a new monastery at Tewkesbury. The church and monastic buildings were on a grand scale, only possible with the patronage of such a wealthy founder. Writing soon after 1125, the well-travelled monk, William of Malmesbury, was evidently impressed by the new monastery recording that 'the splendour of the edifice and the hospitality of the monks, attracts the eyes and captivates the minds of visitors'.[2] The generous endowments of Tewkesbury were further increased by Robert Fitzroy, the illegitimate son of Henry I, who married Mabel, the eldest daughter of Robert Fitzhamon, and was created earl of Gloucester. His bequests included the priory of St. James in Bristol which he founded as a cell of Tewkesbury in 1137. The new monastery was thus endowed with widespread additional estates to those already possessed by the existing priory. In 1102 the building work was sufficiently advanced for Abbot Gerald and his monks to transfer from Cranborne to Tewkesbury,[3] leaving only a prior and two monks at Cranborne which was to become a dependent cell of Tewkesbury. The number of monks at Tewkesbury increased rapidly, and 57 are recorded in 1105.[4] Apart from being within the territory controlled by Fitzhamon, Tewkesbury, with its strategic crossing of the Severn, with its important water-borne trade and at the junction of roads, was a much more important and frequented place than remote Cranborne.

Gerald was to prove an ideal choice as the first abbot of the newly founded monastery. He coped with all the challenges of the continuing building work, the large establishment of monks and servants, the administration of the estates, and also attracted further endowments. These included lands and property in Wales which had been conquered by Fitzhamon, including the rich parish church of St. Mary, Cardiff, with eight dependent chapels.[5] Under the organisation which Gerald established, the new monastery rapidly became one of the foremost Benedictine abbeys in England and by the later Middle Ages had become the richest monastic house in the region.

Not least of his achievements was the introduction of an efficient administrative system whereby responsibility for the successful functioning of the monastery and the maintenance of its regular round of services was vested, under the abbot, in five senior monks, known as 'obedientiaries'.[6] Each of these monks was responsible for a department of the monastery. The cellarer had the onerous duty of overseeing all the complex housekeeping. The chamberlain was responsible for the clothing, footwear, bedding and laundry needs of the brethren. The sacrist and the precentor together directed all the services in the monastic church—they took charge of the music, cared for the vestments, lights and service books, and provided everything necessary for divine service. The almoner's duty was to supervise the distribution of alms to the poor. St. Benedict laid stress in the *Rule* on the importance of monastic almsgiving, and most monasteries devoted part of their income to charity. In time more obedientiaries were appointed at Tewkesbury to oversee other aspects of the monastery's work. These included the infirmarer who cared for the sick and infirm monks, the guest-master or hosteller and a novice-master to educate the boys and young monks. In 1109 Abbot Gerald resigned, possibly as the result of some unspecified disagreement with Henry I over property. He returned to his original monastery at Winchester where he died in 1110.[7]

Much information concerning the establishment of Tewkesbury and the subsequent history of the abbey comes from the Annals of Tewkesbury, the original manuscript now being held in the British Library.[8] Making and keeping a chronicle of events and of the affairs of an abbey was a common method used by monks to preserve the heritage and identity of their house, for it could be used to establish history and rights, and resist encroachments on abbey possessions. The Annals were evidently compiled at the abbey during the 13th century. As well as notices of contemporary events, the Annals record the fortunes of the abbey, the succession of abbots and news of neighbouring abbeys. There are numerous references to disputes with the bishops of Worcester and controversy over the abbey's right to execute criminals arrested on its estates. They give only bare outlines of the early history, but become much more detailed after about 1200, until the entries cease in 1263. A prominent feature of the Annals is the account they give of the successive patrons of the abbey, their births, marriages and burials. It was the continuing patronage of the earls of Gloucester, and the notable families of de Clare, Despenser and Beauchamp which ensured that Tewkesbury remained one of the richest and most influential of the Benedictine abbeys. In return for their patronage, protection and gifts the noble families obtained the unceasing prayers of the monks, the right to approve the appointment of abbots, rights of burial in the abbey and the exertions of the abbots in their interests.

The Latin text is precise in dating the entry of the monks into the new monastery, recording under the date 1102: 'This year we entered into the new monastery for the first time' (*Hic primum in novem monasterium ingressi sumus*).[9] In 1107 the Annals record without comment the death of their founder and generous benefactor, Robert Fitzhamon. A year previously, Fitzhamon had obtained from King Henry I a charter confirming to the abbey all the grants which it had secured from Fitzhamon himself and from other donors. The long list of lands and property in the charter includes extensive estates around Tewkesbury, the church of St. Peter in Bristol and the rents from Fitzhamon's demesne lands in Bristol. Robert Fitzhamon died while fighting in Normandy, but his body was brought back to Tewkesbury for burial in the chapter house. He was the first of a long line of patrons who were buried in the abbey and who enriched it with their gifts.[10]

The Monastic Life

> At midnight I will rise to give thanks unto thee ... Seven times a day do I praise thee because of thy righteous judgements.
> *Psalm 119*

Robert Fitzhamon founded the abbey at Tewkesbury as part of the Benedictine order, which was the monastic rule followed by the monks he brought from Cranborne. Tewkesbury thus became the youngest member of a family of wealthy Benedictine monasteries in the region, which included Evesham (founded *c*.989), Pershore (*c*.972), Winchcombe (*c*.972), Malmesbury (*c*.965) and St. Peter's at Gloucester (*c*.1017). Tewkesbury was one of the last major Benedictine foundations, since new orders such as the Cistercians and the Augustinians were to become dominant in the 12th century.

Within a Benedictine monastery the monks followed a closely ordered and regulated existence based on the detailed Rule written by St. Benedict (*c*.480-534). The monks took vows of poverty, chastity and obedience; they abandoned personal possessions, and were pledged to remain within the monastic community. Their day was filled with an unchanging routine of prayer, work and study, of which the most important was the service of God through the liturgy. The monastic day varied from winter to summer, and according to the seasons of the Church's year, but was based on seven services each day, together with the daily celebration of the Mass.[11] The earliest service, Matins, was soon after midnight, and was followed by Lauds. The monks then returned to the common dormitory before rising again for Prime at 6 a.m. in summer or daybreak in winter. As well as the daily Mass, the succession of services throughout the day followed the accustomed course—Terce, Nones, Vespers and Compline. The principal meal of the day was at noon. This was eaten in silence whilst one of the monks read from the Bible or from some theological or devotional work. After the meal the monks had a period of relaxation before Nones. This was followed by a period of study. After Vespers there was a light meal. The last service was Compline and the monk's day ended by 8 p.m., or earlier in winter.

The services were accompanied by elaborate chant and ceremonial which the monks performed from memory. On Sundays and on numerous other days the length and elaboration of services was increased by festivals, saints' days and the commemoration of benefactors. The great festivals of the Church were observed with pomp, ritual and complex liturgy. This maintenance of an unceasing daily routine of prayer and praise to God was the principal function of a monastic community, to which all else was secondary. It was to supply and enhance this that monasteries were endowed and enriched, and it was in order to share in the spiritual benefits of the monks' prayers that bequests were made, endowments given and that burial within a monastery was so highly prized.

Fig.5.1 The processional door from the cloister into the nave of the church used by the monks

For the Benedictine monk the life within the monastery was not one of great austerity, although there were few comforts; but absolute obedience to the abbot, the life-long commitment, celibacy, the total lack of privacy and the long daily services were not a burden to be assumed lightly. The Rule did not impose intolerable demands on a monk: in return for his acceptance of the monastic life, he was assured of clothing, shelter, regular—if not lavish—meals, health care in the monastic infirmary and eventual burial within the monastic precinct. St. Benedict's Rule forbade the eating of meat or game by the monks, except by the sick and infirm. This regulation was relaxed during the later Middle Ages, although flesh was still not eaten during Lent or on fast days.

The Benedictine Rule is insistent that 'idleness is the enemy of the soul', and therefore the monk's day was filled with activities. Time not taken up with the daily performance of the services was spent in reading, the copying of manuscripts or craft work. These activities took place in the cloisters which could be cold, damp and uncomfortable, especially in winter. For most of the day silence was to be observed in the cloisters and during meals in the refectory. The monks assembled daily in the chapter house where a chapter of the Rule was read, monastic business discussed and faults were reproved. The abbot's power within the monastery was absolute, and increasingly abbots of Benedictine monasteries lived apart from their monks and maintained separate households. At Tewkesbury, for example, as well as a separate establishment inside the monastic precinct the abbots enjoyed the use of manor houses at Stanway and Forthampton (see below). The abbot's household staff included a retinue of servants and attendants. As well as periods spent in the manor houses, abbots were frequently absent on monastic business, estate administration, national concerns or royal commissions. During these times the government of the abbey was the responsibility of the prior.

Life within a medieval monastic community was not always peaceful and undisturbed. Many monks entered monasteries as children, and not all were motivated by enthusiasm for an ascetic or religious life. The unchanging routine could be boring, internal feuds were not uncommon, and the daily services must often have been interrupted by building work, pilgrims and eminent visitors. Nonetheless, the number of monks at Tewkesbury remained high. Throughout the 12th and 13th centuries there were some 60 monks in the monastery. During the mid-14th century there was a decline, partly due to the devastating effect of the Black Death of 1348-9 and subsequent outbreaks of the plague. The chance survival of an account roll (Compotus) for 1351 reveals the sharp drop in numbers; there were only 20 monks at Tewkesbury, with a further three at Cranborne and six at St. James, Bristol. By *c.*1400, however, the numbers had once more grown considerably, although they never again reached the pre-plague figures. The number of monks remained at about 40 during the 15th century, and there were 37 monks in 1534. The abbot and 39 monks were awarded pensions when the house was suppressed in January 1540.[12]

The Abbots

As with most monasteries, the history of Tewkesbury abbey is largely known through the succession of abbots on whom the prosperity of the house depended. It was their ability, sanctity of life and political skill that ensured the reputation of the house and a continuing stream of endowments. Among the abbots of Tewkesbury, a few were outstanding for piety, scholarship, organisational skills or for the legacy of fine building work which they left. The success of Gerald has already been noted. Abbot Benedict (abbot 1124-37) left a reputation for sanctity and instituted a Mass in honour of the Blessed Virgin, to whom the monastery was dedicated.

Also exceptional was Abbot Alan, who ruled over the abbey during the years 1186 to 1202. Born in Kent about 1140, Alan was educated in Paris and was pursuing a promising church career in Italy when, in 1174, he turned his back on promotion and entered the ordered life of the Benedictine monastery of Christ Church,

Canterbury, as a novice. At Canterbury he prepared a collection of the letters of Archbishop Becket, who had been murdered in the cathedral church in 1170. His scholarly edition of these letters helped promote the massive surge of interest in Becket and the fervent belief in his sanctity and 'martyrdom' that was to bring so many pilgrims to Canterbury. Alan rose rapidly to be the prior of Christ Church by 1179, and in 1186 he was elected abbot of Tewkesbury. He was highly respected as a scholar, and was employed on various royal commissions, but we know little of his impact upon his monastery. He died in 1202 (Fig.5.2).[13]

Abbot Peter (abbot 1216-32) was particularly aggressive and litigious in pursuit of the abbey's interests. Owing to disturbances in Wales and Ireland, he faced problems over the abbey's lands there, and in 1224 he sold some of the Irish properties to the bishop of Dublin. He was involved in a series of controversies with the bishop of Worcester over rights of episcopal visitation and property disputes. These were described in the Annals as 'many persecutions by the bishop'.

Fig.5.2 Tomb slab of Abbot Alan (as depicted in Sepulchral Slabs and Crosses of the Middle Ages *by E.L. Cutts)*

One cause of complaint by the abbot was that the bishop burdened the abbey with excessive expenses by holding many of his ordinations and synods in the abbey church.[14] In 1224 the abbot travelled to Rome to put his case in person to the pope and, according to the Annals, received absolution. Not until 1226 did the abbot return, and was received with great honour by the monks. He was then involved in a long dispute with the bishop over the appropriation of the parish church at Fairford by the abbey. When the abbot refused to relinquish the church he and his whole monastic community were excommunicated in 1231. With the dispute unresolved, Abbot Peter died in 1232 and was buried by the monks within the monastic church at Tewkesbury. The bishop then ordered that the abbot's body should be removed from the church and issued a further sentence of excommunication. The matter was finally resolved through the conciliation of Hubert de Burgh, guardian of the abbey's patron, Richard de Clare, who was a child, and the abbot's body was allowed to remain in the church.[15]

One of the most notable abbots was Robert III of Forthampton (abbot 1232-1254) who was a fierce defender of the abbey's rights, and active in developing the resources of its estates. Unlike the neighbouring abbey at Hailes, Tewkesbury had few relics with which to attract pilgrims and their offerings. In 1235, through the efforts of Abbot Robert, the abbey was given a curious assortment of relics by Isabel of Gloucester. These included a stone from Calvary, a bone of St. Wulstan, the blood and hair of St. Thomas the Martyr, and most remarkable of all, the stake or base into which the Cross of Christ had been fixed (*... de stipite in quo crux Christi fixa fuit*). Thereafter a Feast of the Holy Relics was celebrated each year on 2 July. The Feast grew rapidly in popularity and in the revenue it generated. Several miracles were reported to have taken place as a result of pilgrimages made to the relics.[16]

Few of the later abbots left much indication of their personality. Like the monks, many came from the district and bear the names of local towns and villages, such as Norton and

Cheltenham, Kempsey and Strensham (Worcs.), and Chesterton (Warks.). Not all maintained the strong rule established by the early abbots. The entries in the Annals were allowed to cease during the abbacy of Richard Norton who died in 1282. He was severely criticized during a visitation by Bishop Giffard in 1278, who ordered the abbot and other monastic officials to fulfil their duties with more care.[17] Criticisms were also made during the abbacy of Thomas Kempsey (abbot 1282-1328). Kempsey did have the initiative to go to Rome in 1316 where he successfully pleaded Tewkesbury's cause in a long-running struggle to appropriate the parish church of Fairford. For the hazardous journey he was provided with letters of safe conduct by King Edward II. A major reason for desiring the income from Fairford was to finance the continuing expense of building work. In spite of episcopal criticisms and failure to maintain a consistently high standard of monastic life, costly additions continued to be made to the abbey church and to its furnishings.[18]

Abbot Thomas Chesterton, who died in 1389, was harshly criticised by Bishop Henry Wakefield during a visitation in 1378. Chesterton passed most of his time at his manor house at Stanway, and spent large sums on rebuilding and enlarging the house, barn and other buildings. Abbot Thomas Parker (abbot 1389-1420) was responsible for erecting a chapel over the tomb of the founder, Robert Fitzhamon, and may have built the abbey gatehouse which survives. Abbot John Strensham, who died in 1480, was abbot at the time of the Battle of Tewkesbury in 1471 and protected the Lancastrian fugitives who fled to the abbey for sanctuary.[19] Later he led his monks in procession to welcome the victorious Edward IV who came to the abbey church to give thanks for his triumph. Abbot Richard Cheltenham (abbot 1480-1509) spent much time at Stanway where he greatly enlarged and virtually rebuilt the manor house. The eventful career of the last abbot, John Wiche or Wakeman, with its unexpected twists and turns of fortune, is described in Chapter 7.

Episcopal Visitations

For our knowledge of daily life in the monastery we are dependent upon the brief entries in the Annals or upon the registers of the bishops of Worcester and the accounts of their visitations of the abbey. It is clear from the evidence of the visitations that, like many other monastic institutions, St. Mary's Abbey fluctuated between periods of austerity when the Rule was carefully observed, the estates and endowments profitably managed and the buildings well maintained, and periods when human weakness and the inevitable tedium and tensions of monastic life led to slackness, indiscipline and neglect. It has to be remembered, however, that bishops during their periodic visitations were concerned with finding fault and reproving abuses, and that the careful performance of daily services, appropriate conduct of the brethren and charity towards their neighbours never provokes any comment. Faults are meticulously recorded, but praise is never given. Most of the monks remain as shadowy figures, only appearing in the surviving records when admonished for some fault or when involved in some scandalous conduct.

It is notable that when Bishop Walter Cantilupe visited the monastery in 1251 and again in 1253, he found nothing amiss. The Annals proudly comment that in spite of careful inquiry (*maximum scrutinium*), examining each of the monks in turn, the bishop could find nothing wrong. The mid-13th century was a prosperous and well-ordered period in the life of the abbey. As already mentioned, during the years 1232-54 the abbey was under the energetic rule of Abbot Robert of Forthampton, an able administrator who devoted himself to the interests of the abbey.[20] The well-ordered life of the monastery which was reported in the bishops' visitations did not long survive his death in 1254. A visitation made in 1279 by Bishop Godfrey Giffard, found much to criticize. The bishop was indignant at the waste of resources, the failure of the obedientiaries to perform their duties and, above all, at the gluttony and drunkenness of the monks. Instant reform was ordered, and the bishop reminded the community that 'they should eat to live and not live to eat'. A few weeks later he wrote to the abbot to reinforce the message. Clearly the bishop was concerned about the state of the abbey, and made further triennial visitations in 1284, 1287 and 1290.[21]

Although Benedictine abbeys such as Tewkesbury were subject to periodic visitations by the bishop of the diocese, the monastic communities were protective of their rights and resisted all attempts to undermine them. When Bishop Giffard died in 1302, the prior of the monastic cathedral of Worcester demanded to exercise his right of visitation during the episcopal vacancy. When he arrived at Tewkesbury he was refused admission on the grounds that the monastery had recently been visited by the bishop. A typical ecclesiastical dispute ensued, with the prior of Worcester excommunicating the abbot and principal monks, an appeal to Canterbury, inquiries, court proceedings and finally a compromise settling the dispute. In another episcopal vacancy during 1308, the prior of Worcester came again to Tewkesbury, and this time was admitted peaceably.[22]

Interesting light is thrown on the democratic process of electing an abbot in 1347 and again in 1361. In August 1347 the prior of Tewkesbury, together with 39 monks, met in the chapter house to elect a successor to Abbot John Coles. A full account is given in the register of Bishop Wolstan de Bransford (1339-49). Thomas Leigh, the prior was unanimously elected. Approval was obtained from Hugh III Despenser, the patron, and from the bishop. After enquiries had confirmed that Thomas Leigh was 'in priest's orders, legitimate, circumspect, adequately lettered, of praiseworthy life and character', he was formally installed as abbot.[23] When Abbot Leigh died on 7 October 1361, the monks then had to seek the permission of their patron, Lord Edward Despenser, to elect a new abbot. This secured, the monks met in the chapter house on 24 November for the election. After a reading from the bible, the hymn *Veni Creator* was sung and there was a long discussion of possible candidates. A committee of senior monks was then appointed to elect that day an abbot 'from themselves or others of the monastery' before 'the darkness of the night'. Eventually the cellarer, Thomas de Chesterton, was elected. This was announced in the chapter house, approved by all the monks, who individually gave their assent, and the election was welcomed with the singing of *Te Deum Laudamus*.

Fig.5.3 The high altar table, with the 13th-century Purbeck marble slab or mensa, *the largest medieval altar slab surviving in England*

The next stage in the process provides a rare glimpse of the way in which the atmosphere of a medieval monastery differed from the modern notion of appropriate behaviour in church. During the singing of the *Te Deum* the new abbot was lifted up by the monks and carried triumphantly into the church. There he was placed upon the altar, while the sub-prior announced the election to 'a great multitude' of clergy and laity assembled in the nave. The abbot was a major landowner in the district, with great influence over the lives of people living in Tewkesbury and the locality, so that the election of a new abbot was a matter of immense local interest. Finally, the bishop of the diocese was asked to confirm the election, and this was duly granted on 10 December 1361.[24]

Thomas de Chesterton remained as abbot until his death in 1389. He was evidently not a forceful head of the house, and under his rule the abbey's affairs appear to have greatly deteriorated. This emerges strongly from the record of a visitation conducted in 1378 by Bishop Henry Wakefield, who found a scandalous neglect of some aspects of the monastery's affairs. No yearly record of the abbey's finances was kept. The obedientiaries were not even-handed or equitable in their treatment of the monks, favouring some and disciplining others. The monks were badly fed, with poorly-made bread and inferior ale. The infirmary was neglected, there was no doctor and sick monks were inadequately cared for. Visitors to the abbey, including relatives of the monks, were not properly welcomed or looked after. The education of young monks was unsatisfactory. The abbey bell-tower was in a dangerous condition and likely to fall. The bishop also condemned the practice whereby the monks were given an annual break from the monastic regime. They were allowed to go to the nearby abbey property at the Mythe from Sunday to the following Friday. The bishop declared that this was too long and ordered a much shorter annual holiday. Faced with such an unsatisfactory situation at the abbey, the bishop ordered that the worst excesses should be improved within ten days.[25] There is no evidence as to whether the bishop's orders were obeyed.

An Account Roll 1351-2 & the Kitchener's Roll 1386

Most of the records relating to Tewkesbury and its estates have vanished. The following two stray accounts are therefore of great value in shedding light on daily life in the monastery. The first is a brief Latin account or Compotus kept by the chamberlain, William of Bristol, in 1351-2. This appears to relate primarily to the priory or cell of St. James in Bristol. Nevertheless it gives some indication of the way in which Tewkesbury Abbey and its dependencies continued to function in the aftermath of the Black Death of 1348-9. The number of monks at Tewkesbury had shrunk to 20, with a further six at Bristol and three at Cranborne; the Roll records payment for 29 brothers now in the monastery (*Soluti xxix Fratribus tam in Monasterio*). The chamberlain's income amounted to £71 18s. 11d., derived from manors, lands, parish churches and some sales. The sum of £7 13s. 4d. was received for 115 wether sheep sold for 16d. each; a horse was sold for £2. These were sold at Bristol fair, the valuable site of which belonged to the priory of St. James. The expenditure of £71 5s. 10d. included clothing for two boys, perhaps the only ones remaining at the abbey after the plague. A vicar choral was paid 8s. for his year's salary, and two cobblers were paid 8s. each. Drinks for the servants at Christmas cost 2s. Repairs were made to the kitchen and a rope was bought for the well. A workshop was set up in the cloisters for the cobblers; thread and other things were provided (*In filo pro sartoria videlicet sutoria et cetera vs iiid*). No doubt leather for the cobblers came from the abbey tannery. Malt, hemp-seed and bran for the monastic horses were purchased. A major expense was the sum of £10 5s. paid for 120 wether sheep bought at Bromyard (Worcs.). The incomplete and difficult medieval Latin of the account at least illustrates that life at the abbey was proceeding normally in spite of the catastrophic impact of the plague.[26]

The Kitchener's Roll survives for the year ending Michaelmas 1386 and records the business of providing food for the monks and their numerous servants.[27] It also lists foodstuffs brought to the abbey and later sold in the town. The long Latin Roll provides a remarkable insight into the produce of the monastic estates, the sales of surplus foodstuffs, the purchase of additional supplies for the monks' kitchen, and gives an indication of the diet of the monks and the large number of monastic servants. The kitchener (*coquinarius*) was Thomas Carsyntoun (or Carsington). His income was derived from property rents, sales of wool, lard, tallow, livestock, skins and the profits of the abbey's tannery. The rent from the manor of Great Washbourne was specifically assigned to the costs of the monks' food. Expenses included large purchases to supplement the produce of the monastic manors. It can be assumed that there were some 40 monks and possibly as many servants employed in and around the monastery. In addition there was the separate establishment of the abbot, and possibly some scholars and visitors who would have to be fed, and some food would have been given to the poor at the abbey gate. Even so, the amounts listed in the Roll are prodigious. During the year the kitchener accounted for 73 bullocks, 3 cows, 18 calves, 216 sheep, 135 hogs, 29 porkers and 60 sucking pigs. Great numbers of poultry were consumed, as well as pigeons and more than 70,000 eggs.

Although it is of great interest in giving details of the domestic life in a major monastery, the Kitchener's Roll also provokes several questions. The monastic establishment alone could not have consumed all this food. Was some food sold in the town, perhaps at the market outside the abbey gate? Some may have been given to the poor, but there is no evidence of this. Most puzzling of all is the fact that only eight years earlier Bishop Wakefield's visitation had complained that the monks were badly fed. The contemporary evidence provides no answers to these questions.

No doubt large quantities of salmon were provided by the abbey's own fisheries on the Severn, but in addition there were many purchases of eels, herrings, cod, ling, plaice, hake and other fish. Salt fish was purchased in Bristol. Spices purchased for the kitchen included pepper and saffron, although there is no mention of salt. Many supplies came from the abbey's own granges or farms at Stanway, Forthampton, Ashton, Walton, Fiddington, Ampney Crucis and Washbourne. Other payments were made for cheese, firewood, utensils, repairs to the pigsties and for servants' wages. The servants mentioned included the convent cook, the household cook, the abbot's cook, the keeper of the larder, the gardener, porter, scullion, cook's boy, the keeper of the vineyard and servants employed in the bakery, brewery and mill. The variety of items purchased, the amount of foodstuffs consumed and the number of servants employed about the kitchen show clearly the size and complexity of the monastic establishment and the expertise required in its efficient administration.[28] It also shows that whatever austerities the monks endured, they did not go short of food.

It is clear from the Kitchener's Roll that the Tewkesbury granges, especially Stanway, supplied great quantities of food to the abbey kitchen. Even so, Abbot John Coles must have been straining credulity when he complained to the Crown in 1340 that 11 named individuals from the locality had broken into his grange at Stanway and stolen 20 horses, 20 mares, 100 oxen, 40 bullocks, 100 cows, 40 heifers, 150 swine and 1,000 sheep, worth a total of £300.[29] By the 15th century, most of the granges, except Stanway, had been let to tenants, and the monks depended for their livelihood almost entirely upon rents rather than upon direct farming.

Income and Appropriations

The two main sources of the abbey's income were the rents from the ancient endowment of estates, lands and properties, and from the appropriation of parish churches. Many of the estates formed part of the original endowment of the abbey and are listed in the charter of 1102. Property included the manor of Stanway, lands at Toddington, Washbourne, Ampney Crucis, Fiddington and elsewhere in the district, lands in Wales at Llantwit Major (Glam.) and Cardiff, mills at Tewkesbury, fisheries on the Severn, and town properties in Tewkesbury and Bristol. Parts of two of the abbey's farms or 'granges' still survive. One is at Llantwit Major, where there are the well-preserved remains of a circular dovecote and a gatehouse (Fig.5.4); the other is at Stanway, where the abbey maintained a large sheep flock, and there was a fulling mill, three corn mills and a large 14th-century barn, as well as the manor

Fig.5.4 The 13th-century gatehouse at Llantwit Major. The passage has been blocked

The other major source of income came from the parochial tithes of churches appropriated by the abbey. By this arrangement the abbey became the rector of the parish and received the greater part of the tithes, while appointing a vicar or secular priest at a modest salary to minister to the spiritual needs of the parishioners. Like many other abbeys, Tewkesbury had an insatiable appetite for appropriation, and many ingenious reasons were put forward. For example, in order to justify the appropriation of Fairford in 1276, the abbot and monks complained to Pope Gregory X of the heavy expenses of hospitality and the dangerous condition of their buildings. Such complaints were used by many monastic houses when pleading for additional income and are not necessarily to be taken at face value. In 1314 they were given licence to appropriate

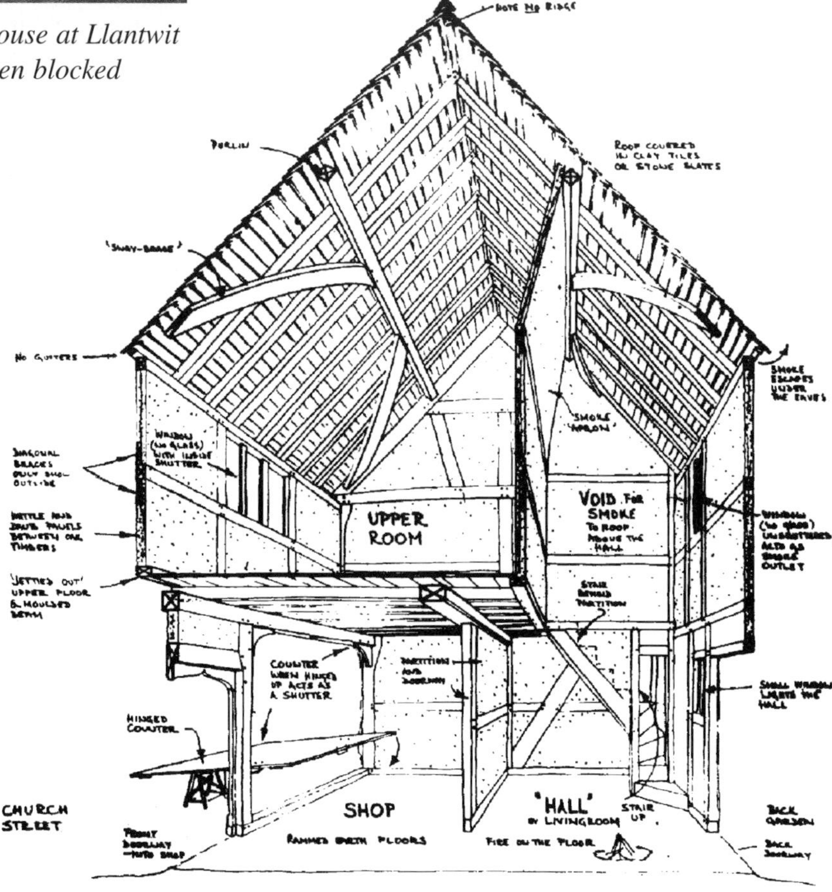

Fig.5.5 Cut-away reconstruction of a typical interior in one of the medieval shops in Church Street, Tewkesbury

house which provided an occasional residence for the abbot. Only the barn survives; the mansion was rebuilt on the foundations of the abbot's house by the Tracy family (Fig.7.1). An example of the way in which the abbey exploited all possible sources of revenue is the row of 24 cottages to the south of the abbey precinct, built about 1450 as a speculative development to produce income for the monastery (Fig.5.6). Erected against the abbey precinct wall, they were fitted up as shops facing the street and were let to merchants and traders who clustered at the abbey gate. The restored counter and shutters can now be seen within one of the timber-framed buildings (Fig.5.5).[30]

Fig.5.6 The former medieval shops at Nos 41-48 Church Street as they are in 2003

Thornbury on the grounds of losses by fire, heavy debts and attacks on their rights by enemies. Llantrisant (Mon.) was appropriated in 1345, Tarrant Monkton (Dorset) in 1439 and Sherston in 1471. There were numerous others, many at a distance from Tewkesbury, so that the only contact the parishioners would have had with the abbey was the diversion of the major part of their tithes for the benefit of the distant monks.[31]

Tewkesbury also possessed three dependent 'cells' or subsidiary houses. Cranborne remained part of Tewkesbury's possessions until the suppression. The wealthy priory of St. James in Bristol, founded in 1137, remained a cell of Tewkesbury until the end. In 1442 Tewkesbury acquired the alien priory of Goldcliff in Monmouthshire, but in 1450 it was granted by Henry VI to his new foundation at Eton. In 1462 Tewkesbury was compensated for this loss by a grant of the priory of Deerhurst by Edward IV. These subsidiary houses were served by monks from Tewkesbury and contributed valuable revenues to the mother house.[32]

Finally, there is little surviving documentary evidence concerning the abbey during the last decades of its life. In October 1498 Roger Church, acting as deputy for the prior of Worcester, carried out a visitation of the abbey. He recorded the names of Abbot Richard Cheltenham and 32 monks. No serious faults were found, but the abbot was criticised for failing to provide an inventory of the goods, chattels and jewels and he was ordered to supply these before Christmas. Abbot Cheltenham had been in office for 18 years and was possibly not as energetic or enthusiastic as he had once been, although he remained as abbot for another 11 years.[33]

Throughout the early 16th century the life of the abbey appears to have continued without provoking any comment in the contemporary records. The number of monks increased slightly, and had reached 39 by 1534. Outside the walls of the monastery, however, theological views and attitudes were changing rapidly. In universities throughout Europe the teaching of the Church on matters such as purgatory, pardons, veneration of the saints and Masses for the dead was being questioned. The Gloucestershire man, William Tyndale, was beginning his life's work on translating the New Testament and part of the Old Testament into English, a work which was to have profound effects throughout Britain. Meanwhile, the Crown and the gentry were casting envious eyes upon the wealth of the monasteries and upon their widespread estates. The impact of these significant new trends upon the future of the monasteries, and in particular upon Tewkesbury, will be explored in Chapter 7.

CHAPTER 6

The Founders' Book *by* Julian M. Luxford

As one of England's wealthiest and most populous religious houses during the later Middle Ages, Tewkesbury Abbey is likely to have possessed a large and diverse library. Unfortunately, we know practically nothing about it: just 11 manuscripts—a number of them fragmentary—and two printed books are attributable to it, and the antiquarian bibliophile John Leland recorded only five additional titles when he visited the monastery sometime between 1535 and 1540.[1] Three of the surviving manuscripts were displayed at the abbey in 2002, in an exhibition organized by Carolyn Methven: the book that is the subject of this chapter; an early 12th-century copy of St. Jerome's commentary on Jeremiah;[2] and an unillustrated missal of the 13th century with early 14th-century additions.[3] The other Tewkesbury books that have come down to us, roughly in order of age, are as follows: a later 12th-century theological collection, mostly writings of St. Anselm of Bec, once possessed by the renowned Abbot Alan (1186-1202);[4] a liturgical calendar and annals of *c.*1200, once part of a larger book;[5] a fragment of an early 13th-century book of English history and topography;[6] another liturgical calendar, of the mid-13th century, with a 15th-century metrical list of English kings (fol.5r) and notes concerning services (fol.5v);[7] a psalter of *c.*1260 with nine historiated initials of high quality;[8] the Tewkesbury Annals and cartulary of the 1260s;[9] a late 13th-century copy of Alexander of Bath's moralizing commentary on the writings of the Evangelists;[10] a genealogical roll with chronicle, which is discussed below; a copy of Bartholomew the Englishman's encyclopedic *De proprietatibus rerum* ('On the Properties of Things'), printed in Strasbourg in 1480;[11] and a large volume of John Duns Scotus' works, printed in fascicles at Venice in the 1490s.[12] While these few volumes reveal most of what we know about the history and liturgical life of the abbey, they represent a mere sliver of Tewkesbury's medieval textual culture.

Fortunately for posterity, the Tewkesbury manuscript now bearing the shelf mark MS. Top. Glouc. d.2 in the Bodleian Library at Oxford numbers among these survivals, and this ranks as one of the most interesting and colourful of all late medieval English monastic books. The text represents our single most important source of information about the abbey during the 14th and 15th centuries and, as a homegrown product written and illustrated by local monks, it has a particular claim on the attention of those involved with Tewkesbury today. It will be referred to throughout this chapter by its familiar name, the Founders' Book, as it does not carry a medieval title.[13] While the Founders' Book is known to historians and art historians alike, it has never received the analysis it deserves.[14] It is hoped that this chapter will in some way redress this state of affairs.

Physical description and dating

Like all other surviving Tewkesbury manuscripts, the Founders' Book is written in Latin on parchment. It is relatively short, containing only 46 folios, the first and last of which are flyleaves. All folios have been individually mounted on cards, probably at the last binding, and there are no quire signatures: a collation of the gatherings is thus impossible. The leaves measure 24.5 x 17.5cm., with the exception of fols.12, 16 and 38, which are smaller. The binding, in brown morocco leather, is of mid-19th century date. The manuscript contains five distinct 'books' (*libri*), which will be called chapters for the sake of clarity, and was written by four different but contemporary scribes. All of the writing is cursive except for the illustration titles of chapter 4, which are in a red textualis (i.e. 'Gothic' script).

Chapters 1 (fols.2r-5r), 2 (fol.5r-v) and 5 (fols.42v-45v) are historical narratives, the last two based substantially on abbey muniments. All are currently unpublished. Chapter 1 is written in a casual anglicana hand, and chapter 2 in a neater 'archaizing' script imitating 12th- and 13th-century writing (Fig.6.1).[15] Chapter 5 begins in this same old-fashioned hand, but the scribe gives up after two sides and finishes off in the cursive script to which he was more accustomed. Chapter 3 (fols.6r-7v) is a document—the 'great charter' of Tewkesbury. It is written in a neat secretary script. Chapter 4, the illustrated chronicle of the abbey's founders and benefactors (fols.8v-42r), is mostly written in an anglicana hand distinct from that of chapter 1 (Fig.6.4). However, the secretary script of chapter 3 also occurs, and actually completes the chronicle (fols.37r-40v). It has been thought that the passages in secretary were added later, but both scribes of chapter 4 were obviously working closely with the illustrator.[16] In total there are 24 figure illustrations and 121 coloured coats of arms. The colours employed are white, black, red, yellow, blue, grey-blue, two shades of green, brown, and pink. All of the illustrations are in chapter 4 except for the representation of William, second earl of Gloucester, in chapter 3.

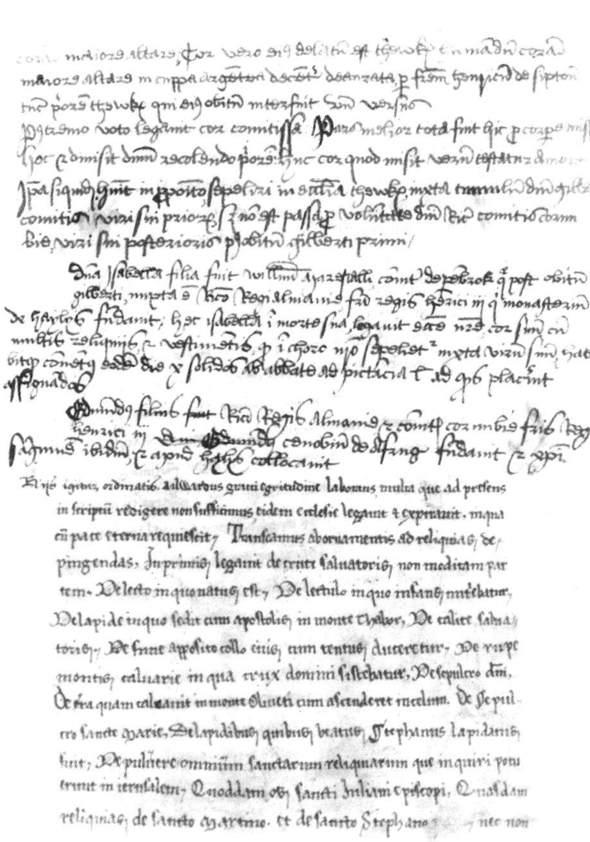

Fig.6.1 Oxford, Bodleian Library MS. Top. Glouc. d.2, fol.5r. Here, the casual anglicana script of chapter 1 gives way to the archaizing hand in which chapter 2 and the beginning of chapter 5 are written

Although there is a lack evidence for precise dating, it is most likely that the Founders' Book was compiled during the first quarter of the 16th century. A *terminus a quo* is provided by the notice in chapter 4 (fol.37v) of the appropriation to Tewkesbury by Henry VII of the church of Great Marlow in Buckinghamshire, which occurred on 11 August 1494.[17] The styles of handwriting are all consistent with a date *c*.1500-25 as are the costumes represented in the figure illustrations. For example, the feathered bonnet of Robert Fitzhamon and the gabled hood of his wife Sybil, hanging well down over her shoulders behind, with embroidered lappets falling to breast-level in front, are typical of the early 16th century, but not so of the later 15th (Fig.6.2). The very full sleeves of Sybil's gown, slashed at the

Fig.6.2 Oxford, Bodleian Library MS. Top. Glouc. d.2, fol.13r. Robert Fitzhamon and Sybil, his wife, holding a model church symbolic of their patronage of Tewkesbury Abbey's reconstruction

shoulders and elbows, and her studded belt tipped with metal, reinforce the impression.[18] Explicitly similar costume appears in contemporary manuscripts such as the Westminster Tournament Roll (1511) and, closer to home, the pedigree roll of the Gloucestershire family of Dennis (*c*.1520), both now kept at the College of Arms, London.[19]

The 'family' of the Founders' Book

The Founders' Book was not *sui generis*. It belonged to group of cognate manuscripts, and setting it in context will suggest the importance of its material to Tewkesbury's monks. This, of course, informs our evaluation of the manuscript, and our understanding of its makers. To begin with, it seems reasonable to posit the existence of a now lost chronicle containing facts about the abbey's founders and benefactors out of which the surviving texts evolved. The 13th-century Annals and cartulary do not contain enough information:[20] some other record must have been kept. In all likelihood, chapter 1 constitutes a part of it. Chapters 2, 3 and 5 are obviously early compilations as well, containing no post-13th-century information.

The earliest surviving written evidence for the development of the chronicle of chapter 4 lies in a parchment armorial roll (Oxford, Bodleian Library MS. Lat. misc. b.2 (R), dorse), once the property of the abbey.[21] This was produced by a single artist not earlier than 1475, as it includes the arms of Edward Plantagenet, son of George duke of Clarence, born in February of that year. There is also an armorial 'key' in the left-hand margin of the fourth and fifth membranes, provided to explain the complicated quarterings of Edward's arms (Pl.5). The 38 coats of arms here were the basis of those included in the Founders' Book. Edward Plantagenet's arms and the armorial key—the latter an exceptional feature—were both copied, probably directly, from one to the other. The roll also contains an abbreviated version of the chronicle, which breaks off at 1400.[22]

British Library MS. Cotton Cleopatra C.III, fols.210r-228r, is an unillustrated Latin chronicle of the founders and foundation of the church of Tewkesbury copied out *c*.1550. It is through printed editions of this manuscript that the abbey's later medieval history has become widely known.[23] The text of Cleopatra C.III must have been at Tewkesbury before the monastery's dissolution because John Leland extracted the account published in his *Itinerary* from it.[24] Yet it is not the same as the text of the Founders' Book. It lacks chapters 1, 2, 3 and 5, and includes two items—a 22-line metrical epitome of the chronicle (fol.225r), and a list in Latin and Middle English of those killed in the Battle of Tewkesbury (fols.226r-228r)—not occurring in the Founders' Book.[25] The chronicle is largely identical to chapter 4, but its first sentence differs, naming King Coenred of Mercia (d.716) as well as Æthelred (d.*c*.716) and Æthelbald (d.757),[26] and it omits two sections altogether: a descent of the earls of Normandy from pre-Christian times (fols.11v-12v), and the passage mentioning the battles of Barnet and Tewkesbury, and the grant of Great Marlow (fol.37r-v). There are many other minor discrepancies. Thus, there were at least three versions of the chronicle (roll, Founders' Book and the text represented by Cleopatra C.III) existing at the abbey before the Dissolution.

There is ample evidence that the Founders' Book remained important after the Dissolution. There exists, for example, an incomplete copy made *c*.1550-75 (British Library MS. Additional 36985), which contains chapters 1, 2, 3, and 4 down to 1442, plus all but two of the figure illustrations and most of the armorials.[27] Excepting certain corrections and condensations, the scribe copied his exemplar word for word. His figure illustrations, too, are passable imitations of the originals (cf. Figs.6.2 and 6.3), although neither they nor the heraldry are coloured. This was not the only copy made. In 1697, Sir Henry St. George possessed a 'Register of Tewkesbury, following the truly and thoroughly examined original' (*Registrum Tewkesburiense, secundum originale vere et perfecte examinatum*): the same title appears, in a small post-medieval hand, on fol.1v of the Founders' Book, perhaps placed there by the writer of Sir Henry's copy.[28] And there were other manuscripts which, if not exact copies, were nevertheless closely related. The Elizabethan historian John Stow used a 'Liber Theauxbury' when compiling his *Annales* that included information found in chapter 4 of the Founders' Book, while James Bennett had access to a copy of a Tewkesbury chronicle that was close to but definitely distinct from the Chronicle of Cleopatra C.III.[29] A third manuscript was destroyed in the Cotton Library fire of 1731.[30] Other Tewkesbury 'registers' (so called) noted by past historians may have constituted further copies.[31] Thus the chronicle at the heart of the Founders' Book has never fallen into disuse, and while this particular manuscript was not known publicly until 1892, when it was advertised for sale at £84, the bulk of its text has always been considered important.[32]

Fig.6.3 London, British Library MS. Additional 36985, fol.12r. A mid-16th-century copy of Figure 6.2, showing Robert Fitzhamon and Sybil, his wife

Text

The following textual outline does not question the historical veracity of the information contained in the Founders' Book, but aims simply to convey an impression of content.[33] Not that the Founders' Book contains copious misinformation: generally, indeed, it is reliable enough. Though various claims concerning the monastery's early history—for example, the 8th-century foundation, the Tewkesbury burial of Beorhtric, king of Wessex, and the patronage of the nebulous Hugh, 'great Mercian duke'—cannot be taken at face value, it is important to remember that as time-honoured traditions, they will have gone unquestioned by those who produced the manuscript. In general, it is bias rather than invention that the reader encounters.

While the heart of the Founders' Book is its illustrated chronicle, it must not be thought that the other chapters are mere accretions, unrelated to the whole. They are closely related, for the information they contain underlines the impression of antiquity, authority and *esprit des corps* that chapter 4 is designed to convey. A system of cross-referencing in the manuscript between chapters 1 and 4 demonstrates the practical connection between the various parts. In both chapters, the scribe of chapter 1 has added five marginal symbols in rubric. In chapter 4 these are accompanied by the note 'search in the first book where you encounter [for example] ØØ' (*quere in principio libri ubi inueniet ØØ*).[34] Sure enough, in each case the material indicated in the first chapter supports claims made in the fourth. As a whole, therefore, the Founders' Book is best described as an historical compendium rather than simply a chronicle with extraneous additions. It is most definitely not a register, although commonly described as such.

(i) Chapter 1

Chapter 1, which contains a largely unexploited fund of information concerning Tewkesbury's early history, merits searching and individual study.[35] This précis can only adumbrate its essentials. First mentioned are benefits bestowed on the church of Tewkesbury by Æthelweard Maew's wife Ælfgifu, and son Ælfgar.[36] In particular, lands in Dorset are listed: 55 hides (*mensas*) at Cranborne, 5 at Wimborne, 20 at Dewlish and 25 at Ashton. Beorhtric, Ælfgar's successor as patron of Tewkesbury (then a cell of Cranborne), also advantaged the monks but fell foul of Matilda, future queen of William I, by refusing to marry her: he died in prison in Winchester. The honour of Gloucester then passed to the crown (fol.2r). Meanwhile, the monks of Cranborne, labouring under a disagreeable abbot, petitioned for a new leader. On the advice of Lanfranc, archbishop of Canterbury, and Osmund, bishop of Salisbury, King William II sent them Gerald, former chaplain to Hugh, earl of Chester, and monk of Winchester, a man of surpassing qualities (fol.2v).[37] The text contains nothing about Gerald's rule at Cranborne. Indeed, it implies that he set off for Tewkesbury, 'land of abundance' (*terra pinguedine*), without delay. It is said that this relocation carried royal, archiepiscopal and monastic sanction. Gerald was accompanied by 'several' monks (*nonnullis fratribus*), one named Alfred, and took with him certain church ornaments (*de quibusdam ornamentis ecclesiasticus*). Tewkesbury's monks received him with joy. At that time, the chronicler records, there stood an ancient and imposing church at Tewkesbury. In this, Gerald and his brethren remained for almost three years until the 'coming of Robert Fitzhamon' (fol.3r).[38] It is said at this point that the monk Alfred was afterward (*in processu temporis*) made master of the rebuilding works (*magistrum operis*): thus we learn something of the official who oversaw the erection of the great Norrnan church.

An important historical point arises here which it is worth pausing to emphasize. From this information an approximate date for the relocation of Gerald to Tewkesbury, that is more precise than the traditional date of 1102, can be extrapolated. Chapter 1 later implies that the 'coming' of Robert Fitzhamon to Tewkesbury coincided with his agreement to fund construction of a new monastery. This, we learn elsewhere, was habitable by 1102;[39] suggesting that building had commenced some years previously. Supposing that the works took a minimum of five years and thus were begun around 1097 (and it cannot have been much later, for the new monastery had to accommodate an abbot and 57 monks, plus all of their servants), this gives a date of *c.*1094 for Gerald's relocation. Thus, the monks remaining at Cranborne (i.e. the majority) apparently lived without their abbot for some eight years.

Robert Fitzhamon and his wife Sybil are introduced at this point. Robert, it is said, was wealthy and well connected, but he lacked heirs (he was *prolis inops*), which depressed his spirit. He gave generously to churches and monasteries in the expectation of heavenly succour. In particular, Sybil travelled to Glastonbury to supplicate St. Benignus. She was vouchsafed a sign, but deceived in her expectation of giving her first husband an heir. Sybil did have children, but by a second husband (described as *plebeius*, 'a commoner') taken after Robert's death (fol.3r-v).[40] This is a digression, for we are next told of Robert's reconfirmation of Tewkesbury's rights and privileges, of his marriage, and of his desire to increase the number of monks at Tewkesbury by 15. Gerald replied that the ancient monastery was too small for this. Thus Robert, confirmed in his course by Sybil's petitions, funded construction of a new monastery, giving lands, silver and gold. The decision to rebuild was not taken lightly: a council of nobles and knights was assembled to discuss the matter. Many other gifts given by Robert and Sybil to the enrichment of the monastery are mentioned (fols.3v-4r).

Chapter 1 ends with a brief summation of the more important benefits bestowed upon Tewkesbury by William, second earl of Gloucester, his wife Hawisa and Mabel, his mother. The patronage, death and burial of Earl Gilbert I is noted (his marble 'mausoleum' is mentioned), and also the generosity, death and heart-burial of Isabel, Gilbert's wife. A passage here, including a verse of four lines, is also found in the 13th-century Annals.[41] This is fitting, because chapter 1 plainly belongs to the same historiographical genre.

(ii) Chapters 2 and 3

The brief chapter 2 returns to Æthelweard Maew's gifts. These were so many and great, it is suggested, that they cannot all be recorded. Fortunately, however, the scribe does catalogue the relics Æthelweard gave, recording a fascinating sidelight into Tewkesbury's devotional culture, a subject about which regrettably little is known.[42] Fifteen major relics are listed individually, including a large part of the True Cross, the bed on which Christ was born, the cradle in which he was nourished in infancy, stone from Mount Tabor whereon he sat with his disciples, the Holy Grail, the rope with which he was bound and led away when arrested, and rock from various sources, including the spot on Calvary where the Cross stood, the Holy Sepulchre, and the Virgin Mary's tomb (fol.5r-v). Further grants of real estate by Ælfgifu, Ælfgar and Hugh, son of Grippa, are then mentioned (fol.5v).

Chapter 3 is also relatively brief. The 'Magna Charta Theokusburiæ', as it is called, is a comprehensive reconfirmation by the second earl, William Fitzcount, of the lands, rights and privileges enjoyed by Tewkesbury Abbey. It also includes new grants made for the good of the earl's soul, that of his wife Mabel, and those of all his predecessors and successors (fol.6r). It is an impressive document, demonstrating the wealth commanded by the abbey at an early stage in its history. A representation of the earl at the head of the charter is designed to emphasize its significance and verity. It ends not with a witness list but in the word 'amen' (fol.7v).

(iii) Chapter 4

The chapter 4 chronicle, approximately 7,500 words long, is difficult to classify. It is not a domestic monastic history like the Annals, nor is it wholly secular, as are, for example, the history of the earls of Warwick produced by John Rous, the Mohun chronicle or the metrical narrative of the so-called Clare Roll.[43] Nor is it a 'benefactors' book' of the type produced at St. Albans during the late 14th century.[44] It is a combination of all three. Behind the veneer of secularity created by the decoration, the peculiarly monastic interests and assumptions of its writer assert themselves: this work was clearly written by a monk for monks. Most noticeably, the writer employs the first person plural throughout, as in 'our father St. Benedict' (*sancti patris nostri Benedicti*; fols.9r, 11v, 14r), 'Gilbert ... gave to our church' (*Gilbertus ... contulit ecclesiæ nostræ*; fol.22r), and 'we have a daily prayer' (*habemus quotidie orationem*; fol.22r). Gifts and privileges bestowed upon the convent by its patrons, episodes demonstrating abbatial dignity, the minutiae of chantry ordinances, and in particular illustrious burials—a matter of honour for any monastic community—are also emphasized. There is much more here about the patron-client relationship than there would be in a straightforward genealogical chronicle. All things considered, chapter 4 is best described as a history of the reciprocal relationship between a series of illustrious individuals and the illustrious institution they oversaw.

To begin with, it is stated that Oddo and Doddo, two quasi-saintly Mercian dukes, constructed in 715 a Benedictine monastery of the Virgin Mary. This conflicts with the earliest surviving account of the foundation, in Bodleian Library MS. Lat. misc. b.2 (R), which gives the date as 717 (a fact not hitherto noticed).[45] It is said that the hermit Theocus had lived on the spot previously; whence the name 'Tewkesbury'.[46] Both dukes, however, were eventually buried at Pershore. Thereafter the glass darkens, for civil war and invasion rent England, the monastery twice being burned. Hugh, a great Mercian nobleman, is said to have buried King Beorhtric at Tewkesbury *c*.800. Hugh himself was buried there in 812, after which the chronicler tells us nothing more until the introduction of Æthelweard Maew, who founded Cranborne as an abbey, and subjected Tewkesbury to it *c*.980. Ælfgifu and Ælfgar, already encountered in chapter 1, succeeded him as patrons, being followed by Beorhtric, victim of Matilda's vengeance (fols.9r-11v).

Post-Conquest, Matilda held the honour of Gloucester. She died in 1083, and her obit is noted in an anglicana formata script found nowhere else in the Founders' Book (fol.11v). Robert Fitzhamon, descendant of Rollo, first duke of Normandy, succeeded her. To emphasize his illustrious pedigree, Rollo's descent from pagan times is provided (fols.11v-12v). Tewkesbury's rebuilding and Cranborne's subjugation are duly noted. Fitzhamon died in 1107, and was buried in the chapter house 'as was then normal practice among great men'. Around the year 1242, during the rule of Abbot Robert III (Forthampton) his body was translated to the presbytery, where in 1397, it is said, Abbot Parker erected a chantry chapel 'of astonishing workmanship' over his grave. Robert Chandos, founder of Goldcliff Priory in Monmouthshire, is mentioned next (fol.14r-v). Goldcliff did not become a Tewkesbury cell until 1442, but Chandos nevertheless stands among the pantheon of early benefactors praised by the chronicler. Robert the Consul, a bastard son of King Henry I, and son-in-law of Fitzhamon, became first earl of Gloucester after 1107 (Fig.2.1). He founded St. James's Priory, Bristol, and annexed it to Tewkesbury. His successor, William Fitzcount, also benefited the abbey greatly, as well as founding the Augustinian canonry of Keynsham (Som.). John, later king and 'called "Lack land"' (*dicto sine terra*), next obtained the earldom but no direct gifts from him to the abbey are mentioned.

The chronicler then notes Geoffrey de Mandeville, earl of Essex and Amauri de Montfort, son of William Fitzcount's eldest daughter Mabel, as sometime holders of the honour of Gloucester, without further discussion (fols.15v, 17r).[47] Neither produced an heir, and thus the honour devolved upon William Fitzcount's second daughter Amice, wife of Richard I de Clare, earl of Hertford. Amice's son Gilbert I became the first earl of Hertford and Gloucester. He bequeathed Mythe wood to the monks, died in 1230, and was buried at Tewkesbury (fol.17r-v).[48] Richard II de Clare ratified the grant of Mythe wood, and other gifts of his father. His tomb was ornamented like a shrine by his wife, with gold, silver, precious stones and his sword and spurs (*uxor eius ornauit tumula eiusdem auro et argento et lapidibus preciosis, cum gladio et calcaribus* [*eius*]). Gilbert II, called the Red Earl 'because his hair was red and beautiful to behold', and Gilbert III are then briefly discussed.

Hugh II Despenser became lord through marriage to Gilbert III's sister. Of him it is learnt only that his execution was 'wicked, damnable, cruel and illegal' (fol.21r-v). The descent of kings Edward IV and Richard III from the Red Earl is then explained in a manner intended to reflect royal dignity upon the monastery (fols.21v-22r).[49] Hugh III Despenser, a great warrior, appropriated the parish church of Llantrissant in Glamorgan to the monastery. After his death in 1349, his wife Elizabeth married Guy de Bryan (Lord Welwyn), from whom more benefactions flowed. Their chantry ordinances are set out at length (fol.23r-v). Elizabeth chose burial next to Hugh III, however; his tomb was 'very beautiful' (Fig.13.5).

Edward Despenser, nephew of Hugh III, was next created lord. More is said of his family connections than of him. Dying in 1375, his wife Elizabeth raised a stone chapel 'constructed with amazing skill' (the Trinity Chapel) above his grave (Fig.13.9), while he bequeathed a cup of pure gold and a 'most precious jewel made with surpassing workmanship' (fol.25r).[50] Elizabeth, who died in 1409, also bequeathed sumptuous gifts, including 15 copes. Thomas Despenser's succession and murder at the hands of 'commoners' in Bristol (in fact he was executed by Henry IV's agents) are noted, and also the death of his son and heir Richard Despenser in 1414.[51] Isabel Despenser, Richard's sister, is then introduced. She is important to the writer, and one of only two individuals to be depicted twice in the Founders' Book. She married Richard Beauchamp, lord of Abergavenny and Worcester. When this earl was killed in 1421 he was buried at a spot upon which Isabel constructed a chantry chapel (the Warwick Chapel)—'a beautiful chapel built with astonishing skill' (Pl.13); this was dedicated early in 1423 (fol.28r). In fact, the year 1433 (MCCCCXXXIII) is given, but as the chapel is subsequently (fol.28r) said to have been raised one year and ten months after Earl Richard's death, it is clear that the scribe has accidentally inserted an 'X' too many.[52] She then married Richard Beauchamp, earl of Warwick, and in 1424 they produced Henry Beauchamp. On Earl Richard's death in 1439, Isabel had six extra chantry monks installed at Tewkesbury. She left riches to the abbey, established a sophisticated chantry for the health of her soul and the souls of her forebears and followers, and was buried under a marble tomb of 'remarkable craftsmanship' (fol.32r).[53]

Henry Beauchamp became lord, and annexed Goldcliff to Tewkesbury (fols.32v-33r); the reader now realizes why the little priory's legal rights have been mentioned repeatedly to this point. There follows much discussion of Tewkesbury's possessions and privileges (fols.34v-36r), during which Baron Henry's death is recorded. Night burial was necessary, for throngs of mourners would otherwise have damaged the monastery. Henry's sister and daughter being dead, Richard Neville, earl of Warwick ('The Kingmaker'), assumed the lordship of Gloucester and, *inter alia*, appropriated Sherston church to the convent. He was killed at Barnet in 1471 along with his brother and many other supporters of King Henry VI (fol.37r-v), and was buried at Bisham Priory (Berks.). Edward IV's triumphs at Barnet and Tewkesbury are impartially mentioned, although Henry VII is then called, unspecifically, *victoriosus*. At the petition of the next lord, George, duke of Clarence, the monastery obtained the manors of Kinver and Stourton in Staffordshire (1475), these later being exchanged for the revenues of Great Marlow (fol.37v).[54]

Finally, the chronicler records the births of the duke of Clarence's children—Margaret (1473), Edward (1475) and Richard (1476), the last in the abbey infirmary. Richard's baptism in the parish church was elaborate, but both he and his mother Isabel soon died. She lay 35 days unburied beneath her hearse in the choir (fol.40r). Isabel's sister Anne, who had wed the late Prince Edward, son of Henry VI, then married Richard of Gloucester, later King Richard III. The chronicle ends halfway down fol.40v, with the birth of Anne's son, Edward, at Middleham Castle (Yorks.) in 1476.

Chapter 4 reveals much of interest concerning Tewkesbury, but it is disappointing in one significant respect. Whilst not too much should be expected of the author, a cloistered monk—the contemporary political intrigues in which the lords were involved lay outside his compass—one can feel justifiably cheated in not learning something of the building and embellishment carried out at Tewkesbury during the 14th and 15th centuries. Responsibility for the great church's remodelling has been ascribed to the 14th-century lords, commencing with Hugh II Despenser.[55] As the chronicler's aim is to extol these individuals with special reference to their generosity to his abbey, and as he mentions both their monuments and their other material gifts, this silence is both puzzling and disappointing. Perhaps it implies a larger monastic role in the works than has previously been thought.

(iv) Chapter 5

Chapter 5 is an extract from a narrative cartulary, which aims to establish the 12th-century foundations of Tewkesbury's wealth and power. It begins with a recapitulation of Abbot Gerald's complaint that Tewkesbury's old church was insufficient, and of Fitzhamon's gifts of gold, silver and land annexed to the reconstruction (fol.42v).[56] Thereafter it is occupied with discussion of other endowments and real estate purchases.[57] There is also an interesting list of the churches whose revenues belonged, partially or wholly, to the abbey, beginning with All Saints in London (fols.44v-45r).

Decoration

The decoration of the Founders' Book stands with that of the Warwick rolls of John Rous and the Salisbury roll of arms of *c.*1463 as a rare example of a more-or-less comprehensive heraldic *and* pictorial pedigree. In fact, its unique roll of armorials is apparently incomplete, for on a number of pages escutcheons have been outlined but not filled in (fols.21v, 22r, 23v, 24v, 29r-30v, 32v). This is also the case with the roll, Bodleian Library MS. Lat. misc. b.2 (R) from which the Founders' Book derives its heraldry. Some of the early armorials are *post mortem* attributions, such as Oddo and Doddo's golden cross engrailed on a red field (also the abbey's arms), and Robert Fitzhamon's *rampant guardant* lion on a field of blue (Pl.4 and Fig.6.2).[58] At the end of the roll the same phenomenon occurs in the arms of Edward Plantagenet, which include a number of attributed quarterings imported from the Warwick pedigree: the diagonal ragged staff on a black field of the Briton consuls of Warwick, the gold cross entwined with a serpent in a red radiance on a silver field for Sir Eneas Chyvaler, the 'Swan Knight', and others no less fanciful (Pl.5, copied in Founders' Book fol.41r).[59] Among Edward's quarterings are the bearings of Oddo and Doddo, Fitzhamon, Robert the Consul and William Fitzcount, Prince John, Geoffrey de Mandeville earl of Essex, the de Clares, the Despensers and the Beauchamps. This final escutcheon epitomizes in heraldic splendour what the chronicle of chapter 4 labours to demonstrate in words.

Fig.6.4 Oxford, Bodleian Library MS. Top. Glouc. d.2, fol.24r. Edward Despenser presenting a seven-branched candlestick, perhaps symbolic of his celebrated knightly prowess. He is clad cap-à-pie in armour, just as he is atop the Trinity Chapel in the abbey church

Turning to the figure decoration, one is struck by its good condition and vividness, but also by its relatively low artistic quality. The representations of people and objects demonstrate a meagre understanding of perspectival, linear and painterly values, a limited repertoire of pose and gesture, and a lack of control in the application of colour. Physiognomies are distorted: for example hands, eyes and noses are too large, and faces charmingly but unnaturalistically supplied with rosy cheeks and lips (Fig.6.4). The most successful figures are Robert Fitzhamon and Sybil, over which more care has clearly been taken, along with those of Oddo and Doddo and Isabel Despenser (Fig.6.2; Pls.4, 6).

There are reasons for this mediocrity. The artist was not a professional illuminator, but a Tewkesbury monk named John of Evesham (*Ewisham*). On fol.1v, an erased inscription, legible under ultra-violet light, reads 'John of Evesham had this book made' (*Johannes Ewisham hunc librum fecit fieri*). While this apparently indicates only the manuscript's commission, we find Evesham's name repeated several times in brush-trials on the flyleaves (fols.1v, 46r), in yellow, red and brown; three of the colours used throughout. John of Evesham, it seems, wielded a brush laden with these colours, presumably to decorate the manuscript. A John of Evesham, who was among the monks pensioned off at the abbey's dissolution,[60] may well have been this artist.

A second reason concerns the source of the illustrations. John of Evesham did not invent the figures, but copied them from elsewhere. His main source was a series of statues representing founders that stood somewhere within the abbey church,[61] fragments of which were discovered in the area of the medieval high altar during the 19th century. These now reside in the abbey collection (Figs.2.1, 2.2). Like the figures in the Founders' Book, the statues were apparently limited to frontal or three-quarter profile poses. One torso has a leafy branch against its breast, while another shows traces of the same; both wear surcoats with de Clare chevrons. They correspond precisely to the figures of Gilbert I and Richard II de Clare in the Founders' Book. Another torso with de Clare surcoat holds a staff, broken off halfway down, representing Gilbert III, who is shown in the Founders' Book inverting a long-handled torch. A fourth figure boasts a Garter badge as does the illustration of Thomas Despenser (Pl.15), and a fifth (now lost) held a hawk to which he was pointing, as Hugh II Despenser does (Fig.13.12, no.4).[62] Evesham's illustrations manifest the weaknesses of an amateur copyist craning his neck to view statues set up above him.

The Founders' Book has 18 single figures, two paired figures standing, three seated couples, and one deathbed scene with two figures—30 figures in total. Altogether, 28 individuals are represented (William Fitzcount and Isabel Despenser appear twice), one of whom is a 15th-century abbot (William of Bristol), the rest patrons of the monastery or their wives—'founders' in the medieval sense. The seated figures occupy stone benches, while nearly all of the standing ones surmount small grassy knolls. All of the secular male figures wear stylistically uniform plate armour which, although not very well understood, corresponds to that of the later 15th and early 16th centuries. With two exceptions—the Mercian duke Hugh and Robert Chandos—the figures wear heraldic surcoats or tabards as well. All but four of the male lords have full-length mantles, coloured either brown or red, with white lining. Three of them wear helmets of the sallet type with visors, the rest bonnets of brown, red or blue, of the style seen in Figure 6.2. Often, these are flourished with purple, red, yellow or blue feathers. Eight of the lords bear swords, either sheathed or drawn, and some hold unusual symbolic attributes. These will be mentioned below.

Of the six female figures, four are dressed in gowns drawn at the waist with a belt or length of rope, and sporting very full sleeves. The same four wear gabled hoods with embroidered lappets, and one—Hawisa—has prayer beads at her waist. The illustrations of Isabel Despenser are different. In one (Pl.6) she wears a long heraldic surcoat emblazoned all over with the arms of de Clare, Despenser and Warwick, a blue gown beneath, and a caul of blue and gold embellished with foliate embroidery. The other is her deathbed scene, where she wears a white bed-garment and simple brown headdress. The abbot wears the standard Benedictine cowl, though brown rather than black, so that in habit, he resembles a Franciscan as much as a Benedictine. He is bareheaded and tonsured.

Collectively, these illustrations constitute an example of what Kathleen Scott has called the 'iconography of power'. Groups of founders and benefactors, whether represented as figures or vicariously through heraldry, were popular with religious patrons of art during the late Middle

Ages as demonstrations of the strength and authority on which ecclesiastical rights stood, and by which they were protected.[63] In the Founders' Book there are both figures and heraldry; the manuscript thus exemplifies a pictorial tradition arising out of a combination of pride and insecurity, both qualities endemic in English monasticism during the 15th and early 16th centuries.

As for the figures themselves, William Fitzcount is represented on fol.6r, holding a rolled parchment which may symbolize the 'Great Charter of Tewkesbury' set out beneath. Next, Oddo and Doddo (Pl.4) appear on fol. 8v as a frontispiece to chapter 4, Oddo presumably being the figure on the left. Each holds a model church, the standard medieval iconographic designation of an architectural patron. These symbolize Tewkesbury church and another, either Pershore or the chapel at Deerhurst which Doddo supposedly had consecrated for his brother's burial (cf. fol.9r). Between them is a tree of uncertain species, perhaps a pomegranate, symbol of Christian unity and heavenly joy (cf. Deuteronomy 8:8).

The Mercian duke Hugh occurs at fol.10r, followed by Æthelweard Maew and Ælfgifu at fol.10v, who between them support a model church intended to suggest Cranborne Abbey.[64] Robert Fitzhamon and Sybil come next, on fol.13r, holding a model advertising their patronage of Tewkesbury Abbey (Fig.6.2). Robert Chandos appears on fol.14r, with Goldcliff Priory church in miniature. On fol.15r Robert the Consul with his wife Mabel display three diminutive churches: one for St. James's Priory, Bristol, a second for a Lady Chapel which they built from every tenth stone annexed to Bristol Castle's construction (cf. fol.15r), and a third either for Tewkesbury, or for the Cistercian abbey of Margam (Glam.) founded by Robert in 1147.

William Fitzcount appears again, this time with Hawisa, on fol.15v. The model they hold expresses their foundation of Keynsham Abbey. Prince John occupies fol.16v, which is one of the small leaves. His inverted sword hangs redundant before him. However, Richard I de Clare (fol.17v) displays his upright in the next illustration, thus pronouncing the advent of a new dynasty (cf. Richard Neville). On fol.18r, comes Gilbert I, holding a branch with leaves sprouting from it, to symbolize the gift of Mythe wood to the monks which is mentioned in the adjacent text. On fol.18v, Richard II clutches a similar branch in his left hand and a document in his right, as a reminder that he reconfirmed his father's valuable gift. Gilbert II is shown on fol.19v with brick red face and hands: an obvious way of distinguishing the 'Red Earl' from his counterparts. Gilbert III, on fol.20r, holds an inverted torch with bristle-like flames at the end. Among the flames is a small golden orb, the de Clare sun extinguished at Bannockburn. This illustration is of particular interest, for the use of an inverted torch to symbolize the end of a line is very rare in English medieval art, occurring primarily in classical and Renaissance funerary contexts.

Hugh II Despenser appears on fol.21r. Staring at the reader, he points to a hawk perched upon his unprotected left hand. Here the hawk may not be simply an aristocratic accoutrement. The most likely interpretation is that it represents Hugh II's soul, recalled at death to its proper abode. Religious poetry of the 15th century likens the soul of man to a hawk which is called back to Christ by the promise of redemption.[65] Hugh III Despenser, on fol.22v, holds a more conventional symbol—another miniature church, which recalls his annexation of Llantrissant church to Tewkesbury. On fol.24r Edward Despenser, the only figure other than Oddo and Doddo to be shown clad *cap-à-pie* in armour, presents a seven-branched candlestick with burning tapers (Fig.6.4). A plausible reading of this unusual attribute is that it typologizes him with Judas Maccabeus, who erected a new *menorah* in the Temple after routing the gentiles who had overrun Jerusalem (I Maccabees 4:49).[66] Judas Maccabeus, as one of the knightly exemplars known as the 'Nine Worthies', was an immensely popular chivalric role model during the later Middle Ages.[67] Edward Despenser was a model knight: this is recognized by the Flemish chronicler Froissart.[68]

The badge of the Order of the Garter is displayed by the left shoulder of the next figure, Thomas Despenser (fol.25v). The motto *Honi soit qui mal y pense* ('Shame on him who thinks evil of it') on a garter surrounding the arms of St. George declares his membership of a chivalric élite to which his father had also belonged. Isabel Despenser follows, in the surcoat and caul described above, kneeling in prayer before a representation of the Virgin and Child (Pl.6). Her will mentions such an image, suggesting a special devotion to the Mother of God.[69]

On fol.27v, Richard Beauchamp, lord of Abergavenny and Worcester, appears and on fol.28v, Richard Beauchamp, earl of Warwick, brandishes an over-sized sword in his right hand—perhaps the clumsiest illustration of all. Fol.31r shows Isabel Despenser *in extremis*: she lies in a luxurious bed dignified by a green tester trimmed in yellow and brown, and hung with great green tassels. Isabel hands a testament emblazoned with the Despenser arms to the kneeling William of Bristol (whose identity is confirmed by the large golden crozier he holds). Underneath the image part of the text contained in her will is set out, detailing sumptuous gifts to Tewkesbury—a perfect illustration of the intimacy with which text and image combine in the Founders' Book. The final two figures illustrated are Henry Beauchamp (fol.32r), again displaying a hawk on a bare left hand (the interpretation suggested above may be offered again here), and Richard Neville on fol.36v, adopting an aggressive stance with sword held vertically upward, and face framed by grey hair. By later medieval standards, however, George duke of Clarence, Richard duke of Gloucester (both fol.38r), Edward son of King Henry VI (fol.38v), and Edward Plantagenet (fol.41r) are no less present in the manuscript for being represented by armorials only (Pl.5).[70]

Conclusion

The Founders' Book is a product of its time and its collection of texts, heraldry and figure decoration is the colourful result of a marshalling of historical resources for self-promotion and self-defence. Here is the monks' pride in their ancient foundation and illustrious associations expressed large. Here also, at a time when the lordship of Tewkesbury had finally expired, their insecurities concerning the future are implied, and their nostalgia for a lost period under the protection of devoted and reliable patrons. The mutability of the times, of which the Battle of Tewkesbury was a signal indication, engendered uncertainty and anxiety throughout the late medieval monastic domain, for by this period, wealthy religious houses had much to lose, but could expect to gain very little in the way of new endowments. In such an environment, the Founders' Book will have functioned to educate monks about their abbey's glorious past, thus enabling them to speak in its defence, and to prove to visitors from outside what the statuary, stained glass, tombs and chantry chapels also demonstrated: the glorious, incorruptible and indisputable authority on which Tewkesbury Abbey's rights were founded. It is primarily to these ends that the Founders' Book was made.

CHAPTER 7

The Final Years of the Abbey and the Dissolution *by* Joseph Bettey

With the benefit of hindsight it is possible to discern that the various factors which together were to bring about the downfall of the monasteries were already gathering for some years before the final dissolution. But during the first decades of the 16th century few contemporaries would have predicted that by 1540 all the religious houses would have been suppressed and that all their property, wealth, lands and buildings would be confiscated by the Crown. Even in 1530 the abbey at Tewkesbury must have seemed secure against all assaults. Its wealth was immense, its widespread estates and other profitable assets provided a large annual income, the monastic buildings dominated Tewkesbury, and the abbey's influence extended throughout the town and the surrounding region. The abbey owned much property in the town, and the townspeople worshipped in the nave of the abbey church.

By *c.*1500 there were signs of change; as elsewhere, the abbey's wealth and possessions provoked the envy of local gentry and attracted the interest of the Crown. Gloucestershire was notable for the number of gentry families which actively supported reform in the Church and questioned the usefulness of the monasteries.[1] Some of these men were involved in the administration of the abbey's estates and prominent among them were the Tyndales. It was during his return to Gloucestershire in 1522-23 that William Tyndale took the momentous decision to translate the Bible into English, with such far-reaching consequences for the Church.[2] William's brother, Edward Tyndale, a wealthy and influential man, was steward of Tewkesbury abbey lands and leased the manors of Pull or Pull Court (Worcs.) and Burnett (Som.) from the abbot.[3] Another supporter of church reform was Sir William Kingston of Painswick, a ruthless opportunist, who had risen in the favour of Henry VIII through his strength and skill at jousting. In 1528 he was appointed by the Crown to be chief steward of the town and hundred of Tewkesbury. He became constable of the Tower of London in 1530 and arranged the execution of Anne Boleyn there in 1536. He was rewarded by the grant of the site and lands of Flaxley Abbey in 1537.[4]

Even more significant was the involvement of the Tracy family in the affairs of Tewkesbury. The Tracys were an ancient family which had for many generations been settled on lands around Toddington, a few miles east of Tewkesbury. They were actively involved in the affairs and estate management of local monasteries. In 1533, after applying considerable pressure on the abbot and with the help of Thomas Cromwell, Richard Tracy was able to lease the manor of Stanway, one of the best of Tewkesbury's properties (Fig.7.1).[5] Richard Tracy's father, William, had achieved national prominence following his death in 1530 because of the Protestant opinions

Fig.7.1 Stanway House, with the medieval barn of the abbey's former grange in the foreground

expressed in his will, and his body was dug up and burnt as a heretic by the Church authorities.[6] Richard Tracy fully shared his father's opinions and expressed them in several pamphlets. As a member of parliament he pressed for an apology from the Church for the dishonour done to his father. He was to become a dependable local agent of the Crown, and a supporter of Hugh Latimer, the reforming bishop of Worcester. On 25 October 1538 Richard Tracy helped to dismantle the shrine of the Holy Blood at Hailes and took the relic, the phial which was alleged to contain the Blood of Christ, to London. Later he was to be richly rewarded with grants of monastic land.[7] It was supporters of reform like Tyndale, Kingston and Tracy who took an increasingly important part in the affairs of Tewkesbury Abbey.

Other influential local gentry families who actively supported reform in the Church included the Poyntz family of Iron Acton and Sir John Walsh of Little Sodbury, in whose household William Tyndale found shelter. Walsh was married to Anne Poyntz and was steward of the Berkeley estates in Gloucestershire as well as administering some of Tewkesbury Abbey's lands. Members of the Wye family of Tewkesbury, who were related to the Tracys, were also enthusiasts for church reform.[8]

The surviving evidence suggests, however, that the majority of the inhabitants of Tewkesbury did not share the Protestant views exhibited by many members of the gentry. The few incidents which are recorded suggest support for traditional beliefs and practices rather than for reform. An unnamed priest, described as 'of little reputation and less discretion, of no promotion or learning', was in trouble with the royal commissioner, Thomas Evance, in 1536 for criticising the royal policy while in a Tewkesbury alehouse. Later, in February 1540, following the suppression of Winchcombe, Hailes and Tewkesbury abbeys, William Wodlow was reported for predicting that the king would soon likewise strip the possessions from every rich man. 'Sirs, now beware and take heed, for all will away'.[9] But these seem to have been isolated and uncharacteristic incidents. Unlike some towns which were dominated by a wealthy monastery such as Bath, Cirencester, Edington (Wilts.), Shaftesbury (Dorset) and Sherborne (Dorset), there is little evidence of conflict between monks and townspeople at Tewkesbury during the final decades of the abbey's life.

Like the gentry, some of the monks at Tewkesbury were also influenced by the pressures for change within the Church. It had for long been the custom to send monks from Tewkesbury for prolonged periods of study at Oxford. Most went to Gloucester College (now Worcester College) where Tewkesbury Abbey maintained rooms. At Oxford they would have been exposed to all the latest humanist learning and theological thinking coming from Europe, and to the pressures and arguments for reform. Robert Cisseter or Cirencester, a monk of Tewkesbury, studied logic, philosophy and theology at Oxford for nine years before graduating in 1523. Later he became prior of St. James, Bristol. Another monk, John Beeley, spent the years 1530-8 at Oxford, returning to become the last prior of Tewkesbury. Notwithstanding their monastic vows, young monks studying at Oxford were not always models of decorum. In 1538, for example, Philip Wyatt or Cardiff, another monk of Tewkesbury at Gloucester College, was charged with a breach of the peace by the university proctors.[10]

Monks from different monasteries who had been at Oxford maintained contact with one another, encouraging the continuing study of theology and philosophy as well as interest in European movements for church reform. Nothing is known of the provision for study by the monks at Tewkesbury, although the abbey possessed its own library and there is no reason to suppose that it differed from the neighbouring Benedictine houses of Winchcombe and Evesham. At Winchcombe during the 1520s Abbot Kidderminster arranged an elaborate system of theological lectures, giving some himself. Indeed, the house was described as 'a little university'.[11] At Evesham, during the years 1530-37 a former head of Gloucester College, the Benedictine monk Robert Joseph, kept up a scholarly correspondence with former students in west-country monasteries, including monks at Tewkesbury.[12]

Nonetheless, even when the problem of Henry VIII's marriage became critical and the Reformation Parliament was called in 1529, few would have predicted the speed and scale of the upheavals which were to follow. During the early 16th century the abbot of Tewkesbury was regularly summoned to sit in the House of Lords (Fig.7.2). In July 1530 Abbot Henry Beeley was one of 21 abbots who unsuccessfully petitioned the pope to grant the king's divorce.[13]

Final Appropriations

During the final decades of its existence the abbey maintained its appetite for the appropriation of parish churches and the diversion of the major part of their parochial tithe income into the monastic coffers. In spite of its large estates, the expenses of building work and the costs of maintaining a large household with many monks and an army of servants meant that Tewkesbury, like other monasteries, was always looking for new sources of income.

The means of persuading bishops to grant the necessary licences for appropriation were many and remarkably inventive. In addition to the parish churches already appropriated, the abbot and monks of Tewkesbury successfully petitioned the bishop of Lincoln in 1494 for licence to appropriate the church and tithes of Great Marlow in Buckinghamshire. The reasons given were that valuable fields, meadows and pastures which the abbey possessed on the Sussex coast had been inundated by the sea and lost.[14] In 1500 they obtained permission to appropriate Taynton (Oxon.) and Eastleach Turville on the grounds that the bell-tower, cloister and other parts of the abbey were in a ruinous condition, and that various farms and barns needed to be rebuilt. They also complained that because of their position on a major highway, the costs of hospitality were a heavy burden.[15] In 1505 the abbey was granted licence to appropriate Preston-upon-Stour (Warks.) and the wealthy parish church of Wotton-under-Edge.[16] At the Dissolution the abbey possessed 25 appropriated churches, together with portions of the tithes and other annual payments from numerous others.[17]

The Prelude to Suppression

When Thomas Cromwell replaced Cardinal Wolsey as the king's chief minister in 1529, he immediately took an active interest in the election of abbots. No doubt his aim was to install as many ecclesiastics as possible who were sympathetic to his views and ready to do his bidding. Cromwell also influenced the leases of monastic property, ensuring that his supporters were rewarded, but at no cost to himself. Thus in 1532-3 he put pressure on Henry Beeley, the abbot of Tewkesbury, to lease the manor of Stanway to Richard Tracy. Recognising Cromwell's importance in royal counsels, countless abbots sought to secure his goodwill by gifts. In July 1532 Beeley sent Cromwell a gift of 'a cast of Lanners'—hawks used in falconry, a sport to which Cromwell was much addicted.[18]

In the months before Abbot Beeley died at Tewkesbury in March 1534, Cromwell was busy making plans for the election of a successor who could be relied upon not to oppose his plans. In April 1533 he sent two of his commissioners to Tewkesbury to find the most amenable candidate and secure the necessary support from the monks. The following March the commissioners, John Tregonwell and Thomas Bayard, reported to Cromwell that they had secured the election of John Wakeman (sometimes known as John Wyche) who had been the prior.[19] Cromwell and his commissioners, however, were not the only laymen who sought to influence the monks in the election of their abbot. Sir William Kingston, crown steward of Tewkesbury, was also involved, and supported Wakeman's election. In April 1534 Wakeman wrote to Kingston to thank him for his support, even before his installation on 10 June 1534.[20]

Wakeman had been in office for only a few weeks when he was called upon to make a momentous decision. The Act of Supremacy passed by Parliament in 1534 declared boldly that:

> The King our Sovereign Lord, his heirs and successors kings of this realm, shall be taken, accepted and reputed the only Supreme Head in earth of the Church of England called *Anglicana Ecclesia*.[21]

All monks and nuns were required to take an oath upon the Holy Scriptures that they accepted the royal headship of the Church, thereby repudiating the power of the pope. On 28 August the assent to the Royal Supremacy was signed by Abbot Wakeman and 37 monks, assembled in their chapter house.[22] No doubt many of the monks had misgivings about the oath they were required to take, but following the lead of their abbot, and faced with the power of the Crown supported by the local gentry, all the Tewkesbury

Fig.7.2 Abbot Beeley in the procession to Parliament of the lords spiritual and temporal, 1518. (Trinity College Cambridge, MS 0.3.59, membrane one)

monks put their signatures to the Act as they were bidden. Having accepted that the king was now Supreme Head of the Church, the abbot and his monks had no grounds on which to oppose any of the changes to be proposed by the Crown. Henry VIII himself, accompanied by a large number of courtiers, including Thomas Cromwell, stayed at Tewkesbury Abbey from 23 July until 27 July 1535. Later Abbot Wakeman wrote to Cromwell to thank him for 'your loving commendations to the king when he was at Tewkesbury'. In gratitude the abbot sent Cromwell a horse together with £5 'to buy you a saddle'.[23]

During 1535 Cromwell sent two groups of commissioners to monasteries throughout England and Wales. One group was required to enquire carefully into the property, value, income and expenses of all the houses, the other to search for scandal, for evidence of laxity, abuses, neglect of duties and sexual misconduct by abbots and monks. The first group completed their amazingly complex undertaking, the *Valor Ecclesiasticus*, in a remarkably short time by the end of 1535; the detailed returns of which will be considered shortly.

Of more immediate use to Cromwell was the information from the second group, as this could be used to justify at least a partial suppression and confiscation of monastic property. One of the commissioners who came to Tewkesbury during August 1535, searching for material to serve Cromwell's purpose, was a young priest, Richard Layton. Layton was keen to rise in Cromwell's service, and his reports to Cromwell from elsewhere in the West Country are lively, colourful and amusing, though hardly to be taken at face value. He had a contemptuous attitude towards the monks, a fine aptitude for the discovery of salacious gossip and a careless disregard for the truth of his allegations. In return for providing Cromwell with the sort of 'evidence' he required, Layton was rewarded with a succession of lucrative benefices, and became dean of York in 1539. About Tewkesbury in 1535, he was completely silent. He wrote to Cromwell from Evesham on 1 August 1535 to announce that he was going to Tewkesbury, yet presumably found no abuses or failings to report. If he had done so, it is certain that he would have recorded them with relish.[24]

The Valor Ecclesiasticus

The careful enquiries of Cromwell's first group of commissioners revealed that the annual income of Tewkesbury, including the subsidiary priories of Cranborne, Deerhurst and St. James, Bristol, amounted to £1,598 10s. 3d. This made it one of the wealthiest of all the west-country monasteries. The income maintained a large and opulent establishment, with nearly 40 monks and no less than 144 servants. As initiated by Abbot Gerald in 1105, the abbey's income was divided between the various officers or 'obedientiaries' in charge of the different departments. The abbot himself received £253 14s. 7¼d. He maintained a separate household with a large staff and enjoyed the use of the manor houses at Stanway and Forthampton. He also received the income from several appropriated churches. The abbot kept the office of cellarer in his own hands, and this brought him an additional income of £842 18s. 11d., reinforcing his dominance within the establishment. It is noted in the *Valor* that he alone had the right of appointing and removing all the officials of the house. Other major officials receiving an income included the following:

	£	s.	d.
Abbot & Cellarer	1,096	13	6¼
Kitchener	32	13	1
Chamberlain	83	1	6
Sacrist	42	4	7
Master of the Lady Chapel	12	3	1½
Prior	9	9	8
Almoner	35	13	4
Hosteller	3	5	2
Master of the Frater	1	4	4½
Master of the Spices	42	13	11
Cook	32	13	1
Prior of Deerhurst	134	8	0½
Prior of St James, Bristol	55	7	4
Prior of Cranborne	37	19	0

Although imported spices were always expensive, the expenditure on them seems remarkably high. Conversely, the expenditure on alms is low, since the almoner's income included £15 6s. 4d. for clothing 16 poor scholars and for the maintenance of boys who were clothed, fed and educated at the abbey. Other officers may, however, have devoted some of their income to charity, and surplus food may have been distributed to the poor.

The *Valor* also provides a detailed list of all the abbey's property, the appropriated churches and other parish churches from which pensions were paid to the monastery from their tithe income. Other sources of income included £18 10s. per annum from the abbey's corn mill at Tewkesbury and £3 per annum in tolls from the ferry across the Severn at Overlode.[25]

The Suppression

The *Valor* revealed for the first time just how extraordinarily wealthy many of the monastic houses were. It made opponents of the monasteries even more eager to accomplish their downfall. Many gentry families, in particular, could hope to profit greatly by a dispersal of the monastic estates. Tewkesbury was well outside the provisions of the Act for Suppressing the Smaller Monasteries of 1536, and monastic life continued throughout 1537, 1538 and 1539, even though more and more monasteries were 'voluntarily' surrendering to the Crown in return for pensions to the abbot and monks. In 1538 all the friaries in England had been closed, and increasing pressure was used by Cromwell and his commissioners to secure the closure of the remaining abbeys. Finally, in 1539 Parliament passed the Act for the Dissolution of the Greater Monasteries, ordering all the property of the few remaining monasteries to be transferred to the Crown. Tewkesbury held out for as long as possible, and was the last Gloucestershire monastery to surrender. A group of seven commissioners received the surrender of Hailes on 4 January 1540 and wrote to Cromwell telling him that they would proceed to Tewkesbury 'and conclude with this shire'.[26] On 9 January Abbot Wakeman and 39 monks, including the priors and monks of Cranborne, Deerhurst and St. James, Bristol, signed the deed transferring the house and all its possessions to the Crown, in return for receiving pensions.[27] At Tewkesbury, as elsewhere, the pension awarded to the abbot was extremely generous. Abbot Wakeman received an annual pension of £266 13s. 4d., together with the manor house at Forthampton and the demesne lands and tithes there. The monks received pensions ranging from £13 6s. 8d. per annum for senior monks, to £6 13s. 4d. per annum for the younger men. It is a measure of the status of the abbot that his pension was almost equal to the combined total of all the monks' pensions which together amounted to £284 13s. 4d. In addition, no less than 144 servants were employed in and around the abbey. These were paid any wages owing and dismissed.[28]

The Survey of 1540 and the Demolition of the Buildings

Immediately after the suppression of the abbey, a detailed survey was made of its buildings. This reveals the opulence of the architecture, the splendour of the furnishings and the separate establishment kept by the abbot. The 'records and evidences belonging to the said late monastery' remained in the Treasury and were in the custody of the two commissioners, Sir John Whittington and Sir Richard Poulet. Most of the domestic buildings, including the abbot's lodging, together with the barns, bakehouse, brewhouse, slaughter house and malting house were 'assigned to remain undefaced'. All the other buildings including the church, infirmary, cloisters, library, chapter house and two dormitories were 'deemed to be superfluous'. The early 15th-century cloisters were a particularly grievous loss, since they were reputed to be 'as fine' as the near-contemporary examples which survive at Gloucester Cathedral (Fig.12.7).[29] The nave of the monastic church was saved from destruction because it had been used by the parishioners, but the eastern Lady Chapel was demolished (Fig.7.3). In 1543 the church was purchased from the Crown by the parishioners for £483, and survives as a fine example of a

Benedictine great church, the spectacular tombs within illustrating the importance and wealth of the successive patrons of the monastery.[30]

Most of the remaining domestic buildings were demolished, however, partly no doubt for the sake of the valuable lead on the roofs. The surveyors in 1540 estimated that 180 fodders (3,510 cwts. or 175.5 tons) of lead could be obtained. The careful survey also recorded eight bells in the tower and 'jewels to the use of the King's Majesty', including two mitres garnished with silver gilt and decorated with ragged pearls and other stones. There was also 1,431 ounces of silver plate and quantities of other ornaments and valuable vestments. All of these were taken for the Crown and were delivered to the Master of the Jewel House in the Tower of London in March 1542.[31]

Fig.7.3 The site of the demolished eastern Lady Chapel, showing the lines of its walls marked out on the ground

Fig.7.4 The nave of St. James, Bristol

The Dispersal of the Estates

Some of the former monastic estate was quickly disposed of on behalf of the Crown by the Court of Augmentations which had been set up to handle the administration and sales of the land of dissolved monasteries. As early as March 1540 the priory of Deerhurst with its lands was granted to George Throckmorton of Deerhurst.[32] The priory of St. James, Bristol, and its lands were sold to Henry Brayne and Sir William Kingston, who were eagerly buying former monastic property. They quickly demolished most of the priory buildings for the sake of the lead and when John Leland visited the Bristol site in 1545 he described it as a ruin. As at Tewkesbury, however, the nave of the priory church of St. James at Bristol had been used by the people of the parish and was therefore spared from demolition (Fig.7.4).[33] In July 1541 the former abbey park at Tewkesbury and the mills on the Severn were granted to Henry Jernyngham, and outlying lands in Sussex and Devon were rapidly sold to new owners.

The Diocese of Gloucester

A detailed account of properties in Tewkesbury made for the Court of Augmentations in 1542 shows the demolition of some of the monastic buildings and gives details of the site, including fishponds, orchards, pastures and a duck decoy 'upon the water called the old Avon'. It also shows the way in which two Tewkesbury families, the Pearts and the Reades, were busily acquiring former monastic property. Daniel Perte or Peart was King's Bailiff and William Rede or Reade was 'farmer of the site of the said late monaster'. For a time the Court of Augmentations took responsibility for expenses formerly met by the abbey, including the purchase of bread, wine, wax and incense for the church. In 1542 the Court paid the large sum of £97 6s. 5d. on expenses at Tewkesbury. These included payments to the bailiff of the town and other officials, materials for the abbey church, including a censer presumably to replace one confiscated by the Crown, and the purchase of a cart 'called a Scolding Carte ... for chiding and punishing malefactors'.[34] Following the sale of the abbey church in 1543 such responsibilities passed to the parishioners.

In 1544 part of the abbey site was sold to William Reade, and there are numerous references during 1544 and 1545 to sales of other parts of the former monastic estate.[35] A new era began in the ecclesiastical history of Gloucestershire when the ancient and extensive diocese of Worcester was divided, and a new diocese of Gloucester was created on 3 September 1541. This was part of Henry VIII's restructuring of the Church, by the creation of six new dioceses. Like the other newly created dioceses, Gloucester was endowed with lands and property which had been taken from the monasteries, and a new cathedral was established in the former Benedictine abbey of St. Peter. The last abbot of Tewkesbury, John Wakeman, became the first bishop of the new diocese, and many of the lands of Tewkesbury were granted for the maintenance of the bishop, cathedral clergy and the diocese.[36]

The Career of John Wakeman, the last abbot

The remarkable changes in the career of the last abbot of Tewkesbury mirror the twists and turns in the fortunes of the Church during the reign of Henry VIII. Until he became abbot in 1534, he was known by the name of John Wiche, thereafter adopting the name Wakeman. He came of a Worcestershire family and began his monastic career at an early age. It was presumably from Tewkesbury that he was sent to Gloucester College, Oxford, where he graduated with the degree of Bachelor of Divinity in 1511. There is no record of his life as a monk at Tewkesbury during the following years until he became prior sometime before 1530. He was evidently regarded by the local gentry and by Cromwell's commissioners as conformable and sympathetic to their views. Through their influence he was installed as abbot on 10 June 1534. There appears to have been some reluctance among the monks, but the commissioners, John Tregonwell and Thomas Bayard, exerted pressure on them by fostering the rumour that unless Wakeman was elected Cromwell would impose upon them an abbot from elsewhere.

Wakeman seems to have justified the confidence of his supporters by conforming to the changes which followed, by welcoming the king and court to the abbey in 1535, and by his readiness to surrender the abbey to the Crown in January 1540. He also apparently supplied Cromwell with information, writing for example in May 1539 to accuse one of the priors of the three subsidiary houses of being 'datyve and removabull'.[37] The meaning is obscure, and it is not clear which of the priors was being accused. Presumably he was considered so unsound in his views that he should be removed from office.

Following the Dissolution in January 1540, Wakeman was left in a comfortable situation as a reward for his conformity. The extremely generous pension, use of a manor house and other perquisites put him in the position of a prosperous country gentleman. But he did not long enjoy the comforts of his new status. Henry VIII's foundation of the new diocese of Gloucester in 1541 created the need for a new bishop, and the choice fell on the amenable former abbot, John Wakeman. He was consecrated by Archbishop Cranmer at Croydon in September 1541, but the income from his bishopric meant that his pension as an ex-abbot now ceased. As bishop, Wakeman appears to have accepted without demur all the changes in royal policy. He conducted visitations of his diocese, but avoided stirring up trouble for himself. A recent study concludes that Wakeman appears merely to have presented the image of a conscientious bishop without actually doing very much. Henry VIII's innate religious conservatism probably suited Wakeman well, but in 1547 he conformed without protest to the suppression of the chantries and the confiscation of their property by the Crown during the first year of Edward VI's reign. He seems to have been well regarded as a scholar by Cranmer; when the archbishop proposed to produce a revised translation of the bible in 1549 he chose Wakeman as one of his revisers, allocating to him the difficult Book of Revelation.[38]

Fig.7.5 The de la Zouche monument at Forthampton Court. The effigy was moved from the abbey probably by Abbot Wakeman

After his appointment as bishop, Wakeman continued to occupy the manor house at Forthampton (Fig.7.5) and it was probably there that he died in December 1549. The place of his burial is unknown, and the tomb at Tewkesbury with its well-known effigy of the decaying figure is unlikely to be that of Wakeman, in spite of the popular tradition.[39]

In his will dated 30 July 1549 he left a bedstead and bedding at his house in Gloucester to his nephew, Thomas Wakeman, and to his servant Edward Rubbry he left another bedstead 'which bedd I lye upon in Forthampton'. Wakeman's will reveals his readiness to espouse the new Protestant thinking and follow the official doctrines of Edward VI's government. The bequest of his soul is expressed by Wakeman in thoroughly Protestant terms, confident in eternal life by 'trusting stedfastly my onelye Redemer to be partaker of his eternal Kyngdome and glorious fruycion'.[40] Wakeman's sentiments in the preamble to his will are in line with the concern he showed throughout his career to protect his own position. He conducted his episcopacy in accordance with the rapidly-changing theological temper of the times and retained it until his death by dutiful conformity. Throughout, however, he retained the loyalty of one of his former monks, William Didcot, who had been prior of Cranborne at the time of the Dissolution. Didcot became the bishop's chaplain and was a witness to his will in July 1549.[41]

The Fortunes of the Monks

Like their abbot, the careers of the monks following the dissolution were very different from the unchanging Benedictine routine they envisaged when they made their monastic vows. Although the pensions they were awarded were tiny in comparison to the huge sum provided for the abbot, they were adequate. Most received an annual pension of £6 13s. 4d., which was in line with the current stipend of a parish incumbent or a chantry priest. The subsequent careers of many of the former monks have been traced by Geoffrey Baskerville, and this section is based on his work.[42]

When the abbey was suppressed in January 1540, the numerous chantries and fraternity chapels were still in existence and so continued up to the first year of Edward VI's reign. Many ex-monks therefore found employment as chantry priests. Roger Compton, the former almoner, became a chantry priest in the former priory of St. James in Bristol; Philip Cardiff alias Wyatt, the third prior, served as chantry priest at Newent. Thomas Bristow became priest to the fraternity which met in the crypt or 'crowd' of St. John's Church, Bristol. Other former monks became curates. Richard Compton was curate at Deerhurst, Richard Cheltenham at St. James, Bristol, and Richard Wimborne at Shurdington. Eventually many became rectors or vicars, including those whose careers were abruptly ended for a second time by the suppression of all chantry foundations in 1547. Some married when clerical marriage was permitted by Edward VI's government in 1549, and thus found themselves expelled from their positions for a third time when Catholicism was restored during the reign of Queen Mary (1553-58). John Bromsgrove, the former prior of Deerhurst, became rector of Pendock (Worcs.); Thomas Newport was successively rector of Dodington then Saltford (Som.); John Welneford became rector of Little Comberton (Worcs.) in 1550 and remained there until his death in *c.*1570. John Hartland, rector of Pitchcombe, Thomas Thornbury, rector of Blandford St. Mary (Dorset), and Richard Cheltenham, who eventually became vicar of Wraxall (Som.), were all deprived for marriage during the early months of Queen Mary's reign.

Many of the monks were young men at the time of the suppression of the abbey and several lived on well into the reign of Queen Elizabeth. Thomas Leckhampton, who became vicar of Cranborne (Dorset), lived until 1566 and Henry Worcester, the former abbot's chaplain, was still serving as curate of Dymock in 1559.[43] They had coped with religious changes which would have been unimaginable when they entered the cloistered life at Tewkesbury. They had adapted themselves to Protestant theology, the Bible and services in English, the destruction of images, the reversal of the whole process and the restoration of the Latin Mass under Queen Mary, and finally they had accepted a third English service book and a restored Protestant church in 1559. In their final years, the regular round of seven daily services and the chants, ritual, festivals, commemorations and ceremonies of their former life at Tewkesbury must have seemed like a distant dream.

CHAPTER 8

The Parish of Tewkesbury after the Reformation *by* Anthea Jones

Two facts are of great importance in the story of the parish of Tewkesbury. The first is the foundation of an abbey endowed with the lands and tithe income of an older church whose parish reflected the extensive manor; the abbey community collectively became rector of Tewkesbury church and collected the tithes. The second is that the abbey church was not a parish church; a consequence was that the borough of Tewkesbury, a small enclave within the parish, acquired unusual influence over the church after the abbey was dissolved. A monastery's endowment with the 'church' of the parish where it was situated did not imply that the monastery church became the parish church. At Cirencester, for example, founded by Henry I only a few years after Tewkesbury, two new churches were built, one for the parish and one for the monks.[1] For Tewkesbury there is some evidence that an already existing parochial building continued in use for some time after the foundation of the monastery, but by the time of the Dissolution in 1540, the parishioners certainly used the monastic church as a parish church, and so an enterprising group of inhabitants negotiated with the king to buy the building.[2] They were not able to buy any of the parochial revenues which the monastery had absorbed.

The medieval parish of Tewkesbury comprised 12 townships. Southwick, to the south, including the hamlet of Gupshill and Tewkesbury Park, was most closely associated with the town.[3] Natton, Newton, Northway, Aston on Carrant, Fiddington and Pamington were all served by the chapel of Ashchurch.[4] Other townships were Tredington, Walton Cardiff, Oxenton, Forthampton and Bushley (in Worcestershire). It is surprising to modern eyes that Oxenton, some seven miles to the east of the parish church, and Bushley and Forthampton, on the western side of the Severn, should have been in Tewkesbury parish. Oxenton's name suggests that it supplied hill pasture for the oxen, and a chapel was provided for the servants of the manor, while Bushley and Forthampton were each connected with Tewkesbury by a ferry belonging to the abbey, which thereby controlled the landing places on the farther bank of the river. The abbot of Tewkesbury himself occupied the principal manor house of Forthampton, where the great hall with a splendid roof survives. Four subordinate chapels—Ashchurch, Bushley, Forthampton, and Oxenton—were probably included in the abbey's foundation grant: they were confirmed about 1150 by Simon, bishop of Worcester.[5] Tredington was not mentioned in the foundation grant, although it had a church at least from the Norman period, but it was always treated as an integral part of Tewkesbury parish.

Bishops, whose responsibility was the pastoral care of the people, tried to arrange the permanent endowment of a vicarage where a monastery was the rector, so that there should be a secular clergyman, a *vice* or substitute. Such an attempt was made for Tewkesbury in 1242 by the bishop of Worcester, in whose diocese it was then, but unsuccessfully.[6] When the abbey was dissolved, there was no endowed vicarage for Tewkesbury itself, nor for the chapels for which the abbey was responsible. This did not mean that the townsmen and the inhabitants of the villages were without priests to minister to their spiritual needs. In 1522 there were no less than ten 'secular' clergy in Tewkesbury, including probably a schoolmaster; there was also a chaplain at Oxenton, a curate at Forthampton, and a curate at Ashchurch. The salaries or stipends were £6 13s. 4d. (which was equivalent to 10 marks) for the clerk in Tewkesbury and the curate at Ashchurch, and £5 6s. 8d. (8 marks) for the other chaplains and curate.[7]

The *Valor Ecclesiasticus* in 1535 shows that the sacrist, who collected personal tithes of parishioners at Easter, offerings in Tewkesbury church at the five principal feast days, and fees for weddings and burials, 'by ancient custom' paid the curate who celebrated in Tewkesbury and in Tredington; the prior paid the curate of Oxenton, and the cellarer the curate of Ashchurch.[8] After 1540 the obligation to pay curates' stipends was passed to the purchaser of the appropriate tithes. In the accounts of abbey property in 1540, the 'parish priest' of Tewkesbury occupied one of the Abbey Cottages; the assistant curate, also called the 'secondary', occupied two rooms in the monastic precincts; the schoolmaster had a schoolroom over the Warkhey Gate to the monastery; another cleric had a room near the cemetery stile.[9] The Crown was then paying £10 to the parish priest of Tewkesbury and to the curate of Ashchurch, £8 to the 'secondary' and £6 to the curate of Oxenton. The last abbot of Tewkesbury and first bishop of Gloucester, John Wakeman, leased the Forthampton estate and paid the curate's stipend. James Brandard, who leased the 'Priest House', orchard and garden and part of the tithes of Ashchurch, known as the Rectory or Parsonage estate, similarly maintained the curate and had to keep the house in repair. There was no provision out of the tithes for a curate in the chapels of Bushley and Walton Cardiff. After this date, Bushley and Forthampton were no longer regarded as part of Tewkesbury parish, and when the diocese of Gloucester was created in 1541, Bushley was retained in Worcester diocese.

From the Dissolution, the legal position of each chapel developed differently, although with some common themes.[10] The sale of the tithes to private purchasers tended to break the link with the 'mother' church of Tewkesbury. The curates had no glebe-land or house, and only a stipend fixed at a mid-16th century sum unless the purchaser of the tithes or a benefactor was more generous. William Ferrers, for example, in 1625 gave an endowment to Ashchurch, and Edwin Skrymshire to both Ashchurch and Tredington in 1683. Fulk Read in 1658 endowed Walton Cardiff chapel with the tithes of Southwick and The Park.[11] The most significant endowment was in 1832 when the Rectory estate was given to the curate of Ashchurch; between 1825 and 1851 the income quadrupled and the one-time curate became a 'rector'. In the 18th century, Queen Anne's Bounty, which was founded in 1704 to give financial assistance to just such poor livings using the taxes paid to the Crown by better-off clergy, provided small endowments to Ashchurch, Oxenton, Tredington (four times), and Walton Cardiff (twice).[12]

The break-up of Tewkesbury parish has not been entirely satisfactory. From 1847, the curacy of Walton Cardiff was always combined with Tewkesbury vicarage, and in 1928 was merged with it. Bushley became linked with Chaceley, a nearby but not contiguous chapelry and Forthampton was united with Chaceley in 1923. The curate at Tredington became technically an 'assistant curate', licensed by the bishop as were other clerics without their own churches; he often lived in Tewkesbury, and sometimes combined the curacy with mastership of the grammar school. In 1963 the vicar of Tewkesbury became priest in charge of Tredington. In 2000 only Ashchurch, because of its expanding population, remained a separate parish, with two clergymen.

Owning the church

The Dissolution of the abbey might have left Tewkesbury with no church but, as is well-known, the townsmen decided to purchase church and churchyard from the king. Initially the church had been 'deemed to be superfluous', together with the cloisters, chapter house, and other purely conventual buildings, and would therefore have been demolished.[13] As soon as the monastery was closed, and perhaps even before, there must have been negotiations concerning the purchase between representative townsmen and the royal commissioners—who received £30 which seems like a deposit. The commissioners were persuaded that the nave of the church 'was used as the parish church', and the townsmen paid a further £453 for the choir or presbytery, aisles, chapels (but not the Lady Chapel), vestry, and tower or steeple with the eight bells, for 'the enlarging of the said parish church' which 'shall be had, reputed, and used and taken for and as the parish church of Tewkesbury'.[14]

How was the money raised? There is one fascinating insight in the will of Alexander Pyrry, draper, made in 1542. He gave £115 to the churchwardens

> towards the redemption of the late Abbey church, the leddes and belles of the same, of the king's Majestie for a parisshe church for the parishioners of Tewkesbury, which sum the late Abbot and convent were truly indettyd to me, as appereth by their obligacion under their convent seale.

He also gave £85 more 'in feyre golde'.[15] In taking over the property of the monastery the king became liable for its debts, and so the sale of the church cancelled at least this one. To whom precisely was the church sold? The formal grant named the bailiffs, burgesses and commonalty.[16] At this date, 1542, as a result of several past charters from lords of the manor, Tewkesbury had two bailiffs, representatives of the lord; a charter from the Crown constituting a fully independent

Fig.8.1 The south door into the church after the Dissolution, when the area of the former cloister became private property

Fig.8.2 The reconstructed bay of the cloister and the south door after the Abbey House estate was purchased for the benefit of the church in 1883

council was not obtained until 1575. There was also a select group of about 142 burgesses who owned the burgage plots in the three main streets. The 'commonalty' were the other inhabitants of the town. The word 'parishioners' was used only twice in the grant: firstly

> And that the bailiffs and commonalty of the said town of Tewkesbury and other the parishioners of the said parish church, shall have, use and enjoy the whole aforesaid late abbey church

and secondly, the grant stated that parishioners were buried in the churchyard. Significantly, it noted that the abbots and convent of the monastery had repaired the church hitherto 'at their costs and charges', but now bailiffs, burgesses and commonalty were to be responsible for repairs; otherwise, the king as rector of Tewkesbury might have been liable. The churchwardens' tasks before 1542 had been limited, but from this time were of great importance.

The first churchwardens' book starts in 1563, but noted that money was received from the previous wardens, William Read, gentleman, and John Butler.[17] William Read was tenant of the house called The Vineyard, and in 1544 had purchased the site of the monastery and other buildings including the Abbot's House, the tithes of Oxenton and the former abbey's half of Walton Cardiff; for a short time he also owned the Southwick estate.[18] He was probably an important figure in the purchase of the church. The Abbey House estate passed to Giles Read and then to John Read, who sold it in 1612 to Baptist Hicks, another important figure in the history of the town.

Fig.8.3 The abbey church from Abbey House garden: the south wall was 'decayed' in 1601, probably as a result of demolishing the conventual buildings where the monks lived, which were on this side despite an obvious risk of flooding from the River Swilgate

The churchwardens had four main sources of revenue with which to maintain the abbey church: sales of lead, church ales, taxation of the parish by means of rates, and pew rents. In the mid-16th century the accounts record sales of lead taken from roofs; a merchant of Bristol owed the churchwardens £7 for a ton of lead for 15 years. Some roofs were slated, while others continued to be leaded, most notably the long roof which covered the nave, releaded in 1594-96, and the chancel, releaded in 1603-4; occasional sales of old lead continued to be recorded, as in 1601 for lead 'taken of the sowthe side of the church being sklatted', and 1618-22 'for the ould butterlead out of the south ile'.[19]

The 'church ale' was the Tudor equivalent of the modern church fête. The churchwardens brewed ale and organised sales of

Fig.8.4 Tewkesbury Abbey from the south: the leaded long roof over the nave and that over the chancel were preserved after the abbey church became a parish church, but other roofs were covered with stone slates replaced probably in the 19th century with clay tiles. The nave south aisle roof was leaded in 1983-85

goods. Most colourfully, they presented plays in church, an activity that came to an end after the Canons of 1603 prohibited it. Between 1566 and 1577 five church ales were organised at Whitsun, making profits of between £7 and £27.[20] In 1600 the churchwardens organised a series of plays and markets on the first three days in Whitsun week to build a new battlement.[21] They erected staging, brewed beer, bought 'fruites and spices', and paid for 'cookery', 'meate' for the players, waiters in the cellar, attendants, hire of costumes, three trumpeters and other musicians. With gifts, the income was £45 but left a shortfall of £21 on the cost of building the battlement.

Reroofing the nave necessitated a more substantial means of finance, 'taxation' or 'rates', which were levied at so many shillings or pence in the pound on an assessment of what a property could be let for, and on 'ability' to pay; rateable value depended on negotiation. Those occupying land paid even if they were not personally resident in the parish.[22] The first recorded rate in Tewkesbury is 1594-6, when the churchwardens collected £13 8s. 2d. 'of those summes of money which were imposed uppon the parishe for coveringe the longe roufe over the body of the church'. In 1600 the parish was again taxed and in 1601 a modest rate was raised for repair of walls and windows on the north side, and soon afterwards another 'to supplie the want in the former being too short, and for amending the sowth side & walles of the churche decayed'.[23] Rates continued to be the main source of finance for major projects for the next two and a half centuries; one was levied every few years. By the late 18th century a rate of 6 pence in the pound raised approximately £150. But by then consent to church rates was being undermined by the growing numbers of Dissenters and perhaps, also, by the growing split between High Churchmen wishing to renew what they understood as medieval church practices, and Low Churchmen who wished to continue in the Puritan ways of the previous two centuries.

In 1834, one of Tewkesbury's two MPs, John Martin, presented a 'memorial' to the Whig prime minister, Earl Grey, from 'Ministers and Members of the Baptist and Independent Congregations and others of the Borough of Tewkesbury'. One of their demands was for exemption from church rates and other ecclesiastical demands.[24] Dissent underlay a dispute over the parishioners' choice of churchwarden the following year.[25] So many people attended the traditional parish meeting on Easter Tuesday in the Vestry that it had to be moved into the nave; the election of Mr. Joseph Smith, a Dissenter and a Liberal, was opposed by some of the meeting who demanded a poll. This lasted several days, and ended with 365 votes for Mr. Smith, and 158 for the alternative candidate. It is interesting to note that 'polling' was a misnomer, since it was not a case of one man, one vote, but of larger property owners or tenants having multiple votes. The Dissenters claimed the right 'to control the disposition of funds to which they were *obliged* to contribute', and all agreed that 'the taxing Dissenters to support the Church is alike impolitic and unjust'.[26]

Another poll was demanded in 1836 and the anti-rate committee advised its sympathisers not to resist because of 'the excited state of feeling at present prevailing in the town'.[27] It was expected that the government would tackle the problem, but a bill to abolish church rates was defeated twice, in 1834 and in 1837-8. Events in Tewkesbury paralleled the larger and better-known protests against church rates in Manchester and other large towns.[28] In 1849 the proposal to create an ecclesiastical district for the second and recently erected church in the town, Trinity Church, was opposed by the Town Council because of the effect it would have on church rates. Trinity Church had to wait until 1893 for its district to be approved; in 2000 it continued to be a separate parish in the town.[29] In 1862 the churchwardens were authorised 'to obtain a good legal opinion (at an expence not exceeding five guineas) as to the Grant of the Abbey Church to the Parishioners of Tewkesbury and to the liability of the Corporation to repair the same'.[30] Of course, the council and the 'commonalty' shared responsibility. In 1868, compulsory church rates were abolished by Act of Parliament. It was a severe blow for the financial support of all churches, and was effectively a partial disestablishment of the Church of England.

The fourth source of revenue to the churchwardens, pew rents, also came to an end in the later 19th century. Pew rents were a widely used system of raising money. The first churchwardens' book shows payments for a 'seat', often indicating which row or gallery it was in, and for a 'room', or individual place and the system was already well-developed; writing-up the seat book was recorded in 1568/9. People sometimes paid for life, sometimes for one year, sometimes for several years in advance.[31] A seat book dated 1751 shows payments according to the position of the pew:[32] the prime position was five pews in the fifth row occupied by the Corporation. There were five galleries: the Blue Gallery, the Upper Gallery, the New Gallery, the Pulpit Gallery and the Rood Loft Gallery and a total of 153 pews.[33] Fanny Burney, the diarist, commented on these untidy structures in the church.[34] An entry in the seat book concerning seat no. 13 in the fourth row throws an interesting light on accepted practices:

> This seat was formerly set to the Officers of Excise at 2s. 6d. quarterly. In the year 1731 Mr. John Jones lessened the Payment to 7s. p.a. And in the year 1749 Edward Popham Esq. and Mr. Weston released the said officers from All Payment for the said Seat on Account of their easing the Parish so considerably in the Land Tax.

In 1796 the churchwardens decided to re-pew the church. It was resolved that 'Seats and sittings shall be let in classes': 14 classes had rents ranging from two guineas for eight pews in the best position to one shilling for the 13 in the worst. The number of pews had dropped to 139; they were sited in the chancel, the crossing and the first two bays of the nave; the rood screen separated the rest of the nave which was empty.[35] It was said in 1835 that the abbey church could accommodate 1,200 people, while the population of the parish was 5,780.[36]

Income from pew rents started to fall when Trinity Church was opened, and in 1847 most pews were reduced in price. But in the large-scale replanning of the abbey church, undertaken under the direction of Sir George Gilbert Scott, not only were the pews removed, after less than a century of use, but in 1877 it was resolved 'That the whole of the seats in the parish church be free and open'. Henceforth the upkeep of the church would rely on voluntary contributions.

'Finding' the parish priest

The scene is set for the clergymen of Tewkesbury after the Dissolution of the abbey in the report of the commissioners investigating the chantries in 1545.[37] Thomas Franklyn, 56 years of age, was the chantry priest at a stipend of £4 7s. 9d. The commissioners reported that parishioners had formerly used money given for the maintenance of the parish church

> to founde iij priestes makinge up the residue of their owne devocion & nowe there is founde oone ... the greateness of the seid paroche & villages within the same considered, it is very requisite there shuld contynue some assistaunte from tyme to tyme.

The commissioners noted 1,600 'howselinge people' or communicants ('housel' being a sacrifice) which should represent about 60% of the population, but may be the total; in 1563 the minister said there were 396 households.[38] The second chantry enquiry two years later noted

> the Kinges Majestie is Parson there, and no Vycar endowed. One curate is there founde at the Kinges Highnes Charges, where there is very grete necesssitie of oone Preist more to be allways assystaunt there to the saide Curate.[39]

Initially the king 'found' the parish priest £10, and after the abolition of chantries, the stipend of the former chantry priest was also paid to him so he in turn could pay an 'assistant'; James I increased the stipend by a small amount and it was still paid by the Exchequer in 1828.[40] From 1575, and the purchase of a royal charter, Tewkesbury corporation became effectively the owner of the abbey church but the appointment of the parish priest was in the crown's hands, and has remained so. The names of many clerics officiating in Tewkesbury over the next 250 years are known, but it is not always clear who was the 'parish priest' and who the 'assistant'. The title 'minister' and later 'reader' was sometimes applied to the assistant.

Mindful of the fact that £10 was considered too poor a stipend to attract a learned man who would be qualified to preach, a number of benefactions were made. Baptist Hicks, Viscount Campden, made a significant bequest in 1629 of the rectory of St. Ismael's or St. Ishmael's in Pembrokeshire, near Milford Haven; half the revenues were to be given to the poor and half to support a 'sufficient preacher'.[41] The corporation had the administration of this 'Welsh money' and it may have given them the opportunity to support a preacher they favoured rather than the parish priest nominated by the king. This seems to have happened during the period of the Commonwealth.

Political and religious feeling ran high during the 1640s and 1650s, and it was difficult for any minister to be acceptable to the council and all the inhabitants. John Wells had probably been instituted before the Civil War started; he was an 'independent' in sympathy, and later said to have been 'zealous' for Parliament against the 'Cavaleers'.[42] In 1646, Wells secured an augmentation of £50 from the Committee for Plundered Ministers and another £50 for an assistant; typically they were to be paid by three recusants (Roman Catholics who paid a fine rather than attend the Church of England) from the revenues of three rectories in Gloucestershire which they owned. In 1650 Thomas Burroughs was the assistant and in a survey of church livings was called an 'able preaching minister'; for some reason Wells was not mentioned, possibly because he was absent from the town. It was estimated that the parish contained 1,000 families.[43] The bailiffs petitioned for a 'further' augmentation, and said they had 'for above fifty years, at their own charge, by way of benevolence, maintained pious and learned ministers, who constantly did and still do preach every Lord's Day'.[44] The benevolence was a voluntary collection in which the council assisted, perhaps with rating lists, perhaps with the services of rate collectors, but not, as might be inferred, by paying him out of their own revenues. Burroughs was given £50. The council also repaired the chancel in 1650 and created a pulpit there for a lecture sermon, especially useful 'when the minister hath a low voice', indicating their Puritan sympathies.[45]

There were strong rumblings of discontent against Wells. In July 1654, at the request of the corporation, the assistant's £50 was directed to George Hopkins, 'a godly and painful preacher of the Gospel', and ceased to be paid to John Wells. Wells claimed that he never received the 'Welsh' money, that he had no house, and that he received £37 not £50 for the assistant, and the order was countermanded. The Trustees for the Maintenance of Ministers in December noted Tewkesbury's need for an assistant, 'being a very greate and populous Parish and having severall country villages neere adjoining' and agreed there should be a weekly lecture on 'every Wednesday being the Market day'; George Hopkins, who was also vicar of All Saints, Evesham, was appointed. Wells complained about 'a malignant lecturer put upon me' and the committee's time was taken up with plea and counter plea. Eventually £20 was allotted to Wells and £30 to Hopkins.

After the restoration of Charles II, it appears that Wells was not allowed to continue in the parish, and a more orthodox man was licensed as 'preacher' in Tewkesbury, and later as master of the grammar school.[46] Robert Easton declared his acceptance of the Act of Uniformity in 1662 as 'preacher at Tewkesbury' and Richard Wilkes as master of the free school and curate of Stoke Orchard, Tredington and Walton Cardiff. Francis Wells, possibly John Wells' son, was licensed to 'officiate' in the church in 1670 and in 1677 he was instituted to what for the first time was called the 'vicarage of Tewkesbury'. Like John Wells, his tenure was troubled.

The legacy of the period of Civil War, Commonwealth and Protectorate was vivid divisions between Puritan and Orthodox. Tewkesbury had a strong independent movement, particularly of Baptists who had their own burial ground and chapel. Francis Wells was either triumphant or defiant to state in his return in 1676 to Bishop Compton of London that there were 1,500 Nonconformists in Tewkesbury, for he was shortly to be arraigned by the council in the ecclesiastical court for his nonconformity.

1676: returns known as the Compton Census[47]

	Conformists	*Catholics*	*Nonconformists*
Ashchurch	280	-	30
Bushley	60	-	-
Forthampton	165	-	9
Oxenton	108	-	12
Tewkesbury	500	1	1,500
Tredington	70	-	5

Soon after he became vicar, Francis Wells preached on the sins of the nation and revealed his strongly anti-royalist attitudes. The bailiffs complained to the bishop and Wells was suspended. They said they had 'long suffered great inconveniences for want of an able Orthodox Minister amongst us', but had forborne any complaints 'although he hath justly in many ways deserved it from his Nonconformity' and they complained also of his manner of preaching.[48] To encourage him to resign, the council offered to assist in 'collecting what benevolence he can gett from the Inhabitants of this Towne', but he did not oblige.[49] Later they found 10s. a day for 'each minister that shall be procured to preach here during the present business'. From the articles exhibited against him in 1680 it appears that he refused to wear the surplice. Tewkesbury church had been without a surplice since 1641 when it was torn up, until a churchwarden gave a replacement in 1678.[50] It was a dispute about a symbol which had great significance for what it implied about the general ways and beliefs of the Church of England. Another complaint was that Wells did not employ a clerk, though he maintained that he was not able to both support his family and to provide wages to a clerk.

This case was the background to the most important of the bequests to Tewkesbury corporation respecting the church minister. In 1679 Edwin Skrimshire offered to give the tithes of Fiddington and Tredington, from which the £10 for the curate was already found, 'in order to the better maintenance of a Minister here for the future'; the corollary was an unsuccessful attempt to persuade the Crown to transfer the advowson to Mr. Skrimshire. The deed was dated 1683 and a grateful council went to Staffordshire to thank him.[51] From these revenues the corporation had to pay £12 to the minister of Tredington, £12 to the minister of Ashchurch, and £10 with any surplus to Tewkesbury's minister. This raised the financial position and status of the curate very considerably, and he was properly a 'vicar' because he now had a share of the tithes of the parish, but the council was still responsible for giving him his income. By the earlier 18th century the living was valued at £80 and was no longer rated as a poor one.[52]

Intermittent entries in the diary of a minister, John Matthews, illustrate the uncertain nature of the vicar's income, and even if not the patron, the council certainly attempted to call the tune.[53] In 1685 Matthews took the oaths required of the master of the grammar school, but added a caveat which revealed his High Church attitudes. The bishop wisely cautioned him against 'medling in the town business'. He officiated in the church but does not seem to have become vicar until 1697.[54] Matthews found himself up against the severely Baptist and anti-royalist town clerk, Henry Collett, who complained that he did not 'preach' because he read his sermons. The council in 1705 petitioned the Lord Chancellor to appoint the reader in Matthew's place if he should resign, but he did not.[55] He reflected in his diary:

> I am in great measure at the disposal of my superiors ... But if ordinary mechanics, if the butcher and the baker, the glazier, the grazier and the glover, be suffered to domineer over their orthodox and aged pastor, and stint or alienate at their pleasure a considerable portion of his revenues, I am sure it will do great disservice to the true ends of Religion.

He received some of the money which the council had withheld from him, but did not endear himself to the authorities by refusing to address the bailiffs with the title 'worshipful', and he ended one sermon at which they were present with an 'admonition to do the repairing of our church'. In December 1712 he had to record 'a scanty collection of benevolence from the Town'.

In Matthews' case, the minister was high church and the council apparently dominated by dissenters. In the next major conflict, some 50 years later, the stand-points were reversed. Edward Evanson was inducted as vicar in 1769. He was also perpetual curate of Tredington, a position which the bishop hoped would help him pay for a curate in Tewkesbury.[56] His sermons soon earned him the hostility of Neast Havard, town clerk. On Easter Sunday 1771 'I preached a sermon with a view to begin a Reformation; the time can't be far off ... for the service of the Church of England is such a jargon of inconsistent nonsense, it can't possibly subsist long'. A complicated legal battle began, and in November 1773 articles against him were exhibited in the ecclesiastical court. A meeting at the Swan Hotel in Tewkesbury revealed popular support, and an agreement to subscribe to his expenses was circulated and signed by 305 people, from all walks of life, men and women, but perhaps predominantly the artisans in the town; it raised £204, and Evanson claimed when it was all over that 'the truly generous inhabitants of the parish of Tewkesbury ... defrayed the charges attending my defence against the late malevolent Prosecution'.[57] Just as an ecclesiastical court found largely for Evanson, he resigned.

For a variety of reasons the steam went out of these doctrinal conflicts in the 19th century. The annoyance of tithes was removed by the enclosure of Tredington in 1806 and Fiddington in 1811: the vicar of Tewkesbury received 336 acres in lieu of tithes, from which he paid the traditional small pension of £12 each to the perpetual curates of Ashchurch and Tredington. The Tithe

Commutation Act of 1836 required all remaining tithes to be changed into money payments calculated according to an index based on yearly average prices for wheat, barley and oats. In Tewkesbury little land was still liable for tithes: out of 2,333 acres they were paid on only 66 acres of arable and 266 acres of pasture. The perpetual curates of Walton Cardiff and Tredington were granted a rent charge of £25 and £18 15s. respectively, and three laymen a further £38 18s. 6d.[58]

Another reason was the council's changed political tone after the reforms of the Municipal Corporations Act of 1835: the electorate was enlarged and battles were channelled into who should be elected. Acceptance of dissenting meeting places led instead to disputes over church rates. Civil Registration, introduced in 1837, also seems to have lessened the intensity of feeling over the Church of England. By the time the Oxford Movement roused doctrinal conflict, it was within a much more limited church-going community.

There was also change in the nature of the Church of England's organisation. In 1831 the Whig government had established a royal commission to investigate the revenues of archbishops and bishops, cathedral deans and chapters, and of all parochial benefices. They showed Tewkesbury's vicar receiving on average £376, placing him in the upper half of the 10,500 benefices surveyed. By the time the report was ready, a further royal commission was established to propose reforms, and in 1836 became permanent as the Ecclesiastical Commission. Its powers grew, and localism was gradually eroded along with the ancient anomalies of parochial provision.[59] In the 20th century, the Ecclesiastical Commission (renamed the Church Commission after amalgamation with Queen Anne's Bounty in 1948) took on responsibility for pensions and then for stipends, and the various miscellaneous endowments of individual livings were gradually absorbed into diocesan or central administration. Standardization became the watchword.

Returns to Parliament published in 1835[60]

	Benefice	*Incumbent*	*Patron*	*Population*	*Av. annual income 1829-31 (£)*	*Glebe house*
Ashchurch	PC	F.H. Romney	F.H. Romney	649	50	No
Bushley	PC	W. Prosser	Dean & Chapter of Worcester	113	58	No
Forthampton	PC	R.B. Plumptre (also rector of North Coates, Lincs.)	J. Yorke	459	138	Unfit
Oxenton	PC	E. Beavan (also PC Gt. Washbourne, Glos.)	E. Beavan	166	68	No
Tewkesbury	V	C. White (also PC Deerhurst, & V Hexton, Herts.)	The Crown	5,780	376 (£80 to assist. curate)	Fit
Tredington	PC	R.Hepworth	Bishop of Gloucester	153	54	No
Walton Cardiff	PC	W. Prosser (also PC Chaceley & PC Bushley, Worcs.)	All Souls, Oxford	49	56	No

Note. V=vicar; PC=perpetual curate.

A house for the vicar

Charles White, who became vicar in 1818, was responsible for building the first vicarage house in Tewkesbury, on a site near the abbey church facing Gloucester Road. His predecessor had been absent from the parish for many years on account of the lack of a house, combined with the 'low and damp situation of Tewkesbury' and violent attacks of the gout, so the parish was looked after by his curate.[61] Charles White secured a grant from Queen Anne's Bounty in 1826 of £600 towards the cost of a house which he designed himself—the Bounty was encouraging the provision of houses where none existed—and a mortgage from the same source of £340; voluntary subscriptions added £852: £300 was contributed by the two Tewkesbury members of parliament, and £125 by the bishop of Gloucester.[62] In the 1841 census Charles White, then over 80 years of age, was living there with his unmarried daughter, two children, probably grand-children, a very young boy servant and a female servant. White died in 1845.

His successor, Charles Greenall Davies, made alterations to the house to 'combine a most convenient arrangement for a Parsonage with a thorough and substantial repair'; in 1846 £428 was borrowed on mortgage from the Bounty for the work.[63] Mostly the alterations were to the internal plan and a porch was added; downstairs

Fig.8.5 The front and rear elevations of Tewkesbury vicarage house, as drawn in 1846 by Samuel Whitfield Daukes, architect, of Cheltenham, when alterations were made

Fig.8.6 The vicarage house, built in 1827 to the design of the Revd. Charles White, has been little altered externally since the mid-19th century, but the vicar now lives in the former abbot's house

there was a drawing room, dining room, study, hall, kitchen and butler's pantry. The vicarage house, now called Abbey Lodge, is much as it was then, except that the central decorative gable has been lowered (Fig.8.6).

Hemming Robeson, Davies' successor, shouldered the responsibility for the ambitious restoration of the abbey embarked on by Davies, assisted not only by a local restoration committee but a national one. The abbey reopened in 1879, and the *Parochial Magazine* was also started in January of that year. In 1881 Robeson lived in the vicarage with his wife, mother-in-law, two lady's maids, a cook, a parlour maid and a house maid. In 1883 news started to circulate that under the will of John Martin of Upper Hall, Ledbury (who in 1834 had petitioned against church rates) the trustees were going to sell the old Abbey House.[64] The president of the Society of Antiquaries of London, alerted by the chairman of the national restoration committee, wrote to *The Times* to communicate a resolution expressing the hope that the former monastic site could be purchased for the church. The possibility was particularly welcome locally, it seems, because the meadow and a walk through the gateway and across the south side of the abbey had in the past been 'semi-public' but recently had been more clearly defined as private property. The sale was advertised on 9 June 1883 and the auction took place on 18 July. The estate included the Gatehouse as well as Abbey House, and what later became known as Abbey Cottage, with other cottages and meadow land.

An urgent appeal for funds was launched. Canon Robeson seems to have been the moving spirit, supported by the builder Thomas Collins who had done so much for the restoration of the abbey. The *Tewkesbury Register* reported that on the afternoon of the sale, the large room at the Swan Hotel was crowded. Alfred Healing, who then occupied Abbey House, was one of those bidding for it; he gave up at £10,400, and £10,500 secured it for Hemming Robeson.[65] One oddity of the sale was that it included a room within the abbey itself, in the west bay of the nave south aisle,

Fig.8.7 The memorial to Thomas Collins in the abbey. A well-known builder in the town, he was important in preserving many of Tewkesbury's old houses, in the restoration of the abbey, and in the purchase of the Abbey House estate in 1883

which in the event was given to the church by John Biddulph Martin. The purchase enabled the construction of the Cloister Walk (the north walk of the former monastic cloister), and the opening up of the south door into the abbey church, thus allowing parishioners and inhabitants access to the south side of the abbey for the first time (cf. Figs.8.1, 8.2); this was an important reason for the purchase.[66] Some of the property was immediately sold again; Hemming Robeson bought Abbey Cottage where his sister lived for a number of years, and then Robeson and his wife after he retired.[67] In 1891, when he filled in the census forms, Hemming Robeson was living in Abbey House, which had been transferred to a trust, and his household contained his wife and his son, his mother-in-law and seven female servants. The curate, his wife and two maid servants, were living in the vicarage house, which was retained until about 1968, when it was vested in the Diocesan Trust for the P.C.C.; Abbey House has served as the official benefice house since 1966 (Fig.8.8).

Robeson died in 1912, but he might have been disappointed if he could have read what a later vicar, Ernest F. Smith, announced in the *Parochial Magazine* in September 1919:

> I myself shall move into the Vicarage proper on Michaelmas Day, and I have not the slightest doubt that, in all human probability, I shall be the last Vicar of Tewkesbury to occupy the Abbey House. Thank God, the days are over when the parson was necessarily a man of large means ... Unless the income of this living is increased to at least three times its present amount (- and I don't think there is much likelihood of this), no future incumbent will find it possible to keep up so big a house and grounds. This may be matter for regret, but no one can possibly be sorry that the 'parson' of the town should henceforth be more obviously on the same level as his parishioners.

His forecast was not fulfilled, as the vicar at the beginning of the 21st century continues to occupy the Abbey House. But in some ways the situation has come full circle from the time when the abbey was closed. In 1940 another vicar only

Fig.8.8 After the Dissolution of the abbey, the abbot's house was privately owned. The garden reached right to the south wall of the church. Hemming Robeson, the vicar, and Thomas Collins together purchased the estate in 1883 and transferred it to trustees for the use of the vicar of Tewkesbury. The south front is a Georgian reworking of a late medieval stone and timber-framed house

agreed to stay in Tewkesbury when his parishioners promised him more financial support. Clergymen rely on parishioners for their maintenance, even if this is disguised by the Church Commissioners' system of the 'diocesan quota'.

Fortunately Tewkesbury Abbey is the centre of an active church community, particularly evident in its music and in the welcome given to visitors to the church so imaginatively saved by the townsmen of Tewkesbury in 1540.

CHAPTER 9

The Norman Church *by* Malcolm Thurlby

Tewkesbury is one of the most important and interesting survivals of a Norman great church in the British Isles.[1] Only Durham, Peterborough and Norwich cathedrals are more complete in their Romanesque fabric.

The church was founded by Robert Fitzhamon, who had been given the honour of Gloucester in 1087. This patronage was inspired by his wife, Sybil, and Gerald of Avranches, the first abbot of Tewkesbury. Work on the new church and conventual buildings would have been under way in the 1090s, and in 1102 Benedictine monks moved from Cranborne to Tewkesbury.[2] At this time the eastern arm of the church, the crossing and transepts, and the first two bays of the nave would have been completed. This facilitated the liturgical functioning of the church with high altar and choir, and provided subsidiary altars in chapels.

According to the Chronicle of Florence of Worcester, the church was consecrated in 1121.[3] The Annals of Tewkesbury and *Monasticon Anglicanum* give 1123,[4] but internal evidence invalidates this date. Theowulf, bishop of Worcester, who performed the consecration, died on 20 October 1123, four days before the consecration date given in *Monasticon Anglicanum*.[5] The church would have been essentially completed by 1121 with the exception of the upper parts of the crossing tower. The abbey was severely damaged by fire in 1178.[6]

A large part of the Norman church remains today although no single area has come down to us in an unmodified form. The remodelling of the church in the 13th and especially the 14th centuries presents the historian of the Norman fabric with problems of interpretation. In order to recreate the appearance of the original building, additions and modifications have to be peeled away in the mind's eye. With this done it is possible to reconstitute the form of the Norman church by referring to fragments of evidence in the stonework and through analogy with related buildings. We are then in a position to explore the sources for the design of the church.

Photographic Introduction to the Norman Church

In essence, the plan of the church is that set out in the late 11th century (Fig.9.1). Reading from east to west (right to left)—the order in which construction proceeded—the two-bay, aisled choir had arcades on columnar piers ('columns')[7] that terminated in a semi-hexagonal east end and was surrounded by an ambulatory. The present chapels off the ambulatory and south choir aisle belong to the Gothic remodelling (Masterplan); the Norman church probably had chapels to the east, north-east and south-east, like the north-east and south-east chapels at Gloucester Cathedral.

The crossing is asymmetrical and has piers elongated on the east-west axis and east and west arches wider than those on the north and south. The aisleless transepts are two bays deep and

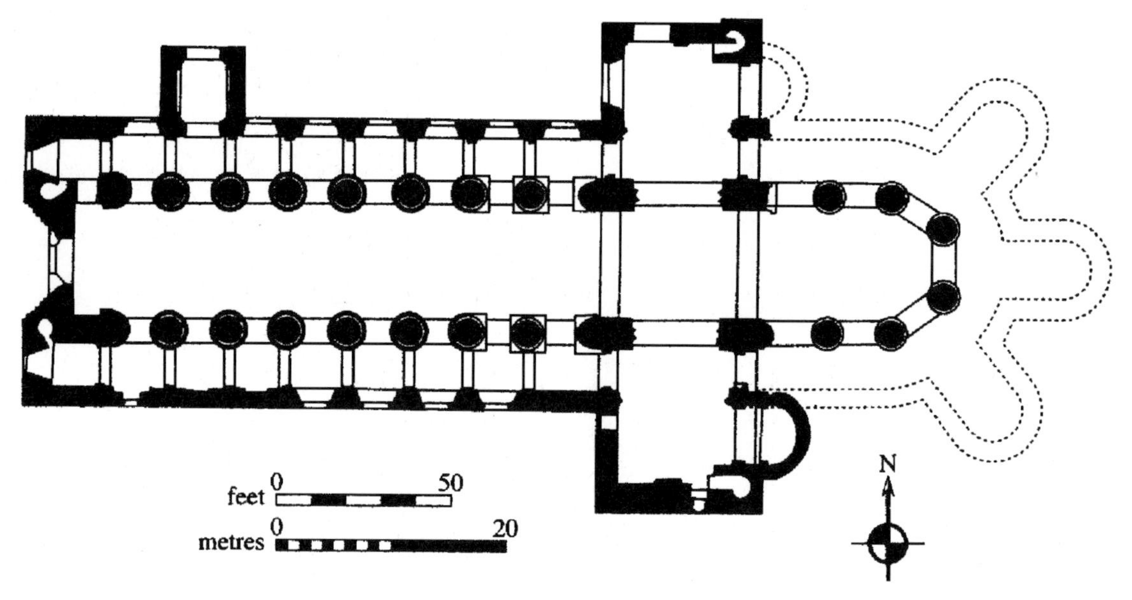

Fig.9.1 Plan of the Norman church (after Fernie)

have spiral staircases in the outer eastern angles that lead to the upper storeys and the roof space. The Norman two-storey apsidal chapel (now the Lady Chapel) survives on the east side of the south transept but its counterpart in the north transept was replaced in the 13th century.

The nave has eight bays carried on columnar piers. The aisles have an 'extra' bay that flanks the westernmost bay of the nave and the cavernous entrance arch. It is from these western aisle bays that there is access to spiral staircases in their inner western angles. A two-storey porch

Fig.9.2 Exterior from the south-east, with the Norman north transept and apsidal chapel in the centre

Fig.9.3 Exterior from the north-west, with the Norman north porch in the centre

Fig.9.4 The west front with the 'triumphal' arch

projects from bay 7 of the north aisle (numbering from east to west).

The tour of the standing fabric of the exterior commences on the south side (Fig.9.2). The south transept, with its apsidal chapel, and the crossing tower remain from the Norman church. The original roof pitch over the choir and south transept is marked by the gables on the east and south faces of the crossing tower. Red scorch marks within the east gable probably result from the fire of 1178.

The exterior from the north-west (Fig.9.3) shows the two-storey Norman porch projecting from bay 7. The clerestory windows are 14th century but the blind arches at this level belong to the Norman fabric.

The massive western 'triumphal' arch of the west front preserves six of its original seven Norman orders (Fig.9.4). At high level the arch is flanked by two tiers of blind arches on cushion capitals, topped by two turrets with conical pinnacles, all surviving from the Norman abbey.

Entering the church by way of the north porch, the doorway has four orders, of which three are plain and one has an angle-roll moulding (Fig.9.5). They are carried on plain cushion capitals and

Fig.9.5 Norman tympanum and barrel vault of the north porch

surround a tympanum of unusual design with stepped radiating stones. There are local affiliates in the north doorway at Twyning and the south doorway at Lower Swell. The barrel vault above is plastered but the ashlar of the walls is not.

Standing in the nave, looking east, the arcades have eight columnar piers, 6 feet (1.83m.) in diameter and 30 feet 8 inches (9.35m.) in height, that carry round-headed arches, with a plain inner order and a roll-moulded outer order (Fig.9.6). Above, there is a triforium with paired arches. The clerestory and vault are 14th century.

The floor rises one step up towards the east between the second pair of piers and this is accompanied by a change in the plinth in pier 2, square to the east and round to the west (Fig.9.7). This marks the western extent of the liturgical choir and the beginning of the liturgical nave.[8] This reading is confirmed upon close examination of the aisle side of the south pier where stepped patches rising from the floor reveal the former existence of a stair which probably led to the medieval rood loft (Fig.9.7).

The vaults and windows of the aisles are 14th century but these are just modifications to the basic Norman fabric (Fig.9.8). From the latter there remain the single-shaft responds and the jambs of wall arches below the windows. A

Fig.9.6 Nave, looking east, with the massive Norman nave arcades

Fig.9.7 Nave south arcade, pier 2 looking north across the site of the former rood screen

Fig.9.8 Nave south aisle, looking east

complete Norman wall arch is visible on the right.

In the transept, giant arches rise through two storeys and are moulded in the arch (Fig.9.9). The left arch leads to the south choir aisle while the upper arch, now filled with later 13th-century tracery, formerly opened to the gallery. The right arches open into two superimposed apsidal chapels of which the ground-floor one (now the Lady Chapel) is vaulted with a three-part rib vault, whereas the gallery chapel has a plain semi-dome in the upper storey decorated with a painted foliage 'boss' surrounded by chevron. The wall of the lower chapel, like the south aisle wall of the presbytery, is faced with small squared blocks of lias stone with levelling courses of limestone ashlar. There is a triforium passage above the gallery which continues behind the south-east crossing into the choir and thereby demonstrates the former presence of the triforium in the Norman choir. Above the triforium there is a change from red, fire-damaged

Fig.9.9 South transept, east elevation

ashlar to partly restored masonry (Pl.7) which is probably contemporary with the present 14th-century vault.

The south (and north) arches of the crossing have an inner order carried on paired scalloped capitals atop twin coursed shafts (Fig.9.10). By contrast, the inner orders of the east and west arches are corbelled out just below the springing point of the arch, originally to facilitate the placement of the choir-stalls flush against the wall. The outer order of each arch rises without interruption from the jambs and has a simple angle roll. Along with the larger size of the east and west crossing arches and the east-west elongation of the crossing piers, these angle rolls subtly emphasize the importance of the sanctuary and liturgical choir over the transepts.

Above the crossing, the interior of the tower was formerly open to the ground but is now hidden by the 14th-century vault (Fig.9.11). There is a low wall passage faced with plain round-headed arches on cushion capitals atop octagonal shafts. This passage gives access to doorways to the four roof spaces above the choir, transepts and nave vaults. Above, there are tall unadorned arches which enclose blind arches and windows on the back plane of the walls.

East of the crossing, much less of the Norman fabric survives. The columnar piers, which bear distinct vertical axe marks and wide mortar joints characteristic of the Norman work, were reduced in height in the 14th century and are now topped with 14th-century capitals (Fig.9.12).

Reconstruction of the Norman Church

With the extant elements of the Norman church established one can begin the process of careful sleuthing for clues to reconstruct the missing

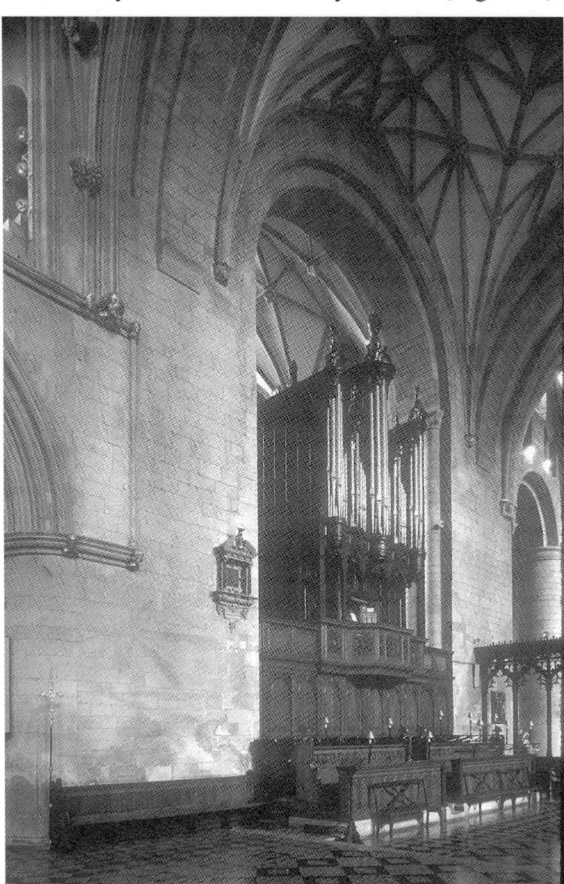

Fig.9.10 South crossing arch and the choir

Fig.9.11 The lantern of the crossing tower

Fig.9.12 Choir and sanctuary, looking east

aspects of the Norman building. The detective work requires an attention to detail of a Miss Marple or a Sherlock Holmes, not least because earlier studies have not reached the same conclusions about the appearance of the Norman church. In particular there has been debate over the number of storeys in the choir and transepts; was there a four-storey, wood-roofed elevation, or a three-storey vaulted scheme? If the latter, were the vaults of the same form in the choir and transepts and were they built of stone or wood? Did the choir have a so-called giant order, that is with piers rising through the ground storey to support the gallery arches, or were the main arcade and gallery quite separate? Were the aisles vaulted? Resolution of these questions is crucial in order to create an accurate picture of the Norman church, for then it becomes possible to understand the proper associations of the design and, concomitantly, the aims of the patrons in having it so built.

The piers of the east arm now carry 14th-century capitals (Fig.9.14) but there is clear evidence above the western responds of both arcades that the piers originally rose higher in the main elevation. On the north side, the eleventh stone above the capital has diagonal tooling to the west but vertical to the east. The same occurs on the second and seventh stone above the west respond of the south arcade, where the change in tooling is accompanied by the curvature of the stone exactly in line with that of the pier below the capital (Fig.9.13). This suggests that in the Norman choir the piers rose probably to the same height as those in the nave, and that the level of the gallery arches would have been the same as in the transepts (Figs.9.9 & 10.8). Turning to the aisle side of the piers, there are chamfered capitals at the same level as the Norman scalloped capitals of the aisle wall responds (Fig.9.14). These would have carried transverse arches of an

Fig.9.13 Detail of wall above the west respond of the south choir arcade

Fig.9.14 West pier in the choir south arcade, detail from the choir aisle

aisle vault as in the choir aisles of Gloucester Cathedral (Fig.9.15). As at Gloucester this would have been a groin vault, the traces of which are still visible in the east bay of the north aisle (Fig.9.16). The capitals at the back of the main arcade piers now carry the ribs of the 14th-century vault and the beginnings of the recessed main arcade arches (Fig.9.14). To the sides of these springers are the hacked-back springers of the Norman recessed arcade arch. The scheme is fundamentally the same as in the arches from the transepts to the choir aisles and gallery (Fig.9.9). Later reflections of this design appear in the eastern bay of the nave at Romsey Abbey (Hants., begun *c*.1120), in the choir of Jedburgh Abbey (Borders, founded *c*.1138) (Fig.9.17) and throughout Oxford Cathedral (c.1160).[9] This creates a giant or colossal order on the principle explained by the Roman architect, Vitruvius, in the 1st century BC in his *Ten Books on Architecture* (*De Architectura*) for the basilica he built at Fanum, Italy.[10]

Fig.9.15 Gloucester Cathedral, south choir aisle to the east, with Norman groin vaults

Turning to the south transept, the ground-floor chapel has an early rib vault dating to *c*.1100 (Fig.9.9). It has been suggested that the ribs were added in the mid-12th century, but the archaeology of the chapel does not support this idea.[11] While chamfers on the ribs are often associated with a later 12th-century date, the transverse arches of the axial crypt chapel at Gloucester Cathedral (begun 1089) are also chamfered. The

Fig.9.16 Trace of former groin vault in the north choir aisle, west bay

use of ribs in the ground-floor chapel suggests that it had a higher status than the semi-domed upper chapel and concomitantly that the main apse in the east arm would also have been ribbed.[12] Support for this interpretation is found in the east arm of Ewenny Priory (Glam.) (1116-26), where the eastern bay is rib-vaulted while the western two bays have a barrel vault (Fig.9.18).[13] Ewenny was a daughter house of St. Peter's, Gloucester, where the Norman east arm had a high barrel vault over the straight bays and a rib vault in the apse. It is likely that the same arrangement was found in Norman Tewkesbury.[14]

The evidence for a high barrel vault in the transepts is unequivocal. The trajectory of the former barrel vault is clearly marked above the south crossing arch by the reddened, fire-damaged masonry that terminates in an arc. This may be followed in the mind's eye behind the springing of the 14th-century vault in the north-east angle of the transept down to the original springing point of the Norman barrel above the triforium. Here there is a break from fire-damaged Norman ashlar to undamaged 14th-century stonework introduced when the Norman barrel vault had been removed. What is most significant is that the fire damage does not always rise to the very top of the Norman ashlar. Instead, it terminates up to an inch below the top of the course of masonry (Pl.7). This came about through the plaster of the underside of the barrel vault encroaching on to the top of the wall in just the same way as in the barrel-vaulted north porch (Fig.9.5), and this served to protect the upper wall from the fire. The restored west wall of the south transept retains nothing to confirm the reconstruction of a Norman barrel vault. However, in the north bay of the west wall of the north transept, the point at which the former barrel

Fig.9.17 Jedburgh Abbey, choir elevation, like that formerly at Tewkesbury

Fig.9.18 Ewenny Priory, interior of the choir looking east

vault sprang is marked by the change from Norman ashlar below to restored stonework above. Throughout the east wall of the north transept there is the same change from Norman ashlar to partly restored 14th-century stonework above the triforium as in the south transept, although without fire damage.

It is significant that on the exterior of the east and west walls of the south transept, and the east wall of the north transept there is an upper blind arcade (Fig.9.19). This motif is especially popular in central, western and south-western France where it usually accompanies a barrel-vaulted interior space.[15] In the east wall arcades at Tewkesbury the third arch from the end was originally open and the restored inner splay of this is seen above the north transept vault at the very top of the wall.[16] Thus it is far too high in the wall to be associated with a clerestory.

Instead, the opening provided air circulation and light above the barrel vault and would not

Fig.9.19 Crossing tower from the north-west

Fig.9.20 Passage to the upper chapel in the south transept, with painted mortar joints

have been seen from within the church, just like the surviving arrangement in the transepts of the former abbey church at Souillac (Lot, France).[17] The barrel vaults simply abutted the wall, as demonstrated by the trajectory of the fire damage across regular courses of Norman ashlar above the south crossing arch, and the absence above the north crossing arch of any trace of a former vault. Whilst it has been suggested that the vaults may have been of lath and plaster this material would not have contained the fire and, therefore, a tufa vault is more likely. Tufa may be classified as either calcareous or volcanic tufa.[18] It is the calcareous type that was used in English medieval vaults, which is much lighter in weight than either limestone or sandstone, a feature that especially recommends its use in vaulting. Fragments of tufa which possibly come from the former Romanesque high vault are used in the jambs of the 14th-century clerestory windows in the Tewkesbury nave.[19] Willis records the use of tufa in the vault of the Norman chapter house at Worcester Cathedral (*c.*1120), and it is documented in the Norman nave of Chepstow Priory.[20]

On the evidence of the barrel vault of the passage leading into the south transept gallery chapel, the plaster of the south transept high barrel vault would have been painted with red lines in the form of imitation mortar joints (Fig.9.20).[21] Something similar appears in the east bay of the presbytery at Ewenny Priory where the ashlar of the walls and ribs of the vault have painted masonry on limewash while the web of the vault is plastered, albeit not painted. Romanesque polychromy appears elsewhere at Tewkesbury, for example in the red chevron painted directly on the abaci of some of the nave north arcade capitals, most clearly on the west side of the first pier (Pl.9). This painted chevron is the same as on the recently revealed 'boss' in the south transept gallery chapel, where it surrounds a foliage pattern that relates to a loose capital in St. Peter at Newnham-on-Severn and generally to the foliage on tympana of the Dymock school churches (Pl.10).[22]

Corroborative evidence for the reconstruction of Norman barrel vaults in the transepts is on hand at the former Benedictine abbey at Pershore (Fig.9.21).[23] Here the elevation of the east wall of the south transept is the same as at Tewkesbury and is even accompanied by the same change in masonry above the triforium that marks the

Fig.9.21 Pershore Abbey. Interior of the south transept looking south-east

Fig.9.22 Detail of the east wall of the eastern crossing arch, with the trace of the Norman vault (centre)

former springing point of the barrel vault (cf. Fig.9.9).[24] This change in masonry is also represented at exactly the same level on the west wall of the south transept at Pershore where in the south-west angle it arcs up on to the stair turret to reveal the trajectory of the former Norman barrel. Moreover, above the present 14th-century vault against the south wall there remain some voussoirs of the former barrel, and the full trajectory of the high barrel still remains in the stump of the north transept, above the north crossing arch.[25]

Returning to Tewkesbury, the trace of the arc of a former high vault over the choir exists above the east crossing arch (Fig.9.22). It has been suggested that ashlar was inserted between the extrados (i.e. outer circumference) of the crossing arch and the arc after the removal of the webbing of the Norman vault (Fig.21.2B,C).[26] Two details indicate that this is incorrect. First, the ashlar is Norman with the characteristic diagonal linear tooling and thick mortar joints. Secondly, the trajectory of the arc descends almost to meet the extrados of the crossing arch at its springing (Fig.9.22). In other words, the section of the putative vault web that was bonded into the wall above the crossing arch is narrower at the bottom than at the top. In terms of vault construction this makes little sense and, even though it has been suggested that the original web would have broadened beyond the trace at the springer of the vault, the notion of having part of the springer within the trace, and part without, is impractical. Instead, the original vault is marked by the masonry immediately outside the trace of the arc (Fig.21.2C, D), and its thickness, or rather relative thinness, at the apex is marked by the horizontal stones which were inserted after the removal of the Norman web. Thus the Norman vault was bonded into the wall in contrast to the transept vaults, in which the web just butted up against the ashlar above the north and south crossing arches. Such variation in techniques of vault construction was not unusual at a time when the technology was in its infancy. Further variation is evident in the junction of the former Norman high vault in the choir of Hereford Cathedral, and in the vaults of Lilleshall Abbey (Shrops.).[27]

The focus of late 20th-century architectural historians on the reconstruction of high vaults in Romanesque Tewkesbury has detracted from the contention that there was a four-storey elevation at Tewkesbury, a forerunner of the classic early Gothic scheme in northern French cathedrals like Noyon and Laon.[28] There could never have been clerestory windows in the barrel-vaulted transepts, but what of the eastern arm? It seems likely that the pitch of the roof over the nave aisles is the original Norman pitch (Fig.9.4). If

Fig.9.23 Western bay of the nave, south elevation

Fig.9.24 Western bay of the nave, north elevation

Fig.9.25 Detail of upper south wall in bay 7 of the nave south aisle

this reflects the arrangement over the former choir galleries, then there could not have been clerestory windows in the Norman choir. The same would be true of the apse even if it was rib-vaulted, as in the south transept chapel, unless the external blind arcade was modified by being extended downwards to accommodate clerestory windows. Any openings in the blind arcade as existing would only have ventilated and lit the roof space above the vault, as in the east walls of the transepts.

It is most likely that the Norman nave of Tewkesbury was also barrel-vaulted as evidenced by the consistent horizontal masonry break above the triforium, as in the transepts (Figs.9.9, 9.23). The quadrant arches that communicate between the transepts and the nave aisles indicate that the nave aisles would originally have had half-barrel vaults (Fig.9.8). These would have sprung from a point just above the tops of the respond capitals that supported quadrant arches. This is seen most clearly in the second and third bays of the north nave aisle and in the western bays of the south aisle in the form of a horizontal break in the wall masonry above, and to either side of, the scalloped capital of the responds (Fig.9.25). Whether these vaults were of masonry or wood has been a matter of some debate.[29] The corbels in the western bays of the nave south aisle and in bay 7 of the nave north aisle have been associated with a wooden vault. However, it is possible that the corbels supported centering for the construction of a masonry vault as in the nave north aisle at Brancion (Saône-et-Loire, France) where the quadrant vault abuts a pointed barrel vault over the nave (Fig.9.26). In the westernmost bay of the nave south aisle there are corbels on both sides which suggests that this bay was originally covered with a barrel vault.[30] In the corresponding bay of the north aisle there is a horizontal masonry break at the right point for the barrel but there are no corbels. The absence of corbels in the other aisle bays may be explained either by the cutting back of stone corbels or the filling in of holes for wooden corbels, of the type still visible in the Brancion nave. If the aisle vaults at Tewkesbury were of stone then there is little reason to doubt a stone barrel vault over the main span. The vertical break in the jambs of the present clerestory windows indicates that the windows were cut through the former Romanesque vault before the present vault was constructed (Fig.9.23).[31]

The capitals of the nave triforium are mainly various standard Romanesque scalloped and volute types but there is also some figurative work.[32] On the north side, the west capital of bay

Fig.9.26 Saint-Pierre, Brancion (France). Eastern bays of the nave aisle vault

Fig.9.27A Western capital of bay N4 in the nave north triforium

Fig.9.27B Eastern capital of bay N7 in the nave north triforium

Fig.9.27C Eastern capital in bay N8 from the south in the nave north triforium

4 has a male head with almond-shaped eyes, a pronounced, almost cylindrical nose, a rope-like moustache, a wide mouth with slightly protruding tongue, and a cleft chin (Fig.9.27A). In bay 7 the east capital has a ram's head (Fig.9.27B), as well as a cat's head shared between two bodies that spread respectively on the south and west sides of

Fig.9.27D Eastern capital in bay N8 from the south-west in the nave north triforium

Fig.9.27E Capital fragment No.79/1C

Fig.9.27F Shaft fragment No.79/1A

the capital. The cat's mouth flares out to reveal crenellation-like teeth that grasp a human head. The east capital of bay 8 has a feline mask at the south-east angle and on the south face a forward-bending male figure who wears three-quarter length ribbed trousers (Fig. 9.27C). His bearded head occupies the south-west angle of the capital and he holds the left side of his long drooping moustache with his left hand. The west face and west half of the north side of

Plate 1. The Battle of Tewkesbury, as depicted in Ghent MS 236

Plate 2. The Execution of Somerset after the Battle of Tewkesbury, as depicted in Ghent MS 236

Plate 3. Edward IV confronting the abbot after his victory at Tewkesbury, depicted in a painting by Richard Burchett

Plate 4. Oxford, Bodleian Library MS. Top. Glouc. d.2, fol.8v. Oddo and Doddo, the saintly dukes of Mercia credited with founding Tewkesbury monastery in 715 (or 717). Their arms, a gold cross engrailed upon a red field, are also those of the abbey

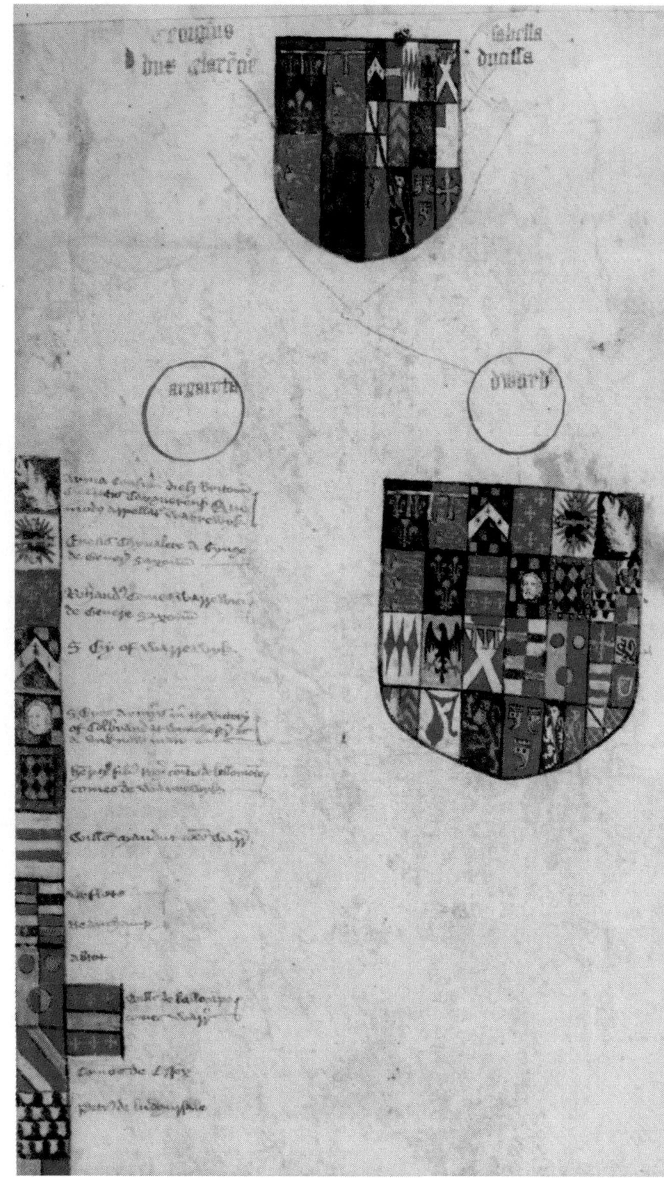

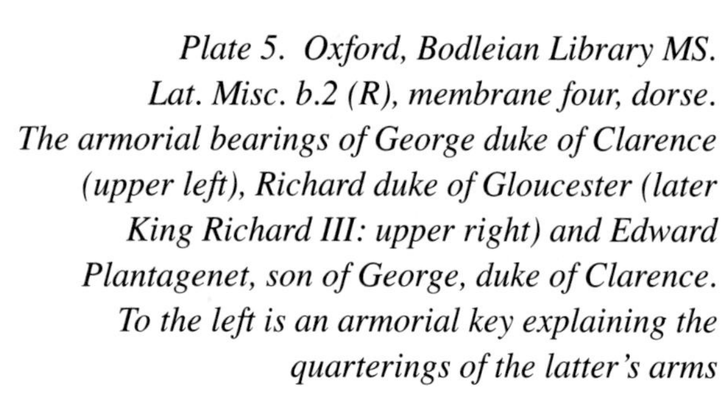

Plate 5. Oxford, Bodleian Library MS. Lat. Misc. b.2 (R), membrane four, dorse. The armorial bearings of George duke of Clarence (upper left), Richard duke of Gloucester (later King Richard III: upper right) and Edward Plantagenet, son of George, duke of Clarence. To the left is an armorial key explaining the quarterings of the latter's arms

Plate 6. Oxford, Bodleian Library MS. Top. Glouc. d.2, fol.27r. Isabel Despenser kneeling in adoration of the Virgin and Child. Her rich surcoat is embroidered with the arms of de Clare, Despenser and Warwick

Plate 7. The east wall of the south transept, close-up of fire-damaged masonry in the upper parts

Plate 8A The north wall of the abbey nave

Plate 8B Wall adjoining the abbey barn by the mill

Plate 9. Detail of medieval painting on a Norman capital in the nave north arcade

Plate 10. A 12th-century painted roundel in the upper chapel of the south transept

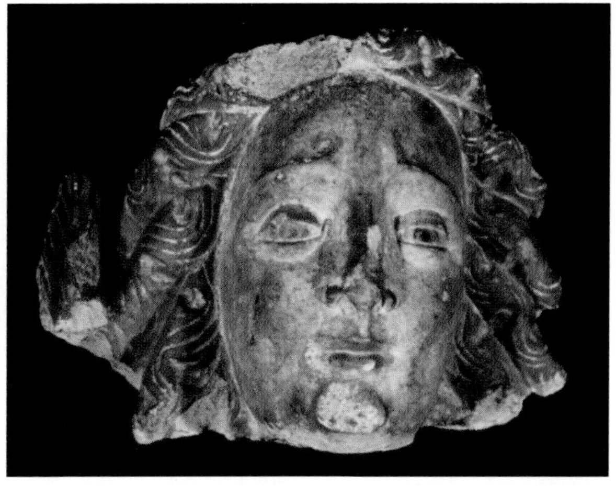

Plate 11. An angel's head, carved and painted in the 15th century, from an altarpiece (height of head 155mm)

Plate 12. 14th-century mural painting of Lord Edward Despenser and his wife before the Trinity, on the east wall of the Trinity Chapel

Plate 14. The 14th-century figure of the 'kneeling knight', Lord Edward Despenser, on the roof of the Trinity Chapel

Plate 13. The Warwick Chapel, viewed from the north choir aisle

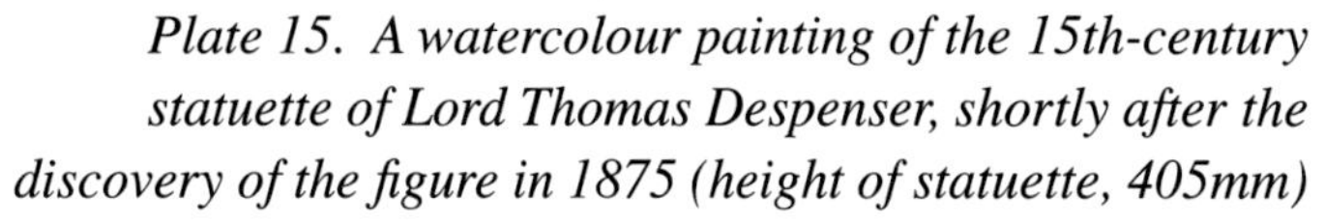

Plate 15. A watercolour painting of the 15th-century statuette of Lord Thomas Despenser, shortly after the discovery of the figure in 1875 (height of statuette, 405mm)

Plate 16. The sanctuary from the nave scaffold in 1996

Plate 17. 14th-century painted carvings in the nave
A, Boss: the Nativity B, Boss: the Resurrection
C, Boss: a Censing Angel D, Male corbel figure from the western transverse arch

this capital are carved with a trefoil-tailed monster who appears to be about to bite the cap-like hair of the angle head (Fig.9.27D).[33]

It is worth mentioning at this point additional survivals of Romanesque ornamental carving in the abbey collection. There is a fragment of a capital carved with a moulded segmental arch with decorated cable pattern; below there is a human head in profile, broken off just below the eye, with striated ribbons of hair (Fig.9.27E). In front of his head there is what appears to be his arm which is covered with ringed cloth. He appears to be in a jockey-like pose on a horse.[34] There are also two fragments of a shaft (Nos.79/1A and 79/1B) now very damaged but enough remains to show that they were richly carved with intertwining foliage (Fig.9.27F). The shaft and capital fragments may come from the Norman cloister.

At the west end of the nave, it was clearly the original intention to build twin west towers, the classic *façade harmonique* of Norman architecture as seen at Durham Cathedral.[35] The scheme was abandoned at Tewkesbury during the building campaign of the nave, and the west front topped instead with a pair of turrets, probably completed by 1121 (Fig.9.4).[36] The evidence that the builders intended twin towers is threefold. First, the responds of the arch into the westernmost bay of each nave aisle have a two-step pilaster rather than the half shaft used in other bays. This would have carried a wide, two-order arch appropriate for the support of the east wall of a tower over the end of the aisle. Secondly, in the roof space above the aisle vault, exactly above the proposed arches, are the stumps of the cross walls of the projected towers (Fig.9.28). Thirdly, the thickening of the wall in the western ends of the nave arcades, most evident to the west of the triforium in the south arcade, also goes with the proposed tower (Fig.9.23). The equivalent area on the north side of the nave reveals that the plan for the towers was soon abandoned (Fig.9.24). Here the thickening of the wall is discontinued at the level of the main arcade abacus, and the westernmost triforium opening is set too far to the west to accommodate the continuation upwards of the thick wall.

Fig.9.28 Stump of east wall of intended north-west tower in the nave north aisle roof space

In the event, the only tower to be constructed was the crossing tower (Figs.9.2, 9.19). The lower section would have been integral with the first campaign of construction as the roofs of the main spans butted up against it. The upper three stages are adorned with lavish decoration that is entirely absent on the lower section of the tower. Construction of the upper stages was probably left until the church was otherwise completed, in other words after the consecration of 1121, and possibly not until the middle of the 12th century. The rich adornment of the crossing tower is only matched in England at Norwich Cathedral, albeit with different motifs. However, the heavily ornamented surfaces of the transept towers of Exeter Cathedral, and the crossing tower of St. Kyneburga at Castor (Northants.) may indicate that the decoration at Tewkesbury was not exceptional. For comparative details one has to go no further than Gloucester Cathedral where the angle turrets of the transepts share a similar range of motifs.

Sources and Affiliations of the Norman Church

The great churches of post-Conquest England never relied simply on models back home in Normandy. The designs were eclectic with elements taken from the Anglo-Saxon tradition,

Normandy, the Loire Valley, major churches on the pilgrimage road to Santiago de Compostela, the Low Countries and Germany, northern Italy, Constantinian Rome, even Byzantium.[37] Ambitious patrons aimed at creating what they believed would be a truly great building, one to vie with the very best buildings both in England and throughout Europe. At Tewkesbury is found nothing less than an attempt to recreate a Roman basilica, one that involved a wide variety of sources.

Half a century ago Jean Bony suggested that the Norman church at Tewkesbury was designed by the master mason who was earlier responsible for the bishop's chapel at Hereford (1079-95), an idea deemed 'entirely plausible' by Richard Gem, and accepted by Richard Halsey.[38] The cavernous west portal of the Hereford chapel reads as a squat version of the great west arch at Tewkesbury (Fig.9.4) and the location of the stair vices in the walls to either side of the portal is the same as at the Hereford chapel. The upper storey of the chapel had a barrel vault in the east and west bays of the 'nave' flanked by quadrant vaults in the aisles, as proposed here for the nave at Tewkesbury. The plain arches of the main arcade of the upper storey of the chapel spring from a lower point in the pier than the transverse arches, in a manner similar to the giant order of the Tewkesbury choir. The wall arches that framed the aisle windows of the upper storey of the Hereford chapel may be read as forerunners of the taller, thinner examples in the Tewkesbury nave aisles where they would also have been topped with a quadrant vault. The extant north wall of the Hereford chapel contains much tufa which may indicate that the vaults there were also constructed of tufa as mooted for Tewkesbury. William of Malmesbury recorded that Robert de Losinga, bishop of Hereford (1079-95), built a chapel modelled on Charlemagne's chapel at Aachen (Germany). Whether or not this was the Hereford bishop's chapel destroyed in the 18th century and known from antiquarian drawings, or another chapel on an octagonal plan by Bishop Robert, is a moot point.[39] Be that as it may, there is a clear resemblance between the giant arch on

Fig.9.29 Speyer Cathedral. West doorway, from the east

the west front of Tewkesbury and its counterpart at Aachen. This imperial association may be extended back to Roman triumphal arches and forward to the west doorway of the German imperial cathedral of Speyer with its multiple orders so reminiscent of the great arch at Tewkesbury (Figs.9.4, 9.29). The polygonal termination of the choir arcade at Tewkesbury is also allied to Aachen especially if, as at Gloucester, there were two transverse arches springing from the back of the piers at Tewkesbury.

Looking to France, the three-sided apsidal termination for the Tewkesbury choir, with its arcade on massive columnar piers, and the proposed high barrel vault, are close to Sainte-Croix at Loudun (Vienne) (Fig.9.30). Sainte-Croix was founded in 1062 as a daughter house of Saint-Philibert at Tournus in Burgundy, a church well-known for the tall piers in the nave, and the upper chapel of the westwork with a high barrel vault and quadrant vaults in the aisles. Moreover, in the lower chapel at Tournus there is differential springing for the arches of the main arcades and transverse arches. How to interpret these parallels is far from straightforward and is further complicated when it is realized that similar features existed at an early date in Normandy. For example, the barrel vault is used in the transepts of Mont St. Michel, probably in the 1050s, and there are large piers in the nave of Breteuil (Eure) and the three-sided east end at Broglie (Eure). It is also interesting that the arches in the apse at Broglie are segmental, like the transverse arches of the central bay of the upper storey of the Hereford bishop's chapel.

The location of Breteuil and Broglie in southern Normandy leads to a reconsideration of Halsey's contention that churches in the border region of Normandy and Maine were significant for the design of Tewkesbury.[40] Halsey cited the abbey church of Saint-Denis at Nogent-le-Rotrou (Eure-et-Loir) in relation to the large piers and triforium design at Tewkesbury. To these may be added the use of a continuous outer order with the inner order on a capital for the responds of the transept screen, in the manner of the transept east elevation at Tewkesbury (Fig.9.9).

Fig.9.30 Sainte-Croix, Loudun (France), interior looking east

Halsey also revived the association made by Sir Alfred Clapham in the 1940s of the Tewkesbury giant order with the destroyed choir of St. Thomas d'Epernon (Eure-et-Loir).[41] Clapham dated Epernon around 1130, but previously Dion had dated it to the 11th century—a more convincing date adopted by Halsey.[42] Halsey noted that Sybil, wife of Robert Fitzhamon, was the daughter of Roger of Montgomery, earl of Shrewsbury and cousin of William the Conqueror.[43] Orderic Vitalis observed that Earl Roger was a 'conspicuous patron of the monks' in Normandy and England.[44] In 1087, the first abbot of Shrewsbury, Fulchred, was brought from Séez in southern Normandy, an earlier foundation of Earl Roger's, and 'two monks of Séez, Reginald and Frodo, came there [Shrewsbury] and began to construct the monastic buildings with the help of Odelerius and Warin and many others'.[45] While these observations do nothing to document exact sources or connections for Tewkesbury with the Normandy-Maine border region, they suggest that associations are at least likely.

The ultimate origin of the giant order lies in the work of the Roman architect, Vitruvius. In his discussion of the giant order at Tewkesbury, Eric Fernie observed that the reconstruction of Vitruvius's basilica at Fanum by the French 17th-century architect,[46] Charles Perrault, shows the latter with a wooden barrel vault (Fig.9.31). Fernie noted that Perrault translated the word *testudo*, used by Vitruvius, as 'vault'.[47] Etymologically this makes perfect sense: *testudo*, a tortoise-shell, and hence, a shell-like covering or vault over a space. Vitruvius also used *testudo* in connection with the vaulted architecture of bath buildings where it is universally translated as vault.[48] However, elsewhere his use of *testudo* is unlikely to mean vault but, rather more generically, covering or roof.[49]

Fig.9.31 Perrault's reconstruction of Vitruvius's basilica at Fanum, with a wooden barrel vault

One wonders whether the connection between Tewkesbury and Vitruvius is textual or established through a masonic tradition. In other words, was it the patron or the mason who proposed the use of the motif? The evidence does not permit a definitive answer but at least some possibilities can be perused. If a mason had copied this idea from an earlier Romanesque building, then variations on the arched form of the giant order appear in a number of places across western Europe in the 11th century, such as in the nave of Speyer Cathedral, the rotunda at Charroux (Vienne), and the exterior of the nave at Saint-Etienne at Caen. Also in Normandy, there is the south nave elevation at Mont St. Michel, where a giant arch rises through all three storeys to enclose the clerestory.[50] Abbot Serlo of Gloucester came from Mont St. Michel and the articulation of the Gloucester nave triforium is indebted to Mont St. Michel. In the presbytery of Cerisy-la-Forêt shafts rise from the ground to the gallery capitals in the east and west responds in the manner of a compound version of Tewkesbury. Any one of these could have inspired Tewkesbury.

Alternatively, it is quite possible that the patron or one of the monks had examined a copy of the text in the late 11th century. The earliest extant copy of Vitruvius' *De Architectura* is a Carolingian manuscript now in the British Library, which may have been made at Charlemagne's scriptorium at Aachen.[51] This manuscript, and apparently the entire tradition of some 80 extant Vitruvius manuscripts, shows 'signs of a derivation from an archetype in Anglo-Saxon script'.[52] The text was probably available in England by the 10th century and quite possibly earlier, and Ker holds that the Benedictine abbey of St. Augustine, Canterbury, had a copy or copies of Vitruvius in the 11th century.[53] One such extant copy is British Library, Cotton Cleopatra D.i, from which many copies descend, including a 12th-century one from northern

Fig.9.32 The nave with painted vault at Saint-Savin-sur-Gartempe (France), looking west

England, probably from Durham.[54] Extracts were made from a text at Canterbury by William of Malmesbury *c.*1130, and around 1150-1175 there was a copy of Vitruvius at Bury St. Edmunds.[55]

Returning to architectural parallels with western France, we have already seen that external blind arcades accompanying barrel vaults are found in Romanesque churches there. In addition, the turrets on the west front of Tewkesbury are closely paralleled by those on the angles of the crossing tower at Sainte-Marie-des-Dames at Saintes. There are tall columnar piers in the nave at Saint-Savin-sur-Gartempe (Vienne) and the painted barrel vault there may indicate that the choice of the barrel vault at Tewkesbury was conditioned by the desire for a painted cycle of biblical scenes (Figs.9.6, 9.32). The painted barrel vault in the chancel of Kempley (Glos.) is possibly a small-scale, local reflection of the Romanesque decoration of the lost high vault in the east arm at Tewkesbury.

Wall arches also occur in western French Romanesque churches, as at Parthenay-le-Vieux (Deux-Sèvres), but none of the western French examples known to me are necessarily earlier than Tewkesbury. The motif appears elsewhere as well as in the transept aisles at St. Maria-im-Kapitol, Cologne (mid-11th century), a building in which the transepts have high barrel vaults and an elevation employing the giant order like Tewkesbury (Figs.9.33, 9.34).

The crossing with its wider arches to the east and west than to the north and south may derive from English pre-Conquest sources, as reflected at Dorchester Abbey (Oxon.) and Wimborne Minster (Dorset).[56] The triangular arches inside

Fig.9.33 Cologne, St. Maria-im-Kapitol. Interior looking to the south of the south transept aisle

Fig.9.34 Cologne, St.-Maria-im-Kapitol. East elevation and eastern crossing arch with high barrel vaults and giant order

the passages of the transept end-walls and the baluster shafts on the west front turrets may also reflect an Anglo-Saxon tradition.[57] On the other hand, the lantern tower with wall passage above the crossing arches and windows flanking the gables of the main spans (Figs.9.11, 9.19) was introduced into England from St. Etienne at Caen. The earliest extant English example is at St. Albans Cathedral after 1077 and subsequently, in the context of west-country Romanesque, it is used at Sherborne Abbey.[58]

Tewkesbury finds many direct analogues in Norman church architecture in the south-west midlands and the West Country. The tall columnar piers relate to Gloucester and Pershore where also there are, or were, galleries in the choir and triforium passages in the nave. Large columnar piers were popular in the region before Tewkesbury, as at Shrewsbury Abbey, Worcester Cathedral and Great Malvern Priory, and subsequently at numerous sites such as Evesham Abbey and Hereford Cathedral.[59] In all of these churches except Worcester Cathedral, the crossing piers are elongated like Tewkesbury, and to this list may be added Sherborne Abbey and Shrewsbury Abbey.[60] The presence of a prominent porch on the side of the nave, rather than at the west end (Fig.9.3), is found earlier at Worcester Cathedral on the north side and subsequently appears on the south at Malmesbury Abbey and Sherborne Abbey. The triforium is witnessed in the transepts at St. Werburgh's at Chester, Ewenny Priory and Gnosall (Staffs.).

With regard to the Romanesque use of high vaults in stone, in addition to Gloucester and Pershore, Chepstow Priory was probably fully vaulted and there was a stone high vault in the presbytery at Hereford Cathedral. On a smaller scale, besides those at Kempley and Ewenny mentioned above, there are the traces of vaults in the east wall of St. John the Baptist at Halesowen (Worcs.) and above the east crossing arch at Usk Priory (Mon.).[61]

Conclusion

The Norman abbey church of Tewkesbury represents a pretentious imperial statement. The founder of the church was Robert Fitzhamon, a Norman lord who had been given the honour of Gloucester in 1087.[62] The chronicle of Tewkesbury records that Fitzhamon's patronage was inspired by his wife, Sybil, and Gerald of Avranches, the first abbot of Tewkesbury.[63] Whether the design of the church was the outcome of this team, or specifically the wish of Robert Fitzhamon in consultation with the master mason, is not recorded.[64] Be that as it may, Fitzhamon's extensive land holdings, which included an 'empire' in south Wales, may well be equated with imperial aspirations in architecture. Bishop Robert de Losinga had already set a precedent for such imperial pretension in his chapel at Hereford, for in addition to the connection with Charlemagne's palace chapel at Aachen, the plan and configuration of the two storeys are intimately related to imperial German chapels of two storeys ('doppelkapellen').[65]

The Norman abbey church of Tewkesbury similarly flaunts an imperial grandeur. The church is entered at the west end through a massive triumphal arch that reflects the glory of ancient Rome, and combines the great scale of the west arch of Aachen palace chapel with the multiple orders of the west doorway of Speyer Cathedral. In the nave and choir the use of 'columns', rather than compound piers favoured in Normandy and even in imperial Germany, recalls Roman basilicas. The giant order in the choir is at once associated with Vitruvius and imperial Germany, and, whether or not the high barrel vaults interpret Vitruvius' basilica at Fanum, such vaults would have recalled the monumental bath architecture of the Roman empire.

CHAPTER 10

The Gothic Church: Architectural History

by Richard K. Morris *with a contribution by* Malcolm Thurlby

Tewkesbury Abbey is justifiably famous as an outstanding example of two periods of English architecture, Romanesque and Decorated, of which the latter is the main focus of this chapter. 'Decorated' is a 19th-century term to describe that inventive and highly decorative period of architecture associated by the antiquarians with the reigns of the first three king Edwards (1272-1377), and arguably the most significant period of English medieval architecture in a European context.[1] It was distinguished in the antiquarian literature from Early English—the purer, French-influenced style of early Gothic which preceded it; and from Perpendicular—the sober, 'national' style of England which came after and continued to the end of the Middle Ages.[2] In fact, both Early English and Perpendicular features are also represented in the fabric of the abbey church and deserve to be better known. Thus all three periods will be considered here, and in the next chapter the development of late Gothic vaulting at Tewkesbury will be explored—an architectural theme which links Decorated and Perpendicular.

Of course, the investment in works of such expense and quality was possible only through high status patronage in the service of God. Thirty years ago I coined the phrase 'the Despenser mausoleum' to characterize the motivation for the new Decorated choir of the abbey, and I shall take the opportunity in this chapter to re-evaluate the relative roles of the lordly patrons and of the monastic community in the modernization of the Romanesque church from the 13th century to the Dissolution.

The 13th century[3]

The first major modifications to the symmetry of the Norman church plan occurred in the early 13th century, when a large north chapel was added to the north transept and, shortly afterwards, the apsidal chapel of the same transept was replaced by a larger rectangular chapel, currently occupied by the abbey shop (Masterplan, A, B, C).[4] It is probable that the finely ornamented north chapel, with Purbeck marble shafts and elaborate mouldings, was dedicated to the Virgin Mary, following the fashion for building Lady chapels at this period. Comparison may be made with with the Elder Lady Chapel on the north side of Bristol Cathedral, also built *c.*1220,[5] which was complemented in the 14th century by a new Lady Chapel at the east end of the church, exactly as happened at Tewkesbury (see below).

The north chapel consisted of an aisle-less nave, demolished after the Dissolution, and a chancel, now occupied by the song school (Masterplan, A, B). Originally the chapel was entered through the archway in the north wall of the north transept (now behind the Grove organ), which has detached shafts, crocket capitals and a richly moulded arch of four orders (Fig.10.1). Scars on the exterior of the transept wall (originally the interior of the chapel) indicate that the nave was rib-vaulted in four narrow bays. The nave communicated with the chancel through an exquisitely detailed double archway, flanked by narrower blind arches with recessed quatrefoils above.[6] Despite its partially blocked state, the details of the double archway—the delicate centre shaft ('trumeau'), its base carved with a grotesque, and the lacy saw-tooth chevron in the arch—evoke the former splendour of this chapel, and the archway deserves to be better presented (Fig.10.2).[7] Chevron of the saw-tooth variety, as here, is not unusual in early Gothic architecture in the West Country, for example at Glastonbury Abbey (after 1184) and at the bishop's palace at Exeter (early 13th century).

In the chancel, the original arrangement is well preserved in the north wall: a continuous dado arcade with a large lancet window above in each bay, all framed with marble shafting on marble crocket capitals (Fig.10.3). The wider eastern wall would have had a double or triple

Fig.10.1 (left) North transept and the site of the nave of the former north chapel
Fig.10.2 (right) Detail of the chancel arch of the former north chapel

group of lancets between the surviving marble shafts. The inserted tracery in all the window openings is 14th century, as is the rib vault in its present form. The shafting and capitals of the vault responds show that a vault was intended as part of the original design, but the heraldry carved on the bosses is that of de Clare and Despenser, inferring a date of *c*.1317-26.[8] The diagonal and transverse ribs have an early Gothic profile and, though it has been suggested that they are reused from the 13th-century vault,[9] they are more likely to be 14th-century replicas, copied from the profile of the original stone springers for the vault. The chancel was probably originally vaulted in wood in imitation of stone rib vaults, an idea used elsewhere in early Gothic architecture in the West Country.[10] Its replacement in stone in the 14th century would explain why buttresses to take the extra thrust of a stone vault have been added to the exterior of the chapel.[11]

The foliage decoration of the chancel's dado arcade is of interest in providing evidence for workshop affinities (Fig.10.3). General analogues for its cusped spandrels carved with stiff-leaf foliage are found in the Elder Lady Chapel of Bristol Cathedral (1218-22) and the eastern arm of Worcester Cathedral (after 1224), but the

Fig.10.3 The chancel interior of the former north chapel, looking west and north (drawing by Roland Paul, 1886; now the Camera Cantorum*)*

Fig.10.4 Pieces of 13th-century coffin lids outside the north transept

particular style of leaf owes more to earlier works, like the north porch of Wells Cathedral, and to the foliate carving of coffin lids.[12] The leaves are rather flat, over-large and with pronounced linear veins, which suggests either that they predate the mature style of stiff-leaf in works of the 1220s as at Worcester, or that they are contemporary work of inferior quality. It seems likely that they were carved by local sculptors who also produced coffin lids decorated with foliated crosses employing the same leaf convention, two examples of which survive in the vicinity at Deerhurst and Didbrook.[13] Recently another product of this workshop has been identified at the abbey itself, amongst pieces from several slabs on top of a stone coffin in the cloister walk (Fig.10.4). It is likely to have come from the tomb of an abbot or important monastic official, by analogy with the (unfoliated) cross slab of Abbot Alan (d.1202, Fig.5.2), and one may conjecture that it was carved at about the same time that masons were working on the north chapel, some time in the first two decades of the 13th century.

After the construction of the north chapel, the two-storey apsidal chapel of the north transept (originally similar to that in the south transept, now the Lady Chapel) was replaced by the large rectangular chapel still present today, filling the space between the north chapel and the north choir aisle (Masterplan, C). It is single-storey and was rib-vaulted in four bays which would have required a central pier for support (Fig.10.5). Very little 13th-century detail survives except for the vault corbels carved with trumpet-scallop or stiff-leaf. It is evident that the new chapel was constructed after the north chapel, because originally the chancel of the latter was freestanding on its south side. High up in the south wall of the chancel there are traces of Early English windows, matching those still extant in the north wall.[14]

The new work should be interpreted as a double chapel with an altar against the east wall in each bay, which would accord well with the entries in the Annals that in 1237 the chapel of St. Nicholas was built anew from the old (*de veteri nova fabricata est ...*) by Prior Henry of Sipton, and that the altars of St. James and St. Nicholas were dedicated in 1238.[15] The rebuilding involved the demolition of the two-storey Romanesque transept chapel, which presumably housed the altars of SS. James and Nicholas, thus satisfying the statement that the new chapel was built 'from the old'.[16] It is possible, too, that the carved torso of an ecclesiastical effigy, fixed by the Victorians in the east wall of the north chapel, might be identified with Prior Sipton (Fig.10.6A). The piece must be one of those found by Thomas Collins in 1879 when he cleared the post-medieval blocking from the double arch of the north chapel,[17] and it represents a rare survival of an early effigy of Tournai limestone.[18]

The Annals indicate some significant works of reordering and fitting-out being undertaken in the

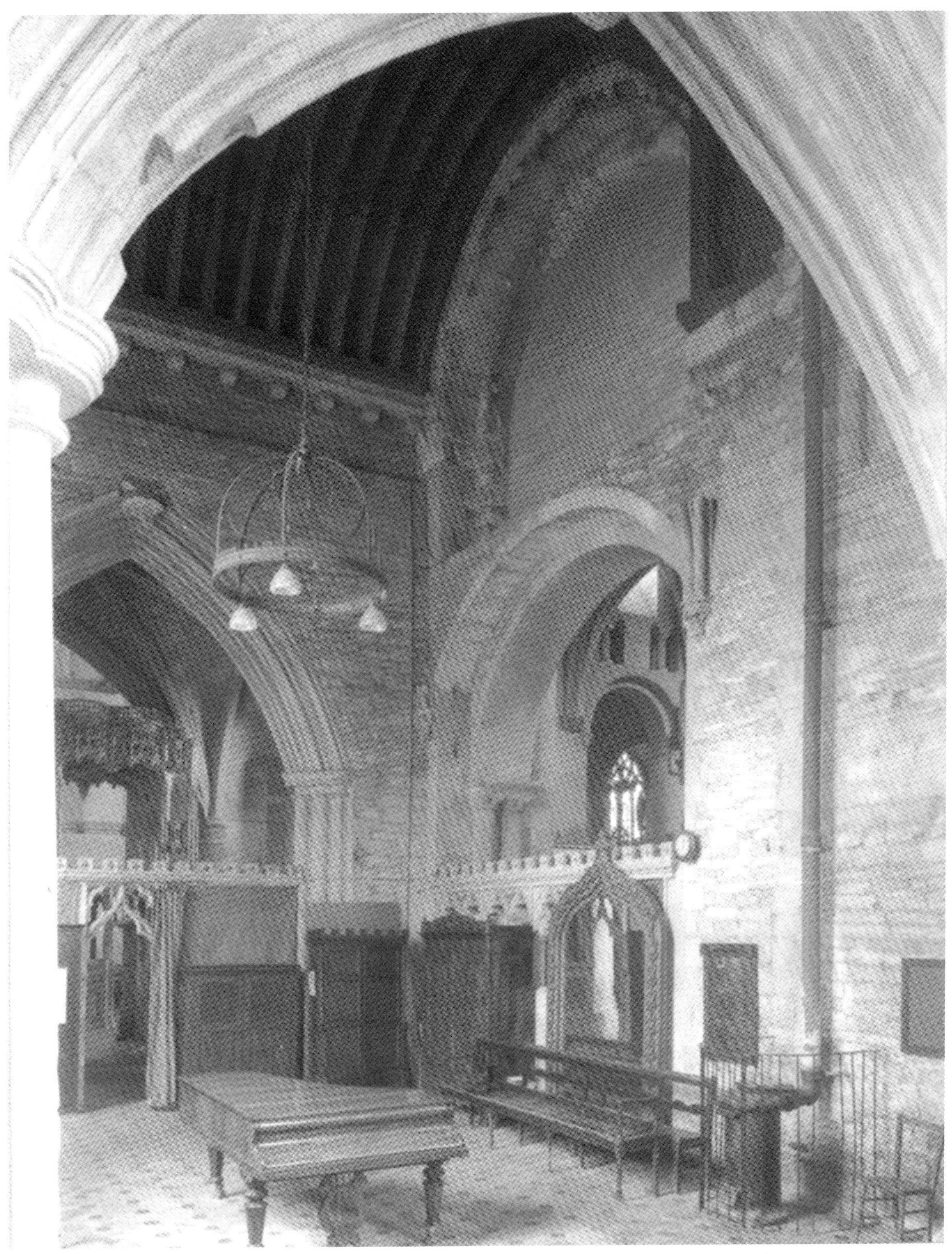

Fig.10.5 North transept, former east chapels, as in 1970 (now the shop)

1230s and 1240s. In 1239 the church was dedicated, with its high altar in honour of the Virgin Mary, by Walter Cantilupe, bishop of Worcester,[19] and it is likely that the abbey's great altar slab (*mensa*) of Purbeck marble—the longest now surviving in England—was made for this ceremony (Fig.5.3).[20] However, there are reasons for thinking that the dedication was merely a tidying-up of past business, for almost immediately, in 1241, the Annals record the monastery launching into further works affecting the choir. In August two great bells were consecrated, followed in October by the translation of the bodies of Robert Fitzhamon and Abbot Benedict from the chapter house to the choir, on the left side of the high altar.[21] In the same year altars were consecrated in honour of the new saints, Wulfstan and Thomas Becket, but of more relevance architecturally is the erection of a chapel of St. Eustace in 1246.[22] Some writers have maintained that this chapel was the one added north of the north transept, but it has been shown above that the style of the fabric is several decades earlier. Rather, it might be one of the eastern chapels off the choir, where other changes in the fabric imply that some remodelling was being undertaken around the mid-century.[23]

Fig.10.6
A (top) Effigy of an unidentified churchman, early 13th century (height 55cm)
B (lower) Purbeck marble effigy of a de Clare lord, ?13th century (scale: 25cm)

The demolition of the north transept two-storey chapel in or before 1237 suggests that the Romanesque gallery and its chapels around the eastern part of the church were falling into disuse, possibly to be replaced by additional chapels on the ground floor. The move to place all altars at ground level was one of the most fundamental liturgical changes affecting many English great churches in the 13th century, of which the complete rebuilding of the east ends of Worcester Cathedral (after 1224) and Pershore Abbey (*c*.1220-39) provide major local exemplars. At Tewkesbury, the process was under way by 1237 and had almost certainly been completed by the 1260s when window tracery was inserted into the former gallery openings in the east walls of the transepts (Fig.10.7). This would have cut off access to the gallery around the Romanesque choir, which obviously had become redundant and probably had had its roof removed.[24]

The gallery windows of the transepts can be dated on the basis of their style. They are in the new French technique of bar tracery, made popular in England by its use at Westminster

Abbey (1245-69), and the curve-sided triangular shape of the south window (Fig.10.7) is also French, copied at Westminster and only rarely elsewhere, as at the cathedrals of Hereford (*c*.1255-68) and Lichfield (after 1258). The details of the Tewkesbury window are closest to the gallery tracery in the east bays of Westminster's nave (*c*.1259-69),[25] and this dating would also fit the reciprocal tracery in the north transept, a circular window containing seven cusped roundels (Fig.10.8)—a design repeated in another Westminster-influenced work, the Angel Choir of Lincoln Cathedral (1256-80), in the head of the great east window. Thus the 1260s provide a terminal date for the conjectural modification of the Romanesque east end, and the two transept gallery windows probably represent the end of a rather piecemeal process of updating through new fenestration. Towards the end of the century the process continued with the insertion of pairs of traceries into the large window apertures in the end walls of the transepts. In each case one design incorporates a small curve-sided triangle in the head and the other is 'Y-tracery' with impaled trefoils (Fig.10.1, left and right), both of which are early Decorated patterns in vogue in works of the later 1280s and 1290s like the eastern arm of Exeter Cathedral and the chapel of Merton College, Oxford (1289-94).[26]

Fig.10.7 South transept, east clerestory window and former Romanesque gallery site

One can only speculate as to the nature and reasons for the mid-13th-century modifications to the choir. Probably the main interior structure remained unaltered, including the high vault, but windows were inserted in the gallery openings—on the general model of those in the transepts —and the upper storeys of the Romanesque ambulatory chapels were removed along with the covered gallery which had provided access to them.[27]

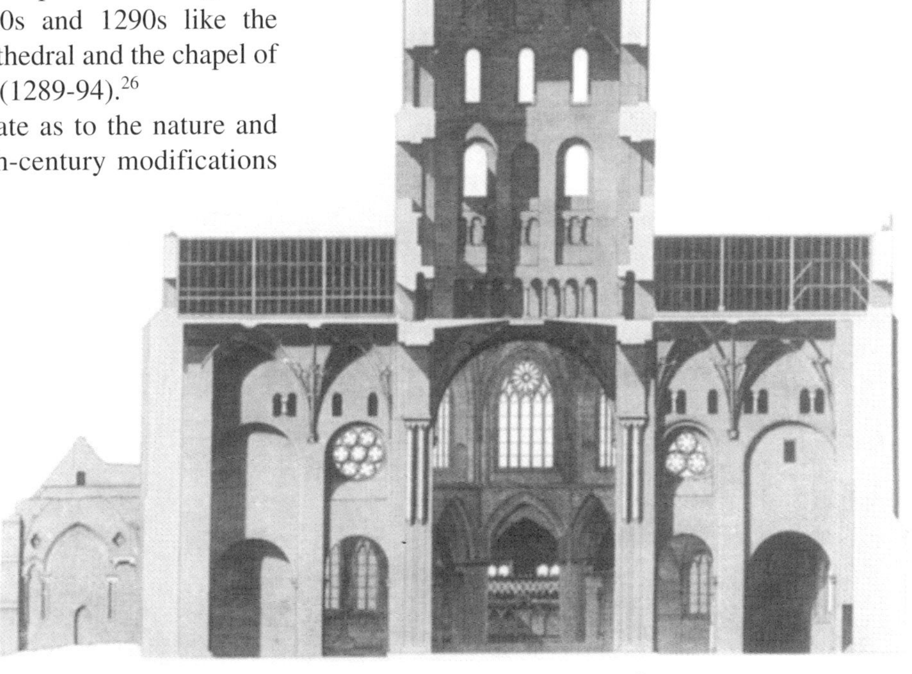

Fig.10.8 Transverse north/south section at the transepts, Vetusta Monumenta, *Vol.V*

A major factor in setting these works in train is likely to have been the start of the burials of the de Clares before the high altar, commencing with Gilbert I (1230) and the heart burial of his widow, Isabel (d.1240), followed by their son, Richard II (d.1262).[28] Gilbert's adoption of the abbey as his burial place was doubtless a great coup for the monastery, and thoughts turned to making the choir a more sumptuous setting for his tomb and that of his successors. The tantalizing fragment of a large Purbeck marble effigy with the de Clare arms in the abbey collection may be part of Gilbert's tomb or his son's (Fig.10.6B).[29] Introducing stained glass windows—the revolutionary new medium of French Gothic—would be the obvious solution, not least because the Romanesque choir would have had little direct illumination if it had been barrel-vaulted.[30]

Whether the de Clare family subsidized such improvements is a moot point. Golding has argued that neither Gilbert nor his de Clare successors were over-generous in their benefactions to the abbey,[31] though the late medieval compiler of the Founders' Book singles out Gilbert for his gift of the Mythe wood, confirmed by his son.[32] Moreover, the monastery benefitted very considerably from the will of Isabel, with grants of land, valuables and especially a reliquary containing hair of St. Elizabeth and relics of SS. Mark and Agnes.[33] In fact, a wish to provide a finer setting for these relics, combined with a concern to secure future de Clare burials at the abbey—there had been a 'tug-of-war' with Beaulieu Abbey over Isabel's body[34]—may well have precipitated the updating of the choir by the monastic community. This would explain the move of Robert Fitzhamon's remains to the sanctuary in 1241, so that the de Clare tombs would be in symbolic proximity to the Norman founder, whose heirs became the first earls of Gloucester.

The monastery, as the real beneficiary, is more likely to have been the prime mover in this programme. The Annals supply incidental evidence that the priors were involved in building two of the chapels in this period: Henry of Sipton with that of St. Nicholas (1237), and Henry of Banbury with that of St. Eustace (1246).[35] But the key figure was probably Abbot Robert III of Forthampton (1232-54), who is recorded in the Annals as the promoter (*agente*) of the translation of the founder's body as well as being associated with the rebuilding of St. Nicholas' Chapel.[36] The

Fig.10.9 Ambulatory, interior looking south, with the Decorated screen and the tomb of Hugh II Despenser in the foreground

chronicle refers to Robert as 'of blessed memory', so he was clearly an abbot of special reputation amongst the later medieval monks.[37]

The 14th Century

Up to the 14th century, Tewkesbury Abbey was essentially the massive Norman church of Robert Fitzhamon, despite the various 13th-century modifications described above. From about 1320 it was to be dramatically transformed to assume the ornate Gothic appearance with which we are still familiar today. The impenetrable effect of the Romanesque walls and barrel vaults was dispelled throughout the church by the insertion of large Decorated windows and elaborate lierne vault patterns (Fig.9.12). The famous stained glass windows of the choir clerestory belong with this programme of works, as well as new fittings such as the choir stalls.[38] For a monk of Tewkesbury who lived through the second quarter of the century—someone like Abbot John Coles (d.1347)—the changes to the liturgical setting would have been sensational.

However, their commissioning and execution are undocumented. The Annals fall silent after 1263, the Founders' Book is unhelpful for architectural works and no building fabric accounts survive. So the chronology needs to be reconstructed by reference to associated historical events and important burials, and to dates provided by heraldry in the glass, tiles and carvings. It is also essential to study the architectural fabric as if it were an historical document, because many changes of detail occurred during the Decorated rebuilding which permit us to recreate its phases of development; and to provide relative dates for them through parallels with contemporary buildings whose architectural histories are better documented or researched.

Such an analysis suggests that the work may be divided into four schematic phases of construction.[39] The first three phases were focussed mainly—but not exclusively—on the remodelling of the monks' church to the east of the former screen in the second bay of the nave. By the second phase it appears that the celebration of the lordly burials had become the primary objective.

The ground floor works in advance of demolishing the choir superstructure constitute Phase I, and were carried out at some time between *c*.1315-*c*.1328.[40] The main feature of this phase was the ring of new radiating chapels (the 'chevet'), sweeping away any traces of earlier fabric in this area, and laid out beyond the Romanesque choir as indicated by the wider ambulatory (Masterplan, E; Fig.10.9). The chapels included a splendid new Lady Chapel on the centre axis, 72 feet long and considerably higher. Unfortunately it was demolished at the Dissolution, but its size can be appreciated from the outline of its plan recently recreated on the lawn (Figs.10.10, 10.11). Contemporaneously, arches with the same mouldings as those of the ambulatory chapels were introduced at the entrances to the nave aisles, demonstrating that the plans for updating extended to all parts of the monks' church. The new windows and rib vaults

Fig.10.10 The eastern chapels from the top of the tower

in the first bay in the south aisle, and the first two bays in the north aisle, also belong to this phase.

At some time between 1317-26—based on the heraldry of the roof bosses—arcade arches of the same design were inserted between the 13th-century north and east chapels of the north transept, to connect them together and to the north choir aisle, and they were revaulted (Figs.10.3, 10.5).[41] This may well have been undertaken early in the programme, because it was probably intended to provide the monks with a temporary space for worship, focussed on the old Lady Chapel: just as the Elder Lady Chapel at Bristol Cathedral was modernized in the 1290s in advance of building the new Decorated east end.[42]

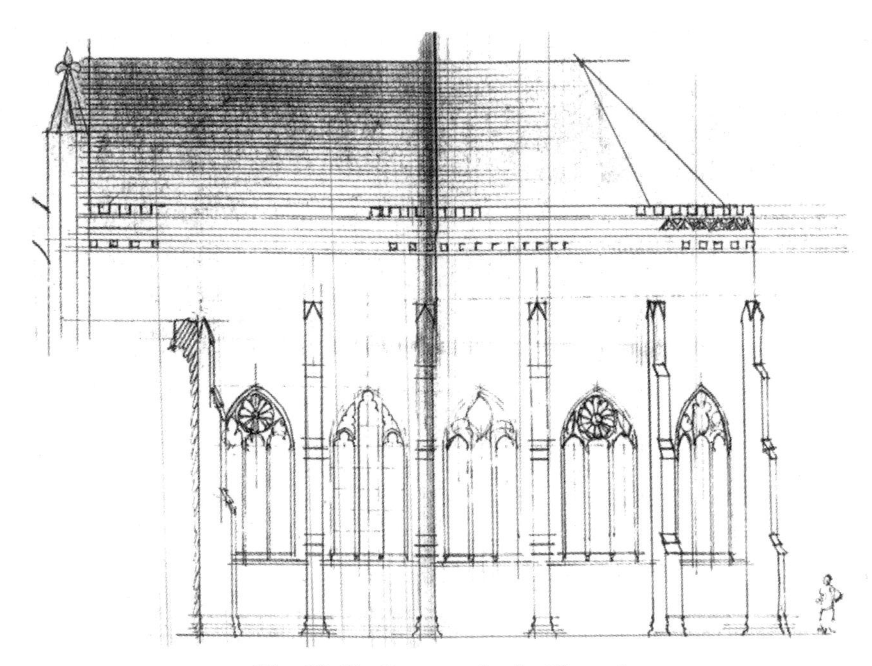

Fig.10.11 Eastern Lady Chapel, reconstruction drawing of the exterior viewed from the south

Phase II spanned *c*.1322-*c*.1337, probably interrupted in the middle and resumed in the early 1330s.[43] It delivered the main objective of the programme, namely the rebuilding of the choir, by demolishing all of the Romanesque superstructure east of the crossing except for the six piers around the sanctuary. These were shortened, given new capitals each with a carved head, and on top of them was constructed the simple two-storey elevation, which maximizes the size of the clerestory windows within a relatively low building (Pl.16).[44] The last work was the construction of the choir vault, the first of the abbey's Decorated high vaults—and the most lavish, which would have been completed before glazing began in the clerestory windows *c*.1340. In the same phase or early in Phase III, each of the transepts was provided with a large west window, a continuation of the piecemeal updating there stemming back to the previous century. Presumably the Romanesque barrel vaults had been removed in the transepts to facilitate this work, so new vaults were probably intended at this stage though not implemented until Phase IV.

In Phase III (*c*.1335-*c*.1349)[45] the fitting out of the choir with non-architectural items like stalls and stained glass windows completed the Decorated remodelling there. To this phase belong the stone screens in the north choir aisle and at the entrance to St. Margaret's Chapel, with Despenser shields and ornate blind tracery patterns comparable to ones found on the choir-stall canopies (Fig.11.12).[46] At the same time architectural work was under way in the nave to insert clerestory windows and erect the new high vault with its famous figure bosses (Fig.9.6). This operation was rather piecemeal and was apparently interrupted when near completion by the Black Death in 1348-9.[47] An equally demanding structural undertaking was the removal of the Romanesque infill wall at the west end of the nave, under the great arch of the west front, and its replacement by a single large window (Fig.9.4). The remaining stonework surviving from this window, around the frame of its 1686 replacement, testifies that it belonged to the 14th century, and not to the 15th as usually stated.[48] It was of a noticeably different design to the 1686 window, divided vertically into two parts rather than three, probably influenced by the early Perpendicular south transept window at Gloucester Cathedral (see further below). It was designed about 1340 but possibly the tracery was not completed until the 1350s or 60s.

Phase IV (*c*.1350-1360s) covers several works of completion which were probably planned before the Black Death interrupted, and which are not overtly Perpendicular in style. These are particularly the new rib vaults in the transept arms, assigned on stylistic evidence to the 1350s or 60s, and replacing Romanesque barrel vaults. In addition, a new rib vault was introduced in the crossing, probably between *c*.1350-60 on heraldic evidence (Figs.11.2, 18.2). Previously the lantern inside the Romanesque central tower had been visible at the crossing, so the insertion of a vault closing off this view was a major alteration to the interior effect of the church, and in keeping with contemporary modifications in some other great churches, such as Worcester Cathedral.[49]

Within the first two phases one can identify numerous inconsistencies which testify to changes of plan, changes of craftsmen and probably some use of piece-work. This is obvious in the chevet chapels, which were evidently all laid out together at foundation level but which developed differently in building, as demonstrated by the contrast in style between the eastern Lady Chapel and the sacristy. The interior of the latter, together with its entrance door and associated tomb recess, is studded with ballflower ornament (Fig.10.12) and closely connected in its details to the local 'Hereford style' of ballflower work at Gloucester Cathedral (1318-29).[50] This ornament (whether fully carved as a ballflower or left as a plain ball) is not used architecturally in the other chevet chapels, and appears elsewhere in the abbey church only in fittings, such as the lower part of the stone screen in the east and north-east bays of the ambulatory (Fig.10.9). This represents a first set of Decorated screens, a second being the finer quality set commissioned in Phase III, mentioned above.[51]

In contrast to the ballflower works, the remains of the eastern Lady Chapel indicate that its connexions lie with the style of the crossing tower at Pershore Abbey (probably finished by 1327).[52] If one stands on the site of the Lady Chapel today, facing its west wall and the

Fig.10.12 The 'Forthampton' tomb recess by the sacristy door

blocked entrance from the ambulatory, enough fabric survives at each side to reconstruct its lateral window apertures (Fig.10.13). These have distinctive bands of miniature foiled figures running across the window frame mouldings at capital level, just like Pershore and ultimately derived from the tower of Salisbury Cathedral (*c*.1300-10), and the mullion profile is also repeated at Pershore.[53]

It is evident from the quality of its mouldings that the Lady Chapel was designed to be the *pièce de résistance* of the chevet, but it seems to have been the original intention to apply some of its details to the ambulatory and chapels as well. For

Fig.10.13 Eastern Lady Chapel, west wall: the upper arch is the vault line, and the lower arch is the blocked entrance to the church

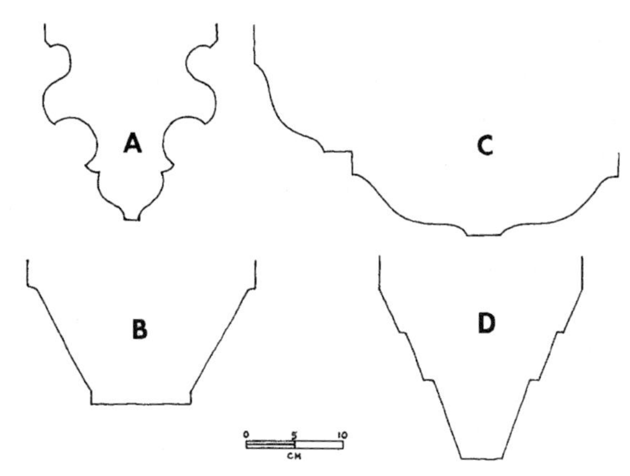

Fig.10.14 Moulding profiles, 14th century. A. choir vault rib; B. ambulatory and chevet chapels, rib with sunk chamfer mouldings; C. choir arcade, ambulatory side, arch with wave mouldings; D. nave, west window, reconstruction of main mullion (interior profile)

example, the immediately adjacent vault springers in the chapels of St. Dunstan and St. Faith are carved with the elaborate rib profile of the Lady Chapel, whereas thereafter the ambulatory and chapel vaults employ a simpler sunk chamfer rib (Fig.10.14 A, B). More obvious is the fact that seven different designs of tracery survive in the chevet chapel windows, indicating the involvement of at least three workshops. Firstly, in the sacristy two of the three windows have patterns found locally in other churches with ballflower work, such as Badgeworth and Bishops Cleeve (Fig.10.15, centre).[54] Second, the standard design in the chapels is a group of three stepped lights, variously treated (Fig.10.15, right), a window tracery common in the first half of the 14th century in Herefordshire and the lower Severn valley (including Pershore), and used later at Tewkesbury in the nave clerestory.

The tracery designs of the main windows of the Lady Chapel are unknown—those in Thomas Overbury's reconstruction are speculative (Fig.10.11)—but the third type is represented by the west clerestory window, which alone survives and is clearly by a different master (Fig.10.16).[55] Its tracery is fussy and metallic in quality compared with the robust patterns in the other chevet chapels, and is one of a tight-knit group of five windows in the same style in the abbey: three in the east bays of the nave aisles (Fig.10.18, centre) and one smaller one in the north choir aisle. The closest local parallel for its tracery pattern is in St. Katherine's Chapel, Ledbury (Herefs.), but the ultimate source lies in the north-west midlands in the west bays of the choir at Chester Cathedral, *c.*1300-20, and at Lichfield Cathedral.[56] So this group of windows represents a secondary phase within Phase I at the abbey, and should be dated no later than the 1320s.

Not all the inconsistencies evident in the fabric today can be blamed on the medieval building campaigns because restorations, commencing in Queen Elizabeth I's reign, have taken their toll. In the choir clerestory windows, the confusion of mullions and the omission of capitals, which I had taken to be evidence for hasty completion of this area in the 1330s,[57] is more likely to be explained by 'reparations' like those of 1566-7. In this year the churchwardens' accounts record payment 'to Hiat the mason for 45 fote of stone for the chauncell wyndow'.[58]

Fig.10.16 West clerestory window of the eastern Lady Chapel

Fig.10.15 Sacristy and St. John the Baptist's Chapel, exterior from the south

Fig.10.17 Parapet frieze with carved heads on the choir clerestory

Fig.10.18 Decorated windows in the north transept and nave north aisle

Despite being characterized by interruptions, the quantity and variety of architectural work executed at Tewkesbury from the 1320s to the 1340s makes it an important workshop site, probably attracting a considerable workforce when building activities were in full swing. The numerous masons' marks in parts of the church, such as the ambulatory chapels and the east bays of the nave vault, imply the rapid recruitment of masons at various stages of the construction.[59] The abbey's works yard acted as a link—a receiver and a transmitter—for architectural ideas especially between the Cotswolds and the Welsh Marches, as well as showing an acquaintance with the north midlands and south-west England. It permits us to appreciate traits of Decorated architecture in the local area which must once have been employed in buildings at other monastic sites like Evesham and Winchcombe, destroyed at the Dissolution.

The above information allows a broad-brush reconstruction to be attempted of the main activities of the various master masons (or architects), who have been given short fictional titles for reference.[60] The first one ('Pershore') to be involved in Phase I designed most of the new Lady Chapel, in a style closely related to the choir vault and crossing tower at Pershore Abbey. The Lady Chapel fits well between these two works, in the second decade of the 14th century. The vocabulary of mouldings is essentially local, as similar loose carved stones have been found at the monastic sites of Evesham, Winchcombe and Hailes; but some ideas are influenced by the style of Salisbury Cathedral's crossing tower and, ultimately, from the 'court' style of Kentish masons at the turn of the century.[61]

Work was probably ongoing on the other chevet chapels, especially the north-east ones, when a second master ('Chester') took charge, being responsible for the new fussy style of window tracery (as above, Fig.10.16) and also probably for the introduction of sunk chamfer and wave mouldings in the ambulatory and chevet chapels (Fig.10.14 B, C). Both mouldings first came to prominence in the royal works of King Edward I in the north Welsh castles and at Chester around 1300, and went on to become a characteristic of the Decorated style in the Welsh Marches.[62] At Tewkesbury, the sunk chamfer rib replaced the more elaborate (and more expensive) Lady Chapel vault rib design throughout the vaults of the chevet chapels, ambulatory and east bays of the nave (Fig.9.16). His responsibility continued into Phase II, with the use of multiple wave mouldings for the new arcade arches of the choir and probably for its simple two-storey elevation (Pl.16), for which the choir of Chester Cathedral (*c*.1280-1320) provides a more up-to-date general model than the more local example in the choir of Pershore Abbey (*c*.1225-39).[63] Uniquely at Tewkesbury the arcade arch actually consists of two arches, that on the choir side higher than that to the ambulatory, an arrangement brought about by the junction of a low ambulatory vault with a choir elevation requiring tall Gothic arches (Fig.10.23). This oddity strongly suggests that Phase I was initiated before any detailed designs had been prepared for Phase II.

Meanwhile, still in Phase I, the ballflower decoration of the sacristy and adjacent tomb recess (Fig.10.12) infers the presence of another master ('Gloucester'). The use in the sacristy of the sunk chamfer rib, introduced by Master Chester, proves that ballflower appeared only later in Phase I, not at the start. The local sources of this style have already been mentioned, and in addition loose carved stones from Winchcombe Abbey, found at Sudeley Castle in 1996, demonstrate the existence there of very similar work with little grotesque heads amongst the ballflowers. The Winchcombe parallels continue in the sedilia in the sanctuary (Fig.11.6) and in a collection of loose stones (probably from a screen) carved with ballflowers, hanging shields and grotesques (Fig.13.4, the 'tomb-chest'), all of which could date to the 1320s and, in the case of the sedilia, take us into the rebuilding of the choir in Phase II.[64]

The main decorative features of Phase II are a profusion of carved heads and bold Decorated tracery patterns, both of which are continued in the design of the choir vault (Fig.9.12).[65] The window tracery is different to any of the three types described above and a new master mason ('Banbury') seems to have arrived to take charge of Phase II. The windows in the choir clerestory include unusual wheel shapes in the heads of the three east windows (Pl.21) and S-curving ogee arches, a trait of mature Decorated tracery which links them with the main type of nave aisle windows in the same style (Fig.10.18, right).[66] The curvilinear heads of their three-light designs find close parallels from Yorkshire to Somerset by the 1320s but, when viewed in combination with a fondness for carved heads and friezes, the likely source narrows to North Oxfordshire, where the churches around Banbury are well-known for these features between *c*.1310-40.[67] In the choir, human heads depicting various classes from contemporary society—kings, great ecclesiastics, monks, knights and ladies, merchants, jesters and grotesques—inhabit the pier capitals, junctions of mouldings and the exterior parapet, without any discernible iconographical scheme (Figs.10.17, 9.14).[68] Some of the facial types resemble those on the figure capitals of nave arcades at Bloxham and Hanwell near Banbury.[69]

Moving to Phase III, the nave vault is devoid of useful detail for attribution, but the triple stepped chamfer mouldings (Fig.10.14 D) of the new west window perhaps provide enough evidence to speculate on a new master mason ('Ludlow') engaged in the 1340s. Stepped chamfer window mullions feature in a group of church works around Ludlow (Shrops.) *c*.1340-70, which also show influence from the early Perpendicular style at Gloucester Cathedral.[70] Likewise Tewkesbury has relationships with Gloucester in the engineering of its large west window and, in Phase IV, in the fan-vault techniques of its transept vaults, suggesting that Master Ludlow may have continued working at the abbey in the third quarter of the century. The focus for this master's work in the Welsh Marches may indicate that he is a successor in the next generation to Master Chester.

When I wrote almost 30 years ago about the 'Despenser mausoleum', I envisaged the Decorated rebuilding of the eastern arm as being heavily resourced by the royal favourite, Hugh II Despenser, and thus that its chronology was determined by the rapid rise and fall of his fortunes.[71] Hugh had married Eleanor, the de Clare heiress, and the presumed intention of the work would be to provide monumental expression to the prestige of the previous lords of Tewkesbury and the legitimacy of the Despensers as their successors. In this scenario, building could not have commenced before 1318 and would have been at its peak in Hugh's boom years from 1322 until his execution in 1326, after which a break occurred until his widow redeemed the family fortunes in the early 1330s.[72]

Fig.10.19 South choir aisle, looking east, with the abbots' monuments

Inevitably the real picture is more complicated than this, both historically and architecturally. No proof exists that Hugh's wealth directly paid for the work, though the likely involvement of Eleanor and her son Hugh III in the iconography of the choir glass and in the disposition of the Despenser tombs may well have extended to funding as well. Significantly Hugh III's monument is sited directly to the north of the high altar and adjacent to Fitzhamon's tomb, in the position of a second founder (Pl.12). Both Eleanor's husbands, Hugh II and William de la Zouche (d.1337), are depicted in the west bay of the clerestory (Pl.23, Fig.14.4), though Brown questions whether Eleanor is the kneeling figure in the east window, and oddly the site of her burial in 1337 is unknown.[73] Possibly her remains were interred in the choir, like those of Gilbert III de Clare's widow, Maud de Burgh, whose slab for a monumental brass still exists; or with those of her second husband, Lord Zouche, in the new Lady Chapel. The only survivals from this chapel are his single effigy, now at Forthampton Court (Fig.7.5), and probably a group of loose floor tiles which are heraldically unhelpful for attribution (Fig.15.6).[74]

With regard to a break in construction which could coincide with Despenser's downfall, and which I identified in 1974 with the half-finished state of the chevet chapels, there appears to be no single major disruption which lends support to this argument. It has been shown above that Phase I is characterized by the comings and goings of various masons, but if Master Chester's work belongs in the 1320s,[75] then almost certainly Phase II—the choir rebuilding—was under way in this decade; and quite possibly its architectural shell was complete. That there might be a break in the later 1320s could be as much to do with the death of the long-lived Abbot Kempsey (1328) as that of Despenser the younger. In which case the most likely major work at a resumption would be the choir vault, which sits more easily as a design of the 1330s both architecturally and symbolically. The radiating flower-like patterns of the vault may be read as symbolizing the Paradise garden, enclosing the tombs of the lords of Tewkesbury and their painted depictions in glass. Its symbolism reflects the chivalric imagery fashionable at court and more explicitly is an essential attribute of the iconographic programme attributed to Eleanor and Hugh III in the 1330s.[76]

Another facet of my former argument linking Hugh II to the remodelling was that his influence would explain the presence of features apparently of court derivation in the architecture of this provincial abbey. These range from the unusual choice of a chevet plan for the east end, with precedents in royal burial churches like Westminster and Hailes, to details like the band of miniature battlements along the choir parapet (Fig.10.17).[77] As the royal favourite, Hugh was in a position to attract master masons from the royal works to his own commissions, and indeed Master Thomas de la Bataile from Kent and the royal carpenter, William Hurley, are documented as working on his great hall at Caerphilly Castle in 1326.[78] One can only speculate whether Thomas gave advice at Tewkesbury too, but it is worth noting that masters with experience of the royal works were active in the area before Despenser came on the scene. Master Walter of Hereford (fl.*c*.1277-1309), a key figure in Edward I's Welsh castles campaigns and documented as working also at Winchcombe Abbey, is a notable example of a master who could have facilitated a knowledge of the latest Kentish court style in this area around the turn of the century.[79] Overall, it is clear that the Decorated work at Tewkesbury does not reveal the close attentions of a royal mason, in contrast to the incontravertible evidence for the king's master mason, Thomas of Canterbury, as designer of parts of the remodelled south transept at Gloucester Cathedral (1329-37).[80]

Against the potential involvement of the early Despensers must be set the far more likely engagement of Tewkesbury's abbots, priors and monastic community in the fabric of their own abbey. Doubtless they would have noted with envy how local monastic rivals had been updating their churches in the later 13th century. At the old Benedictine establishments of

Winchcombe and Evesham, new Lady Chapels had been erected after *c*.1275, Winchcombe and Pershore had received new choir vaults around the turn of the century, whilst the Cistercian newcomer, Hailes Abbey (f.1246), added a chevet with radiating chapels in 1270-77 to celebrate its newly acquired relic of the Holy Blood.[81]

The remodelling of Tewkesbury's eastern arm must be viewed as much as a response to these works as a concern to retain the favour of the new lords of the manor at the extinction of the de Clare male line. Thus the Tewkesbury chevet, with its elaborate vaults and varied plan (Masterplan), upstages that at Hailes, and the priority placed on completing the new Lady Chapel infers that it was a reaction to similar chapels at Winchcombe and Evesham. Indeed, judging by the relatively naturalistic foliage carving of its remaining capitals, there is no impediment to placing work on the Lady Chapel earlier than the arrival of Hugh II Despenser.

Overall the new chevet is likely to have been commissioned by monastic patrons, who seem to have favoured the choir aisles and chevet chapels for burial. As has been shown, already in the 13th century the Annals record the involvement of priors Henry of Sipton and Henry of Banbury in the rebuilding of chapels. Several abbatial tombs are found today in the south choir aisle and some chevet chapels, and although the situation is complicated by the movement of coffins apparently since the Dissolution,[82] the monuments of abbots Cheltenham (d.1509) and Wakeman (pre-1540) in the chapels of St. John the Baptist and St. Edmund are testimony to the continuity of this practice to the end of the Middle Ages.[83] Thus, the so-called 'Forthampton' recess, stylistically of the early 14th century (Fig.10.12), virtually certainly housed the body of an abbot—given the splendid quality of the recess and its associated sculpture—who was the benefactor of the adjacent sacristy.[84] On grounds of date, the only candidate is Abbot Thomas Kempsey (1282-1328) and, indeed, if an abbot was the main promoter of Phase I of the rebuilding, it could only be him, given the longevity of his abbacy. The monument takes its lead from the two earlier gabled recesses in the south choir aisle (Fig.10.19), one of about 1300 and now empty, the other of *c*.1240 and perhaps always intended to house Abbot Alan's tomb which now occupies its space (Fig.5.2).[85]

So far, the monks' church has dominated the discussion, but the Phase III works in the nave warrant brief mention on account of the vault sculptures and the relevance of some of the 14th-century features there to the debate about the nave as parish church. In the vault, the ridge rib at the apex is flanked by two lateral longitudinal ribs, lending a strong processional accent from west to east (Fig.11.5). This triple arrangement provides an armature for the famous carved figure bosses, which on the ridge rib depict scenes from Christ's Infancy, Passion and Ascension. They are accompanied on the lateral ribs mainly by angels playing musical instruments and swinging censers, but with the four evangelical symbols and the instruments of the Passion in the two east bays—the part of the vault within the monks' church.

The main series of 15 bosses commences with the Nativity in the centre of the west (eighth) bay. It then moves to the Passion cycle with the Entry into Jerusalem at the start of the fifth bay, and culminates in the Crucifixion, Resurrection and Ascension in the third bay, below which appropriately would have stood the nave altar dedicated to the Holy Cross (Pl.17 A, B, C).[86] The last three bosses represent the Pentecost, the Coronation of the Virgin, and the Divine Judge seated on an orb, probably symbolizing the Day of Judgement. This iconographical sequence forms a natural preface to the choir vault, read as the vault of Paradise, and thus served the purpose of embellishing the processional route for the monastic community from the nave west door to the choir on great feast days.

Though often illustrated in books on sculpture,[87] the carving of these bosses is actually fairly rudimentary, with much of the detail made up in paint:[88] their quality compares unfavourably with the mid-14th-century bosses of angel musicians in the choir vault of Gloucester Cathedral. Less frequently noted, however, are the monumental head corbels at the springers of the nave vault, which seem to be a continuation of the Oxfordshire group of carvings under Master Banbury in Phase II (Fig.9.6). With them belong the two larger figure corbels supporting the transverse arch at the west end of the nave, traditionally identified as 'Adam and Eve' or, less probably, Robert Fitzhamon and his wife.[89] A biblical context is likely, so the female might be Eve. However, the male figure could as well be Isaiah, whose Messianic prophesies are highly appropriate to the iconography of the bosses above; or Jesse, the subject of Isaiah's prophesy concerning the genealogy of Christ (Pl.17 D).[90]

The one physical feature which could testify to a parochial function in the nave in the early 14th century is the font. This is now a composite piece, in that the bowl was replaced in 1878-9, the stem and its capital are 14th century, and the base is in 13th-century Early English style (Fig.10.20). The medieval sections fit together well, which suggests that this should not be interpreted as an assemblage of pieces brought together after the Dissolution.[91] The ballflower ornament of the stem places it in Phase I or early in Phase II, probably in the 1320s, and overall a case may be made that in the early 14th century a new font was commissioned reusing the base from its Early English predecessor.[92] This could indicate that the rite of baptism in the nave extends back at least to the early 14th century, but it has been suggested that the font has been moved here later: this font stem and base cannot be proven to be sited in the nave until two centuries after the Dissolution (see Fig.16.1).[93]

Fig.10.20 The font in the nave

It seems reasonable to speculate that the rood screen and pulpitum, which delineated the boundaries of parish nave and monks' choir, were replaced in the first half of the 14th century, with the new choir stalls (*c.*1340).[94] Fourteenth-century examples elsewhere show that a new pulpitum frequently accompanied the commissioning of choir stalls, as for example at Exeter and Wells cathedrals. Nothing now survives of these screens and authorities differ on their positions, but all the evidence of vault bosses, floor levels and post-medieval usage points to a rood screen standing between the western piers of nave bay 2 (Masterplan).[95] Traces of medieval painting can be discerned on the east face of each of these piers, possibly linked to the images of Our Lady of Pity and St. Clement recorded in this area in the late 15th century.[96] According to Hope, the most likely arrangement was that another screen (the pulpitum screen) stood between the eastern piers of bay 2, linked to the rood screen by a loft as at St. Albans.[97] Some parts of the arrangement may have survived the Dissolution and thus appear in John Coney's early 19th-century engraving (Fig.16.1), before they were finally removed in the 1875 restoration.[98]

The Late Middle Ages

By about 1370 the great renovation of the Norman church was completed and the story of its medieval architecture is normally considered to have come to an end. Such works as were carried out in the 15th century receive scant attention—the new processional door from the nave to the cloister,[99] and the new niche over the Romanesque north porch, with a statue of the Assumption of the Virgin (Fig.9.3).[100] The image was probably copied from the iconography of the 15th-century seal of the abbey.[101] Instead, the attention of the guidebook writers turns to the fine collection of tombs and cage chantries which arose in and around the choir from the mid-14th century onwards.[102] However, the chantries are legitimately works of Perpendicular architecture in miniature, as well as representing the continuation of themes integral to the architecture of the previous Gothic periods, and are considered as such below.

The only Perpendicular style window in the abbey, just west of the nave north porch, should probably be placed in the late 14th century or *c.*1400. Its insertion seems to represent a catching-up on the one aisle bay which had escaped refenestration in the Decorated period, probably because of the greater constructional difficulties caused by the Romanesque passage to the porch upper chamber running through this wall. The 'alternate' units in the head of the window, each sub-divided into panels ('sub-reticulated'),[103] suggest a designer familiar with the later 14th-century tracery of St. Mary Redcliffe, Bristol (Fig.10.21).

Another work of Perpendicular tracery, rather neglected in the literature, is the monumental openwork screen in the south bay of the choir west of the Trinity Chapel (Masterplan, G; Fig.10.22). Exact parallels for this fussy design are elusive, but in general it shares the use of alternate, sub-reticulated tracery with the north aisle window, whilst both screen and window have nothing in common with the Oxford-derived patterns of the Trinity, Founder's and Warwick chapels (cf. Figs.10.22, 10.23). Rather the screen looks to Gloucester Cathedral for its inspiration, where such features of its design as Y-tracery impaling a central panel (termed 'sub-arcuated, through-reticulation') and the row of 'Venetian' shouldered arches were all in use before the mid-14th century. Such motifs remained popular in the region in the first half of the 15th century, for example in the sub-arcuated through-reticulated tracery of the abbey's cloister (Fig.12.6) and in the Beauchamp Chapel at St. Mary's, Warwick (1443-*c.*1450).[104] But the design of the screen possesses a gawkiness which sets it apart from these examples, and suggests that it is a significant work of early Perpendicular design probably dating to the third quarter of the 14th century. For instance, the row of shouldered arches which threads its way across the mullions recalls the mannered row of hexagons in the same position in the great south transept window at Gloucester (*c.*1335), which established the Gloucester style of tracery design.[105] The screen should thus precede the erection of the Trinity Chapel in the next bay, and would appear to be roughly contemporary with the fine unidentified tomb recess of *c.*1360 now in the south-east ambulatory, which also employs a prominent shouldered arch (Masterplan, F; Fig.13.4). It is unclear whether the screen functioned as a barrier, or whether the aperture in it is original and permitted access into the sanctuary.[106]

Fig.10.21 Nave north aisle, window west of the porch

Fig.10.22 Screen to the south choir aisle

The commissioning of the Trinity Chapel (*c*.1380) by Edward Despenser's widow, and of its virtual replica, the Founder's Chapel, by Abbot Parker (1397) continued the combination of aristocratic and monastic patronage which seems to have resourced the Decorated remodelling of the church. Specifically, Abbot Parker's action in making the founder's burial place a fitting complement to the new Despenser monuments almost certainly represents a conscious emulation of Abbot Robert of Forthampton's initiative in translating Fitzhamon's body to this site in 1241 to accompany the early burials of the de Clares.[107]

The openwork grid of 'super-mullioned' tracery for both chapels reflects the monumental elegance of early Perpendicular windows of a kind derived from sources other than Gloucester (Fig.10.23, right). It also contrasts with the later elevation of the Warwick Chapel (after 1422), with its exaggerated four-centred arches and rows

Fig.10.23 The north side of the choir: the Warwick and Founder's chapel and Hugh III Despenser's tomb

of canopied niches (Fig.10.23, left). The latter is a ground-breaking example of the refinement of Perpendicular style in the 15th century, in which nichework dissipates architectural solidity. Oxford and the north Cotswolds is the likely source area for the craftsmen for both designs, and it is notable that in each case the date of the Tewkesbury work sets it at the cutting edge of architectural fashion. The 14th-century chapels are related to the work of the royal master, William Wynford, at New College, Oxford (1380-86), and the Warwick Chapel to the style associated with the major Cotswold master, Richard Winchcombe, as in the Divinity School, Oxford (*c*.1424-39).[108] In a national context, the fantastic canopies of the Warwick Chapel anticipate such outstanding royal monuments as the chantry chapels of King Henry V at Westminster Abbey (*c*.1438-48), Duke Humphrey of Gloucester at St. Albans (1443-*c*.1447) and Cardinal Henry Beaufort at Winchester Cathedral (after 1447).[109] This is remarkable even if the chapel dates to the 1430s, and the more so if a date in the early 1420s is accepted, based on the Founders' Book.[110]

The Warwick Chapel was founded by Countess Isabel Despenser after the death in 1422 of her first husband, Richard, earl of Worcester, and constitutes the main survival of a new initiative for fitting out the sanctuary in the 1420s and 1430s. Isabel (d.1439) was a generous benefactress to the abbey and it is likely that she assisted with these works, thus continuing the theme of major artistic patronage by widowed noblewomen at Tewkesbury.[111] Another recurring theme is represented by the commissioning of a new cycle of the lords of the manor, complementing the 14th-century stained glass figures in the choir clerestory with a series of painted sculptures placed in the niches of the Warwick Chapel, discussed further by Phillip Lindley in Chapter 13.[112] The works apparently also extended to a new high altarpiece, which presumably would have replaced an earlier tall altarpiece because the plain west face of the ambulatory arch behind the high altar was clearly designed to be hidden by such a fitting in the 14th century. The 15th-century altarpiece may have incorporated a representation of the Tree of Jesse, another theme pre-existing in the clerestory stained glass and an iconography known from late Gothic altarpieces at Christchurch Priory (Hants.), Abergavenny Priory (Mon.) and St. Cuthbert's, Wells (Som.).[113] The fragments to be identified with the new altarpiece are the head of an angel, from a figure originally about four feet high, and pieces of carved foliage to the same scale.[114] The head is amongst the finest examples of painted sculpture surviving from late medieval England—the black pupils and blue irises of the eyes are particularly striking (Pl.11).[115]

The refurbishment of the choir for the Despensers is not quite the end of the story. The house of York was to have the last word, when its supremacy after the Battle of Tewkesbury (1471) was celebrated by the embellishment of the choir vault with the Yorkist badge, the sun in splendour (Fig.11.1).[116] This must have happened in the early 1470s, during the lordship of George, duke of Clarence, and involved not only fixing the wooden sun bosses but also superimposing large new foliage bosses of wood over some of the original 14th-century ones of stone (Fig.21.3).[117] As this would have necessitated scaffolding—probably cantilevered out from the clerestory passage—it must be virtually certain that the opportunity was taken to repaint the vault at this time. A parallel for updating and personalizing a pre-existing vault with new bosses occurs in the choir vault of Winchester Cathedral, renovated for Bishop Fox *c*.1503-09.[118]

This is one of several ways in which the architectural development of Tewkesbury Abbey in the later Middle Ages mirrors those of many English monastic great churches. A massive Romanesque superstructure was remodelled in the 14th century, especially in its eastern parts and especially with new fenestration and vaulting. Later building activity, insofar as it involves the church, was restricted to minor works and private chapels. What sets Tewkesbury apart from this stereotype is the quality of its later Gothic fabric, no more so than in its vaulting, which is the main subject of the next chapter.

CHAPTER 11

The Gothic Church: Vaulting and Carpentry

by Richard K. Morris

Vaulting

English rib vaulting of the later Middle Ages represents the culmination of the master mason's skills, combining intricate linear design with the complexities of constructed three-dimensional form, carved with precision and assembled in physically difficult locations. Masons in the south and west of England played a particularly important part in this development, encouraged by the availability of good freestone and light-weight tufa in the Cotswolds and elsewhere, and Tewkesbury Abbey is the best place—together with Wells Cathedral—to study a representative range of their achievements.

In England, the three main types of later medieval vault with decorative rib patterns are, in order of appearance, the lierne vault (from *c.*1300), the net vault (from *c.*1320) and the fan vault (from *c.*1350). All are found in Tewkesbury Abbey. The first is characterized by numerous extra ribs (called 'liernes', e.g. Fig.11.1) and the second takes the form of a mesh of diagonal ribs (e.g. south transept, Fig.11.2).[1] In both types the ribs are normally separate stones from the infill ('rib and panel' construction). The fan is distinguished from these by having all its spreading ribs of equal length in a radial pattern (Fig.11.3) and by incorporating ribs cut from the same stones as the infill ('jointed masonry' construction).[2] The fan is typified as the characteristic vault of the Perpendicular style, but in fact the other vault types remained equally popular.

Underlying the design of the most important Decorated vaults at Tewkesbury is a mason's formula for dividing a square into thirds, which modern scholars have termed 'the one- and two-bay diagonal'. For example, the chamfer profile of the nave rib was set out using this geometry

Fig.11.1 Choir Vault

Fig.11.2 South transept vault

(Fig.11.4A). The application to vault patterns is most clearly demonstrated in the nave, where the traditional diagonal ribs intersecting in the centre of a single rectangular bay are overlaid by diagonals stretching across two bays (a 'double' bay, Fig.11.4A). Another mason's formula—rotated squares—underlies the pattern of the crossing vault (Fig.11.4D).[3] This method was commonly used by medieval masons across Europe for establishing the proportions of everything from ground-plans to pinnacles,[4] and it lends itself naturally to the square bay of a tower vault. However, parallels for the Tewkesbury design in towers are scarce,[5] though the pattern appears in the near-contemporary north transept vault at Gloucester Cathedral (1367-73).

A trait very specific to Decorated vaults in the lower Severn valley is the 'triple ridge rib', which was used to good effect in the nave to multiply the number of vault bosses, and its influence continues in the vaults of the transepts (Figs.11.5, 11.2). It also features at Gloucester Cathedral in the choir vault (1337-*c*.1350), which is a direct

Fig.11.3 Fan vaulting in the Founder's Chapel

successor to the Tewkesbury nave vault, and in the later vault of the north transept.[6] However, it has a wider frame of reference in that it is an embellishment resulting from the division of the vaulting field into thirds, using the 'two-bay diagonal' formula (Fig.11.4A). The earliest one- and two-bay diagonal vault with a firm documentary date is the small-scale example in the pulpitum screen at Exeter Cathedral (1317-25), but the principle was already being applied to high vaults in the Tewkesbury area before this, as shown by a reconstruction of the geometry underlying the choir vault of Pershore Abbey (*c*.1300-10, Fig.11.4C).[7]

This was evidently the inspiration for the lost vault of Tewkesbury's eastern Lady Chapel, which used a tri-partite sub-division longitudinally and had diagonal ribs on a two-bay align-

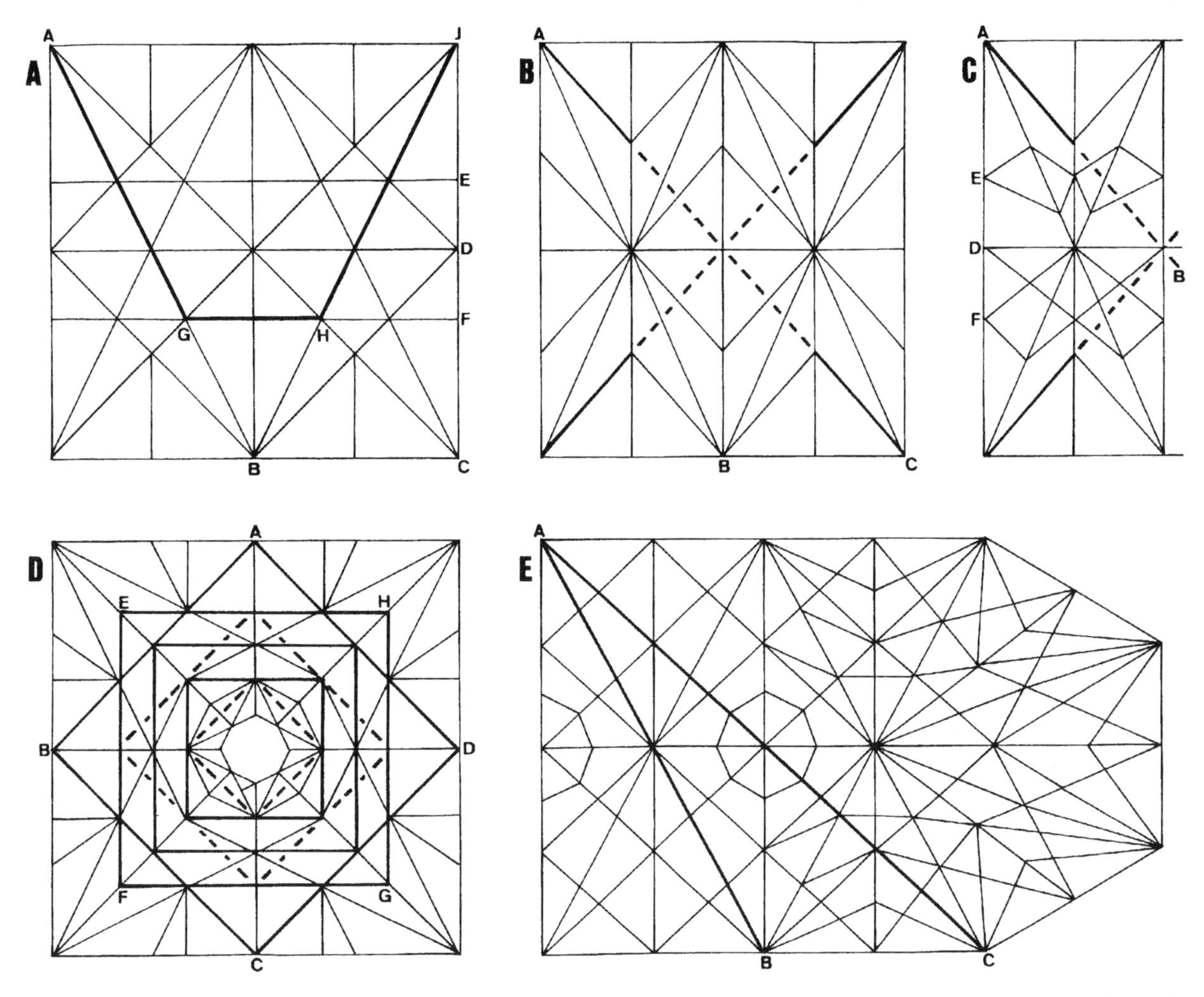

Fig.11.4 A-E Diagrams of vault patterns. A, Tewkesbury nave (two bays), with one-bay (a-b) and two-bay (a-c) diagonals, triple ridge ribs (d,e,f), and the geometry for a section of the nave rib (a-g-h-j); B, Pershore Abbey choir (two bays), with one-bay diagonals (a-b), and two-bay diagonal geometry partly reconstructed (a-c);
C, Tewkesbury eastern Lady Chapel (west bay), two alternatives for reconstruction (top, bottom), both based on geometry from two-bay diagonals (a-b) and triple ridge ribs (d,e,f);
D, Tewkesbury crossing, with two schemes of rotated squares superimposed (a-b-c-d and e-f-g-h);
E, Tewkesbury choir (with cusping and some minor ribs omitted), one-bay (a-b) and two-bay (a-c) diagonals

Fig.11.5 Nave vault, looking east, showing the triple ridge ribs and the many carved bosses

Fig.11.6 Sedilia in the sanctuary, showing the miniature vault

ment, as indicated by the western vault springers and the wall-bosses still extant (Fig.10.13). Not enough survives to reconstruct the vault pattern definitively (Fig.11.4C), but it must have borne a resemblance to the miniature vault in the sanctuary sedilia, with a row of lozenge-shaped panels running on each side of the ridge rib (Fig.11.6). As Pershore choir is noted as one of the two earliest lierne vaults known in England,[8] recognition should be given to the Tewkesbury Lady Chapel vault, which clearly was another early example, probably designed in the second decade of the 14th century.

The next major vault is the choir vault, assigned to Master Banbury in Phase II of the 14th-century reconstruction—a highly eclectic design which is the *pièce de résistance* of the series (Fig.11.1). On the one hand it is indebted to the previous vaults in the underlying framework of one- and two-bay diagonals (Fig.11.4E). On the other, the overriding impression is of radial patterns of ribs, grouped around the springers and hanging in the centre of the vault like large flowers, filled with cusping like window tracery (Fig.11.1). Indeed, the fondness for bold cusping in the choir clerestory and the rose pattern in the head of the east window suggests a coherence of design between the windows and the vault (Fig.9.12).

The breaking down of barriers between different architectural features in this way would be consistent with the Oxfordshire background of Master Banbury, where we find novelties like the introduction of sculpture and architectural gables into window tracery, at Merton College chapel, Oxford (1289-94) and Dorchester Abbey (1320s).[9] The Tewkesbury vault is one of three in which cusped panels appear for the first time, the others being the choir vaults of Bristol and Wells cathedrals, all in the 1330s. After the choir vault, the nave vault returns to a more minimal grid of one- and two-bay diagonals, reflecting its relatively less prestigious location in the church (Fig.11.5). However, the radial patterns and conical shapes of the choir vault were to have a profound effect not only on other later Gothic vaults in the abbey but further afield, culminating in the famous fan vaults of Tudor England like King's College chapel, Cambridge.

The Tewkesbury choir vault, in effect if not in detail, is a prototype fan vault on a monumental scale. Unlike many other high vaults of this period in the west of England, it does not take the form of a pointed barrel vault (as, for example, the nave vault) but rather deploys delicate conoidal-shaped springers to produce a fuller integration between windows and vault (cf. Figs.9.6, 9.12). The high vaults of Exeter Cathedral (from *c*.1300) provide the general source of inspiration, but Tewkesbury incorporates new ideas which anticipate real fan vaults of the next generation: for example, the cusped heads to the panels between the radiating ribs, and the staggering of the springing of the ribs—every other rib springs from a head corbel. An interest in vaults with radiating patterns seems to have been alive locally in the early 14th century. The lost polygonal chapter house of Evesham Abbey (1295-1317) must have had some radial arrangement of ribs in the centre of its vault, because unusually it had no central pier, and a reflection of this idea appears at Tewkesbury in the ring of ribs in St. Margaret's Chapel encircling the centre boss depicting the saint (Masterplan, D).[10] Of equal significance are the miniature vaults in the canopies of contemporary monuments, notably those adorning the tomb of Hugh II Despenser (after 1330) which show symmetrical radial patterns and conoidal springers from the same decade as the completion of the choir vault (Fig.13.1).

The tomb canopy of the next Despenser, Hugh III (d.1349), provides the best evidence not just locally, but nationally, that the true fan vault had been perfected around the middle of the century.[11] The part of the canopy which frames the two effigies comprises a series of regular conoids with flat spandrel panels in between, and on the conoids are faint traces of radial ribs added in paint to create a regular panelled effect (Fig.11.7). Thus, as all the visual characteristics of fan vaulting are replicated here, but in a non-structural form, one must assume that real fan vaults were available to be copied by the 1350s, the date of the tomb. The most likely model locally would be the first fan vaults in the east cloister walk of Gloucester Cathedral (1351-77).[12]

At Tewkesbury the partial application of fan vault techniques in monumental architecture can be observed in the transept and crossing vaults, in their panelled springers (Figs.11.2, 18.2) of a kind also used at Gloucester Cathedral north transept (1367-73) and Worcester Cathedral nave (*c*.1377). Beyond the springers the transept vaults

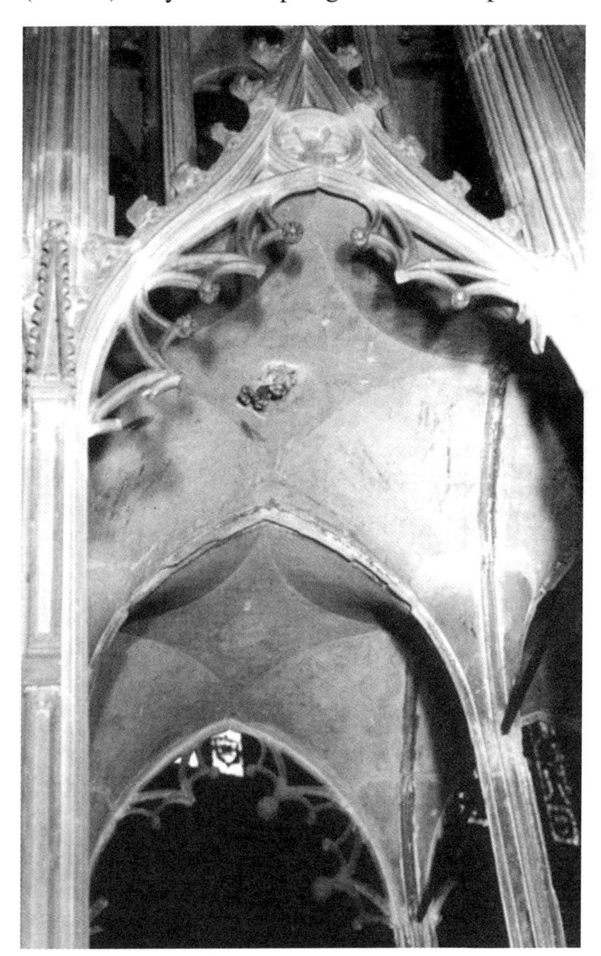

Fig.11.7 The vault conoids of the canopy above the tomb of Hugh III Despenser

Fig.11.8 Fan vault in the west bay of the Warwick Chapel

revert to a net pattern and the crossing vault to an elaborate lierne—the ability to construct a full-size fan vault is not evident from surviving vaults until the next century, at Sherborne Abbey (Dorset, *c*.1425-37).[13] The Tewkesbury transept vaults may be dated to *c*.1360 on account of the very close similarity of their carved bosses to ones in the south-east transept of Hereford Cathedral, documented to Master Thomas of Cambridge, 1364-71.[14] Three bosses of the crossing vault bear the arms of Sir Guy de Bryan (d.1390) and it is thus usually dated post-1375, after the death of Edward Despenser. However, the occurrence on another boss of De Bryan's arms impaling Montacute makes it more likely that it was erected in the period of Guy's marriage to Elizabeth Montacute, Hugh III Despenser's widow, 1350-59, and that it slightly predates the transept vaults.

It is in the Trinity Chapel about 1380 that true fan vaulting makes its first appearance in the abbey, followed shortly afterwards in the Founder's Chapel, and in the 15th century in the east walk of the cloister.[15] The Trinity Chapel vault is of considerable significance as one of the two or three earliest surviving fan vaults,[16] displaying all the textbook features – conoidal fans each describing a semi-circle and flat spandrel plates at the apex, all of jointed masonry construction; copied almost in replica in the Founder's Chapel (Fig.11.3).

In addition, the Trinity Chapel fan vault is the first to incorporate pendant bosses, used here for the springers between the two bays of vaulting. Their inclusion has been explained functionally, to produce two exactly square bays best suited for fan vaulting, but it is surprising that the double square was not established initially in the ground-plan of the chapel, and they may be consciously decorative: to draw attention to the miraculous suspension of the vault over the chapel (Fig.11.3). Master William Wynford was making use of the

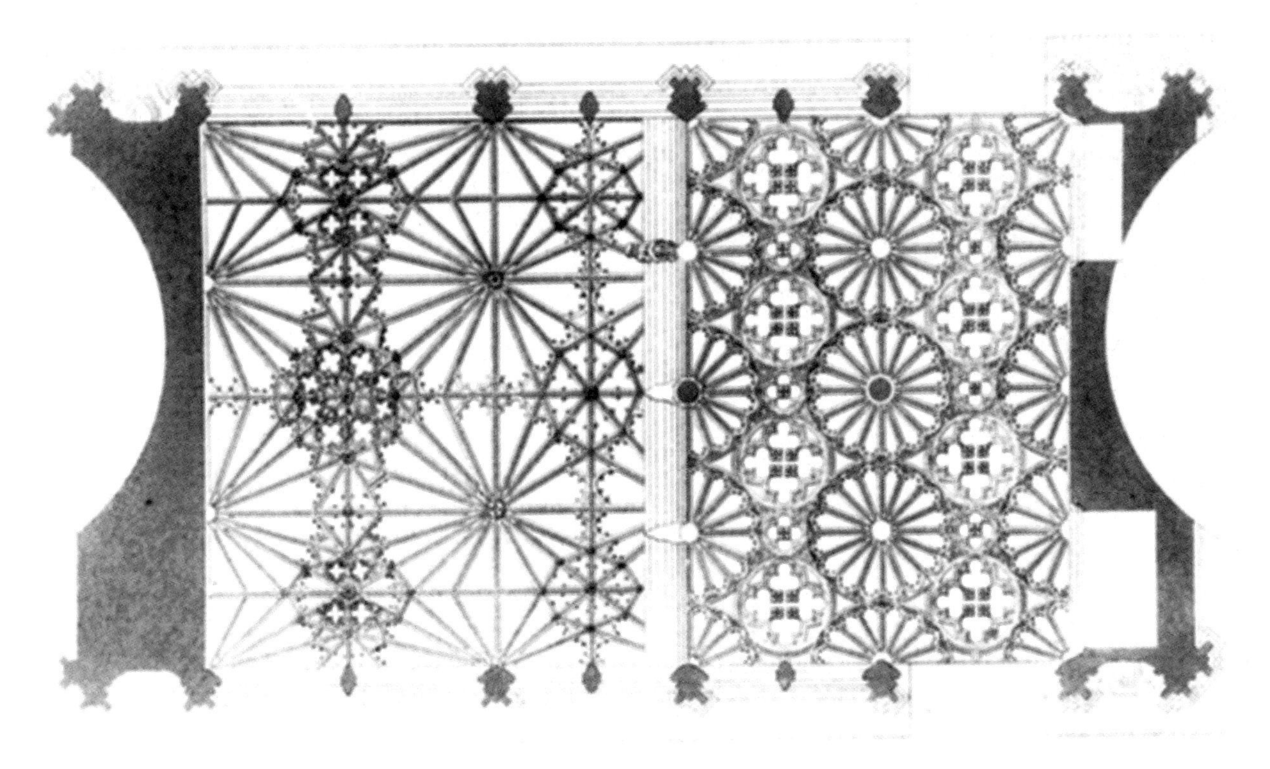

Fig.11.9 The vaults in the Warwick Chapel, from Vetusta Monumenta, *Vol.V*

pendant boss at New College, Oxford (1380-86), thus emphasizing the likely Oxford pedigree of the Trinity Chapel, and the ultimate source for the pendant appears to be in the crossing arches and high vault of Gloucester Cathedral choir (1337-*c*.1350).[17]

By 1400 the masons of the Cotwolds—an area loosely straddling a line drawn from Gloucester to Oxford—had established a reputation for advanced vault patterns and techniques, mixing features from fan vaults and elaborate lierne vaults. The Warwick Chapel (after 1422) represents a showcase of their skills, taking advantage of the two-storey arrangement to display two different vault designs (Fig.10.23, left). Under the west gallery is a fan vault, with the amazing feature of three conoids in the centre, one springing from a column and the others suspended like stalactites (Fig.11.8): the first known usage of this invention, to be copied in the 1440s at the Beauchamp Chapel, Warwick.[18]

The main vault of the Tewkesbury chapel is a lierne by definition, but exploiting fan vault ideas in its radial patterns of ribs and its use of jointed masonry construction, to create an incredibly flat vault more akin to a wooden ceiling (Fig.11.9, left half). Pendant bosses were a major feature of both vaults,[19] demonstrating how the classic simplicity of early fan vaulting—which eschewed the clutter of carved bosses associated with lierne and net vaults—was overtaken again by decorative impulses in the 15th century. The lierne vault is also loaded with cusped panels, and overall the Warwick Chapel vaults are appropriate successors to the pioneering design of the choir vault above, and were almost certainly detailed with this reference in mind.

In the later 15th century and the early 16th century, the vaulting experiments tried in miniature in the Warwick Chapel were brought to fruition in the superlative vaults of the Divinity School, Oxford, St. George's Chapel, Windsor, and Henry VII's Chapel, Westminster, in which Cotswold masons like the Janyns family played a key role.[20] Tewkesbury possesses an exquisite miniature cameo of these Tudor vaults—not in the abbey, but in the little known vault of the oriel in Abbey House (now the vicarage), commis-

Fig.11.10 Trusses in the north transept roof space

sioned by Abbot Henry Beeley (1509-1534).[21] The influence particularly of the choir vault at Windsor (1506-09) manifests itself in the details of the star patterns with pendant bosses (Fig.12.16), whereas the closest parallel overall appears in Worcester Cathedral, in the chantry vault of Prince Arthur (d.1502), a work of metropolitan quality. Thus it is evident that Abbot Beeley acquired the services of a master mason of outstanding ability for his oriel, and in so doing he was following in a long tradition of architectural patronage at Tewkesbury.

Medieval carpentry and timber fittings

No account of a medieval church would be complete without mention of its timber roofs and fittings, even though their survival at Tewkesbury is meagre in comparison with the riches still to be seen in some other great churches such as Winchester Cathedral. The roofs of the abbey have been almost entirely rebuilt in the post-medieval period, and the choir-stalls were so dispersed after the Dissolution that the Victorian reassemblage is more of a collage. Nevertheless the stalls repay a closer study and the abbey also possesses two more unusual objects, a winding wheel and a wooden canopy perhaps from a Sacrament house.

The carpentry of great church roofs is difficult to appreciate because it is hidden in dark voids above the stone vaults, and yet it can contribute invaluable evidence to a church's history.[22] At Tewkesbury, the nave roof is typical of the high roofs, with its low pitch indicating that it is a later replacement for the medieval roofs which have left their outlines on the tower (Fig.9.19). The king-post trusses and other details of the existing roof suggest that it was replaced shortly after 1720: 'the Roof being so much decayed and rotten that the whole must be taken off and new framed, and the lead work new cast ...'.[23]

It is surprising therefore to find that the carpentry of the north transept roof has been judged by Cecil Hewett to be substantially medieval (Fig.11.10). He characterized it as a remarkably eclectic roof system which had survived on account of its efficiency, and he noted similarities of technical details elsewhere which could place it either in the 13th century (*c*.1260) or in the 14th (*c*.1330-45).[24] The latter is the more likely date, in view of the preparations for revaulting the transept arms *c*.1340, finally implemented around 1360.[25] However, his analysis does not appear to have taken account of the low pitch of the roof which, in the context of the history of the abbey roofs, would incline one to place its final form after the Dissolution—and which might explain the eclecticism of its structure. Amongst the various clues suggesting a later date are the use of tenoned purlins, which are unlikely to predate the Tudor period; post-medieval brickwork around the wall-plate areas; and the incorporation of timbers which are clearly reused. However, other features like the notched lap joints, as seen at the tops of the queen posts (Fig.11.10), are less easily dismissed as post-medieval, and obviously the north transept roof requires a fresh survey to resolve this issue.

Where an opportunity has presented itself to investigate the lower roofs of the church, as around the ambulatory and chevet chapels, their associated details show that they have been rebuilt in the 18th or early 19th century, and subsequently retiled in the Scott restoration (Fig.10.15).[26] Numerous timbers display redundant joints and have evidently been reused, though whether from the later medieval roofs or from early post-dissolution roofs is not always clear (Fig.21.4). However, in one instance a large beam reused to support the lean-to roof below the choir clerestory may conceivably be as early as the 12th century.[27]

To haul the many loads of stone and timber needed for the construction of the upper stages of great churches, medieval masons had at their disposal large winding wheels (or windlasses) from a relatively early date.[28] Extremely few survive today, but Tewkesbury has one hidden away in the top stage of the tower (Fig.11.11). It would originally have stood in mountings, with a rope around the barrel connected to pulleys, and it could have lifted considerable weights. The rim, 12 feet in diameter, would have had rungs through the holes to allow two men to operate it manually or by standing on it, like the only other comparable example in this country in the north-west tower of Peterborough Cathedral.[29] Hewett thinks that it is 12th century and had been employed to construct the Romanesque tower,[30] but it is as likely to be later in the medieval period, when it could have been equally useful in hauling loads to the upper level of the four arms of the church. A windlass is mentioned more than once in the churchwardens' accounts for 1563-1624, though whether referring to this wheel is not certain.[31]

The choir-stalls take us from the work of the master carpenter as engineer to that of joiner and carver. The surviving medieval stalls are the present back stalls of the choir, 12 on the north and 11 on the south, which were brought together from the south aisle and transepts during the Victorian restoration. In addition, there is a set of three loose stalls against the south-west crossing pier, found in a garden in Tewkesbury in 1908, and one loose stall inside the chancel screen on the south, presented in 1924.[32] In their later medieval arrangement the fuller complement of stalls may have extended further west, one bay into the nave, depending on where the pulpitum screen was sited.[33]

Only on the north side of the choir can one now appreciate something of the original effect with the stalls backed by a screen and canopies (Fig.11.13), though this superstructure is a somewhat arbitrary reassemblage of components.[34] It is evident that the stalls were made around 1340, presumably for the new-built choir. In their general design they belong in date between the cathedral stalls at Wells (*c.*1335-40) and Hereford (*c.*1340-55),[35] and specifically their miniature tracery patterns use the same vocabulary as those in the Decorated stone screens created for the

Fig.11.11 The former winding wheel in the crossing tower

abbey in Phase III of the 14th-century remodelling (Fig.11.12). The apposed mouchettes of the canopies appear in the section of screen by St. Margaret's Chapel, and the curve-sided triangles of the spandrels appear in the section in the north choir aisle: an interesting instance of shared patterns in two different media.

The best known features of the stalls are the 17 misericords, despite the mutilated and worn condition of many of them. All the north stalls and the loose stalls have misericords, but only one exists in the south stalls.[36] As far as they can be deciphered, the subjects are mainly grotesques, mythical beasts, animals and birds derived from illustrated Bestiary manuscripts, a popular source for the carvers of misericords.[37] The north stalls have an amphisbaena, a beast with an extra head on its tail to enable it to move backwards as well as forward (Fig.11.14B). On the loose stalls, a human figure gesturing to its

Fig.11.12 St. Margaret's Chapel, 14th-century stone screen with blind tracery and the Despenser arms

Fig.11.13 Drawing of a choir-stall on the north side (by Roland Paul in 1886)

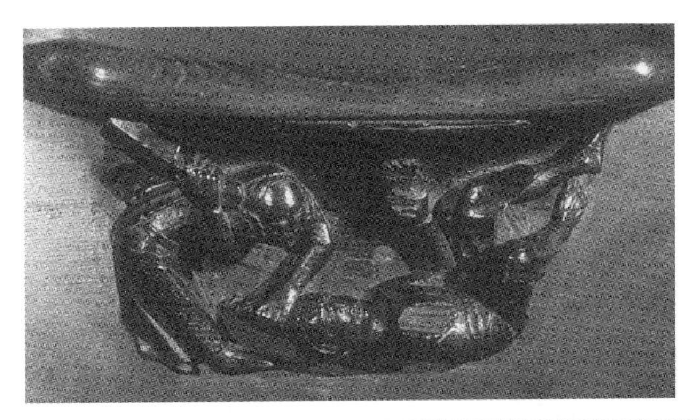

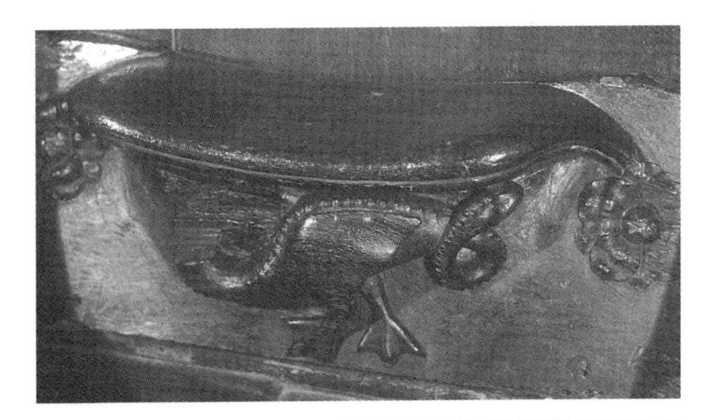

Fig.11.14 Top: misericords on the choir stalls: A, woman beating a man; B, an amphisbaena
Bottom: C, frieze with the initials of Abbot Henry Beeley

bottom probably refers to the devil—farting was associated with the sulphurous smells of hell. Grössinger has observed that some of the designs are repeated at Great Malvern Priory (*c*.1350-80) and much later at Fairford parish church (*c*.1500), such as the misogynistic scene of a woman beating a man with a washing beetle (north stalls, bay 2, Fig.11.14A) and the sick-bed scene (south stalls, bay 5); showing how patterns continued to circulate locally over a long period.[38]

High on the north wall of the choir to the east of the stalls is a finely detailed wooden canopy with traces of gilding, which stylistically probably dates to *c*.1330-1380 (Pl.16). It is about 4 feet high (plus pinnacles) and takes the form of five sides of an octagon, with Decorated openwork tracery filling the front and canted sides.[39] The stained glass canopies over the figures in the choir clerestory windows possess some general similarities to it (Fig.14.2), and so does the canopy over the kneeling knight on the Trinity Chapel (Fig.13.9). Its provenance and function remain uncertain, but it does not belong with the plain stone corbel on which it now sits; the latter is pierced to take the rope for a medieval sanctus bell.[40] Most recent authorities interpret it as the canopy from a Sacrament house or hanging pyx, possibly from the 14th-century high altar.[41] The only certain example surviving in England of a hanging pyx cover is the 13th-century one at Wells Cathedral, completely octagonal in shape and with simple openwork tracery.[42]

Another little known wooden fitting is a length of frieze bearing the initials of Abbot Henry Beeley (1509-1534), similar to those carved in stone on his oriel in Abbey House (Fig.12.15). Its various pieces run to over 10 feet in length, all carved as openwork vine-scroll inhabited by jaunty little birds (Fig.11.14C).[43] The Roman capital 'H' for 'Henry' has a 'cranked' cross-bar, suggestive of Renaissance influence and a date probably no earlier than the 1520s.[44] The pieces are thought to have come originally from a screen, but this could not have been from the rood screen of the abbey, as usually inferred; the latter would have been a substantial stone structure. In fact, the frieze could be from various types of ecclesiastical or secular fittings, not necessarily a screen.[45] Moreover the possibility should be considered that its provenance might be in Abbot Beeley's work in the abbot's lodging rather than in the church. This hypothesis has received some support when several more pieces of the frieze were kindly returned to the abbey in 2003 by a private donor in south Wales, whose ancestors are said to have removed them from Abbey House in the early 19th century.

It has also been noted recently that a monogram with the initials 'h b' appears on six remounted panels on the chancel screen of Ripple church (Worcs.), five miles north of Tewkesbury.[46] Though the style of the letter 'h' is Gothic, rather than Roman like the examples at Tewkesbury, these panels might also be assigned to Henry Beeley and have found their way from Tewkesbury to Ripple at some time after the Dissolution. Indeed, an origin at the abbey might solve the mystery of the source of the late medieval choir stalls at Ripple.[47] Certainly the return of the pieces of the 'Beeley screen' and the discovery at Ripple draw attention to the potential for finding more fittings from the abbey dispersed around the local area and further afield.

CHAPTER 12

The Monastic Buildings *by* Richard K. Morris

Shortly after the Dissolution of the abbey in 1540, the monastic buildings deemed to be superfluous—and that amounted to virtually all of them—appear to have been demolished. In 1875, Blunt reported that 'many foundation walls existed a few years ago, but they were removed to level the field'.[1] So a chapter devoted to this subject would hardly seem justifiable, and yet this is precisely why it should be undertaken. Nothing of substance has ever been published on the accommodation and service buildings of what was one of England's wealthier monasteries.[2]

Of course, there are a few survivals of architectural distinction, notably Abbey House, the gatehouse and part of the cloister; and further afield, some medieval elements of the manor house at Forthampton and the granges at Stanway and Llanwit Major (Glam.) (Figs.5.4, 7.1).[3] Also, valuable physical evidence about the service buildings has become available from an archaeological excavation in the meadow south of the abbey in 1992. Beyond that, some additional clues exist in the documentary sources and the fabric of the church where the monastic buildings adjoined it, combined with comparative information from other better preserved monastic sites. For example, the former Benedictine priory buildings around the cloisters at Gloucester, Worcester and Chester cathedrals provide some idea of the form and scale of what has been lost at Tewkesbury.

The Claustral Buildings

The obvious starting point is the survey of the abbey's buildings made immediately after its suppression in January 1540. The commissioners listed the 'houses and buildings' in two groups, the first to be kept ('to remain undefaced') and the second 'deemed to be superfluous'.[4] For our purposes I shall rearrange these entries to reconstruct a tour around the main areas of the monastery, commencing with the cloister and then moving outwards to the courtyards and precinct. The cloister was at the heart of the monks' 'cloistered' world, usually adjoining the south side of the church as at Tewkesbury, and enclosed on its three other sides by ranges of buildings. The main rooms in these ranges follow a predictable pattern from the 12th century onward.[5]

Unfortunately the survey does not specify rooms by ranges and it has other limitations. For instance, some room names are omitted which we should expect to find, such as the 'slype' (a passage through the east range to the monastic cemetery) and the warming room (Fig.12.1). The omission of these ground-floor rooms also occurs, for example, in the 1539 inventory of monastic buildings at Rievaulx Abbey (North Yorks.), and may well have been a standard procedure.[6] Thus, the scribe at Tewkesbury is evidently adhering to a formula for such stocktakings, but their sequence appears to based on a more or less logical route, commencing at the east range. The list of superfluous buildings, after the church, starts:

> ... cloister, chapter house, misericord, the ii dormitories
> The Infirmary with chapels and lodgings within the same
> The workeheye, with one other house adjoining to the same
> The convent kitchen.[7]

Thus on the ground floor the chapter house is visited, followed by the misericord, another ground-floor room in which sick monks were permitted in the later Middle Ages to eat meat.[8] The exact location of the misericord varied, but it is assumed here that it was off the south-east corner of the cloister, in a position somewhat analogous to that at Jervaulx Abbey (North Yorks.) (Fig.12.1).[9]

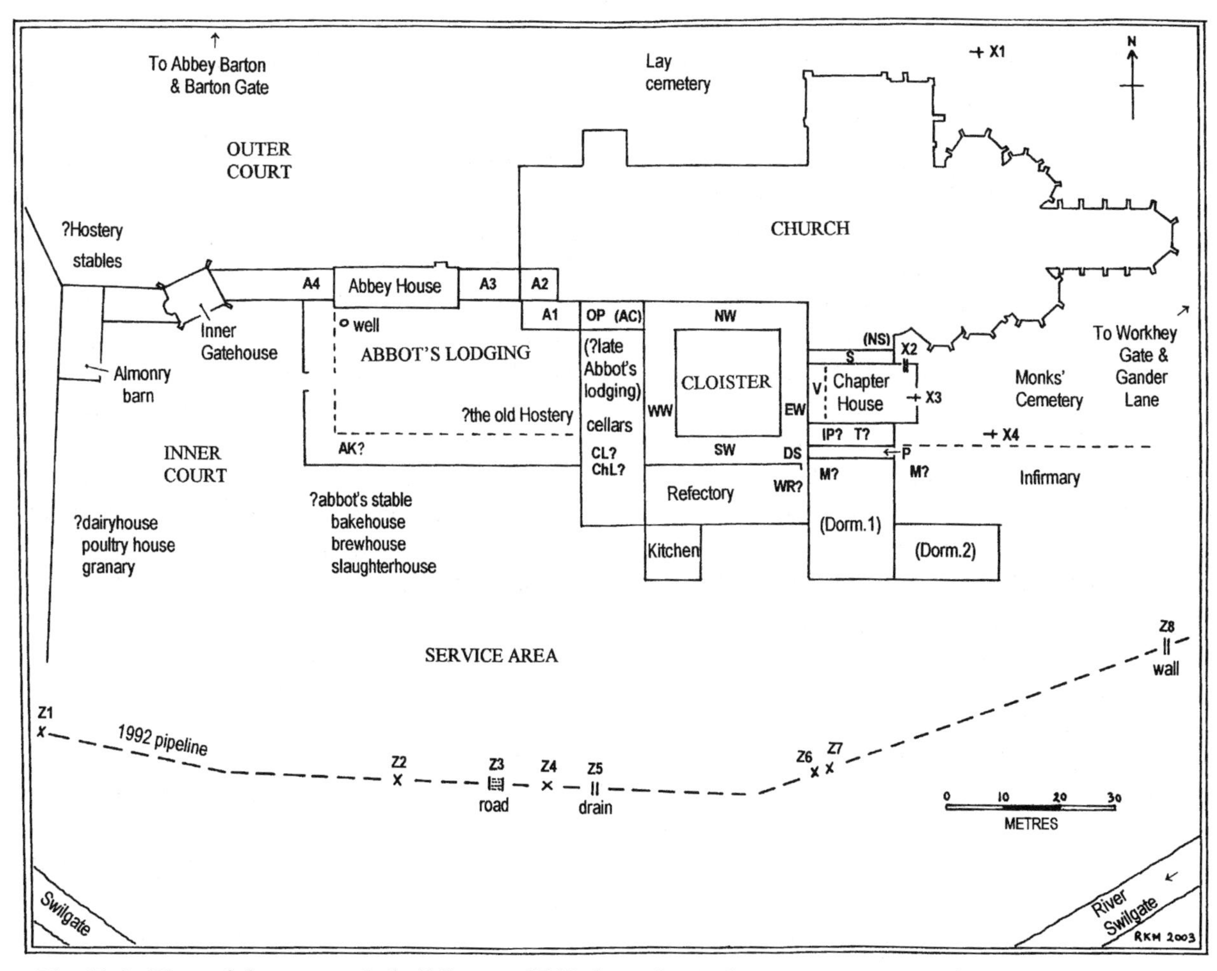

Fig.12.1 Plan of the monastic buildings c.*1540, hypothetical reconstruction with some relevant finds from recent excavations.*

A1-4	*rooms in the abbot's lodging*	*DS*	*day stair*	*P*	*passage*
AC	*abbot's chapel*	*EW*	*cloister east walk*	*S*	*slype*
AK	*abbot's kitchen*	*IP*	*inner parlour*	*SW*	*cloister south walk*
CL	*cellarer's lodging*	*M*	*misericord*	*T*	*treasury*
ChL	*chamberer's lodging*	*NS*	*night stair*	*WR*	*warming room*
Dorm.1	*dormitory, room 1*	*NW*	*cloister walk*	*WW*	*cloister west walk*
Dorm.2	*dormitory, room 2*	*OP*	*outer parlour*		

X1-4 archeological finds 1996-2000 *Z1-8 Abbey Meadow pipeline finds*

( ) denotes rooms at 1st-floor level

Next the first-floor dormitories are visited, presumably by way of the day-stairs found typically at the south end of the cloister east walk. The fact that two dormitories are mentioned may mean that architecturally this accommodation was provided in two large rooms or that the second was actually the 'reredorter', the monks' latrine block which always adjoined the dormitory.[10] Returning to ground level, the survey moves east beyond the cloister to the infirmary complex,[11] and then further east to the 'workeheye', which is likely to be the Workhey gate in the wall on Gander Lane (Fig.12.1).[12]

Finally in this sequence comes the monks' kitchen, which would have been close to the refectory (Fig.12.1). It seems odd that a refectory is omitted in the list, but this is probably because the Workhey accessed the service area of the monastery, adjoining the kitchen, and thus the survey has gone directly to it, bypassing the south walk of the cloister. Confirmation that a refectory existed is found in the inclusion of 'frater' (the medieval term for refectory)[13] in the separate list of buildings with lead remaining on their roofs.

As to the date of these buildings, their origins must go back to the Norman foundation of Robert Fitzhamon, and presumably a cloistered enclosure, with its main rooms probably constructed in stone, awaited the arrival of the monks from Cranborne in 1102. Documentary confirmation of the early existence of the chapter house is provided by the burial of Fitzhamon there in 1107,[14] and some rearrangement of the abbots' burials took place in it in 1241.[15] More specifically architectural is the account in the Annals that in 1219 the dormitory collapsed as the monks were re-entering it after Matins, but miraculously only one monk, Gilbert, was injured.[16] Substantial rebuilding must have been necessitated in the east range after this accident.[17] Regarding the infirmary we learn that the duchess of Clarence gave birth to her son, Richard, there in 1476,[18] an interesting insight in to how far monastic life had been infiltrated by laymen and women in the later Middle Ages; and perhaps a commentary on the relative quality of healthcare in a monastery. Presumably the birth took place in one of the infirmary 'lodgings' listed in the suppression survey. With regard to the monastic kitchen, the Compotus Roll (1351-2) includes a payment for stone to build a shelf in it for lights (*pro cresettis*).[19]

The monastic buildings suffered several times from fires, though the extent of the damage is usually impossible to determine. Major fires are recorded in 1178; in 1234, which destroyed service buildings but which also 'threatened' the abbey; in 1256, which destroyed service buildings 'outside the gate'; and in 1292 in the bell-tower.[20] In 1314, the bishop of Worcester approved a licence to appropriate Thornbury church on grounds which included the havoc wrought by fire amongst the abbey's monastic buildings.[21] Evidence for these fires may still be seen in patches of stone burnt pink on the south side of the nave and the south transept, but nowhere is the damage more evocative than on the south wall of the transept, where large areas of the burnt stone surface have scaled off.

This elevation of the transept is especially significant for understanding the history of the east range of monastic buildings which directly adjoined it (Fig.12.2). Some major changes have occurred to the wall masonry since the Dissolution, such as the refacing and thickening of the wall at ground-floor level,[22] but some telling medieval fabric still survives.

The most striking feature is the absence of any traces of a tall single gable running across the width of the upper area, which should appear there if the east range had had a single roof with its ridge running north-south and abutting the transept. The gable line for such an arrangement may still be seen, for example, in the ruins of Croxden Abbey (Staffs., Fig.12.3).[23] Instead, at Tewkesbury one sees at least two horizontal creases to receive the flashings for roof coverings, and below them a line of projecting corbels, to support the timber frame of a roof (Fig.12.2B, C, D). These features indicate that the ridge of the roof immediately adjacent to the wall ran east to west, and thus that the first-floor dormitory could not have adjoined the transept. The east-west roof covered a two-storey structure which almost certainly contained a vaulted slype passage on the ground floor, and above a space the functions of which can only be surmised; they may well have altered over time. The space connected to the first-floor door (Fig.12.2E), which gave access to the church interior and the Norman gallery chapels by way of the spiral stair in the transept (Masterplan, J). Thus, the space may have incorporated a corridor from the dormitory to the church, and it may also have housed a muniment room. At its west end it has been heightened by a roof running north-south (Fig.12.2A), which is clearly a later modification because the gabled weathering is cut into fire-damaged masonry and across a horizontal roof crease. This may have provided an additional second-floor room, possibly for a library, as in the later medieval additions over the slype at Gloucester Cathedral (Fig.12.4).[24]

Immediately south of the slype we should reconstruct the chapter house. This almost certainly stood to the full height of the east range, because the absence of a gabled roofline on the transept implies that the first-floor dormitory commenced only beyond the chapter house (Fig.12.1), as happened, for example, at Gloucester.[25] What form the chapter house took is unknown, for both rectangular and centralised spaces are found in Benedictine usage; but on balance the former is more likely at Tewkesbury, quite possibly with an eastern apse as at Gloucester.[26]

A tall chapter house created the problem of whether the monks retained the conventional 'night stairs' access to the church, directly from the first floor of the east range into the transept, for their early morning services.[27] At Tewkesbury, it is possible that the chapter house had a single storey vestibule in its west bay, as can still be seen at Bristol and Chester cathedrals, thus permitting a passage over the vestibule to link the dormitory to the first-floor door above the slype (Fig.12.1). Otherwise all the monks' journeys from the dormitory to the church would take the normal daytime route, descending a 'day stair' located towards the south end of the cloister walk, then processing along the east walk and into the church through the east processional door (Fig.5.1; Masterplan, L).

Fig.12.2 South transept of the abbey

Fig.12.3 Ruins of the east range at Croxden Abbey (Staffs.)

Fig.12.4 East range of the former monastic buildings at Gloucester Cathedral

Of course, the original Norman fabric of the east range will have been remodelled more than once during the monastery's existence, to take account of fire damage and of the changing requirements of the monastic community. However, virtually no firm architectural evidence survives to guide us. One possibility is that the chapter house was enlarged to the east in the 12th or 13th century. A recent archaeological watching brief noted a massive wall foundation about 1.8m (6 feet) east of the east wall of the east range (Fig.12.1, X2).[28] The foundation would appear to be on the alignment of the presumed wall running east-west between the chapter house and the slype, and implies that the chapter house extended beyond the width of the east range; probably as the result of a rebuilding, because reused moulded stones were incorporated in the foundation.[29] The reason for the enlargement could be to take account of the increase in the number of monks in the early 12th century,[30] or for purposes of prestige, or it might be related to one of the relevant documented events described above—possibly the rearrangement of abbots' burials in 1241.

Further evidence for partial rebuilding is preserved in the south wall of the transept, in which all the main features relating to the east range post-date the fire-damaged masonry except possibly the upper roof creasing (Fig.12.2B).[31] The fire in question is usually taken to be that of 1178, but others are recorded (see above). The upper creasing could represent a Norman roof level, though it is unlikely to be primary (i.e. *c.*1090-1102) because it covered the lower slit window lighting the spiral staircase (Fig.12.2F). The line of corbels supported a different roof, which may be the same one signified by the lower creasing (Fig.12.2C, D). It was probably a response to an earlier fire or incident—possibly the collapse of the 'dormitory' in 1219. The monks were returning from Matins, so if this was the night stairs route, it could conceivably be the site of the accident—in an area actually preceding the dormitory. Then the gabled weathering to the left (Fig.12.2A) probably post-dates this roof: it would be in line with and above the proposed passage between the dormitory and the night stairs. The four-centred head of the night stairs door (Fig.12.2E) indicates that it is a later

Fig.12.5 South aisle of the nave showing remains of monastic buildings

medieval modification, though framing a Norman aperture inside.

The west range is harder to reconstruct because this area of the claustral buildings was subject to more variation and alteration during the Middle Ages. The survey supplies the following possible constituents from the list 'deemed superfluous', following on from the 'convent kitchen':

The library
The old Hostery
The chamberer's lodging
The new hall
The old parlour adjoining to the Abbot's lodging
The cellarer's lodging.

Hardly any of the rooms and buildings in this part of the list can be guaranteed to be in the west range. Some were almost certainly located in the inner courtyard of the monastery, which backed on to the west range, or in the service area to the south (Fig.12.1). The cellarer's lodging would probably have been in the west range originally to administer the monastery's stores in the 'cellars', and the accommodation for the chamberlain ('chamberer') might have been there too; the chamberlain looked after the monks' clothing and other necessities.[32] The 'old Hostery' (guest house) almost certainly stood in the inner court, and the same may well be the case for 'the new hall'.[33] On the other hand, the library would definitely have been located within the claustral buildings for the monks' use, on an upper floor, but whether in the east or west ranges or in a room above a cloister walk cannot be predicted.[34]

Mention of the 'old parlour' directs our attention to the one surviving area of standing fabric which relates to the west range, namely the features incorporated in the wall of the church's south aisle. Outside bays 6-7 of the aisle are the remains of a barrel-vaulted room at first floor level, with a plainer room beneath (Fig.12.5, left) which is in the right position to be the outer parlour, where monks were permitted to talk to lay people. Perhaps this may be identified as the 'old parlour' in the survey.[35] The room above is likely to have been the abbot's chapel in the Norman period, though whether it continued in this function up to the Dissolution cannot be certain.[36] The group of three attached shafts in its east corner is the north side of an arch leading to a small sanctuary beyond (Fig.12.5, centre). Judging by the simple Romanesque capitals and bases, this work would probably have been complete by the church consecration in 1121, and thus it constitutes the only significant survival of the Norman monastic buildings.[37]

For reconstructing the cloister, the survey is of little assistance except to record that it was roofed in lead, but in compensation more of its architecture is still visible than for any other structure. The evidence comes predominantly from a late medieval rebuild, and is confined to standing fabric from the east and north walks, against the walls of the north transept and nave south aisle respectively (Fig.12.5, right). Comparison is always drawn with the famous fan-vaulted cloister at Gloucester Cathedral, and indeed the blind tracery pattern at Tewkesbury and its mouldings are essentially identical with those of the north, west and south walks at Gloucester, 1381-1412 (cf. Figs.12.6, 12.7).

The only medieval fan vault now extant in the cloister area at Tewkesbury is the miniature one in the entrance passage of the east processional door (Fig.12.8, right).[38] However, provision for vaulting was made in the east walk, and it seems likely that fan vaults were constructed here because a stone cusped panel remounted at Gupshill Manor, Tewkesbury, is the central spandrel for a bay of a fan vaulting of the right size for the abbey cloister (Fig.21.20).[39] In the north walk the blind tracery against the church wall is incomplete and this walk could only have been ceiled in wood (Fig.12.5). Nothing is known about the west and south walks, but the monks claimed the cloister was in ruinous condition in 1500, and a donation toward its reconstruction is recorded in 1503.[40] Its remodelling in the Perpendicular style was evidently never finished.

The new work probably started in the east cloister walk, as the most significant processional route,[41] probably in the first quarter of the 15th century, given the close similarities to Gloucester. An additional signpost to the date is provided by the splendid new entrance from the east walk into the church, a work of the highest quality to vie with Isabel Despenser's Warwick Chapel (Fig.5.1).[42] Even devoid of the statues which once stood its the niches, the doorway still presents a virtuoso display of tabernacle work and miniature vaults (Fig.12.9). Like the Warwick Chapel it appears related to the style associated with the early 15th-century Cotswold master mason, Richard Winchcombe, but the closest parallels for particular details are found in the Beauchamp Chapel at Warwick (*c.*1440-50), the burial place of Isabel's second husband. The

Fig.12.6 Blind tracery in the cloister east walk

Fig.12.7 The cloister west walk at Gloucester Cathedral

Fig.12.8 Tomb recess and processional door (drawing by Roland Paul, 1886)

unusual idea of diagonally inclined canopies around the door arch (Fig.12.9), which causes the statue to be carved in a bent posture, occurs in the frame of the Beauchamp Chapel east window;[43] and the sideshaft mouldings of the door frame are replicated in the chapel's blind arcading. Moreover, it appears that the tiny quadruped carved at the apex of the arch is a bear (Fig.12.9, top left), presumably a reference to the badge of the Beauchamp earls of Warwick, and thus likely to refer to Isabel's second marriage, or to her son, Henry, duke of Warwick (d.1446). So the door should date to the second quarter of the 15th century, and as it belongs with the adjoining cloister masonry, into which it is bonded, it indicates how far the cloister work had progressed by this date.

Practically no physical evidence survives from any earlier cloister structure, except for part of the Norman processional doorway into the east walk, preserved inside the nave south aisle (Fig.12.8, right).[44] More tenuously, there are the fragments of a Romanesque historiated capital and a decorated shaft in the abbey collection which Malcolm Thurlby has suggested might derive from a 12th-century cloister (Fig.9.27E and F).[45] Then, inside the west wall of the south transept is a passage of unknown purpose which originally would have led into the north-east bay of the cloister, by-passing the processional door (Masterplan, L). Its mouldings suggest a later 13th-century date, and it was blocked by the 15th-century refacing of the cloister.

The plan of the cloister raises a number of problems. The first is its remarkably small size for an establishment of Tewkesbury's importance. The north walk extends for not much more than half the length of the nave, and consists of only five bays, discounting the corner bays (Masterplan); compared with the equivalent of 10 bays at Gloucester. This anomaly cannot be explained by markedly different widths for the walks—Tewkesbury and Gloucester are comparable;[46] nor by the Perpendicular remodelling

Fig.12.9 Canopy work over the processional door to the church

reducing the size of the Norman cloister—the north walk is fitted in between a Norman transept to the east and a Norman outer parlour to the west. Moreover, the position of the Norman east processional door argues for a Romanesque east walk at least as wide as the Perpendicular one (Fig.12.8). The matter is not easily resolved, except to suggest that provision from the beginning of a substantial west range to include an abbot's lodging may be the reason for the small Norman cloister. A corollary of this is that if the cloister followed the norm in being approximately square,[47] thus extending only about 30m (98 feet) to the south, there would be very little length in the east range in which to fit the main rooms (especially the dormitory) without a long extension to the range (Fig.12.1).[48] But without further investigation, there is no way of knowing whether the east and west walks were of the same short length as the north walk.

Another anomaly is that no door exists in the customary position between the church and the west walk of the cloister, for use as a processional entrance into the west end of the nave (Masterplan, M).[49] Perhaps this purpose was served by the smaller door in the outer parlour, blocked at an unknown date, which communicated into bay 8 of the nave south aisle (Masterplan, N).[50]

The Outer Buildings

Moving out beyond the conventual buildings, several courtyards or enclosures would formerly have existed within the monastery's precinct.[51] To the west of the cloister was an inner court, which is the only one of these areas with substantial architectural remains (see further below). Somewhere to the east of the cloister we should expect to find the monks' cemetery (Fig.12.1).[52] Between the south range of the cloister and the River Swilgate was an extensive service area, some tantalising traces of which were recorded in the Abbey Meadow excavation of 1992. To the north of the monastic buildings and beyond the existing gatehouse stood an outer court, dominated by the west front of the church. In one enclosure of the outer court, by the later Middle

Ages, was the lay cemetery (churchyard) on the north side of the church, with a bell tower.[53] To the south, around the abbey mill on the Mill Avon, lay the area called 'the Barton', the home grange of the abbey (Fig.1.2).[54]

A number of buildings which stood in the precinct are named in the survey, though the precise site of each is not specified. Setting aside for the moment buildings relating to the abbot's accommodation, the survey lists the following to remain undefaced:

> The hostery
> The great Gate entering into the Court with the lodging over the same
> The Abbot's stable, bakehouse, brewhouse, slaughterhouse
> The Almery barn
> The dairyhouse
> The great barn next Aven
> The maltinghouse
> The ox house in the Barton
> The Barton Gate and the lodging over the same;

and the following at the end of the list 'deemed superfluous', continuing on from the cellarer's lodging:

> The poultry house
> The garner
> The almery.

The 'great Gate' is the surviving gatehouse at the entrance to the inner court, and the shell of the 'Almery' (almonry) barn still exists on the western boundary of this court (Fig.12.1). The 'almery', where alms were distributed to the poor, should probably be placed in its vicinity and may be identified with the adjoining cottages on the site today.[55] The great barn is definitely the stone structure next to the mill on the Mill Avon, of which five bays of the north wall survive (Fig.1.6). The detail of its buttresses suggest it was constructed in the later 14th or 15th century.

One can only guess at the locations of the other buildings from their relative positions in the survey lists. Thus the dairyhouse, following the entry for the almery barn, is probably in the inner court or the service area to the south, as well as the poultry house and the garner (a granary or store) (Fig.12.1). The 'maltinghouse with garner', following the great barn, is more likely to have been in the area of the mill, together with the ox house 'in the Barton'.[56] Other service buildings are known from other sources. The Kitchener's Roll (1386) refers to a tannery ('*tanneria*'), also thought to be in the Barton, and a pig-house ('*porcarie*');[57] and earlier documents refer to the abbey mill.[58]

The Abbey Gatehouse

The monastery is known to have had three gatehouses, two of which are clearly named in the survey as the 'Barton Gate' and the 'great Gate', and the third is probably the building called the 'workeheye'. The context suggests that the Barton Gate was the main entrance to the monastery, the gate of the outer court, adjacent to the abbey barton (Fig.1.2). This was presumably the 'principal' gate which was burnt with two stables in 1234.[59] It was 'assigned to remain undefaced' in the survey, but it has not survived. The Workhey (or Warkhey) Gate in the precinct's east wall has been characterised as the 'tradesmen's entrance' by Anthea Jones,[60] leading to the service areas by the River Swilgate (Figs.1.2, 12.1). This gate had a room over it, being used as a schoolroom in 1540, and was scheduled for demolition in the survey.[61]

The 'great Gate' is the only one to survive, originally serving as the inner gatehouse (Fig.12.1).[62] It was a roof-less shell by the later 18th century, made habitable again in the mid-19th century and conserved most recently by the Landmark Trust.[63] It is a monumental two-storey building, which impresses the visitor by its relative austerity and its fine quality limestone construction (Fig.12.10). The main ornament of the façade is a niche, which presumably originally housed a figure of the Virgin Mary and which echoed the niche with statue over the north porch of the church (Fig.9.3).[64] As an inner gate, one would not expect it to show the greater elaboration of form and display often found on the public façades of outer gatehouses, such as those still to be seen at Worcester Cathedral (the Edgar Gate, *c*.1370), Llanthony Secunda at Gloucester (1494-1500) and Bristol Cathedral (*c*.1500).[65] The passage of the Tewkesbury gatehouse is divided into a gateway and gatehall by a cross-wall, which contains both a pedestrian door and a larger 'vehicular' door—a typical arrangement for inner gatehouses.[66] These gave access to the inner court, the boundary of which apparently had no stone walls in this section but rather was defined by the timber-framed buildings adjoining the gatehouse.[67]

The gatehouse is Perpendicular in style and almost certainly 15th century, but dating it more closely is difficult. The prominent gargoyles below the battlements are typical of Cotswold parish churches in this century, such as Winchcombe, whereas the vaults of the gateway and gatehall have been restored in the 19th century with a pattern which is probably simpler than the original (Fig.12.11, upper).[68] Bennett reports various antiquarian speculation that the gatehouse was erected in the abbacy of Thomas Parker (1389-1420), and served as the abbey prison.[69] Stylistically it is conceivable that the present structure could have been erected in the later years of Parker's abbacy; but there is no evidence of a prison.[70] On the other hand, Haslam and Morriss both prefer a date around 1500, following the report to the bishop in that year that some of the monastery's houses and buildings, unspecified, were 'ruinous'.[71] However nothing about the style of the gatehouse need be so late,[72] nor do the circumstances surrounding the Battle of Tewkesbury (1471) apparently necessitate a new gate to be built. The existing gatehouse has no special provision for defence, the battlements being primarily for display.

Fig.12.10 The Abbey Gatehouse, front façade

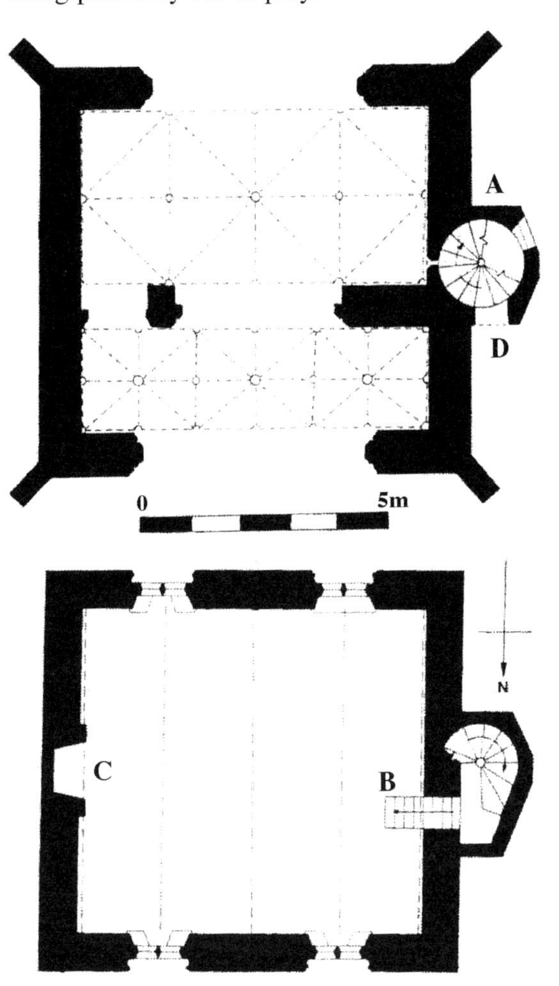

Fig.12.11 The gatehouse, upper ground-floor plan (top) and first-floor plan (bottom)

The only accommodation in the gatehouse is the large chamber of good quality on the upper floor, lit by the pairs of windows in the front and rear façades (Figs 12.10, 12.11). It is approached from the ground-floor gatehall by a stone newel staircase attached to the west wall, which originally fitted inside the adjoining timber-framed building to the west (Fig.12.11A).[73] The newel leads by way of a small lobby and a straight flight of stairs into the first-floor chamber, with a fireplace on the opposite wall (Fig.12.11B, C). The interior and roof were restored in the mid-19th century and again in 1990, but the three ceiling beams appear to follow the medieval configuration, running north-south (Fig.12.11, lower). Haslam suggests that the chamber may have been used by one of the abbey's officials, perhaps for transacting business. To function as a lodging—as it is called in the suppression survey—Morriss points out that it would need to be linked to additional rooms on the first floor of the building adjoining to the west, by way of a second door near the top of the newel stair (Fig.12.11D).[74]

The Abbot's Lodging

To the east of the gatehouse and within the inner court lay the abbot's lodgings, with the residential accommodation and essential services probably grouped around a courtyard of their own (Fig.12.1).[75] The main constituents of his establishment are listed in the survey, under buildings to remain undefaced:

> The lodging called the New Warke leading from the Gate to the late Abbot's lodging with buttery, pantry, cellar, kitchen, larder and pastry there adjoining
> The late Abbot's lodging
> The Abbot's stable, bakehouse, brewhouse and slaughterhouse.

The inference of the survey, combined with evidence from the fabric, is that the abbot's accommodation was originally sited in the west range of the claustral buildings. This arrangement may well date from as early as the time of Abbot Gerald, judging by the former Romanesque barrel vault of the abbot's chapel in this location (Fig.12.5).[76] The original abbot's lodging was presumably adjacent to this chapel, but by the later Middle Ages it had been extended westward into the inner court (see below). At some monasteries, such as St. Peter's, Gloucester, when the abbot moved to new accommodation in the later Middle Ages, the prior occupied the abbot's former lodging in the west range.[77] However, this does not appear to have happened at Tewkesbury. The account of the dormitory accident in 1219 mentions the prior,[78] who was presumably housed with the monks in the east range, and the survey does not list a separate prior's lodging.

Abbey House is the main surviving part of the later medieval extension to the abbot's lodging (12.13). There can be little doubt that it is 'the lodging called the New Warke [Work]', and it constitutes one of the best preserved survivals of this type of building in England. Its main features date from two phases, the first in the late 15th century and the second in the early decades of the 16th century. This was a period typified by the amplication and elaboration of lodgings for great churchmen, for purposes of prestige and for guest accommodation, like those still to be seen at Benedictine Muchelney (Som.) and Cluniac Wenlock (Shrops.). Tewkesbury deserves to be as well known as these examples,[79] but Abbey House has never received a thorough study and only a preliminary assessment can be attempted here.[80]

For the purpose of description, the house may be said to have seven bays, based on the articulation of the late Georgian south façade (Fig.8.8) which roughly corresponds to the medieval bay divisions in the roof. The five easternmost bays (bays 1 to 5, counting from the east) retain a coherent medieval principal rafter roof,[81] with each open truss linked by clasped purlins at the upper collar, and with diminished principals above that level (Fig.12.12A, B).[82] Such features are parallelled in roofs dated to the 15th century in the west midlands.[83] Moreover the roof has a second set of purlins at the lower collar level, which are tenoned into the trusses (Fig.12.12C), an advanced technical detail which suggests that it is no earlier than the late 15th century.[84]

An unusual feature of each open truss is what appears to be a pair of curved struts descending from the lower collar to connect with the tiebeam (Fig.12.12D). Struts linking two horizontal timbers in this way are apparently unprecedented, which suggests that the tiebeams and the ceilings they support are secondary; and that probably the curved struts were originally arch braces which have been cut off at wall-plate level when the tiebeams were inserted (Fig.12.12E). We can be fairly certain that this conversion happened before the Dissolution—probably in Abbot Beeley's time—from the fact that one of the first-floor medieval windows has been inserted in a position where originally one of the arch braces would have descended.[85]

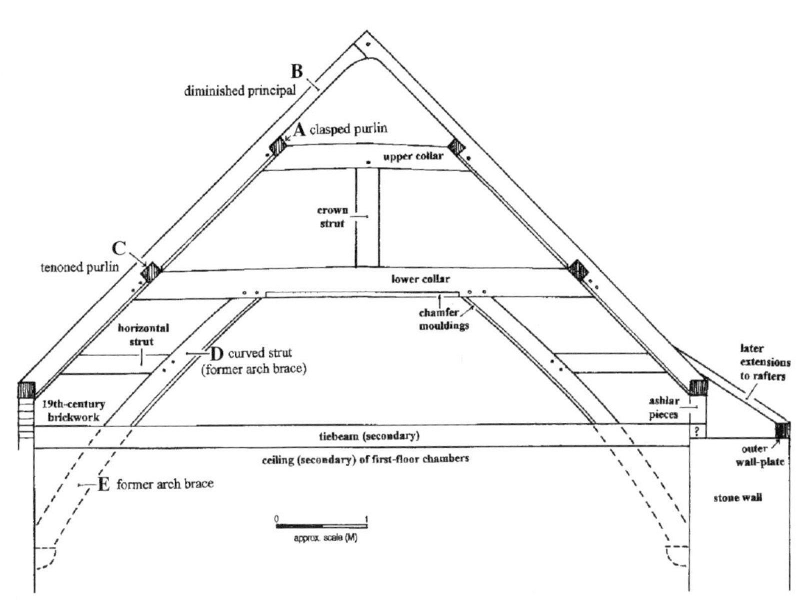

Fig.12.12 Abbey House, drawing of an open roof truss

In this 'Jekyll and Hyde' of a building, the north wall of the house, facing the churchyard, contains all the surviving medieval features in stone, whereas the south elevation to the garden evokes a Georgian country house (cf. Figs.12.13, 8.8).[86] At the first stage of development, the north wall, of coursed lias stone, may have had no

Fig.12.13 Abbey House, north side seen from the churchyard

Fig.12.14 Abbey House, east wall

major windows in it because it formed the exterior wall of the inner court.[87] Instead, the show side of the range would have been the south elevation facing into the court, with most of the windows. The south wall is also of lias stone at ground-floor level, with a medieval entrance (now blocked) just to the right of the Georgian door (Fig.8.8).[88] The first floor externally is now entirely brick of *c*.1825,[89] which looks at first sight to be a veneer in front of a medieval timber frame. However this does not explain why the corner post is set back from the front plane of the ground-floor wall (Fig.12.14, left), so possibly the wall was stone-faced to its full height originally.[90]

Internally the divisions of the ground floor indicate that the seven-bay building was designed as a hall of three bays in the centre, with services to the west and a chamber block in the two bays to the east.[91] The south door in bay 5 was the entrance into the former screens passage of the hall. The hall is now only a ground-floor room, with a modest fireplace and two late medieval windows in the north wall, but when first built, this space was presumably the full height of the building. The first-floor chambers at each end were likewise open to the roof.[92] Subsequently, it would appear that the hall was ceiled over at ground-floor level to provide two large rooms one above the other, and that the first-floor rooms in bays 1-5 were also ceiled, hiding the roof.

The dating of the house can be estimated from the details of the roof construction (as above) and from the carvings of the oriel window in the north elevation. Externally the latter bears shields with the arms of the abbey and of Robert Fitzhamon, flanking a mitre with the monogram 'H B' for Abbot Henry Beeley, 1509-1534 (Fig.12.15).[93]

Fig.12.15 Abbey House, detail of the oriel window, showing Abbot Beeley's initials

Fig.12.16 Abbey House, the vault of the oriel window

This attribution is supported by the close similarity in design between the exquisite miniature vault of the oriel (Fig.12.16) and the vault canopy of Prince Arthur's chantry chapel in Worcester Cathedral (*c*.1502-1516). The oriel is clearly an insertion into the north wall—externally it interrupts the main eaves cornice and internally the roof timbers at wall-plate level have been adapted to receive it. Thus, it appears that the second phase (probably the 'New Warke' of the survey) should be credited to Abbot Beeley, whilst the original five-bay building is likely to have been constructed under his predecessor, Abbot Cheltenham (1481-1509), whose reputation as a builder was noted by Leland.[94]

With regard to the other medieval features of the north elevation, the two prominent windows on the first floor west of the oriel belong to Beeley's work. The three large ground-floor windows, originally all cross-mullioned like those above, are also more likely to be secondary (Fig.12.13).[95] In its final form this façade was apparently intended to carry a battlemented parapet, creating a visual reference to the neighbouring gatehouse (Fig.12.10).[96]

The purpose and functioning of the house in its final form before the Dissolution can be reconstructed in general and in some details. Almost certainly it combined additional private chambers for the abbot with good quality guest accommodation, a form of building found also, for example, in the western range of the Cluniac priory of Castle Acre (Norf.) as remodelled about 1500.[97] The 'hostery' listed as a separate building in the Tewkesbury survey would have provided accommodation for lesser visitors. The house was a late medieval extension from the core of the abbot's lodging at the north end of the claustral west range, which the survey refers to as 'the late Abbot's lodging' (Fig.12.1).

If we were to have taken a tour of the abbatial accommodation about 1540, commencing in the old lodging over the cloister, we would have found that it included a two-storey block west of the cloister (Fig.12.1, A1). This was connected by a first-floor door to a room at the west end of the south aisle, now the Holy Cross Chapel (Fig.12.1, A2).[98] We know that the abbot's lodging incorporated the west bay of the church because it only became part of the parish church again after the purchase of Abbey House in 1883.[99]

In order to gain access from this block to the New Work, a two-storey linking structure must have existed between the west wall of the south aisle and the present east wall of Abbey House (Fig.12.1, A3).[100] The evidence for this lies in the provision for a door (now blocked) in the timber-framing of the east wall (Fig.12.14, right), formerly leading to the oriel chamber apparently by way of a lobby, lit by the small window high up in the north wall to the left of the oriel (Fig.12.13). At the church end, access to the first floor of the link building was probably through the lower part of the aisle west window, which explains why it has a horizontal transom, unlike its counterpart in the north aisle (Fig.9.4).[101] This adaptation to a door is unlikely to have taken place before the later 14th century at the earliest.[102]

The culmination of this first-floor route from the old lodgings was the oriel chamber, which would have been the abbot's withdrawing chamber or study, like the chamber with oriel at Castle Acre Priory. These were fashionable appendages of the period for great churchmen's lodgings, often personalized with carved heraldry and devices, like the splendid oriel added by Dean Gunthorpe (1472-98) to the Deanery at Wells.[103]

The abbot's oriel chamber occupied the two easternmost bays of Abbey House at first-floor level.[104] Beyond, the next three bays constituted a great chamber (now subdivided into a gallery and three bedrooms), and bays 6 and 7 each housed a chamber over the services.[105] The great chamber was the finest apartment in the range, with the best fireplace flanked by the two large windows in the north wall, with internal seats (restored), glazed tracery above the transoms and rebates for shutters below. Presumably it could serve as a great chamber where the abbot entertained guests, or as the main chamber of a guest suite.

Continuing our tour, descending to the ground-floor, the timber-framed west wall of the hall incorporates the remains of three medieval doors connecting to bays 6 and 7. If the lateral doors accessed the buttery and pantry of the New Work, then the better door with a four-centred arch may have led to the low-end chamber in bay 7, denoted externally by a good cross-mullioned window.

It is likely that the kitchen was probably free-standing from the range and that cooked food was delivered via the exterior entrance to the screens passage.[106] An unexpected discovery in 1996, which tends to corroborate placing the services at the west end of the house, was a well-shaft about 4m south of bay 7 and about 4m deep (Fig.12.1).[107] It was unlined and thus probably not medieval, but its existence suggests a medieval water source in this vicinity. Other services listed in the survey—larder, pastry and cellar—were presumably housed in a timber structure, since removed, between the house and gatehouse (Fig.12.1, A4). The abbot's stable, bakehouse, brewhouse and slaughterhouse were probably to be found further away in the inner court.

Abbey Meadow Excavation

The only knowledge of the fabric of the ancillary buildings in the service areas south of the claustral buildings and abbot's lodging comes from excavations by the Gloucestershire County Council's Archaeology Service in Abbey Meadow in 1992.[108] This was no more than 'keyhole' archaeology, restricted by the width of the pipeline route for the Severn-Trent re-sewerage works, but nonetheless it represents the only extensive excavation undertaken anywhere on the abbey site and produced significant evidence of monastic occupation from the 12th to the 16th centuries. What follows is my summary of interpretations which are still provisional until full post-excavation analysis has been undertaken by the county's Archaeological Service. Pending such a report, three broad phases have been used for the monastic occupation between the 12th century and 1540: early-, mid- and late-monastic.[109]

The evidence for buildings extended from a line approximately south of the existing almonry barn all the way following the River Swilgate eastwards to a point south-east of the present abbey church (Fig.12.1, Z1–Z8). At this point stood the most impressive architectural feature surviving *in situ* from the early monastic phase, part of a large well-constructed wall still about 2.5m high (Fig.12.1, Z8). It dates from the 12th or early 13th century, on the basis of the style and tooling of its external face which includes a chamfered set-off of hard green sandstone (Fig.12.17).[110] Its monumentality suggests that it might be a section of the precinct wall running roughly north-south,[111] but more probably it represents the eastern boundary wall of an enclosure containing the monks' infirmary and cemetery (Fig.12.1).

Evidence was uncovered all along the terrace in the early- and mid-monastic phases for a repetitive process of dumping soil and rubble, constructing walls for substantial buildings, then dumping again both inside and outside the buildings, to raise the ground level above the flooding of the River Swilgate. A small coin hoard found in a floor make-up in the eastern part of the excavation has a date-span of 1154-1247 (Fig.12.1, Z6). Towards the western part of the site a large drain was located, perhaps originally connected to the reredorter or to the monastic kitchen, and a section of metalled roadway running north in the general direction of the inner court (Fig.12.1, Z5, Z3). Further west some insubstantial wall footings from the latest monastic phase probably supported timber superstructures, one of which appears to have housed a charcoal store.

Fig.12.17 Meadow excavations 1992, east face of 12th- or early 13th-century wall

The small finds added fascinating information about other activities in the service area, and indicated the presence of some high-status buildings. Two pieces were found from a stone chimney (Fig.12.1, Z7), and also fragments of decorated ceramic louvres to draw out the smoke from under roofs. Preliminary analysis of the pottery sherds has identified an imported French green-glazed jug, of a type which has been noted at other sites in the Bristol Channel area, and a high proportion of specialized cooking vessels, such as dripping dishes for a spit roast, condiment trays and aquamaniles.[112] Such evidence has led Alan Vince to suggest that the excavation disturbed parts of a medieval kitchen.[113] The monastic kitchen south of the refectory would seem more likely than the abbot's kitchen, because of the distance of the trench from the abbot's lodgings (Fig.12.1).

The bones from cattle, pigs, sheep or goats, domestic fowl and fish were found in relative profusion, and further analysis of them will be a valuable supplement to the documentary information in the 14th-century Kitchener's Roll.[114] There were considerable deposits of deer bones in various contexts along the site from the western boundary to as far east as a point about level with the claustral east range. The consumption of venison could relate primarily to the entertainment of guests, but in the later Middle Ages the monks of Westminster, for example, consumed special 'pittances' of venison, game birds and swan on saints' feast days.[115] The source of all these bone deposits might well be pits close to the slaughterhouse, dug specifically for the purpose of disposing of animal waste, like those discovered in the excavations at Eynsham Abbey (Oxon.).[116]

The animal remains also included cats' bones, presumably from the abbey's ratters. The bones from a falcon found to the south of the inner court (Fig.12.1, Z2) hint at a more worldly life-style, probably centred around the abbot's lodging. In 1532 Abbot Beeley sent Thomas Cromwell a gift of hawks for use in falconry.[117]

Necessary service industries for the monastic community were represented by slag from secondary iron-smithing and a stone mould possibly for metal-working, whilst a high concentration of fragments from Droitwich ceramic floor-tiles has raised speculation as to whether the abbey had a kiln site in the later Middle Ages.[118] The excavators found very few human bones and therefore, not surprisingly, no trace of the monastic cemetery or of new evidence relating to the Battle of Tewkesbury.

After the suppression, some of the buildings may have remained in use for a while, but others were soon demolished and their stone removed, as the robber trenches testified. Poignant evidence of destruction appeared in an area of shallow hearths where the remains of windows from high-status buildings had been burnt in order to collect the metal from their lead cames (Fig.12.1, Z4). A 13th-century stone base, about 0.75m in diameter, had been turned over and carved with a shallow cavity, to be reused as a hearth for this activity. Elsewhere there were fragments of high quality stone carvings, which are considered to have come from the destruction of fittings or possibly monuments.[119] The most likely provenance for these is the best of the conventual buildings, such as the chapter house and refectory.

The finds from the 1992 excavation have demonstrated the extent of the physical evidence for the abbey's monastic buildings below the ground, despite the efforts of the Dissolution to efface them and their memory from the landscape. The potential has yet to be realised for much more information to become available from field archaeology in the future.

CHAPTER 13

The Later Medieval Monuments and Chantry Chapels *by* Phillip Lindley

Introduction

Samuel Lysons, addressing the Society of Antiquaries of London in November 1801, stated: 'There are few of our churches which contain a greater number of antient tombs, or such as are more likely to be interesting to an antiquary, both on account of the richness of their decorations, and eminence of the persons to whose memory they have been erected, than the abbey church of Tewkesbury'.[1] He was right. The church houses one of the finest series of late-medieval tomb-monuments and chantry chapels in England (Fig.13.1). They include, in the 'Warwick Chapel', one of the most spectacular examples ever constructed.

The architectural context in which the monuments are located requires some initial scrutiny, for their spatial organisation reflects both the hierarchy and the chronology of power.[2] The rebuilding of the east end of the church was part of a large-scale reconstruction programme, most of which took place in the second quarter of the 14th century.[3] The iconography of the clerestory glazing scheme has been influential in the evocative designation of this part of the church as the 'Despenser mausoleum', but some reservations about this title may be suggested.[4] Most importantly, it is the post-medieval destruction of the de Clare monuments which has made it appear solely a Despenser burial space. In the early 1340s, the location of the de Clare tombs in the centre of the sanctuary and the glazing programme above them emphasized the descent of the lordship through the distinguished de Clare line from the founder. By the middle of the 15th century, it is true, the retrospective celebration of the lords of Tewkesbury in the glazing had been augmented and updated by monuments for the later lords. Despenser tombs and chapels—as well as a new, monastically funded, chantry chapel for Robert Fitzhamon—now clustered round the high altar. The original focus of the sanctuary had thus been modified by the accumulation of the later monuments. If the meanings of earlier monuments might be nuanced by their successors, reciprocally the specific locations of the later tombs and their relationships with their predecessors were sometimes key determinants of their architectural forms and helped shape their sculptural repertoires.

The Despenser tombs' deployment round the high altar symbolically emphasizes the power and status of the secular patrons of the abbey;[5] but it should not obscure the fact that other monuments of great importance and interest, mainly ecclesiastical ones, are gathered round them, on the far side of the ambulatory. A further group of tombs, generally—but not exclusively—of less important individuals, children and babies, was located in the eastern Lady Chapel, destroyed after the Dissolution.[6] In addition, following the Battle of Tewkesbury in 1471,

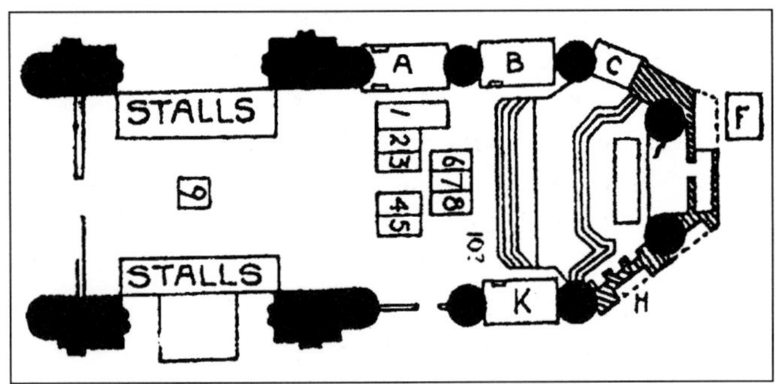

Fig.13.1 Plan of the choir with the secular burial sites and chantry chapels located (after Massé, with additions)

Burials
1. Maud de Clare (d.c.1320)
2. Gilbert III de Clare (k.1314)
3. Gilbert II de Clare (d.1295)
4. Gilbert I de Clare (d.1230)
5. Richard II de Clare (d.1262)
6. Richard Despenser (d.1414)
7. Thomas Despenser (k.1400)
8. Isabel Despenser (d.1439)
9. Henry Beauchamp (d.1446)
10? Elizabeth Burghersh (d.1409)

Chapels and Monuments
A. Warwick Chapel (Richard, earl of Worcester, d.1422)
B. Founder's Chapel (1397)
C. Hugh III Despenser (d.1349) & Elizabeth Montacute (d.1359)
F. Clarence Vault (1476)
H. Hugh II Despenser (ex.1326)
K. Trinity Chapel (Edward Despenser, d.1375)

a whole group of Lancastrian notables was buried in the church, the more important of them in the north transept with a second group in the nave, close to images of Our Lady of Pity and St. Clement, by the rood screen.[7]

Architecturally, the Tewkesbury monuments and chapels include some of the most precocious designs of their period, a pioneering employment of fan vaulting and some revolutionary deployments of figure-sculpture. Although all the monuments are damaged, some fragments of the original sculptural programmes can be reunited with them and there are significant survivals of medieval polychromy. It is surprising that they have received so little attention from recent scholarship.[8]

Early monastic tombs and the de Clare monuments

The first three monuments to concern us are not those of the secular lords of Tewkesbury, but of monastic officials, in the south choir aisle. The first is that of Abbot Alan. A trefoil-arched wall-tomb of *c*.1230-40 has had inserted into it a coffin and Purbeck marble slab for Abbot Alan (1187-1202).[9] This high quality monument with remains of a crucifix on the finial is one of the earliest examples of the newly resurgent format of gabled and arched wall-tombs, an arrangement which was to be extremely important for the rest of the Middle Ages.[10] Its location, in the south aisle (Fig.10.19), demonstrates that important monastic officials might now, for the first time, be buried within the church. It is overlapped to its west by a pinnacled and crocketed late 13th-century wall-tomb which possesses a fine vaulted canopy but has lost its tomb-chest altogether (the excellent head stops are by two different sculptors). To the east of the sacristy door (opposite the Trinity Chapel), the important wall-tomb often called that of Abbot Robert of Forthampton dates, probably, to the 1320s, with its cusped, ogee-headed arch, ballflower-encrusted mouldings, luxuriant foliate finial and large flanking pinnacles (Fig.10.12). The cusping of the arch features a fight between a man (sometimes misidentified as Abbot Forthampton) and a dragon in one cusp, with a grinning devilish 'green man' in the other.[11] The figure sculpture is again of high quality, with distinctive inset eyes. On the low tomb-chest has been placed a dark stone slab and a foliate cross with a figure of an abbot in the head. The coffin and slab do not originally belong together or in this wall-recess, but this lavish wall-tomb was doubtless an abbot's burial place: two later abbots' tombs are in analogous positions, round the periphery of the ambulatory aisle. It may well be the tomb of Abbot Kempsey (d.1328), who was so significant in the rebuilding of the church.[12]

The dominant position within the sanctuary was early reserved to the secular lords of the abbey. Gilbert I, Earl of Hertford and Gloucester (d.1230) and son of Richard I de Clare, was buried '*ante majus altare*' as the Tewkesbury chronicler records, '*in medio presbiterii*'.[13] His son, Richard II (d.1262), was interred, Leland states, on 'the right hond of his father and there lay his image yn sylver' (Fig.13.1).[14] The chronicle relates: '*Uxor ejus ornavit tumbam ejusdem auro et argento et lapidibus pretiosis, cum gladio et calcaribus quibus utebatur vivus*'.[15] This must have been a monument of enormous expense. It seems to have inaugurated the custom of suspending arms near the grave of a knight and may well have been influential in other ways.[16] The evidence that Richard II was given a precious metal effigy serves to undermine recent claims that such precious materials were ideological signifiers of royalty in this period. It was the visual reference to precious and sacred objects and the sheer expense of such effigies—rendering them out of reach for all but the wealthiest élite—which explains the choice of materials.[17]

Richard's son, Gilbert II (d.1295), the 'Red Earl', was buried on the left of his grandfather.[18] Gilbert III de Clare, Gilbert II's son by his second wife—Princess Joan (d.1307), daughter of Edward I—was killed at the Battle of Bannockburn in 1314, and was entombed on his father's left.[19] His wife, Maud de Burgh (d.*c*.1320), was buried beside him (Fig.13.1); the indent of her splendid brass still survives.[20] Gilbert III died without surviving male issue and this decisively changed the fortunes of Hugh II Despenser: the patronage of the monastery of Tewkesbury and a third of the de Clare estates now descended to his wife Eleanor (d.1337), one of Gilbert's co-heirs.[21] However, Hugh II was hanged, drawn and quartered in the overthrow of Edward II and it is his monument which constitutes the first significant survival of the later aristocratic tombs at Tewkesbury.[22]

Hugh Despenser the Younger

Leland relates that 'one of the quarters of [Hugh II] was buried by the lavatory of the high altare'.[23] The tomb stands behind the sedilia, on the south side, facing into the ambulatory (Fig.13.2). It cannot antedate 15 December 1330 when Hugh's friends received permission to collect up his scattered remains from London, York, Bristol, Carlisle and Dover.[24] This action, which followed Edward III's coup against Mortimer and Queen Isabella, presupposes a strong desire to commemorate Hugh and the monument will have followed very shortly thereafter. The design of this unusual wall-tomb depended for its screen-like effect on its lost sculptural programme. A central arched recess is surmounted by two tiers of niches, and is flanked by pairs of canopied niches in two tiers. Above the depressed arch, decorated with large vine leaves and grapes, and with dragons in the spandrels, are 13 smaller niches, perhaps for statues of Christ and the Apostles. Above them were six more large statues and on the left (western) side of the tomb, are two further small niches.[25] The only positively identifiable one of the large upper figures is a damaged image of St. John the Baptist, discovered in the excavations beneath the high altar in 1875 and now fixed on a bracket in the chapel opposite (Fig.13.3); its dimensions, style and depth all fit it for one of the niches.[26] The saints represented were intended to perform an intercessory function for the dishonoured and

Fig.13.2 Monument of Hugh II Despenser in the ambulatory (photo c.*1870)*

dismembered Lord Despenser. The programme must be understood within the context of contemporary belief in the powers of images to mediate good and ill. There is evidence that Hugh himself was particularly superstitious. In September 1323, he complained to the Pope that he was threatened by magical dealings; later, it transpired that John de Nottingham, a necromancer living in Coventry, had spent several months making wax images of the king, the Despensers and others, with the malevolent intention of murdering them by harming their images.[27]

Hugh II's monument was not accorded a dominating position on the south side of the sanctuary. Its relatively discreet positioning may bear witness to the still recent dispute at Worcester, where Bishop Giffard's monument offended the monks, who complained to the archbishop that it occupied the position intended for the sedilia and towered over the high altar.[28] This is not to say that Hugh's monument is a modest structure: the return to his widow of her dower lands after April 1328 gave her the financial ability to fund a monument of considerable size and scale.[29] Its design has no precise Westminster or 'Canterbury school' precedents, abandoning the favoured gabled arch design for a massive superabundance of sculpture niches arranged like a screen: unlike the monument of Bishop de Luda at Ely, it cannot be viewed as a direct derivation of work at Westminster.[30] It is probably the product of a local west midlands master mason. What is striking is that there are so many problems of coordination in the construction: this suggests a lack of tight control over a workshop brought together for a 'one-off' commission. However, this is not just a feature of this monument, and similar problems are seen elsewhere in the Tewkesbury monuments. One key feature, not hitherto noticed, deserves attention. The flanking niches have varying vaults to the canopies: those on the lower right have fan vaults, where the ribs were evidently painted onto the conoids. These are decorative proto-forms: fan vaults had not yet been constructed on an architectural scale.[31]

Fig.13.3 Statue of St. John the Baptist from Hugh II Despenser's monument

No effigy of Hugh II Despenser survives *in situ* though the size and depth of the recess suggests that there was one. Its space was later filled by the coffin-shaped Purbeck marble slab for Abbot John Coles (1328-47): it is of superb quality, decorated with a low relief cross with trefoil terminals; on its southern chamfered side is the indent for an inscription in separately inlaid brass Lombardic capitals (unevenly spaced and situated, suggesting the sculptor was not highly literate): '*Iohannes abbas huius loci*'.[32] Lysons recorded that the coffin below was opened in 1795, 'when on removing the lid there appeared to be nothing remaining in it except some pieces of rich gold tissue, ornamented with the arms of de Clare, probably part of some of the sacerdotal habits, the gift of one of the Clares'.[33]

Despenser's terrible punishments had included the humiliation of execution in a robe bearing his coat of arms reversed, so that his arms would be discarded for ever.[34] The absence of heraldry on the tomb may reflect the historical context in 1331, straight after Despenser's scattered remains were gathered together; by *c*.1340, Hugh II could be again depicted in the clerestory windows bearing Despenser heraldry on his jupon. One should be careful of arguing dogmatically from an absence of evidence: there must surely have been an effigy and it will doubtless have been identified heraldically. Nevertheless, the base of Hugh II's tomb does not use shields as decoration, by contrast with the two sections of what appears to be a low tomb-chest recently mortared into the neighbouring monument to the east with ballflower-encrusted quatrefoils containing shields suspended inside them.[35] The moulding designs are unlike Hugh II's monument and the very lavish deployment of ballflower tends to associate it with an earlier phase of the 14th-century remodelling.[36]

Fig.13.4 Tomb recess of the later 14th century in south-east ambulatory

The monument in which this tomb-chest is now located dates, perhaps, to the late 14th century (Fig.13.4). It has a crocketed ogee cinquefoil arch with blind panelling above, surmounted by quatrefoils and crenellations. Stylistically, it seems far too late to be the tomb of Eleanor de Clare, for the site of whose grave there is neither documentary nor archaeological evidence.[37] Blunt's statement that she was buried with her second husband, in the Lady Chapel, seems to be based on nothing more than antiquarians' guesswork.[38] Recently mortared onto the tomb-chest are two parts of a very damaged 15th-century Assumption of the Virgin/Madonna in Glory with flanking angels and a part of a lion foot-rest from a *c*.1325-50 effigy of a knight, perhaps originally from Hugh II Despenser's effigy. At the rear of the monument it can be seen that part of the screen wall behind the high altar has been removed to its eastern face, and it appears that a larger reorganisation of the area behind the high altar may have been envisaged, or actually have taken place when the Clarence vault was constructed.[39]

Hugh III Despenser and Elizabeth Montacute

The title of earl of Gloucester was given to Margaret de Clare's husband, Hugh Lord Audley, following the decease of her elder sister Eleanor in 1337. The lordship of Tewkesbury, however, descended to Hugh III Despenser. Through his military service to Edward III—he was with the king at the great victories of Sluys in 1340 and Crécy in 1346—Hugh rose to the title of Lord Despenser and succeeded in recovering a portion of the family's fortunes.[40] Hugh died on 13 February 1349 and was buried '*juxta summum altare in dextera parte*'.[41] His widow, Elizabeth Montacute, married Sir Guy de Bryan, but after her decease on 31 May 1359 was buried with Hugh III. The 1875 examination of the tomb revealed that Hugh's corpse had been buried in the vault prior to the monument's erection but hers was inserted only after construction; so, the tomb must have been erected before her death in 1359 and seems likely to be a work of the early

1350s (Fig.13.5).[42] The chronicler describes the tomb as remarkably fine with white marble (actually alabaster) effigies (Fig.13.6).[43]

The monument, on the north side of the high altar is not a direct counterpart to that of Hugh II Despenser on the south, as a view of a ground-

Fig.13.5 Monument of Hugh III Despenser and Elizabeth Montacute from the ambulatory

plan might suggest. The later monument stands in a location typically associated with founders or major patrons on the north side of the high altar, symbolic of a place on God's right hand, and is visible both from the sanctuary and the ambulatory, dominating the area beside the altar. It was the first step in the century-long process of encircling the sanctuary with major monuments. On the ambulatory side, the tomb-chest is raised on a tall sub-base, with numerous holes drilled into it, for a later iron screen. Figures of 'weepers' (all are lost and their particular identification is unknown) formerly stood in the niches of the tomb-chest.[44] Both sides have six niches and there are four on the western return (Fig.13.5).

The three-tiered freestone canopy places this monument amongst the most ambitious and ostentatious of its period. It has been compared to that of King Edward II in Gloucester Cathedral on which the three bay design and tiered superstructure must be loosely based, though it has here been radically enlarged vertically and logically flattened into a series of planes.[45] The canopy and superstructure are of freestone, and Purbeck marble makes no appearance on the tomb, although both effigies are, as at Gloucester, of alabaster, a material which was fast becoming the favoured choice for three-dimensional effigies of the élite.[46] The canopy consists of no fewer than four tiers of open arches, diminishing upwards and richly decorated. The fan vault above the effigies has six bays of conoids (the traceried designs were painted on), supported by shafts between the effigies (Fig.11.7). It is exactly contemporary with the first large-scale exposition of fan-vaulting, in the east walk of the cloisters of Gloucester Cathedral, and belongs to the same moment in the genesis of this most distinctive contribution of English Perpendicular architecture.[47] Above this level are three openwork niches, both to north and south, large enough to have contained figures. Then there is a trio of niches, with a further small one at the apex. There is copious evidence of the extensive and rather crude 1828 repair-work to the canopies, pinnacles and cusping, but the numerous adjustments to the canopy at the east end, where it abuts the earlier wall, are medieval.[48]

The monument seems originally to have been intended as fully (or largely) freestanding from evidence of an important change during its erection on site, revealed when it was dismantled for conservation in 1992-3. The lowest section of the canopy comprised three enormous blocks of limestone, one spanning the tomb transversely at one end and the other two running longitudinally, side by side. Morris noted that 'it was evident from carved details subsequently hidden between the canopy blocks that the design had been changed during execution, and that it was probably intended originally that the canopy should be visible at its east end', a decision which was revised to leave the original screen in place (Fig.13.7).[49] The monument was designed and manufactured off-site. Adjustments would have been necessary if the originally intended location of the monument was elsewhere or, more likely, when it was realised that destruction of the earlier screen would necessitate the building of a replacement in order to maintain the security of the high altar.

Hugh's effigy is a precocious example of what was to become a standard type for alabaster effigies: 'a close casing of mail and plate with the body covered by a tight-fitting jupon, and a uniform facial type ... with clean-shaven chin and long moustachios drooping over the mail aventail' (Figs.13.1, 13.6). His head lies on his great helm with a griffin crest, his hands together in prayer on his chest, and at his feet is a lion. Elizabeth is 'similarly constricted by the fashion of the day, which dictated a symmetrical U-shaped arrangement of the hair on a wire frame and a close-fitting kirtle that hugged the body'.[50] She has a small lap-dog at her feet.

By the 18th century, the correct identification of the tomb—recorded by Dingley in the 17th century—had been lost and it had been mis-assigned to Thomas Despenser, or even to George Duke of Clarence and Duchess Isabel.[51] When the

Fig.13.6 Effigies of Hugh III Despenser and Elizabeth Montacute

Fig.13.7 A canopy block from the monument of Hugh III Despenser

antiquary John Carter sketched Hugh III's effigy in 1788, he saw the Despenser arms on the tabard and was able to re-identify the effigies correctly.[52]

Sir Guy de Bryan

Sir Guy de Bryan's monument stands opposite that of Hugh III and Elizabeth Despenser, at the entrance to St. Margaret's Chapel (Fig.13.8). Sir Guy, standard bearer to King Edward III at the Battle of Crécy, married the widowed Elizabeth Despenser. Though she was buried with Hugh III, her effigy also lay, in effect, next to Sir Guy, separated only by the ambulatory (Masterplan). He appropriated rents from Bristol properties to pay for chantry masses for his soul and that of his wife at the chapel's altar.[53] The establishment of a chantry—an endowment for the performance of specified masses and other charitable works for the spiritual benefit of particular individuals—led to a structural alteration of the fabric, reflecting the privatized nature of the intercession.[54] Like the Despenser monument, the de Bryan tomb has been intruded into an earlier screen; this one separated the chapel from the ambulatory (Fig.11.12).[55] The tomb's placing economically demarcated a chantry chapel without construction of a separate building within a church, such as chantry chapels were often becoming in the later 14th century.[56]

The tomb-base is separated into three by pairs of diagonally turned pinnacles, supporting a net-vaulted canopy above the effigy; it is surmounted by a group of five pinnacled openings, above which are a further three openings, with another one at the top. It is modelled on that of the Despenser monument opposite. The selection by patrons of a specific feature to emulate, or even wholesale quotations from models, was characteristic of the Middle Ages, although these borrowings might be transmuted by the artist in the copying.[57] Thus the canopy of Sir Guy's

Fig.13.8 Guy de Bryan's monument, north side

monument is not a direct copy of the Despenser one.[58] It is less deep, covering only a single effigy, the vault is of a different type and the proportions and architectural details differ markedly. When the monument was dismantled for conservation, the canopy was found to comprise four large stones set transversely.[59] The technical and stylistic differences between this and the Despenser monument are so great that it is impossible that they are the work of the same designer. Stylistically, the monument must presumably antedate the Trinity Chapel (*c*.1375-85), with which it has nothing in common, and so should probably be dated to the 1360s. Like Hugh III's monument, it was subjected to a rather drastic restoration in 1828.[60] The huge clumsy finials obtrusively inserted into some of the canopies—originally intended to hold statues—date from this restoration.[61]

Fig.13.9 The Trinity Chapel and the kneeling knight

Sir Guy's tomb-chest has heraldic decoration not weepers: the arms of his wife, Elizabeth Despenser (née Montacute) impaling de Bryan on either side of his own arms.[62] The damaged freestone effigy shows a knight in early plate armour, his head resting on his great helm, his feet on an alert lion turned towards the east (Fig.3.2): the characteristics of the armour also suggest an early date for the whole monument.[63] There are now few traces of its originally lavish surface decoration and colouring. Carter noted the colours of the heraldry on the knight's jupon and Stothard states that 'The whole of the armour, plate and mail, has been once covered with silver leaf' and argued that the mail was produced by stamps impressed onto gesso, which was also the method used to diaper the surcoat.[64] Stothard's superb engravings and his vignette of the effigy's polychromy restored provide the best available evidence for its original paintwork and remind us that that all the medieval monuments were once lavishly coloured.

The Trinity Chapel

Hugh III and Elizabeth had no surviving children; on her death in 1359 her nephew Edward succeeded to the lordship. Edward's parents were Edward I (d.1342) and Ann Ferrers. Edward the Younger held high command under the Black Prince.[65] He had three sons, two of whom died in infancy, and four daughters by Elizabeth Burghersh.[66] Edward died at Cardiff Castle on 11 November 1375 and was buried '*ante ostium vestiarii juxta presbiterium*'.[67]

The Trinity Chapel (Fig.13.9)—the first chantry chapel of the so-called 'stone cage' type to be constructed at Tewkesbury—stands on the south side of the sanctuary, west of Hugh II Despenser's tomb.[68] Such chapels were designed as locations in which chantry priests would offer prayers on behalf of the deceased. There are doorways at the west end on both south and north sides and it seems possible it functioned as a thoroughfare to the high altar, perhaps replacing an earlier screen doorway in this approximate location. This suggests that there was never a tomb-chest at the west end of the chapel.[69]

Lawrence Stone argued that the chapel had been built before 1375 because Edward made no provision for building any tomb or chantry in his will.[70] Despenser's will does indeed require 'my body to be buried ... on the south side, near to the bodies of my ancestors'.[71] However, whilst a reference to an existing tomb is certain evidence for its prior construction, the absence of any mention proves nothing.[72] Other documentary evidence unequivocally credits construction of the chapel to Edward's widow, Elizabeth. The Tewkesbury chronicler writes: '*uxor ejus aedificavit capellam ex lapidibus arte mirifica constructam, quae dedicata est in honore Sanctae Trinitatis*'.[73] Lady Despenser remained a widow for 33 years and died in 1409, so the chapel dates between 1375 and 1409.

If Edward's tomb was located within the chantry chapel, it was not to be joined by Elizabeth's. She chose burial in the sanctuary 'betwixt my lord and husband, Edward Lord Despenser, and my son, Thomas le Despenser ... I desire that ... a stone of marble be placed over my grave, with my portraiture thereon'.[74] The chronicler confirms that this was carried out (although no trace of the slab or of her grave has been discovered).[75] Her monument was the second in the Despenser colonisation of the sanctuary floor area, as they joined their de Clare ancestors in front of the high altar, to the adornment of which they were major benefactors (Fig.13.1).[76]

The Trinity Chapel is articulated in two bays. The base level comprises a large canopied statue niche, flanking each entrance doorway from north and south, and six smaller niches (the canopies and bases are severely damaged and all the images have been removed).[77] One of the most striking features is the lack of co-ordination between the base section and the two five-light traceried openings above: only one canopy is linked to the central bracket between the windows (Fig.13.9). The mullions of the openings are not articulated as extensions of the pinnacles from the image niches below. Of the many possible explanations for this anomalous treatment, the likeliest seems that—highly unusually—the specific sculptural programme was more important than the systematic co-ordination of architectural elements.

Three features of this chapel have attracted considerable attention. The first is the fan vault with its pendant bosses.[78] Secondly, the east end has a remarkable series of devotional wall-paintings (perhaps retouched) above a blocked squinch to the high altar (Pl.12). At the apex is the Trinity, housed in a painted niche and censed by angels. To the sides of the angels are, to the left, Edward Despenser, and to the right Lady Elizabeth, praying towards the Trinity. Beneath them, under architectural canopies are, to the left, the Resurrected Christ, another subject largely defaced, and, on the right, the Coronation of the Virgin.[79] The style of these paintings is quite close to that of the main artist of the mid-14th-century Fitzwarin Psalter in features such as the borrowings from Italianate art (e.g. the emphasis on three-dimensional recession so evident in the throne of the Trinity); the elaborate fictive architectural structures within which the individual subjects are located; and the details of that architecture.[80] The date of these paintings (*c*.1375-85) suggests a long-lived florescence of the style.

The flooring of the chapel has been entirely replaced and there is now no evidence for a tomb—whether freestanding or set level with the floor (Fig.15.3).[81] Instead, attention has focused on the canopied niche on the roof with its life-sized kneeling effigy of Lord Despenser praying towards the altar (Fig.13.9). It does not seem to have been generally noticed that the canopy itself is the result of early 19th-century restoration. It is not shown in Carter's excellent plate nor in Richard Gough's *Sepulchral Monuments*; Bennett states, 'the fragments of it lay scattered ... and broken into upwards of two hundred pieces, until the year 1827 ... more than one third of the buttresses and pinnacles were entirely lost'.[82]

Lawrence Stone thought the statue, which was cleaned, repaired and regilt in 1937-8, was 'evidently a London work inspired by the similar figures painted on the wall of Saint Stephen's Chapel, Westminster, some twenty years earlier', and viewed it as an 'isolated experiment'.[83] The functional specificity of the St. Stephen's Chapel paintings makes them very unlikely to be a direct model.[84] A pertinent question might be whether there were any antecedents at Tewkesbury itself. The apparently total loss of all the figure sculpture—other than the effigies—from Hugh III's tomb renders any argument speculative but it is suggestive that there is a single niche at the apex of its canopy, which could easily have housed a small kneeling image of Hugh III (Fig.13.5). The same point applies to the de Bryan monument. It could be objected that the depiction of the same man twice on the single monument would be redundant, but the greatly reduced scale of the praying figure would dispel the sense of tautology.[85] The potential for representational conflict inherent in depicting the deceased in two separate life-sized sculptures must, though, have been evident and the Trinity Chapel may have featured a single three-dimensional representation to avoid any such issues.[86]

The Founder's Chapel

The chantry chapel of Robert Fitzhamon, the abbey's founder, stands opposite the Trinity chapel and is closely related to it in style. Fitzhamon (d.1107) was first buried in the chapter house.[87] Leland records '*in camera Sacelli*' the epitaph, '*Hic jacet Robertus filius Haymonis hujus loci fundator*', together with other epitaphs to Robert Consul and their wives.[88] It seems evident, therefore, that the chapter house, in which the abbots might also be buried, was then the most honourable location for secular benefactors' tombs. However, in 1241 Fitzhamon's remains were translated to the presbytery, reflecting the new importance of this area as the location for secular graves.[89] In 1397, Abbot Parker erected this chantry chapel on the same site.[90] This is a clear example of monastic provision for the abbey's founder so as to provide an up-to-date physical and liturgical counterpart to the Trinity Chapel opposite. The initiative occurred at the same time that Thomas, the youngest son of Edward Despenser and Elizabeth Burghersh, had succeeded in becoming earl of Gloucester, reuniting the lordship with the earldom for the first time under the Despensers.[91] It was a peculiarly auspicious moment in the history of the secular patrons, and by reflection, shed increased glory on the monastery.

Like the Trinity Chapel, Fitzhamon's is a chantry-chapel of the 'stone-cage' type (Fig.10.23, centre).[92] If it was designed as a copy of the Trinity Chapel, it also differs in numerous minor ways. It has a single opening, from the south. Each bay has a five-light traceried opening closely modelled on that of the Trinity Chapel but the base section and tracery are carefully synchronised and there is no place here for a programme of sculpture. The design of the fan vaults is so close as to suggest that the same workshop was responsible (Fig.11.3).[93] Analysis of the chapels' close stylistic relationship highlights the problems of dating late medieval architecture. The historical circumstances make a date of *c.*1397 for Fitzhamon's chapel perfectly plausible and there is no reason to doubt the veracity of the monastic chronicler. Though a date in the second half of the 1370s is probable for the Trinity Chapel, a slightly later one cannot be ruled out.[94] The changes between the two chapels suggest that the Founder's Chapel is an intelligent critique of the earlier monument.

Above the sculptural frieze on the chapel's exterior was once a painted inscription reading: '*In ista capella jacet Dominus Robertus filius Hamonis hujus loci fundator*'.[95] Inside, on the east wall, there are painted architectural niches,

Fig.13.10 The tomb-chest and indent for Fitzhamon's brass in the Founder's Chapel

reminiscent of those in the Trinity Chapel, though very badly effaced. The remains of the figure painting are of the very highest quality. Bennett records a tradition that the story of St. Thomas Becket was painted inside the chapel.[96] The devotional imagery of the Trinity Chapel seems here to have been substituted by a narrative series, doubtless modelled on Abbot Alan's 12th-century history of the archbishop, an unusual scheme in wall painting of this period.

The tomb-chest of the founder is set against the west end (Fig.13.10). Most interestingly, the north side of the tomb-chest is entirely plain, because it was hidden from view. The monument was opened at least once in the 18th century.[97] A Purbeck-marble indent for the lost brass shows that Fitzhamon was depicted as a knight, a lion at his feet, under a gabled canopy with two coats of arms.

This was not the only retrospective monument in the church: there was a tradition that King Beorhtric had been buried at Tewkesbury by Hugh, earl of the Mercians, patron of the church, in 812.[98] Leland also saw Hugh's tomb on the north side of the nave.[99] The Founder's chapel with its quotidian service in memory of the founder and his wife is a distinguished example of the care taken by the monastery to ensure commemoration and prayer for their founder in line with current liturgical fashions. It was an impressive expression of piety; a celebration of the illustrious past, which is also manifested in monastic chronicles - particularly the Tewkesbury one, with its obsessive interest in the secular lords; and an encouragement to contemporary benefactors.[100]

The Warwick Chapel

Thomas, son of Edward II Despenser, was created earl of Gloucester on 29 September 1397, but retained his title for little more than two years.[101] One of King Richard II's supporters, he joined the plot to seize Henry IV and was executed in January 1400, predeceasing his mother by nearly a decade. He was buried in the middle bay of the choir, under the lamp which burned before the Sacrament (Fig.13.1).[102] No trace of his grave was apparently discovered in the 19th-century restoration but it is probable, given its original position, that he had a memorial brass set level with the floor.[103] Thomas's son, Richard, died aged 18 and was buried to the left of his father in October 1414.[104] With Richard, the male line of the Despensers came to an end. His young sister, Isabel, then succeeded to the lordship. In 1411, she had married Richard Beauchamp, lord of Abergavenny, who was created earl of Worcester in 1421 but killed at the siege of Meaux in 1422. Isabel married, secondly, her husband's cousin, also called Richard Beauchamp, earl of Warwick, in 1423. On his death at Rouen in 1439 she had his remains brought back to England for burial in the Beauchamp Chapel at St. Mary's, Warwick.[105] The countess died the same year but chose to be buried at Tewkesbury.[106]

The chantry chapel (Pl.13) which Isabel erected for her first husband on the north side of the sanctuary, in the bay west of the Founder's Chapel, has acquired the name of the Warwick Chapel; it might more properly be called the Abergavenny and Worcester chapel, since these were her first husband's titles. The chronicle relates that Isabel constructed a beautiful chapel '*arte mirifice fabricatam*', dedicated to the Virgin, Mary Magdalene and St. Leonard, where the earl was buried, and gives a dedication date of 2 August 1438.[107] Julian Luxford argues the date is a scribal error and that the correct date is 1423.[108] The issue is a complex one which ultimately depends on the relative weight one ascribes to the Founders' Book and chronicle texts (BL MS Cotton Cleopatra C III). The chapel's painted inscription provides the date 1439 for Isabel's death but need not imply anything about the date of the chapel itself. Given the difficulties of accurately dating late medieval architecture, it would be unwise to be dogmatic, but Luxford's dating of 1423 is accepted here.[109]

*Fig.13.11 Cut-away section of the Warwick Chapel, looking west (*Vetusta Monumenta*, V, pl.XLV)*

The chapel set new standards for aristocratic magnificence.[110] Unlike its Tewkesbury predecessors, it is constructed in three bays. At the west end only (Fig.13.11), it is of two-storeyed construction—ultimately reflecting the impact of Bishop William of Wykeham's innovative chantry chapel in Winchester cathedral—the lower section being fan vaulted (Fig.11.8).[111] The upper vault is a lierne, of similarly superb quality, and also featuring (lost) pendant bosses. The sides of the chapel are constructed as traceried stone screens featuring shield-bearing angels, with a doorway in the west end, surmounted by four-light tracery (Pl.13). All the angels have been defaced and the canopies above them severely damaged.[112] The treatment of the eastern bays shows the same disregard for carrying down the mullions of the windows through the niche pinnacles found on the Trinity Chapel, though the other bays are co-ordinated (Fig.10.23, left).[113] The difference between the numbers of angels in the eastern bays of the south and north sides demonstrates that heraldry rather than symmetry was the key concern of the patron. At the west and east ends of each side, three empty image niches stand between the pinnacles, making 12 niches in all. Above the open tracery is a wide moulding surmounted by a distinctive 'palm' foliage cresting which curves upwards in the central bay, the moulding being substituted, at the west end, by six coats of arms. The cresting above is missing on the north side but is shown in the *Vetusta Monumenta* engraving published in 1835. All the extant heraldry was recorded by Carter in 1788 and published by James Bennett and by Richard Gough.[114] The scheme is an heraldic celebration of relatives and ancestry selected to be at its most impressive. The moulding contains a painted inscription, reading:

> Mementote D[omi]n[a]e Isabell[a]e
>   LeDespenser cometissae de Warrewyk
> qu[a]e hanc cappellam fundavit in
>   honore[m] B[ea]t[a]e Mari[a]e
>   Magdalen[a]e
> et obiit Londinis apud minores a[nn]o
>   d[omi]ni mccccxxxix die S[an]c[t]i
>   J[o]ha[nni]s Evangel[is]t[a]e

et sepulta est [in] choro in dextra patris
sui: cuius an[ima]e p[ro]p[itietu]r deus
amen.[115]

The upper storey is open—except for the image canopies at the west and east ends and the buttress-mullions carried up though the screens from the base below—and terminates in a series of three-dimensional image canopies. At the west end of the chapel, there is a clumsy abutment with the Romanesque pier (Fig.11.9, right). The planned opening to the west on the north side was blocked, leaving just a squinch to the high altar:[116] the southern 'opening' backs straight onto the pier (Fig.13.11). It looks as if there was an intention to provide access from the west end, or stairways to the upper floor here. Such anomalies suggest that a decision to change its location was made after the chapel's components had already been constructed off site.[117] The fan vault had numerous (lost) pendants and terminated to the east in three elaborate projecting brackets with angels holding scrolls. Only one survives *in situ* (Fig.11.8, top left).

The purpose of the upper chapel has long been a matter for debate because there is no means of access to it. It seems impossible that it was intended as an elevated private location for the countess to observe services. The two southern recesses in the west wall (Fig.13.11) appear to have housed kneeling images of the earl and countess looking towards the high altar, an example of the importance of family precedent in this expanded and updated homage to the format of the kneeling image of Edward Despenser on top of the Trinity Chapel.[118]

It is conspicuous that the exterior sculptural programme of the chantry chapel, other than the shield-bearing angels just mentioned, is missing. One thing which is striking about the chapel is the survival of its original paintwork, which includes a cycle of painted figures inside and on the east wall of the chapel (including the Last Judgement) and fictive tracery on the pinnacles. Dingley records 'sundry inscriptions in paint and gold so imperfectly discern'd and abus'd as not to be made anything of. In the whole I judge them to be prayers: over the heads of the 12 Apossles richly painted and gilded is often, and in other places repeated Mercy lord: Mercy lord'.[119] The subject matter powerfully represented the primary function of chantry chapels, to gain through the chanting of masses and prayers, the alleviation of the pains of Purgatory, before the Resurrection.[120]

The 12 image niches have spaces in the paintwork where separately carved sculpted images have stood: the surviving paintwork indicates that the niches and the rest of the architecture were (unusually) painted before the images were put in place, but with the full knowledge of their dimensions. Remarkably, a large number of pieces from the 12 statues which formerly stood in the exterior niches can be reunited with the chapel (Fig.13.13). In 1824, according to George May's article in the *Gentleman's Magazine*, three fragmentary torsos and a head from these sculptures were found in the space at the rear of the 18th-century altar-screen, in a rubble flooring two feet deep (Fig.13.12).[121] The three large fragments then disinterred were painted with the arms of Hugh Despenser the Younger (Fig.13.12, no.4) (it was unclear whether the head belonged with the figure); Robert the Consul (Fig. 13.12, no.5); and Gilbert I de Clare (Fig.13.12, no.6).[122] The author perceptively noted that the figures—two of which are now lost—must have formed part of a tomb or chantry chapel and correctly suggested that they came from the Warwick Chapel.

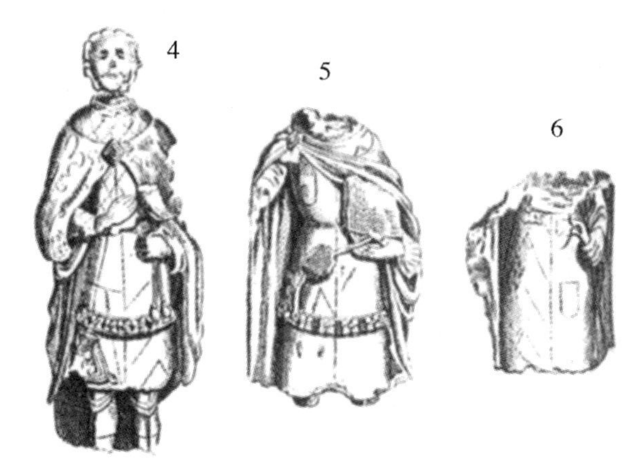

Fig.13.12 Figures of the lords of the manor discovered in 1824
(Gentleman's Magazine, *1824)*

In February 1875, as manuscript notes from J.H. Blunt reveal, the soil under the altar place from which the 18th-century altarpiece had been removed, was excavated to the depth of four feet. Many fragments of painted sculpture were found, which Blunt wrongly conjectured to have come from the ancient reredos because of the location in which they had been discovered.[123] He identified pieces of six figures from inscriptions on the bases or from the heraldry painted on the figures as representing the following: Robert Fitzroy; William Fitzcount; Gilbert II de Clare; Richard II de Clare; Thomas Despenser (Pl.15) and Gilbert III de Clare.[124] In total, this means that there were, in the 19th century, at least nine fragments from the chapel's 12 niches. The inscriptions give the clue to the figures' identities (Figs.2.1, 2.2): they constituted the lords of the manor from Robert Fitzhamon to Richard Despenser (d.1414). In 1910, the Revd. C.H. Bickerton Hudson suggested the provenance for these figures, adding, 'my own impression is that the ... decoration of the [Founders'] Book was derived from the decoration of the chapel. The chapel was 'The Founders' Book' in stone'.[125] In addition a head exhibited in a recent exhibition at Leeds as from a separate ensemble is from one of the 12 figures, as is another head in two pieces in the abbey collection, which exhibits the same stylistic features.[126] The fact that these clearly secular figures have been smashed suggests that iconoclasm took place in the 17th century, during the Civil War conflict, as it was relatively rare for secular imagery to be targeted during the Reformation.[127]

Fig.13.13 Statuette of Robert Fitzroy placed in an upper niche in the Warwick Chapel

The chapel's figure-sculpture constituted a remarkable celebration of the descent of the lordship of the manor, the direct ancestry of Isabel Despenser, who had brought the lordship to her first husband through marriage. Obviously, it was directly influenced in its format by the stained glass scheme which stretched round the sanctuary's clerestory; but, as a sculpted celebration of inheritance it transfers to the chapel's superstructure the type of scheme associated with the tomb-chests of monuments.[128] King Richard II's late 14th-century remodelling of the great hall at Westminster Palace included a cycle of the English kings since the Conquest, a scheme which was to have important successors in the 15th and 16th centuries, and may have influenced the Tewkesbury chapel, just as the latter seems directly to have influenced the design and iconography of Duke Humphrey of Gloucester's chapel in St. Alban's Abbey, datable to *c.*1441-3.[129] Whatever its specific model, the chapel's programme of secular figures celebrating the descent of the lordship was highly distinctive: it was effectively retrospective in its nature, celebrating the illustrious inheritance of the earl of Abergavenny and Worcester. By contrast, the tomb of the earl of Warwick, Isabel's second husband, in St. Mary's, Warwick, is a tomb of descent essentially prospective in its programme of 'weepers'.[130]

Isabel Despenser's Monument

Isabel and her first husband only had a single daughter, and the latter might, of course, have been represented on his monument, whether it was three-dimensional or brass. The chronicle places his burial in the chapel; but there is no apparent evidence for his monument. By contrast, there is considerable documentary evidence for the countess's, which, as the painted inscription intimates, was located away from the chapel. Her remarkable will specified:

> my body to be beryed In the Abbey of Tewkesbury, yn such place as I haue assyngned. And that my grete templys [fillets or head bands] with the Baleys [pale rubies] be sold to the vtmest pryse, and delyueryd to the sayde Abbat and the howse of Tewkesbery, so they groche not with my lyenge, and with such thyng as y woll haue done a-bowt my body. And my Image to be made all naked, and no thyng on my hede but myn here cast bakwardys, and of the gretnes and of the fascyon lyke the mesure that Thomas Porchalyn hath yn a lyst, and at my hede Mary Mawdelen leyng my handes a-crosse, And seynt Iohn the Evangelyst on the ryght syde of my hede; and on the left syde, Seynt Anton, and at my fete a Skochen of myn Armes departyd [impaled] with my lordys, and ij Greffons to bere hit uppe; And all a-bowt my tumbe, to be made pore men and wemen In theire pore Array, with their bedys In theire handes ...[131]

The chronicle provides details of how she revised the chantry for her first husband: she left vestments, precious stones and other gifts to the value of 300 marks and endowed six more monks to pray for herself, her predecessors and her successors. It also confirms the accuracy of the painted inscription that she was buried '*in dextra patris sui*'.[132]

Isabel's decision to be buried near her father and close to her first husband, rather than with her illustrious second husband at Warwick, is comprehensible, for she was the last in the direct line of the Despensers, and a widow. Bannister notes that when the sanctuary graves were opened during the restorations of 1875-9, 'her stone grave was uncovered and disclosed, the body was found in good preservation ... on the underside of the covering slab was a long cross, in shallow lines, across the upper part of which in deeply-cut black letter characters, was the inscription: *Mercy Lord Jesu*.[133] It seems certain, then, from the documentary and archaeological evidence that countess Isabel was buried where she had wished. The chronicle further relates that within a year of her death a superbly made marble tomb was erected over her grave.[134]

The reference in the will to an agreed design, with the tomb's dimensions indicated, proves that it directly reflected Isabel's intentions. What is equally clear is that this monument, if it was constructed in the form she wished, was unique. Perhaps the most remarkable feature was the cadaver or *transi* effigy (by which is meant a representation of the deceased as a corpse, generally in a shroud pulled open to reveal the dead or decaying body).[135] The imagery of the corpse effigy was a novelty in English effigial sculpture, the first example being the 'double-decker' tomb of Archbishop Chichele (d.1443) in Canterbury Cathedral.[136] Chichele's monument, complete by 1426, had an effigy of the deceased in his archiepiscopal vestments, above another effigy representing him as a naked cadaver. The genre was an alien import, just like the Dance of Death, which John Lydgate must have seen in 1426, newly painted on the cemetery walls of the Franciscan Convent aux SS. Innocents in Paris, after which he produced Middle English 'translations' of its verse inscriptions.[137] The almost exact contemporaneity of the English assimilation of both these mordant reflections on mortality testifies to the expressive potency of their formulation and to the impact of French models at a time when the English had conquered so much of France. The sudden death of both her husbands in the French wars may also have endowed Isabella's choice of a cadaver effigy with quite personal and specific meanings.

An all-encompassing explanation of the *transi* effigy's meaning is probably illusory, for the genre was various and multi-valent. Endemic plague mortality may be the *conditio sine qua non* but recurrent plague is not by itself a sufficient explanation for the genre. Though cadaver effigies articulated an orthodox Christian view of the mortality of the human body as the result of Original Sin,[138] their invention, towards the end of the 14th century, reflects a new manner of articulating that view in sculpture. In one sense, their first appearance can be construed as a by-product of a fascination with realism, the same interest evinced by the first painted portraits in the west since classical antiquity.[139] Yet, as the (Latin) inscriptions round Chichele's monument indicate, cadaver effigies could also be powerfully didactic. On the upper slab, alongside his archiepiscopal effigy, the inscription outlines his career. Beside the cadaver, on the southern side, it reads: 'I was born a poor man: and afterwards raised to be Primate here. Now I am cast down: and turned into food for worms. Behold my grave, and see in it a mirror of your true self'.[140] In a sense, the two effigies visually express the contrast drawn by preachers such as John Bromyard between magnificent funerary monuments and the putrefaction of the corpses they contain.[141]

One focus of *transi* tombs is on the inevitability of the death of the individual, on the need to prepare oneself, as the tomb's viewer, for a good death. It would be tempting to view Isabel's cadaver effigy as a realistic depiction of her corpse designed to stimulate such reflections on the part of the spectator.[142] Yet construing this effigy as realistic is problematic when it also featured sculpted representations of three saints as intercessors, with Mary Magdalene actually folding the countess's arms across her body (presumably to mask her breasts). This is a case of what one might term 'symbolic realism', with different levels of 'reality' functioning simultaneously. The presence of the saints at the head of the representation of the dead body was intended to symbolise their intercessory aid to the deceased, through the pains of Purgatory, prospectively anticipating the bodily resurrection at the Last Judgement: 'I believe that my Redeemer lives and that on the last day I shall rise from the earth. And in my flesh I shall see my Saviour'.[143] On Chichele's effigy, the inscription at the west end of the upper effigy refers to the images placed in the piers at the head and foot of the effigy: 'This company of saints is prayed to together, that God may have mercy on this man for the sake of their merits'.[144] So, at Tewkesbury, the representation of saints as intercessors is not to be understood as conflicting with the realistic rendition of the corpse. The complex of messages articulated by Chichele's double-decker tomb and its associated imagery and inscriptions—effigy in pontificals, corpse effigy, sculpted saints in niches on the flanking piers—was in effect condensed round Isabel's corpse figure on the tomb-chest with her noble estate also represented by her elaborate coat of arms, supported by griffins, at her feet.[145] Her heraldic bearings were represented as identifiers of the nude corpse, even without an inscription (there must presumably have been one), and emphasize that the cadaver effigy is certainly not 'desocialised', removed from the duchess' social position. The spiritual intercession of the three saints was augmented by the presence of sculpted bedesmen and women on the tomb-chest, symbolically standing for those who would pray for Isabel's soul, perhaps at the altar of her first husband's chantry chapel as well as evoking the prayers of those who saw this monument. The monument thus combined different levels of reality but it also derived its meaning from the liturgical context and the intercessory prayers that once resonated around it and from the chapel nearby.[146]

Consideration of Isabel Despenser's lost monument presents a counter-example to the thesis that the whole genre of the cadaver effigy was essentially a clerical one, the sentiments behind it a 'donnish conceit'.[147] This monument's imagery, and its location in front of the high altar, like the rich bequests left by the countess, were designed to elicit the prayerful memory of the monks. The pains Isabel took to ensure that the abbot and monks did not complain ('*groche*') about the tomb indicates that it was not solely its prominent position—obstructing access to the altar—which she envisaged as a potential cause of complaint. It was also the very novelty of the monument, with its unprecedented focus on her naked corpse. At the time it was produced, this was an image designed to shock the viewer into reflection and prayer.[148]

The description of the monument as 'marble' poses other questions. If Purbeck marble was the medium of the effigy too, this would have been a unique example of the genre in that material.[149] If alabaster was indicated, then that too would have been highly unusual: there is only one other alabaster cadaver effigy, the later one to Alice, Duchess of Suffolk (d.1475) at Ewelme (Oxon.).[150] But, of course, the effigy may have been two dimensional, a brass. It is just possible that a fragment of the monument survives reset into the wall of the *Camera Cantorum*; it comprises three bays of a late medieval Purbeck marble tomb-chest, deprived of its 'weepers', with mouldings close to those of the chapel (Fig.13.14).[151] The choice of Purbeck marble for the tomb-chest in this period immediately defines it as part of an élite monument. There are several possibilities if this is from a mid-15th-century monument: it is either a surviving section of Isabel's lost monument or it is from the tomb of her first husband, about whose grave we otherwise know nothing. On the other hand, it could be from one of the later 15th-century monuments, of which there were once a considerable number at Tewkesbury.

Fig.13.14 Panel from a late medieval tomb-chest, probably of Isabel Despenser

Burials and Tombs 1446–*c*.1510

Countess Isabel's only son, Duke Henry Beauchamp, died aged only 22 in 1446 and was buried in the choir of the abbey church (Fig.13.1).[152] His death precipitated a dispute over the right to the lordship of Tewkesbury which was decisively resolved in favour of Richard Neville, the 'Kingmaker'. In 1469 he married his daughter Isabel (d.1476) to George, duke of Clarence, brother of Edward IV, but his interventions came to an end when he was killed at the Battle of Barnet in 1471.[153] A few weeks later, the Lancastrians were crushingly defeated at the Battle of Tewkesbury.

Rushforth's analysis of the Lancastrian burials showed that Prince Edward of Lancaster, son of Henry VI, was buried in the middle of the conventual choir;[154] the duke of Somerset, and his brother, together with John Courtenay, earl of Devon and Sir Humphrey Audley, were buried in the north transept, immediately opposite the Warwick Chapel.[155] Sir Thomas Tresham was buried to their north. Another group of notables was buried 'in the body of the said monastery church called the parish church', the nave as distinct from the eastern, monastic part of the church.[156] No trace of their monuments has been discovered.

Nothing is said in any of the chronicle accounts of the burial at Tewkesbury of John Lord Wenlock, to whom early antiquaries such as Atkyns ascribed an effigy in a wall tomb in the eastern bay of the nave north aisle (Fig.13.15).[157] Although Lysons rightly disputed this attribution of the tomb on the grounds of the heraldry on the jupon, he still thought the effigy might be that of another nobleman slain in the battle;[158] instead, as Carter realised, this is a much earlier effigy.[159] It is a mid-14th-century knight resting his head on his great helm, and housed in a contemporary wall-tomb. It is amongst the first knights to be represented straight- rather than cross-legged, comparable with one of the mid-century pair at Abergavenny Priory (Mon.). The tomb's positioning, to the east of the site of the pulpitum, places it within the monks' church and implies that this was the effigy of an important nobleman.

Diagonally opposite, to the east of the entrance door from the cloisters, is another recess with its ogee arch and angel finial, which early antiquaries ascribed to Edmund Beaufort, duke of Somerset (Fig.12.8, left). Lysons again disputed this, noting that 'the style of this tomb does not, in any respect, agree with the time of his interment ... there are two shields of arms on the tomb, neither of which has any relation to the duke of Somerset. That on the right side has a lion rampant, that on the left the arms of Clare'.[160] A corbel to the east was the location for a statue. Both of these monuments emphasise the range of high-quality work being produced at Tewkesbury even after the Black Death but have nothing to do with the aftermath of the Battle of Tewkesbury.

Fig.13.15 Wall tomb with military effigy in the east bay of the nave north aisle

Fig.13.16 Scallop shells and monogram from the tomb of Abbot Richard Cheltenham

After the Kingmaker's death, his wife Anne Neville should have been entitled to the lordship of Tewkesbury, which Edward IV instead assigned to his brother, George, duke of Clarence, in right of his duchess, Isabel.[161] Isabel died in 1476 aged 25, and Clarence himself was executed in 1478, aged 28. Both were buried in a vault behind the high altar (Fig.4.4).[162] The 15th century seems to have been the first time when sizeable vaults were constructed beneath tomb-monuments; this was apparently Edward IV's intention at Windsor.[163] Since Isabel's body lay in state in the choir for 35 days, it seems highly probable that the vault's excavation and construction took place at this time. The vault's location is precisely identified in the monastic chronicle as 'a vault behind the High Altar, before the door of the Virgin Mary's chapel, and opposite the door of St. Edmund the Martyr's chapel'.[164] Michael Hicks links payments of £373 with provision for a tomb which would have stood over the vault. If it did cost this sum, the lost tomb monument must have been magnificent. No trace of it has been discovered and it was doubtless a victim of 17th-century destruction. An analytical account of the bones and vault is provided in Chapter 4.

After Clarence's death, political circumstances ensured that countess Anne Neville only had her rights returned to her at the price of disinheriting her heirs. Neither Edward, earl of Warwick, executed in 1499, nor Margaret, countess of Salisbury, executed in 1541, was buried at Tewkesbury. The only two 16th-century tombs in the abbey are both ecclesiastical. The first is that of Abbot Richard Cheltenham (1481-1509), housed at the entrance to St. John the Baptist's Chapel. It is a freestone altar-tomb with four panels decorated with quatrefoils bearing shields, and surmounted by a vaulted and arched canopy. The spandrels are carved with shields bearing the letters 'RC' entwined round a crozier, a chevron between scallop shells and a palmer's staff (Fig.13.16); evidence that the abbot had been a pilgrim or, perhaps, funded a pilgrimage on his soul's behalf in his will.[165] It has been conjectured that there was once a recumbent effigy of the abbot, but there is no evidence for it.[166]

The Wakeman Cenotaph

The only monument at Tewkesbury to have attracted much modern attention is, like the Cheltenham tomb, an abbot's monument, housed at the entrance to one of the ambulatory chapels, continuing the ring of ecclesiastical monuments round the ambulatory. The luxurious 'Wakeman cenotaph' (Fig.13.17) straddles the entrance to the double chapel of SS. Edmund and Dunstan. The superstructure is composed of a trio of niche canopies modelled on those at the west end of the Warwick Chapel, above a pointed multi-cusped arch with pierced spandrels. A heavily moulded ogee arch in the centre of the monument rises from the two lateral piers, and surmounts two arches with irregular pierced tracery and a complex multi-cusped opening between them, terminanting in a central pendant.[167] A cadaver effigy of a tonsured priest (Fig.13.18) rests on a flat table above an openwork screen, comprising three eight-pointed star shapes, and decorated with small shields of the Passion, only four of which remain intact. To the east is a section of Perpendicular traceried screenwork (Fig.13.17, right); another part of the screen has evidently been removed on the western side, as have the statues from the small niches flanking the central screenwork and those in the niches to the east

Fig.13.17 The Wakeman monument, from the ambulatory

and west of the effigy. It seems evident that the monument formed part of a screen which closed off the chapel for the performance of chantry masses, just as did Sir Guy de Bryan's monument to the west. There are no coats of arms or inscriptions to help identify either the monument or the effigy.

From inside the chapel, it can be seen that the screenwork below the cadaver effigy fronts an open recess. This suggests that the monument may have been intended as an example of the double-decker tomb type—like Archbishop Chichele's at Canterbury—with a representation of the deceased in his high social position above an effigy of the decaying corpse. The suggestion that the cadaver was intended to be placed in the lower recess has been rehearsed before. In Lionel Gough's guidebook, for instance, the corpse effigy is claimed to have been originally behind the 'stone screen: the upper slab would have been occupied by the figure of John Wakeman, last Abbot of Tewkesbury, had he died here. But Wakeman surrendered the abbey to King Henry VIII in 1540 and became Bishop of Gloucester'.[168] In this formulation, no other effigy of Abbot, later Bishop, Wakeman was ultimately produced and the monument remained an incomplete cenotaph when he was buried elsewhere. However, it is also possible that a now-missing upper effigy was carved, but later destroyed by iconoclasts—no other abbatial effigies survive intact at Tewkesbury—and the lower, cadaver effigy was subsequently raised onto the table slab. The effigy is covered in 17th-century graffiti, suggesting it was already at this level by the 1620s (Fig.13.18); one graffito, on the left arm, is dated 1625. That the effigy is not in its original position is indicated by the fact that its front surface is entirely made up in modelled concrete. It clearly belonged originally to the lower recess and this side must have been cut back to fit it against the openwork screen.[169] In masking the cadaver from the viewer on the outside of the chapel, the design subtly enhanced its power symbolically. The screen through which the viewer here contemplated the corpse effigy was itself studded with the arms of the Passion: Christ's sacrifice pointed the way to the believer to transcend the death of the body. Inside the chapel, the cadaver was open to the view of the priest at the chantry altar; so the monument evidently had two separate audiences.

Recently, Pamela King re-examined the original meaning of this *transi* effigy.[170] She distinguished between different types of cadaver iconography but believed this example to be unique.[171] It shows a shroud, opened to reveal a corpse with several different vermin crawling on it. King hypothesized that each of the specific creatures represented stood for one of the seven deadly sins; but that two may be missing from the lost right arm or have been otherwise defaced, since there are only five represented.[172] The need to postulate missing extra vermin and

Fig.13.18 Cadaver effigy from the Wakeman monument

the unverifiable claim that each creature stood for a specific sin rather than, for instance, being associated with decomposition and the grave, perhaps undermine these fascinating conjectures.[173] If the effigy did belong in the lower recess, it would have been virtually impossible for even the most attentive spectator to recognize each of the vermin. Their appearance must surely have been more generally keyed to the corruption of the flesh than specifically related to the seven deadly sins. In fact it is the decoration of the openwork screen—in the small, separate, deconstructed elements of the Passion, placed on shields which normally bore secular arms—which is the arena for the viewer's focus on the contemplation of specific symbols (Fig.13.17).

It seems impossible that the monument could be a 15th-century one as is often stated.[174] It is clearly from the phase of Tudor Perpendicular which follows the model of Henry VII's Chapel, Westminster Abbey, in its luxurious virtuoso effects, pierced tracery, layered planes of decoration and tracery style. A date *c*.1510 would be likely if one were judging purely by typology, but a date in the 1520s or 1530s cannot be ruled out.[175] An early tradition, which goes back at least to the time of Bishop Godwin's *De Praesulibus Angliae* of 1616, assigning the effigy to Abbot Wakeman (1534-40), may be correct.[176]

The *memento mori* meaning of the cadaver effigy and the invocation of prayer may not be the only reasons for the popularity of this genre, but they were certainly the most potent, right up to the Reformation.[177] It is perhaps not too fanciful to interpret the unusual iconography of Wakeman's cadaver effigy as obliquely commenting on the earlier figure of Isabel Despenser. Her effigy comprised a unique combination of corpse effigy with saints as intercessory protectors at her head, and her husband's and her own arms at her feet. If the 'realistic' effigy of her corpse was glossed by the monument's concurrent insistence on her rank and status, Wakeman's tomb returned, in a sense, to the origins of the *transi* tomb in England in Archbishop Chichele's monument at Canterbury. What one might term the self-abnegating aspect of the cadaver is even accentuated by the appearance of vermin. However, the meaning of the cadaver effigy, even without an accompanying recumbent figure of the abbot above, has to be construed within the opulence of its architectural context, not divorced from it. The design of the monument with the screened cadaver, seems to have been intended to induce thanatopsic reflection on the part of the viewer outside the chapel—contemplation of the effigy of the decaying corpse to which we are all inevitably reduced—but also reflection on the death of the body in the light of the bodily resurrection in Christ. In a characteristically late medieval manner, the effigy is both emotive and designed to elicit contemplative prayer: its message was forged in the empathetic relationship demanded between the viewer and the deceased, between the living and the dead, mediated via the effigy.[178] So, the work's original meaning was actually situated between the abbot's effigy and the viewer, in the reflective and prayerful processes it evoked.

CHAPTER 14

The Medieval Stained Glass *by* Sarah Brown

The medieval stained glass of Tewkesbury Abbey is among the best-known and most frequently illustrated in England.[1] The windows have attracted the interest of visitors from an early date, largely thanks to the combination of heraldry and figures of secular lords for which they are justifiably famous.[2] Medieval stained glass is preserved in seven choir clerestory windows (I, NII, NIII, NIV, SII, SIII, SIV,

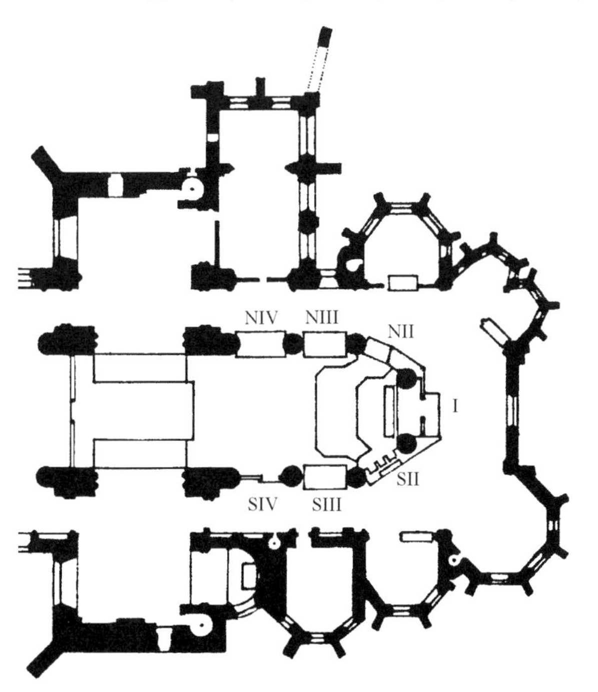

Fig.14.1 The windows of the choir clerestory numbered according to the notation of the Corpus Vitrearum Medii Aevi (CVMA)

Fig.14.1), with a few pieces *in situ* in small tracery openings in the ambulatory chapels and an assemblage of miscellaneous fragments glazed in 1923 into a 'museum' window in the sacristy. The greater part of the glass dates from a single glazing programme of *c.*1340, associated with the beautification of the choir following the completion of the rebuilding campaigns (see Chapter 10). A single figure of an angel and a shield of arms survive from 13th-century building works. A few fragments of painted glass, none of them figurative, were excavated on the site of the demolished 14th-century Lady Chapel, the glazing of which otherwise remains a mystery.[3] The Lady Chapel windows were presumably Marian in character and are thus likely to have been destroyed at the Dissolution, as part of the demolition of the building for which they were made.

The condition and extent of the surviving medieval glass

The condition of the seven choir clerestory windows reflects their chequered history in the years since their creation in the second quarter of the 14th century. It is likely that even in the Middle Ages these windows would have suffered some damage as a consequence of their relative accessibility from clerestory passages. The head of a prophet figure (NII, panel 3b), for example, is in a style distinct from the other heads in the clerestory windows and this may represent a medieval repair.[4] The sharp and sudden decline in demand for stained glass following the Reformation, together with a decline in the expertise of post-Reformation glaziers meant that maintenance of stained glass was often entrusted to relatively unskilled craftsmen, a process which took its toll. From the 1560s onwards new glass was being purchased for the abbey church. In 1566-7 the windows of 'Seyncte Katheryns chappell' were stopped up.[5] In the same year Hiat the mason was paid £45 for the remaking of a chancel window and in the late 1960s Richard Morris recorded ovolo mouldings in window SIV.[6] As the glass in window SIV is relatively well-preserved, if the tracery was indeed remade, it suggests that Robert Collins and his fellow glaziers retained a reasonable level of competence in handling the medieval glass. Between 1572 and 1574 500 feet of new glass, the bulk of it for the chancel, was purchased from Robert Collins and this must have resulted in the loss of most of the glazing of the side chapels.[7] In 1576 the chapels of St. James and St. Nicholas were walled off from the main body of the church for use as a free school, only to be returned to ecclesiastical use in the 19th century.[8] Any medieval figurative glazing is unlikely to have survived this conversion. The fate of any medieval nave glazing is unclear, although on 18 February 1661 the tracery of the west window was blown in, and was completely replaced in 1686.[9]

The earliest account to refer specifically to the releading of old stained glass occurs in the accounts for 1611-15, when John Paynter was paid £6 15s. 1d.[10] The earliest antiquarian description of the glass in the clerestory windows, made in April 1623, suggests that they remained in good order, and the author was able to trick 35 shields in the lower panels without any difficulty.[11] A late 17th-century restoration of the windows, by an unnamed glazier of the town, was recorded by Thomas Dingley, and his account of the glass suggests that some transposition of panels had resulted.[12] The Virgin Mary in the east window, for example, was located in the extreme right-hand light of the window, which cannot have been its original position. The 18th-century churchwardens' accounts record a constant stream of repairs to the east end of the church and its windows, although none of the references are specific as to their location or extent. In the period 1720-22 the sum of £1,792 was spent on repairs to the choir and Rudder and Bigland both record the gift of £50 for window repairs.[13]

Despite this steady flow of expenditure, by the early 19th century the windows had clearly suffered extensive disturbance, particularly in their lower panels. The shields of arms were described as being 'in a wretched state'. In March 1820 Thomas Hodges submitted his accounts for the removal and repair of the choir windows—in fact, the glass had already been removed and the windows boarded up in December 1819.[14] A series of new shields of arms were made, described in 1903 as 'dreadful', while deficiencies in the medieval stained glass were made good with fragments of old glass brought from elsewhere in the church. In 1828 the glazier William Collins of the Strand in London, presumably a descendant of the 16th-century glazier of the same surname, donated new painted heads for the east window figures of the Virgin Mary and St. Michael (Fig.14.2).[15] These, subsequently described as 'glaring blots', have since been removed and have not survived. The somewhat jumbled order in which Hodges left the windows can be seen in the small number of photographs taken before the 1923 restoration.[16]

Lack of funds meant that the medieval windows were omitted from the restoration of 1824-30 and from Scott's restoration of the 1870s, although exterior protective glazing was installed in 1879.[17] Nothing more was done until 1923 when the windows were restored in commemoration of the 800th anniversary of the consecration of the abbey. It is this programme that has determined modern understanding of the windows. The work was undertaken by the London firm of Kempe & Co., under the direction of Walter Tower, nephew of the firm's founder, C.E. Kempe. The eminent stained glass scholar Gordon McNeil Rushforth acted as historical consultant and wrote the article which remains the principal account of the scheme and the main record of the approach adopted by the restorers. This can be augmented by the text of a lecture delivered by Tower to the Society of Antiquaries of London.[18] The restorers laid a number of charges at Thomas Hodges' door, accusing him of careless jumbling of the panels. The Kempe craftsmen removed from the windows any early 19th-century glass, together with any medieval glass believed to be alien to them, fragments now found in the so-called 'museum window' in the sacristy. In fact, it is clear that the restorers mistakenly removed some original glass and

Fig.14.2 The east window, prior to restoration in 1923 and the removal of the painted heads installed in 1828 by William Collins

despite Rushforth's claim to the contrary, undertook some rearrangement of original glass, disrupting authentic medieval cut-lines. Areas of lost glass were made good with modern stippled fragments, emulating the approach first championed by the 19th-century glass historian, Charles Winston.[19] Rushforth's main contribution was probably in the interpretation of the subjects of the windows and at his advice the figures were reordered in the combinations that we see today.

During the Second World War the windows were temporarily removed for safety. Only in 1974 was further conservation undertaken. The glass was cleaned and all but one of the figures (Hugh Despenser in NIV) was releaded. A small number of pinky flesh-toned insertions were removed and new faces were painted for the figures of knights in NIV (the heads of Robert Fitzroy and Gilbert de Clare). The conservation was otherwise conservative, and left the windows as Rushforth and Tower had envisioned them in 1923.[20]

Fig.14.3 The east window. Detail of the damned being led off to torment

The subject matter

At the heart of the scheme is the five-light east window with its twelve-petalled rose tracery, depicting the Last Judgement, surmounted by the Coronation of the Virgin surrounded by angel musicians (Pl.21). In the main lights is Christ the Judge displaying his five wounds and enthroned on a rainbow. On Christ's right hand is the Virgin Mary, also seated on a rainbow, whilst on His left hand stands St. Michael, holding a shield now filled with miscellaneous fragments. St. John the Baptist, so often occupying this position, has been consigned to one of the rather cramped groups of apostles in the first light (light a) and can be identified by his camel-hair robe and the *Agnus Dei* he holds. A second group of apostles is depicted in the fifth light (light e). Among the apostles St. Peter, St. Paul and probably St. John the Evangelist can also be identified. Beneath the feet of the Judge and His heavenly companions are scenes of the general resurrection and the division of the resurrected souls into the saved and the damned. Angels with trumpets summon the dead to rise from their tombs, their shrouds slipping from their shoulders. On Christ's right hand the saved are led to paradise by angels, while the damned are driven to the left by an angel with a flaming sword reminiscent of the expulsion of Adam and Eve from the garden of Eden. They are duly dragged off in chains by a grotesque demon (Fig.14.3). In the extreme right-hand panel is the kneeling naked figure of a woman, her hands raised in prayer, presumed to be the donor of the window, represented as a penitent soul at the feet of the Divine Judge (Fig.14.5).

The heavenly company is extended into the side windows of the choir. The south-east, south, north-east and north windows (SII, SIII, NII and NIII) contain figures of prophets and kings from the Old Testament (Pl.22). These figures were originally labelled with inscriptions in Lombardic capitals, of which only eight legible names remain. The number of prophets considerably outnumber the four kings, so the restorers were

Fig.14.4 Window SIV.
William, Lord Zouche of Richard's Castle (d.1337) and three de Clare earls of Gloucester and Hertford

undoubtedly correct in placing a king in the central light of each window, with two pairs of prophets on either side.

The outermost window on each side (SIV, Fig.14.4, and NIV), depict successive secular lords of Tewkesbury, from the abbey's founder, Robert Fitzhamon (d.1107, Pl.23), through Robert Fitzroy (d.1147), the three de Clare earls of Gloucester, to the notorious Hugh Despenser the Younger (ex.1326, Pl.24), whose family helped to promote the ambitious remodelling of the abbey church (see further Chapter 10). The most recent figure to be represented in the gallery of Tewkesbury's secular lords was William, Lord Zouche of Richard's Castle (d.1337), second husband of Despenser's widow, Eleanor de Clare. The figures can be identified by the armorial bearings on the heraldic surcoats worn over their armour.

The enigma of the 'donor' figure

Rushforth and the 1923 restorers were particularly intrigued by the naked female figure with hands raised in prayer, now positioned in the bottom right-hand corner of the east window (Fig.14.5). They identified her as Eleanor de Clare (d.1337), widow of Hugh II Despenser and William Zouche and assumed her to be the donor of the windows. The figure is undoubtedly female—the naked breast can be glimpsed below the raised left arm. The nakedness of the figure is

Fig.14.5 The east window. The naked figure of a female ?donor, possibly Eleanor de Clare (d.1337)

certainly suggestive of an association with the depiction of the Last Judgement. There are, however, reasons for questioning these assumptions and the positioning of the panel in the base of the east window. In the late 17th century Thomas Dingley was able to recognise quite clearly the small figures in the east window's traceried head and described the contents of its main lights in some detail. He made no mention of the 'donor' figure and instead described the depiction of the damned that now occupies the bottom right-hand panel.

The figure has been restored. Her lower arms and her legs from below the knee have been replaced, although the angle of her thighs suggests that her kneeling posture is authentic. While her posture and her nakedness are thus suggestive of a figure present at the Last Judgement, the scale of the figure and its framing makes for an uncomfortable fit in its present location. The banded background to the figure is a unique design in a window that otherwise employs balanced and repeated background designs. The use of a backdrop not otherwise found in the east window may not, of itself, be sufficient reason to 'depose' the figure from the window; the figure of Robert Fitzhamon in NIV also has a distinctive background, presumably to give honour to a founder figure (Pl.23). The fact remains, however, that the figure fits uncomfortably into its panel, a fact acknowledged by Rushforth, even though he then dismissed the possibility that the panel was an insertion. The background has been patched and heavily restored, especially along the left-hand edge of the panel, where miscellaneous unrelated architectural fragments have been inserted. The woman's head is uncomfortably close to the panel's upper edge. All four other figurative panels in this row are framed under an arch and are divided from the heavenly 'zone' above by a pronounced battlemented parapet (Fig.14.3). Its omission in the 'donor' panel is a conspicuous break in the symmetry of the window's otherwise balanced design and is a further reason for caution in accepting Rushforth's attribution.

These observations have implications for the identity of this figure, suggesting that either it does not represent Eleanor de Clare, or that the figure is Eleanor, but does not belong in the east window and perhaps not in the clerestory at all. An alternative female candidate worthy of consideration is Elizabeth Montacute, Eleanor's daughter-in-law, whose family heraldry appears in the clerestory windows (see below). It is very unlikely, however, that a naked figure in this position would have been conceived during the lifetime of the person depicted. Elizabeth survived her husband Hugh III Despenser (d.1349), marrying Guy de Bryan, whose arms appear in the vault of the central tower. She died on 31 May 1359.[21] On stylistic grounds the 'donor' figure is unlikely to be this late in date. The possibility that the figure originated elsewhere in the abbey cannot de discounted. On the basis of the few remaining *in situ* fragments, it is clear that the ambulatory chapels were glazed in the same period, although we know nothing of their content. The 'donor' figure remains a tantalizing enigma.

The heraldry

The aspect of the glazing which has consistently attracted the attention of antiquarian visitors to the abbey from the 17th century onwards is the display of heraldry. A shield of arms was positioned in the base panel of each light, each shield framed in a cusped quatrefoil and set into diamond quarries (Fig.14.6). Only four shields survive out of a possible 33, although the 1623 description enables the scheme to be reconstructed with some confidence. The heraldic surcoats of the knights have also attracted notice and heraldic devices decorate the outer borders of some of the lights as well.

While some of the families represented by the heraldry were of sufficient local and indeed national importance to be included in almost every stained glass heraldic display of the period, closer examination reveals that a high proportion of the shields allude specifically to the dynastic alliances of successive lords of Tewkesbury and to the de Clares and Despensers in particular.[22] A few examples will suffice. The arms of Berkeley, originally in the east window, might reasonably

Fig.14.6 The east window.
The arms of Munchensi (barry of 12 argent and azure), recorded in window SIV in 1623

be expected in every Gloucestershire display of the first half of the 14th century. There were, however, specific connections to both the de Clares and Despensers. In 1316 Isabel de Clare married Maurice de Berkeley, while in 1338 his grandson, also Maurice, married Elizabeth Despenser.[23] In 1270 the marriage of Roese de Clare, daughter of Richard de Clare, brought about an alliance with the Mowbrays, whose arms appeared on the south side of the clerestory.[24] The husbands of Eleanor de Clare's sisters, Hugh Audley and Roger d'Amory, were also included.[25] The Despenser arms formerly appeared twice in the east window, flanking the arms of the king in the centre light. Many of the shields displayed had been chosen to emphasise the more advantageous connections of the family. The Despensers, while certainly noble, were not especially distinguished or prominent before the 14th century. The transformation of the family's fortunes and status had been occasioned by the meteoric rise of Hugh Despenser the Elder, created earl of Winchester by Edward II, and the advantageous marriage of his son, Hugh the Younger, to Eleanor de Clare in 1306. Through his wife, Hugh acquired the largest portion of the de Clare inheritance following the death of her brother at the Battle of Bannockburn in 1314, taking possession of it in 1317.[26] The creation of a 'Despenser mausoleum' had been a major impulse in the transformation of the architecture of the abbey's eastern arm.

By the time the windows were being installed, another Despenser lord, Hugh III, son of Hugh and Eleanor (Fig.3.3), held the principal manor and would have been looked to for patronage and protection. The arms of Beauchamp of Warwick, for example, were probably included as a reference to his maternal great grandfather.[27] The arms of Hastings probably refer to the marriage of Isabel, Hugh's aunt, to Sir John de Hastings.[28] Some of the alliances alluded to were of more recent vintage. In 1330 both William de la Zouche and his step-son, Hugh Despenser, had been implicated in a plot instigated by Edmund, earl of Kent, whose arms were displayed in a choir clerestory window.[29] The arms of de Warenne and Fitzalan are probably in reference to the marriage of Isabella Despenser to Richard Fitzalan, earl of Arundel, whose mother was Alice de Warenne.[30]

This does not mean, however, that the heraldry was exclusively concerned with the fortunes of the de Clares and Despensers. The arms of several prominent local families were also included. Thomas of Bradestone, for example, was constable of Gloucester Castle in 1330 and again between 1338 and 1360.[31] The Tracys of Stanway, retainers of the Berkeleys, held the manor of Toddington near Hailes, while the Bures family held Boddington manor between Tewkesbury and Winchcombe.[32] Whether the inclusion of these shields reflects donations to the fabric will probably never be known.

The date and patronage of the glazing

The first phase of the rebuilding of the eastern arm extended from *c.*1315 to *c.*1328, with work resumed in the early 1330s, following the political rehabilitation of the Despenser family, to which period the clerestory belongs (see further Chapter 10). The inclusion of historical figures in the glazing scheme is immediately helpful in dating it. The inclusion of a figure of William de la Zouche, whom Eleanor de Clare married without royal license early in 1329, means that the scheme cannot have been conceived before that date, and probably only after the couple were reconciled with the king in January 1331, with their confiscated lands, including Tewkesbury, restored to them.[33] The inclusion of Zouche in the heavenly realm would have been inconceivable before his death on 28 February 1337. The fact that the gallery of lords goes no further, places its installation before the death of Eleanor's son, Hugh, in 1349.

The heraldry is even more instructive, confirming that the glazing was installed either immediately as the building was completed or very soon afterwards, and certainly by 1340. This is rather earlier than the date of *c.*1340-44, proposed by Rushforth in his 1924 article, a chronology quoted in all accounts of the glazing published since.[34] Rushforth's discussion of the heraldry relied on a second-hand 19th-century transcript of a lost and supposedly earlier antiquarian account reproduced in James Bennett's *History of Tewkesbury*.[35] Rushforth's estimate of the date hinged on his assertion that the display included the quartered arms of England, as adopted by Edward III in 1340.[36] A single surviving quarter of this shield is now located in the east window. However, the 1623 description of the heraldry makes it clear that the only royal arms in the choir clerestory windows were those in use before 1340.[37] The fragment of a quartered coat in the east window is not, in fact, original to the clerestory glazing scheme and is painted in a different style. Rushforth's cut-off date was based on the dissolution of the marriage of Isabella Despenser and Richard Fitzalan, in December 1344.

Other shields also confirm a date of before 1340. A number of those commemorated had died by the time the windows were installed. Edmund Woodstock, earl of Kent, for example, had died in 1330 and his heir, a minor, died in the following year.[38] John of Eltham, earl of Cornwall died in 1336 and Thomas de Brotherton, earl of Norfolk, died in 1338.[39] The posthumous depiction of heraldry is, of course, well attested in medieval art. Perhaps more significant for dating the glass are the arms of Hastings, which were changed to a quartered form when Laurence Hastings was made earl of Pembroke in February 1339.[40] Of greatest interest is the inclusion of the arms of Grandison and of Montacute. This is surely a reference to the parentage of Elizabeth Montacute, daughter of William de Montacute and Katherine de Grandison. Elizabeth married III Hugh Despenser, son of Eleanor and Hugh Despenser the Younger. Elizabeth's first husband (Sir Giles Badlesmere) only died in the late spring or early summer (sometime between 7 April and 22 June) of 1338 and she would have been unable to remarry for 12 months after his death, early in the summer of 1339 at the earliest.[41] She had certainly become Hugh III's wife by 27 April 1341.[42]

As discussed above, since 1923 the scheme has been attributed to the patronage of Eleanor de Clare and the so-called 'donor portrait' has been identified as an image of Eleanor herself. Despite the appearance of both of Eleanor's husbands in the stained glass, there are reasons for questioning this 'donor portrait' as an original feature of the east window, and the role of the abbot and monks of Tewkesbury in its conception cannot be discounted. A shield of arms of the abbey survives in the east window and in their subject matter the windows serve a monastic agenda. This shield, although of glass of *c.*1340, is slightly smaller than its companions. This difference might be explained by the loss of a bordure, a device often added to the arms of a cathedral or abbey to denote the arms of a bishop or abbot, in this case, perhaps, denoting Abbot John Coles.

Fig.14.7 The east window. Christ displays his wounds

The message and the meaning

The seven windows represent a coherent iconographic scheme, one in which traditional subjects have been subtly altered to accommodate new devotional images. The Last Judgement in the east window has been given a particular Eucharistic significance appropriate to its position directly above the high altar. The seated figure of Christ (Fig.14.7) displays his five wounds (the prominent wound in his side, formerly revealed through a gap in his tunic, has since been replaced by a restorer's insertion of green glass). Devotion to the wounds of Christ was increasingly important in late medieval Europe, as a response to His human suffering. The most spectacular example of this devotional empathy was, of course, St. Francis's receipt of the stigmata. The wounds served as a reminder of Christ's redeeming sacrifice, commemorated in the Mass. The side wound was of particular significance in an Eucharistic context, for from it flowed a mixture of blood and water, recalling the mixing of wine and water in the Mass. At Tewkesbury an emphasis on the wounds may have received particular encouragement from the proximity of the Cistercian abbey of Hailes, a building to which the plan of Tewkesbury's east end was indebted. Hailes possessed an important relic of the Holy Blood, the gift in 1267 of Edmund of Cornwall, son of the founder, Richard, earl of Cornwall, brother of Henry III.[43]

Christ the Judge was commonly accompanied by the Virgin Mary, normally seated on His right hand, as in the Tewkesbury east window (Pl.21, Fig.14.8). Her role as heavenly intercessor at the Last Judgement was well established by the end of the 13th century. In the Psalter of William de Brailes, for example, she intercedes together with St. John the Evangelist. It is this role that is emphasized here and it is hardly surprising that the saint to whom the abbey church was dedicated should be given particular prominence in its principal window. However, the designer has included a further dramatic and uncommon detail, for the Virgin has bared her breasts, which she offers to her Son as a reminder of her special

Fig.14.8 The east window.
The Virgin Mary as heavenly intercessor

status as His earthly mother and her rights to claim pre-eminence as a heavenly intercessor. This motif was established in England by *c*.1280, included in manuscripts such as the Huth Psalter (British Library Add MS 38116, fol.13v.) and the early 14th-century Queen Mary Psalter (British Library MS Royal 2.B.VII, fol.302v).[44] It also features at the base of the Hereford Cathedral *Mappa Mundi* of *c*.1280-90.[45] It appeared in wall paintings at an early date. A mid-13th-century depiction in St. John's church in Winchester has been lost, but 14th-century examples survive at Chalgrove (Oxon.) and Ickleton (Cambs.).[46] This is probably its earliest appearance in English stained glass. Thus, by the middle of the 14th century the Virgin Mary has been elevated by virtue of her motherhood to the role of 'Maria Mediatrix'. In the *Speculum Humanae Salvationis* (The Mirror of Man's Salvation), composed *c*.1310-24, the Virgin and Christ are jointly celebrated as intercessors, defending mankind from God's wrath, she offering her breasts, He his wounds: in the words of the 15th-century Middle English translation of the Latin text:

> Christ to his Fadere shewes his cicatrices for mercy,
> And til hyre son hire bristes shewes for us swete Marie.[47]

It would be usual for the Virgin to be matched on Christ's left hand by St. John the Baptist. As has been noted, however, in this window the Baptist has been relegated to one of the outer lights, where he can be identified among the apostles. This adjustment is in order to accommodate a full-length figure of an angel, probably St. Michael, who supports a shield (Fig.14.9). Although now filled with miscellaneous restorers' fragments, it is clear from Dingley's 17th-century account that this was originally the shield of the Passion, the *Arma Christi*, a shield on which the instruments associated with Christ's passion were displayed.[48] A fragment of what is undoubtedly the original shield, with the handles of two scourges, is preserved in the 'museum window'. The instruments of the Passion were

Fig.14.9 The east window.
The archangel Michael supporting a shield, flanked by a group of apostles and St. Paul

'signs' of Christ's authority as Judge and were commonly depicted around Him in 12th- and 13th-century depictions of the Last Judgement.[49] The gathering of the instruments onto a shield was a relatively new departure, although perhaps not surprising given the ubiquity of heraldic display by the end of the 13th century.[50] It was not uncommon for heraldic devices to be attributed to the saints and to Christ himself and the *Arma Christi* had received papal sanction at the Council of Lyons in 1245. Probably its earliest appearance in England was in a Franciscan context, engraved on the seal die of the vice-warden of the Cambridge Grey Friars of *c*.1300.[51] The earliest datable English manuscript example is found in Walter of Milemete's illuminated copy of Pseudo-Aristotle's *De Secretis Secretorum*, made *c*.1326-7 for the young Prince Edward (BL Add Ms 47680, fol.14).

The representation in the east window of Tewkesbury Abbey must have been one of the earliest images in a monumental medium, and is certainly the earliest surviving in English stained glass. This would explain the somewhat awkward reordering of the standard iconography of the Last Judgement and its inclusion perhaps reflects a personal devotion on the part of one of those involved in the window's creation. The *Arma Christi* became inextricably linked with the concept of protection, even gazing on it conferred spiritual benefit. Indulgences were soon attached to it and scraps of parchment bearing its image were carried as talismans. It is no accident that this image in the east window is borne on a shield carried by St. Michael, for in Jacobus de Voragine's *Legenda Aurea*, the archangel is described in chivalric terms as Christ's standard bearer, 'and it is he who will present the cross, the nails, the spear, and the crown of thorns at the Day of Judgement'.[52]

Prophets and kings in windows SII, SIII, NII and NIII, Christ's ancestors and those who foretold His birth and ministry, are witnesses to the Last Judgement (Pl.22, Fig.14.10).[53] Figures like these have a long pedigree in this sort of elevated position in the windows of a monastic choir. The clerestory windows of the eastern arm of Canterbury Cathedral, for example, originally accommodated over 80 such figures, glazed *c*.1180-1200.[54] This is a theme frequently explored in a Tree of Jesse, and while the Tewkesbury figures are framed in architectural niches, vine foliage is copiously used to fill the tracery openings. The concept of lineage and descent is continued in the south-west and north-west windows (SIV and NIV), probably the best-known of the Tewkesbury windows, with their figures of successive secular lords under canopies. This is not, strictly speaking, a family

Fig.14.10 Window NII. King Solomon accompanied by four prophets, including Jeremiah and Joel

tree, although it has genealogical overtones, being an account of the legitimate descent of the lordship of Tewkesbury. This theme, of the uninterrupted descent of legitimate secular authority, would have had considerable appeal following the upheaval of the early years of Edward III's reign. While there is no suggestion that these are saintly figures, they are represented on the same scale and in the same heavenly zone as the sacred figures in the adjoining windows.

As lords of Tewkesbury and benefactors of the abbey, those depicted would have been commemorated in the daily prayers of the monks celebrating the offices in the choir below. Seven of the eight figures represented in the windows (Robert Fitzhamon [Pl.23], Gilbert I de Clare, Richard II de Clare, Gilbert II de Clare, Gilbert III de Clare, Hugh II Despenser [Pl.24] and William de la Zouche [Fig.14.4]) were all buried in the abbey church, four of them in the choir and directly beneath the windows.[55] Analogy may be drawn with the treatment of tomb-chests of the period, such as the lost paintings of armoured knights holding spears decorating the tomb-chest of Edmund Crouchback, earl of Lancaster (d.1296) in Westminster Abbey.[56] A number of other monastic churches contained a similar display of figures of benefactors—in the 14th-century Lady Chapel of St. Augustine's Abbey at Bristol of *c*.1340-50; in the mid-14th-century choir glazing of St. Peter's Abbey in Gloucester; in the Augustinian church of St. Mary Overie in London and in the Augustinian priory church at Warrington (Lancs.), for example.[57] These schemes underline the importance of stained glass as a vehicle for historical record, a striking and monumental expression of the written chronicle. In the early 16th century a similar series of images of abbey benefactors were depicted in the illuminated Founders' Book and it is likely that the windows were an important source for the compilers of this book (see Chapter 6).[58]

The windows thus served as a repository of memory, holding the images of the abbey's greatest benefactors in the minds and prayers of the monks in perpetuity. They were both an acknowledgement of past patronage but also a promise to future patrons. While images of Hugh III Despenser (d.1349) and his successors could not be accommodated in the clerestory windows, their monuments continued to be made for positions in the choir.

The Glass-Painters

No documentary sources survive to identify the team of glass-painters responsible for the Tewkesbury clerestory windows. Examination of the craftsmanship leaves no doubt that it was one of the leading ateliers of the day.

The windows contain ample evidence of economical and well-ordered working methods and in particular the use of the glaziers' tables described by Theophilus in the 12th century, an example of which survives in the cathedral treasury at Gerona in Catalonia.[59] While the scheme necessitated a unique design for the east window, the other six windows were executed from a limited range of cartoons, skilfully deployed in such a way that this is not immediately apparent. This is particularly true of the windows depicting the prophets and kings (SII-SIII and NII-NIII). Of the four kings, two are from the same cartoon. For a total of 16 prophet figures, 13 of which are substantially medieval, five cartoons are used. The armoured figures in SIV and NIV are also drawn from small variants of the same basic cartoon.

This is not to suggest that the glass-painters were cutting corners. The cartoons are executed with variations of palette and posture, and the repetition of figure designs ensures that the windows have a balanced and harmonious rhythm. There are numerous instances in which the labour-intensive nature of glass-painting is demonstrated to good effect. Amongst the decorative elements, for example, seven intricate rinceau designs are used as backdrops to the figures, and eight different border motifs are employed. Many aspects of the glass such as extensive back-painting, are well-nigh invisible once the panels were installed at height—there is extensive back-painting, for example, a detail visible only when

Fig.14.11 Window NII. Detail of the head of the prophet Jeremiah c.*1340*

Fig.14.12 Bristol, former abbey church of St. Augustine. Lady Chapel east window, head of a prophet, c.*1340-50*

the panels are examined at close quarters. Without it, however, the windows would be diminished in their impact, a fact well-understood by these masters of the glass-painters' craft.

There is little doubt that the glass-painters were locally based. The stylistic similarities between Tewkesbury and glazing schemes at nearby St. Augustine's Abbey in Bristol (Fig.14.12) and St. Peter's Abbey in Gloucester have long been appreciated, although the Tewkesbury windows can now be demonstrated to be earlier in date than both of these other major west-country glazing schemes.[60]

Conclusion

The Tewkesbury choir clerestory glazing is a sophisticated and subtle blend of devotional imagery and history. It is indebted to both the background of current devotional literature and the long-standing tradition of monastic chronicle. It presented an image of the monastic choir and its community under the spiritual protection of Christ and His holy mother, and the secular patronage and protection of the lords of this world.

CHAPTER 15

The Medieval Floor Tiles *by* Alan Vince

A moderate quantity of floor tiles survive at Tewkesbury Abbey. Some are still *in situ* but most are either relaid or loose. They provide some indication of the former wealth of the abbey's internal furnishings, but it is clear that the majority has been lost. Excavations outside the church in the 1940s and again in the 1990s have produced tile types not previously known from the abbey and it is likely that further excavation would allow a more balanced view.

Academic interest in medieval floor tiles in the Severn valley began in the mid-19th century, stimulated not only by the upsurge of interest in all things Gothic but specifically by the discovery of tile kilns at Great Malvern[1] and Droitwich.[2] The recording of tile designs also started in the 19th century. Early published records tend to have been idealized and, in any case, published at too small a scale for individual dies to be identified. An exception, however, is a note by Hall.[3] This paper forms our first definite evidence for the history of the abbey's floor tiles. Subsequently, the tiles of Gloucestershire have been systematically recorded by Anne Kellock.[4] This work has been undertaken as part of the Census of Medieval Floor Tiles, supported by the British Academy, but is not yet in print. This chapter is therefore an interim statement on the Tewkesbury tiles and, hopefully, one day will be surpassed by the sort of study which is now available for Wales.[5]

Traditionally, floor tile studies were based almost entirely on the designs and the dies used to produce them. This allowed the assignment of tiles to art historical 'schools' and the charting of influence of the work of one group of tilers on another. The recognition of wear and breakage on the dies and the subsequent replacement of one die by another could be used to establish the order of production of different pavements. However, such methods could not distinguish between the movement of tiles and the movement of tilers, and if a previously unknown die was found it was not possible to do more than hazard a guess as to its makers. The use of ceramic petrology and chemical analysis of clays, however, has provided another dimension to this study. For the Great Malvern school, for example, a study of the fabric of the tile can now differentiate between a tile made at Great Malvern[6] and one decorated with a Great Malvern die but made elsewhere, at for example Lenton Priory (Notts.).

The Tewkesbury floor tiles

There were until recently four separate tile pavements in the abbey. The first pavement is that which surrounds the monument to the founder of the abbey in the Founder's Chapel (Fig.15.1). This chapel is ascribed to the late 14th century and the tiles themselves are consistent with this date. Furthermore, apart from a few clear areas of repair it seems that this pavement has not been relaid and preserves its original layout. As such it is an important cornerstone in the chronology of

Fig.15.1 Floor tiles in the Founder's Chapel

14th-century floor tile use in the Severn valley, comparable to that provided by the Singing School pavement at Worcester Cathedral[7] which was constructed in the 1370s. The tiles were laid diagonally and include heraldic panels consisting of four tiles making up the arms of the founder. A single fleur-de-lys pattern was used alternating with these panels (Fig.15.1).

The second pavement is that in the Warwick Chapel which was constructed in the 1420s or early 1430s.[8] The tiles here have undergone more wear and substantial areas of the pavement have been replaced or relaid (Fig.15.2). Nevertheless, the original design survives. It, too, was laid diagonally, but consisted of panels of 16 tiles alternating with panels of four repeating tiles. The central tile of the 16-tile pattern is not that originally designed as part of this set, but a rose. Whether this was substituted at the time the pavement was laid and, if so, whether this was because of damage to the original die or to some symbolic significance of the rose to the family is unknown. However, no example of the missing centre design survives in the pavement, either *in situ* or relaid and it is fairly certain that it was never present.

The third pavement used to lie in the Trinity Chapel (Fig.15.3), but was removed and replaced

Fig.15.2 Floor tiles in the Warwick Chapel

by a stone floor in 1982-83.[9] The tiles were laid at right-angles to the chapel walls and were heavily worn, so that it was unclear whether they had ever been decorated. Furthermore, the floor had been disturbed so that it was not apparent whether the tiles formed part of the original pavement of the chapel or were inserted later.

The fourth pavement, which may be a medieval pavement still *in situ*, lies in the Clarence vault in the east bay of the ambulatory (Fig.4.4). The decorated tiles are laid in a cross with arms only one-tile wide, which results in tiles originally designed for 4- or 16-tile patterns being used out of context. This might suggest that the arrangement is post-medieval, which is

Fig.15.3 West half of the pavement in the Trinity Chapel before its removal in 1982-3

Assemblages of medieval patterned floor tiles, relaid at various locations in the abbey

Plate 18. Details of the tile pavement in the nave south aisle

Plate 19. Tile pavement in the south choir aisle

Plate 20. Tile pavement in the south transept

The 14th-century stained glass of the choir clerestory (this page and opposite)
Plate 21. The east window. The Last Judgement and the Coronation of the Virgin Mary

Plate 22. Window SII. King Rehoboam accompanied by four prophets

Plate 23 Window NIV. Robert Fitzhamon (d.1107), founder of the abbey

Plate 24 Window NIV. Hugh II Despenser, 'the younger' (ex.1326)

Plate 25. Modern stained glass by Tom Denny window in St. John the Baptist's Chapel, commemorating the 900th anniversary of the arrival of monks from Cranborne (2002)

Plate 26. Christ in Majesty from the Victorian stained glass of the great west window, by Hardman of Birmingham (1886)

certainly a possibility, but a 'variegated pavement' of decorated 'bricks' was observed when the vault was partly opened in 1826, and the cross pattern was reported in existence when the vault was reopened in 1876.[10] As far as can be ascertained, the tiles would fit a date in the 1470s when the vault was created: the heraldic designs include the arms of the Newburgh earls of Warwick.[11]

Our knowledge of the medieval choir and sanctuary pavements is based on very limited evidence with regard to surviving tiles. During the investigation of the foundations of the tomb-chest of Hugh III Despenser in 1993, a decorated floor tile was discovered *ex situ* about 15cm below the 19th-century sanctuary pavement (Fig.15.4). It seems that the tile was part of a 16-tile pattern and possibly of early to mid-14th-centry date.[12] An invaluable source of information is Hall, who describes how decorated floor tiles were discovered in 1875 in the choir and that those tiles, together with others found at the same time, were used as models for the new floor tiles, made by Godwin of Lugwardine (Pl.16).[13] Hall illustrates 30 of these designs, together with the four-tile coat of arms from the Founder's Chapel (Fig.15.5). With one exception, the earliest of these are likely to be of mid 14th-century date but the majority are of the later 14th to early 15th century and some of an even later date.

It can be surmised, therefore, that if the choir had been tiled in the early/mid 14th century this

Fig.15.4 The decorated floor tile, to the left of Hugh III Despenser's tomb-chest, as found during the restoration of 1992-3

floor was comprehensively removed and the area retiled. Examples of mid-15th and later 15th/early 16th-century tiles were also included in Hall's note and these probably indicate limited reflooring during those periods, perhaps associated with the insertion of monuments or chapels.

A patch of relaid tiles in a tomb recess in the south choir aisle (Pl.19; Masterplan, H) is composed mainly of well-preserved square tiles of similar dimensions (10-13cm square), which include several of the designs published by Hall (Fig.15.5). These are probably tiles discovered in the area in 1875. It includes a few plain, dark glazed tiles.

There are further patches of relaid tiles in two recesses: at the west end of the nave south aisle and in the west wall of the south transept (Pls.18, 20; Masterplan, K, N). Hall mentions two tiles which were found too late for incorporation into Godwin's floor, and one of these was said to be 'in a recess on the west side of the Norman chapel in the south transept'. Although complete tiles are present, these collections are much more fragmentary than those relaid in the choir and include fragments of larger early to mid-14th-century tiles, made for quarries ranging between 16 and 19cm square. The low frequency of complete tiles in these patches suggests that they were recovered from rubble rather than intact pavements.

A group of loose heraldic tiles in the abbey collection has been established as coming from an early 14th-century step in the now demolished Lady Chapel (Fig.15.6).[14] They appear to have been discovered in 1940 and from the absence of this type in other collections it is likely that they were never disturbed, merely buried. Other tiles in this collection show signs of wear and had been used as flooring, whereas the heraldic tiles had been set vertically. Some, if not all, of these tiles probably also came from the excavations on the eastern Lady Chapel site and were mainly also of 14th-century date.

Finally, a collection of tiles was recovered by Gloucestershire County Council's Archaeology Service in 1992 at Abbey Meadow (see Chapter 12).[15] Whether these tiles were once laid in the church or in one or more of the other abbey

Fig.15.5:
A, Late 13th- / early 14th-century Nash Hill?
B and C, Mid-14th-century Droitwich-type?
D and E, Late 14th-century Droitwich type?
F and G, Late 14th-century Droitwich-type from the Founder's Chapel (F is a 4-tile pattern);
H, I and J, Mid- to late 15th-century Great Malvern tiles;
K, L, M, N, O, Late 15th- to early 16th-century Canynges-type tiles;
P, Q and R, ?16th-century Malvern Chase tiles (none extant)

All drawings are taken from those made by H. Hall in 1904 of tiles found c.1875. They are not to scale buildings is unknown. They add to the range of types known from the abbey, however, and serve to emphasize how partial our knowledge of the abbey's floor tiles still is.

Tile Groups

There are no floor tiles known from Tewkesbury Abbey which date to the 12th or 13th centuries. Such tiles occur elsewhere in the region, for example the relief-decorated tiles at Abbey Dore (Herefs.)[16] which are probably late 12th- or early 13th-century, or the tiles of the Wessex School from Hailes Abbey which might date from its foundation in the 1240s. Hailes, together with Evesham, Halesowen and sites in Warwickshire, also produced tiles of late 13th-/early 14th-century date of the Chertsey-Halesowen school: Chatwin listed Bordesley Abbey (Worcs.) and Coventry, Kenilworth, Maxstoke and Tanworth in Arden in Warwickshire.[17] Similarly, there is a group of tiles known from Gloucester and sites further south in the Severn valley and Severn estuary which is not represented at Tewkebury, of which the best-known example is at Cleeve Abbey (Som.).[18] Ward-Perkins argued for a late 13th-century date for this group, on the basis of the heraldry, and this is consistent with the sites in which the tiles were found. It would appear, therefore, that Tewkesbury Abbey was not in the forefront of floor tile use in the region.

Probably the earliest group of tiles known from the abbey is a group found in the 1992 excavations which are identified as coming from the Nash Hill tilery, at Lacock (Wilts). This tilery seems to have been established in the late 13th century and belongs to the Wessex School whose early products were made at Clarendon (Wilts.) for use in the royal palace in the 1240s and 1250s. However, again, heraldry suggests that the Nash Hill tilery began several decades later than this and probably continued well into the 14th century.[19] In the Severn valley Nash Hill tiles have been found at the Blackfriars house in Gloucester as well as at various sites in Wales and the Marches, probably all supplied via Bristol (for example, Goodrich Castle, Herefs.). The Tewkesbury fragments are too small to establish the patterns or dies used but include pieces scored before firing and snapped into small squares and triangles for use in borders. This suggests that the Tewkesbury pavement was probably quite elaborate and laid out in panels orthogonal to the walls of the building. A single design which is probably from this group was published by Hall in 1904 (Fig.15.5A). It consists of a griffon within a circular band with fleurs-de-lys in the corners.[20]

The heraldic tiles from the east end of the church have been studied in detail elsewhere.[21] They were probably made in Herefordshire, perhaps at Hereford itself, although the heraldic designs seem to relate to a Despenser marriage held at Ludlow Castle in the early 1320s. The collection of heraldic tiles at Abbey Dore, by contrast, represents a much earlier group of heraldry, probably from a roll drawn up in the 1260s or 1270s. This is extremely unlikely to be

Fig.15.6 Heraldic tiles from the former eastern Lady Chapel, in old showcases in the nave (c.1980)

the actual date of manufacture of the tiles, however, since the non-heraldic tiles from Abbey Dore were clearly based on designs used in the Chertsey-Halesowen school *c*.1300. They probably represent the output of the industry in the first two decades of the 14th century and the absence of similar non-heraldic designs at Tewkesbury suggests that all the Tewkesbury Abbey examples post-date the early 1320s. Mostly, these were 4-tile patterns based loosely on Chertsey-Halesowen designs, such as those known from Kenilworth and Maxstoke priories (Warwks.). Such tiles are present in the abbey collection and in the relaid nave aisle pavement. At Bredon parish church (Worcs.) and St. Oswald's Priory in Gloucester the heraldic risers were accompanied by a pavement consisting of 12 panels, each of which had a circular central tile surrounded by four square tiles with a quarter-circle cutout bearing the name of the month in Lombardic script. Another tile of this group is now relaid in the wall of the parish church at Colwall (Herefs.) where presumably another pavement of this type once existed. No tiles of this group have been found at Tewkesbury.

At least one heraldic tile from the abbey collection was produced in a clay containing abundant fragments of Malvernian rock. This group seems to have been made at Hanley Castle (Worcs.) in the Malvern Chase, between Great Malvern and Upton on Severn, where there was already a thriving pottery and roof tile production centre. Only one pavement constructed entirely from these Malvern Chase tiles survives, at the Greyfriars in Gloucester. Some of the tiles used there were stamped with crude copies of the original dies and presumably they date from a period after the closure of the Herefordshire tilery. Without examination of broken edges it is not possible to say whether any of the relaid early to mid-14th-century tiles are from this source, but the quality of the design cutting suggests that most were of the earlier type.

The 1992 excavations in abbey meadow produced a group of 40 Malvern Chase tiles. Only one of these was definitely of this Herefordshire-related type and the remainder included a number of tiles with a quarry size of *c*.14cm compared with the 16.5cm square size of the Bredon-type tiles. Tiles of this size and fabric occur widely in the Severn valley and are probably of slightly later date, say 14th to 15th century. Some had been scored diagonally and snapped into large triangles whereas small border tiles were used with the Bredon-type tiles; although none are known from Tewkesbury Abbey.

The two main pavements in the abbey are both paved with Droitwich-type tiles. This tile factory is named after the tile kiln found at Droitwich, but it is likely that the centre of the industry was in Worcester, which documentary sources indicate had a large and successful medieval tile industry, although those documents do not specify that floor tiles were amongst its output. The Founder's Chapel pavement (Fig.15.1) is typologically amongst the middle products of the industry, produced in the late 14th and early 15th centuries, whereas the Warwick Chapel pavement is typical of the latest known products, of mid- to late 15th-century date.

The earliest tiles made in this industry, judging by their typology, were small—only 10cm square—and decorated with a range of designs used in the later 13th century in the London area (the Westminster Tiler group). However, they are also found at Worcester Cathedral Singing School in the later 14th century, although they may have been reused from an earlier pavement. No examples of this early type have been found at the abbey, although they are known from Holm Castle,[22] along with a collection of mosaic tiles which are also typologically of late 13th- to early 14th-century date, and two examples were published by Hall (Fig.15.5B, C), suggesting that they were originally present in the choir area.[23] Some of the larger tiles recorded by Hall also belong to this late 14th- to early 15th-century group. Over half of the 1992 tiles are of Droitwich-type and are of two sizes, *c*.12cm and *c*.13cm square. Similar tiles also occur in the relaid nave aisle pavement (Pl.18). In most collections of medieval floor tiles from monastic sites in the Severn valley, Droitwich-type tiles form the majority of the finds and this is likely to have been true at Tewkesbury as well. This reflects a general increase in the use of decorated floor tiles in the area in which, clearly, Tewkesbury took part.

A single example of a Great Malvern tile was present amongst the 1992 finds, three tiles with Great Malvern designs were published by Hall and examples are present in the nave aisle and south transept pavements, albeit only represented by small fragments. This tilery operated from the 1450s to the 1480s when the floor of the Lady Chapel at Gloucester Cathedral was made. At several sites where Great Malvern tiles have been found they occur singly or in very small numbers, as at St. Oswald's Priory, Gloucester,[24] and Hailes Abbey. This may be because they were never used at those sites in large quantities—they may have been used, for example, to form the paving over a grave. It is always possible that larger buried pavements await discovery, but on present evidence it seems that the abbey floors contained small patches of Great Malvern tiles rather than whole floors, as in the choir of Gloucester Cathedral. However, the three examples published by Hall are all of 4-tile designs which were used in the Gloucester choir pavement and may have been made specifically for it (Fig.15.5H–J).[25]

Finally, all the relaid pavements, and Hall's illustrations, include a number of tiles of the type first noted at Bristol in a pavement from a merchant's house, erroneously identified as that of William Canynges.[26] Subsequent work has established that these tiles are probably of early 16th-century date and were produced somewhere in Worcestershire, quite likely at Worcester again. This concentration around Worcester is shown well by Lewis' distribution map of his Group 24.[27] The designs present at Tewkesbury include heraldic designs commemorating local families (such as Somerville of Gloucestershire and Warwickshire)[28] as well as stock patterns, including 16-tile patterns (Fig.15.5K–O). Such tiles would only be used in extensive areas of paving and imply some early 16th-century reflooring was carried out.

Discussion and Summary

For the period from the late 13th to the mid-16th century floor tiles were widely available in the Severn valley and it is therefore possible to compare what tiles have been found at the abbey with what might be expected. Floors could be laid as part of major building works, as with the eastern Lady Chapel and the chantry chapels, but floors needed constant repair and renewal, and therefore provide a source of information about investment in the abbey fabric at times when there were no new structures being built. It must be remembered, though, that the surviving tiles are probably a small fraction of those once used in the abbey and it may well be that they are not representative of those originally present.

The lack of late 13th-/early 14th-century tiles does seem to be significant. Floor tiles were enjoying a period of popularity during this period and other local houses, such as Evesham, Halesowen, Hailes and various houses in Gloucester, were all using decorated floor tiles of types which have not been found at Tewkesbury. It may be that late 13th-/early 14th-century pavements were present but were comprehensively replaced in later periods, but this would not explain why they are rare even in the 1992 excavated collection from abbey meadow.

It seems as though the first substantial use of floor tiles at Tewkesbury was probably in the 1320s. The large number of designs found, within quite a small collection, is possibly an indication that there were once extensive tile pavements of this period, perhaps covering substantial areas of the church. Repair of these floors seems to have fallen to tilers working at Hanley Castle, who used some of the same dies used in the earlier industry, together with some inexpertly cut dies of their own. A few of these have been found at Tewkesbury, suggesting that the pavements were maintained and repaired into the middle of the century at least. Later in the 14th century Droitwich-type floor tiles of 10cm and 12cm quarries were widely used throughout the area, including at Holm Castle, Tewkesbury. The abbey seems to have received some of these tiles, but not a great number.

There does, however, appear to have been some other tiling carried out at about the same time as the Founder's Chapel was constructed, and this is consistent with the 1875 finds. Whether this was within further chantry chapels or more extensive flooring is not known, but the presence of 16-tile and 9-tile patterns suggests a large and significant pavement, such as might be expected in the transepts or choir, just a few decades later. The small number of such pavements known, and the status of the places where they occur, suggests that a sizeable investment was made in the abbey structure in the late 14th to early 15th centuries. Few of the relaid or loose tiles from the abbey parallel those used in the Warwick Chapel and it is likely that by this time large-scale reflooring had been completed. Similarly, the presence of a small number of Great Malvern (or Malvern school) tiles may indicate tiling over a single grave or in a chapel.

There is no other tiling known from Tewkesbury until the early 16th century. Canynges-type tiles are quite common within the relaid tiles in the nave aisle and these examples include 16-tile patterns, some quite heavily worn. This suggests that part of the central area of the church, perhaps the nave, was repaved at this time. Several unprepossessing parish churches in the Severn valley still retain extensive areas of early 16th-century paving, albeit almost always heavily worn and relaid. This seems to indicate that floor tiles were less expensive than previously, or perhaps a general rise in prosperity. Specially commissioned pavements were produced for several Severn valley sites both religious and secular, as at Thornbury Castle, but no such tiles have been found at Tewkesbury. Finally, the Hanley Castle tilers were again active in the 16th century, producing some large decorated tiles for Ewenny Priory (Glam.), for example. Some of the small unidentified fragments relaid in the nave aisle may be of this type, although none can be positively identified.

This takes the story of the paving of Tewkesbury Abbey to the Dissolution when, unlike many religious houses, the church survived. The fashion for decorated earthenware floor tiles, however, had passed and it was not until the Victorian restoration of the 1870s that new decorated tile flooring was provided for the abbey (Pl.16). It has been stated that the designs used for the 19th-century choir floor are based on medieval examples found on the site—in some cases the actual prototypes are known, whereas in others Hall's illustrations and the replica tiles are the only surviving evidence. The choir pavement includes 16- and 4-tile patterns laid diagonally with dark borders surrounding the 4-tile patterns. This is a standard later 14th- to 16th-century layout and is consistent with the surviving evidence. It may well be that the choir pavement provides a good model for the appearance of the east end of the church from the end of the 14th century onwards.

CHAPTER 16

The Fabric from the Dissolution to the 20th Century *by* David Aldred

The general fabric of Tewkesbury Abbey has changed little since the townspeople inherited it in 1543. There have been no great building campaigns to change the outward appearance, and so it is to the monuments and the written sources that the historian has to turn to understand the place of the abbey in the hearts and souls of the townspeople over the following 400 years. Of the written sources the most useful is an almost unbroken sequence of churchwardens' accounts which survive from 1563 to 1921. They form the backbone of this chapter, which has as its theme the transformation of the abbey from a conventual church to a world-famous historic building which has continued to serve the spiritual needs of a parish. When the bailiffs, burgesses and commonalty purchased the church for £483 in June 1543, they took possession of both an asset and a liability. The asset was, of course, a magnificent, purpose-built house of worship, but the disappearance of its monastic incomes turned it into a liability. Since that day in early summer 1543 the building has devoured money endlessly and the churchwardens have had to seek their funds ever further afield. The lack of substantial funding is the most obvious reason why there has been so little change to the main fabric.

For the first 250 years after the Dissolution, alterations were largely occasioned by changing fashions in worship and by not wholly successful attempts to keep the edifice in good repair. The churchwardens were always walking a tightrope between income and expenditure. Income came from burial fees, pew rents, property rentals and the levying of rates on the town. Thus the whole town, in theory, had a stake in their abbey. The relatively small numbers of worshippers were willing to pay for changes to their worshipping area, so they funded the high altar of 1726, the Milton organ of 1737 and part of the re-pewing of 1795. They were less willing to spend money on the rest of the building and so, for example, a subscription list was opened to pay for the general repairs of the 1820s.

Standing in the interior today, it is very difficult to appreciate that the church was actually divided into two until the restoration of 1865-79 by Sir George Gilbert Scott. A stone wall stretched across the nave interior at the second piers from the crossing (Fig.16.1). The origin of this stone wall remains uncertain. It existed before the Milton organ and gallery were constructed in 1737 because the parish meeting minutes refer to where 'the screen stands to separate the Chancel from the Church'.[1] There is no record of the building of this screen in the churchwardens' accounts after 1563, so it is possible that at least parts of the medieval screen had remained, to which door frames with English Renaissance details had been added subsequently (Fig.16.1). These may well be associated with the purchase in 1617-18 of a bar for a door in the screen and keys for a lock, again testifying to a

Fig.16.1 John Coney's engraving of 1820 shows the wall dividing the chancel from the nave with a glimpse of the Milton organ. The font, with 17th-century bowl, stands in Bay 5

pre-existing barrier.[2] Such measures suggest that the chancel to the east of the wall was regarded as private property by the élite of Tewkesbury society who worshipped there. This arrangement led to the anomalous situation of a privatized cramped chancel accessed through a much larger nave empty of both people and furnishings.

If this comes as a surprise to many modern worshippers and visitors, so also will the type of worship conducted in the abbey. Until Scott's restoration it possessed a strong streak of Puritan preaching and nonconformity. In 1650 the bailiffs claimed they had paid a minister for more than 50 years 'to preach twice every Lord's Day'.[3] As if to emphasise this, in the same year they provided a new pulpit.[4] The communion table stood in the middle of the chancel, an arrangement dating to the Commonwealth period, until the remodelling of the high altar in 1726.[5] Edward Evanson, vicar from 1769 to 1777, was accused of being a Unitarian and eventually resigned, despite enjoying the support of many in his congregation.[6] From such evidence it would seem that the spread of Nonconformist places of worship in the town, and its reputation as a stronghold of Dissent, came as much from the lack of seats for those not identified with the town's élite who filled the chancel as from any doctrinal differences. Strength for this interpretation comes from the evidence that between 1684 and 1687 some 300 burials took place in the abbey churchyard, but only 29 elsewhere.[7]

The need to pay pew rent not only excluded most townspeople from worshipping in the abbey, but it also led to inconvenient overcrowding in the chancel. Galleries were built to provide more seats to ensure a steady revenue. The earliest reference is to a Blue Gallery, built in 1607 in front of the high altar and containing 14 rows.[8] Two years later John Payntor was paid £5 for making a 'new gallery'.[9] In 1618 a gallery was built for the scholars of the free grammar school, which had been founded in 1576, in the former east chapels of the north transept.[10] Eight

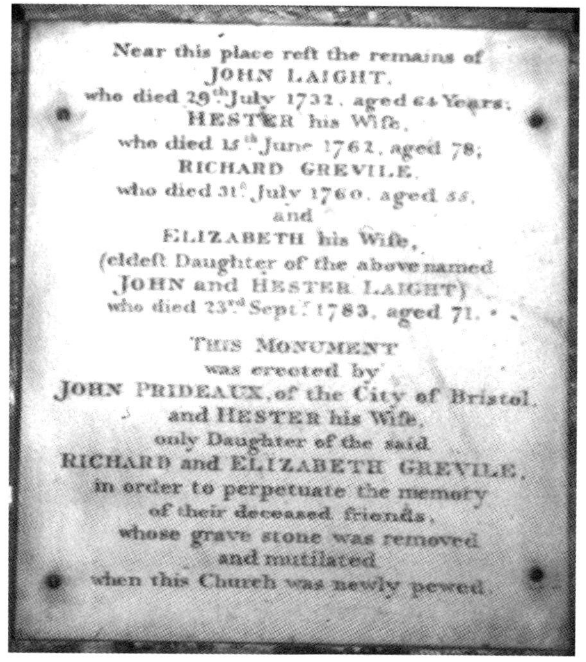

Fig.16.2 The wall tablet to John Laight and others, recording strong opinions on the re-pewing of 1795

scholars were paying the pew rents in the following year.[11] Elevated galleries were also built in the north and south transepts and in the north and south aisles as far as the stone screen.[12] Unfortunately there is no way of knowing how many the galleries seated. The 1784 rental book identifies 199 rentals producing £26 8s. 3d. each year to the abbey, but as most rentals were family or household rentals, it is impossible to calculate the number of seats, especially as there was subletting to provide the pew owners themselves with an income.[13] Thus the town's ruling élite had moulded their chancel according to contemporary fashion, regardless of any damage caused to the historic fabric. In 1788 the famous novelist and diarist, Fanny Burney, commented how the nave (presumably she meant the chancel) was disfigured by 'irregular pews'.[14] However, when the worshippers swept them away in 1795 there was considerable opposition (Fig.16.2).[15] A new pulpit built under the tower in the same year evidenced the continuing preaching tradition. This is the arrangement caught by George Rowe (Fig.16.3) before the pulpit was moved to the north-east pier of the nave in 1849.[16]

In the early 18th century two major developments had further emphasized the exclusiveness of the chancel to the detriment of the historic fabric. At the east end the sedilia was mutilated to accommodate a new Doric altarpiece erected in 1726 to replace the central Commonwealth communion table (Fig.16.4).[17] The latter was the original medieval altar slab (*mensa*), 13ft. 4ins. long, buried at the Dissolution, to be dug up in 1607 and reinstated in the chancel. In 1726 it was cut into two to provide seats in the porch and only returned to its original position at the Scott restoration (Fig.5.3).[18] Blue steps were

Fig.16.3 The cramped nature of the chancel is caught in George Rowe's lithograph of 1830, after the extensive work of the 1820s. The print captures well the nature of the chancel as a preaching box. It also shows the high altar of 1726, the fronts of the transept galleries and the paved floor

Fig.16.4 The pelican from the 1726 altarpiece survives in St. Margaret's Chapel

laid to the altar, with blue and white tiles on the chancel floor.[19] The second development saw the visual exclusiveness of the worship area enhanced by the erection of the Milton organ from Magdalen College, Oxford, above the dividing screen in 1737.[20] Thus the worshippers were further isolated from the bare, empty nave. However, not only did the living appropriate the chancel to themselves, but so did the dead. Despite the Puritan form of worship, Tewkesbury's élite demanded burial in this holy place, as had their monastic forebears. The first burial recorded in the chancel in the churchwardens' accounts was that of a Mr. Pert who paid 6s. 8d. in 1566—the first of many similar useful sources of income.[21] The last recorded in the accounts was in 1819.[22] When an unfortunate unnamed 'Officer in the Army' was killed in a duel at the White Hart in 1725 he provided a rare example of a 'foreigner' being granted the privilege.[23] Such burials provide clear evidence that the building was serving the needs of the present, with no respect for its historic fabric. This reached its nadir in 1709 when Samuel Hawling, bailiff in 1677, appropriated the Clarence vault for his own burial, to be followed by his wife and son John, also a bailiff. The Clarence burials were pushed behind a new wall leaving most of the vault for the 'perriwigged-pated aldermen', where they remained until 1829.[24]

The burials in the chancel were allowed not only to bestow status on the dead, but also to provide an income for the living, despite the damage they caused. They seem to have reached a peak in the early 18th century, for between 1726 and 1730 over 23,000 bricks were purchased to line graves and make good the floor, although how many were cut into the chancel floor compared to the nave floor is not known.[25] Grave cutting on such a scale inevitably created prob-

Fig.16.5 The emptiness of the nave is reflected in this engraving published in 1825. The uneven floor, caused by frequent burials, is shown immediately before the work of the 1820s

lems for the general maintenance of the building as a whole. In 1724 the abbey's surveyor, Francis Smith, declared no new grave was to be cut within three feet of a wall or pillar, and from 25 March 1729 every grave was charged an extra 8d. to guarantee the stone was laid flush to the surrounding floor (Fig.16.5).[26] When Ralph Bigland conducted his survey of monuments in the county, he recorded 346 post-medieval examples at Tewkesbury, many of which no longer survive.[27] The Scott restoration destroyed evidence of these chancel burials, so consequently the churchwardens' records alone remain as a reminder of this phase of the abbey's history.

The gravecutting, and the damage this caused, is just one example of the worshippers' lack of concern for their historic church. Outside their worshipping area, very little was done that was not forced upon them. It might have been bad luck that the steeple blew down on Easter Day 1554, but it took until 1602 to replace 'a beautiful wooden battlement' destroyed in the fall. The stone for the new battlements came from Coscombe Quarry on Stanway Hill and in order to meet the cost of £54 13s. 7d. without a charge on the worshippers or rates, a variety of methods was used. Three plays were performed with ale, fruit and spices sold to the audiences. Even so there was a shortfall of £10 which the bailiffs met by diverting rents from town properties, unusually hitting themselves in the pocket.[28]

Another disaster struck in February 1661 when the great west window was blown in. It showed the repairs carried out in 1654 to have been inadequate, possibly because of the reticence of the worshippers to spend money outside their chancel.[29] Consequently the churchwardens levied three rates on the town, but it took until 1686 (the date is on the window) to pay all their bill to the contractors Abraham Farmer and Jonathan Butler.[30] In the rebuilding, the inner order of the seven original surrounding arches was concealed (Fig.16.6). Of the other repairs caused by natural hazards and recorded in the accounts, one which has resonance with today took place in 1664 when John Parrett was paid £1 for mending the floor badly damaged by the great

Fig.16.6 Samuel Lysons' view of 1795 of the west front shows the window of 1686 and the wall separating the public graveyard from the private grounds of Abbey House. The abbey appears dilapidated whilst the print itself reflects the growing antiquarian interest which was to lead to improvements in the abbey's fabric

flood.[31] In 1770 and 1786 it was again so damaged.[32]

Keeping the building watertight was a constant struggle and work was generally only carried out in reaction to chronic neglect. The original weather-mouldings on the tower show that the medieval roof lines have been lowered (Fig.9.19). The nave roof was repaired in 1593-94 and the chancel roof was rebuilt at a lower pitch in 1603-04.[33] Neither action was successful. By the time the chancel roof was lowered, the new long roof over the nave had already largely been repaired after a storm had blown much of it off in 1597;[34] two years later the lead had to be recapped.[35] By this time the walls were in such a poor state that part of the wall of the north aisle had collapsed. This must have involved a considerable area of the wall as 240 feet of stone was purchased and the equivalent of 300 man days was spent on the repair.[36] At the same time the south aisle was refurbished: payments were made for pulling out weeds from the wall, repairing the roof and 'makinge the battlement'.[37] The roofing continued to cause major concerns; in 1640 over £85 was spent, including 5s. expenses to 'the man sent by the bishop to view the church in what repair it was'.[38] In 1686 a rate of 9d. in the pound was levied 'to take speedy care' to repair the long roof over the nave.[39] In 1713 a brief was requested to rebuild the same roof 'which is now in great decay and want of Repairs'.[40] The brief was repeated seven years later, resulting in the present roof structure.[41] In 1752 two pinnacles on the tower were repaired; the next year repairs to the nave roof were requested 'in the best manner they can' and in 1756 the weathercock was also repaired.[42] Even further evidence of the problems of the roofs can be found in the frequent references to large numbers of slates purchased and also the construction of buttresses to shore up the fabric: two flying buttresses to the east end of the chancel above the ambulatory (1680), a flying buttress to the north aisle (1723) and an unidentified buttress in 1785.[43] All the references to windows in the accounts seem to suggest repairs rather than new creations, apart from the new window cut high in the south wall of the south transept in 1608 to light the roof void (Fig.12.2). The reactionary spending on the main fabric in these years contrasts starkly with the monies spent more liberally on the decorative furnishings of the sanctuary.

By the end of the 18th century the structure of the abbey appeared much as today, although in the churchyard the ground level was higher.[44] In it stood a small tower, generally held to have been a medieval campanile, converted into the borough gaol in 1582 before its demolition in 1817 to make way for the National School.[45] The actual appearance of the abbey, however, was very different, for all the stone surfaces were lime-washed. The accounts have regular references to the liming campaigns from 1571-2, when Edward Cooke was paid for 22½ days' work for white liming.[46] The details recorded for the campaign in 1618 provide a valuable insight into the process. It was organised by builders Thomas Hickes and Richard Kinges. Three horse-loads of charcoal were used to fire the temporary limekilns set up in the churchyard, and at least 105 barrels of lime were used (the manuscript is damaged). Two long ladders, costing 11s., and boards costing 6s. were used for the scaffolding, and the pews in the chancel were covered to prevent damage from splashing. Church life was disrupted for over a year.[47] Between 1624 and 1627 a further 379 barrels of lime were used.[48] Did this further campaign reflect a chancel/nave or interior/exterior division of the work? In 1636 more was done.[49] The accretion of years of liming led a visitor to complain in 1822 that the whole interior had been 'defiled', but by then tastes in church interiors were changing and the camouflaging of historic

Fig.16.7 The walls on the north side of the abbey still have traces of limewash which once covered the whole structure

features was increasingly regretted (Fig.16.7).[50] Yet despite the monochromatic internal appearance, there were still splashes of colour. In the 1618 campaign, oils and colours were purchased for a star and its surround.[51] After the Restoration of Charles II in 1660, the church was decorated every Christmas at a cost of 2s.[52] There are occasional references to payments for painting the royal coat of arms: on the 'new gallery' in 1616 (James I) and in an unspecified location in 1691 (William and Mary).[53] Those of Queen Anne can still be seen by the choir screen.

So, after two and a half centuries in the hands of the people of Tewkesbury, how did the fabric of the abbey appear? Externally there was little architectural change except lower roofs behind new classical parapets, and the spire had gone. Internally the town's élite had created their own private preaching box approached through the cold, damp empty space of the nave, the stone floor uneven from numerous burials; the walls and ceilings washed in lime; light filtering through the many small panes of glass and the whole enlivened only by a number of wall monuments of varying degrees of taste. The only source of heating throughout this early period was in the vestry, where the parish meetings were held; in 1609 a new grate was purchased.[54]

Beyond the stone screen, with doors locked against unwelcome visitors, lay the cramped chancel with its box pews, galleries and burials. The system of pew rents precluded visitors from partaking in services so that although the preaching continued to reflect Puritanism and nonconformity, the congregation reflected the *status quo* of the town's ruling élite. In their hands the fabric had been moulded to serve their own needs, with little regard to its historicity. From 1795 this prevailing attitude changed.

The end of the 18th century was a period of growing interest in antiquities nationally. Locally William Dyde published the first guide to the abbey in 1790 and in 1791 Ralph Bigland began his recording of the county's ecclesiastical monuments, including Tewkesbury. In 1795 the first recorded investigation into Tewkesbury Abbey as an historic building took place. Samuel Lysons, the antiquary, opened a number of the famous medieval tombs during a programme of repairs. His most spectacular discoveries lay in Abbot Alan's tomb where the body crumbled to a skeleton before his eyes, leaving the burial clothes, boots, a wooden crozier and part of a chalice.[55] Thus began another phase of the abbey's history; a phase which brought conflict between the needs of the worshipping community and the desire to conserve an historic monument.

In the same year as Lysons' investigations, the worshipping community started to renew the pews. When the new pews did not fit the space, the medieval stone pillars were cut, not vice-versa. The pews cost over £2,000 which was raised by a variety of methods, including £800 on mortgages on pew rentals; evidence that the abbey was held by its community as a source of revenue as well as spiritual succour.[56] Yet Lysons had started a movement and in the same year the vicar, the Revd. Robert Knight, himself an antiquarian, placed a brass plate in the chancel to commemorate the supposed burial place of Prince Edward, killed at the Battle of Tewkesbury in 1471.[57] In 1821 the Society of Antiquaries of London published the first detailed prints of the abbey fabric, drawn by Frederick Nash. Although somewhat stylised, they provide the earliest detailed visual evidence of the structure of the building (Fig.16.9). The *Gentleman's Magazine* praised their accuracy and, reflecting the new spirit of the age, declared that any ambiguities could only be settled by archaeological investigations.[58] The engravings were reissued in volume V of *Vetusta Monumenta* (1835), and their accuracy is such that they are still used by modern scholars (Figs.10.8, 11.9, 13.11).

Nevertheless, decay and damage continued. In 1814 Mr. Reede's family from Cheltenham was charged £21 for his burial in the chancel, 'he being a stranger'.[59] By 1820 the general fabric was in a critical state. The worshipping community through the churchwardens had to act. A subscription list raised £700, but over £3,000 was needed, so a series of rates was levied on the townspeople by the worshippers sitting as the

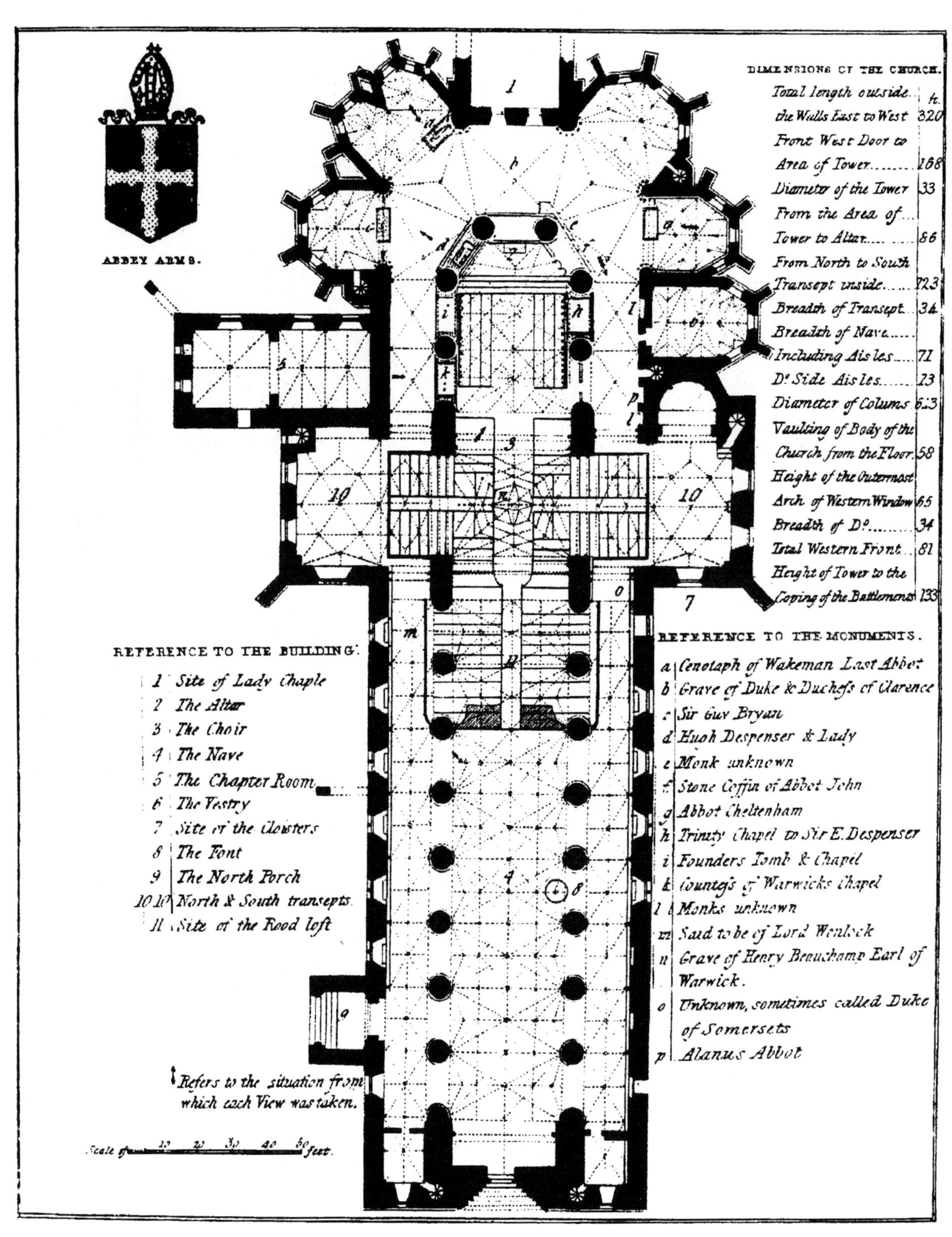

Fig.16.8 Ground plan of the church in 1825. It provides evidence for the seating arrangements before the Victorian 'restoration', as well as illustrating growing antiquarian interest in the abbey by listing its main features, monuments and dimensions

Fig.16.9 Longitudinal west-east section of Tewkesbury Abbey, from Vetusta Monumenta, *vol.V (1835), pl.XXXIX. This analytical section of the fabric, first published in 1821, is evidence that the abbey was being recognized as an historic building of national importance*

vestry meeting.[60] The work provides more evidence of the tension between contemporary needs and the integrity of the historic fabric. Repairs to the roof and windows were made, one of the tower pinnacles was rebuilt and those at the west end extensively repaired. Much of the existing floor of Painswick freestone with blue insets was laid down and the whole interior was coated in yellow distemper to appear 'decently and in good order'.[61] Proposals to place draught curtains above the organ screen and across the aisles, thus creating the 'front of a puppet show' in the words of a critic, were rejected. Also rejected were proposals to raise the galleries to within 20 feet of the transept ceilings, evidence that the conservationists were having some influence.[62] Although there are indications that the worship was becoming more Anglican than Puritan by this time, the older tradition remained very much alive when the vicar, the Revd. Robert Knight, wrote a vitriolic attack in 1818 on popish ritual with its 'almost pantomimical' vestments.[63]

As in 1795 the repairs went hand-in-hand with antiquarian investigations. In 1824 stone fragments from the monuments and fittings were rescued from two feet of rubble and rubbish behind the altar screen.[64] Such discoveries reached a national audience through the *Gentleman's Magazine* as did the opening of the Clarence vault: 'In the north-west corner were found two sculls [*sic*], and other bones, of a man and a woman, but there was nothing by which these relics could be identified as belonging to the unfortunate Duke and Duchess of Clarence'.[65] This scepticism, together with the condemnation of the Hawlings' appropriation of the vault, is clear evidence of increasing respect for the historic fabric of the abbey. Some repairs were carried out on the tombs and it was said that the canopy over the tomb of Hugh III Despenser was rebuilt from over 200 pieces.[66] Yet there was still much to be done. When the British Archaeological Association visited in 1846, they reported the Warwick Chapel as 'falling rapidly into decay' and they heavily criticized the reformed interior: 'an abominable altar screen of pseudo-Italian fashion, with pews to match, sadly mar the general effect ... It is to be hoped that a time will not elapse before a reformation be attempted here'.[67] No doubt they were pleased when the Wakeman monument was extensively repaired four years later.[68]

This ongoing debate between those who worshipped and those who valued the historic fabric can be seen as one between local and national interests. Two years after the British Archaeological Association's visit, the local writer of a guide to the abbey, the Revd. J.L. Petit, could write: 'It is true that a ruinous effect in the interior, or indeed any part of the church, is painful to our religious feelings ... and therefore such restorations as are necessary to ensure stability, or prosperity of appearance, must be fearlessly undertaken ... Till we can work as the medieval artists did, surely we ought to attempt none but necessary restorations?'[69] A generation later the 'restorers' felt they could work as the medieval artists and it was a Tewkesbury builder, Thomas Collins, who began to bring together the two attitudes towards the fabric. In making the abbey a more convenient place of worship, he also conserved its historic fabric as he worked under the direction of Sir George Gilbert Scott, the foremost architect of the day.

Scott had made his name at Ely Cathedral in the mid 1840s. He was appointed architect to Westminster Abbey in 1849 and went on to have a hand in the restoration of 39 cathedrals and minsters and 476 churches. He was heavily influenced by the renewed enthusiasm for medieval liturgy and the archaeological study of Gothic architecture, stemming from A.W.N. Pugin and the Cambridge Camden Society (founded 1839). He became the leading apologist for these values in the High Victorian period, as well as the main target of criticism for excessive restorations. Yet, as one recent commentator has remarked in relation to his work at Chester Cathedral, '... his tracts show him to have been a sensitive and knowledgeable restoring architect'.[70]

At Tewkesbury, though Scott's work is called a 'restoration', in fact he did not restore to a former state but created a new one which had never previously existed. The 'restoration' cut the abbey from its post-Dissolution Puritan past and swept away the enclosed preaching box. It democratized the interior space through making the neglected nave the congregational area with the chancel becoming the preserve of choir, priest and ritual. In so doing the fabric was extensively repaired and conserved—but not without opposition.

The story of the restoration, from an inaugural meeting in 1864 to the rededication in 1879, is well known.[71] The need for further work had become pressing. The walls were streaming with moisture and there was a damp, musty atmosphere throughout the interior.[72] The vicar, Canon C.G. Davies, chaired the first meeting in the Town Hall on 7 May 1864. It was agreed that restoration should take place and as the Gothic Revival swept through the south-west midlands bringing Scott to work at Gloucester, Great Malvern, Hereford, Pershore and Worcester, it is not surprising he was approached. He agreed and set out his plans—to open up the length of the church by removing the screen and Milton organ,

Fig.16.10 Scott's proposals for changing the abbey emphasize the historic stonework which would appear once the coats of limewash, wall monuments and other post-medieval accretions had been removed

and to replace them with an open screen two bays nearer the altar (the present position). The interior would be stripped of its distemper, the 18th-century pews removed and the remaining monastic stalls resited in the chancel, where they are still located. There would also be practical repairs, especially to strengthen the fabric in the south aisle. Scott concluded that: 'the Church, if carefully restored, will be one of the noblest, as it is one of the most interesting, in the kingdom' (Fig.16.10).[73]

Another subscription list was opened, but work already under way at Gloucester and Worcester cathedrals meant funds were not forthcoming and nothing happened until Thomas Collins took the initiative in 1872 by moving the monks' seats to the chancel, removing the wooden galleries in the transepts, taking out pews and restoring the piers damaged when the former were installed. This breathed life into the moribund campaign. Scott was again approached, a faculty was gained and Collins was instructed to clear all the pews from the chancel.[74] Temporary arrangements were made for worship to continue in the nave.

The opening of a subscription list was an acknowledgement that neither the worshippers, nor the wider town community could afford to fund the full restoration. The setting up of a national appeal, supported by the archbishop of Canterbury, was a firm indication that Tewkesbury Abbey had become an historic building of national importance. Over £9,000 was raised and, as time moved on towards the rededication in September 1879, a further meeting took place in March at Lambeth Palace. Here it was agreed to open another subscription list to raise a further £6,770. A London committee was established to help raise it and although the vicar of Tewkesbury, Canon Hemming Robeson, and his sister, Mrs. E. Glynn, headed the list with £500, the report of the meeting leaves no doubt that the wishes of a wider, national community were now driving the changes to the fabric.[75] The worshipping community of the leaders of Tewkesbury society was being swept along by the High Church movement grounded in Victorian interpretations of medieval ritual and decoration. How the Revd. Robert Knight must have turned in his grave!

Hemming Robeson was vice-chairman of the National Committee, Charles and Frederick Moore of the old-established family firm of estate agents and auctioneers were the treasurer and secretary respectively, and Thomas Collins was the contractor. All the other members of the committee were national figures. Lord Sudeley (High Steward of Tewkesbury), Earls Beauchamp, Bathurst and Dudley and local M.P.s Sir Edmund Lechmere, J.R. Yorke and J.T. Agg Gardner, were names necessary to give prestige to the appeal, but they were not regular worshippers in the abbey.

The restoration gave substantial opportunities for archaeological investigations. As the floors were relaid, the step before the monastic screen was revealed between the second and third bays of the nave.[76] In the chancel, the present pavement was laid with close copies of some remaining medieval tiles, produced by Godwin of Lugwardine who had already provided Scott with tiles for Gloucester and Hereford cathedrals.[77] Great skill was needed in the designing and firing, but they were dismissed by Massé as 'stiff printed' as he bemoaned the fact they totally covered the evidence for the medieval burials.[78]

Before the tiles were laid in 1879, the medieval chancel burials were investigated (Fig.13.1). A memorandum of February 1875, apparently written by one of the best-known historians of the abbey, the Revd. J.H. Blunt, gives a first-hand account of the extent of the investigations: 'The soil under the Altar place was dug out to the depth of 4 feet until the virgin earth was reached, the excavation extending from pier to pier, & for 24 feet from East to West'.[79] This produced a large number of fragments of painted sculpture, identified at the time by Blunt as depicting some of the medieval lords of the manor as well as religious figures like St. John the Baptist.[80] The search for the coffins of the famous produced yet further evidence that earlier generations had paid scant regard to the historic fabric in moulding it to their needs. The late 13th-century coffin of Gilbert II de Clare had been broken up to provide foundations for the walls of the pews. Only the bottom 3 inches of stone of the coffin of his grandfather, Gilbert I, survived.

Other coffins were hardly identifiable, being full of rubble, but the coffin of Isabel, Countess of Warwick, was a welcome exception, as her body was found complete in its linen shroud. There can be no better evidence of how attitudes towards the abbey were changing than the action of Blunt and Sir Edmund Lechmere before the burial was resealed. They placed a signed brick at the head of the grave inscribed: 'This grave was opened during the restoration of 1875, and, after being inspected, was reverently closed again and restored to its original condition'.[81] Interestingly, no mention is made of the countless more recent burials which the churchwardens' accounts recorded through to the early 19th century. Presumably they were not considered of historical worth.

The vaulting also received special attention. The restoration centred on the bosses of the high vaults, which had been covered in distemper 50 years earlier. On discovering fragments of the original colouring, the bosses of the chancel vault and those of the first two bays of the nave were recoloured during Scott's time, but this was not considered a success and so the work stopped. Leaving alone also proved to be unsatisfactory and so Thomas Gambier Parry, who had previously recoloured the nave roof and octagon in Ely Cathedral, was called from Highnam Court (near Gloucester), and he employed a more conservative approach to add colour to draw out the medieval features (Pl.17A–C).[82] There is little doubt he was allowed, and took, a free hand in his interpretations; for example, the carving of the crucifixion boss lacked a crucifix, so he added one in gold paint beneath the crucified figure. 'There was a great deal left so vague that one had to follow one's own idea of what was intended', he later remarked.[83] However he respected the original medieval fabric, unlike the earlier attempt. In 1914, a fine painted reredos, 'A Witness to the Crucifixion', incorporating ten panels painted by Thomas Gambier Parry in early Italian Renaissance style, was placed behind the high altar. It was the work of Thomas' son, Sidney, and had been previously in the chapter house at Gloucester Cathedral. In 1934 it was removed to the east chapels of the north transept where it still stands, currently dividing the abbey shop from the song school.

Now for the first time the high altar could be viewed from the nave. Scott placed the division between nave and chancel in its present position. It was marked only by the low wall until 1892 when the present wooden screen was added by J. Oldrid Scott, who had taken over after his father's death in 1878 (Fig.16.11).[84] The east chapels of the north transept were extensively repaired with the adjoining north chapel at the expense of the Freemasons. They had previously been divided from the church as part of the grammar school and were now reunited by demolishing a wall. Four feet of rubbish was removed from the floor. Outside, the churchyard was lowered again in the mid-1880s and approached through Lord Gage's gates, a gift from 1750 which had previously formed the gates to the north porch of the church.[85]

Many people showed their benevolence through a variety of gifts which led to a wealth of furnishings to enhance the new High Church atmosphere which was being so successfully created. Earl Beauchamp paid for the reinstatement of the original stone altar table (Fig.5.3), and the Revd. Charles Grove of Mythe House presented the lectern, the glass in the west window of the nave and that in the north and south aisles in memory of his wife (Pl.26), and the organ which carries his name. The parishioners paid for a new Jubilee clock in 1887 to replace one of 1750.[86]

The abbey had been refashioned into High Anglicanism and this did not pass without opposition. Many parishioners fought to continue the right to occupy their chosen pew, although pew rentals had long since ceased to provide significant incomes. In 1872, the last year of recorded pew rentals, they provided only £59 out of a total offertory for the year of £218 11s. 6d. However, they no longer had the power to control the social order inside the chancel. Only 296 out of 600 seats were allocated to named worshippers at the reopening.[87] Thus the restoration swept away the control of the worshippers over their own seat of spiritual power in the community (Fig.16.11). It brought the church into the mainstream of contemporary trends of Anglican worship and it made many necessary repairs to the fabric—but it also provoked criticism. On 10 March 1877 William Morris, pioneer of the Arts and Crafts movement, wrote a letter to the London paper, *The Athenaeum*:

> My eye just now caught the word 'restoration' in the morning paper, and on looking closer I saw that this time it is nothing less than the Minster of Tewkesbury that is to be destroyed by Sir Gilbert Scott. Is it altogether too late to do something to save it?[88]

Fig.16.11 The restoration complete! This print of 1894 shows how much the present arrangements were the creation of Scott in the 1870s. Compare with Figs.16.3 and 16.5 to appreciate how the 'restoration' changed the post-dissolution appearance of the church interior

Out of this letter arose the national Society for the Protection of Ancient Buildings. Not surprisingly, Scott defended himself:

> The thick coats of whitewash, which would have suggested to our ancestors that the stately fabric was doing penance in a white sheet, the immuring pews and stilted galleries, which would have reminded them of the convict's cell and the felon's scaffold, are gone ...[89]

Tewkesbury Abbey was now established as an historic church of national reputation. Consolidation continued to take place. In 1883 the room at the west end of the south aisle of the nave (now the Holy Cross Chapel) was purchased and reunited with the church, at the same time that Abbey House was bought at auction to be the vicarage.[90]

The former processional doorway into the cloister was restored by Thomas Collins in 1892, outside which he reconstructed in *c*.1898-99 a bay of fan-vaulting in the north-east corner of the former cloister walk. Plans to rebuild the complete north alley came to nothing.[91]

Yet the criticisms continued. H.J. Massé wrote in 1900 in his guide book:

> During the last twenty years little has been done to the fabric. Windows and other decorations have been lavished upon the interior, and money expended to several thousand of pounds, a sum which might have been spent with more benefit to the fabric.[92]

No doubt the author would have also criticised the present entrance lobby and west doors, built in 1915 as a memorial to Canon Wardell-Yerburgh who had followed Hemming Robeson in 1899. Conversely he might have approved the incorporation of the cloister garth to the south of the abbey in the same year.[93] The building continued to need attention. In 1906 the west front was repaired and in 1923 £2,000 was needed to restore the windows in the chancel in advance of the 800th anniversary of the abbey's consecration.[94] An important development for future funding was the setting up of the Friends of Tewkesbury Abbey in 1932 by the vicar, the Revd. Pountney Gough.[95] One of their first acts was to open an appeal for £25,000 to repair the tower for 'every high wind brings stones crashing down':[96]

> We are therefore asking all England to help us, and not only England, but the Dominions and America as well. For we believe that the great task of saving Tewkesbury Abbey for posterity is not the concern of one town or one county or even one country alone, but of the whole of our generation.[97]

A Friends' letter in 1938 listed some of the recent changes to the fabric: electric lighting and floodlighting; foundations of piers strengthened; the parapet round the chancel roof made secure; the tower repaired; and the walls strengthened in the roof space.[98] A year later Abbey Lawn was presented to the abbey, and the church was at last reunited with its immediate landscape from which it had been separated since the Dissolution.[99] The creation of Tewkesbury Abbey as a medieval icon in a modern world was now complete. The abbey had completed its transformation from a parish church to an historic building and centre of worship of international importance.

CHAPTER 17

The Post-Reformation Monuments and the Churchyard *by* Jane Birdsall *with contributions by* Richard K. Morris

Tewkesbury Abbey is justly famous for its medieval tombs and chantries, but it also possesses an interesting and representative selection of monuments and memorials ranging in date from from the early 17th century to the 20th century. The majority are wall monuments, of which more than 40 survive, but there are also ledger slabs in the church floor and various memorials in the churchyard. Although they cannot stand comparison with, say, the collection of wall monuments in Gloucester Cathedral,[1] nevertheless they hold a fascination for the social insights they offer, as commemorations of individuals and families in the town and its hinterland, as well as giving historical information about their deeds and about works undertaken in the abbey.

Some of the more ornate monuments can be considered as miniature works of art, comparable to sculptures in galleries and museums. As a whole, they are a representative illustration of the evolution of monumental design through the centuries in a provincial centre such as Tewkesbury. They are made of a large number of different materials, ranging from Italian marbles to local limestone and stylistically encompassing complex and finely carved monuments to simple inscription panels.

Monuments have come under threat throughout history, and never more so than when destruction was fashion driven—for example during the 19th-century Gothic Revival when many churches were 'restored' and 'improved' by being rebuilt and stripped of their original furnishings. Monuments are also in danger through neglect and accidental damage, in addition to the hazard of being over restored, badly repaired and repainted. In recent times awareness has grown of their potential deterioration, from the loss of pieces or worn inscriptions, so that their conservation and recording need to be actively pursued. Indeed, as long ago as 1933, Robert Holland-Martin, in his presidential address to the Bristol and Gloucestershire Archaeological Society, made a plea for better consideration of the 17th- and 18th-century monuments in our churches.[2]

The Wall Monuments

Church monuments such as those seen today first appeared in an ecclesiastical setting as floor slabs, a direct precursor of ledger-slabs, with inscriptions and often a figure depicted on the stone (e.g. Figs.5.2, 10.6A). This developed over time into a high relief carved effigy, often erected on a freestanding tomb-chest with a canopy over (e.g. Fig.13.5).

A significant development in the later 16th century was the invention of the hanging wall monument, completely free from the floor.[3] During the 17th century the form became common because of its appeal and relative cheapness, and carried on to the mid-19th century. Nigel Llewellyn has described how monumental

Fig.17.1 John Roberts d.1631

Fig.17.2 Ann Slaughter d.1640

tombs of the 16th and 17th centuries communicate to the public through four systems of signification: the effigy, the architectural frame, the inscription and the heraldry.[4] In the case of wall monuments of the 'middling classes' effigial sculpture was rare, and instead striking architectural surrounds framing the inscription and heraldry were the main features (e.g. Figs.17.5, 17.7).

Monumental Styles

During the 16th century, Renaissance influence slowly superseded medieval Gothic forms in church monuments, especially from Queen Elizabeth I's reign. Northern European craftsmen tended to deploy classical details in a more decorative fashion, in contrast to the closer correlation between architecture and the style of monuments which had existed in the Middle Ages. This period of design was characterised by the use of columns, strap-work, and painted and gilded work, a good late example being that to Ann Slaughter (d.1640) <40> [< > referring to the location on Fig.17.3] in the choir (Fig.17.2).

The Elizabethan and Jacobean period was the only time in which effigial sculpture often appeared as a component of modest wall monuments. Typically the deceased was represented in a kneeling pose, the precedent for which was probably a type of late medieval monumental brass depicting kneeling figures, which were

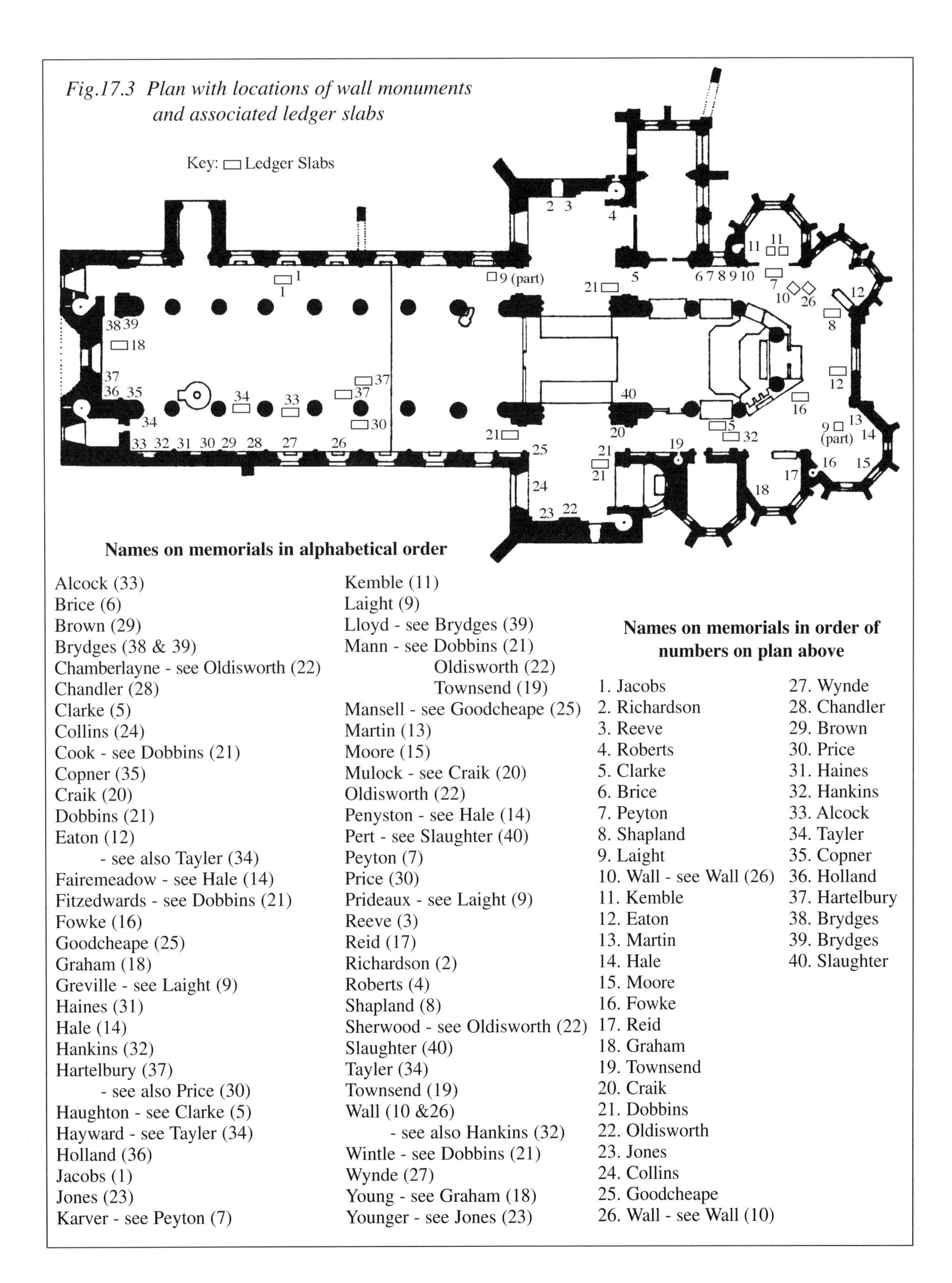

Fig.17.3 Plan with locations of wall monuments and associated ledger slabs

Fig.17.4 Elizabeth Townsend d.1685

Fig.17.5 Laetitia Hale d.1700

fixed vertically to a stone slab or matrix at the back of the tomb. Three-dimensional effigies were virtually never represented kneeling in the Middle Ages; the exception which proves the rule surviving right here at Tewkesbury, in the 'kneeling knight', Edward Despenser (Pl.14). The abbey possesses no wall monuments with kneeling figures, but the trend after *c*.1600 to a frontal demi-figure is represented by the monument to John Roberts (d.1631) <4>, rather unfortunately hidden away behind the Grove organ (Fig.17.1). This is the earliest post-Reformation monument surviving at the abbey, and indeed it is curious that none is extant from the reigns of Elizabeth I or James I.

The second half of the 17th century witnessed the development of the 'cartouche design', in which an inscription, typically oval in shape, was set within a frame which is less architectural and more decorative.[5] The most common motifs are acanthus foliage and elongated scrolls or volutes. Tewkesbury possesses a good sample of this style of monument—though none is strictly 'cartouche' in shape: that to Elizabeth Townsend (d.1685) <19> is a typical example (Fig.17.4).[6] The monument comprises a rectangular inscription panel between fronds of acanthus, volutes and scrollwork, surmounted by the feminine form of the family's coat of arms. The inscription panel rests on a motif of a draped skull and cross-bones.

Fig.17.6 Charles Wynde d.1716

Above the inscription is a small female bust which, if it represents the deceased woman, is a rare example of an idea that was more prevalent in the 18th century. The classical influences typical of this time can be seen in the style of the segmental broken pediment on top in addition to the stylised acanthus foliage and the volutes. There is a great deal of polychrome present on this and other monuments in the abbey, mainly on the coats of arms but also to emphasize different areas and details, in addition to a lot of examples of gold leaf, of which the inscription on the Townsend monument was once formed.

The influence of the Baroque—in so far as this essentially continental Catholic style had much following in England—was felt in monuments in the opening decades of the 18th century, lingering on in memorials rather longer than in architecture. The presence of twisted salomonic columns in the monument of Laetitia Hale (*c*.1700) <14> may reflect this influence

Fig.17.7 George Peyton d.1742, attributed to Thomas White of Worcester

Fig.17.8 Mrs. Mann and the Dobbins family c.1749, by Richard Squire of Worcester

(Fig.17.5),[7] though in other aspects the general form has altered little from the Townsend monument. Very popular at this time was the depiction of cloth draped over marble, as in the Baroque curtains with gilt hems which are drawn back to reveal the inscription to George Peyton (d.1742) <7> and his wife on their memorial in the north choir aisle (Fig.17.7). The monument in memory of Charles Wynde, 'High Bayliff' (d.1716) <27>, illustrates another popular trend of the period, the classically inspired portrait bust set on a pedestal (Fig.17.6).

During the 18th century came a more restrained ideal of monumental design, with greater accuracy in classical details, reflecting initially the popularity of Palladian architecture and, later in the century, a greater enthusiasm for anything Greek. In this respect, the monument to Mrs. Esther Mann (d.1749) <21> and her family makes a telling comparison with that to George Peyton <7>, only a few years earlier. The inscription of the Mann monument is firmly framed by a Roman order of fluted pilasters and Corinthian capitals (Fig.17.8).[8] The arrival at Tewkesbury of ideas associated with ancient Greece is marked by Flaxman's sombre monument to Lady Ann Clarke (d.1800) <5>, with mourning female figures, anthemion ornament at the apex (where earlier monuments had a Roman-derived pediment), and amphorae and Greek key pattern below (Fig.17.9).

Various forms of neo-classicism dominate the relatively numerous wall tablets of the Regency

Fig.17.9 Lady Ann Clarke d.1800, by John Flaxman

period (*c*.1800-1840) in the abbey, to be found now mainly towards the west end of the nave. The large flat pyramid shape was commonly used as a backing, as in the memorial to Thomas Hartelbury (*c*.1800) <37>. The monument to Kenelm Chandler (*c*.1833) <28> is an elegantly simple study in classical forms, bordered by tapering fluted pilasters, with a band of guilloche ornament crowned by a funerary urn. Designs based on antique sarcophagi were also popular, as seen in the memorials to D'Avenant Hankins (erected 1837) <32> and Robert Wall (d.1847) <26>.

The Gothic Revival was the most distinctive style of the High Victorian period, especially in ecclesiastical architecture and fittings, and the abbey has two very representative examples in wall monuments—those to Sir Robert Graham (d.1853) <18> and Humphrey Brown M.P. (d.1860) <29>. Graham's monument is a spirited revival of medieval Gothic by the local

Fig.17.10 Sir Robert Graham d.1853, detail, by Thomas Collins

Fig.17.11 Mrs. Craik (Dinah Mulock) d.1887, by Hugh H. Armstead (1890)

contractor, Thomas Collins, especially in the treatment of the pinnacles, which appear to have drawn their inspiration from the 14th-century 'Forthampton' tomb recess close by (cf. Figs.17.10 and 10.12). Another aspect of the Gothic Revival was that the fashion for recumbent effigies on tomb-chests re-emerged for grander monuments, a medieval format which had disappeared during the 17th century.[9] Archdeacon Hemming Robeson, vicar of Tewkesbury from 1877 to 1892, (d.1912), is appropriately commemorated by such a memorial, which is medieval more in form than in detail. Much of the great Victorian restoration to the medieval fabric was carried out during his incumbency.[10]

In the late 19th century a renewed interest in classical art developed as an alternative to Gothic, and one strand of this taste which found a following in monumental art was a revival of Italian Renaissance style, especially of the Quattrocento. In this context the memorial to Mrs. Craik (d.1887, erected 1890) <20> is a typical product of the period (Fig.17.11). In comparison, in the slightly later memorial to Thomas Collins (d.1900, erected 1906) <24>, Gothic detail has been mixed with Renaissance—perhaps to signify his role in restoring the medieval fabric of the abbey—and his portrait bust stares out of the medallion with an uncanny realism (Fig.8.7). After this date, the few wall monuments erected in the church are tablets commemorating persons with exceptional associations with the abbey, such as Victoria Woodhull Martin <13> and Arthur Brice (both d.1927) <6>.[11] On the Martin tablet, the Renaissance inspired details of the frame and the Roman lettering are in tune with the neo-Georgian architectural taste of the period (Fig.22.7).

Social History Portrayed

The value of these monuments from a social point of view is the amount of information that the inscriptions and even the style, materials and details can tell us about the individuals, their lifestyles, their position in society and how others perceived them. The wall monument was unlike all other kinds of monument in that it was designed to be separate from the point of burial; and therefore often tended to proclaim the virtues of the deceased.[12]

Monuments were generally paid for personally, or by the families, or their supporters and friends. Examples of this can be seen on a number of inscriptions, for example that to the Revd. Joseph Shapland (d.1887): 'This tablet was erected as a tribute of regard by his affectionate sister, Lucy Shapland'. Many tablets assert similar affection and admiration, and state that bereaved close relatives have erected them. Others, however, were commissioned by a wider social group such as that to Humphrey Brown M.P. (d.1860) <29> which 'was erected by the subscriptions of many of the Inhabitants, as a testimony of their appreciation of his unwearied efforts for the benefit of the poor and the welfare of the Town'. There are also a number to soldiers and naval officers that have been erected by colleagues, showing that it was not just the families of the deceased who felt obliged to pay for a monument and have their generosity recorded.

Members of notable local families would typically choose to be buried in their ancestral church even if it was not where they were living or had died. Robert Wall Esq., magistrate, of Tewkesbury Park <26>, came from such a family: his inscription records that he died at Cheltenham (1847) and that he lies buried with his father Colonel John Wall <10> in the family vault in the abbey. There are a number of monuments to individuals who have died abroad, the most dramatic example being that of Kenelm Chandler <28>, who drowned in a shipwreck in the Indian Ocean in 1809 and whose memorial tablet is here because his family lived locally.

The monuments also illustrate both the movement of people in the late 18th century from the colonies to England, and the attraction of the abbey as one of the prestigious burial sites in the vicinity of Cheltenham Spa in the early 19th century. Lady Ann Clarke was born in Jamaica, died at Cheltenham (1800) and is buried at Tewkesbury (Fig.17.9) <5>; likewise John Reid (d.1813)<17>. In this connection it is interesting to note that the list of subscribers to Bennett's *History of Tewkesbury* (1830) include persons from as far off as Bengal, Madras, Australia and St. Kitts.[13] According to the voluminous inscription on Sir Robert Graham's memorial (Fig.17.10) <18>, he was born at Battle (Sussex), lived at Esk (Cumberland) and died in 1853 at Dursley, claiming a Scottish ancestry which included a daughter of King Robert II, the dukes of Montrose, the earls of Mentieth and a gentleman of the horse of King James I (of England).[14]

Inscriptions can tell us a great deal about the social and historical backgrounds of the individuals commemorated, beyond details such as the years of birth and death, occupation and the number of children that they had. Mary Oldisworth (d.1684) <22> '... lived a Virgin 29 yeares, a Wife 5 and a Widow 39 ...'. In addition, her monument makes great show of her own and her descendents' marriages, something that does not have the same cachet now, but the good marriages of two daughters to gentlemen was obviously deemed important enough to be stated on their mother's memorial. More effusive is the fine inscription to Elizabeth Townsend <19>:

> She was a person of true & unaffected piety
> of a Modest and Sweet Behaviour
> of a Generous and Exemplary Charity
> For by her last Will and Testament
> she gave two hundred pounds to be layd
> out for the Benefitt of the Mnr of Gods
> Word in this parish, and his Successours
> for ever
> Shee died July 29 1685
> Aged 33.
> *Let her own works prais her in ye Gates Prov. 31. 31.*

The inscription to Catherine Price <30> states that she died aged 23 in 1787 and had four daughters who died under the age of 19.

References to the town and the abbey are frequent. The memorial to Mrs. Craik (Dinah Mulock, d.1887) <20> (Fig.17.11), records 'She wrote John Halifax Gentleman, the well-known classic book' (published 1857), which brought fame to various buildings in Tewkesbury, such as the Abbey Mill (Abel Fletcher's Mill in the book).[15] The abbey, of course, is mentioned most frequently on the memorials. The tablet to John Copner <35> states that he was '... well Skill'd in Church Musick ...' and '... Designed and built the Altar Piece in this Church the Year he died' of smallpox in 1726, 70 years before Jenner's first use of the vaccine. In a different vein, Arthur Brice (d.1927)<6> '... by his pen helped to make known the glories of this Abbey at the time of its octocentenary ...'. The finest of this genre of memorial is that to Thomas Collins (d.1900)<24>, who was so instrumental in implementing the restoration of the abbey and other properties in the town in the Victorian era (Fig.17.12).[16] The inscriptions on his monument, executed in 1906 by R.L. Boulton, are worth quoting at length:

> To perpetuate the memory of 'a wise master builder', five times mayor of Tewkesbury ... always zealous in preserving the ancient beauty of his native town ... and the restorer of this venerable Abbey. The friends of Thomas Collins J.P., born 1818, died 1900, have placed this tablet and stained glass window in the church he loved.

Fig.17.12 Thomas Collins d.1900, by R.L. Boulton (1906)

On the alabaster frame is inscribed, 'A workman that needeth not to be ashamed', and the inscription in the window above reads, 'Every house is builded by some man, but He that built all things is God'.

A more oblique reference to the history of the building is found in the tablet commemorating John Laight and family (d.1732) <9>, erected in the early 19th century by John Prideaux, in which the latter laments that their 'gravestone was removed and mutilated when this church was newly pewed' (Fig.16.2). The date of the re-pewing is not stated, but it is likely to be that of 1795. Pieces of this disfigured gravestone can be seen in the floor of St. Faith's Chapel and by the stove at the east end of the nave north aisle.

Symbolism and Allegory

Fig.17.13 The figure of Charity on the monument to Lady Ann Clarke by Flaxman

In the earlier monuments the emphasis of their symbolism is placed on resurrection and immortality, connoted particularly by the presence of cherubs or putti. These were standard in various adaptations and poses from the start of the 17th century to the end of the 18th.[17] Cherubs' heads adorn, for example, the monuments of Joseph Reeve (d.1651) <3>, Elizabeth Oldisworth (d.1684) <22> and Robert Eaton (d.1687) <12>. Putti hold trumpets (one now missing) at the top of the monument to Maria Tayler (d.1762) <34>, to signify the corpse awaiting the Day of Judgement. On the monument to Laetitia Hale (d.1700) <14>, two large putti hold a trumpet, a palm frond, an hour glass and a skull (Fig.17.5). The skull is an obvious symbol of death, but it could also symbolize immortality in combination with olive branches or crowned with a laurel wreath, as in the monument to Elizabeth Townsend (Fig.17.4). Urns can be seen to be very popular figurative symbols of death, especially if closed or draped, but they could be modified into an image of immortality by turning them into flaming urns, as in the Dobbins memorial <21> (*c*.1749) (Fig.17.8)

A trend which has been identified in monuments during the later 18th century is the portrayal of family relationships and emotions, especially regarding the deaths of women.[18] The memorial which approaches closest to this ideal at Tewkesbury is, not surprisingly, one of the few wall monuments with figure sculpture—that to Lady Ann Clarke by Flaxman <5> (Figs.17.9, 17.13). This severe monument is relieved by the personifications of the female virtues, Faith and Charity, made more pertinent to the subject of the deceased by the inscribed lines: 'But the greatest of these is Charity' (I Corinthians, 13.13), and, 'As a wife and mother, she [Lady Clarke] was tender and solicitous; and as a Christian remarkably pious and charitable'. Figures illustrative of 'Truth', Purity' and 'Charity' are also prominent later on Mrs. Craik's memorial (Fig.17.11) <20>.

Other less ambitious tombs of the early 19th century are also made more poignant or meaningful by additional sculpted symbols. On the top of the monument to Edward Brydges (d.1834) <39> and his wife a cross is carved above the word 'HOPE'—they lost their two sons Richard and Charles in a drowning accident on the River Severn in 1818, as recorded on an adjacent tablet to them <38>. On the monument of the Revd. Joseph Shapland (d.1837) <8>, it is presumably the scholarly qualities of the deceased which are signified by the scroll, quill, inkstand and book depicted. The choice of the Quattrocento style, associated with Renaissance humanism, for the memorial to the writer, Mrs. Craik (d.1887), was intended to indicate 'the noble aim of her work' according to the commission. Amongst the eminent members of the committee formed shortly after her death to advise on the form of the memorial were Lord Tennyson, Robert Browning, Matthew Arnold, Sir Frederick Leighton and Sir John Millais, and it was executed in 1890 by the fashionable London sculptor, H.H. Armstead R.A. (Fig.17.11).[19]

Since the early 20th century, the few monuments erected inside churches have generally been those to important individuals or have taken the form of war memorials. No significant development of the art form has occurred and symbolic attributes are rare. As Nigel Llewellyn has remarked, 20th-century culture has tended to understate the need for ritual complexity in death, in contrast to the public display of death and mourning in the Victorian era.[20]

Construction, Materials and Sculptors

In the 17th century and before, wall monuments were usually sturdily constructed and depended largely on corbels for support, which were often built some way into the wall. At this date, unambitious wall monuments were still carved from freestone, which at Tewkesbury is typically limestone from the Cotswold quarries, as for the monument of Joseph Reeve (d.1651) <3>. Other techniques were used, however, when marble became fashionable.

At Tewkesbury, marbles first feature as a significant element in the monument to Laetitia Hale (d.1700, Fig.17.5) <15>, and during the first half of the 18th century the use of veined white marble characterizes the Peyton <7> and Mann family <21> monuments by the Worcester sculptors Thomas White and Richard Squire respectively (Figs.17.7, 17.8). Marble has great inherent strength and large sheets can be used with little support. Marble monuments were therefore merely hung on the wall with the use of metal pins and this method was stretched to its limit in larger and more extravagant monuments. Large sheets of marble are prone to warping and bending because of their weight if insufficiently supported. In addition, the iron pins used to support them corroded over time because of dampness in the wall. This can be seen with the memorial to Copner (d.1726) <35>, where the rusty iron pins have expanded and pushed the marble apart. Eventually cracks occur, and pieces can fall off. For example, in 1983 the moument to Laetitia Hale <14> was threatening to come away from the wall, and so it was completely dismantled, the damp problem remedied and then re-rected as we see it today (Fig.17.5).[21]

Often monuments are composed of several different stones. It is not uncommon to find several different pieces of various sizes and thicknesses, fashion and economy prevailing over long-term structural stability. Marble was an expensive commodity, especially the highly coloured or pure white varieties, so these were sliced as thinly as possible and all small scraps used. The surface can look opulent and as if it is one sheet, but in reality many thin, small pieces have been used for economy. Behind the surface is often a very rough backing of lime, limestone, plaster of Paris or rubble stones (especially if the monument is deep). The monument to Lady Clarke is obviously more expensive and highly crafted than many of the other examples here (Fig.17.9). Sizeable pieces of pure white Carrara marble have been carved in quite high relief and this quality and the lavish use of a costly commodity show the relative wealth of her family.

On many monuments, close inspection reveals that small areas of the surface have been tooled in a pock-marked pattern. These are where an individually carved element of a monument, such as a cherub's head or rosette, has fallen off. The pocked surface was created to provide a key so that the element could be attached to the main surface of the monument with, most probably, a small wooden dowel and plaster of Paris. The latter is not an adequate adhesive, especially if the details have later been knocked or wetted, and many elements have become detached because of this and broken or lost. This can be seen, for example, on the monument to Thomas Hartelbury (*c.*1807) <37>.

It is also important to note that a number of the wall monuments have been moved from their original locations, which could result in missing features and have implications for their conservation. This probably occurred mainly during the great Victorian restoration of the 1870s and 1880s, presumably to reinstate the purity of the medieval architectural features of the church, especially the arcades and the setting of the high altar, freed from later accretions. For example, the memorial to D'Avenant Hankins, erected in 1837 on a Norman pier in the south ambulatory and photographed in this location in *c.*1870 (Fig.13.2), is now found on the south aisle wall in the eighth bay of the nave <32>.[22] Similarly the monuments in the same location to Charles Wynde (d.1716, Fig.17.6) <27>, Robert Wall (d.1847) <26> and Richard Alcock (d.1829) <33> have all been moved, the first two from the chancel in prestigious positions close to the high altar and the third from a pier in the nave.[23]

One aspect of the post-Reformation monuments which is more rewarding than the study of their medieval counterparts is that the names of their craftsmen are recorded in numerous instances, usually by an abbreviated signature carved on the work. The 17th century retains the relative anonymity typical of the Middle Ages, and stylistic parallels still provide the best clues to attribution. For instance, it has been observed that the Roberts monument (Fig.17.1, 1631) <4> is similar to those of William Ferrers (d.1625) at nearby Ashchurch and Alderman John Jones (d.1631) in Gloucester Cathedral, and it has been suggested that they are all imported works from the Southwark marblers' workshops in London.[24]

It is in the 18th century at Tewkesbury that the names of individual craftsmen begin to appear, providing evidence for the significance of Worcester as a centre for better quality tombs in the lower Severn valley area. The George Peyton monument (d.1742) (Fig.17.7) <7> is firmly attributed to Thomas White of Worcester (*c.*1684-1748), and the consoles supporting the Mann family monument <21> are inscribed 'SQUIRE' 'WORC'—for Richard Squire (1700-86), 'one of the best of the Worcester statuaries', according to Gunnis.[25] On first inspection, the Mann monument (Fig.17.8) is perplexing because it carries dates from 1712 (the death of Henry Dobbins, Esther Mann's first husband) to 1825 (the death of John Wintle, her great-grandson via Henry Dobbins), so the known working career of Richard Squire is helpful in localizing the date to *c.*1730-60. In fact, the original monument was erected in or about the year of death of Esther Mann (d.1749), and a difference in hands can be discerned in the later inscriptions.

The 19th century opens with the only monument in the abbey by a sculptor of international fame, the Clarke monument by John Flaxman.[26] More representative of the Regency period are the fairly standardized tablets produced by local monumental masons, such as that to Joseph Shapland (d.1837) <8> by Lewis of Cheltenham (signed 'Lewis Chelt sc');[27] and those to Richard Alcock (d.1829) <33>, Kenelm Chandler (*c.*1833) <28> and the Price family (*c.*1844) <30>—all by 'Gardner of Tewkesbury'.[28] A more inventive work by a local craftsman is the Gothic Revival monument to Sir Robert Graham (d.1853) <18> by Thomas Collins (Fig.17.10), and Collins' own memorial (1906) <24> by R.L. Boulton of Cheltenham (who was responsible for the choir screen, 1892) is also a work of character carved in fine alabaster (Fig.17.12).

This revival of interest in a wider range of monumental stones, especially indigenous ones, is a feature of the modern period. In contrast to the Italian marble of Mrs. Craik's memorial (1890) (Fig.17.11) the elegant tablet to Victoria Woodhull Martin (d.1927) <13> (Fig.22.7) appears to be of polished Hopton Wood sand-

Fig.17.14 Archdeacon Hemming Robeson d.1912; detail, signature of P. Bryant Baker (1914)

stone from Derbyshire, carved by the London sculptor, G. Kruger Gray R.A. C.B.E., in 1939.[29] In contrast, French Caen stone is considered to be the material used for the recumbent effigy of Archdeacon Hemming Robeson, the work of another London-based royal academician, P. Bryant Baker, in 1914: his signature is lightly carved in cursive script at the foot end of the effigial slab (Fig.17.14). Baker was a regular exhibitor at the Academy between 1909 and 1916, his exhibits including busts of royal subjects like King Edward VII, and his model for the completed Robeson effigy appeared in the 1915 exhibition.[30]

Ledger Slabs and Churchyard Monuments[31]

The floor of the abbey church incorporates a considerable collection of ledger slabs which have survived various repavings. Ledger slabs—floor slabs with an inscription and, where appropriate, an heraldic achievement—appeared in the 16th century in response to changing religious attitudes at the Reformation, replacing medieval incised slabs and monumental brasses.[32] The only medieval slab of this type to survive is that to Leger de Parr (*c*.1300), in bay 3 of the nave south aisle. Unfortunately it is now largely hidden by the pedestrian ramp put down there in about 1960, but the 17th-century drawing in Dingley shows the full slab (Fig.17.15).[33] Today the words 'DYEVX : DE' of the Norman-French inscription are still visible, together with the crudely cut initials 'T H' of the person who reused the slab for his own grave probably in the 16th century.[34] The lack of evidence in the church for medieval and 16th-century monumental brasses and incised slabs to laymen of Tewkesbury is a curiosity for which various reasons have been put forward: for example, that the medieval parish church was elsewhere in the town.[35] However, this should certainly not apply in the 15th and 16th centuries—the most prolific period for such memorials—when the parish church was definitely in the nave. More probably extensive repavings of the church floors have taken their toll. The only old brasses in the abbey now are three 17th-century inscriptions.[36]

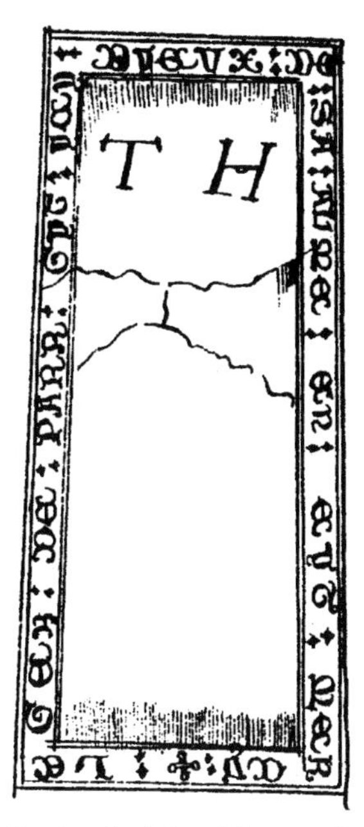

Fig.17.15 Incised slab of Leger de Parr c.*1300 (from Dingley,* c.*1680)*

Ledger slabs were particularly popular between the mid-17th and mid-19th centuries, which is the approximate datespan of the surviving examples in the abbey.[37] Some of the slabs appear still to be in their original locations, such as the enormous stones in the north ambulatory near the de Bryan tomb marking the graves of Frederick, son of Joseph Longmore of The Mythe (d.1819) and Philip Godsall Esq. (d.1826).[38] Inscriptions of other slabs, since lost, are known from the surveys by the 18th-century antiquary, Ralph Bigland, (fl.*c*.1750-84), and his 19th-century continuators. There we find, for example, the only record of the Hawlings family who usurped the medieval Clarence vault in 1709, and whose slab was lost in the repaving at the great restoration of 1875.[39] In 1897 the verger, Mr. W.G. Bannister, completed lists of all the slabs then extent in the church floor, and of many of the memorials in the churchyard as well.[40]

Amongst the more unusual ledger slabs is one celebrating a family servant, situated in bay 6 of the nave north arcade. The epitaph commemorates Gilbert Insall (d.1765) and his wife Elizabeth (d.1798), and continues:

Also of Ann Reynolds
who died Oct the 26th 1800
Aged 62 years
who lived servant with the above
Gilbert and Elizabeth Insall
upwards of 40 years
Well done thou good and faithful servant
Enter thou into the joy of the Lord[41]

A slab of particular interest in documenting the changing pattern of burial in the abbey during the 19th century is that to the Banaster family under the fifth bay of the nave south arcade. Its inscription is worth quoting at length as poignant testimony to the anguish brought to some families as a result of the 1850s Burial Acts.[42] After listing the early deaths of his children—William (d.1818), Mary Ann (d.1829) and Sarah Frances (d.1840)—and of his wife Elizabeth, aged 70 (d.1850), the inscription records:

... George Banaster Esq. the husband of the above
named Elizabeth Banaster died 24th March 1858
aged 83 years.
His earnest wish to be laid in
this Grave beside the remains
of his beloved Wife and Children
was frustrated by an act of the
Government prohibiting interment
within the walls of this Church
His mortal remains lie in his
Father's vault in the Chur[chyard][43]

One of the effects of the Burial Acts was to bring to an end the practice of burials within churches, and unfortunately for George Banaster the local application of this change came about between the death of his wife and his own decease. One would like to think that some of his annoyance with central authority may be reflected in the fact that most of the lettering of the word 'Government' has been recut: was it misspelt originally through ignorance or out of sympathy for the plight of the deceased?

In the churchyard, the digging of new graves ceased in 1857 when the town cemetery was opened. The churchyard extends on the north and west sides of the nave, the monastic buildings and monks' graveyard having occupied the area to the south (Fig.12.1). The use of the north churchyard for parish burials probably dates back to the 15th century at least, when the phrase 'parish church' was applied to the nave.[44] Wills of the early 15th century specify burial in the churchyard of the monastery, a wording which, Jones argues, indicates that previously the parish church and burial ground had been located elsewhere.[45] An early record of burial in the 16th century is that of Jeffrey Goughe who, by his will of 1525, bequeathed his body to the churchyard;[46] and the matrix for an early Tudor brass, apparently *in situ* externally on the north nave wall facing the churchyard, is further evidence of usage (Fig.10.18, centre).[47] Attempts were made in 1820 to enlarge the churchyard westward, to accommodate the pressure of burials for a populous parish, but the idea was rejected for financial reasons.[48]

Almost all the extant memorials belong to the 18th and first half of the 19th centuries, disposed each side of the main path from Church Street to the north porch. The path was first paved in 1750 and an avenue of trees planted.[49] Two pairs of new wrought-iron gates were set up, one standing at the entrance to the church porch and the other at the entrance from Church Street, of which the fine Gage gates—one of the abbey's treasures—are the survivors (Fig.21.18).[50] Lining the west edge of the path are several antiquities and curioisties in stone. On the corner nearest to the porch is a large moulded stone about two feet square, which is thought to be the base of a medieval cross,[51] but which looks as likely to be 17th or

Fig.17.16 The 'Norman' altar in the churchyard

Fig.17.17 The north-west churchyard, photograph c.*1855*

Cotswolds—notably at Painswick—which may in part be explained by the levelling of Tewkesbury churchyard in 1878, resulting in the loss of many monuments. Photographs before this date show the area to the north-west of the church packed with tombs, especially 19th-century headstones (Fig.17.17): which contrast with Lysons' earlier view of this area (Fig.16.6). The extent to which parts of the churchyard were lowered may be gauged in the area alongside the north aisle where, for example, the ground-course moulding on the pier of the 18th-century

18th century. Nearer to Church Street, an ashlar stone chest with massive top slab is labelled 'Traditionally the Norman altar' (Fig.17.16), and close-by a very weathered stone chest is known as 'the Saxon altar'.[52] The latter had a stump of stone fixed vertically in its 'altar' slab until recently, said to be the preaching cross associated with the 7th-century hermit, Theocus.[53] Far-fetched as these claims appear to be, the two items are not easily explained away as chest tombs and warrant further research.

A scattering of reasonable chest tombs is still to be seen in the churchyard, one of which was singled out for illustration by the conservation architect, Walter Godfrey, in his *English Mural Monuments and Tombstones* as an exemplar of 'the square built table tombs at their best' in Cotswold churchyards.[54] On the opposite side of the path is an example of a Cotswold chest tomb with characteristic lyre ends to the memory of Adyey[*sic*] Hoskins (d.1715, aged 25). However, one must admit that Tewkesbury pales before much richer collections elsewhere in the

flying buttress now stands several feet above ground level (Fig.10.18).[55]

Several of the surviving 19th-century monuments in the western section of the churchyard may be picked out for their associations. Best known is the headstone to John Hart (d.1800) because, as the inscription proclaims, he was 'the 6th descendant from the poet Shakespeare'. Hart (1753-1800) was a turner and chair-maker in Tewkesbury, and was of the sixth generation of lineal descendants from Shakespeare's sister, who had married William Hart, a hatter.[56] The Gothic-style headstone, by the northern boundary of the churchyard, carried this lament from his widow, Mary, stated to have died in 1830:

Here lies the only comfort of my life
Who was the best of husbands to a wife
Since he is not no joy I eer shall have
Till laid by him within this silent grave
Here we shall sleep, and quietly remain
Till by God's pow'r we meet in Heaven again
There with Christ eternally to dwell
And until that blest time, my love, farewell!

It appears to have passed previously unnoticed, however, that this cannot be the headstone of *c*.1800. The investigations of Pat Webley have revealed a number of textual changes—for example, according to the burial register, Mary died in 1814. These indicate that the present stone is a copy of the original, with some additions and minor mistranscriptions, and was set up towards the end of the 19th century by John Hart's descendants, well-off and still living locally.[57] The style of Gothic decoration on the headstone is not dissimilar to Boulton's work on the abbey choir screen of the 1890s.

Loose against the brick wall of Abbey Lodge, which forms the western boundary of the churchyard, is a headstone to the Bennett family. The first named is James Bennett (d.1856), bookseller of Tewkesbury, who was proud to have been a churchwarden at the 1828 restoration of the church, and whose *History of Tewkesbury* (1830) is such an important source for historians of the abbey and town. His memorial deserves to be more securely sited in the churchyard.[58]

Close to the southern boundary with Abbey House stands the simple, classically inspired chest tomb commemorating the family of Samuel Healing (d.1883), from Samuel his son, who died young in 1848 (aged 19), to his daughter Helen who died in 1915 (aged 75). She was the last person whose body was interred in the churchyard, by special dispensation.[59] Samuel Healing was a well-to-do mill owner in Tewkesbury, and another member of the family, Alfred Healing, was living in Abbey House at the time of its sale in 1883.[60] The family developed significant associations with the abbey church during the 20th century: Peter Healing was chairman of the Friends (1966-88) and also of the committee for the major restoration appeal of the 1970s, which included the Grove organ.[61]

The land encircling the eastern chapels of the church was given in 1939, and established the Abbey Lawn Trust.[62] Before this, an area of land to the south of the chancel was consecrated as an addition to the churchyard in November 1914, having been conveyed from the trustees of Abbey House to the parish earlier in the year.[63] Memorials additional to those in the churchyard have subsequently been set up in this area, the earliest and most prominent dating to 1916. This is to the memory of Elizabeth Smith (d.1916), the mother of the then vicar, the Revd. Ernest F. Smith, and takes the form of a freestanding Calvary—the first of two monumental cross memorials in the churchyard. The other is in the north churchyard, by the Gage gates, erected to commemorate Major James B.F. Cartland, killed in France in 1918, and other members of the Cartland family, relatives of the novelist, Barbara Cartland.

The other memorials are all tucked discreetly into the flowerbeds against the south-facing chapels, and are to 20th-century incumbents and other persons closely associated with the abbey. The Revd. Edward Pountney Gough (vicar 1930-42) and the Revd. Brian Purefoy (1942-63), with his wife, are commemorated by slabs here: that to Gough taking the medieval form of a Gothic cross-slab with a chalice and paten carved in the head, reflecting his Catholic disposition in matters of ritual.[64] Others with small slabs in this area include Henry Gordon Kitching (d.1946), 'a friend of this abbey and a chorister for 69 years'; and the most recent to Richard ('Dick') Chorley (d.1999), steward of the abbey (1993-98), in whose time major restorations like the cleaning of the nave ceiling were undertaken. His epitaph reads simply, 'He loved and cared for this abbey'. These words surely speak for many of those commemorated at Tewkesbury, whose memorials have been the subject of this chapter.

CHAPTER 18

The Bells *by* John Eisel

The story of the bells of Tewkesbury Abbey is dominantly post-Reformation, because from Queen Elizabeth's reign onwards the churchwardens' accounts and other documentation provide a plethora of details. In contrast very little information is available for the Middle Ages. The medieval abbey had provision for bells in the central tower of the church, and it is assumed that a former detached tower to the north was also a campanile (see below).

The first mention of bells at Tewkesbury Abbey occurs in the Annals in 1224, when the Bishop of Killaloe dedicated two large bells (*majora signa*) in the tower. Seventeen years later two other new bells (*magna signa*) were dedicated in the choir.[1] The first entry must refer to the central tower of the abbey (*in turri*) . This was originally of lantern form and the two internal stages above the lantern would have contained the bells in the upper stage with a ringing loft below. The lierne vault closing this in was added in the 14th century and was decorated with badges after 1471. In the middle of the vaulting is a bell hole, designed to raise bells into the tower (Fig.18.2).

The detached tower, which was demolished in 1817,[2] is known from a series of 18th- and early 19th-century views of its exterior, of which the most familiar is the engraving in James Bennett (Fig.18.3). The evidence for its medieval use as a bell-tower derives from post-Dissolution references to 'the belfrey', especially in 1582 when it was converted into a house of correction.[3] Detached bell-towers often occurred as adjuncts to great churches in the Middle Ages, such as the fine surviving example from Evesham Abbey.[4] By such standards the Tewkesbury tower appears relatively small and unostentatious, and more appropriate parallels may be sought in parish church examples like those at Richards Castle and Holmer (both Herefs.).[5] Bennett was of the opinion that the central tower of the church was not intended originally for bells, hence the existence of this campanile.[6] However, judging from old views of the latter—of which the Turner drawing and painting of *c.*1794 may be the most reliable—the windows and battlemented parapet of the top stage look 14th-century or later (Fig.18.4).[7] It is possible that these features are secondary, and that the simple unbuttressed form of the tower indicates that it was built earlier, but there is no proof that it is contemporary with the Norman church, which it would need to be to validate Bennett's hypothesis.

No records for actual bells in the campanile have come to light. At the Dissolution there were eight bells 'in the steeple there', weighing a total of 14,2001b. This steeple must be identified as the central tower of the church and no other bells are mentioned in the survey. It therefore seems very likely, following another suggestion of Bennett, that the campanile had ceased to function before

Fig.18.1 The bell 'Helen' added in 1992, the gift of Eric and Helen Taylor

the end of the Middle Ages and any bells had been removed before the Suppression.[8] Large cracks are shown in one wall in the engraving in Bennett (Fig.18.3), and if these are medieval then it would appear that vibration from bell-ringing had damaged the unbuttressed structure.

The eight bells from the central tower were bought by the townspeople from the king's commissioners for £142, at a rate of £1 per 100lb.[8] Three or four of these were probably sold on again, as the surviving churchwardens' accounts from 1563 onwards indicate that there were then only four bells, together with a small or sanctus bell.[9] In 1563 the 'greate' or tenor bell received attention at a total cost of 1s., including a key, probably for the keyed fittings (a method of fixing before the use of screw threads). A bald-erick or leather strap for suspending the clapper was also bought. Maintenance of the bells in 1564 totalled 16s. 5d., out of a budget for the abbey of about £25. A one-off payment in 1570 was for a similar amount:

> Paid to iiii men to ryd the dunge owt
> of the steple for viiii dayes vi a
> daye a peace xvis.

This was quite a high rate of pay for the time, and the fact that it took four men eight days to clean out the tower was an indication of the amount of work that was necessary.

At this period the sexton was John Cole, and he was paid 26s. 8d. per year for ringing a bell 'morning and evening, winter and summer', and for 'ryning of the Bowbelle at Crystmas'.

The little bell—probably the sanctus bell—cracked in 1587 and was sent on a barge to Worcester, where it was recast at a cost of £1 2s. The whole bill for the transaction, including transport, was £1 6s. 5d. Although the founder is not mentioned, it may have been an early bell by John Green, whose surviving bells date from 1595 onwards.[10]

In the Register of Baptisms which covers the years 1607 to 1629, there are two verses relevant to the bells:

> William Dixon and Thomas Hoare
> Made us that Bell which wee ringe before
> Which men for that good deede: praie we they
> maie thrive:
> For we hauinge but foure Bells: they made them
> Five
> And out of the grownde this Bell they did delue
> The 24th of Julie Anno Dom 1612.

Below this is a drawing of a bell with the name of 'Willm' Ward upon it and below again is written in a different hand:

Fig.18.2 The bell 'Helen' being raised through the bell hole in the middle of the crossing vault, 1992

The Bell Speakes
Wm. Dixon and Thomas Hoare
Did sell me away though I runge befor
Wch men afterwards did never thrive
For making us foure being once made five
And sould me to Wales as I doe weene
About Anno Dm 1613[11]

These verses imply that a smaller or treble bell was added to the ring in 1612, and infer that that Dixon and Hoare were the founders—casting the bell on the spot. Their names have not been recorded elsewhere as founders, but neither do they seem to have been local inhabitants.[12] However, the second verse suggests that after being used for a short while at Tewkesbury the new bell was sold to somewhere in Wales, a rather dubious transaction. There is no record of this casting in the accounts, which lump the years 1611 to 1615 together, but one item of interest is the payment 'to a messinger that went to Farmer to Evesham abought the staple of the greate bell', which may establish where Henry Farmer was resident.[13]

For the next few years there is little of interest. The bell loft was planked out in 1624 at a cost of 2s. 8d. and in the same year the first of a series of annual payments 'for ringing the

Fig.18.3 The engraving in Bennett of the tower

Fig.18.4 J.M.W. Turner's drawing of the former bell-tower, c.*1794*

sermon bell xviiid.' was recorded—this was to give warning that a sermon was about to be preached. In 1626 the payment for ringing the sermon bell for a whole year was 6s.

In 1632 repairs were carried out and the bells recast—the whole costing £124 11s. 11d. No clue is given as to the bellfounder who did the work, but it is assumed that the work resulted in them being augmented to a ring of six, as the accounts of the following year record a payment of £1 1s. 3d. for six ropes. In the same year there is the first of a long series of annual payments of 2s. 6d. for ringing on 5 November.

The 'Great Bell' or tenor bell cracked in 1648 and had to be recast. The accounts show that a bargain was made with the bellfounder at Worcester, articles of agreement were drawn up at Gloucester, and the bell was sent to Gloucester where it was recast. During the recasting 420lb. of extra metal were added to the bell and at 7d. per lb. this cost £13 13s., which contrasts with the £14 that John Barnwood was paid for casting the bell.[14] The whole operation cost £37 0s. 3d.

During the 1650s the bells were rung regularly for occasions of national rejoicing. There seems to have been a keen band of young ringers, for in 1650 there is the entry 'received of the younge ringers towards buyinge ropes 6s. 6d.' At that period ropes were bought by weight, and in 1660 five ropes weighing 52lbs. were bought at a cost of 5d. per lb.—a total cost of £1 1s. 6d. Normally a new set was obtained each year, and it may be that the old ropes were considered perks of the outgoing churchwardens, as they were at other places.

On 24 December 1653 the ringers were paid 8s. for the proclamation of the Lord Protector,[15] while on Coronation Day in 1660 the ringers were paid 10s., and from 1663 they were also paid for ringing on 29 May (Oak Apple Day)—a custom that continued at the abbey until modern times.

In 1670 the fourth bell became cracked, and an unnamed bellfounder in Gloucester was contacted, but the work was eventually given to John Martin in Worcester. The bell was sent there by water—the total bill for transport, recasting and adding extra metal being £24 8s. 10d. This was followed by more trouble with the bells in 1678/9 when a subscription was raised to enable the fifth and sixth bells to be recast. They were sent to 'Cleave'—Bishop's Cleeve—the bill totalling £1 6s. 8d; the unnamed bellfounder was paid £10 for casting the bells, while Abraham 'Riddle' was paid £6 for hanging them.[16] Yet more trouble was recorded in the accounts for 1679/80 when another bell was taken down and the accounts show that Abraham 'Ridell' was paid 10s. 6d. and the bellfounder £4 1s., so probably the same combination was again at work.

Despite all this, the bells were rung regularly and continued to be rung for occasions of national significance. Thus, in 1684, the ringers were paid 10s. 'on news of the hopes of the recovery of King Charles the second'. The defeat of Monmouth's rebellion in 1685 was celebrated, as was the coronation of James II, and his later defeat at the Battle of the Boyne in 1690. William of Orange, the successor of James II, pursued a war in Flanders from 1691 to 1697 and events connected with this were also marked by paid ringing.

In 1695 the surrender of the castle of Namur (Belgium) only attracted a payment of 2s. to the ringers, while the ringing in 1697 when peace was proclaimed cost 5s. In between these occasions the six bells then in the tower were recast into a ring of eight bells—the work being carried out in 1696 by Abraham Rudhall I who had added bellfounding to his skills in 1684. A total of £68 2s. was subscribed by local residents towards the cost, and the final bill was £72 3s. 3½d. A page in the accounts dated 6 April 1697 gives the weights of the bells, that of the treble as 5cwt. ½qr. 0lb. and that of the tenor as 22cwt. ½qr. 08lb. For his work Abraham Rudhall received £51 2s. and surplus metal owing to the parish was still in his hands. There were problems with the work carried out, and the following was recorded at a meeting on 4 June 1697:

> It is unanimously agreed by the inhabitants at this meeting that the metal that was remaininge in Mr. Rudhalls hands which amounted to one hundred and a half and fifteen pounds should be forgiven and allowed him by reason of the recasting of trible and seaventh bells.

The accounts for 1697/8 record a number of items relating to the movement of bells between Tewkesbury and Gloucester, but no payment to Abraham Rudhall, apart from the surplus metal. The recasting continued in 1700, when Rudhall received £3 10s. for the fourth bell, adding 71lbs. of metal on which he reproduced the inscription 'ABRA RVDHALL CAST VS ALL' recording his work, but without the date of recasting. In 1717 the seventh bell was recast once again, having lasted only 20 years, and there was a payment of £6 16s. to 'the Beffounder for wast of Mettle and Mettle added'. The work was carried out by Abraham Rudhall II, son of Abraham I. He also recast the second bell in 1725, and he was paid £10 10s. for the work he had done and for the extra metal.[17]

The treble bell cracked in 1742 and was recast by Abel Rudhall, son of Abraham II, at the cost of £9 13s. 9d. As the bell was sent to Gloucester twice it seems that the first attempt at recasting was unsuccessful. There was obviously concern about the continual cost of maintaining the bells, and no doubt Abel Rudhall's work was closely scrutinised by the churchwardens, for the parish meeting in that year ordered the churchwardens to take proper care about the casting of the newly-cracked treble bell.

Following this there was something of a break in the recasting of the bells, although on 6 July 1771 one William White of Gloucester put the seventh and eighth bells in order, for which he was paid £15 7s. 9d.,[18] and on 19 November 1773 Mr. 'Radall'—Thomas Rudhall, son of Abel Rudhall—was paid £3 3s. for rehanging the third bell. In 1783 Thomas Rudhall rehung the tenor bell and repaired the others.[19]

On 11 July 1795 John Rudhall, youngest son of Abel Rudhall and half-brother of Thomas, contracted to recast the tenor bell at an estimated cost of £59 1s. 6d., with suitable allowances for differences of weight, and this work was completed by 18 June 1796 when he submitted his account. Because the new bell was heavier than its predecessor, the eventual bill was £70 2s. 7d. Not surprisingly the churchwardens were slow in paying, and on 20 December 1796 John Rudhall wrote a pleading letter asking for at least something on account as he was pressed for money.[20]

By the end of the 18th century the work of the following members of the family was represented:

Treble	Abel Rudhall	1743
2	Abraham Rudhall II	1725
3	Abraham Rudhall I	1696
4	Abraham Rudhall I	1700
5	Abraham Rudhall I	1696
6	Abraham Rudhall II	1696
7	Abraham Rudhall II	1717
Tenor	John Rudhall	1796

Throughout the 19th century the bells were rung for national occasions, and the Napoleonic Wars gave plenty of excuse for such celebrations, and mourning as well. When the news of the Battle of Trafalgar reached Tewkesbury in 1805, the bells were rung; the churchwardens' accounts record:

> Pd Ringers for Nelson's glorious victory over the combined fleets of france and spain when that Immortal & Unparaleled Hero fell to the great grief of the Universe, France Excepted. £1 1s.[21]

Clearly the idiosyncratic use of capitals is intentional.

The behaviour of the Prince Regent in the early part of the century and his scandalous relationship with his wife Caroline caused public opinion at first to be on her side, but it later turned against her. When he was crowned as George IV on 19 July 1821 the ringers at Tewkesbury were paid 10s. Queen Caroline attempted to gain access to Westminster Abbey on that occasion but the doors were barred against her. She died a fortnight later, and on 14 August 1821 the ringers at Tewkesbury were paid 10s. for ringing 'when the Queen was taken from England'. It is not clear if they were for or against her.

In 1830 James Bennett stated that 'some of the bells require recasting'[22] and in April 1837 the bells were taken to Gloucester where the fifth and tenor bells were recast, as was the small sanctus bell. John Rudhall, the last of the family, had died in 1835 and the foundry had been taken over by Thomas Mears II of Whitechapel, whose name appeared on the recast bells.[23] While the bells were being removed, an accident with the seventh bell broke the leg of Thomas Wheeler, a journeyman carpenter, and he later died from this injury in Gloucester Infirmary.[24]

A new oak frame was built by James Cull, a local carpenter, with layout Pickford classification 8.2, a type commoner in earlier times.[25] Typical of its period is the use of cross braces, and the detail of the frame, including the inconsistent use of braces, indicates that Cull was not a regular bell hanger. Despite this comment, the frame has only needed minor repairs, including replacement of one of the cross-braces and insertion of two braces in the north elevation, and it continues to give good service today. The frame rests on the floor, mainly supported by two early north-south timbers with braced wall posts from corbels at either end, relaid with three-inch thick softwood boards at this period. It is placed in the north-east corner of the tower, whereas its predecessor is thought to have been nearer the centre. At the same time the floor above the lantern part of the tower was rebuilt, incorporating some of the timbers of the earlier floor, but not necessarily *in situ*, and the ringing chamber moved up to this level, reducing the length of the ropes by about 30 feet. Previous to this the bells had been rung from a floor inserted just above the lierne vault, evidence of this being seen in the form of changes carved on the walls of the tower. The earlier ones may date from the 17th century, and it is tempting to associate these with the young ringers of 1650. For the comfort of the ringers the new ringing chamber was partitioned off in the north-east corner, and this has recently been extended to give the ringers more space.

The net cost of the recasting of the bells and providing them with new clappers was £91 9s. 9d., while the other associated work, including the new frame, hanging the bells and the new floors, was £352, almost £300 of which was raised by public subscription.[26] The final payments for this new work were not made until 1839.

The bells were reopened on 16 October 1837, when bands from Longney, Painswick and Cheltenham attended. The first two named rang touches of Stedman Triples on the restored bells, while the Cheltenham Society rang a peal of 5,184 changes of Kent Treble Bob Major.[27] Another account states that three peals were attempted on the day, but only that attempted by the Cheltenham Society was successful. The band walked over from Cheltenham on an extremely cold day, bringing their own ropes with them.[28] The rehanging of the bells and the details of this peal are recorded on a tablet hung in the ringing chamber.[29]

Then, as now, a new or rehung ring of bells is an attraction to other ringers, and although the band from Gloucester was not present at the opening of the bells, it visited in January 1838, as reported in the *Hereford Journal* of 31 January:

> On Monday last was rung, at the Abbey Church, Tewkesbury, by the Glocester Ringers, a true and complete peal of Grandsire Triples, containing 5040 changes, 190 bobs and 50 singles, brought round in two hours and 57 minutes. Conducted by Mr. Isaac Gaze.

Shortly after this, in 1839, the regular ringers were no longer paid, although they received remuneration for special occasions. There was little done in the way of change ringing until C.D.P. Davies, son of the then vicar of Tewkesbury, born in 1857, got together a band and with much encouragement rang a peal of Grandsire Triples in 1877, also recorded on a tablet in the ringing chamber.[30]

Little was done on the bells for the rest of the 19th century, and in 1904 it was reported that the bells were:

> Rehung by Cull 1837. Slight repairs by local tradesmen at various times since. Rehanging and the addition of two trebles has been recommended to the church authorities, but no steps have been taken owing to the want of funds and other reasons.[31]

However, the work was taken in hand in 1914, and the fifth bell of the ring of eight was recast by Messrs. Mears and Stainbank at the Whitechapel foundry. Two trebles were added to make the ring up to one of ten bells, the frame extended to the south with two oak pits, the old bells were rehung, and the work was rededicated on 6 July. At the service the bells were dedicated by the Revd. C.D.P. Davies who also delivered the sermon. A photograph was taken of all the ringers and clergy present on this occasion.[32]

When the Revd. C.D.P. Davies died in 1931, in such esteem was he held that a proposal was made to augment the bells to a ring of 12. This was carried out in 1933, when the Whitechapel trebles of 1914 were recast, two smaller bells were added and the remaining bells were tuned. Two pits with cast-iron frames were squeezed in between Cull's frame and the east wall. The work was dedicated on 19 May 1933.

Although the work of tuning the old bells was considered a success at the time, the tonal qualities were lacking and by 1960 the bells were in need of rehanging. It was decided to take the opportunity to have a completely new ring of bells, but because of historic interest it was decided to preserve the former sixth bell (Abraham Rudhall II 1725), the seventh bell (Abraham Rudhall I 1696), the eighth bell (Abraham Rudhall I 1700) and the eleventh bell (Abraham Rudhall II 1717) and use them for clock bells.[33] The other bells were recast, the inscriptions of the old fifth and tenth bells being reproduced in facsimile and their inscription bands cut out and preserved, and the weight of the tenor bell being increased from 21cwt. 2qr. 23lb. to 27cwt. 1qr. 5lb. The weights and diameters are given below:[34]

Bell	Diameter (ins.)	Weight cwt.	qr.	lb.
Treble	25½	4	3	22
2	26½	5	0	8
3	27½	5	1	8
4	28½	5	2	13
5	29¾	5	3	4
6	31	6	2	6
7	32¾	7	0	14
8	35½	8	0	27
9	39½	11	2	3
10	42½	13	3	20
11	47	18	3	10
Tenor	53	27	1	5

The final addition to the bells came in 1992, when a flat sixth bell was added, the gift of Eric and Helen Taylor (Fig.18.1). It was cast late in 1991 at Loughborough, weighs 6cwt. 3qr. 6lb. and is hung in an adaptation of the Whitechapel pits of 1914. The provision of this bell completes a middle ring of eight bells, with the ninth bell as tenor, a handy ring of bells on which to learn change ringing on eight bells.[35]

The bells are rung regularly, twice every Sunday and for practice each Thursday, and for weddings. Other notable occasions are marked by peals of at least 5,000 changes. One major event that takes place each year in May is the annual ringing competition for the Tewkesbury Shield, which is competed for by six bands from across the country.[36]

CHAPTER 19

The Milton Organ *by* Kenneth Jones

In 1631 Robert Dallam built a new organ for the Chapel of Magdalen College, Oxford. Thus begins the story of a remarkable instrument which has had an interesting and much-travelled life. That significant parts of this historic organ have survived until the 21st century is almost miraculous.

The Dallam organ had two keyboards and two organ-cases—the main case at which the organist sat and a smaller 'Chaire' case placed behind the organist's back.

The diarist John Evelyn describes the organ still standing (and he heard it played) in Magdalen Chapel in 1654, but shortly thereafter it was dismantled, and re-erected in Hampton Court Palace. The poet John Milton must be assumed to have played it there; the organ's soubriquet derives from this belief.

In 1660 it was dismantled again and in 1661 was returned to Magdalen College Chapel, where it was re-erected by its creator Robert Dallam. In 1690 it was remodelled by Dallam's grandson, Renatus Harris.

The main organ-case, with the organ's main soundboard, keyboard, action and pipes, was sold to Tewkesbury Abbey and set up there in 1737 by Thomas Swarbrick—the third time it had been dismantled and re-erected. The siting was on a screen which spanned the abbey's nave two bays west of the massive west piers of the tower. The Dallam organ-front with its colourfully decorated and embossed pipes faced the crossing and choir, while Swarbrick provided a new second 'front' facing west into the nave. At Magdalen the organ had been set in a side arch, and had a simple panelled back.

The Chaire organ and its case found their way to St. Nicholas' Church, Stanford on-Avon (Northants.), where they were modified and re-erected (again by Thomas Swarbrick) as a small one-manual organ. Much of this instrument has remained there to this day, but with only a handful of internal pipes, and mute for a century and a half (Fig.19.3).

The next major work on the Milton organ at Tewkesbury was executed by John Holland of Bath in 1796; he added a short-compass Swell organ and carried out repairs.

In 1848, Henry Willis, then aged 27 and as one of his first commissions, remodelled the organ considerably. He provided new sound-boards and action and added a number of new stops and pipes. He amended the manual compass and added a pedalboard and two pedal stops. He also deepened the organ-case so as to accommodate the enlarged organ.

In the period of the 1875-1879 restoration of the abbey the Milton organ was moved again, no less than three times. First it was dismantled and taken down from its screen (which was eliminated) being re-erected on the floor in the north aisle. Yet again it was dismantled and re-erected, this time against the south wall of the south transept. Then it was moved to a position under

Fig.19.1 The restored and reconstructed Milton organ. Upper case-front and pipes by Robert Dallam, 1631; new organ-screen and lower organ-case by Kenneth Jones, 1997

the north arch of the crossing—but this time it was not dismantled, being moved bodily, right across the transept, by means of aids such as screw jacks, in an operation described by *Musical Times* as 'an unusual and very clever proceeding'.

To rest at last? Not a bit of it. In 1887, a mere eight years later, when the massive Grove organ was presented to the abbey and set up in the north transept (where it remains) the Milton organ was dismantled once more, and re-assembled exactly opposite on the south side of the choir.

In 1948 a major rebuilding and enlargement of the organ was executed by J.W. Walker & Sons. This included yet another dismantling and re-erection.

By this time the Milton organ had lost virtually all its lower casework—but the 1631 Dallam and 1737 Swarbrick 'fronts' with their pipes had survived. That the complete set of 37 Dallam front-pipes remained intact, although mutilated in their voicing and their nether parts, is particularly astonishing.

In 1995-97 the Milton organ-cases (what had survived of them) were taken down by Kenneth Jones and Associates of Dublin. Exhaustive research was carried out to establish the previous dimensions, architectural and cabinet-work detailing and successive decorative schemes which the organ had enjoyed over the centuries. New casework to replace missing parts was made, and the surviving parts of the ancient cases were lovingly restored; the 1631 front-pipes were repaired and restored. The organ was erected in a raised position on a new screen, at least its tenth setting-up, almost all of which involved a new home or setting. Apart from tiny portable organs, the Milton organ must be the most moved church organ in existence; and it has even been across the Irish Sea to the Dublin workshops of Kenneth Jones and Associates.

The new parts of the organ-cases, and the new screen/gallery, were designed by David Graebe. All work, new and restorative, including the making of the new screen, was carried out by the Kenneth Jones team. Kenneth Jones and Associates also created what is essentially a new organ for the abbey, but which incorporates the best of the surviving pipes of various eras, fully restored.

The Instrument

Robert Dallam's instrument of two manuals and thirteen stops was to a specification which may be considered old-fashioned for its day. It had chromatic keys from Cl to d51. But it was pitched at what is called 'Choir Pitch', which means that when playing on the Principal stops it sounded a fourth higher than today's unison stops—the bottom key sounded 'five-foot' F. But Dallam's organ had two sub-unison stops, one with stopped pipes and the other (the largest pipes seen in the front) open; the central pipe originally sounded 'ten-foot' F. Thus was defined the size of the organ-case.

Renatus Harris rearranged the pipes, lowered the pitch a semitone and provided new keyboards the sounding compass of which started at the G below today's bottom C. Apart from certain conventions at the bass end the keys now played the pipes not at a transposed pitch but as today — key c sounded note c. I ignore in this discussion the fact that overall pitch has varied over the centuries as against today's A=440 cycles.

While Renatus Harris altered the tonal specification it is more likely that he re-regulated and transposed his grandfather's work rather than altering its basic tonal character to any great degree. It is unlikely that Swarbrick altered the tonal qualities either, possibly apart from the effect resulting from lowering the pitch another semitone; or for that matter Holland in 1796, as far as the Great Organ is concerned.

We cannot know what the Dallam sound was like, but we can make a reasonable guess from the technical evidence of the surviving Dallam pipes—not their present actual tone, for they have been greatly altered and mutilated over the past century and a half. These surviving pipes, including the front-pipes, have a very high tin content (*c*.93%) and thin walls. There is enough information to enable the making and voicing of replicas of the stops as originally made. Every possible piece of information was gathered from every individual surviving pipe, including hundreds of macro photographs—a daunting mass of material to catalogue, tabulate and evaluate.

Swarbrick and Holland both altered the keyboard compass in the fashion of their times, as did Willis in 1848, when the compass started again from today's 'eight-foot' C. But while Willis' work was well done and conservative for all the new stops, the altering of the compass caused further distress to the old Dallam pipes. Most of the front-pipes were cut down at the back, where such work is not visible when looking at the organ, and made to sound notes altogether higher than those for which they had been designed originally.

The 1948 rebuild compounded this further, and the largest pipe in the front was found to have been cut to sound C, no less than six semitones higher than its musical Dallam design, and a similar fate had been suffered by those of the other front-pipes which were still speaking. The revoicing of the surviving internal Dallam pipes (and to a degree the Holland and Willis) at this time involved much cutting and harm, in the context of seeking to obtain from these pipes the power considered appropriate for the volume and needs of the abbey.

The 1948 work, in which the Walker firm collaborated in the tonal design with Huskisson Stubington (then the abbey's organist), has a curious tonal history. The original concept was to make the (Willis) Milton organ and the (Michell & Thynne) Grove organ playable by electric action from a single console in a raised position within the north screen. This would provide the organist with the contact and control which was not available at the consoles of either instrument, while also eliminating running to-and-fro. As far as I know it was not intended that the two organs be played together so much as alternately. The concept was not realised for various reasons, including pitch differences, Grove action requirements, and financial constraints. Eventually it was decided to augment the limited resources of the Milton organ by adding two divisions sited in the apse chamber above the Lady Chapel. The new parts and pipes for this composite compromise were competently made, especially if one considers the immediate post-war era, but many of the stops used second-hand pipes from other sources, not with entirely happy results. While I have not had access to all the correspondence and documentation on this subject, I am persuaded that Huskisson Stubington has been quite unfairly maligned for what appeared to be a grandiose and unfocussed concept, but one which was much more influenced by other circumstances than by his artistic wishes or guidance.

While the Milton organ had had tracker (mechanical) key-action and mechanical stop-action from 1631 to 1947, the new scheme unfortunately replaced this with electro-pneumatic action, connected to the new console in the north screen. By the 1990s the action of the organ had become tired, worn out and unreliable.

Fig.19.2 The rear case of the Milton organ by Swarbrick, 1737

Specification of the new Milton Organ in 1997

The new pipe organ of four manuals and pedals, with 68 stops and 4,611 pipes, includes certain of the best of the pipes of the previous organ, carefully restored and revoiced.

Great Organ

No.	Stop	Pitch
1.	Double Diapason	16′
2.	Open Diapason No 1	8′
3.	Open Diapason No 2	8′
4.	Claribel Flute	8′
5.	Principal	4′
6.	Wald Flute	4′
7.	Twelfth	$2^{2}/_{3}$′
8.	Fifteenth	2′
9.	Sesquialtera	III ranks
10.	Mixture 2′	IV ranks
11.	Cymbal $^{1}/_{2}$′	II ranks
12.	Trumpet	8′
13.	Clarion	4′

Swell Organ (enclosed)

No.	Stop	Pitch
14.	Open Diapason	8′
15.	Stopped Diapason	8′
16.	Salicional	8′
17.	Voix Celeste TC	8′
18.	Principal	4′
19.	Open Flute	4′
20.	Flageolet	2′
21.	Mixture 2′	III-IV ranks
22.	Double Trumpet	16′
23.	Cornopean	8′
24.	Hautbois	8′
25.	Clarion	4′

Choir Organ

No.	Stop	Pitch
26.	Stopped Diapason	8′
27.	Quintadena	8′
28.	Dulciana	8′
29.	Principal	4′
30.	Chimney Flute	4′
31.	Nazard	$2^{2}/_{3}$′
32.	Fifteenth	2′
33.	Flute	2′
34.	Tierce	$1^{3}/_{5}$′
35.	Larigot	$1^{1}/_{3}$′
36.	Sharp Mixture 1′	IV ranks
37.	Cremona	8′

Solo Organ (enclosed)

No.	Stop	Pitch
38.	Harmonic Flute	8′
39.	Violoncello	8′
40.	Traverse Flute	4′
41.	Piccolo	2′
42.	Orchestral Oboe	8′
43.	Voix Humaine	8′
44.	Horn	16′
45.	Trumpet	8′
46.	Clarion	4′

Apse Organ (enclosed except Tuba)

No.	Stop	Pitch
47.	Cor de Nuit	8′
48.	Dolce	8′
49.	Unda Maris TC	8′
50.	Fugara	4′
51.	Flute	4′
52.	Harmonia Aetheria	III ranks
53.	Corno di Bassetto	8′
54.	Tuba (high pressure)	8′

Pedal Organ

No.	Stop	Pitch
55.	Open Wood	16′
56.	Open Diapason	16′
57.	Subbass	16′
58.	Pedal Bourdon (Apse)	16′
59.	Quint Flute	$10^{2}/_{3}$′
60.	Principal	8′
61.	Flute	8′
62.	Nazard (ext. No.59)	$5^{1}/_{3}$′
63.	Fifteenth	4′
64.	Mixture $2^{2}/_{3}$′	IV ranks
65.	Double Horn (ext. No.44)	32′
66.	Trombone	16′
67.	Horn (No.44)	16′
68.	Trumpet	8′

Couplers for Solo to Swell, Solo to Great, Solo to Choir, Swell to Great, Swell to Choir, Choir to Great, Apse Sub-octave, Apse Octave, Apse Unison Off, Solo to Pedal, Swell to Pedal, Great to Pedal, Choir to Pedal.
Tremulants to Solo, Swell, Choir and Apse.

The organ is provided with a comprehensive combination system, with eight pistons per division and eight general pistons, also reversible pistons for the couplers. The combinations on all pistons are adjustable by setter piston and there are 16 separate levels of memory for divisional pistons, 99 for general pistons. A ‘stepper’ facility progresses through the general pistons and level by level, giving nearly 800 sequences, and a memory-card facility can store the settings of the entire system.

The heart of the organ consists of the Great Organ, Swell Organ and Pedal Organ (in the Milton organ-case) with the Choir Organ within the screen, to the west. These divisions have tracker (mechanical) key-action. The Solo Organ and Pedal Basses (also within the screen) have electro-pneumatic action, as does the remote Apse Organ. All unison coupling is mechanical, including from electro-pneumatic divisions.

The Restoration of the 1990s

The foregoing gives some idea of the nature of the instrument which faced us when we undertook its restoration in the mid 1990s. There were pipes from 1631, 1690, 1796, 1848 and various years in the 20th century—these last mostly by Walker, 1948, but also recycled pipes by several other builders, including Robert Hope-Jones. The most recent additions to the team came in the 1970s, when pipes which had been borrowed from the Grove organ, including the Solo Tuba, had to be returned to that instrument, and replaced.

It was decided to create an essentially new organ of three manuals (Great, Swell and Choir) and pedals, with tracker action, housed in (and beside, not in line of sight) the Milton organ-case in its raised position on the new screen, thus restoring to the organ the position of dignity which it enjoyed from 1631 to 1875 and from where it can speak authoritatively through the building. The *en-fenêtre* console, with its ambo, places the organist in an excellent position for visual and musical contact with the choir and with everything occurring in the liturgy. In this new tracker-action organ we undertook to incorporate all of the old pipework which could be restored or voiced to serve in the context of a cohesive and balanced tonal scheme, completing this scheme with new pipework which has been scaled and designed to complement and blend; and to create an articulate, flexible and resourceful organ for the accompaniment of choir, liturgy and congregation. Consideration was given to the alternative of a more strictly historic instrument, but there were many difficulties. To what period does one go? Could such an organ even attempt to serve the repertoire enjoyed in the abbey today, with demands which include contemporary music and the leading of large congregations? Could the received state of the sadly altered old pipes justify their further alteration and punishment in an attempt to retrieve a more original tonal quality? We were also conscious of the affection and respect that those who worship in the abbey have for their historic Milton organ, whether evaluative or purely sentimental; and that this was coloured by some of the sounds it has made over the past 50 years.

The Dallam front-pipes required special attention. They have been physically restored and repaired conservatively, and where collapsing the feet have been stiffened (at the back). The areas cut out of the backs of the pipes have been refilled, using metal of similar composition to that used by Robert Dallam. The upper lips have been lowered and regularised. Thirty-five of the 37 Dallam front-pipes now speak in this organ, the other two were too physically distressed to be able to serve. They sound notes which are very close indeed to the notes they originally sounded—for example the largest frontpipe now sounds 'ten-foot' G, whereas it originally sounded between F# and G at today's pitch, and is part of the new Double Diapason 16-foot of the Great Organ. Parts of the Dallam ranks of pipes have been reunited so as to recreate a substantially Dallam stop: the Open Diapason No. 2 of the Great Organ, which from 'five-foot' G up has only occasional pipes not belonging to a single original rank (one of the original Principals as far as we can ascertain). Inserted pipes, and the bass, have been made as Dallam replicas, in 93% tin.

To enhance the resources of the organ in the more romantic/symphonic areas, and to enable continuation of service and enjoyment of the considerable number of pipes to which that description can be applied, a fourth manual has been provided in the organ, with electro-pneumatic action, playing the Solo and Apse organs. All inter-manual and -pedal coupling, including from this keyboard, remains mechanical.

The Archaeology, Restoration and Conservation

Exhaustive examination of the organ and its case included raking-light examination, photography and macro-photography, the taking of microscopic paint scrapes and samples and their examination under the microscope, with section photographs having up to x500 magnification. Kenneth Jones Associates photographed and measured every part of the composite organ-case and the individual front-pipes. We also took all physical dimensions of the historic internal pipes.

As a result, we were able to establish the physical and decorative history of the organ-case and its front-pipes. Further work on the old parts of the case and front-pipes has involved conservation rather than full-scale restoration. While our discoveries suggested the exciting prospect of being able to return the case to the appearance it had when first set up in the abbey by Thomas Swarbrick, or to restore parts of the decorative scheme so as to illustrate the history of the organ, it had already been decided that the casework would be finished overall in a near-matt, near-black uniform finish, over a shellac coat so as to make the process reversible. This decision was not revised and the result is as you see it; while the front-pipes remain gilt, the aged gilding as received having been laboriously restored and repaired with careful matching.

In addition to repair, we completed missing parts of the old case (including carved work) and made the new lower casework. We also made in our workshops the new oak screen, with its ambo and carved pierced panels.

In Magdalen College Chapel the organ-case was in natural oak, oiled, with a painted blue background to the cherubs' heads and strapwork on the impost immediately below the front-pipes, and with four 'suns in splendour' in blues and gilt in the circular panels or cartouches higher up the front casework.

The front-pipes were elaborately decorated in pigments and gilt, with varied patterns, giving a very rich appearance, in a manner similar to the decoration which may still be seen at Stanford-on-Avon (Fig.19.3).

Thomas Swarbrick left the four blazing suns untouched, an appropriate gesture for Tewkesbury Abbey's historic associations. Otherwise he primed the entire case, including

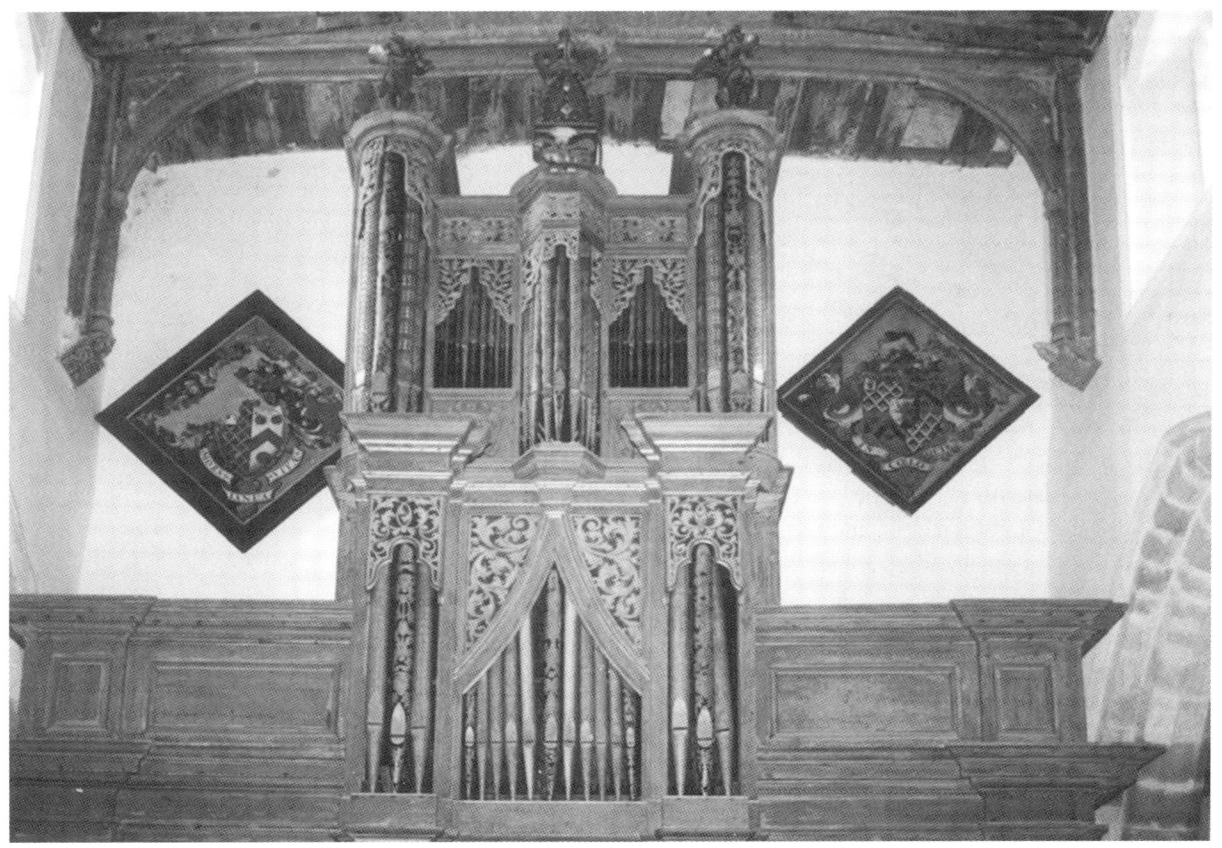

Fig.19.3 The organ at Stanford-on-Avon, Nothamptonshire

his new 'nave' case-front, with a red oxide primer or raddle, and over-painted this with an umber colour. This appears to have included a glaze, giving a mild effect of false-graining. The cherubs' heads were gilt, as were the falcons on the outer towers and finials on intermediate towers. The crown was illuminated with vermilion, blue, white (ermine) and gold. The new nave case had painted designs with arabesques and floral images; two major panels depicted musical trophies.

At the time of John Holland's work, the entire organ-case was painted in a mahogany false-grained finish, including the previously decorative areas. The front-pipes were gilt all over: while this could have been done by Swarbrick, it is unlikely in view of the fact that he did not cover the decoration on the Stanford-on-Avon front-pipes.

At the time of the Willis work, the entire organ was painted in an oak false-grained finish. At some time then or later, the front-pipes were re-gilded.

In 1923, as recorded in the *Tewkesbury Parish Magazine* of February 1924, the then sacristan 'Mr. Bannister has (without any cost but that of the materials) himself replaced the hideous paint of the organ-case with a dark stain which brings its colour into harmony with the ancient choir-stalls; for this he deserves the warmest thanks of all lovers of the Abbey'—words which will be forever engraved on my memory. It is this crudely-applied finish, darkened to near-black by the effects of light, which covered the organ until recently. It had been quite erroneously attributed to the 18th-century style associated with John Holland, and is the reason for the present near-black finish.

CHAPTER 20

The Grove Organ *by* Michael Peterson

'Surely the greatest British Organ of its day'[1]

The History

The Grove organ was presented to the abbey in 1887 by the Reverend C.W. Grove to commemorate the Golden Jubilee of Queen Victoria. It was originally built by the short-lived firm of Michell & Thynne for the Inventions Exhibition of 1885, held in South Kensington, where it was awarded 'the Silver Medal and Diploma for superior Voicing and Specialities in Tone Colour'. It was subsequently displayed at the Liverpool Exhibition in 1886, where the distinguished recitalist W.T. Best pronounced it to be the finest organ of its kind that he had ever played upon. In spite of this commendation no home could be found for it until the Revd. Grove bought it for about £800. The firm had already incurred considerable expense brought about by some confusion with the authorities over the siting of the instrument at the original exhibition, and so it is hardly surprising that, soon after, 'the firm failed', and Michell and Thynne went their separate ways.

Probably bought specifically for the abbey, though there is an unsubstantiated myth that it might have been meant for Cheltenham, the Grand organ, as it was at first known, was set up, uncased, as it still is, in the north transept. Its early existence was not always free from criticism, at least on the part of the abbey authorities, who sometimes found themselves embarrassed by such a generous gift since there was an understanding that all expenses in connection with the removal of the organ and its re-erection in the abbey should be borne by the parishioners. Hydraulic engines to operate the organ's blowing apparatus had to be purchased, and the necessary water supply arranged—'a dead rent of £2 10s. per quarter with an allowance of 50,000 gallons'. In addition the Milton organ had to be moved from its position on the north side of the choir to the south side and its pitch raised to agree with the high pitch of the Grove. Three years after the arrival of the Grove there was still some £229 owing and it was announced 'that the churchwardens would be happy to receive gifts'. More drastically, on account of the heavy water rate, now £19 a year, it was thought best 'to discontinue the use of the Great Organ at the Sunday services'. In the end, it seems that the donor himself may have had to come to the rescue.

The opening recital on Tuesday, 27 September 1887, was given by George Riseley, the organist of Bristol Cathedral. There were links with Bristol, since the vicar at the time, Hemming Robeson, was also archdeacon of Bristol, the diocese then being that of Gloucester and Bristol. The occasion appears to have attracted widespread attention, and it was advertised that 'the 9.40 train from Tewkesbury will enable persons from a distance (not holding Excursion Tickets) to attend Mr. Riseley's recital'. An audience of over 2,000 people is said to have assembled in the abbey. The *Tewkesbury Register*, though noting that 'the programme was not quite so suited to popular taste as might have been wished', agreed that 'the playing was all that could have been desired' and commented on 'Mr. Riseley's wonderful skill as a pedalist'. The main items were Mendelssohn's First Sonata, Bach's Fantasia et Fuga in G minor, and Neukomm's Storm Fantasia, together with pieces by Wesley, Guilmant and Haydn, and vocal solos by Mrs. Hemmingway (the abbey organist's wife), 'whose powerful voice is always heard to great advantage in the abbey', and the Revd. F.R. Carbonell, lately precentor of the abbey. The proceedings were opened and closed with hymns and prayers. An auspicious beginning!

The hydraulic blowing apparatus, however, always seems to have been a matter of some concern. The *Parish Magazine* of April 1898 drew attention to 'strange unearthly preliminary sounds from the Great Organ, which indicate that its internal arrangements are also very unsatisfactory. Mr. Bath (the organist), soon converts these strange mutterings into sweet harmonies, but modern appliances would make them vanish entirely'. In 1905 the organ was cleaned and the then organist, Mr. Vine, reported that:

> A new hydraulic starter will be placed at the keyboard so that the wind will be under the immediate control of the organist. Several of the pipes the present organist has never yet heard. In one case a large quantity of hay had been left in the pipe - the remains of a bird's nest in another. Some of the wooden pipes still contained the little supports that were used by the makers - these had never been removed. Other defects have been found in the conveyance pipes and wind trunks, the cause of much waste of wind and water. It is hoped that the work will be finished by Christmas.

Alas, hope was not realised!

In 1924 the blowing apparatus was again under attack. Work was being done on the Milton organ, and while this was going on the vicar wrote, somewhat testily, in the *Parish Magazine*:

> We have had to endure the accompaniment of Divine Service on the Grove Organ, and this has greatly taxed the patience of the congregation; for not only is the big organ too far away from the choir to permit of absolute synchronisation, but the engine is so intolerably noisy that an unaccompanied service would have been preferable. The Grove Organ is, in many respects, a 'white elephant', and it can never serve its purpose until it is provided with electric action and in conjunction with the Milton Organ, played from a single console placed in the chancel at the east end of the choir stalls.

A month later, when repairs to the Milton Organ had been completed, he was able to report: 'We may well be thankful that our two months purgatory is at an end ... we may hope that the music will once more be brisk and crisp, which is impossible when it is accompanied on the Grove Organ'.

As it turned out, these views narrowly escaped being prophetic, for in 1948, although the problem of the intolerably noisy engine had been resolved by the provision of an electric motor, an ambitious scheme was proposed whereby the Grove organ was to be enlarged from 35 to 70 stops, the Milton organ moved to the north side of the choir with solo and echo departments added in the former gallery chapel of the south transept, and all were to be played from an elaborate five manual console in a new loft, with a two manual console provided in the choir to play the Milton organ alone for service accompaniment. Much discussion and indeed argument followed, but what finally emerged from the fracas was a five manual console, a two manual console, a rebuilt Milton organ with its solo and echo departments, and, miraculously, the Grove organ untouched; money had run out! The 1948 scheme was certainly imaginative and ambitious but hindsight and an increasing awareness of the Grove's unique distinction have made it abundantly clear that to have tampered in any way with Michell & Thynne's masterpiece could only have been disastrous. It is not often that one can be thankful that funds were insufficient.

By 1972 some money was available, and Messrs. Bishop & Son were approached with a view to restoring the Grove organ on strict 'conservation' lines. A tiresome hiatus occurred when a difference of opinion in the parish as to the siting of the organ necessitated holding a consistory court. The outcome was that the Chancellor of the diocese rejected all the petitions and granted a faculty only for the restoration of the organ *in situ*. Work finally began in 1980, and in the early stages presented the appearance of an archaeological dig; 90 years' accumulation of parochial paraphernalia dumped under the organ and the removal of dust and ash thrown up by the abbey's two Gurney stoves occupied a fortnight. In some cases the mouths of pipes were completely blocked. Thereafter work, under the supervision of Mr. John Budgen, proceeded smoothly, a testimony to the original builders' work.

Finally on 2 February 1981, the Feast of Candlemas, Canon C.G.R. Pouncey, at his last service as vicar before retirement, was able to rededicate the organ: 'To the glory of God and in memory of Brian Purefoy, Vicar of Tewkesbury Abbey, 1942-1963'.

The Instrument

Though the instrument today is substantially as Michell & Thynne left it, it does not fully reflect their original intentions. A letter published in the *Musical Opinion* for October 1885 and signed 'X.Y.Z.', amongst other things accused the new firm of 'poaching' workmen and ideas from elsewhere in order to acquire knowledge of 'improved principles', and altering their original plan to incorporate those principles. 'X.Y.Z.' was presumably T.C. Lewis, a leading organ builder, who had employed Thynne and who, no doubt, was aggrieved at losing him and one or two other employees who defected at the same time. Michell & Thynne replied that:

> Our original design, a model one, remains as at first laid out, with this difference [which bears importantly on "X.Y.Z.'s" statement], the solo organ is in a different position, a change made, not by our own choice, but in compliance with an order from the authorities of the exhibition, which required us to raise our platform several feet higher than at first agreed upon when the allotment was made for our exhibit.
>
> Practically this entailed the cutting down our frame-work, the lowering all the sound-boards, the finding a new position for the solo organ, besides the rearranging the whole action, - alterations which (the organs having been planned to stand in tiers one above the other) not only injured the symmetry of our design, but seriously impeded the progress of our work, and caused us to incur heavy additional expense.

The solo organ now projects, rather uncomfortably, at the treble side of the organ, as does the console. Curiously, no mention was made of the position of the latter, which one might expect to have been in a more conventional position at the front of the instrument, below the choir organ. The additional expense must have contributed to the ultimate bankruptcy of the firm, and the organ, in fact, was only completed towards the end of the exhibition's run.

The builders' stated aim in creating what they referred to as their 'Model Organ' was:

> an attempt to place in the hands of the player a grand and complete organ, reduced to the smallest possible dimensions as regards the number of its slides. It will be found to contain all the solidity, dignity of tone, and refinement of detail, which should characterise a good church organ, with many novelties in tone and construction, and to possess unusual capacity for orchestral effects.[2]

The phrase 'smallest possible dimensions' certainly does not include the general lay-out, which is generous, but for a mere 35 stops spread over four manuals and pedals the effect is spectacular.

The commonly expressed opinion of the organ is that it combines a bold and commanding Schulze-type diapason chorus with high pressure Willis-type reeds. Stephen Bicknell has pointed out, though, that both may be more properly derived from the work of T.C. Lewis.[3] Lewis was himself an admirer of Schulze and, as has been said, Thynne worked for him before combining with Michell, also a Schulze admirer. Be that as it may, the Great chorus is certainly bold and commanding, in the Schulze style, and the big Mixture arrives with considerable éclat, as do the reeds. In later writing Michell stated that in his opinion the basic Great organ should consist, as here at Tewkesbury, of a Diapason chorus from 16ft. to 2ft., topped by a Mixture and Reeds on higher pressure, the only additions here being an 8ft. Claribel and a 4ft. Flute Octaviante.

The basic wind pressure for the organ is 3½ ins. for the flue work, with the trebles of the Great a little higher, on 4ins., a French characteristic. The Great and Swell chorus reeds are on 5¾ ins. and the Solo Tuba and Pedal Bombarde on 12ins.

On the Swell Organ the Viole de Gambe and Voix Celestes were claimed to be 'of novel construction' and are early examples of modern string tone. The Swell-box itself is thick, made of three one-inch boards sandwiched with felt and lined. The shutters have limited movement, and the organ builder the late Roger Yates suggested that this was deliberate in order to send the sound down to blend with that of the Great.

At the other end of the dynamic scale is the unenclosed Choir Organ. If the tutti supplied by the Great and Swell is spectacular, the exquisite voicing by Thynne and the balance of the choir stops is incomparable. Commentators' opinions have ranged from the well-nigh poetic to refusal to attempt to describe their charm! Placed right at the front of the organ—a Michell characteristic judging by his subsequent work in America—the subtlety of these stops can make its full effect. Again, four were claimed to be 'of novel construction', amongst them being the Zauberflote, a stopped pipe overblown to the second harmonic and so three times the normal length.

On the Solo Organ, the Harmonic Flute, the Voix Humaine and the Tuba had been transferred to the Milton organ's echo department in the south transept in 1948. Some modifications were made, (minimal in the case of the flute), but when they were returned to the Grove in 1981 they were left as they were rather than attempt a conjectural restoration. Also on the Solo is a Violoncello, originally a two rank stop of wood and metal. At some time during the rebuilding of the Milton organ in 1948 the wooden rank disappeared. The remaining rank, though fine in itself, would be more effective as a solo stop with some filling out. Another 'loan' to the Milton was the central tower of nine pipes from the Great Open Diapason, which was used to to form a front to the Echo deparment. They were painted gold and are clearly visible, now returned to their rightful home.

For the modern player, the Pedal Organ is, perhaps, the least satisfactory department. The five pedal stops can cover most of the dynamic range and the Dolce Bass, more positive than the usual Bourdon, is an unusual stop which seems to grow to meet whatever is asked of it. However, a 16ft. rank to bridge the gap between the Dolce and the Great Bass would be helpful and even a conventional Bourdon might have a place. But bearing in mind the fact that in 1885 there was less of a demand for an independent pedal line, the five stops are remarkably successful; pride of place perhaps going to the Dolce. The Bombarde is apocalyptic, especially for the player—some notes a few feet from his right ear! The bottom five notes of the 32ft. Harmonic Bass have now been replaced by full length pipes from the former Willis organ in Christ Church Cathedral, Oxford.

Of the three forms of action applied, tracker for the Choir, Barker lever for the Great, and pneumatic for the Swell and Solo, that to the Choir is excellent, that to the Great good; only that to the Swell and Solo leaves something to be desired. But considering the horrendous amount of redesigning that must have been required when the organ arrived at the exhibition, it is surprising that anything works at all!

As to playing aids, there are conventional composition pedals—four each to Great and Swell, and a system of ventils operated both by stop knobs and by buttons beneath the appropriate manuals. The Tremulants to Swell,Choir and Solo are in fact the same and operate on all 3ins. wind, including the Pedal Dolce! There are also remains of a *Prolongement Harmonique*, a form of sustaining device, though John Budgen doubts that it ever worked. One of the 'many novelties' perhaps!

All in all, it is hard to see how Michell & Thynne could have met their stated aims more successfully: 'solidity, dignity of tone, refinement of detail, capacity for orchestral effects', all are here.

Before quoting the specification of the organ it is interesting to note that a specification published in the *Musical Opinion* for May 1885—the month in which the exhibition opened—reveals that changes must have been made at some time before the organ's eventual arrival, via Liverpool, in Tewkesbury. They include: a 16ft. Trombone added to the Great, the Swell Piccolo transferred to the Choir and renamed Flautina, an Open Diapason added to the Swell, and the scale of the Swell Geigen increased. Also, the positions of the Choir Clarionet and the Solo enclosed Voix Humaine may have been reversed—difficult to envisage, though just possible, if the Swell Piccolo had not been transferred from the Swell to the Choir.

The Builders

Carlton Cumberbatch Michell was born in 1835, the son of the curate at Lymington (Hants). According to an obituary by Vincent Willis, who had known him for 45 years, Michell's interest in organ building began early: 'He made the pedals and applied them to a small organ before he, yet a boy, could begin to study organ playing'. His career began in the accountants' office of the Bank of England, but interest in the rebuilding of the organ of the church where he was organist led him to take up organ building seriously. He was greatly impressed by the famous Schulze organ in Doncaster, and this may have brought him to T.C. Lewis, the English builder who came under Schulze's influence and who employed Thynne as a voicer. When Thynne left Lewis, Michell saw his chance and in partnership with Thynne set about building the Inventions Exhibition organ. Shortly after the collapse of the firm, Michell went to America, where there were several other English builders at work and his

Specification of the Grove organ

Great
Barker Lever Action

Violone	16
Great Open Diapason	8
Small Open Diapason	8
Claribel	8
Octave	4
Flute Octaviante	4
Quint Mixture 12.15	II
Great Mixture 19.22.26.29	IV
Trombone	16
Trumpet	8

Swell to Great
Choir Suboctave to Great
Ventil - Flue to Quint Mixture
Ventil - Great Mixture & Reeds

Choir (unenclosed)
Tracker Action

Spitzflote	8
Gedact	8
Viole Sourdine	8
Zauberflote	4
Gemshorn	4
Flautina	2
Clarionet	8

Choir Octave
Swell to Choir
Ventil-Wind to Choir

Pedal
Pneumatic Action

Harmonic Bass	32
Great Bass	16
Dolce	16
Great Flute	8
Bombarde	16

Great to Pedals
Swell to Pedals
Choir to Pedals
Solo to Pedals

Swell
Pneumatic Action

Open Diapason	8
Flauto Traverso	8
Viole de Gambe	8
Voix Celeste	8
Geigen	4
Mixture 15.19.22.	III
Contra Posaune	16
Horn	8
Oboe	8

Tremulant
Swell Octave
Ventil-Flue to Mixture & Oboe
Ventil - Swell Reeds

Solo (unenclosed)
Pneumatic Action

Harmonic flute	8
Violoncello	8
Voix Humaine (enclosed)	8
Tuba	8

Tremulant
Solo Octave
Ventil - All except Tuba
Ventil - Tuba

Accessories
Thumb pistons for all ventils
Four composition pedals each to Great & Swell

Wind Pressures
Manual flue-work $3^{1}/_{2}$in. except Great Trebles 4in.
Manual Chorus Reeds $5^{3}/_{4}$in.
Tuba & Bombarde 12in.

All stops metal except: Great Claribel, Choir Gedact (Bass), and Pedal flue-work
Manual compass: 61 notes
Pedal compass: 32 notes

influence there was considerable. He returned to England in 1902 and set up business in Wakefield as 'Tone Specialist, Voicer, Expert Finisher and Consulting Expert'. He died in 1921 aged 86.

Michell's importance as a designer and his influence on organ building has recently become clearer. Research by Stephen Bicknell on organs in America in which Michell had a hand show him to have been more influential than perhaps has been realised. And the fact that he lived to a considerable age links him to some of the major 20th-century builders in this country.[4]

William Thynne was born in 1839 at Bishop Wearmouth (Durham), the son of a glass cutter. His marriage certificate describes him as 'Professor of Music', and he was also said to be a competent organist. He was employed by Lewis from 1869 to 1881. After the collapse of the partnership with Michell he joined Casson's Patent Organ Co., before becoming a partner in the firm of Beale and Thynne. His claim to fame rests upon his undoubted skill as a voicer of string and flute stops, some invented by him. He died at his voicing machine in 1897, aged 58.

Sadly, after Michell and Thynne had parted company, and Michell had gone to America, a certain amount of acrimonious correspondence broke out in the columns of the *Musical Opinion*. Michell wrote a letter published in August 1897, in the course of which there were references to 'my Tewkesbury organ', giving the impression that Michell had been responsible for the design of all the stops. Thynne felt obliged (September 1897) 'to state most emphatically that Mr. Michell had no hand in this whatever; every stop having been designed and every pipe scaled and voiced by Yours, &c. W. Thynne'. Worse followed after Thynne's death. Obituaries claimed that Thynne had been trained by Schulze, though Thynne himself never made this claim. In February 1898, Lewis pointed out that Thynne had, in fact, never met Schulze, and until employed by Lewis in 1869 'had no practical knowledge of organ building'. Michell then weighed in with a letter (April 1898) supporting Lewis, denigrating Thynne, and claiming that the Tewkesbury organ 'was practically set out, entirely toned and finished by Mr. Michell'. Thynne was described as 'a good workman, with a correct ear, but he had no creative faculty'. This letter would either seem to be true, in which case Thynne can be 'written off', or, frankly scurrilous. In May, Casson, Beale and others leaped to Thynne's defence. Though accepting that the Thynne-Schulze pupilage story was untrue and should never have been allowed to grow, and suggesting that Michell himself may have been the originator of the story for publicity purposes, they disputed most of the other statements made in Michell's letter. Michell never responded. Whatever the rights and wrongs of the case, Thynne's claim to fame as a voicer remains secure.

The Donor

The Reverend Charles William Grove, B.D. was a notable benefactor of both the abbey and the town. He was born in 1817, the only son of William Grove of Swansea, a member of a family firm of merchants having connections with the East India Company. He took his degree at St. David's College, Lampeter, and was ordained deacon in 1841. He served for 14 years in the Forest of Dean and came to Tewkesbury in 1856. He seems at this time to have given up any official position in the Church. His gifts to the abbey include the lectern, the glass of the great west window, of five windows in the north aisle and six in the south, a set of communion plate and also the east window of the ambulatory, representing the Parable of the Pharisee and the Publican. Grove himself is said to be depicted as the publican, and his wife is portrayed in the top right hand corner of the window. He died in 1896 and is buried in a mausoleum in Tewkesbury cemetery.

It appears that he may have had some skill as an organist. The *Carmarthen Journal* for 7 July 1854 notes that at the Lampeter Day Commemoration Service that year 'The Rev. C.W. Grove B.D. presided at the organ with great ability and taste'. He evidently knew a good organ when he saw one!

CHAPTER 21

Recent Architectural Works & Archaeology

by Neil Birdsall *and* Richard K. Morris

Tewkesbury Abbey has had an architect charged with the maintenance of the fabric probably for at least a century, but the archaeological consultant was a more recent appointment in 1990. The architects in charge of the Victorian restoration were Sir George Gilbert Scott, then John Oldrid Scott, who was succeeded by W.D. Caröe after 1910.[1] In 1933 Thomas Overbury became the architect,[2] followed until 1954 by his son of the same name, to be succeeded by Anthony B. Chatwin of J.A. Chatwin & Son (Edgbaston).[3] In the following year, the *Inspection of Churches Measure 1955* was introduced, which provided the main impetus for the sort of regime that obtains today. Neil Birdsall, the present architect, succeeded Chatwin in January 1978, and undertook what appears to have been the first formal quinquennial inspection of the abbey church early that year.[4]

There had been practically no formal archaeological investigations at the abbey prior to the late 20th century, the one exception being the excavation of the site of the eastern Lady Chapel in 1940 by Sir Charles Peers and the architect Thomas Overbury senior (Fig.21.1).[5] The Parochial Church Council (hereafter P.C.C.) appointed Richard K. Morris as their archaeological consultant in 1990, for a term to coincide with the quinquennial appointment of the present architect.[6] This arrangement was approved by Gloucester D.A.C. (Diocesan Advisory Committee on Faculties and the Care of Churches), and at that time Tewkesbury Abbey was the only parish church in the diocese to have its own archaeological consultant.[7] Nationally, however, there are other churches of non-cathedral status which retain their own archaeologist, such as St. Mary Redcliffe, Bristol, and Selby Abbey in the Greater Churches Group. The appointment of Dr. Morris formalized an association with the abbey, relating to art-historical and archaeological matters, going back to the late 1970s and to about the time of the appointment of the present architect. Thus this chapter presents a selection of works, relating to both appointees, undertaken at the abbey in the last two decades or so.

Architectural Conservation

In the first half of the 20th century, following the great Victorian restoration, relatively few major architectural works were needed. Probably the most interesting from an archaeological perspective was the extensive masonry repairs and associated works to the central tower in 1936-37, commemorated by the plaque on the south-west crossing pier. At that time, the main piers supporting the tower were underpinned in sections. Their foundations, particularly on the south side, were found to be remarkably shallow—only about 2 feet below the ground, beneath some of which vaults and burial chambers had been dug.[8]

When the present architect was appointed, the work of repairing and conserving the choir

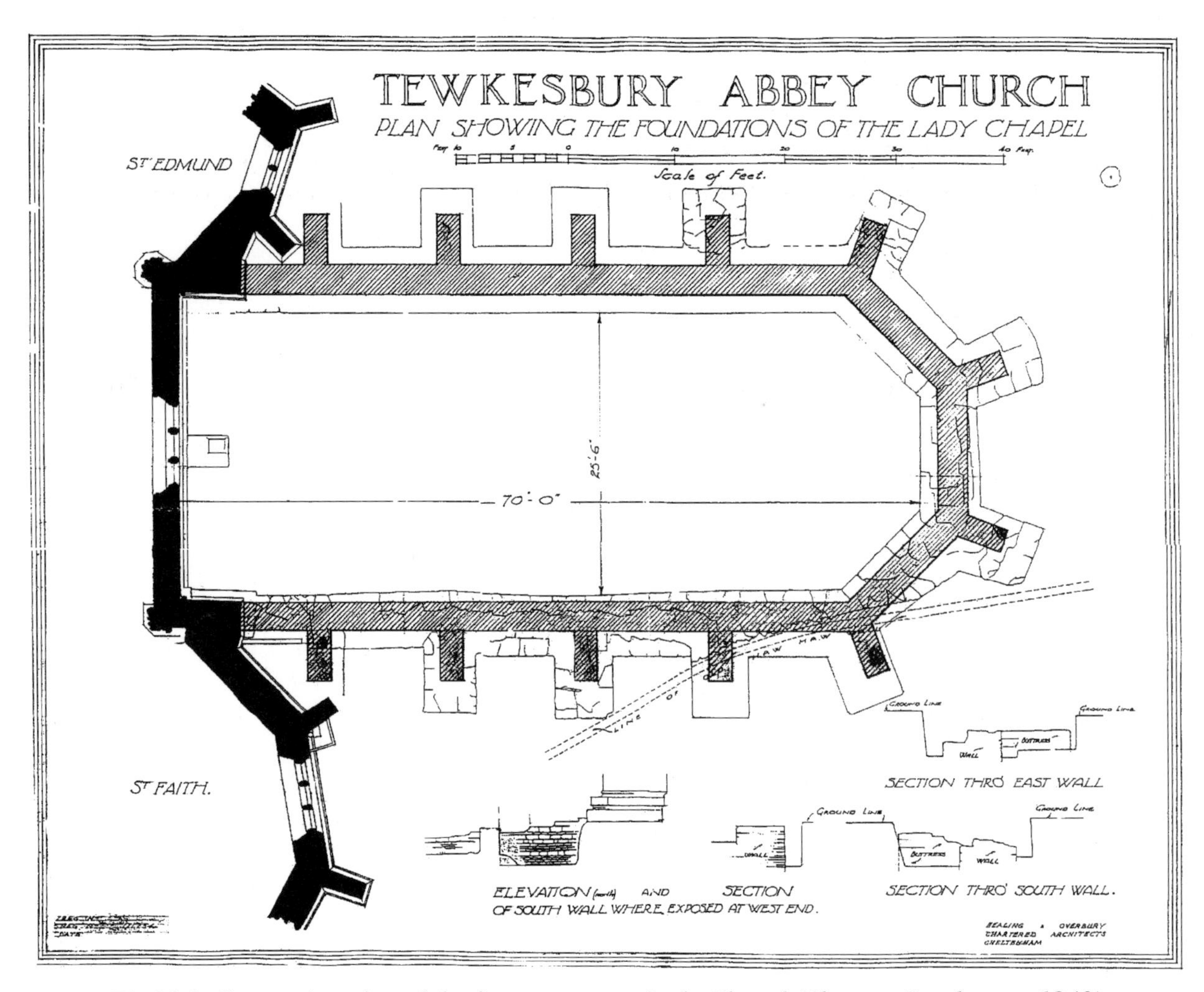

Fig.21.1 Excavation plan of the former eastern Lady Chapel (Thomas Overbury, c.*1940)*

clerestory windows was nearing completion, as one of the final phases of the restoration appeal launched in 1972 during the incumbency of the Revd. Cosmo Pouncey, and supervised by the then architect, Anthony Chatwin. The famous Decorated glass was cleaned and conserved by Dennis King at the studios of G. King and Son (Lead Glaziers) Ltd. of Norwich, and some replacement window masonry was executed by John Hopkins of Tewkesbury.

By comparison, this left the Victorian painted decoration of the choir vault looking decidedly faded. The polychromy was in a poor state, presumably because of water penetration at some time in the past, and one of the rib-stones could be seen to have broken away from the vault. So in 1984 a scaffold was erected over the sanctuary, cantilevered out from the wall passage at the foot of the clerestory windows, to facilitate a programme of repair and redecoration. It had been the Architect's intention to replicate the existing colours, but the Bakers[9]—who were engaged on conserving one of the chantry chapels—intervened during the work. They persuaded the P.C.C. that brighter colours would have been the medieval intention, resulting in the decorative scheme existing today (Fig.11.1). As an extension of the programme, the crossing and transept vaults were also cleaned and redecorated.

The choir scaffold permitted excellent access not only to the vault but also to the east face of the eastern crossing arch. Here the scar of the Romanesque choir vault was recorded, forming a semi-circular line beneath the 14th-century vault and very difficult to see from ground level. The parts of the surviving arc delineated the lower surface of a vault, probably a barrel vault (Fig.21.2C).[10] It was also possible to see for the first time the extent to which the original carved stone foliage bosses of the 14th-century vault had been hidden by wooden foliate bosses in a 15th-century style, as an accompaniment to the gilt sun bosses added to the vault after the Battle of Tewkesbury in 1471 (Fig.21.3).

Concern for the state of the abbey roofs led to some of the major works undertaken between 1978 and 1985. The architect's first quinquennial inspection in 1978 identified inadequacies in the roof trusses of the chancel and transept, in that huge blocks of brickwork had been built underneath them to shorten their span, probably in the 18th or early 19th century. These blocks were sitting on top of the haunches of the medieval vaults, and in some trusses the main tiebeam was also resting on the crown of the vaults. It was recommended that the sides of the beams should be plated with steel supports, the underside of the beams eased clear of the vault crowns, and then total or partial demolition of the brickwork carried out.[11] This solution was implemented in the roofs affected between 1980 and 1982.

In the same quinquennial report the deficiencies of the roof over the north porch were also identified. Hitherto this curious roof comprised three parallel tile-covered ridges running north/south, with four gutters in between which inevitably leaked, irrespective of the amount of repair carried out.[12] Thus the roof

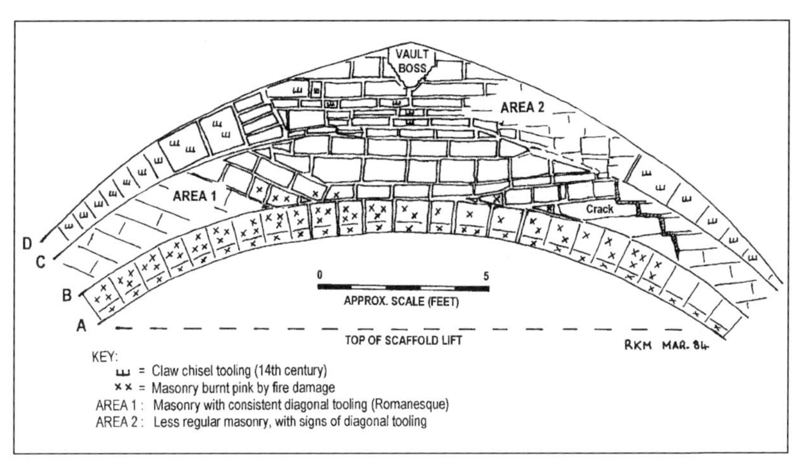

Fig.21.2 Crossing arch, east face, from the choir scaffold. A, the inner arc of the crossing arch; B, the outer arc of the crossing arch; C, the inner arc of the former Romanesque vault; D, the line of the present vault

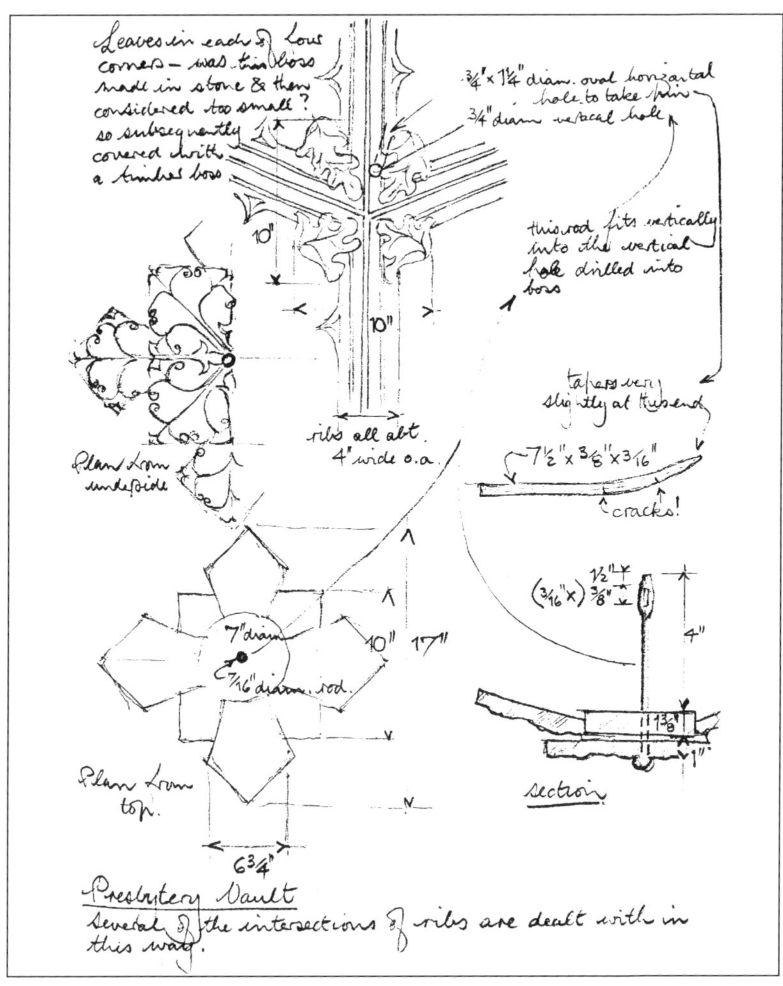

Fig.21.3 A 15th-century wooden boss covering a 14th-century boss (top) in the choir vault (drawing by Neil Birdsall)

was stripped off and an almost flat roof covered in lead was substituted in 1978-80. In 1983-85 the covering of the nave south aisle roof was changed from tiles to sand-cast lead (Fig.8.4). The red clay tiles had been of the same type as those still on the ambulatory chapel roofs (Fig.10.15), but they were vulnerable to storm damage and access for repair was possible only by erecting scaffolding.

The last decade has seen a series of important and interesting architectural works. Between 1994 and 1996, the roofs of all the eastern chapels were stripped, repaired and relaid,[13] and at the same time substantial changes were made to the roof drainage, including reforming the gutter over the ambulatory and choir aisles. Hitherto, all the water from the roofs of the tower, the choir, the chapels and the east sides of the transepts had flowed into this gutter, from where it discharged through three outlets, one of which ran through a chapel roof and blocked periodically. Consequently, all the gutters associated with the ambulatory chapel roofs were relaid so that as much water as possible flowed directly to the outside perimeter of the church, and thence to part of a new ring drain and collecting pit (see further below).

Watching briefs on the roof works were maintained by the City of Hereford Archaeological Unit (subsequently Archaeological Investigations Ltd.), and analytical reports produced for the P.C.C. by Richard Stone and Richard K. Morriss.[14] Potentially the most interesting roof was that over the Romanesque vault of the gallery chapel above the Lady Chapel, because this roof void was inaccessible and no record existed of its structure. As anticipated, the roof underneath the clay tiles turned out to have been constructed in the post-dissolution period (probably in the 17th or 18th centuries) largely from reused medieval timbers, not necessarily from the previous medieval roof over the chapel (Fig.21.4).[15] No additional evidence was noted on the exposed exterior of the stone vault for the fire which burnt off the original Norman roof, though part of a monumental Romanesque stone sculpture—apparently depicting a bull's head—was found unstratified in the roof void (Fig.21.6).[16]

Fig.21.4 South transept apsidal chapel roof trusses during restoration in 1995

Fig.21.5 Scaffolding in the nave for the conservation of the vault decoration in 1996

Fig.21.6 Romanesque carving of a bull's head, height 36cm

The stripping and investigation of the other roofs provided an understanding of how the eastern chapels and ambulatory were roofed after their reconstruction in the 14th century. As the chapel roofs were higher than that of the ambulatory, rainwater from the latter ran off through a network of stone troughs inside the chapel roof-spaces, some of which still survive.[17] The present roofs should all be dated to one campaign in the 18th or very early 19th centuries on the basis of the brickwork underpinning them and other constructional details;[18] again with substantial reuse of medieval timbers, possibly from their 14th-century predecessors.

The renovation of the decoration of the abbey's high vaults continued in 1996 with the cleaning and conservation of the nave vault paintings by Ruth Davis of Bristol and her assistants.[19] An impressive scaffold was erected along the entire length of the vault, cantilevered out from the triforium passage with extensions down to the vault springers, providing the best opportunity for close inspection since Victorian times (Fig.21.5). The paintings were substantially the work of Gambier Parry after 1878, except for the two eastern bays which experienced a more intrusive treatment in 1877-78 during Scott's restoration. The initials 'J D' and the date '1878' were found carved behind one of the angel bosses in the eastern bays, where considerable Victorian recutting of the medieval faces was detected.[20] In the other bays some traces of medieval pigment were found, but the visible decoration is essentially by Gambier Parry. He used his innovative spirit fresco technique in the vault cells, as at Highnam church near Gloucester, but applying the stencilled lines direct to the ribs and painting the bosses with a stone-coloured oil-based paint.[21]

Access to the nave clerestory and vault provided a lot of valuable new data for the architectural history of the nave. It was already established that the Romanesque nave had lacked a clerestory because some sort of tunnel vault had sprung from the top of the triforium level. In the Decorated period, clerestory windows were inserted and the new rib vault swept away whatever had been there before (Fig.11.5).[22] In 1996 we were able to detect a significant number of Romanesque stones reused by the 14th-century builders.[23] The presence only in the eastern bays of reused tufa stone, favoured for vault construction, raised the possibility that the Romanesque vault over the monks' church was of stone and that a wooden tunnel vault or coved ceiling covered the rest of the nave in this period. Two fine Romanesque capitals carved with foliage, together with pieces of scalloped abaci, were discovered reused in the frames of the 14th-century windows (Fig.21.7). No precise parallels for the detail of the capitals have been found elsewhere in the church, but a possible provenance for them would be the centrepiece of the Romanesque west front, removed to make way for the new 14th-century west window.

The most notable feature of the vault when seen close-up was the large number of masons' marks, the distribution of which suggests a tripartite phasing for its construction. Work commenced in the eastern bays 1 to 3, thus prioritizing the monks' church, then bays 4 to 6 were done, and finally the two western bays (with work on bay 8 preceding that on bay 7).[24] This proposed sequence of execution runs in the opposite direction to the west-to-east narrative of the main vault bosses and demonstrates that their iconographic programme had been established from the start.[25] Even by the very modest quality of craftsmanship exhibited in the vault as a whole, the stone-cutting and assembly, especially in bay 7, were almost amateurish. If this was the last bay to be finished, work may have been caught by the arrival of the Black Death in 1348, so that the poor execution reflects the difficulty of finding skilled labour in this period. It is also

Fig.21.7 Romanesque capital reused sideways in the nave clerestory

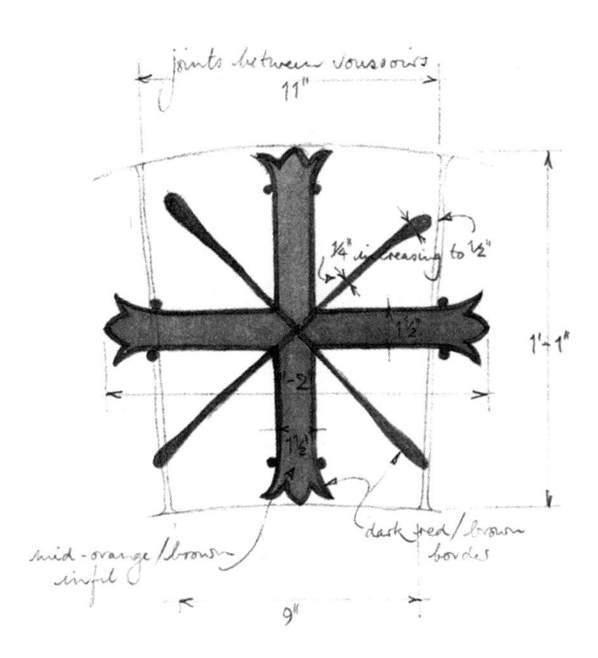

Fig.21.8 Medieval painting of a cross in bay 7 of the nave north arcade (drawing, Neil Birdsall)

conceivable that the painted cross, discovered on the north arcade arch of bay 7 during the 1996 programme (Fig.21.8), may commemorate the completion of the vault in this bay during the plague years.

Another medieval painting revealed in 1996 was the foliate 'boss' on the barrel vault of the south transept gallery chapel, part of the 12th-century decoration of this remarkably well preserved Norman chapel (Pl.10). The painting had been noted in Victorian times,[26] but the vault had been in a parlous state for some time such that in about 1950 a layer of hardboard had been inserted directly beneath it to prevent debris falling into the organ pipes which filled the chapel—the so-called 'apse organ', part of the Milton organ. Once the exterior roof of the chapel had been repaired (see above) and the pipework of the Milton organ removed in 1996,[27] the underside of the vault was conserved by David Perry and the Romanesque painting is now visible again.

An inspection of the upper part of the great west window from the nave vault scaffold indicated that both the masonry and the glazing of the window tracery were in poor condition. Some attention was also required to the west turrets and their pinnacles, so in 1999 a specification was prepared to carry out the necessary works, to include scaffolding the whole west elevation (Fig.9.4). In the event, the programme had to be implemented in two phases, of which the first—the turrets—was completed in 2002, and the second—the west window—is ongoing at the time of writing (2003).

From the 1996 inspection of the west window, it was clear that the medieval forerunner of the existing 17th-century window had a completely different tracery design and belonged to the late Decorated period, not the Perpendicular. A crucial detail is a stub of the medieval mouldings returning to form one of two super-arches, surviving internally high up on the frame, visible only close-up from scaffolding: (Fig.21.10). Thus the 14th-century window was apparently of 'Y-tracery' pattern, with an even number of lights in each half, probably eight lights in total. The window finished in 1686 was to an entirely new design, of remarkably convincing Gothic character for its period and probably taking as its model the great Perpendicular east windows of Gloucester Cathedral. Its tri-partite arrangement provided two enormously thick main mullions to resist the forces of the westerly winds which had weakened its predecessor, reinforced by horizontal wrought iron bars, one running along each of the three transoms. The bars were observed in

Fig.21.9 Inscription commemorating the mayor and churchwardens of 1686 in the nave west window

Fig.21.10 Detail of 14th-century stonework in the arch of the nave west window

1996 to be seriously corroding in places. One of two stone inscription plaques placed high up in the head identified the builders of the new window—'Francis Reeve James Hill Master Builders 1686'. James Hill (fl. 1675-1734) was a Cheltenham-based master mason who specialized in Gothic church repairs.[28] The other plaque records the names of the mayor and churchwardens in 1686 (Fig.21.9), and their respective arms appear on carved and painted shields on the window's stonework.[29]

The initial architectural problem with the west turrets was that, being open, pigeons were able to get into them, and also rain and snow blew in and damp was percolating through the stonework below. So the work involved fitting netted panels to all openings, and lining the inside of the turrets with lead to conduct water to new gargoyle chutes, decorated in traditional manner with dragons' heads. At the same time repairs and some stonework replacement were undertaken to the pinnacles.

Fig.21.11 North-west turret to the nave after restoration in 2002

The high level scaffold for this work proved valuable for archaeological inspection of the tooling and other details of the stones. This confirmed that the fabric of both turrets is predominantly Romanesque right up to the top stringcourses ('collars') around the pinnacles (Fig.21.11). Above the collars, the design of the 'cones' had been modified and Gothic finials added at their summits, probably contemporaneously with the major modifications to the Norman west front in the 14th century. The turrets appear in essentially this form in the earliest known view of the church, in Thomas Dingley's notes, *c.*1680 (Fig.21.12). The actual fabric of the cones above the collars had been almost entirely replaced after the Middle Ages, probably during the major reroofing of the nave after 1720.[30]

Of particular historic interest is the authenticity of the baluster-shaped shafts in the upper apertures of the turrets, because they represent a feature associated with Anglo-Saxon rather than Romanesque architecture (Fig.21.11). Close study of the balusters indicated that their existing stonework derived from the 1720s restoration, but there is no way of telling whether the 18th-century masons invented the form or copied what was already there. Certainly the medieval monastery was conscious of its pre-Norman pedigree, as evidenced in the Founders' Book,[31] and would have had good reason to incorporate Anglo-Saxon features in its façade.

Some of the ground works in the last decade or so have required a watching brief by field archaeologists. In 1987 the drainage around the church was found to be in a sufficiently poor state that a decision was taken to create a 'ring drain', taking all the water from downpipes and gullies to a new collecting pit, and from thence to connect to an existing culvert in Abbey Meadow. The work was to be implemented in stages, and the circuit around the eastern parts of the church has yet to be completed. The excavations, under archaeological supervision, to the south of the south transept and south chapels, provided some valuable information, albeit restricted by the 'keyhole' nature of the operations. In 1996 artic-

Fig.21.12 The earliest known view of the church, from the south, c.*1680 (Thomas Dingley)*

ulated human remains were detected—but not disturbed—at the base of the collecting pit, and from the depth of burial (1.25m.) the skeleton was considered to be medieval.[32] Four years later another interment, on an east/west axis, was located when digging a drain south-east of the south transept.[33] Both these burials are likely to relate to the monks' cemetery which traditionally lay to the east of the claustral buildings, though the second one might lie within the chapter house (Fig.12.1, X3).[34]

A separate excavation on Abbey Lawn Trust land, and therefore not the domain of the abbey's archaeological consultant, also revealed skeletal remains in 1998.[35] During the rebuilding of a collapsed garden wall east of the north transept chapels, a watching brief by the Gloucester and District Archaeological Research Group recorded four adult inhumations in an east/west alignment, at least one of which dated from the 12th to 14th centuries on the basis of associated finds (Fig.12.1, X1). Whether these are further monastic burials or burials relating to a lay cemetery is not known.

The Conservation of Monuments

The maintenance of an internationally famous set of medieval chantries and monuments, retaining considerable traces of painted decoration, provides an additional challenge—and privilege—to the abbey's architect. Occasional records survive of earlier restorations, particularly between 1824 and 1830 when the tombs were cleaned and the more elaborate tomb canopies partly rebuilt 'by a local mason';[36] and again, for example, in 1937-38 when the kneeling figure of Edward Despenser on the Trinity Chapel was cleaned, repaired and regilt.[37] It has been characteristic of the conservation of the monuments that, firstly, they tend to take a back seat to the vastly more expensive and usually more pressing works to the architectural fabric; and secondly, that it is generally done by specialist contractors who—however good their work—have tended in the past not to produce adequate reports as a record, making the writing of this section more difficult.

Recent conservation work began in earnest in the 1980s. It was found that the Wakeman monument was held together laterally by two iron rods, perhaps inserted after the medieval stone screen which originally abutted its western end had been removed (Fig.13.17). These rods, one below the cresting and the other below the cadaver, were found to be rusting badly and breaking up the stonework, so in 1983 they were removed and replaced with stainless steel.

In the previous year the conservation of the Trinity Chapel was undertaken, the first of several chapels to be worked on by the Bakers (Fig.13.9).[38] It had a largely cementitious floor which did not breathe, causing the rising damp to migrate into the chapel walls and exfoliate the stonework, so this floor was taken up. There were no clues as to the tile arrangement of the original medieval floor: 'the tiles and quarries are of all dates and sizes—indeed, the floor appears to have been hurriedly disturbed and put back' (Fig.15.3).[39] However, Robert Baker was of the view that the altar step was a later modification when a floor piscina was added; originally there had been no step.[40] The stonework was poulticed and minor repairs carried out, then the whole structure was shelter-coated with limewash and a new stone floor and altar introduced. The Trinity painting on the east wall was consolidated and cleaned, and Robert Baker remarked on its translucent quality to give the appearance of a gold and enamel altarpiece (Pl.12).[41] The polychromy of the kneeling effigy was also treated, to remove the wax paint applied by Gambier Parry and to reveal medieval colours beneath (Fig.3.2).[42] The roof of the chapel was thoroughly cleaned, and an estimated one-and-a-half hundredweight of 'rubbish' was removed from it which, when analysed, was found to be 40% coal dust—presumably a deposit from the Gurney stoves.

Following the completion of the Trinity Chapel, the Bakers returned to carry out similar works, as appropriate, in the Founder's and Warwick chapels (1984-87; Fig.10.23, Pl.13). Stonework was conserved, the roofs cleaned and considerable conservation of the polychromy was undertaken in the Warwick Chapel; new altars were designed by the abbey architect (1986) but neither of the floors was taken up.[43] Two new metal gates, decorated with shields from the Beauchamp arms and designed by the abbey architect, were hung in the Warwick Chapel.[44] After these works, the Bakers went on to clean the polychromy and make modest repairs to the sanctuary sedilia (1987), which proved to be their swan song at the abbey (Fig.11.6).[45]

In 1992-93 work on the monuments was resumed with the dismantling by Bruce Induni (Bournemouth University) of the canopy of Hugh III Despenser's tomb, followed by the whole of the Guy de Bryan monument.[46] Such drastic action was necessitated by the corrosion of iron straps and clamps splitting the stonework, and by continuing salt damage, caused by capillary action through the porous masonry of the tomb-chests. Weaknesses in the original design were also noted by Bruce Induni, who described the de Bryan monument as 'a *tour de force* of structural optimism'![47] The deconstruction and re-erection of the Despenser canopy was found to be almost a more complicated feat of engineering than making the original in the Middle Ages, because its lowest level proved to consist of just three enormous carved blocks of limestone (Fig.21.13). However, this work and the small accompanying excavation to one side of the tomb-chest provided valuable new information about the archaeology of the tomb which has helped inform several chapters in this book (Figs.13.7, 15.4).[48]

The state of the de Bryan monument required it to be taken right down to the ground, revealing a tomb-chest filled mainly with lias stone and scraps of medieval worked stone: de Bryan's body rests in the floor (Fig.21.14, cf. Fig.13.8).[49] The main canopy consisted of four large stones set transversely and was original, but the upper canopies revealed many crude repairs, suggesting that they had collapsed and been rebuilt since the Middle Ages—probably 1824-30 (see above). Bruce Induni returned in 1996 to repair the westernmost gabled tomb recess in the south choir

Fig.21.13 Bruce Induni (left) and assistant dismantling the canopy of the Hugh III Despenser monument in 1992

aisle (Fig.10.19, right), which had been shored up since 1993 and was included in the £2 million restoration appeal of that time. To correct the problem, the western pinnacle was taken down and rebuilt with stainless steel cramps tying it into the ambulatory wall.

New Works and Fittings

During the last 25 years, the abbey architect has had to provide solutions to numerous problems which challenge those charged with the care of historic churches in the modern world. These have varied from essential works to one-off projects which facilitate maintenance, aid visitors and inspire worshippers—from electrical rewiring, upgrading the sound system and rationalizing locks and keys, to a new shop, a new song school and new settings for liturgy.

One of the recent schemes, which has immeasurably changed the architect's life for the better, has been the design and implementation of the walkway and lighting in the roof space above the nave vault (completed 2002). The walkway was made by Phil Hughes of Tewkesbury, and provides a safe, quick link at high level between the crossing lantern and the west end of the nave, where previously anyone working there had to traverse an unlit obstacle course through the roof trusses. An additional unforeseen benefit is that it has opened up a significant area of the church for archaeological recording, namely the tops of the nave walls within the roof space. Preliminary inspection of the pattern of fire damage on them appears to substantiate the thesis that the Norman nave was stone-vaulted only in its east bays.

Fig.21.14 The site of the Guy de Bryan tomb, after dismantling in 1993

Quite a lot of the abbey architect's attention to new works has been spent designing new fittings and fixtures for liturgical use. One of the first questions he was asked at Tewkesbury was what to do with the immediate surroundings of the high altar. At that time there was a dossal (hanging curtain) surmounted by a tester, all covered in a buff/grey material. The architect's view was—and still is—that the best solution would be an English altar, of the more emphatic kind currently seen at the high altar of Ripon Cathedral designed by Sir Ninian Comper, with figures and other embellishments. However, this idea found no favour at Tewkesbury so, in 1994 he designed a beam spanning the arch behind the high altar from which a two-sided dossal curtain is hung: one side gold for general use and the other purple for the penitential seasons.[50]

One of the earliest refitting works undertaken at the abbey in this period was the development of a choir song school, the *Camera Cantorum*, in the former north-east chapel of the north transept (1981). The scheme was under discussion in 1979, together with the relocation of the shop from the nave to the transept's former east chapels. The chapels had been used as the choir vestry (Fig.10.5), and on their east wall was the Gambier Parry altarpiece, which had been moved to this location only a few years after it had been donated to the abbey in 1914 as the reredos for the high altar.[51] The P.C.C. was minded to dispose of it in 1979, but approaches to the Victoria and Albert Museum and other institutions met with the unanimous response that it ought to be kept at Tewkesbury. Thus it has been incorporated into the new screen between the shop and the song school (Fig.22.14). New cassock cupboards were designed for the song school, set against the screen and in front of the east wall, where they conceal important medieval carvings which had been reset into this wall in the late 1870s (Figs.10.6A,13.14).[52] A large hanging light fitting (Fig.10.5), originally a gasolier said to have hung in the nave, was moved from the east chapels, restored and rehung in the song school.

In 1989 a donation permitted the design of a new verge[53] in memory of Douglas Hawkes, former head chorister (d.1988). It is surmounted by a square head, on opposite faces of which are enamelled shields with the arms of Canterbury province and Gloucester diocese (predominantly blue), and on the other two faces the arms of England and the abbey (predominantly red, Fig.21.15). A glass case was made for it, with a commemorative plaque bearing the quotation from Paul's letter to the Philippians, 'I thank my God upon every remembrance of you'. It is a salutary tale that the word 'remembrance', mis-spelt on the drawing, was approved without comment by the Vicar, Churchwardens, Fabric Committee, P.C.C., D.A.C., the Registrar and the Chancellor before the mistake was spotted![54]

Fig.21.15 Design for the new verge (drawing by Neil Birdsall, 1989)

Discussion began in 1991 about the making of a sacrament house in the abbey. The first idea was to have a pelican in her piety on a freestanding column, with a lockable drawer in the pelican's breast to contain the wafers. However, by the end of the year the idea had changed to a pendant sacrament house of octagonal shape (Fig.21.16), owing something of its inspiration to the medieval wooden fitting (perhaps from a sacrament house) mounted on the north wall of the choir, and to the surviving medieval example at Wells Cathedral.[55] It was decided to house the pyx in St. Margaret's Chapel, where a hole discovered through the medieval boss over the altar facilitated the implementation of the hanging form (1993). The wooden sacrament house, with its colouring and gilding, was executed by Dan Windham of Hackford (Norf.), and the pyx and its metal cage was made by Keith Jameson of Winchcombe.

The room over the sacristy, formerly housing a museum and library (see below), had degenerated into a general store, and in 1993 it was proposed to refurbish it as a chapel, which has become known as 'the upper room'. In 1995 various works were done to the roof and walls, including the conservation of some traces of medieval polychromy by David Perry, and internal shutters were made for the windows where there was evidence for hanging shutters previously. A sculpture of Our Lady of Tewkesbury was set into a former fireplace recess, and in 1997 a large crucifix painted by Peter Murphy was fixed into the roof timbers above the high altar. The crucifix was inspired by the one in Assisi which reputedly spoke to St. Francis, and is a memorial to E.F. (Ted) Potter, sometime Abbey Steward; his middle name was Francis.

In 2000, plans were set in train to commemorate the 50th anniversary of the accession of Queen Elizabeth II in 2002 with a new wrought iron gate to be

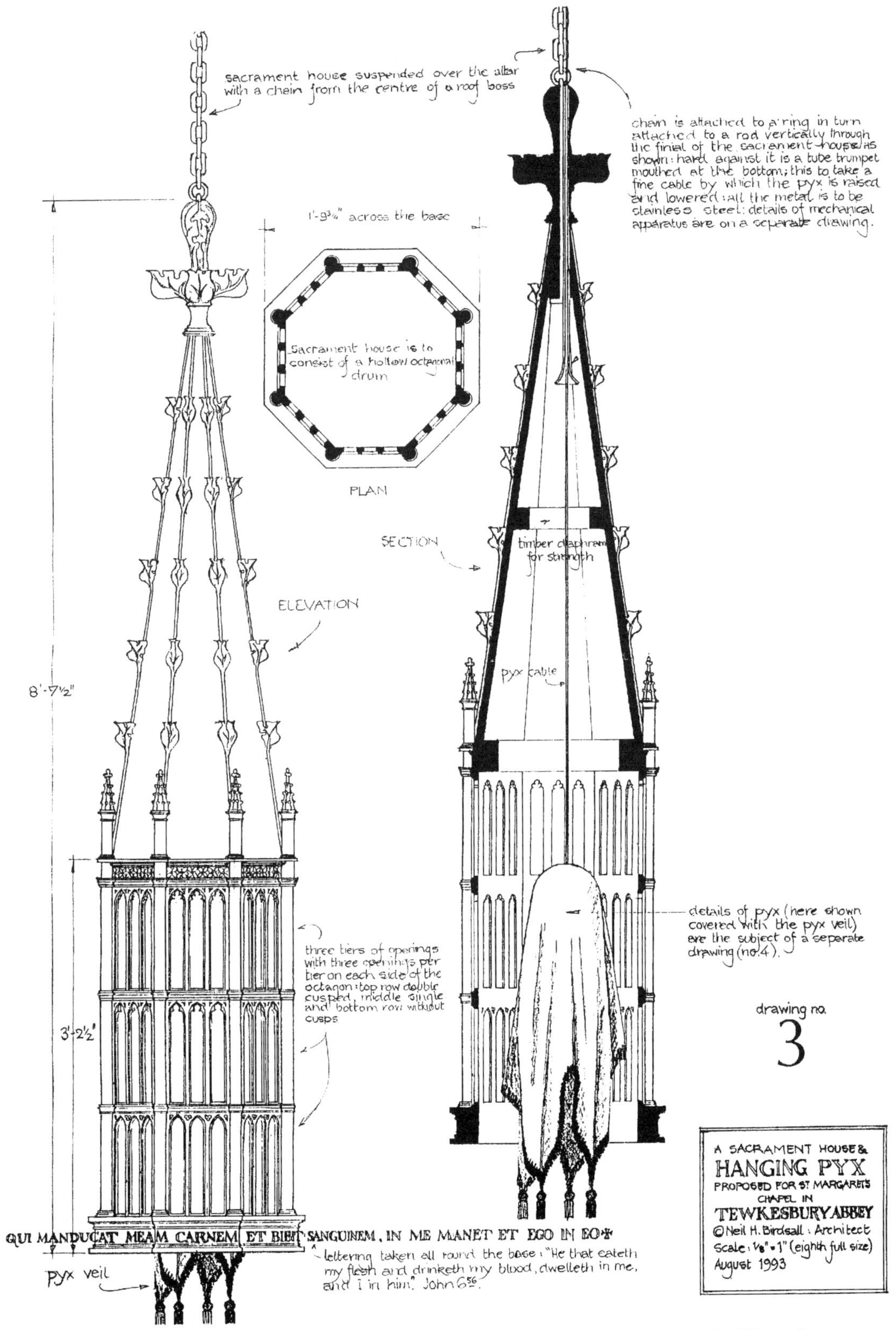

Fig.21.16 Design for a hanging sacrament house for St. Margaret's Chapel (drawing by Neil Birdsall, 1993)

placed in the medieval aperture in the screen behind the high altar (Fig.10.9). The abbey architect's design of a close-set grid of iron bars incorporates a bronze shield with the arms of England facing into the ambulatory, and a shield with the commemorative inscription on the reverse (Fig.21.17). The gate was made by Peter Crownshaw of Tenbury Wells (Worcs.), and is the most recent of a series of metal gates which the architect has designed for the abbey.[56] The very latest work of art in the eastern part of the church is the wonderfully coloured stained glass windows by Tom Denny in St. John the Baptist's Chapel (Pl.25).

At the west end of the church, several fittings have been commissioned in the area of the north door, the main public entrance to the church. In 1985, a holy water stoop, designed by the abbey architect, was made by Keith Jameson for a recess of unknown purpose in the Norman nave arcade pier immediately adjacent to the door. Above it was set a stone slab carved with the legend, 'NIΨON ANOMHMA MH MONAN OΨIN' ('wash my sins and not my face only').[57]

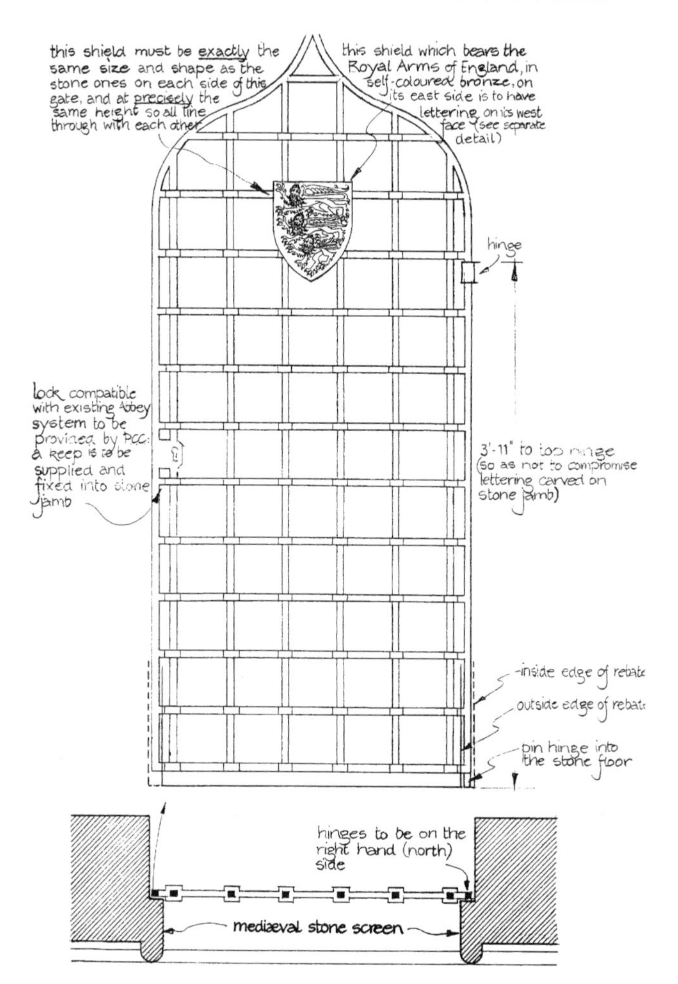

Fig.21.17 Design for a metal gate behind the high altar (drawing by Neil Birdsall, 2000)

In 1994 it was deemed that the accommodation for prayer and hymn books adjoining the door was inadequate, and a new cupboard was commissioned. Details of the abbey architect's design were based on a small organ case in Great Walsingham parish church (Norf.), by A.W.N. Pugin. The organ case is painted black whereas the Tewkesbury cupboard is dark blue, both with red and white details in a matt finish. The words 'read, mark, learn, digest' are picked out in gold on the cupboard's frieze, from the Collect in the Book of Common Prayer. The joinery, painting and gilding were the work of Dan Windham.

Of works outside the church, the only new building to be erected at the abbey in this period was the Visitor Centre (now called the Abbey Centre), added to the revamped Abbey Halls at the north-east corner of the churchyard. The project was executed in 1996 to a design by the Beswick Partnership of Tewkesbury, and provides new accommodation for the abbey office, meeting rooms, toilet facilities and a refectory.[58]

In 1999 the 18th-century Gage gates were in a poor state of repair and were taken down, including the gate-posts and the overthrow, and expertly conserved. When they were re-erected, matching railings were added as a partial replacement for those removed during World War II, but not extending along the full length of the boundary to Church Street which, it was considered, would create too invasive a visual barrier between the church and the town (Fig.21.18). The new railings, designed by the abbey architect to compliment the gates, were finished with specially designed end-posts incorporating details copied from the originals. The blacksmith who undertook all this work was Peter Crownshaw.

Fig.21.18 The Gage Gates (c.1750), restored 1999

The Abbey Collection

One of the duties which the archaeological consultant had commenced before his appointment was to collect and curate the many loose carved stones and other artefacts around the abbey church and its direct environs. The core of this collection (the 'abbey collection') comes from the showcases and larger loose stones formerly in what is now the Chapel of St. John the Baptist, made up primarily of items discovered when the sanctuary floor was lifted in 1875-77,[59] together with a small number of items donated to the abbey in the following decades (Fig.21.19). Evidently, it was intended that this chapel (then of no known dedication) should become a town museum in the late 19th century,[60] as borne out by the nature of some of the donated objects—several Georgian and Victorian police truncheons, a horseshoe and a spear-head thought to derive from the Battle of Tewkesbury, and a stone tea-caddy carved by Henry Daffurn, abbey stonemason (1845-1905).[61] Perhaps the most bizarre item is a grey earthenware pot formerly said to be a 14th-century flagon from the monks' refectory, but which the British Museum has identified as a Chimú-style vessel from Peru which could not have come to England before the mid-16th century![62]

Between 1979 and 1984, this collection—together with numerous fragments rounded up from other areas inside the church—was catalogued and transferred to one dedicated repository within the abbey, for its better preservation and management.[63] Its quality and potential significance may be judged by some of the items used to illustrate various chapters of this book (e.g. Pls.11, 15; Figs.9.27E and F, 10.6B, 11.14C, 15.6). Most of the items are medieval and derive from destruction to buildings, monuments and fittings at or after the Dissolution of the monastery. Not all are loose—some pieces have

Fig.21.19 A museum case with items from the abbey collection, in the early 20th century

been reset in walls, such as the fragments of an early ecclesiastical effigy and of a tomb-chest (perhaps of Isabel Despenser) in the east wall of the *Camera Cantorum*, probably from Thomas Collins' clearance of this area about 1877 (Figs.10.6A, 13.14);[64] and numerous mainly architectural stones in the cloister garden wall outside, from the opening up of the cloister walk after 1883.[65]

Not surprisingly, from what is known about the dispersal of monastic materials at the Dissolution, stonework and other artefacts formerly belonging to the abbey appear at other locations in the vicinity. Perhaps the best known example is the effigy of William de la Zouche, taken to Forthampton Court probably by Abbot Wakeman *c*.1540 (Fig.7.5). However, the other stones which make up the present composition there cannot be from the Zouche monument and were probably not moved from the abbey until the late 18th or early 19th centuries.[66] Other examples of stones which can be matched with stonework at the abbey are reset in the interior walls of Gupshill Manor public house, just south of the town, including pieces from the Perpendicular cloister (Fig.21.20). Recently pieces apparently from the demolished eastern Lady Chapel have been found built into a chimneystack at Manor Farm, Tredington, about three miles from Tewkesbury.[67]

Fig.21.20 Fan-vault stone from the abbey refixed in the bar of Gupsill Manor, Tewkesbury

A little appreciated section of the collection is a large group of plaster casts made in 1853 for the Crystal Palace at Sydenham. The full-size 'casts'—which are really hand-finished copies rather than casts—are mainly of the figurative bosses of the nave vault, but also include other carvings around the abbey. This work was contracted on 20 January 1853 between Thomas Collins the builder, of Church Street, Tewkesbury, and M. Digby Wyatt of the Crystal Palace Company, and an appendix indicates that the commission was to include a full-scale 'perfect facsimile' of the Wakeman monument, 13 feet high, though no trace of this copy exists in the abbey today.[68]

The collection continues to grow, particularly with items found during restoration works on the chantry chapels and monuments in the 1980s and 1990s (see above). A recent initiative is to retain samples of stone from architectural repairs for geological identification, and to start a database of stone-types used at the abbey. The main fabric of the medieval church, for ashlar facings and carved features, is oolitic limestone (Pl.8A), but little is known specifically about its quarry sources.[69] The most obvious general location is the Inferior Oolite beds at the nearest points of the Cotswold escarpment around Stanway and Cleeve, but quite conceivably quarries on Bredon Hill (Worcs.) were employed too.[70] Some years ago the Geological Museum in London assessed a 'representative' sample of building stone from the church as Yellow Guiting limestone emanating from the Jackdaw Quarry on Stanway Hill,[71] and the churchwardens' accounts record payments in 1602 for the purchase of stone from the neighbouring Coscombe Quarry and 'for hallinge over stones from Stanwey hill'.[72] Given the monastic property at Stanway, it seems likely that the abbey had owned a quarry there. Painswick stone from further south down the escarpment does not appear to have been employed at the abbey until the 18th century, especially for paving and decorative carving such as the 1725 altarpiece and the Victorian pulpit.[73] No evidence has been found to substantiate the tradition that Caen limestone from Normandy was used on the Norman church in Robert Fitzroy's time,[74] and it seems inherently unlikely. In the 20th century, however, the effigy of Archdeacon Hemming Robeson is said to be carved from this stone (Fig.17.14).

The other main historic stone for walls is the local Lower Lias, used sporadically in the eastern parts of the Norman church when apparently the supply of limestone was inadequate (Pl.8A), and more extensively in non-ecclesiastical buildings such as Abbey House (Fig.12.13).[75] For the infilling of stone vaults, porous tufa limestone was preferred on account of its relatively light weight (Pl.8B).[76] Other stones employed in the medieval abbey include Highley green sandstone occasionally for walls, brought down the River Severn from beyond Worcester, and Purbeck 'marble' (a polishable limestone) for smart 13th-century architectural details, as in the north transept north chapel (*Camera Cantorum*), for the great altar *mensa* and for tombs (e.g. Figs 5.3, 10.6B, 13.14).[77] The latter was a prestigious material, having to be brought by water transport from the Isle of Purbeck (Dorset). From the 17th century on, the variety of decorative stones available to monumental masons increased considerably, to include foreign marbles, as shown in the post-medieval wall monuments described in Chapter 17 (e.g. Fig.17.8). Likewise, the availability of building stones from a growing diversity of sources in the 19th and 20th centuries has seen the appearance in the abbey of Bath, Doulting (Som.) and Clipsham (Rutland) stones for repairs.[78] The current work on the west front of the abbey is using Bath stone from the Stoke Ground quarry.

A recent visit to the abbey by Professor John Prentice, at the invitation of the Archaeological Consultant, demonstrates the historical value of making geological identifications. He examined a large base-block designed to carry a group of five shafts, standing *ex situ* in the east bay of the ambulatory, which is unconvincing as the base for an architectural support like a pier and which might derive from a fitting such as a lectern of the later 12th century.[79] He confirmed that the block had diagnostic features associated with Wenlock 'marble' (Silurian Wenlock Limestone from near Much Wenlock, Shropshire) and so is likely to belong with a series of three other lecterns in this unusual stone, of which the most complete is at Crowle church (Worcs).[80] Thus it can be shown that the abbey possesses the base probably of one of the very few medieval stone lecterns known in this country and, judging by its size, the most monumental.

Postscript

At the start of the 21st century, at a time of escalating rules and regulations concerning buildings and of an ever-increasing sensitivity to saving our heritage, there is plenty to occupy the minds of the abbey's architect and the archaeological consultant. Apart from preparing specifications for essential future works to the architectural fabric, such as the stonework of the tower, and for appropriate archaeological recording of the same, there are always ideas in mind for new works, should permissions and resources ever combine to allow them to proceed. For example, with regard to architectural works, the new Visitor Centre was intended to move the shop out of the church and to provide a dedicated exhibition room, but in the end financial and operating restraints have prevented these objectives being delivered and other solutions will need to be investigated. The more significant items in the abbey collection are deserving of public display, but many require specialist treatment beforehand. A valuable start was made in 2002, with the conservation of six of the best pieces of medieval painted sculpture in advance of their temporary loan to an exhibition at the Henry Moore Institute Gallery at Leeds.[81]

With regard to archaeology, numerous non-intrusive scientific methods are available nowadays to increase our knowledge of the history of the church, its environs and its contents. These range from dendrochronology to date roof timbers and the winding wheel; to D.N.A. testing of the 'Clarence' bones; and to a radar-based resistivity survey of the abbey grounds and meadow.[82] Beyond these potential initiatives, however, some research excavation is desirable, especially south of the church on the site of the monastic conventual buildings, given the almost complete dearth of field archaeological information about this area and the abbey's plan to develop a Garden of Remembrance in the former cloister. Further south the abbey meadow excavation took place in 1992, which highlighted the need for better liaison between Tewkesbury Borough Council, the Abbey Lawn Trust and the abbey concerning archaeological matters.[83]

Tewkesbury Abbey is in an anomalous position as an historic building. It is larger than a number of English cathedrals and more richly endowed with medieval fittings than many, but as a parish church it is obviously ineligible for the English Heritage grant aid scheme to cathedrals and is not bound by the *Care of Cathedrals Measure 1990* to retain an archaeological consultant; though the P.C.C. has voluntarily engaged one. As with any great historic church, there is a perception that a potential discord exists between on the one hand, a need for change, as represented in liturgy, usage and replacement of fabric, and on the other, conservation and archaeology—especially if they compete for resources.

At the abbey in the past two decades such matters have generally followed a cautious route to a successful resolution, but the occasional impasse has arisen. In 1986 a faculty was granted to replace the doors at the bottom of the three spiral stairwells around the ambulatory, to provide ventilation in the east end of the church, aimed at overcoming the considerable problems associated with dampness there. The installation of the first door, fitted with a grille, in St. Faith's Chapel was sufficient to demonstrate a substantial improvement in ventilation, but thereafter English Heritage objected in the strongest terms to replacing the other doors because of the loss it entailed of historic carpentry: and there the matter has rested since.

A number of chapters in this book will have informed the reader that archaeological investigation is not restricted to excavations in the ground. Indeed, Dr. Warwick Rodwell reminds us that:

> church archaeology must embrace the whole range of material available for study: the church building and its site, the furnishings, fittings and monuments, the graveyard and its boundaries and ancillary structures. ... Then almost everything becomes significant; in particular there is no rule which decrees that the older or rarer an object is, the more absolute importance it accrues.[84]

Thus, the Milton organ is discussed from an archaeological perspective in Chapter 19 much as the archaeological development of the architectural fabric of Abbey House is analysed in Chapter 12.

An example of how the even slightest changes to architectural fabric can destroy valuable historical evidence is provided by the replacement of stone mullions in the choir clerestory in 1976. Some of those removed were almost certainly Elizabethan replacements of 14th-century originals, with Renaissance ovolo mouldings as the evidence for their post-medieval date. They were the only testimony to disprove the assertion by Caroline Litzenberger that the churchwardens had 'added a large new chancel window in the mid-1560s'.[85] In fact, they had carried out major repairs to an old one. Thus the church's architecture, fittings and surroundings are not only an inspiration to those who worship at the abbey, but also potential sources for its history which continue to require sensitive understanding and preservation.

CHAPTER 22

Tewkesbury Abbey in the 20th Century

by Michael Tavinor

The abbey 1900-1930

A person entering Tewkesbury Abbey in the year 1800 would have found the interior to be very different from that in 1900. The church at the earlier date would have been in a poor state of repair, with peeling plaster and with a great variety of box pews and galleries throughout the east end of the building. Worship would have taken place in the chancel, separated from the unused nave by a screen of poor construction, on which sat the Milton organ. The chancel was dominated by a huge central pulpit, which provided a much greater focus than the Communion table, insignificantly placed at the east end (Fig.16.3).

However, by 1900 the interior of the church had taken on most of the features with which we associate it today. The building had been restored by Scott, the walls were scraped of plaster, the Milton organ had been placed in a south position and the original medieval altar had been restored to a commanding position at the east end (Fig.16.11). In effect it was a well cared-for church which became an even greater focus for parish life in the early years of the 20th century.

As in many churches, parish magazines give a fascinating glimpse into contemporary life and worship. Letters from the century's first vicar, Canon Wardell-Yerburgh (1899-1913), discuss burning issues of the day—a contemporary Education Act, possible disestablishment of the Welsh Church—as well as more day-to-day parish activity. For instance, in 1908, Christmas and Easter communicants numbered 403 and 570 respectively. The magazines show a parish with many regular activities: the annual parish tea and Sunday School outing, the observance of Empire Day, the Renewal Bank and Shoe Club. Also

Fig.22.1 Oswald Pryor Wardell-Yerburgh, vicar 1899-1913

Fig.22.2 The chancel on the day of the funeral of King Edward VII in 1910

recorded are the visits of dignitaries to the parish: Princess Victoria of Schleswig-Holstein came to the abbey in October 1908. Significant national events were observed at the abbey with great splendour. There were special services on the day of King Edward VII's funeral, when 2,500 people crowded into the church, and for the Coronation of King George V and Queen Mary.

The restoration of the abbey in the 19th century led to an increase in interest in the abbey's history, and each year the anniversary of the re-opening of the restored church (23 September 1879) was marked by a week of festivities and services. As Wardell-Yerburgh wrote in September 1908:

> The abbey is the pride of all Tewksburians and we may truly say it has a deep hold upon their affections. Those who have once worshipped within its hallowed walls feel that no other place makes quite the same appeal to their religious feelings. Letters written by those who have lived here and joined in the uplifting services of the abbey often contain expressions of regret that they are no longer able to share the privileges of those who worship here.[1]

Services during this period were clearly reverent and well executed but certainly not ritualistic. Numbers were respectable and the following list of services for Easter Day 1911 reminds us that festival observance was a strenuous business!

4.45 a.m. Holy Communion
6.00 a.m. Holy Communion
7.00 a.m. Holy Communion
8.00 a.m. Holy Communion
10.00 a.m. Holy Communion
11.00 a.m. Matins
11.45 a.m. Choral Eucharist and Sermon
Preacher: The Vicar
3.15 p.m. Children's Service and Procession
Preacher: Rev. E.P. Amphlett
3.45 p.m. Litany
4.00 p.m. Holy Baptism
6.30 p.m. Evensong, Sermon and Procession
Preacher: Rev. N.D.M. Crossman

A note in the *Parochial Magazine* for May 1911 says of the 4.45 a.m. celebration: '... we were pleased to see that some of the Post Office officials, for whom the service was chiefly arranged, made use of this opportunity ...'.[2]

After the intense activity of abbey restoration during the 1870s, the early 20th century saw relatively little added to the fabric. A new stained glass window was installed in St. Margaret's Chapel in 1908 but otherwise the period gives the impression of stability and consolidation. All this was about to be shattered.

On 14 November 1913, Canon Wardell-Yerburgh died suddenly and the black-edged December issue of *Tewkesbury Parochial Magazine* was full of tributes to a vicar who had clearly won a place in the hearts of Tewkesbury people. Wardell-Yerburgh's memorial is the impressive inner north door, with its elaborate carving by W.D. Caröe, and this, together with new west doors and a memorial to another former vicar, Archdeacon Robeson, was dedicated in 1915.

Scarcely had the new vicar, Ernest Smith, been inducted in February 1914 than hostilities were declared and Tewkesbury, like so many other communities in the land, felt the terrible effects of the Great War. Many local men were called up and service patterns were changed, with music greatly reduced. Ernest Smith's letters during the war years focused on a number of issues: days of National Prayer, sermons searching out the meaning of the war, heart-searching over the government's insistence that clergy be exempt from active service. In one letter in 1915, the following appears:

> The Easter Festival was a very happy one, and never before has its note of consolation and victory been more needed: never before have we been able to enter so fully into the significance of its message of the triumph of Right over Might, Self-sacrifice over Self-seeking, Love over Hate ...[3]

As the war ended, its tragedy and sacrifice were commemorated by three structures in Tewkesbury: the 'Cross' in the centre of the town, the 'Calvary' at the entrance to the churchyard and the war 'shrine' in the abbey, designed by the abbey's architect W.D. Caröe and executed by the local firm of Collins and Godfrey.

Fig.22.3 Ernest F. Smith, vicar 1914-30

Parish life continued, with Ernest Smith keeping those parishioners who remained 'up to scratch'. He wrote and spoke in a forthright manner and had firm ideas about churchmanship. Although he wore a cope for the first time at Christmas 1914, and approved the installation of the Gambier Parry reredos at the high altar, in other matters he was clearly less prepared for more advanced ceremonial. Writing in March 1918 of the practice of genuflecting during the Nicene Creed, he wrote:

> To 'genuflect' at those words when you only *bow* at the Sacred Name itself shows a curious lack of proportion. The fact is, of course, that the geneflecting is only a 'corrupt following' of Roman Catholic custom: and to do a thing simply because Roman Catholics do it is neither more or less sensible than to wear a pig-tail because Chinamen wear one! ...[4]

Smith was, however, open to change, and during his incumbency a Choral Eucharist became a regular feature of parish worship, at which full eucharistic vestments became the norm.

In his parish letters are seen glimpses of change in the wider Church. The introduction of parochial church councils was a major development in Church government and seems to have found immediate favour in Tewkesbury. Smith also became very involved in the controversy over the revision of the Prayer Book in 1927-28, and regaled his parishioners with his often caustic views on the proceedings. He clearly admired the philosophy which lay behind the changes, not least the (unsuccessful) attempts at simplifying the services as requested by so many war chaplains, but he also agreed with the spirit of moderation which the bishops felt was so clearly seen in their new book:

> The very fact that the Revised Book is disliked by both extreme Anglo-Catholics and extreme Protestants ought to convince the great central

body of Churchmen that it is sane and reasonable; but this central body which includes at least 80% of the members of the Church of England is apt to be silent and unaggressive (not to say apathetic), and at the present moment silence is most certainly not golden! ... [5]

As in the life of today's abbey, finances were a problem. Of particular concern was the question of whether or not to charge admission for entrance to parts of the building. In the early 1920s, Dean Bennett of Chester achieved fame by his decision to abolish charges in his cathedral, thus bringing into question a practice which had become almost universally common. Yet the vicar of Tewkesbury was not to be swayed by such changes, and wrote at length on the issue. He cited two reasons, firstly that:

> Tewkesbury Abbey was deprived of all its endowments by the rapacity of Henry VIII (unlike the Cathedrals, which still possess rich endowments), and if it were not for the amount received in visitors' fees, it could not possibly be kept open, or clean, or warm: even as it is, the fees barely pay for half the cost of this, the rest being contributed by the worshippers.[6]

The other reason also deserves quoting, not least for its contemporary view of society and of a very different view of tourism from that adopted today:

> No one knows so well as our Sacristan the utter lack of reverence shown by the average 'tripper': left to wander at their own sweet will, these trippers would (as they often do) 'behave themselves unseemly', and do irreparable damage to the monuments, etc. The fact is, the English 'lower middle class' have very little appreciation of the unique and priceless glories of such a building, and still less conception of what a House of God is ... I myself deplore that necessity for a fee as much as anyone, but until our 'trippers' are all Christians in fact as well as in name, there is, I fear, no practical alternative ...[7]

The great event of the 1920s was the celebration of the octo-centenary of the abbey's consecration in October 1923. On the Feast of Consecration itself the archbishop of Canterbury, Randall Davidson, preached in the abbey and the service was followed by a great luncheon at the Town Hall and by the presentation to the parish of the Compotus Roll of Henry VIII. This had formerly been kept in the Chapter Library at Winchester.

The major fabric project associated with the 800th anniversary was the restoration of the seven 14th-century windows in the chancel. They were systematically releaded and some of the glass rearranged. The work was completed by 1925 and dedicated on 25 March in that year, the final cost being £1,400.

Other events during the 1920s included a major commemoration of the centenary of the birth of the writer Dinah Maria Craik (author of *John Halifax, Gentleman*), including a lecture given by Sir Arthur Quiller Couch.

In 1930 Ernest Smith moved from Tewkesbury to become vicar of Yate, in the Bristol diocese. He wrote at length of all that had been achieved during his time as vicar:

> It was no light charge to which God called me at the close of 1913, for the care and custody of such a church as the Abbey involves weighty responsibilities of more than one kind, but when I recall the equipment of the Abbey and its services when I was instituted on February 21 1914, and compare it with what they are today, I am filled with humble thankfulness to God, Who has enabled me to do so much to His honour and greater glory.[8]

Canon Smith's time at Yate was, however, short and sad, for in March 1933 he was found dead in his vicarage, having shot himself after filing his petition for bankruptcy. At the coroner's inquest, his financial difficulties at Tewkesbury were mentioned:

> ... a living of great importance, but with little income - under £300 a year, with a house that needed three or four times that amount to maintain. It was a living that could only be kept up by a man with private means ...[9]

The incumbency of Edward Pountney Gough, 1930-42

Ernest Smith was succeeded as vicar by Edward Pountney Gough. He had served curacies in London and Hitchin (Herts.) and was successively vicar of Downham Market (Norfolk), Spalding (Lincs.), Chiswick (London) and Brown Candover (Hants.). His work at Tewkesbury may be divided into four areas: churchmanship, drama, the Friends of Tewkesbury Abbey and the restoration of the fabric.

Within a year of his becoming vicar, incense had been introduced at the main Eucharist and many other 'catholic privileges' restored. The Blessed Sacrament was reserved and much done to the interior of the abbey to emphasize the church's now pronounced Prayer Book Catholic tradition. The high altar received a new dossal; the south transept chapel, formerly known as the Norman Chapel, became the Lady Chapel, with a statue of the Virgin and Child carved in Cotswold stone by Alec Miller. The gift of 19th-century silver staves carried before the Governor of Bombay provided an opportunity to convert these into fine acolyte torches, and the gift of a 16th-century Italian cope added to the abbey's collection of vestments. Canon Gough's sense of history and liturgy found fine expression in 1939, when the 600th anniversary of the Consecration of the High Altar on 18 June 1239 was marked by the re-hallowing of the huge Purbeck marble slab at a High Mass, at which the celebrant was the Abbot of Nashdom, near Burnham (Bucks.).

But not all were happy with the advances in ceremonial. The annual meeting in January 1932 proved very stormy, with one member insisting: 'I cannot follow the service as at present used. To me it is almost like a pantomime'.[10] Canon Gough was adamant and his reply, reported in great detail in the local paper, insisted on his position:

> There is nothing done in the services of the abbey and its ceremonial that is not justified in the Book of Common Prayer as historians and liturgists now understand it ... I am placed here in authority. I don't want to Lord it over anybody, but I regard myself as definitely put here to lead and to teach. On these matters the last word will rest with me.[11]

The churchmanship of the abbey soon became a focus for the wider church and in 1935 the first pilgrimage to Tewkesbury Abbey was held, attended by clergy and laity from many parts of the country, under the auspices of the Church Union. A report in the *Church Times* on the second pilgrimage, in September 1936, speaks of the size and splendour of the event:

> It would be impossible to describe suitably the superb sight of this great procession, with its clouds of incense, its richly embroidered vestments and banners, its crowds of laymen, quite half of whom were of the younger generation, making its way, singing the Litany, down the main street to the entrance of the churchyard, and winding slowly into the vast Norman nave

Fig.22.4 Edward Pountney Gough, vicar 1930-

Fig.22.5 Tewkesbury Pilgrimage passing through the abbey gatehouse, September 1936

> after being received at the west door by the Vicar of Tewkesbury, with other priests and servers ... A demonstration of this kind serves to point a moral, which is that the Catholic Movement is making greater strides in the Midlands than is commonly supposed. The laity are not so apathetic as many think. The really astonishing success of the second Tewkesbury Pilgrimage should prove beyond all contradiction that people will travel long distances and pay quite a lot of their weekly wages to meet their fellow-Catholics, to show their proud enthusiasm and their unity, and to say their prayers together.[12]

The Priests Convention held at Tewkesbury in 1938 saw the presentation of papers on a variety of subjects including: *The Daily Mass* and *Use of the Reserved Sacrament*, *The Parish Mass*, and *The Setting of the Liturgy*, by such eminent liturgists as Dom. Gregory Dix. These were published in book form by SPCK.

In such ways, under Canon Gough's leadership, by the end of the 1930s Tewkesbury was established as a centre of well-ordered Catholic liturgy.

Prominent in the ecumenical movement of his day, Canon Gough invited Orthodox prelates to preach. For the Dedication Festival in 1938, Great Archimandrite Nicholas was invited to preach 'and by his presence with us all day will testify to our virtual unity with the Holy Orthodox Church of the East'.[13] In the event, due to a series of misunderstandings, the Great Archimandrite never turned up for his preaching engagement:

> This was my fault, I admit it and was caused by a mistake about the date in the letter I wrote. At first we thought, as we met train after train at Gloucester, that he had tried to get to Tewkesbury direct and had got lost somewhere on the railway![14]

A disciplinarian, Canon Gough often berated his flock for their luke warmness in attendance. Thus, of regular reception of the Sacrament in April 1939:

> In France ... we should probably find that the Communion would be nearer 3,000 than 2,000 on Festivals. How marvellous it would be on

> the Great Festivals to see our glorious church absolutely crowded (as at the British Legion Service) with communicants. How should we deal with such numbers! Of course, it could only be done by reception in one kind, and at a very great number of services beginning, as they do in such places, at incredibly early hours. However, alas! we need not consider that at present.[15]

Glimpses of later liturgical developments are found during the 1930s, and Canon Gough's lack of enthusiasm is not hard to see!

> The Bishop of Gloucester ordained three priests and four deacons in the abbey at 10.30 on Sunday December 19th. By his wish a nave altar was placed before the screen in order that the solemn act by which the Church commissions her ministers might be witnessed by as large a number of people as possible and that they might feel their proper share in this act as members of Christ's Church. The service in consequence lost something of the beauty which our magnificent choir and presbytery would have given it, but it gained in intimacy and intelligibility.[16]

Certainly, Canon Gough seems to have experienced no hostility from the diocese through his adoption of more advanced Catholic ceremonial. Indeed, he was made an Honorary Canon in 1939, although the editor of the *Parish Magazine* remarked:

> We offer him our congratulations and are pleased that recognition has now been given to all the work that he has done, not least in the matter of architectural improvements ... we have always felt that the vicar of such a church as this should automatically be given a canonry from the moment of his appointment ...[17]

As mentioned, another area of Canon Gough's work was in the field of drama. 1931 saw the production of the Tewkesbury Pageant, a sequence of historical dramas held on the meadow to the south of the abbey, depicting:

The Consecration of the Abbey
The marriage of Richard Beauchamp, Lord Abergavenny to Isabel-le-Despenser in July 1411
The Battle of Tewkesbury
The Dissolution of the Monastery
The Purchase of the Abbey by the townspeople
King Charles I at Tewkesbury, 1643
King William III's Charter, 1698
Mr. Pickwick's visit to Tewkesbury, July 1828

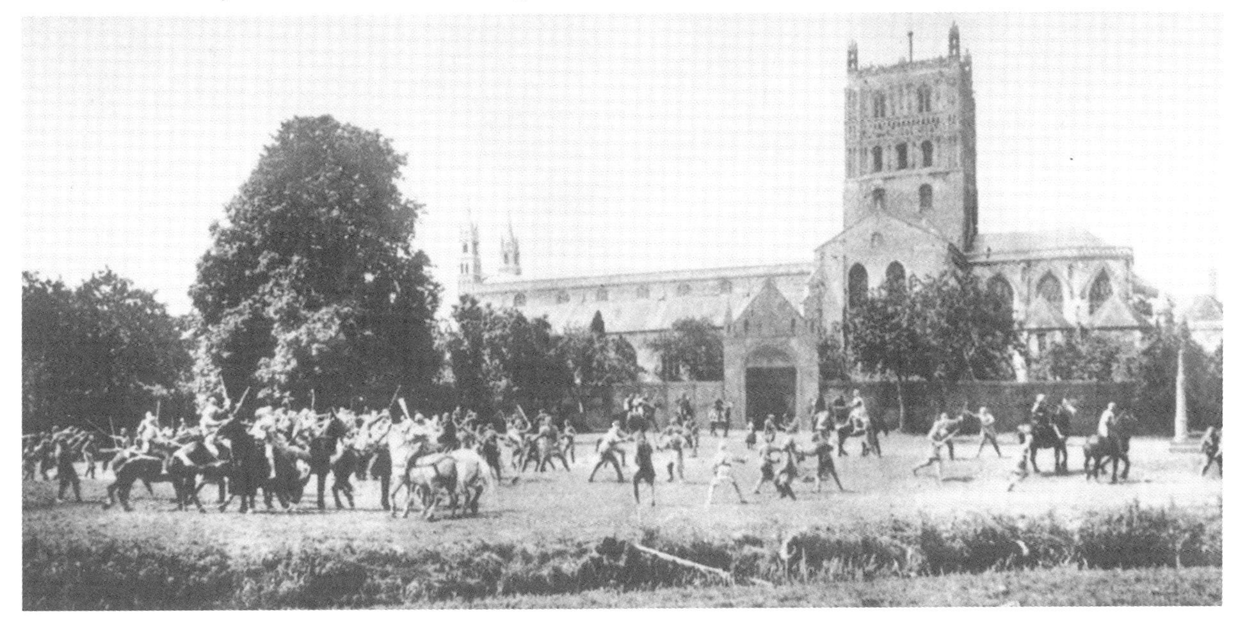

Fig.22.6 Tewkesbury Pageant on Abbey Meadow, 1931: The Battle of Tewkesbury

The finale featured a large 'Choir of Angels' singing from the abbey tower—a part of the Pageant long remembered by Tewkesbury residents. Canon Gough himself appeared in the Pageant, as 'The Abbot of Tewkesbury' in the opening section and as 'The Vicar of Tewkesbury' in the episode featuring King William's charter.

Canon Gough's interest in drama continued throughout the thirties with the regular production of plays at the west end of the abbey: T.S. Eliot's *Murder in the Cathedral*, Bernard Shaw's *Saint Joan*, excerpts from the *York Mystery Plays* and Milton's *Samson Agonistes*. For the 1939 festival, a play *The Tower*, by Christopher Fry, was commissioned, to coincide with the completion of the 1930s period of restoration.

On 27 October 1932, a public meeting was held at which it was decided to form a company of the Friends of Tewkesbury Abbey and approval was given to the draft constitution. The first annual report was produced in 1934 and early projects included the re-binding of the churchwardens' accounts books from 1563 to 1703 and the restoration of the Warwick Chapel.

It soon became clear that the Friends' energies would need to be used on far bigger projects, for a survey by the abbey architect, Thomas Overbury, in 1935 showed that urgent work was required on the tower, eastern chapels, nave, crossing and choir parapet, at a total estimate of some £25,000.

Through the success of a public appeal, the work of the Friends, and the contribution of proceeds from successive years of the Tewkesbury Festival, the target was reached and in July 1939 the abbey bells were rung again, and a plaque commemorating the restoration was unveiled.

An important development was the gift of land at the east end of the abbey, now known as Abbey Lawn, which began the process of opening up the view of the abbey from Church Street. In 1940 Miss Zula Woodhull of Norton Park, Bredon's Norton, left a large legacy, enabling the purchase of Abbey Lawn House and gardens. The gift was in memory of Miss

Fig.22.7 Memorial to Victoria Woodhull Martin

Woodhull's mother, Victoria Woodhull Martin, a prominent American and to date the only woman candidate for the Presidency, and it was stipulated that a memorial should be placed in the abbey for the promotion of friendship between Britain and the United States (Fig.22.7).

Canon Gough's letters during 1938 speak of the gathering storm clouds over Europe:

> Yet God is merciful and it may be that in spite of our sins - both corporate and individual - He may yet give us time to amend our ways. Whatever comes, God give us all grace to play our parts worthily of our Christian profession and of our great nation.[18]

Similar letters on the subject of the war appear frequently, and Canon Gough regularly encouraged people to attend the weekly service in the Lady Chapel for dedication, intercession and self commendation, during which the names of men serving or about to serve were read and prayers made for them. Canon Gough often made reference to the plight of others during the war, and wrote to the Provost of Coventry after the bombing of the cathedral in 1940.

Parish life continued, even though the interior of the abbey seemed duller, with the boarding up of the clerestory windows, and social life became curtailed through the use of the Parish Hall as a British Restaurant run by the Womens Voluntary

Service. But Canon Gough expected no less from the flock and even the introduction of the black-out resulted in a veiled reference to the importance of Catholic discipline in difficult times:

> It was generally desired that we should continue our Sunday Evensong at the usual hour of 6.30pm, but lighting restrictions make this impossible. Evensong will therefore be at 3.30 and end at 4.30pm. To those who make the Holy Communion their first Sunday duty the black-out presents no difficulty of course.[19]

The war, however, and increased pressure of work, took its toll on Canon Gough's health, and

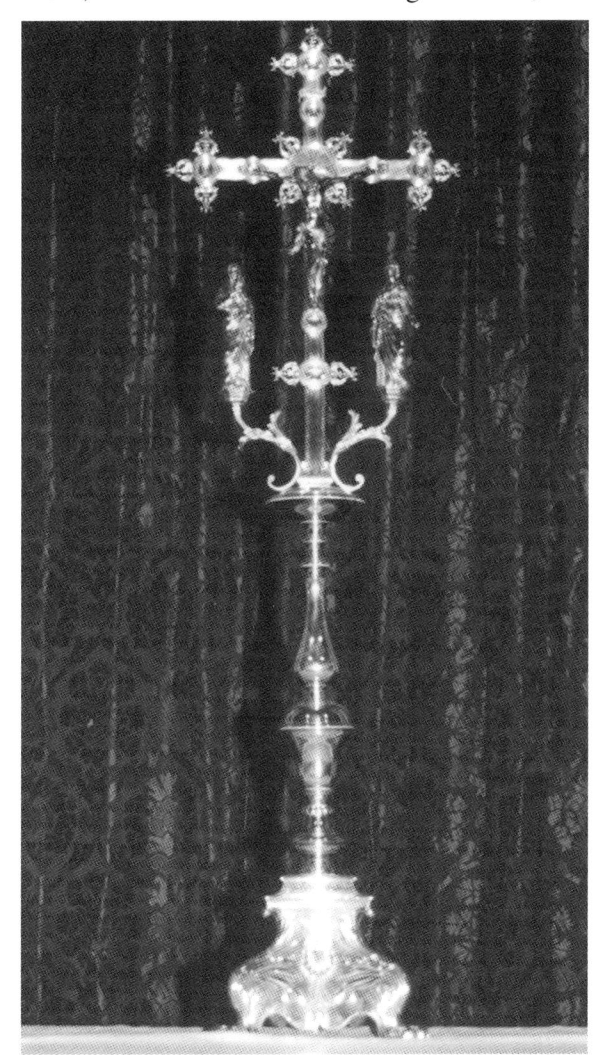

Fig.22.8 High Altar Cross, designed by Ninian Comper, given in memory of Canon Gough

in April 1940 he tendered his resignation to the bishop and Lord Chancellor, as patron of the living. In the May *Parish Magazine*, he reported that he had been urged to reconsider his decision, but that he had declined. By the June magazine, however, the decision had been reversed:

> As you all know, I have decided to postpone my resignation indefinitely. The whole situation has so changed since I last wrote to you and become so much more dangerous that I feel I ought to remain in the place where, at any rate, I can perhaps be more of use to you than a stranger, however good he might be.[20]

Canon Gough eventually retired in 1942 and his last letter gives valuable insight into his ministry:

> I will ask you to remember me not merely as the custodian of the fabric of this glorious church, which I love so dearly, but also as one who has tried to be a good parish priest and to teach you the Catholic Faith without fear or compromise. I have always believed that this teaching expresses the true mind of the English Church and can be given and practised in loyalty to our Prayer Book and to our doctrinal belief.[21]

Canon Gough's retirement was sadly short, as he died only three years later, aged 66. He is buried on the south side of the abbey and is commemorated within the building by the high altar cross, designed by Ninian Comper (Fig.22.8). As a keen watercolourist, his paintings are today displayed in the present Visitor Centre, in a room named after him.

The incumbency of Canon Brian Purefoy, 1942-63

Canon Gough was succeeded by Brian Mews, who, within months of his induction had changed his surname, for family reasons, to Purefoy. A farmer for 20 years in the Burford area, he was trained at Chichester Theological College. After a curacy in Northleach and an incumbency at Farmington, he came to Tewkesbury in 1942. A man large both in personality and stature, he was both outspoken and highly popular. In a *Parish Magazine* he betrayed his keen sense of humour:

> I want to thank all the kind people who have sent me Christmas cards. I had one from one of our visitors in the summer who apparently couldn't remember my name but apparently was impressed with my bulk. It was addressed, 'His Rotund Reverence' ... I'm afraid I can't find a suitable answer to this leg-pull!![22]

At the end of the war Canon Purefoy began a series of improvements to the abbey. The Milton organ was rebuilt under the direction of organist Huskisson Stubington and, with the magic of electrical action still a great novelty, the modest two-manual instrument was transformed into a five-manual giant, with plans laid for the linking of the Milton with the even larger four-manual Grove organ, installed in the 1880s. Lack of money prevented the larger scheme being brought to fruition, but the daring and originality of the rebuild soon became legendary.

Fig.22.9 Brian Purefoy, vicar 1942-63, with Mrs. Molly Purefoy

Fig.22.10 Statue of the Virgin and Child over north porch by Darsie Rawlins (1959)

In Canon Purefoy's time, new chairs to his own design were provided for the nave; another appeal was launched, for £50,000, to deal with deteriorating stonework, lead roofs and the ravages of death-watch beetle. Smaller projects included the placing of a new statue of the Blessed Virgin Mary above the north porch—a replacement of the weathered medieval statue, to a new design by Darsie Rawlins (Fig.22.10).

Fig.22.11 The liturgy during the 1950s

During the late 1940s Prior's Park estate expanded greatly, and the parish sought ways in which this large new population could be ministered to. By 1957 a Mission Hall had been built on the estate, served by abbey clergy, and it continued its ministry there until it was destroyed by a fire in the late 1980s.

In the early 1960s attention was focused on the abbey bells, and in 1962 a new peal by Taylors of Loughborough was placed in the central tower. This was one of Canon Purefoy's last projects, for in September 1963 he retired, moving to his beloved Oxfordshire. His retirement was, however, to be tragically short, as he died suddenly that December. In an appreciation of his life the Revd. Peter Brett, one of Canon Purefoy's last curates, spoke warmly of his humanity:

> And if one were to be asked for one word to describe him, it would be that he was a generous man—generous in every way. What he gave away would fill a book, and what he did had always the hallmark of generosity. Praise would go where it was due—and so would a necessary reprimand![23]

The incumbency of Canon Cosmo Pouncey, 1963-81

During the incumbency of Canon Cosmo Pouncey several important developments took place—developments which still remain strong at the beginning of the 21st century and which are a lasting legacy to a much admired incumbency.

One of the first projects of Canon Pouncey was to begin a fund to restore the ailing Grove

Fig.22.12 The Royal Maundy, April 1971: HRH Queen Elizabeth and Prince Philip received at the Gage gates by the Very Revd. Basil Guy, bishop of Gloucester, and Canon Cosmo Pouncey

organ in memory of his well-loved predecessor—a project which was finally realised in the early 1980s.

In worship, the abbey continued to present a model to the wider church, and improvements in transport led to the development of an eclectic congregation showing that people were prepared to travel to find fine traditional, Catholic worship.

While the traditional Sung Eucharist continued on its weekly basis, the needs of younger families began to be better met by the establishment, in the mid-1960s, of a Parish Eucharist, using a nave altar and simpler ceremonial. Alongside the fellowship engendered by the new service was a post-service parish breakfast—whose regular menu of rolls and sausages continues 40 years on!

The huge space of the abbey was exploited by the introduction of an annual Advent Procession in 1967, and at about the same time the abbey began its now traditional week of *Musica Deo Sacra*—fine music of all periods performed within the liturgy, and drawing worshippers from all over the world.

Of national importance during Canon Pouncey's incumbency was the establishment of the Abbey School. In a report to the Friends of Tewkesbury Abbey in 1971 the vicar wrote:

> An able schoolmaster, who is also a lay clerk in the choir of one of the English Cathedrals, is exploring the possibility of establishing an independent preparatory school, with a musical bias, in Tewkesbury. He has it in mind that this might serve as a choir school for the Abbey.[24]

The school, founded by Miles Amherst, started in April 1973 with seven boys and has grown in numbers and influence. It now provides daily choral Evensong in the abbey on weekdays, the parish choirs singing all services on Sundays—a unique choral establishment and one which further enables the breadth and flexibility of the abbey's ministry and outreach.

No period of the abbey in recent history has shirked its responsibility to keep the fabric of this peerless building in good repair and 1972 saw the launching of another appeal, this time for £200,000, for repairs to stonework and the roofs.

No description of Canon Pouncey's incumbency would be complete without mention of the great celebrations of 1971—a year commemorating the 850th anniversary of the consecration of the church in 1121 as well as the 500th anniversary of the Battle of Tewkesbury in 1471. A huge programme of events was arranged: *Son et Lumière*, concerts, festival services, plays and lectures, with the climax of the year being the distribution of the Royal Maundy by Her Majesty the Queen in the abbey.

The last two decades

The last two decades of the 20th century show a trend to achieve *balance*—balancing the demands and traditions of an ancient church with those of a church 'on the move', ministering to an ever-changing world.

Tewkesbury Abbey is larger than 14 of the English cathedrals, and thus shares many of their

Fig.22.13 Michael Anthony Moxon, vicar 1981-90

Fig.22.14 The shop and the Gambier Parry altarpiece, in the former north transept chapels

problems and opportunities. For this reason, in 1991 an association of similar churches—the Greater Churches Group—was formed to provide a forum where the 19 member churches could share concerns. Like cathedrals, the abbey has to minister to a wider community than just the parish, and so the building is often used for concerts and other events. In 1990, 200,000 visitors to the abbey were recorded. It is very much a focus for community activity, and the development of tourism has led, of necessity, to the development of very different and more positive attitudes to visitors than the views expressed by Canon Smith during the 1920s!

Following the lead of English cathedrals, the abbey has seen the value of modest commercial development. The abbey shop (in the former St. James' Chapel) was opened in 1983 and a refectory (in the new Visitor Centre) in 1996. Both play their part, not only in providing much-needed revenue but also in emphasizing the abbey's Benedictine roots of welcome and hospitality.

During the past 20 years there has been continual care for the fabric of the abbey. The vaults of the church have been thoroughly cleaned and restored: the chancel in the 1980s, the nave in the 1990s. Roofs have been repaired and opportunities taken to beautify the church and to enhance its atmosphere of prayer.

In addition, during the past few years, the abbey has consciously sought to commission works of art as focuses for devotion—whether in

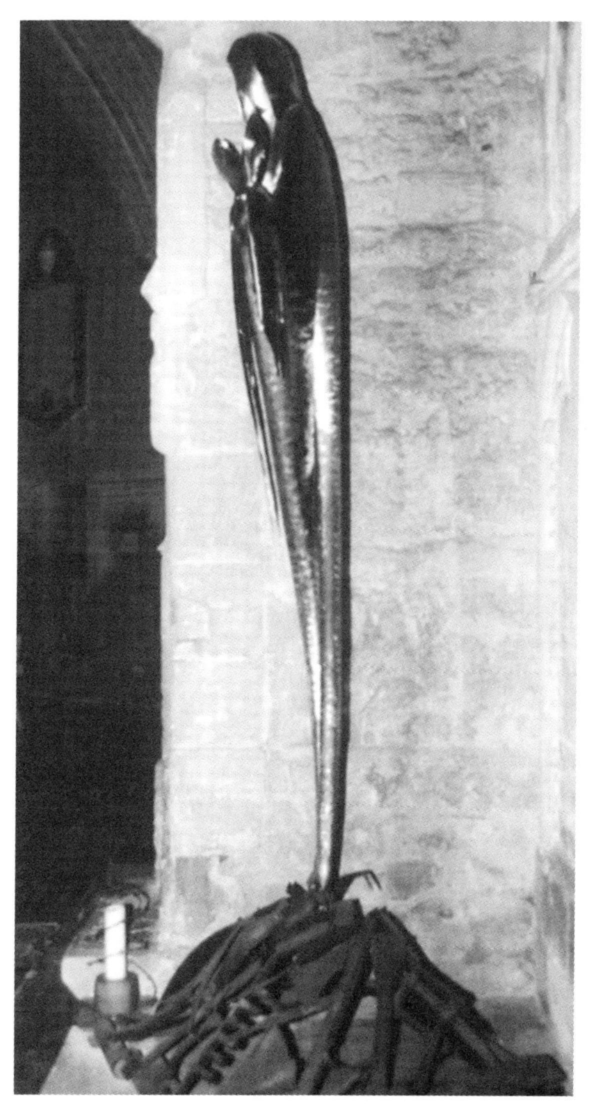

Fig.22.15 Our Lady Queen of Peace by Anthony Robinson

Fig.22.16 Michael Edward Tavinor, vicar 1990-2002, with HRH Princess Margaret at the Thanksgiving Service for the Appeal, April 1997

a traditional mould (icons, and the hanging pyx) or more contemporary form (*Our Lady Queen of Peace* or the altar *I am that I am*) (Fig.22.15).

Another parallel which the abbey shares with cathedrals is the development of a paid staff: vergers, shop and refectory staff; but, important as the staff are, the church relies very much on the faithful and unstinting help of volunteer helpers.

In 1999 the parish of Twyning (population 1,600) was added to the abbey parish, thus creating a united benefice, with the Lord Chancellor and Christ Church Oxford as joint patrons. This addition, together with large new estates on the perimeter of the parish, has led to a massive increase in population with its attendant pressures on clergy time. The development of lay ministry has been partly in response to this but also a response to a re-awakening in the wider church to the unique ministry of each—lay and ordained.

Amidst all these changes and developments the abbey continues—its serene, often brooding presence keeping watch over the community. The people of Tewkesbury have a huge regard and affection for 'our Abbey', and it seems certain to provide a focus for worship, wonder, community and mission in the years that lie ahead.

In 1939 Dorothy L. Sayers wrote a play, *The Zeal of Thy House*, for the Friends of Canterbury Cathedral. In it she presents the joys and sorrows of life in a great church, and she ends with words put into the mouth of the Archangel Michael, which seem to sum up the paradox of worshipping a God so huge that He cannot be put into words, and yet so small that He is closer to us than the very air we breathe. St. Michael says:

> Praise Him, that He hath made man in His own image, a maker and craftsman like Himself, a little mirror of His triune majesty. And whatsoever ye do, do all to the glory of God.[25]

References

Abbreviations used

Atkyns — Atkyns, R. *The Ancient and Present State of Glostershire* (London, 1712; repr. 1974)

BAA Trans — *British Archaeological Association Conference Transactions*

BAA Trans VII — T. Heslop and V. Sekules (eds), *Medieval Art and Architecture at Gloucester and Tewkesbury*, *BAA Trans* VII (Leeds, 1985)

Bennett — J. Bennett, *The History of Tewkesbury* (Tewkesbury, 1830; repr. Stroud, 1976, with an Introduction by C. Elrington). All references are to this edition unless stated otherwise

Bennett/*TYR* — J. Bennett, *The Tewkesbury Yearly Register and Magazine,* vol.1, 1830-39; vol.2, 1840-49. See also *TR*

Bettey — J.H. Bettey, *The Suppression of the Monasteries in the West Country* (Gloucester, 1989)

BGAS — Bristol & Gloucestershire Archaeological Society

Bigland — *Ralph Bigland: Historical, Monumental and Genealogical Collections relative to the County of Gloucester*, B. Frith (ed.), 4 vols, BGAS (1989-95). All references are to this edition unless stated otherwise

BL — British Library

Blunt — J.H. Blunt, *Tewkesbury Abbey and its Associations* (London and Tewkesbury, 1875; 2nd edn. 1898). All references are to the first edition unless stated otherwise

Complete Peerage — G.E. Cokayne, *The Complete Peerage of England,* H.V. Gibbs (ed.), 13 vols (London, 1910-59)

CPR — *Calendar of the Patent Rolls*, PRO

Dingley — Thomas Dingley, *History on Marble: compiled in the reign of Charles II, Vol.II*, J.G. Nichols (ed.), Camden Society, old series vol.97 (London, 1868)

DNB — *Dictionary of National Biography*

GCL — Gloucester City Library

GDR — Gloucester Diocesan Records, in GRO

Gent. Mag. — *Gentleman's Magazine*

GNQ — *Gloucestershire Notes and Queries*

GRO — Gloucester Record Office

Handbook — W. North, *New Handbook and Guide to Tewkesbury Abbey* (Tewkesbury, 1878, numerous subsequent editions)

Hannan — A. Hannan, 'Tewkesbury and the earls of Gloucester: excavations at Holm Hill, 1975-5', *TBGAS*, CXV (1997), 79-232

Hockaday — Hockaday Abstracts, GRO/D3439/369/Tewkesbury

JBAA — *Journal of the British Archaeological Association*

Jones — A. Jones, *Tewkesbury* (Chichester, 1987)

Jones and Grenville — A. Jones with archaeological discussion by J. Grenville, 'Some new Suggestions about the pre-Conquest history of Tewkesbury and Tewkesbury church', *Southern History* 9 (1987), 9-33

Lehmann-Brockhaus — O. Lehmann-Brockhaus (ed.) *Schriftquellen zur Kunst in England, Wales und Schottland vom Jahre 901 bis zum Jahre 1307*, vol.II (Munich 1956), 560-3

Leland — *The Itinerary of John Leland in or about the years 1535-43*, L.T. Smith (ed.), 5 vols (London, 1906-10)

Litzenberger — C. Litzenberger, *Tewkesbury Churchwardens' Accounts 1563-1624* , BGAS (Stroud, 1994)

Luard — H.R. Luard (ed.), *Annales Monastici Vol.I*, Rolls Series, vol.36 (London, 1864), 'Annales de Theokesberia A.D. 1066-1263', 41-180

Lysons — S. Lysons, *A Collection of Gloucestershire Antiquities*, 2 vols (London, 1803)

Lysons/Tombs — S. Lysons, 'Observations on some Tombs in the Abbey Church at Tewkesbury', *Archaeologia*, XIV (1803), 143-53

Massé — H.J. Massé, *The Abbey Church of Tewkesbury, with some account of the Priory Church of Deerhurst, Gloucestershire* (London, 1900; numerous subsequent reprints with corrections). All references are to the first edition unless stated otherwise

Monasticon — *Monasticon Anglicanum*: *a History of the Abbies and other Monasteries in England and Wales; originally published in Latin by Sir William Dugdale, Kt.; a New Edition*, J. Caley, H. Ellis, B. Bandinel (eds), vol.II (London, 1819). All references are to this edition and volume unless stated otherwise

Morris — R.K. Morris, 'Tewkesbury Abbey: the Despenser Mausoleum', *TBGAS* XCIII (1974), 142-55

PRO — Public Record Office

Rudder — S. Rudder, *A New History of Gloucestershire* (Cirencester, 1779; repr.1977)

Rushforth — G.McN. Rushforth, 'The glass in the quire clerestorey of Tewkesbury Abbey', *TBGAS* XLVI, (1924), 289-324

TBGAS — *Transactions of the Bristol and Gloucestershire Archaeological Society*
TBR — Tewkesbury Borough Records, in GRO
Tewkesburian — Tewkesburian, *They Used to Live in Tewkesbury* (Stroud, 1991)
TPM — *Tewkesbury Parochial Magazine*, subsequently *Tewkesbury Abbey Parish Magazine*, now *Abbey News*
TR — *The Tewkesbury Register* (continuation of Bennett/*TYR*)
Valor — *Valor Ecclesiasticus*, J. Caley and J. Hunter (eds), Records Commission, 6 vols, (London, 1810-34)
VCH Glos — *Victoria County History, Gloucestershire*, vol.II (1907), VI (1965), VIII (1968)
Verey — D. Verey, *Gloucestershire: the Vale and the Forest of Dean*, Buildings of England Series (Harmondsworth, 1970)
Verey & Brooks — D. Verey & A. Brooks, *Gloucestershire 2; the Vale and the Forest of Dean*, Buildings of England Series (3rd rev. edn., New Haven and London, 2002)
Vet. Mon. — *Vetusta Monumenta*, Society of Antiquaries of London, vol.V (1835), 33-46

Chapter 1 Tewkesbury before the Normans

1. Hannan, 79, 83-4.
2. *VCH Glos,* VIII, 115.
3. *VCH Glos*, VIII, 112.
4. Hannan, 88 and 222, though fig.38 shows the Mill Avon appearing only in the 13th century.
5. *VCH Glos,* VIII, 139.
6. I am grateful to Toby Clempson, of Tewkesbury Borough Council, for discussing the problem of the Mill Avon. The subject needs further research and elucidation. Jones, 5, suggests that the cut might be Saxon or Roman.
7. A. Hannan, 'Excavations at Tewkesbury 1972-74', *TBGAS* 111 (1993), 21-75.
8. *Ibid.*, 23, fig.1, nos. 3, 20, 21, 28, 31; J. Hoyle, 'Tewkesbury Abbey Meadow', *Glevensis* 26 (1992), 31; Bennett, 17; information from survey of Tewkesbury by Gloucestershire County Council.
9. *VCH Glos*, VIII, 110 n.14. In 1967 '7 burials and pottery of 3rd-4th century' were found; Hannan 'Excavations 1972-4', 43.
10. A. Williams, 'An Introduction to the Gloucestershire Domesday', *The Gloucestershire Domesday* (Alecto Historical Edition, London, 1989), 10-13. It is possible that Tewkesbury was part of Winchcombshire; Julian Wybra, *A Lost County: Winchcombshire in the 10th and 11th centuries*, Studies in Anglo-Saxon History 1 (Woodbridge, 1990). It is usually thought to have been part of Gloucestershire, e.g. D. Hill, *Atlas of Anglo-Saxon England*, map 178. It was certainly in an area where the boundary history was particularly complex.
11. *Glos. Domesday* (Alecto), ff.163, 163v; A. Williams, 'A West-Country Magnate of the Eleventh Century: the Family, Estates and Patronage of Beorhtric Son of Ælfgar', in *Family Trees and the roots of politics*, ed. K.S.B. Keats-Ronan (Boydell, 1997), 46-7, 50-52.
12. A.H. Smith, *Place Names of Gloucestershire*, English Place Name Society vol.39 part ii (Cambridge 1964), 66, gives 'old fort' or 'old manor house'; but the phrase 'old fortified place' or 'enclosed place' is to be preferred, pers. comm. Michael Hare.
13. Hannan, 'Excavations 1972-4', 38-9.
14. K. Lilley, 'Historical Analysis of the Plan Form of the Town', in Hannan, 89-91; and also Hannan, 223.
15. See Appendix.
16. *Glos. Domesday* (Alecto), f.163; A. Williams, 'Beorhtric', 50, n.37.
17. Hannan, 224.
18. *Ibid.*
19. Deerhurst, which might have been a potential candidate for an early market, has too little land above the flood level, and a similar situation might disqualify Twyning (or Ripple) as an early market site. I am grateful to Michael Hare for making this point.
20. Williams, 'An Introduction', 9.
21. *Glos. Domesday* (Alecto), f.163v; Hannan, passim.
22. *VCH Glos*, II, 62; *VCH Glos,* VIII, 158.
23. Williams, 'Beorhtric', 50-51.
24. *VCH Glos*, VIII, 154; Williams, 'An Introduction', 20-21; *Glos. Domesday* (Alecto), f.153, 163v.
25. Hannan, 223.
26. J. Blair, 'Parish Churches in the eleventh century', in *Domesday Book Studies* (Alecto Historical Editions 1987), 65.
27. C.S. Taylor, 'Origin of the Mercian Shires' in H.P.R. Finberg, *Gloucestershire Studies* (Leicester, 1957), 39.
28. P. Sims-Williams, *Religion and Literature in Western England 600-800* (Cambridge, 1990), 173.
29. *Monasticon,* 59-60. Dugdale was using a post-dissolution version of the chronicle: see P.B. Pepin, 'Monasticon Anglicanum and the History of Tewkesbury Abbey', *TBGAS* 98 (1980), 95-97, and ch.6, this volume. I am grateful to Julian Luxford for his comments.
30. Atkyns, 725-37: Atkyns' 'translation' actually abbreviates some of the text.
31. *Ibid.*, 726; with some standardisation of spellings and punctuation.
32. *hostium*, which in medieval Latin is usually translated 'door' rather than 'gate'.
33. S. Bassett, *The Origins of the Parishes of the Deerhurst Area*, Deerhurst Lecture 1997 (Deerhurst, 1998). See also ch.6, this volume.
34. Rudder, 734.
35. A. Williams, *Land, Power and Politics: the family and career of Odda of Deerhurst*, Deerhurst Lecture 1996, (Deerhurst, 1997).
36. Bassett, *Origins*, 12; Michael Hare, pers. comm.
37. Referring to the chapel itself; D.Parsons, 'Odda's Chapel, Deerhurst: place of worship or royal hall?', *Medieval Archaeology* 44 (2000), 225-28.
38. The inscription was subsequently discarded, and was dug up in a nearby orchard in 1675; it is now in the Ashmolean Museum, Oxford. A replica is in the chapel today. Michael Hare informs me that the fabric of Odda's chapel shows no sign of disturbance where the inscription might originallyhave been, though the chapel has been heavily restored.
39. Bassett, *Origins*, 12.
40. *Ibid.*, 11-12, 19.
41. Williams 'An Introduction', 22; Williams, 'Beorhtric', 43.
42. Bassett, *Origins*, 10-12, 19.
43. H.P.R. Finberg, *Early Charters of the West Midlands* (Leicester, 1972), 35, no.22.
44. *Ibid.*, 35.
45. Bassett, *Origins,* 8.
46. Jones and Grenville, 10-15.
47. *Ibid.*, 12.
48. *VCH Glos*, II, 63; *VCH Glos*, VIII, 135.
49. A.H. Smith, *Place Names of Gloucestershire*, 61-62.
50. *VCH Glos,* VIII, 134. Williams comments ('Beorhtric', 43, n.4) that there is no evidence that any part of Twyning belonged to Tewkesbury before the time of Domesday.
51. J. Grenville, 'King John's Castle, The Mythe Tewkesbury: a preliminary survey', in Jones and Grenville, 19-31.
52. Jones and Grenville, 17; *VCH Glos*, VIII, 135.
53. Jones and Grenville, 32, n.40.
54. *VCH Glos*, VIII, 154.
55. Bennett, 355-6. Augmentations: '... the body of the said church there which heretofore was the only parish church to the parishioners of the town of Tewkesbury'. Grant: 'That whereas the body or the nether part of the late abbey church of Tewkesbury ... at the time of the dissolution of the late monastery of Tewkesbury aforesaid, and continually before the same dissolution, was the parish church of the same town of Tewkesbury ...'. For an alternative interpretation, see ch.8, this volume.
56. Bennett, 132.
57. Proceedings at the annual summer meeting at Tewkesbury 8, 9, 10 July 1902, *TBGAS* 25 (1902), part 1, 26-39.
58. *TBGAS* 25 (1902), 29.
59. *VCH Glos*, VIII, 126.
60. Jones and Grenville, 16.
61. *CPR* Edward III, 1367, 13, 379, 380, as cited by Hockaday. One might

expect an entry in the bishop's register for this year, to explain the record further. I am very grateful to John Rhodes, who has searched the Register of Bishop Whittesley in Worcestershire Record Office, but found no relevant entry around this year.

62. 'Plaint of the abbot and convent of St. Mary of Tewkesbury against the Bishop, touching the church of St. Mary of Tewkesbury, AD 1301': J. Willis Bund (ed.), *Register of Bishop Godfrey Giffard 1268-1301*, Worcestershire Historical Society (1902), 542; original in register of Geoffrey Giffard, Bishop of Worcester, Worcestershire Record Office BA 1648/1 (i) f.462. I am very grateful to John Rhodes for transcribing and translating this entry, and to Robin Whittaker, Assistant County Archivist, for his help and advice and for providing a copy of the relevant folio.
63. Alternatively, the appropriation of the parish church to the new abbey foundation need not mean that it became the abbey church; see ch.8, this volume.
64. *Glos. Domesday* (Alecto), 163v.
65. Williams, 'An Introduction', 7. She adds (29) that the two churches of Tewkesbury are analogous to the two at Deerhurst: one church the minster, one the secular church. But the churches at Deerhurst are close together. The two at Tewkesbury are Stanway and Clifford Chambers, 10 miles and 22 miles from Tewkesbury repectively: Clifford Chambers is clearly an estate church (*ibid*., 7). This cannot have been the only estate church in this vast possession.
66. D. Verey and A. Brooks, *Buildings of England Gloucestershire I: The Cotswolds* (1999), 632.
67. C.S. Taylor, *Analysis of the Domesday Survey of Gloucestershire* (Bristol, 1889), 147. I am grateful to Dr. John Blair for discussion of this point.
68. A modern edition of the relevant materials would be very valuable.
69. *VCH Glos* VII, 125
70. A considerable medieval north-south wall was found on this line, with medieval monastic remains existing to the east of it but not to the west: I am grateful to Jon Hoyle, Gloucester County Council, for his information on the excavations of 1992.
71. As suggested by Lilley, 'Plan Form'.
72. See discussion in A. Palmer, 'Contour Survey of Tewkesbury 1987', Manuscript at Archaeology Section, Shire Hall, Gloucestershire County Council.

Chapter 2 The Early Lords: Robert Fitzhamon to the de Clares

1. *Complete Peerage*, V, 682-3; F. Barlow, *William Rufus* (London, 1983), 73, 93, 172-3, 192, 321, 353, 436; Luard, 44-5.
2. *Complete Peerage*, V, 683-6. The fullest account of his role in Stephen's reign is now contained in D. Crouch, *The Reign of King Stephen 1135-54* (Harlow, 2000).
3. M. Altschul, *A Baronial Family in Medieval England: the Clares 1217-1314* (Baltimore, 1965), 25-26; R.B. Patterson (ed.), *Earldom of Gloucester Charters*, (Oxford, 1972), nos. 45, 50, 107, 165.
4. *VCH Glos*, VIII, 114.
5. *Ibid*., 110; *Pipe Rolls, 3 – 13 John* , Pipe Roll Society (PRS), n.s. 14 (1936) – 28 (1952), passim; T.D. Hardy (ed.) *Rotuli de Liberate ac de Misis et Praestitis Regnante Johanne*, (London, 1844), 120; *Calendar of the Liberate Rolls 1226-0*, 193, 216, 228, 231, 320-3; *1240-5*, 66; W.L. Warren, *King John* (London, 1961), 139.
6. S.J. Madge (ed.), *Abstracts of the Inquisitiones post mortem for Gloucestershire*, IV, *1236-1300*, (British Record Series xxx, 1903), 32.
7. *VCH Glos*, VI, 185-6; VIII, 146.
8. *Ibid*., VIII, 112, 172, 196, 228; Madge, *Abstracts*, 180.
9. *VCH Glos*, VI, 187-8.
10. *Ibid*., 137; Madge, *Abstracts*, 189; PRO, SC 11/ 249.
11. PRO DL 29/ 638/ 10362 m.1; see also PRO E 142/54/1.
12. *VCH Glos*, VIII, 110; PRO SC 11/249.
13. Madge, *Abstracts*, 180; DL 29/638/10362 m.1; see also *VCH Glos*, VIII, 125.
14. Hannan, 79-232, esp. 95-6, 109-120, 122-5.
15. *Pipe Rolls 4 John* (PRS n.s. 19, 1941), 93; *Cal. Lib. Rolls 1226-40*, 254.
16. E.A. Fry (ed.), *Abstracts of the Inquisitiones post mortem for Gloucestershire*, v, *1301-58*, (British Record Society xl, 1910), 90-3, 148.
17. *VCH Glos*, VIII, 112; *Rotuli de Liberate*, 61; Hannan, 206; *Pipe Rolls 13 John* (PRS n.s. 28, 1951-2), 68; *Cal. Lib. Rolls 1226-40*, 385.
18. *Pipe Rolls 4 John* (PRS n.s. 19, 1941), 103; *Rotuli de Liberate*, 88.
19. GRO D184/ M15/ 8; DL 29/ 638/10362 m.1; *Cal. Lib. Rolls 1226-40*, 249; *VCH Glos,* VIII, 125.
20. Altschul, *Clares*, 25-6; Luard, 113.
21. T.B. Pugh (ed.), *The Victoria County History of Glamorgan*, III, *The Middle Ages* (Cardiff, 1971), 59.
22. Altschul, *Clares*, 80-91.
23. *Ibid*., 95-120.
24. *Ibid*., 148-9.
25. N. Denholm-Young (ed.), *The Life of Edward II* (Edinburgh, 1957), 52-3.
26. *Ibid*.

Chapter 3 The Later Lords: The Despensers and their Heirs

1. J.R. Maddicott, *Thomas of Lancaster 1307-22: A Study in the Reign of Edward II* (Oxford, 1970), 261.
2. *Monasticon*, 61-2; see also N.M.Fryde, *The Tyranny and Fall of Edward II 1321-6* (Cambridge, 1979); for succinct modern biographies of the Despensers, see M.A. Hicks, *Who's Who in English History 1272-1485* (London, 1991), 62-5.
3. See chs 10 and 13.
4. *Complete Peerage*, V, 271-81.
5. *Monasticon*, 62-3 ; M.A. Hicks, 'An Escheat Concealed: The Despenser Forfeitures 1400-61', *Hampshire Studies* 53 (1998), 185-7.
6. GRO D184/M15/1 m.2.
7. W.H. Courthope (ed.), *The Rous Roll*, (London, 1859), no. 50.
8. *Ibid*.; GRO D184/M15/1.
9. M.A. Hicks, *Warwick the Kingmaker* (Oxford, 1998), pp.31-4; *id*., 'Between Majorities: The 'Beauchamp Interregnum' 1439-49', *Historical Research* 72 (1999), 32-3.
10. Hicks, *Warwick the Kingmaker*, ch.3.
11. *Ibid*., chs.4, 6, 7, 9, 10; J. Bruce (ed.), *Historie of the Arrivall of Edward IV in England* (Camden Society I, 1838), 22.
12. Unless otherwise stated, this section is based on *The Arrivall*, 22-31. For the author, see L. Visser-Fuchs, 'Edward IV's "Memoir on Paper" to Charles Duke of Burgundy: the so-called "Short Version of the Arrivall"', *Nottingham Medieval Studies* 36 (1992), 167-227.
13. *The Arrivall*, 28. For recent reconstructions of the terrain, all inevitably requiring extensive speculation, see C.D. Ross, *Edward IV* (London, 1974), 141 ; P.A. Haigh, *The Military Campaigns of the Wars of the Roses* (Stroud, 1995), 129-33; P.W. Hammond, *The Battles of Barnet and Tewkesbury* (Gloucester, 1990), 93-9.
14. C.L. Kingsford, *English Historical Literature in the Fifteenth Century* (London, 1913), 376-7.
15. L.M. Matheson (ed.), *Death and Dissent: The Dethe of the Kynge of Scotis and Warkworth's Chronicle* (Woodbridge, 1999), 113-14.
16. Kingsford, *Historical Literature*, 377.
17. See Besançon, Bibliothèque Municipale MS 1168 f.4v, conveniently reproduced in A. Sutton and L.Visser-Fuchs, *Richard III's Books* (Stroud, 1997), plate 9.
18. PRO SC 2/194/108 m.1.
19. N. Pronay and J.C. Cox (eds), *The Crowland Chronicle Continuations 1459-86* (London, 1986), 133; M.A. Hicks, *False, Fleeting, Perjur'd Clarence: George Duke of Clarence 1449-78* (rev. edn. Bangor, 1992), 99-103, 108-12; M.A.Hicks, 'Descent, Partition and Extinction: The "Warwick Inheritance"', *Bulletin of the Institute of Historical Research* lii (1979), 120-3, repr. in *id*., *Richard III and his Rivals* (London, 1991), ch.18.
20. Hicks, *Clarence*, ch.4; Hicks, 'Warwick Inheritance', 123-5; C.H. Williams, 'The Rebellion of Humphrey Stafford, 1486', *English Historical Review* xliii (1928), 183.
21. Hicks, 'Warwick Inheritance', 125-6; W. Campbell (ed.), *Materials for a History of the Reign of Henry VII*, ii (Rolls Series, London, 1873), 66, 211-2.
22. E. Stokes (ed.), *Abstracts of the Inquisitiones post mortem for Gloucestershire*, VI, *1359-1413* (British Record Society xlvii, 1914), 95 (1409); PRO DL 29/638/10362.
23. GRO D184/ M15/ 1, 5, 6.
24. Hannan, 133-7; E.A. Fry (ed.), *Abstracts of the Inquisitiones post mortem for Gloucestershire*, V, *1301-58* (British Record Society xl, 1910), 148.
25. Hannan, 217-19.
26. GRO D184/ M15/ 1-8.
27. *Rous Roll*, no. 54; *Monasticon*, 62; Hicks, *Warwick the Kingmaker*, 123; William Worcestre, *Itineraries*, J.H. Harvey (ed.) (Oxford, 1969), 218-19.
28. Hicks, *Warwick*, 82, 85, 89, 64.

29. Historic Manuscripts Commission, *Rutland* I, 2; C.L. Scofield, *The Life and Reign of Edward the Fourth* (2 vols. London, 1923), ii, 184n.
30. M.A. Hicks, *Richard III* (Stroud, 2000), 144.
31. *Monasticon*, 64.
32. PRO DL 29/638/10362 m.1.
33. Hicks, *Warwick the Kingmaker*, 32, 34, 60-1; *id.*, *Clarence*, 151.
34. *Monasticon*, 64.
35. Hicks, *Clarence*, 128.

Chapter 4 The Bones in the Clarence Vault

1. M.A. Hicks, *False, Fleeting, Perjur'd Clarence* (1980), 142, cites a letter of 20 Feb. 1478, from J.B. Sheppard (ed.), *Christ Church Letters*, Camden Society, new series, XIX (London, 1877), 36-7: 'Ther be assignyd certen Lords to go with the body of the Dukys of Clarence to Teuxbury, where he shall be beryid ... '. See also ch.3.
2. W.H. Courthope (ed.), *The Rous Roll* (London, 1859) repr. with a new introduction by C. Ross (1980), no.58: '... the fourth lord Rychard born at Tewkysbury and lyvyd not a quarter of a yere and dyed anon aftyr hys lady modre at Warrewik and there buryed ... '.
3. Hicks, *Clarence*, 204; P. Tudor-Craig, *Richard III*, National Portrait Gallery exhibition catalogue (London, 1973), 81-2.
4. Hicks, *Clarence*, 138-9.
5. The bones at Windsor, identified in 1789 as those of Edward IV, indicated a male more than six feet tall; M. Duffy, *Royal Tombs of Medieval England* (Stroud, 2003), 258-9.
6. The text of Chapter 4 is drawn from a report submitted to the P.C.C. in 1985, following the examination – 'Report on the Examination of the Bones in the Tewkesbury Vault reputed to be those of George, Duke of Clarence, and his wife, Isabella Neville': Part I (The Bones) by Dr. M. Donmall, Part II (Historical Context) by Dr. R.K. Morris. The authors gratefully acknowledge a grant from The British Academy to facilitate that project.
7. i.e. where the left and right sides of the pelvis join centrally at the pubis. This is described in T.W. Todd, 'Age changes in the pubic bone', *American Jnl. of Physical Anthropology* 3 (1920), 285-334; T.W. McKern and T.D. Stewart, *Skeletal Age Changes in Young American Males*, Technical Report, Headquarters Quartermaster Research and Development Command (Natick, Mass., 1957); and others.
8. D.R. Brothwell, *Digging up Bones* (London, 1972).
9. M. Trotter, 'Estimation of stature from intact long limb bones', in T.D. Stewart (ed.), *Personal Identification in Mass Disasters* (Washington, 1970), 71-83.
10. Also, a single jaw fragment may warrant some further attention in order to determine the age at death of the individual to whom it belonged.
11. Translation from BL MS. Cotton Cleopatra C.III in *Gent. Mag.*, XCVI pt. I (1826), 629.
12. See J. Goodall and L. Monckton, 'The Chantry of Humphrey, Duke of Gloucester', in M. Henig and P. Lindley (eds.), *Alban and St. Albans: Roman and Medieval Architecture, Art and Archaeology*, *BAA Trans*, XXIV (Leeds, 2001), 234-6.
13. Hicks, *Clarence*, 142; see also Michael Hicks in the previous chapter.
14. Duffy, *Royal Tombs*, 254.
15. Possibly the confused arrangement now of the screens at the back of the high altar, facing into the ambulatory, may be related to the plans for a monument.
16. *Gent. Mag.*, XCVI pt. I (1826), 628.
17. Atkyns, 722; Rudder, 746.
18. Lysons, II, pl.LXXII.
19. Bennett, 179.
20. Bigland, III, section 268, describing inscriptions on their ledger stone (post 1829), lost in the repaving of the Victorian restoration (1875-9).
21. *Gent. Mag.*, XCVI pt. I (1826), 629.
22. Bennett, 179.
23. *Ibid.*, 179-80; the coffin had been dug up in 1775 between the sacristy door and the Trinity Chapel.
24. Handwritten notice, by J.H. Blunt or F. Moore, bound into Frederick Moore's special large format edition of Blunt, opp. p.84, in the abbey's book collection formerly in the room over the sacristy, where it was seen by Richard Morris about 1980.
25. Massé, 62, notes that the grill, and the brass inscription plaque (still there on the step near the entrance to the vault), were made in 1876.
26. Mr. R. Mulcuck, former head verger, pers. comm. to Richard Morris. However, a wooden-framed case would probably not last long in the damp atmosphere of the vault, so it is more likely that the 1876 case was metal-framed, and that the existing one is either this case or a replacement made *c.*1930-36.
27. Pers. comm. about 1980, from Professor E.B. Ford (All Souls College, Oxford) who was with de Beer at the time (about 1936). No notes from their visit seem to have survived.
28. The bottom half of the lid is from a tapering coffin, designed to go against a wall. On the bottom and side chamfered edges of the lid is an inscription, which has never been deciphered, in Lombardic characters, suggesting a date in the 13th or early 14th century.
29. See further ch.15.
30. For 1876, see handwritten notice bound into F. Moore's special large format edition of Blunt, opp. p.84.
31. *Gent. Mag.*, XCVI pt. I (1826), 629. That their account notes that the tiles 'were placed with little order' may be explained by the fact that only 'a small portion' of the pavement was accessible to their correspondent for inspection.
32. Bennett, 178. As a local man, presumably he had more time to check the vault than the correspondent in *Gentleman's Magazine*; or perhaps he is conflating information from the 1826 and 1829 openings.
33. The child's stone coffin with a shaped cavity for the head, though it might be 15th century, is probably earlier and thus unlikely to be original to the vault; Julian Litten, pers. comm. to Richard Morris, Oct. 1986.
34. *Ibid.* Richard Morris is most grateful to Julian Litten for his advice, received after our report (1985) was submitted, and which significantly changes the preliminary findings about the coffin handles on p.32 of that report.
35. Handwritten notes, apparently by the Revd J.H. Blunt, in GRO P329 CW 4/30.
36. The one concern about the integrity of the two assemblages in 1826 is that holes were 'perforated' in the Hawling burial chambers to ascertain the full extent of the medieval vault, and there were 'many hundred visitors'; *Gent. Mag.*, XCVI pt. I (1826), 629.
37. Thin-section bone samples are tested for changes which occur to the outer (cortical) layer of bone in all individuals of advancing age. The authors are grateful to Dr. William White for discussion of this and other methods.
38. For Edward IV's burial and its opening in 1789, see Duffy, *Royal Tombs*, 255-9.
39. Richard Morris is grateful to Mark Duffy for this suggestion, and to Dr. Eileen Scarff, the Archivist at St. George's Chapel, Windsor, for additional information.

Chapter 5 The Benedictine Foundation and Monastic Life

1. For an alternative view, that the pre-1087 church at Tewkesbury was independent, see ch.1.
2. J.A. Giles (ed.), *William of Malmesbury's Chronicle of the Kings of England*, (London, 1847), 433.
3. Luard, 44.
4. *Monasticon*, 81.
5. C. Johnson & H.A. Cronne (eds), *Regesta Regum Anglo-Normanorum 1066-1154*, vol.2, (Oxford, 1956), No.847.
6. D. Knowles, *The Monastic Order in England*, (2nd edn, Cambridge, 1963), 437.
7. Luard, 44; Knowles, *Monastic Order,* 182.
8. Luard, xv-xxvii.
9. *Ibid.*, 44.
10. S. Wood, *English Monasteries and their Patrons in theThirteenth Century*, (London, 1955), 123-9; Luard, 113, 159, 169.
11. Knowles, *Monastic Order,* 448-53.
12. F.W. Potto Hicks, 'A Tewkesbury Compotus', *TBGAS* 55 (1933), 249-55; J.C. Russell, 'The Clerical Population of Medieval England', *Traditio*, 2 (1944), 188-90; *Letters & Papers of Henry VIII*, XV, 1540, 139(iv).
13. M.A. Harris, 'Alan of Tewkesbury', *Studia Monastica,* 18 (1976), 77-94, 299-345.
14. Luard, 82-4.
15. *Ibid.*; *VCH Glos*, II, 62.
16. Luard, 84-6; *VCH Glos,* II, 62.
17. J. Willis Bund (ed.), *Register of Bishop Godfrey Giffard 1268-1301*, Worcestershire Historical Society (1902), 104-6.
18. J. Willis Bund (ed.), *Registrum Sede Vacante 1301-1435*, Worcestershire Historical Society (1897), 62-3.
19. *VCH Glos*, II, 64-5.
20. C.R. Cheney, *Episcopal Visitation of Monasteries in the Thirteenth Century* (Manchester, 1931), 89-90.
21. Willis Bund, *Register of Bishop Giffard,* 104-6.

22. Willis Bund, *Registrum Sede Vacante*, 62-3.
23. R.M. Haines (ed.), *Register of Wolstan De Bransford 1339-49*, Worcestershire Historical Society, n.s. 4 (1966), Nos 927-43.
24. Willis Bund, *Registrum Sede Vacante,* 214-7.
25. W.P. Marrett (ed.), *Register of Henry Wakefield 1375-95*, Worcestershire Historical Society, n.s. 7 (1972), No. 844.
26. Potto Hicks, 'Tewkesbury Compotus', 249-55.
27. T. Wakeman (ed.), 'On the Kitcheners' Roll of Tewkesbury Abbey', *JBAA* 15 (1859), 318-32.
28. *Ibid*.; *VCH Glos*, VI, 232-7.
29. *CPR, 1340-43*, 87.
30. *VCH Glos,* VI, 223-232; VIII, 196-208; D. Clark, 'The Shop Within? An Analysis of the Architectural Evidence for Medieval Shops', *Architectural History* 43 (2000), 64, 67, 78, 82, passim.
31. *VCH Glos*, II, 63.
32. *Monasticon,* 64, 664, 1021.
33. Hockaday, vol.368, 1498.

Chapter 6 The Founders' Book

1. All but one of these books are listed in N. Ker, *Medieval Libraries of Great Britain* (London, 1964), 188. For Leland's catalogue see R. Sharpe, J.P. Carley, R.M. Thomson and A.G. Watson (eds), *English Benedictine Libraries: The Shorter Catalogues* (London, 1996), 595-6.
2. Hereford Cathedral Library MS. P. IV. 6: see R.A.B. Mynors and R.M. Thomson, *Catalogue of the Manuscripts of Hereford Cathedral Library* (Woodbridge, 1993), 92.
3. Cambridge University Library MS. Gg. 3. 21: see H.R. Luard *et al.*, *A Catalogue of the Manuscripts Preserved in the Library of the University of Cambridge* (5 vols, Cambridge, 1856-67), III, 67-8.
4. BL MS. Cotton Claudius E.I. Ker, *Medieval Libraries*, 188, questions the Tewkesbury provenance.
5. Paris, Bibliothèque Nationale MS. Lat. 9376, fols.21-31: see L. Delisle, *Inventaire des Manuscrits conservés à la Bibliothèque Impériale sous les numéros 8823-11503 du fonds Latin* (Paris, 1863), 31.
6. Lambeth Palace Library MS. 188, fols.168-74: here identified as a Tewkesbury book for the first time.
7. BL MS. Royal 8 C.VII, fols.5-8: see G.F. Warner and J.P. Gilson, *Catalogue of Western Manuscripts in the Old Royal and King's Collections* (4 vols, London, 1921), I, 234.
8. Princeton University Library MS. Garrett 34. The evidence of Tewkesbury ownership is the inclusion of Abbot Richard Cheltenham's (1480-1509) obit in the calendar. The manuscript had earlier belonged to members of the Beauchamp family, and was presumably a gift to the abbot (or abbey) by one of them. See N.J. Morgan, *Early Gothic Manuscripts [II] 1250-1285* (London, 1988), 122-3 and ills 195-6.
9. BL MS. Cotton Cleopatra A.VII, fols.7-103; the Annals printed in Luard.
10. Oxford, Trinity College MS. 50, fols.7-407r. Until very recently, this work was ascribed to the polymath bishop of Lincoln, Robert Grosseteste (d.1253): see H.O. Coxe, *Catalogus Codicum MSS. qui in Collegiis Aulisque Oxoniensibus hodie Adservantur* (2 vols, Oxford, 1852), II:4, 20.
11. Gloucester Cathedral Library shelf mark H.3.7. See also Gloucester Cathedral Library MS. 36 articles 4 and 5, two leaves of a 13th-century gradual from Tewkesbury that were taken from the binding of H.3.7. Effectively they constitute another fragmentary manuscript from the abbey. See S.M. Eward, *A Catalogue of Gloucester Cathedral Library* (Gloucester, 1972), 5, 20.
12. Cambridge, Trinity College shelf mark Grylls 2.179. The volume contains the name of Abbot Richard Cheltenham, and also that of a 16th-century Durham monk, Richard Denand (many times over). Further, there is an indication of ownership by St. Albans Abbey (Ker, *Medieval Libraries*, 301): perhaps this book circulated at Oxford.
13. The title *Chronica de Fundatoribus et Fundatione Ecclesiae Theokusburiae* (Chronicle of the Founders and the Foundation of the Church of Tewkesbury) stamped on the 19th-century cover evidently derives from the chronicle of British Library MS. Cotton Cleopatra C.III, which carries this title (fol.210r) and is printed under it in *Monasticon*. In the Middle Ages the legal patrons and significant benefactors of churches were often called founders, no matter how far removed they were from the original foundation. Hence the title given to our manuscript.
14. Only one short article has ever been written on it: C.B. Hudson, 'The Founders' Book of Tewkesbury Abbey', *TBGAS* 33 (1910), 60-6. See also M. Clapinson and T.D. Rogers, *Summary Catalogue of Post-Medieval Western Manuscripts in the Bodleian Library at Oxford: Acquisitions 1916-1975* (3 vols, Oxford, 1991), II, 1260 (no. 54301), for brief notes and full provenance; O. Pächt and J.J.G. Alexander, *Illuminated Manuscripts in the Bodleian Library at Oxford* (3 vols, Oxford, 1966-73), III, 101 (no. 1177) and plate CVIII, for brief notes.
15. A relatively common late medieval practice.
16. Hudson, 'The Founders' Book', 65. However, the most remarkable heraldic illustration comes at the end of chapter 4, and relates to individuals mentioned only in the secretary hand. Moreover, the two scribes shared the task of writing fol.22r.
17. *CPR Henry VII, 1485-94*, 472.
18. See for example C.W. and P. Cunnington, *Handbook of English Costume in the Sixteenth Century* (London, 1954), 40-3, 60, 70-3.
19. College of Arms, *Heralds' Commemorative Exhibition 1484-1934* (London, 1970), plates VI-IX, XLIV.
20. Luard, xv-xxvii, 41-180; the cartulary is not printed in Luard.
21. F. Madan (ed.), *Summary Catalogue of the Western Manuscripts in the Bodleian Library* (7 vols in 8, Oxford, 1895-1953), V:2, 835, no. 30561 (with erroneous dating).
22. For another illustration of the roll see C. Platt, *The Abbeys & Priories of Medieval England* (London, 1984; 1995 edn.), 108 (with erroneous dating; *c*.1435).
23. *Monasticon*, 59-65; Atkyns, I, 725-37.
24. Leland, III, 150-63. Cleopatra C.III is not, however, in Leland's hand, as suggested in Blunt (1898 edn.), 5.
25. See *Monasticon*, 65 (poem); C.L. Kingsford, *English Historical Writing in the Fifteenth Century* (Oxford, 1913), 376-8; Bennett, 328-31 (list).
26. Leland's account has this opening sentence, and the list of the slain, indicating that he used this text rather than the Founders' Book.
27. *Catalogue of Additions to the Manuscripts in the British Museum in the Years MDCCCC-MDCCCCV* (London, 1907), 271. Fol.30 is missing.
28. E. Bernard (ed.), *Catalogi Librorum Manuscriptorum Angliæ et Hiberniæ* (Oxford, 1697), part 2, 112 (no. 4225).
29. Kingsford, 'Historical Writing', 376; Bennett, 328.
30. This formed part of MS. Cotton Otho D.I. See G.R.C. Davis, *Medieval Cartularies of Great Britain* (London, 1958), 109 (no. 956).
31. *Ibid.*, 109 (nos 956A [1-3]). 956A (1) is the Founders' Book unrecognized.
32. For the advertisement of the manuscript, see Anon., 'Tewkesbury Abbey', *GNQ*, V (1892), 325-7.
33. Unless otherwise indicated, all of the information contained in the following chapter outlines appears in the text.
34. *Sic* in MS. See fols.2r, 3r, 3v, 4v (x2); cf. fols.11r, 13v (x2), 17v, 18r. The symbol 'ØØ' is actually used.
35. Blunt (1898 edn.), 27-30, occasionally draws upon it via BL MS. Additional 36985. See also D. Knowles, *The Monastic Order in England* (Cambridge, 1963), 129 note 4, 182 note 2.
36. While the gifts will have been given to Cranborne, Tewkesbury is designated in the manuscript.
37. Cf. M. Chibnall (ed.), *The Ecclesiastical History of Orderic Vitalis* (6 vols, Oxford, 1969-80), III, 226-9.
38. *Erant ibi tunc temporis vetera aedifica et augusta: in quibus cum fratribus fere triennis deguit ante adventum Roberti filij Hamonis*. For chronological reasons, this 'coming' appears to be a different event to the grant of the manor to Robert Fitzhamon *c*.1087.
39. Luard, 44. In chapter 4 (fol.13v) of the Founders' Book, it is stated that Tewkesbury's rebuilding and the translation of Gerald and his monks from Cranborne both occurred in 1102. Chapter l's version of events is to be preferred, because it is fuller, was written closer in time to the matters described, and makes better sense: the new monastery cannot have been habitable in the same year it was begun.
40. This notion horrified Blunt, who refuted it (Blunt, 30).
41. See Luard, 113.
42. While the relics were originally given to Cranborne, the majority of them (given their importance) must have ended up at Tewkesbury.
43. W. Courthope (ed.), *This rol was laburd & finished by Master John Rows of Warrewyk* (Gloucester, 1980: the Middle English version of the Warwick Roll); E. Lega-Weekes, 'The Mohun Chronicle at Haccombe', *Devon and Cornwall Notes and Queries*, IV (1906-7), 17-22; *Heralds' Commemorative Exhibition*, 37 and plate XLII; *Monasticon*, VI:3, 1600 (Clare Roll).

44. H.T. Riley (ed.), *Chronica monasterii S. Albani* (12 vols; London, 1862-76), IV, 427-64; X, 451-80.
45. MS. Lat. misc. b.2 (R), membrane one, dorse, column a, line 13.
46. There is no hint here of Theocus as Geoffrey of Monmouth's legendary 6th-century bishop of Gloucester, on which see J.S.P. Tatlock, *The Legendary History of Britain* (New York,1974), 249.
47. On the tenures of these earls, see E.B. Fryde *et al* (eds.), *Handbook of British Chronology* (Cambridge, 1996), 463.
48. Cf. Luard, 76-7.
49. The chronicle of Cleopatra C.III does not trace the pedigree as far as Richard III.
50. His will describes this as a ewer reserved for the feast of Corpus Christi, given to him by the king of France. N.H. Nicolas (ed.), *Testamenta Vetusta* (London, 1826), 99.
51. The chronicle of Cleopatra C.III locates Thomas Despenser's 'murder' at Tewkesbury.
52. Note that in reality Richard Beauchamp was killed in 1422; the chronology of the Founders' Book is faulty in this respect. Also the mistake with the dedication date is repeated in BL MS. Additional 36985, fol.30v (the chronicle of Cleopatra C.III says 1438, which has misled a number of scholars).
53. F.J. Furnivall (ed.), *Fifty Earliest English Wills in the Court of Probate*, (London, 1882), 116-17. It has long been doubted whether this tomb was ever made: our chronicler's testimony suggests that it was. Her will describes it as an iconographically complicated 'cadaver' tomb.
54. Cf. *CPR Edward IV, Henry VI, 1467-77*, 530.
55. For the lords' role in the remodelling see R.K. Morris, 'Tewkesbury Abbey: The Despenser Mausoleum', *TBGAS* 93 (1974), 142-55. See also Morris, ch.10.
56. A certain gold cross and silver 'table'—perhaps an altar adornment—mentioned in chapter 1 appear again.
57. Among the real estate mentioned is the village of Weston (Wilts.) purchased for 56 pounds of silver; 5 hides of land at Pulton (Glos.); 1 hide in Chettle (Dorset) purchased from Walter de Camel; 2 hides in the Isle of Purbeck bought from Robert de Clevilla; the village of Ampney Crucis (*Amenel*) by Cirencester, bought from Winnebald the bailiff; two watermills on the Avon and one on the Severn, etc. Much of the material can be cross-referenced with entries in the surviving Tewkesbury cartulary, and the *Valor Ecclesiasticus* of 1535.
58. The latter are also found in the 14th-century clerestory glass: see G.McN. Rushforth, 'Glass in the Choir Clerestory of Tewkesbury Abbey', *TBGAS* 46 (1924), 312 and plate VIII (iv).
59. Cf. A.R. Wagner, *A Catalogue of English Mediaeval Rolls of Arms* (London, 1950), 117. J.A. Goodall is currently editing the roll MS. Lat. misc. b.2 (R) for the Society of Antiquaries of London's *Aspilogia* series (forthcoming). This will provide the best possible description of its armorials.
60. Bennett, 352-3; *Monasticon* , 83.
61. Most probably on the Warwick Chapel. On these fragments, see Phillip Lindley in ch.13; and R.K. Morris with J. Luxford, 'Fragments from Tewkesbury Abbey', in S. Boldrick, D. Park and P. Williamson (eds.), *Wonder: Painted Sculpture from Medieval England* (Leeds, 2002), 86-91.
62. Tewkesbury Abbey collection, nos.79/25J, 79/25K (Gilbert I, Richard II de Clare); 79/25I, 79/25L (Gilbert III, Thomas Despenser). For the lost figure of Hugh II Despenser, see 'Georgius', 'Effigies, &c. from Tewkesbury Abbey', *Gent. Mag.*, 1824, plate II fig. 4 (facing 305).
63. K.L. Scott, *Later Gothic Manuscripts 1390-1490* (2 vols, London, 1996), I, 61-2, 78 note 62.
64. Hudson, 'The Founders' Book', plate I, illustrates this leaf.
65. Cf. M.D. Anderson, *Drama and Imagery in English Medieval Churches* (Cambridge, 1963), 1-2. Here, the motif cannot possibly symbolize envy, as it does in some contexts.
66. Cf. H. Strauss, 'The History and Form of the Seven-Branched Candlestick of the Hasmonean Kings', *Warburg and Courtauld Institutes Journal*, 22 (1959), 6.
67. See M. Keen, *Chivalry* (New Haven and London, 1984), 121-4. The Nine Worthies were represented in art at, for example, the monasteries of Glastonbury, Gloucester, Westminster and Worcester during the later Middle Ages.
68. Jehan Froissart, *Chroniques*, G.T. Diller (ed.), (Geneva, 1972), 107-09.
69. Furnivall, *Earliest English Wills*, p.117.
70. Cf. M. Michael, 'The Privilege of Proximity: Towards a Redefinition of the Function of Armorials', *Journal of Medieval History*, 23 (1997), 55-74.

Chapter 7 The Final Years of the Abbey and the Dissolution

1. K.G. Powell, 'The Beginnings of Protestantism inGloucestershire', *TBGAS* 90 (1971), 141-57; *id.*, 'The Social Background to the Reformation in Gloucestershire', *TBGAS* 92 (1973), 96-120; J.H. Bettey, 'Early Reformers and the Reformation Controversy in Bristol and South Gloucestershire', *TBGAS* 115 (1997), 9-18; N. Saul, 'The Religious Sympathies of the Gentry in Gloucestershire 1200-1500', *TBGAS* 98 (1980), 99-112.
2. D. Daniell, *William Tyndale* (1994), 61-79; J.H. Cooke, 'The Tyndales in Gloucestershire', *TBGAS* 2 (1877), 29-46.
3. *Letters & Papers, Henry VIII*, 1529-30, (ii), 6301 (21).
4. Bettey, 135-6.
5. *L & P Henry VIII*, V, 1531-2, 1724.
6. J. Craig & C. Litzenberger, 'Wills as Religious Propaganda: the Testament of William Tracy', *Journal of Ecclesiastical History* 44 (1993), 415-31.
7. Bettey, 'Early Reformers', 14; *L & P Henry VIII*, 13, (ii) 710.
8. Powell, 'Reformation in Gloucestershire', 112-4.
9. *L & P Henry VIII*, 1540, 183.
10. A.B. Emden, *Biographical Register of the University of Oxford 1501-40* (1974), 643.
11. H. Aveling & W.A. Pantin, *The Letter Book of Robert Joseph 1530-33*, Oxford Historical Society, n.s. 19, (1967), xlix.
12. *Ibid.*, 100, 114, 255-6, 265.
13. *L & P Henry VIII*, 1529-30, (iii), 6153.
14. *VCH Glos*, II, 64.
15. *CPR*, Henry VII, V (i), 200.
16. *CPR*, Henry VII, V (ii), 353.
17. *Valor*, II, 471-86; *VCH Glos*, II, 65.
18. *L & P Henry VIII*, V, 1531-32, 1799. Henry Beeley died in 1534 and was succeeded by John Wyche *alias* Wakeman, *L & P Henry VIII*, VII, 1534, 419 (23). Note: the list and dates of the last three abbots given in *VCH Glos*, II, 65, is incorrect.
19. *L & P Henry VIII*, VI, 1533, 328.
20. *L & P Henry VIII*, VII, 1534, 460.
21. 26 Henry VIII, C1, *Statutes of the Realm*, iii, 492.
22. *L & P Henry VIII*, VII, 1534, 1121 (54).
23. *L & P Henry VIII*, VIII, 1535, 989; IX, 1535, 677.
24. *L & P Henry VIII*, IX, 1535, 3.
25. *Valor*, II, 471-86.
26. *L & P Henry VIII*, XV, 1540, 19.
27. *Ibid.*, 139 (iv).
28. *Ibid.*, 49.
29. PRO, E315/494; Bettey, App. XIV. See further ch.12.
30. GRO TBR/B2/1, June 1543; Blunt, 99-100.
31. PRO E315/494.
32. *VCH Glos*, VIII, 36.
33. Leland, II, 53, 57; IV, 134-7, 150-61.
34. PRO, Augmentations Office, Misc. Vol. 444, 1542, f.13.
35. *Ibid.*
36. Bettey, 111-2.
37. *DNB*, John Wakeman; C. Litzenberger, *The English Reformation and the Laity* (Cambridge, 1997), 44-7, 58-61.
38. *DNB*, John Wakeman.
39. G.McN. Rushforth, 'Tewkesbury Abbey: The Wakeman Cenotaph and the Starved Monk', *TBGAS* 47 (1925), 150-2. For an alternative interpretation, see ch.13.
40. G. Baskerville, 'Some Ecclesiastical Wills', *TBGAS* 52 (1930), 290-2.
41. G. Baskerville, 'The Dispossessed Religious of Gloucestershire', *TBGAS* 49 (1927), 84-6.
42. *Ibid.*
43. *Ibid.*

Chapter 8 The Parish of Tewkesbury after the Reformation

1. A. Jones, *A Thousand Years of the English Parish* (Moreton-in-Marsh, 2000), 116-17. Another local example is Hailes, where the parish church dates from about 1130 and remained the parish church after the monastery was founded in 1246.
2. The case for Tewkesbury parish church being on a different site from the monastery is argued in Jones & Grenville, 9-18, where it is suggested that 8th-century charters relating to *Tweonaeum* should

be interpreted as placing the church in the area in Tewkesbury parish later known as the Mythe, not in Twyning as previously thought.
3. An anomalous area to the north of the town at the confluence of the Severn and the Avon, called the Mythe, was also in the parish.
4. GRO/P19/VE1/1-5 defines the township boundaries. The church was in Northway; the 'Rectory Farm' was in Fiddington, where perhaps an earlier church had been situated.
5. W. de Gray Birch, 'General documents relating to Bristol and the neighbourhood', *JBAA* 31 (1875), 289-90; William the chaplain of Tewkesbury witnessed the confirmation.
6. *VCH Glos*, VIII, 154.
7. R.W.Hoyle (ed.), *The Military Survey of Gloucestershire* (BGAS, 1993).
8. *Valor*, II.
9. GRO/P329/M1/1.
10. Accounts based on *VCH Glos*, VIII.
11. Walton Cardiff had baptism rights from 1677; people went to Ashchurch for burials, which might make for a high burial rate in Ashchurch relative to baptisms. Bennett, 273; and Bennett/*TYR*, II, 287.
12. Jones, *English Parish*, 155-59.
13. Bennett, 125-6.
14. Documents as transcribed in Bennett, 354-59.
15. Hockaday 369.
16. Bennett, 354-59.
17. The early part of the first book has been transcribed and published in Litzenberger.
18. *VCH Glos*, VIII, 136.
19. Litzenberger, 77, 88, 97, 130.
20. *Ibid*., 10, 14, 22, 26, 40.
21. *Ibid*., 93-94; the churchwardens noted the battlement was damaged through the spire falling 'on Easter daye in the first yeare of the Queenes Maris raigne which was a beawtifull woodden battlement'; the date was 2 April 1554. (Mary's first year was 19 July 1553 to 5 July 1554). Bennett/*TYR*, I, 463, isthe origin of the mistaken date 1559. Did he misread his hand-writing, 1553 instead of 1558, adjusting for Easter in the first year of Elizabeth's reign (17 November 1558 to 16 November 1559)?
22. E. Cannan, *The History of Local Rates in England* (London, 1927), 14-16, 71.
23. Litzenberger, 77, 82, 88, 98.
24. Bennett/*TYR*, I, 174-5.
25. It was the practice at least from 1733 for the vicar to nominate a churchwarden for the parishioners to elect, and the parish to nominate the other;GRO/P329/CW2/3.
26. Bennett/*TYR*, I, 226-8.
27. *Ibid*., I, 273-4.
28. G.F.A. Best, *Temporal Pillars* (Cambridge, 1964), 193; W.R. Ward, *Religion and Society in England 1790-1850* (London, 1972), 178-83.
29. Bennett/*TYR*, I, 243, II, 388; *VCH Glos*, VIII, 156.
30. GRO/P329/CW2/4.
31. Litzenberger, 19, 20, 34. The irregular series of payments is explained by this, not by an unusual system of life payment for all pews as suggested by Litzenberger, *xii*.
32. GRO/P329/CW3/1.
33. GRO/P329/CW2/3, CW3/3.
34. Bennett/*TYR*, II, 243.
35. GRO/P320/CW2/3.
36. Bennett/*TYR*, I, 243.
37. J. Maclean, 'Chantry Certificates, Gloucestershire', *TBGAS* 8 (1883), 281-82.
38. *VCH Glos*, VIII, 120.
39. Bennett/*TYR* , II, 411.
40. GRO/GDR V5/302/T2 (1807) & T3 (1828).
41. The vicar of St. Ismael collected one-third of the tithes so, of the total, one-third went to the poor of Tewkesbury and one-third to the preacher.
42. Hockaday 371.
43. C.R. Elrington, 'The survey of church livings in Gloucestershire, 1650', *TBGAS* 83 (1964), 90.
44. *VCH Glos,* VIII, 155; Bennett, 181, 186.
45. GRO/TBR/Geast Charity Book.
46. Bennett, 186, referred to Wells' ejection but doubted it was correct.
47. A. Whiteman (ed.), *The Compton Census* (London, 1986) 178, 538.
48. GRO/D747.
49. GRO/TBR A1/4 (6 Feb. 1678).
50. Bennett, 188.
51. GRO/TBR A1/4 (4 Nov. 1679; 15 April 1684).
52. J. Fendley (ed.), *Bishop Benson's survey of the diocese of Gloucester 1735-1750,* (BGAS, 2000), 98-9.
53. I. Gray, 'Records of four Tewkesbury Vicars, *c*.1685-1769', *TBGAS* 102 (1984), 159, 162, 165, 167-69.
54. Hockaday 371.
55. Bennett, 188.
56. *Ibid*., 190.
57. Papers concerning the case are in GRO/PA329/52, particularly No.5 & No.7; GCL, Hyett collection series C vol.IV.
58. Bennett/*TYR*, II, 287-88.
59. Jones, *English Parish*, 163-9.
60. *Parliamentary Papers* 1835 (22).
61. Hockaday 371.
62. Bennett, 194.
63. GRO/GDR/F4/Tewkesbury.
64. John Martin (1805-1880), M.P. for Tewkesbury 1832-34 and 1837-59; W.R. Williams, *The Parliamentary History of the County of Gloucester* (Hereford, 1898), 225.
65. *TR*, 21 July 1883.
66. 'One of the chief ends in view in the purchase of the estate was to secure to the Abbey authorities absolute control of the exterior of the church building on its south side. This was provided for by the construction of the way now called the "Cloister Walk", and which with the "vaulted chamber", were separately conveyed so as to become part and portion of the church and churchyard'; Blunt, 137-38.
67. GCL, Hyett collection series C vol.IV (North's*Handbook* n.d.), 44-8.

Chapter 9 The Norman Church

1. On the Norman church, see in particular, E. Fernie, *The Architecture of Norman England* (Oxford, 2000), 160-165; M. Thurlby, 'The Romanesque Elevations of Tewkesbury and Pershore', *Journal of the Society of Architectural Historians*, 44 (1985), 5-17; J.P. McAleer, 'The Romanesque Choir of Tewkesbury Abbey and the Problem of a Colossal Order', *Art Bulletin* 65 (1983), 535-559; J.P. McAleer, 'The Romanesque Transept and Choir Elevations of Tewkesbury and Pershore', *Art Bulletin* 64 (1982), 549-563; J. Bony, 'Tewkesbury et Pershore: deux élévations à quatre étages de la fin du XIe siècle', *Bulletin Monumental* 96 (1937), 281-290, 503-504. The following articles in *BAA Trans* VII (1985)—E. Fernie, 'A Note on the Historiography of Tewkesbury Abbey', 1-6; R Halsey, 'Tewkesbury Abbey: Some Recent Observations', 16-35; P. Kidson, 'The Abbey Church of St. Mary at Tewkesbury in the Eleventh and Twelfth Centuries', 6-15; M. Thurlby, 'The Elevations of the Romanesque Abbey Churches of St. Mary at Tewkesbury and St. Peter at Gloucester', 36-51; C. Wilson, 'Abbot Serlo's Church at Gloucester: Its Place in Romanesque Architecture', 52-83.
2. See further chs 2, 5 and 6. Chapter 6 presents a more detailed version of these events, based on the Founders' Book.
3. *The Chronicle of Florence of Worcester*, trans. T. Forester (London, 1854), 234.
4. Luard, 45 and *Monasticon,* 54.
5. *VCH Glos*, VIII, 158 n.90.
6. Lehmann-Brockhaus, 560, no.4357.
7. For a discussion of 'column' v. 'pier' in English architecture, see E. Fernie, 'Technical Terms and the Understanding of Medieval Architecture', *Architectural History* 44 (2001), 16-17. 'Columnar pier' has been preferred here for editorial reasons, but this is not to deny its symbolic association with the classical column.
8. Fernie, *The Architecture of Norman England*, 162.
9. M, Thurlby, 'Jedburgh Abbey Church: The Romanesque Fabric', *Proceedings of the Society of Antiquaries of Scotland* 125 (1995), 793-812.
10. Vitruvius, *The Ten Books on Architecture*, I.D. Rowland and T.N. Howe (eds,) (Cambridge, 1999), Book V, chapter 1.
11. Kidson, 'Abbey Church', 11.
12. On the iconography of rib vaults in Anglo-Norman architecture, see M. Thurlby, 'The Romanesque Priory Church of St. Michael at Ewenny', *Journal of the Society of Architectural Historians*, 47 (1988), 281-294; M. Thurlby, 'The Roles of the Patron and the Master Mason in the First Design of Durham Cathedral', in D. Rollason, M. Harvey and M. Prestwich (eds.) *Anglo-Norman Durham 1093-1193*, (Woodbridge, 1994), 161-184; M. Thurlby,

'The Romanesque Apse Vault of Peterborough Cathedral', in D. Buckton and T.A. Heslop (eds) *Studies in Medieval Art and Architecture presented to Peter Lasko*, (Stroud, 1994), 171-186.
13. Thurlby, 'Ewenny'.
14. Thurlby, 'The Elevations of Tewkesbury and Gloucester', 44-47. At Christchurch Priory (Dorset) the transept crypts have a barrel vault in the nave and ribs in the apse.
15. To cite just a few examples that accompany high barrel vaults: Geay (Charente-Maritime), see R. Rozet, *L'art romane en Saintonge* (Paris 1971), pl. XXVb; Rétaud, Rioux and Talmont (all Charente-Maritime), *Congrès archéologique* 114 (1956), 134-5, 114 and 187/193 respectively.
16. Illustrated in *BAA Trans* VII, pl.VIC.
17. Illustrated in *BAA Trans* VII, pls.VIF, VIIA.
18. *The Oxford English Dictionary* (Oxford, 1933), vol.11 452.
19. R.K. Morris and D. Kendrick, 'Tewkesbury Abbey nave: cleaning and recording 1996', *Church Archaeology* 3 (1999), 18-20.
20. R. Willis, 'The Crypt and Chapter House of Worcester Cathedral', *Transactions of the Royal Institute of British Architects*, 1st ser., 13 (1862-3), 213-225 at 222, reprinted in R.Willis, *Architectural History of Some English Cathedrals*, II (Chicheley, 1973); G. Ormerod, *Strigulensia: Archaeological Memoirs relating to the district adjacent to the Confluence of the Severn and the Wye* (London, 1861), 82. See also, C. Lynam, 'Notes on the Nave of Chepstow Parish Church', *Archaeological Journal* 62 (1905), 270-278. It has been suggested that the Roman legionary fortress baths at Caerleon (Gwent) were either groin- or barrel-vaulted using tufa. Tufa is also used for the vault web in the chapter house at Much Wenlock Priory (*c*.1160) and, after 1185, in the great church at Glastonbury Abbey; J.D. Zienkiewicz, *The Legionary Fortress Baths at Caerleon* (Cardiff 1986), 103-114. M. Thurlby, 'The Lady Chapel of Glastonbury Abbey', *Antiquaries Journal* 65 (1995), 107-170.
21. Whilst the ashlar wall of the passage bears no trace of plaster or paint, the chapel side of the doorway, the west jamb, part of the arch and also the adjacent jamb of the arch to the transept, imitation mortar lines are painted in red on lime-washed ashlar not corresponding with the real mortar joints.
22. E. Gethyn-Jones, *The Dymock School of Sculpture* (Chichester 1979).
23. M. Thurlby, 'The Abbey Church, Pershore: An Architectural History', *Worcs Archaeol. Soc. Trans* 3rd Series, 15 (1996), 146-209.
24. For additional illustrations of Pershore, see Thurlby, 'Tewkesbury and Pershore', figs.17-22.
25. Thurlby, 'Tewkesbury and Pershore', figs.20-22.
26. Halsey, 'Tewkesbury', 18-20, fig.1.
27. Thurlby, 'Tewkesbury and Pershore', fig. 25.
28. Bony, 'Tewkesbury et Pershore'.
29. M.F. Hearn and M. Thurlby, 'Previously Undetected Wooden Ribbed Vaults in Medieval Britain', *JBAA* 150 (1997), 48-58.
30. It is also possible that this bay was treated differently because of the adjacent abbot's lodging; see further ch.12.
31. See ch.21 for an alternative interpretation of the vaulting.
32. M. Thurlby, 'Romanesque Sculpture at Tewkesbury Abbey', *TBGAS* 98 (1980), 89-94; M. Thurlby, *The Herefordshire School of Romanesque Sculpture* (Logaston, 1999, reprinted with additions 2000 and 2002), 17-18, 126-127.
33. See ch.21 for fragments of more carved capital reused in the 14th-century nave clerestory, recorded during the 1996 cleaning of the nave vault.
34. Possibly a depiction of Christ's entry into Jerusalem.
35. J.L. Petit, *The Abbey Church of Tewkesbury* (Cheltenham, 1848), 18; J.P. McAleer, *The Romanesque Church Façade in Britain* (New York, 1984), 721.
36. See further ch.21.
37. Fernie, *Architecture of Norman England*; R. Gem, 'The Romanesque Cathedral of Winchester: Patron and Design in the Eleventh Century', in T. Heslop and V. Sekules (eds.), *Medieval Art and Architecture at Winchester Cathedral, BAA Trans* VI (Leeds, 1983), 1-12; R. Plant, 'English Romanesque Architecture and the Holy Roman Empire', unpublished Ph.D. thesis, University of London, 1998.
38. J. Bony, 'La chapelle épiscopale de Hereford et les apports lorrains en Angleterre après la conquête', in *Actes du XIXe congrès i nternational d'histoire de l'art* (Paris 1958), 36-43; R Gem, 'The Bishop's Chapel at Hereford: the Roles of Patron and Craftsman', in S. Macready and F.H. Thompson (eds.), *Art and Patronage in The English Romanesque* (London 1986), 87-96 at 94; Halsey, 'Tewkesbury', 29.
39. H. Böker, 'The Bishop's Chapel of Hereford Cathedral and the Question of Architectural Copies in the Middle Ages', *Gesta* 37/1 (1998), 44-54. Professor Böker kindly informs me that he now prefers to attribute the Hereford bishop's chapel to Robert de Losinga rather than to Gilbert Foliot as in the article.
40. Halsey, 'Tewkesbury', 25-27, 29.
41. Halsey, 'Tewkesbury', 25; A. Clapham, 'The Form of the Early Choir of Tewkesbury and its Significance', *Archaeological Journal* 106 Supplement (1949), 10-15 at 12 n.1, pls.VIIIB & IXA.
42. A. de Dion, 'Chapiteaux de Saint-Thomas d'Epernon', *Bulletin Monumental* 37 (1871), 627-635.
43. Halsey, 'Tewkesbury', 27.
44. M. Chibnallm (ed. and trans.), *The Ecclesiastical History of Orderic Vitalis*, (Oxford, 1972), III, 1139-149.
45. *Ibid*., 139; Halsey, 'Tewkesbury', 33 n.74.
46. Fernie, *Architecture of Norman England*, 164, fig. 128.
47. *Ibid*., 164 n.91.
48. *Dictionnaire des termes techniques du* De architectura *de Vitruve*, L. Callebat and P. Fleury (eds.) (Hildesheim, Zurich and New York, 1995), 138.
49. For discussion of this, see *ibid*., 163.
50. Fernie, *Architecture of Norman England*, 164.
51. London, British Library, MS. Harleian 2767; L.D. Reynolds and S.F. Weiskittel, 'Vitruvius', in L.D. Reynolds (ed.), *Texts and Transmission: A Survey of the Latin Classics*, (Oxford, 1983), 440-445 at 441; H.G. McCague, 'Building with God: Anglo-Norman Durham, Bury St. Edmunds and Norwich', unpublished Ph.D. dissertation, York University, Toronto, 1999, 182 fn.464. My thanks to Hugh McCague for generously sharing his knowledge of Vitruvius manuscripts on which the following section is based.
52. Reynolds and Weiskittel, 'Vitruvius', 441.
53. N.R. Ker (ed.), *Medieval Libraries of Great Britain: A List of Surviving Books*, (London, 2nd edn, 1964), 40, 43; M.R. James,*The Ancient Libraries of Canterbury and Dover* (Cambridge 1903), 320.
54. BL, MS Add.38818 fols.49-109; Reynolds and Weiskittel, 'Vitruvius', 443; C.H. Krinsky, 'Seventy-Eight Vitruvius Manuscripts', *Journal of the Warburg and Courtauld Institutes* 30 (1967), 36-70 at 49; J.H. Harvey, *The Mediæval Architect* (London, 1972), 21.
55. Reynolds and Weiskittel, 'Vitruvius', 443; R.M. Thomson, 'The Library of Bury St. Edmunds Abbey in the Eleventh and Twelfth Centuries', *Speculum* 47 (1972), 617-645 at 618 and 639.
56. M. Thurlby, 'Aspects of Romanesque Ecclesiastical Architecture in Dorset: Wimborne Minster, Sherborne Abbey, Forde Abbey chapter house, and St. Mary's, Maiden Newton', *Proceedings of the Dorset Archaeological and Natural History Society* 122 (2000), 1-19 at 1-9, fig. 6; M. Thurlby, 'Anglo-Saxon Architecture beyond the Millennium: Its Continuity in Norman Building', in N. Hiscock (ed.), *The White Mantle of Churches: Architecture, Liturgy and Art Around the Millennium* (Turnhout, Belgium, 2003).
57. See ch.21.
58. M. Thurlby, 'L'abbatiale romane de St. Albans', in M. Baylé (ed.), *L'architecture normande au Moyen Age* (Caen 1997), 79-90; Thurlby, 'Romanesque Architecture in Dorset', 8-9.
59. U. Engel, *Die Kathedrale von Worcester* (Munchen-Berlin 2000), 71-73, 230.
60. M. Thurlby, 'The Romanesque Cathedral *circa* 1114-1200', in M. Swanton (ed.) *Exeter Cathedral: A Celebration* (Exeter, 1991), 37-44; M Thurlby, in F. Kelly (ed.) 'The Romanesque Cathedral of St. Mary and St. Peter at Exeter', *Medieval Art and Architecture at Exeter Cathedral, BAA Trans* XI, (1991), 19-34.
61. M. Thurlby, 'A note on the former barrel vault in the choir of St. John the Baptist at Halesowen and its place in English Romanesque Architecture', *Worcs Archaeol. Soc. Trans* 3rd series, 9 (1984), 37-43.
62. *Monasticon,* 53; *VCH Glos*, II, 62.
63. *Monasticon,* 59-60.
64. The Founders' Book, in its chapter 1, names the monk Alfred as *magistrum operis*; see Luxford, ch.6.
65. Gem, 'Bishop's Chapel at Hereford'; Böker, 'Bishop's Chapel of Hereford'.

Chapter 10 The Gothic Church: Architectural History

1. See further N. Coldstream, *The Decorated Style: architecture and ornament 1240-1360* (London, 1994), and J. Bony, *The English Decorated Style: Gothic architecture transformed 1250-1350* (Oxford, 1979).
2. The terms gained popularity through publications like Thomas Rickman, *An Attempt to Discriminate the Styles of Architecture in England* (London, 1817), which went through many editions during the 19th century; the approximate datespans for the three styles in modern scholarship are: Early English, *c.*1170-1280, Decorated *c.*1280-1360, Perpendicular, *c.*1360-1540.
3. Malcolm Thurlby has contributed most of the text on the chapels off the north transept.
4. The material regarding the north transept chapels is presented in greater detail in R.K. Morris, 'Early Gothic architecture at Tewkesbury Abbey', *BAA Trans* VII, 93-98. The main reconsideration since 1985 is that there was not a late 12th-century rebuilding of the apsidal chapel (p.96). A critique is found in J.P. McAleer, 'Tewkesbury Abbey in the later twelfth and thirteenth centuries,' *TBGAS* 110 (1992), 77-86.
5. For Bristol, see M. Thurlby, 'The Elder Lady Chapel at St. Augustine's, Bristol, and Wells Cathedral', in L. Keen (ed.),*'Almost the Richest City': Bristol in the Middle Ages, BAA Trans* XIX (Leeds, 1997), 31-40. The present Lady Chapel at Tewkesbury, off the south transept, was only so dedicated in 1930.
6. On an adjacent stub of the nave north wall is a fragment of the trefoil-headed dado arcade.
7. The present arrangement seems to date from shortly after 1877 when the chapel was cleared and restored by Thomas Collins, himself a freemason, with funds raised by the Freemasons; see F. Moore, '"The Chapter-House"', *TR* . The suggestion that this room was a chapter house is quite unfounded, though the double archway is a feature also shared with some chapter house entrances: the monks' chapter house was on the south side of the church (see ch.12).
8. Morris, 'Early Gothic', 93.
9. *Ibid.* McAleer, 'Tewkesbury Abbey', note 11, believes that the vault was rebuilt by Sir G.G. Scott, but in fact Scott's restoration applied to the roofs of the north transept chapels, not the vault; see the account in *TR* (27 Sep. 1879).
10. M.F. Hearn and M. Thurlby, 'Previously undetected wooden ribbed vaults in medieval Britain', *JBAA* 150 (1997), 48-58: in the West Country, they note surviving wooden vaults in the transepts of St. Davids and Exeter cathedrals, and reconstruct examples at Abbey Dore, Bristol Cathedral (Elder Lady Chapel), Brecon Cathedral, Llanthony Priory, Pershore Abbey and Wenlock Priory.
11. The mid-buttress on the north wall and the north-east flying buttress have 14th-century mouldings, whereas the east wall buttress between the 'chancel' and the chapels of SS. James and Nicholas is post-medieval in its present form, apparently 19th century.
12. For Bristol, see Thurlby, 'Elder Lady Chapel', 35-6; for Worcester, U. Engel, *Die Kathedrale von Worcester* (Munchen-Berlin, 2000), 159, pls. 154-67; for Wells, H. Brakspear, 'A West Country School of Masons', *Archaeologia* LXXXI (1931), pl.XVI (detail, top left).
13. Richard Morris is most grateful to Moira and Brian Gittos for identifying this group of slabs and making the connexion with the Tewkesbury slab fragments; pers. comm., Oct. 2002. The slabs are loosely dated to the first half of the 13th century, but the link now drawn with the north chapel at Tewkesbury suggests some could be as early as the second decade of that century.
14. For a full account of the evidence, see Morris, 'Early Gothic', 94-6.
15. Luard, 106, 111-12.
16. Anthea Jones prefers to interpret the 1237 entry as referring to a separate parish church, noting that the Annals unusually add that the chapel is '*in ecclesia Theokesberiae*'; Jones and Grenville, 16-17. However, the circumstances will also fit our knowledge of the medieval abbey church satisfactorily, in that these dedications are not found amongst the altars of the ambulatory chapels, and siting them off the north transept accords with the record of burials after the Battle of Tewkesbury being made by the altars of SS. Nicholas and James. The surviving fabric belongs with the sort of date indicated in the Annals, albeit perhaps too neatly, though the the use of trumpet scallop capitals might suggest a starting date a decade or so earlier; for the capitals, see McAleer, 'Tewkesbury Abbey', 80.
17. *TR* (27 Sep. 1879). The stone (abbey collection no.81/1) is hidden behind the panelling of the modern vestment cupboards in what is now the *Camera Cantorum*, and another fragment is loose in the abbey collection (no.79/135).
18. The torso is mentioned in I. Cooper, 'Monumental effigies: the rural Deanery of Winchcombe', *TBGAS* 29 (1906), 240. The inscription on one side of the slab is unhelpful in identifying the deceased. An effigy with some resemblances, including the hand positions, is that of Bishop Anselm, St. Davids Cathedral, *c.*1240; see E. Prior and A. Gardner, *An Account of Medieval Figure Sculpture in England* (Cambridge, 1912), fig.652.
19. Luard, 112.
20. Now 13ft 4ins long (originally 13ft 8ins), and before it was polished at its restoration in 1879 five consecration crosses were visible. For its post-dissolution history, see ch.16.
21. Luard, 119-20. We know that the bodies were brought from the chapter house, because the body of Abbot Robert (presumably Robert I, 1110-24) was moved there to the spot formerly occupied by Benedict, his successor (1124-37). It is not clear why the bodies of these particular abbots are being relocated.
22. *Ibid.*, 118-20, 'Sancti Wlstani' (i.e. Wulstan of Worcester, can.1203) and 'Sancti Thomae martyris' (i.e. Thomas of Canterbury, can.1173); 135 ('Sancti Eustachii'). No location is stated for Wulfstan's altar or Eustace's chapel, but Thomas' altar was '*super vivarium*'.
23. St. Eustace is a military saint associated with hunting, so an altar of this dedication would be appropriate in the vicinity of the aristocratic burials in the sanctuary.
24. Perhaps the 14th-century double chapel of SS. Dunstan and Edmund represents a ground-floor rebuild of a Romanesque two-storey chapel, comparable to SS. Nicholas and James off the north transept.
25. For Westminster, see C. Wilson *et al*, *Westminster Abbey, New Bell's Cathedral Guides* (London, 1986), 28-9, 42 (plate). The placing of a cusp rather than a foil on the vertical axis of the roundel is a particular trait of Westminster.
26. For illustrations, see Bony, *English Decorated*, ch.2.
27. For a fuller account of the likely changes to the choir, see Morris, 'Early Gothic', 96-8; and for how the gallery roofs were adapted, McAleer, 'Tewkesbury Abbey', 82-5. The idea that the choir was modified in the 13th century is not new; see Blunt, 118.
28. See further ch.2.
29. Abbey collection no. 79/22. Only the carved shield section survives, and the most appropriate contemporary comparisons are with the Purbeck military effigies with shields in the Temple Church, London. Julian Luxford, pers. comm., May 2003, is sceptical about identifying this fragment with Gilbert I, noting that in the Founders' Book he is shown bearing the chevronnels of de Clare quarterly with three clarions or; whereas Richard II, Gilbert II and Gilbert III bear chevronells only. For the descriptions of Gilbert I's and Richard II's burials, see further ch.6.
30. See further ch.9, where Malcolm Thurlby reconstructs a barrel vault without clerestory windows in the main elevation, and a rib-vault in the apse which might have permitted small windows.
31. B. Golding, 'Burials and benefactions: an aspect of monastic patronage in thirteenth-century England', in W.M. Ormrod (ed.), *England in the Thirteenth Century* (Woodbridge, 1985), 68-71. On the other hand, the importance of Tewkesbury to the de Clares is emphasized in J.C. Wood, 'Fashions in Monastic Endowment; the foundations of the de Clare family, 1066-1314', *Journal of Ecclesiastical History* 32 (1981), 448; and Hannan, 227sqq. I am grateful to Julian Luxford for advice on this matter.
32. See further ch.6.
33. Golding, 'Burials and Benefactions', 69, citing Luard, 113-14; see also ch.6.
34. Golding, 'Burials and Benefactions', 69, for more detail.
35. Luard, 106, 135. The Annals end in 1263, and this entry of 1246 is the last one relevant to architecture: there is no specific mention of modernizing the choir, but such an explicitly architectural reference would be out of character anyway.
36. Luard, 106, 120.
37. I am grateful to Julian Luxford for advice and information on these points.
38. For the stained glass, see ch.14.
39. There is not space here to incorporate observations about all the changes of details in the Decorated fabric, which will need to be the subject of a separate study.
40. This hypothetical datespan opens with a notional start date for the

eastern Lady Chapel, preceding the arrival of Hugh II Despenser (*c*.1317) and ends with the death of Abbot Kempsey; see further below.

41. See further Morris, 'Early Gothic', 93.
42. R. K. Morris, 'European prodigy or regional eccentric? The rebuilding of St. Augustine's Abbey church, Bristol', in Keen (ed.), *Bristol in the Middle Ages*, 46.
43. For convenience the nominal start date of Hugh II's ascent to full power has been retained, and the death of Eleanor Despenser has been selected as the approximate terminal date. The divide between Phases I and II in this *schema* is almost certainly too neat with regard to the date when the old choir was demolished relative to the various works of Phase I.
44. An internal walkway at the foot of the clerestory windows was reincorporated in the new work to continue to provide an upper-level link across the monks' church from south to north, connecting to the Romanesque triforium passages and spiral staircases retained in the east elevation of each transept arm.
45. The start date signifies that some overlap may exist between the later years of Phase II and the nave work in Phase III. The end date is the death of Hugh III Despenser.
46. These screens are topped with openwork reticulated tracery and miniature battlements, which were also added to the earlier screens behind the high altar and in the bay with the monument of Hugh III Despenser.
47. See further ch.21.
48. *Ibid*.
49. For its possible effect on bell ringing, see ch.18.
50. See R.K. Morris, 'Ballflower work in Gloucester and its vicinity', *BAA Trans* VII, 99-100 (for its meaning and distribution), 110 (for Tewkesbury and Gloucester); and *id*., 'The architectural history of the medieval cathedral church', in G. Aylmer and J. Tiller (eds.), *Hereford Cathedral: a History* (London, 2000), 220-1, 237-9.
51. Possibly the screens behind the high altar originally extended further into the ambulatory to create a small feretory, and the present untidy arrangement is the result of a rearrangement of this area for the Clarence monument in the 1470s.
52. For Pershore's dating and photographs, see M. Thurlby, 'The Abbey Church, Pershore: an architectural history', *Worcs Archaeol. Soc. Trans* 3rd ser. 15 (1996), 198-200; though I would differ from his suggestion that the tower was designed as early as *c*.1290.
53. The profile is unusual, an axial roll moulding flanked by ogee mouldings (or partial wave mouldings). There is some irony that Salisbury tower, encrusted with ballflower carving, should be the source of architectural details for the Lady Chapel, a work apparently devoid of the ornament; demonstrating how its application was optional, a matter of taste, time and money.
54. Morris, 'Ballflower work', 107-09.
55. The window now lights the void under the post-dissolution ambulatory roof to its west, but originally it allowed westerly light into the Lady Chapel to its east, the ambulatory roof being lower and differently configured.
56. See J. Maddison, 'Problems in the choir of Chester Cathedral', in A. Thacker (ed.), *Medieval Archaeology, Art and Architecture at Chester*, *BAA Trans* XXII (Leeds, 2000), 72-8, pls. VIIIA, XVIB, XVIIA; *id*., 'Building at Lichfield during the episcopate of Walter de Langton (1296-1321)', in J. Maddison (ed.), *Medieval Archaeology and Architecture at Lichfield*, *BAA Trans* XIII (Leeds, 1993), 78-80, for Lichfield Cathedral west window (*c*.1310-14) and Ledbury. John Maddison argues persuasively for an earlier date for the Ledbury chapel than the 1330s, where I had originally placed it; the related windows at Tewkesbury should also be moved from the 1330s to the 1320s.
57. R.K. Morris, 'Tewkesbury Abbey: the Despenser mausoleum', *TBGAS* 93 (1974), 147. Another inconsistency which is more likely to be post-dissolution than medieval is the absence of parapets from the sacristy and St. John the Baptist's Chapel; *ibid*., 146.
58. Litzenberger, 11. The accounts imply that it was an upper window – 'for the makyng of a scaffolde' and 'for the carryeng of a loade of sand up into the tracyng howse'; the tracing house was probably in one of the chapel roof voids. The window in question might be the westernmost on the north side of the choir, which has mullions with Elizabethan style ovolo profiles.
59. Morris, 'Despenser mausoleum', 147, for the east end; R.K. Morris and D. Kendrick, 'Tewkesbury Abbey nave: cleaning and recording 1996', *Church Archaeology* 3 (1999), 20-1, for the nave.
60. It is now evident that my original hypothesis of a single architect for the Decorated works, 'the Hereford Master', cannot be sustained on the basis of stylistic analysis; Morris, 'Despenser mausoleum', 150-1; much more data and contextual information for mouldings have become available since 1974.
61. Morris, 'Despenser mausoleum', 151-2, esp. (a), (b). The collections of worked stones from Evesham (Almonry Museum and Evesham Manor) and Winchcombe ('The George' and Sudeley Castle) have yet to be published by the author.
62. See J. Maddison, 'The Choir of Chester Cathedral', *Chester Archaeol. Soc. Jnl* 66 (1983), 31-46; R.K. Morris, 'Later Gothic mouldings in England *c*.1250-1400, Part I', *Architectural History* 21 (1978), 29-34; for the influence of Tewkesbury in the southern Marches in the 1320s, *id*., 'Pembridge and mature Decorated architecture in Herefordshire', *Trans.Woolhope Natur. Fld Club* 42 pt. 2 (1977), 129-47.
63. For Chester's choir elevation and related designs, seeMaddison, 'Problems in Chester Cathedral', 78.
64. Some of the loose stones are illustrated in Morris, 'Ballflower work', pl.XXIC, D. The stones from Winchcombe Abbey are unprovenanced and undated, but the abbey was in serious financial difficulties after 1329.
65. For the vault, see ch.11.
66. The windows in south aisle bays 2-5 and north aisle 3- 6 (numbering from the east).
67. For this group of churches, see J. Goodall, 'A study of the grotesque 14th-century sculpture at Adderbury, Bloxham and Hanwell in its architectural context', *Oxoniensia* 60 (1995), 271-332.
68. A characteristic also of the Banbury group, though John Goodall attempts to decipher their meaning; *ibid*., 323-30.
69. Illustrated in Goodall, 'Grotesque 14th-century sculpture, figs 22, 23, 36, 37.
70. R.K. Morris, 'Late Decorated architecture in northern Herefordshire', *Trans. Woolhope Natur. Fld. Club* 44 pt. 1 (1982), 36-53.
71. Morris, 'Despenser mausoleum', 142-50.
72. For the family history, see further ch.3.
73. See ch.14.
74. See ch.15.
75. Morris, 'Despenser mausoleum', 149, dated to the 1330s the window tracery associated here with Master Chester; but John Maddison's research has shown that this design should be dated earlier.
76. For the Paradise garden theme, see further Morris, 'Despenser mausoleum', 145, 153-5; for chivalric imagery in churches, R.K. Morris, 'The architecture of Arthurian enthusiasm', in M. Strickland (ed.), *Armies, Chivalry and Warfare in Medieval Britain and France* (Stamford, 1998), 78-9.
77. For a full list, see Morris, 'Despenser mausoleum', 151-3.
78. A.J. Taylor, 'Building at Caerphilly in 1326', *Board of Celtic Studies Bull*. XIV/4 (1952), 299-300. For the career of De la Bataile, see J.H. Harvey, *English Mediaeval Architects: a biographical dictionary down to 1550* (rev. edn., Gloucester, 1984), 15; and for his connexions with Gloucestershire churches, especially Badgeworth, see Morris, 'Ballflower work', 109-10.
79. For Hereford's career, see Harvey, *English Mediaeval Architects* (1984), 136-7; he may have hailed from Harford near Naunton in the Cotswolds, rather than from Hereford.
80. For Thomas of Canterbury at Gloucester, see C. Wilson, *The Gothic Cathedral: the architecture of the great church 1130-1530* (London, 1990), 204-6; and R.K. Morris, 'Master masons at Gloucester Cathedral in the 14th century', *Friends of Glouc. Cathedral Annual Report* (2003), 10-17.
81. G. Haigh, *The History of Winchcombe Abbey* (London, 1947), 70; D.C. Cox, 'The Building, Destruction and Excavation of Evesham Abbey: a documentary history', *Worcs Archaeol. Soc. Trans* 3rd ser. 12 (1990), 128; J. Coad, *Hailes Abbey*, English Heritage guidebook (London, 2nd edn. 1993).
82. For the investigation of the contents of various coffins in this area in 1795, see Lysons/Tombs, 152-3. A wooden crozier was found in the coffin attributed to Abbot Alan (d.1202), but no crozier was found in the coffin attributed to Abbot Forthampton (d.1254).
83. See further ch.13, where Phillip Lindley argues that the so-called 'Wakeman Cenotaph' is actually Abbot Wakeman's monument.
84. The stylistic date of the recess is at least 60 years after the death of Abbot Robert III of Forthampton (1254), and cannot be for him unless it is a posthumous memorial. The coffin lid is 13th century and its identification as that of Abbot Forthampton (seemingly

unfounded) derives from Browne Willis in the early 18th century; Massé, 65.

85. Abbot Alan's coffin and slab were designed for a free standing tomb originally, but were moved to this wall recess probably when it was built several decades after his death; the recess appears to have been designed for the coffin. I am most grateful to Brian and Moira Gittos for these observations, in advance of their own publication. The recess can be dated to *c.*1240 from the style of its mouldings and carved Crucifixion (at the gable apex, damaged), so this may be a work associated with the movement of tombs recorded in the Annals for 1241.
86. The full list of main bosses, west to east in bays 8 to 3, according to Cave is – Nativity, ?Circumcision [others have Adoration of the Shepherds], Magi journeying to Jerusalem, Adoration of the Magi, Christ Child in the Temple, Entry into Jerusalem, Last Supper, Betrayal, Scourging, Crucifixion, Resurrection, Ascension; C.J.P. Cave, 'Roof Bosses in the Nave of Tewkesbury Abbey', *Archaeologia* XXIX (1929), 73-84.
87. e.g. L. Stone, *Sculpture in Britain: the Middle Ages* (Harmondsworth, 1955), 174, pl.136A.
88. See further Anon., *Roof Bosses in the Nave of Tewkesbury Abbey*, Friends of Tewkesbury Abbey booklet (Tewkesbury, n.d. *c.*2000), 25 and colour illustrations.
89. Bennett, 137, cites Mr. Fosbroke and Mr. King for these differing interpretations.
90. 'Behold a virgin shall conceive and bear a son', Isaiah 7:14; 'a shoot shall come out from the stump of Jesse, and a branch shall grow out of his roots', Isaiah 11:1-3. Julian Luxford, pers. comm., comments that he knows of no parallels for pairing Eve with Isaiah.
91. In the vicinity of Tewkesbury, font stems decorated with ballflower occur at Teddington (shafted, like Tewkesbury) and Overbury (Worcs.).
92. The font is shown standing under the nave south arcade (apparently in Bay 5) in *Monasticon* (see ch.16); the medieval components are recognizable, but the bowl is presumably a new one mentioned in the churchwardens accounts, 1737/8 and 1781-91 (GRO, CW329, summary, vol.2). The font (probably the bowl only) was moved to the south transept chapel in 1828; Bennett, 147-8.
93. Anthea Jones, pers. comm., has raised the possibility that the font was moved in the Middle Ages from another site; in which case, perhaps the 13th-century base is reused from a font elsewhere.
94. For the choir-stalls, see further ch.11.
95. A rood screen had two doors, one each side of a centrally placed altar, and with the possibility of an additional altar against the extension of the rood screen across each aisle. The record of burials in the nave in 1471 implies that it was the aisle altars of the rood screen which were dedicated to SS. George and John [the Evangelist] in this area; see G.McN. Rushforth, 'The Burials of Lancastrian Nobles in Tewkesbury Abbey after the Battle of Tewkesbury A.D. 1471', *TBGAS* 47 (1925), 142-9 and Fig.1.
96. The painting is more noticeable on the north pier, with scarlet colour and some patterning, but its detail is indecipherable now. See E.F. Smith, *Tewkesbury Abbey*, guidebook (Tewkesbury, rev. edn 1931), 22.
97. W.St.J. Hope, 'Quire screens in English churches, with special reference to the twelfth-century quire screen formerly in the Cathedral Church of Ely', *Archaeologia* LXVII (1916-17), 85, 108. A pulpitum screen had a centre door, with an altar to each side.
98. A. Vallance, *Greater English Church Screens* (London, 1947), 121; see also ch.16.
99. See further ch.12.
100. The carving was replaced in 1960 with the present statue of the Virgin and Child, carved by Darsie Rawlins in 1959; *Friends' Annual Reports*, 1959, 1960; see ch.22 for an illustration. The very weathered original is in the abbey collection (No.79/177).
101. Illustrated in *VCH Glos*, II, pl.I (betw.pp.66-7).
102. See further ch.13.
103. For the terminology of Perpendicular tracery, see J.H.Harvey, *The Perpendicular Style 1330-1485* (London, 1978), 70-1.
104. The shouldered arches occur around the dado arcade inside the Beauchamp Chapel, and sub-arcuated through-reticulated tracery in the 6-light lateral windows.
105. For Gloucester, see further Harvey, *Perpendicular Style*, ch.3.
106. The present stonework of the door aperture probably dates from 1824-30, when the screen was rebuilt (Bennett, 153), but the feature may be medieval.
107. For an association of the Founder's Chapel with Thomas Despenser regaining the title of earl of Gloucester in 1397, see ch.13. Neil Birdsall suggests that the Trinity Chapel may have served as a Sacrament chapel (its aisle door faces the sacristy) and the Founder's Chapel as an Easter sepulchre.
108. For Wynford and Winchcombe, see Harvey, *English Mediaeval Architects* (1984), 352-6, 336-7 respectively; and *id.*, *Perpendicular Style*, chaps 4, 6.
109. For a recent discussion of these works, see J. Goodall and L. Monckton, 'The Chantry of Humphrey, Duke of Gloucester', in P. Lindley and M. Henig (eds.), *Alban and St Albans: Roman and Medieval Art and Archaeology*, *BAA Trans* XXIV (Leeds, 2001), 231-55; also M. Duffy, *Royal Tombs of Medieval England* (Stroud, 2003), 207-15, 233-41.
110. I am grateful to Julian Luxford for discussion of the date in the Founders' Book and its implications; see further ch.6. In support of the earlier date for the Warwick Chapel, it should be noted that a date before 1422 has been proposed for the design of Henry V's chapel; C. Wilson, 'The Medieval Monuments', in P. Collinson *et al* (eds.), *History of Canterbury Cathedral* (Oxford, 1995), 480-1.
111. For Isabel, see further chapters 3, 6, 13. Other widows as patrons are Eleanor Despenser (d.1337) and Elizabeth Burghersh (commisioner of the Trinity Chapel, d.1409).
112. See also R.K. Morris with J. Luxford, 'Fragments from Tewkesbury Abbey', in S. Boldrick, D. Park, P. Williamson, *Wonder: Painted Sculpture from Medieval England* (Leeds, 2002), 86-90.
113. For the glass, see ch.14; for Abergavenny, see R. Deacon and P. Lindley, *Image and Idol: Medieval Sculpture* (Tate Gallery, London, 2001), cat.entry 12.
114. The fragments were found when the sanctuary floor was excavated in 1875, and are now in the abbey collection, Nos.79/50, 79/141A-S. See further Morris and Luxford, 'Fragments from Tewkesbury Abbey', 91; though the two heads assigned there as prophets (Nos.79/25Q; 79/25R-S) are now seen as more likely to derive from the series of secular lords, following further research by Phillip Lindley (see ch.13).
115. Observations of Ann Brodrick in advance of conservation, 2002.
116. The suns in the crossing vault are 'modern': Massé, 74; Smith, *Tewkesbury Abbey* (1931), 26.
117. See further ch.21.
118. C.J.P. Cave, 'The Bosses of the Vault of the Quire of Winchester Cathedral', *Archaeologia* LXXVI (1927), 161-78; the Winchester vault is constructed entirely of timber.

Chapter 11 The Gothic Church: Vaulting and Carpentry

1. See J. Bony, *The English Decorated Style: Gothic architecture transformed* (Oxford, 1979), ch.5.
2. W. Leedy, *Fan Vaulting: a study of form, technology and meaning* (London, 1980), chapters 2, 4.
3. The full complexity of this vault is analysed in Bony, *English Decorated* (1979), 52-3.
4. See N. Coldstream, *Medieval Craftsmen: Masons and Sculptors* (London, 1991), 33-9; L. Shelby, *Gothic Design Techniques: the 15th-century design booklets of Mathes Roriczer and Hanns Schmuttermayer* (Carbondale, USA, 1977). The formula produces the medieval mason's favourite proportion of one to the square root of two.
5. The explicit application of rotating squares seems most popular in vaults in north-east England, e.g. the cathedral crossing towers of Lincoln (?later 14th-century) and York (1471-3, in timber). The contemporary vault of the crossing tower of Worcester Cathedral and those of the church towers of Coventry bear no obvious affinities to Tewkesbury, but a national survey would be worth while.
6. Its influence continued locally in the 15th century, e.g. Gloucester Cathedral (west bays of nave, Lady Chapel), Great Malvern Priory (crossing tower vault).
7. Based on measurements taken by the author on site; allowance must be made for some distortion between the original two-dimensional design and its projection onto the three-dimensional form of the vault. For the Exeter pulpitum, see R.K. Morris, 'Master Thomas of Witney at Exeter, Winchester and Wells', in F. Kelly (ed.), *Medieval Art and Architecture at Exeter Cathedral*, *BAA Trans* XI (Leeds, 1991), 57-8.
8. For example Bony, *English Decorated*, 47, the other being the undercroft vault in St. Stephen's Chapel, Westminster Palace. The

third example given by Bony, the choir vault of Bristol Cathedral, has been redated from 1298 to the 1330s; R.K. Morris, 'European prodigy or regional eccentric? The rebuilding of St. Augustine's Abbey church, Bristol' in L. Keen (ed.), *'Almost the Richest City': Bristol in the Middle Ages*, *BAA Trans* XIX (Leeds, 1997), 42-5.

9. The Merton east window has gables, the chancel windows at Dorchester have carved figures and gables. It is unfortunate that no significant vaults survive from this period in the Oxfordshire and north Cotswolds area.
10. The vault of York Minster chapter house (*c*.1280-90) provides an idea of how the Evesham vault would have been arranged; for an illustration, see Bony, *English Decorated*, pl.86.
11. For a full account of the origins of the fan vault, see Leedy, *Fan Vaulting*, chap. 2.
12. Leedy's post-1377 date for the Gloucester vaults is nowgenerally discounted; *ibid*., 166-9. There is no convincing evidence that Hereford Cathedral chapter house (*c*.1340-71), the other reputed early example, was fan-vaulted; *ibid*., 172, and R.K. Morris, 'The architectural history of the medieval cathedral church', in G. Aylmer and J. Tiller (eds.), *Hereford Cathedral: a History* (London, 2000), 227-8.
13. L. Monckton, 'The late medieval rebuilding of Sherborne Abbey: a reassessment', *Architectural History* 43 (2000), 102-03.
14. Morris, 'Hereford medieval cathedral church', 227, passim.
15. For discussion of the cloister, see ch.12.
16. The others are in the east walk of Gloucester Cathedral cloister (1351-77) and in the north porch of Exeter Cathedral façade (probably 1376-94).
17. The New College example is in the vault of the hall porch; both Oxford and Gloucester are lierne vaults.
18. In the dean's chapel, off the Beauchamp Chapel; Leedy, *Fan Vaulting*, pl.35.
19. All the pendant bosses are now missing.
20. For the Janyns family, see J.H. Harvey, *English Mediaeval Architects: a biographical dictionary down to 1550* (rev. edn., Gloucester, 1984), 159-60.
21. For Abbey House, see further ch.12.
22. For the wider context, see J. Munby, 'Cathedral carpentry', in T. Tatton-Brown and J. Munby (eds.), *The Archaeology of Cathedrals* (Oxford, 1996), 165-72.
23. *Brief for the Repair of the Abbey Church*, GRO TBR B1/55. C.A. Hewett, *English Cathedral Carpentry* (London, 1984), 46-7, thought the nave roof was 17th century. However, David Yeomans, pers. comm. (1977) and *id*., *The Trussed Roof: its history and development* (Aldershot, 1992), 152, considers that details such as bolts secured with a cotter (not a threaded nut) and the absence of metal strapping is acceptable for *c*.1720 in a regional context.
24. The trusses incorporate scissor-bracing, queen posts, arched soulaces and curved braces to the ridge piece. The roof is drawn and discussed in C.A. Hewett, *English Historic Carpentry* (Chichester, 1980), 110, 158-9, and in *id*., *English Cathedral and Monastic Carpentry* (Chichester, 1985), 37-8, 242.
25. Alternatively, if replaced as a result of fire damage, one should consider the possible consequences of that of 1292 in *clocherii summitatem*; Lehmann-Brockhaus, II, 563, no.4380 (*Ann. Prioratus de Wigornia*).
26. R.K. Morriss and K. Hoverd, 'Tewkesbury Abbey: an analysis of the roofs of the ambulatory and ambulatory chapels', Archaeological Investigations Ltd, Hereford Archaeology Series 300 (Sept. 1997), sections 5, 6.
27. R. Stone, 'Tewkesbury Abbey: a report on a survey of part of the south transept apsidal chapel and the south side of the choir', City of Hereford Archaeol. Unit, Hereford Archaeology Series 223 (Sept.1994), section 5.3.03.
28. A much reproduced depiction of a tread-wheel type is from Pierpont Morgan Library, New York, MS 638, fol.3r, French, *c*.1240, but they must have been in use in the Romanesque period too.
29. Hewett, *Cathedral and Monastic Carpentry*, 188-90, where both are drawn. Other examples surviving in England are in the cathedrals of Salisbury (combined tread-wheel and compass-wheel), Norwich ('helm'-type wheel), and Canterbury and Beverley Minster (tread-wheels); *ibid*., 191-6. See also W. Backinsell, *Medieval Windlasses at Salisbury, Peterborough and Tewkesbury*, South Wilts. Industrial Archaeol. Soc. Historical Monograph 7 (Salisbury, June 1980, 8pp), which includes a drawing with measurements, fig.3.
30. Hewett, *Cathedral and Monastic Carpentry*, 189, 199; also Backinsell, *Medieval Windlasses*, 3.
31. For example, Litzenberger, 28 (1574-5, 'for shyds [timber pieces] for a wyndles'), 112 (1611-15, 'for the windeing whele and tunbrell', perhaps clock parts).
32. A. Jones, *Tewkesbury Abbey: Church or Ancient Monument?*, Friends of Tewkesbury Abbey (1988), 5; E.F. Smith, *Tewkesbury Abbey*, guide book (Tewkesbury, rev. edn. 1931), 35.
33. For discussion of this, see ch.10.
34. Charles Tracy, the authority on medieval choir-stalls, has tried to effect a reconstruction of the original arrangement, without success; pers. comm., Dec. 1999.
35. C. Tracy, *English Gothic Choir-stalls 1200-1400* (Woodbridge, 1987), 25-7, 31.
36. The misericords are listed in G.L. Remnant, *A Catalogue of Misericords in Great Britain* (Oxford, 1969), 52-3, though he notes only 16. Incised into the seat timbers of the north stalls, from which the misericords are hinged, is a series of Roman numerals which seems to predate the Victorian restoration; the numerals run east to west from I to X (but with IX carved as 'XI') and XII-XIII (carved as 'IIX' and 'IIIX').
37. See further C. Grössinger, *The World Upside-down: English Misericords* (London, 1997), from which most of the following information is derived.
38. *Ibid*., 42-4.
39. Scott's office used it as the basis for the font canopy design; hand written note apparently by Frederick Moore, in his special large format edition of Blunt, opp. p.76, seen by Richard Morris in the abbey book collection *c*.1980.
40. Smith, *Tewkesbury Abbey* (1931), 36, notes that the wooden canopy has a solid bottom and thus could not be the case for a sanctus bell. I have not been able to inspect the canopy to verify this observation.
41. *Ibid*., 36; also D.W. Maclagan, *A Popular Guide to Tewkesbury Abbey*, British Publishing Co. guidebook (Gloucester, n.d. *c*.1960), 11.
42. See C. Tracy, 'Pyx cover', in J. Alexander and P. Binski (eds.), *Age of Chivalry: Art in Plantagenet England 1200-1400* (London, 1987), 233. It currently hangs from the vault under the north-west tower.
43. The pieces are in the abbey collection, Nos.79/161 A-N. Three lengths have been mounted on a plank, probably about a century ago, labelled in hand on the back, 'Fragment of Rood Screen ...'.
44. For the same feature, see the presbytery screen of Winchester Cathedral, with the initials of Prior Henry Broke (1524-36); J. Crook (ed.), *Winchester Cathedral: 900 Years* (Chichester, 1993), 270.
45. For example, late medieval choir-stall canopies incorporate such friezes.
46. The discovery was made by Hugh Harrison, pers. comm. to Neil Birdsall, Nov. 1999.
47. For example, see T. Bridges, *Churches of Worcestershire* (Logaston, 2000), 186. The set of 14 choir-stalls have been assigned to the 15th century, but recently Christa Grossinger has redated their misericords to the early 16th century (Grossinger, *World Upside-down*, 75, 162)—and thus potentially to the period of Beeley's abbacy.

Chapter 12 The Monastic Buildings

1. Blunt, 104-05.
2. The only published plan seems to be inside the front cover of R. Gardiner, *The Story of Tewkesbury Abbey*, booklet for the Tewkesbury Festival (Blandford Forum, 1971), which is an informed and stimulating reconstruction, though containing points of detail with which this author disagrees.Its source appears to be the undated framed plan, signed 'G. Robinson', currently hanging at the entrance to the south choir aisle.
3. For the granges and manor houses, see further chs.5, 7.
4. For the relevant extracts from the inventory, see Bettey, Appendix XIV (source, PRO. E315/494).
5. For a comprehensive analysis of English monastic plans and their constituent buildings, see R. Gilyard-Beer, *Abbeys: an illustrated guide to the abbeys of England and Wales* (London, HMSO, 2nd edn. 1976); also G. Coppack, *The English Heritage Book of Abbeys and Priories* (London, 1990), chs 3-5.
6. Possibly they were omitted because they were stone-vaulted rooms, without wooden roofs and containing nothing of value. For Rievaulx, see P. Fergusson and S. Harrison, *Rievaulx Abbey: Community, Architecture, Memory* (New Haven and London, 1999), 180.

7. This and subsequent extracts are from Bettey, Appendix XIV, with minor amendments; the spelling and use of capital letters is modern, and any punctuation has been omitted. I am extremely grateful to Dr. Bettey for his help with these lists. In this extract, the line about the 'workeheye' [*sic*] was omitted in Bettey, Appendix XIV. 'Convent' is an archaic term for a religious community, not necessarily a nunnery.
8. See further B. Harvey, *Living and Dying in England, 1100-1540: the monastic experience* (Oxford, 1993), 41-2, where the custom is documented from the 13th century at Westminster, and its use by as much as 50% of the monastic community is noted.
9. A curious reference in the Annals for 1253 suggests that the *misericordia iuxta refectorium* was moved to the chamber of Stephen the infirmarer, but moved back again shortly afterwards; Luard, 153.
10. At St. Werburgh's, Chester, the dormitory was in two rooms, the second of which ran eastwards perpendicular to the east range. See Randle Holme's early 17th-century plan, in R.V.H. Burne, *The Monks of Chester* (London, 1962), inside the front cover; the first room ran over ground-floor rooms nos.4, 2, 6, and the second room over no.7.
11. The suggestion in Massé, 24, that Abbey House incorporates parts of the infirmary and misericord is unfounded.
12. Blunt, 99, interprets this word as 'workhouse', which is possibly the origin of the gate's name at Tewkesbury. The *Valor* survey for the nunnery of Wilberfoss (Yorks) includes the entry, 'Item a worke house ...'; Coppack, *Abbeys and Priories*, 103.
13. For the derivation of the term, see W.St.J. Hope, 'Notes on the Benedictine Abbey of St. Peter, Gloucester', in W. Bazeley (ed.), *Records of Gloucester Cathedral*, III (Gloucester, 1897), 94.
14. The Founders' Book, see ch.6.
15. Luard, 120; see also ch.10.
16. Luard, 64.
17. The Annals record that in 1243 Abbot Robert III arranged for an annual donation for the maintenance of the dormitory roof (*ad cooperiendum dormitorium*), perhaps indicating that the roof was new; *ibid.*, 129.
18. The Founders' Book, see ch.6.
19. F.W. Potto Hicks, 'A Tewkesbury Compotus', *TBGAS* 55 (1933), 250. The Kitchener's Roll (1386) provides insights into supplies purchased for the kitchen; see ch.5.
20. For the documentation for all these fires, see Lehmann-Brockhaus, 560-3.
21. *VCH Glos*, II, 63, citing the Register of Bishop Maidstone.
22. The other changes are the lowered gable, in which the segmental headed window dates from 1608 (see ch.16), and the large angle buttress at the south-west corner, which cuts into the line of the former cloister walk. The small segmental-headed door in this wall is post-dissolution, and has a stone plaque above it apparently with the initials of churchwardens. As a door to the exterior, it seems to be a post-medieval insertion, and was known as the 'wedding door' for the discreet admission of wedding parties to the parish church (G. Strawford, *TPM*, June 2003, 9). Inside the transept, the aperture is framed by a Romanesque arch (now hidden) which appears to have given access only to a recess (perhaps a book cupboard or aumbry).
23. As depicted in the reconstruction in Gardiner, *Story of Tewkesbury Abbey*, 27-8.
24. D. Welander, *The History, Art and Architecture of Gloucester Cathedral* (Stroud, 1991), 319-23.
25. *Ibid.*, 303, 323-6.
26. Rectangular chapter houses are standard in Benedictine Romanesque architecture, e.g. Gloucester, Durham and St. Albans; full-height rectangular chapter houses in other monastic orders also survive from the 12th century, e.g. Cluniac Wenlock Priory (Shrops.) and Augustinian Bristol St. Augustine's. Worcester Cathedral Priory is exceptional in the 12th century in using a centralised form, not taken up by other Benedictine houses until the late 13th century, e.g. Evesham Abbey.
27. For the routine of monastic services, see ch.5.
28. N. Appleton-Fox, 'Tewkesbury Abbey: a report on an archaeological watching brief', Marches Archaeology Series Report 202 (Sept.2001), sections 6, 7. The foundation was about 3.5m wide. The suggestion that it relates to a scriptorium is unfounded. No record was made of the 'moulded stones', so their potential evidence for establishing a date *post quem* has not been realised.
29. The watching brief also located a burial which would lie within the extended chapter house, but no other details were recorded; *ibid.*, section 6.
30. See ch.5. Excavations at St. Albans Abbey in 1978 by Prof. Martin Biddle and Mrs. Kjølbye-Biddle revealed that the Norman chapter house had been extended eastwards *c.*1160, probably for the same reason; see D. Kahn, 'Recent discoveries of Romanesque sculpture at St. Albans Abbey', in F.H. Thompson (ed.), *Studies in Medieval Sculpture*, (London, 1983), 71-2.
31. The opportunity for observation of the upper area was provided when scaffolding was erected at the south-west corner of the transept in 2000. The width and depth of the two large window apertures in the south wall has remained almost unchanged since they were built before 1102, so they provide no help in establishing the chronology of the roof creases.
32. For the roles of the monastic officials ('obedientiaries'), see ch.5; for the list of major officials recorded in the *Valor*, see ch.7. The *Valor* indicates that the abbot kept the office of cellarer in his own hands in the late Middle Ages.
33. See further the discussions of the outer buildings (which include 'The hostery') and the abbot's lodgings below.
34. The possibility has been suggested above of a second-floor room in the east range adjoining the transept.
35. *Handbook* (5th edn, n.d. *c.*1891), 79-80, relates that 'a portion of the ancient tile pavement is still to be seen in this area'.
36. For a comparable survival of a former abbot's chapel over the outer parlour, see Chester Cathedral.
37. Also surviving in this area, reset, are the Romanesque fragments of an abacus (or cornice) carved with acanthus scroll, and a corbel or voussoir.
38. The fan vault in the north-east bay of the cloister, reconstructed by Thomas Collins c.1898-99, was evidently copied from Gloucester. W. Leedy, *Fan Vaulting: a study of form, technology and meaning* (London, 1980), 207, gives the incorrect date of 1875-79 for this restoration.
39. Pieces of wall-panelling from the Tewkesbury cloister are also in the assemblage at Gupshill Manor; see further ch.21.
40. See ch.7 (appropriation of 1500); and Leedy, *Fan Vaulting*, 207.
41. For example, at both Gloucester and Worcester cathedrals, the Perpendicular remodelling of their cloister started in the east walks, which linked the chapter house to the church.
42. For the Warwick Chapel, see chs 10, 13.
43. The motif also occurs in his Divinity School at Oxford, which is likely to be part of Richard Winchcombe's design (*c.*1424-39), even if not executed until the vaulting works of 1479.
44. Some of its arch voussoirs have been realigned to create a relieving arch for the 15th-century door.
45. See ch.9.
46. The overall width of the Tewkesbury cloister north walk was about 5.3m (about 17ft); Appleton-Fox, 'Tewkesbury Abbey watching brief', (Sept.2001), section 6.
47. *Handbook* (5th edn, n.d. *c.*1891), 79-80, in the context of 'interesting discoveries during the construction of cloister walk' (after 1883), states that 'within the cloister quadrangle are evident traces of rows of graves ...'.
48. This may add support to the hypothesis that one room of the dormitory ran east-west rather than extending further south.
49. I am grateful to Malcolm Thurlby for first drawing this anomaly to my attention.
50. It is also possible that the north-west corner bay of the cloister has been left blank in the Perpendicular remodelling because thought was being given to piercing through a new processional door into the aisle at this point.
51. For an overview of monastic precincts, see Coppack, *Abbeys and Priories*, ch.5. For a discussion of the Tewkesbury precinct, see ch.1, Appendix.
52. For archaeological evidence, see ch.21.
53. See further chs.17, 18. Maintenance of the bell-tower was the monastery's responsibility, judging from an episcopal visitation in 1378; *VCH Glos*, II, 63.
54. The word 'barton' is often applied to a monastic farm or grange; E. Ekwall, *The Concise Oxford Dictionary of English Place-Names* (4th edn. Oxford, 1960). The evidence for identifying this area as the abbey barton hinges on a grant of 1557; *VCH Glos*, VIII, 125-6.

Barton Street in Tewkesbury, however, seems to derive its name from the grange or barton of the earls of Gloucester which may have stood at the junction with Chance Street; Hannan, 88.
55. *VCH Glos*, VIII, 125.
56. The Kitchener's Roll of 1386 also records the purchase of oxen and bulls from the Barton (*'boves et tauri ... de Bartona'*); T. Wakeman, 'On the Kitchener's Roll of Tewkesbury Abbey', *JBAA*, 15 (1859), 325, 330. An ox-house could be a large structure, like that excavated at Waltham Abbey (Herts.); Coppack, *Abbeys and Priories*, 122-4.
57. Wakeman, 'Kitchener's Roll', 321-332, passim.
58. See ch.1.
59. Luard, 95. In 1256, the stables for the hospice were also in the outer court (*extra portam*), when the Annals recorded that they were destroyed by fire; *ibid.*, 157.
60. Jones, 54.
61. *VCH Glos*, VIII, 125; see also ch.8. The name survived into the 19th century as the 'Warkhay Garden', to the east of the almshouses on the eastern boundary of the churchyard; notice of a parish meeting to discuss the rebuilding of the almshouses, 18 Nov. 1830. I am grateful to David Lees for this reference.
62. The term 'great gatehouse' is often applied to inner gatehouses; P. Fergusson, '*Porta Patens Esto*: notes on early Cistercian gatehouses in the north of England', in E. Fernie and P. Crossley (eds.), *Medieval Architecture in its Intellectual Context: studies in honour of Peter Kidson* (London, 1990), 55.
63. For a history of its restorations, see C. Haslam, 'The Abbey Gatehouse, Tewkesbury: notes on its history', Report for the Landmark Trust (1991), unpaginated; and R.K. Morriss, 'Tewkesbury Abbey Gatehouse: an Outline Analysis', Hereford Archaeology Series 225 (Hereford, Oct.1994), section 2.
64. The church porch statue was an Assumption of the Virgin; see ch.10. The two niches, though generally similar in form and Perpendicular in style, are different in detail.
65. For lists of surviving monastic gatehouses in Britain, see R.W. Morant, *The Monastic Gatehouse* (Lewes, 1995).
66. Fergusson, 'Early Cistercian gatehouses', 47-59. The terminology of 'gateway' and 'gatehall' is derived by Fergusson from Robert Willis; *ibid.*, 55.
67. Morriss, 'Tewkesbury Abbey Gatehouse', section 3.3. This report provides an excellent account of the external fabric, on which I have drawn heavily.
68. The patterns are quadripartite with ridge ribs, not 'sexpartite' as stated in Morriss, 'Tewkesbury Abbey Gatehouse', section 3.5. Originally it is likely that some lierne ribs augmented the pattern in the upper parts of each vault.
69. Bennett, 113, citing Browne Willis and Lysons.
70. For an example of a monastic gatehouse with a small ground-floor prison, see the surviving *Porta* at Ely Cathedral; J. Maddison, *Ely Cathedral: Design and Meaning* (Ely, 2000), 92. Had an abbot's prison existed in the Tewkesbury gatehouse complex, the likely location would have been in the ground-floor room in the building to the east of the gatehouse, close to the abbot's lodging.
71. Haslam, 'Abbey Gatehouse'; Morriss, 'Tewkesbury Abbey Gatehouse', section 2; see also *VCH Glos*, II, 64.
72. Morriss, 'Tewkesbury Abbey Gatehouse', section 4.1, judges that the mouldings are 'debased Perpendicular' and the architectural character 'on the cusp of the medieval and the Renaiscence', but this author is unconvinced; all the mouldings are standard for the Perpendicular period.
73. The crenellated top to the stair turret is a 19th-century addition; Haslam, 'Abbey Gatehouse', illustrates one of several pre-restoration paintings of the gatehouse showing the turret without its crenellated top.
74. Morriss, 'Tewkesbury Abbey Gatehouse', section 4.1. There is no direct access from the gatehouse to the first floor of the adjacent east building nor to the ground-floor of the west building; these floors in both buildings constituted separate units of accommodation.
75. A comparable arrangement is known from St. Werburgh's, Chester, with the former abbot's lodging in its own courtyard between the west front of the church and the gatehouse; see Randle Holme's early 17th-century plan, in Burne, *Monks of Chester*, inside the front cover.
76. In a comparable position to that still surviving at Chester and to the prior's chapel over outer parlour at Castle Acre Priory (Norf.); see F. Raby and P. Baillie Reynolds, *Castle Acre Priory*, English Heritage guidebook (London, 1986; repr.1994), 11-17.
77. For Gloucester, where the abbot moved to new accommodation in the 14th century, see Welander, *Gloucester Cathedral*, 306-10.
78. Luard, 64.
79. For example, its fine oriel window is omitted from the list of oriels in Margaret Wood, *The English Mediaeval House* (Oxford, 1965), 117-21.
80. The very brief account in *VCH Glos*, VIII, 125, 'draws heavily' on 'Outline History of Abbey House', duplicated report (1964) by Paterson and Bishop, chartered architects, undertaking alterations to the house in that year.
81. Curved windbraces link the end trusses to the lower purlins, demonstrating that the roof was erected as a unified work of five bays; the windbraces are used only at the end trusses.
82. For terminology, see N.W. Alcock *et al*, *Recording Timber-framed Buildings: an illustrated glossary*, Council for British Archaeology (York, revd. edn., 1996). I am most grateful to Dr. Alcock for reading a draft of this section and for his comments; any short comings which remain are my responsibility.
83. e.g. Coventry, Spon Street, e.g. No.9; see F. Charles, 'Timber-framed houses in Spon Street, Coventry', *Trans. Birmingham and Warks Archaeol. Soc.* 89 (1978-9), 99-103. These features are apparently absent from the terrace of 15th-century shops in Church Street, Tewkesbury, which probably pre-date the Abbey House; see also ch.5.
84. The roof bears several similarities to the dormitory roof of the Whitefriars at Coventry, recently scientifically dated to 1475 and 1491-4; 'Tree-ring Date Lists 2002: Oxford Dendrochronology Laboratory, General List', in *Vernacular Architecture* 33 (2002), 88. The roof has tenoned purlins, with clasped purlins and diminished principals above, like the Abbey House roof.
85. Today, in the north gallery of Abbey House, the hypothetical position of this arch brace is occupied by a substantial post with jowled end which stands incongruously partly in front of the medieval window aperture, under the fourth open truss (counting from the east). Three similar posts exist against the north wall on the first floor under the third open truss, in the north-west corner of the westernmost room, and on the ground floor under the fourth open truss. These posts are post-medieval reinforcements, introduced to compensate for structural weaknesses at the north end of some of the tiebeams.
86. For the modern history of the house, see ch.8 (A House for the Vicar).
87. It is possible that the wall may predate the 'New Work', as a boundary wall.
88. The Georgian door dwarfs its medieval counterpart because the present exterior ground level is considerably higher than the medieval one.
89. Bennett, 113, states, 'the south front has lately been modernised'.
90. Ashlar pieces and an outer wall-plate, which still survive on the north side of the roof, are not in evidence on the south side; if they had existed originally they could have carried the roof covering over a thicker wall or, conceivably, over a timber jettied first floor.
91. Bays 1 and 2 are narrower east-west than bays 3-5, suggesting that the former constituted a chamber block separate from the latter.
92. The main timbers of the open roof trusses in bays 1-5 are finished with chamfer mouldings, suggesting that they were intended to be seen; that between bay 6-7 is inaccessible.
93. Of the inscription above, only the word 'MISERICORDIA' can still be made out towards the north-west angle. The remainder has been illegible for a long time; see Massé, 24.
94. Referring to Stanway Manor; see ch.5.
95. The oriel, the first-floor windows and the ground-floor windows all have slight variations of detail, such that they could each be by different contractors and not necessarily all executed at the same time within the secondary phase. The disturbed masonry to the east of the oriel suggests it replaces an earlier window in this position. The glazed tracery of the oriel seems to have been restored shortly after the sale of Abbey House in 1883. A photograph in Blunt, opp. p.103, shows the upper lights blocked up, whereas a perspective drawing of the north side of the vicarage by Roland Paul (undated, but almost certainly 1886) shows the window complete; Society of Antiquaries, R. Paul Collection, Box 3 (Gloucs: Tewkesbury).
96. The section of parapet above the central chimney-breast implies that this feature was to be continued along the wall-head. The present overhang of the roof at the eaves seems to be a modification; the rafters have extensions near their feet, carried to an outer wall-plate.
97. Raby and Reynolds, *Castle Acre*, 11-17. Both Castle Acre and

Tewkesbury were developed as extensions of the earlier superior's lodgings in the claustral west range.

98. The existing (blocked) door has a Perpendicular style frame. The link building outside the aisle had been demolished at the suppression or subsequently, because the 1883 sale particulars for Abbey House refer to access to the south aisle chamber ('the Vaulted Chamber') by way of an external staircase; Massé, 24.
99. See ch.8.
100. The link building might have been the full width of the range or just a corridor. A new building was erected in this position in 1886, but has since been demolished and the upper part of the wall against the church lowered; Verey and Brooks, 729. A single-storey side entrance (of 1966?) to the vicarage exists on part of the site today.
101. The south window is shown as largely blocked in older views, e.g. *Monasticon*, between pp.52-3. The north wall of the link building is shown as the same height as Abbey House right up to its junction with the church in 19th-century photographs, e.g. Blunt, opp. p.103.
102. These windows have tracery of the 1330s or 1340s, and the vault of the west bay is uniform with the Decorated remodelling of the rest of the aisle.
103. For Wells, see Wood, *Mediaeval House*, 114-15, pls.8-9.
104. The chamber was probably heated by a fireplace (no longer visible) in the chimney-stack on the end wall; the present stack is of post-medieval brick, but it may replace an earlier one.
105. Bay 6 is now the main stairs and landing, and bay 7 is sub-divided into bedrooms and a bathroom. The roof truss between these two bays changes design from those further east and presumably belongs to a different build, though it continues the system of lower tenoned purlins and upper clasped purlins.
106. Alternatively the better door with four-centred arch accessed a passage to a kitchen within the range.
107. Seen by the author; also mentioned and illustrated in 'Tewkesbury Abbey: A Watching Brief, January 1996', Hereford Archaeology Series 267 (City of Hereford Archaeology Unit, unpaginated), Postscript.
108. The information which follows is derived from my own observations of the 1992 excavation, but predominantly from J. Hoyle *et al*, 'Tewkesbury Abbey Meadow, Gloucestershire: post-excavation assessment', Gloucestershire County Council Archaeology Service, unpublished report, vol. 1 (Dec. 1999); this includes interim specialist reports by other authors, of which those by Ian Baxter, Richard Stone and Alan Vince have proved most useful to me. I am also grateful to Dr. King of the John Moore Museum who first alerted me to this excavation.
109. I am extremely grateful to Jon Hoyle for making this information available in advance of full publication. Brief published summaries are – J. Hoyle, 'Tewkesbury Abbey Meadow', *Glevensis* 26 (1992), 30-31; *id.*, 'Tewkesbury Abbey Meadow', *TBGAS* 111 (1993), 231.
110. Probably from Highley up the River Severn above Worcester. In the 12th century Highley stone was also used in the upper level of the abbey's crossing tower (spiral stairwell lining) and at Worcester Cathedral.
111. If so, it must have turned east at some point north of the trench in order to join the accepted eastern boundary of the precinct along Gander Lane; for the precinct see ch.1, Appendix.
112. A. Vince, 'Medieval pottery and roof tile', in Hoyle, 'Tewkesbury Meadow' (1999), 31-3.
113. *Ibid.*
114. See ch.5.
115. Harvey, *Living and Dying*, 52.
116. A. Hardy *et al*, *Ælfric's Abbey: Excavations at Eynsham Abbey, Oxfordshire, 1989-92* (Oxford, 2003), 401.
117. See ch.7.
118. A. Vince, 'Medieval floor tile', in Hoyle, 'Tewkesbury Meadow' (1999), 38.
119. R. Stone, 'Architectural fragments', in Hoyle, 'Tewkesbury Meadow' (1999), 41-2.

Chapter 13 The Later Medieval Monuments and Chantry Chapels

1. Lysons/Tombs, 143: cf. Massé, 83; G.H. Cook, *Mediaeval Chantries and Chantry Chapels* (London, 1963), 170; and Morris, 142.
2. As another example one might cite the chantry chapels of the bishops of Winchester.
3. Morris, 142-55.
4. The monastic role in the rebuilding of the abbey may have been severely under-rated. See now above ch.10.
5. Morris, 144, cites Westminster and Hailes abbeys as prototypes for the remodelled east end.
6. W.G. Bannister, *Tewkesbury Abbey: as it was – and as it is* (Worcester, 1926), 45, for the date of destruction *c*.1541. Eleanor de Clare's second husband, William de la Zouche, was one of those buried in the Lady Chapel.
7. G.McN. Rushforth, 'The Burials of Lancastrian Notables in Tewkesbury Abbey after the Battle, A.D. 1471', *TBGAS* 47(1925), 131-149.
8. This paper treats the tomb-monuments and chantry chapels together: the tomb-monuments were often associated with chantry foundations, a chief function of all medieval monuments being to obtain prayers for the early release of the deceased from Purgatory.
9. For the opening of the coffin see Lysons/Tombs, 152.
10. C. Wilson, 'The Medieval Monuments', in P. Collinson, N. Ramsay & M. Sparks (eds), *A History of Canterbury Cathedral* (Oxford, 1995), 460 n. 34; L.L. Gee, '"Ciborium" Tombs in England 1290-1330', *JBAA* 132 (1979), 31.
11. L. Gough, *A Short Guide to the Abbey Church of St Mary the Virgin at Tewkesbury* (Tewkesbury, 1955), 18: 'we should notice the spirited carvings of the devil and of the abbot's [Forthampton's] struggles with him'.
12. For the opening of the tomb, see Lysons/Tombs, 153. For a discussion of the recess and a convincing ascription to Kempsey, see Morris ch.10.
13. Luard, 76; *Monasticon*, 61; Leland, IV, 155. Luard, 113, for the heart of his wife Isabel (d.1240), buried in a gilt-silver vase in her husband's tomb; Blunt, 52, says Gilbert's monument was a 'marble mausoleum'. A loose Purbeck fragment of a knight's figure in the abbey collection, No. 79/22, may be from it (Richard Morris pers. comm.)
14. Leland, IV, 140.
15. *Monasticon*, 60.
16. Wilson, 'The Medieval Monuments', 498 and n.208.
17. P. Binski, *Westminster Abbey and the Plantagenets* (London and New Haven, 1995), 110-111. N. Rogers, 'English Episcopal Monuments, 1270-1350 II: The Episcopal Monument', in J. Coales (ed.), *The Earliest English Brasses* (London, 1987), 20-21, for episcopal cast-metal effigies. Henry III commissioned an effigy of Princess Katherine, first of gilt-bronze and then of gilt-silver: see J.D. Tanner, 'Tombs of Royal Babies in Westminster Abbey', *JBAA* 16 (1953), 25-40. In the late 14th century the choice of gilt-bronze for royal monuments did serve to forge a strong association between that material and royal effigies but it was not an unbreakable linkage: for instance, Henry IV and Queen Joan had alabaster effigies and Henry V a gilt-silver one.
18. *Monasticon*, 61. According to Blunt, 62, 'the grave was covered with a plain marble slab, around the margin of which was a narrow band of brass, on which his name and titles were engraved'.
19. *Monasticon*, 61; Leland, IV, 140 and 156.
20. *Monasticon*, 61. Blunt, 64: 'The grave of this last de Clare was uncovered when the modern choir pavement was removed in 1875 ... Under the dust and rubble with which the grave had been filled up in the last century there still remains nearly entire the skeleton of Earl Gilbert ... The Countess Maud's grave is of similar description ... and upon the top of it is the marble slab in which a magnificent brass was once inlaid ...'.
21. Despenser did not receive livery of his portion until November 1317, when the other two Clare heiresses had been married off to Hugh Audeley and Roger D'Amory.
22. *Monasticon*, 62; N. Fryde, *The Tyranny and Fall of Edward II 1321-1326* (Cambridge, 1979), 192-3.
23. Leland, IV, 140 and 156.
24. *Complete Peerage*, IV, q.v.; *Calendar of Close Rolls, 1330-1333* (London, 1898), 175.
25. The total number of niches is 29. The figures are inaccurately given in Blunt, 66.
26. The saints in the east window of the choir may have echoed some of the stone figures.
27. Fryde, *Tyranny of Edward II*, 162-4. See also J.R.S. Phillips, 'Edward II and the Prophets', in W.M. Ormrod (ed.), *England in the Fourteenth Century* (Woodbridge, 1986), 189-201, for some contemporary beliefs.
28. Note also the loss of the upper tier of pinnacles from the tomb.
29. For the wealth of Hugh II and for the redistribution of his lands, see Fryde, *Tyranny of Edward II*, ch. 15 and Appendix I.

30. The sedilia look much closer to metropolitan sources than does the tomb. The 1726 altarpiece damaged the eastern sedile. For Ely, see P. Lindley, *Gothic to Renaissance: Essays on Sculpture in England* (Stamford, 1995), Ch.I.
31. W. Leedy, *Fan Vaulting: a study of form, technology and meaning* (London, 1980), 8, describes the vaults of Hugh III's monument as a 'proto-fan vault' (here he follows F. Bond, *An Introduction to English Church Architecture* (London, 1913), I, 349 and 380) but does not know of those of Hugh II's monument.
32. The coffin and slab are first recorded in this position by Dingley, cccxli. J. Blair, in Coales, *Earliest English Brasses*, 160, suggests that the letters may be Flemish imports or that their designers were 'strongly influenced by Flemish models'.
33. Lysons/Tombs, 151-2. The coffin may not belong with the slab.
34. Fryde, *Tyranny of Edward II*, 192.
35. Hugh's tomb base has fleurons in foiled shapes inscribed within squares. It is possible that heraldry was painted on the bases of the lower flanking niches.
36. There are traces of the painted heraldry on some of the shields. Morris views it as part of a screen of the 1320s. There is some ballflower on Hugh II's tomb but it is very discreet.
37. e.g. BL MS Additional 27, 348, fol.65, where she is listed as buried in the Lady Chapel by Charles Frederick, in 1733.
38. Blunt, 66; he doesn't cite a source. It is possible that she was the occupant of the recess at the east end of the south aisle of the nave.
39. Gough, *Short Guide* (1955), 18.
40. *Complete Peerage* q.v. See also R. Barber (ed. and transl.), *The Life and Campaigns of the Black Prince* (Woodbridge, 1997), 23-4, 29-30ff.
41. *Monasticon*, 62. There is no indication whether he died of the plague.
42. In *Handbook*, rev. edn. (n.d.) by W.G. Bannister, it is noted that the vault under the monument was 'found to be divided into two parts by a longitudinal wall ... The body of Lord Despenser was no doubt lowered into its stone enclosure from above: but the monument being afterwards erected, that of Lady Despenser was placed in the adjoining compartment from the choir ambulatory'. I owe this reference to Dr. Richard Morris.
43. *Monasticon*, 62. Lysons/Tombs, 143, still describes the effigies as marble.
44. The tomb-chest itself is divided into three bays, each with niches for two weepers, divided by panelling. Holes for their fixings are visible in only the three western bays on the north side.
45. In fact there are numerous major differences but the tiered canopy design constructed in three bays was influential. See also Wilson, 'The Medieval Monuments', 468-9, for Archbishop Stratford's (d.1348) monument in Canterbury Cathedral.
46. William of Hatfield's effigy at York Minster cannot be included amongst the earliest alabaster effigies, as French and Routh have shown; e.g. P. Routh, 'Yorkshire's Royal Monument: Prince William of Hatfield', *Church Monuments* 9 (1994), 53-61.
47. Cf. C. Wilson, review of Leedy, *Fan Vaulting*, in *JBAA* 134 (1981), 137-9, and J.H. Harvey, *The Perpendicular Style 1330-1485* (London, 1978), 222.
48. Bennett, 161.
49. R.K. Morris, 'Tewkesbury Abbey', *Medieval Archaeology* 38 (1994), 211-12, reporting the findings of Bruce Induni. During Morris' investigation, a section of stringcourse of the same design as the extant screen was found built into the foundations.
50. L. Stone, *Sculpture in Britain: The Middle Ages* (Harmondsworth, 1972), 182. He follows A. Gardner, *Alabaster Tombs of the Pre-Reformation Period in England* (Cambridge, 1940), 47-8.
51. Dingley, cccxl; Atkyns, 722
52. BL MS Additional 29928, fol.72; For Carter's identification see BL MS Additional 29928 fol.71v; and P. Lindley, 'John Carter at Tewkesbury Abbey', forthcoming. Lysons/Tombs, 144, knew of Carter's work and correctly assigned the tomb for the first time in print. The incised lines for the heraldry can still be seen but no paint is now visible on the effigies, though a good deal survives on the rest of the monument, especially on the south side.
53. *Monasticon*, 62.
54. See H.M. Colvin, 'The origin of chantries', *Journal of Medieval History*, 26/2 (2000), 163-73.
55. See further ch.10. The Despenser arms are on the eastern section. The two sides of the openwork section either side of the tomb do not match.
56. Cook, *Medieval Chantries*, 82. For the fittings of St. Margaret's chapel, see Bannister, *Tewkesbury*, 42.
57. Sir Walter Manney (d.1371), for example—who included Sir Guy amongst his executors—explicitly ordered his monument to be modelled on that of Sir John Beauchamp in St. Paul's, London. See also P. Lindley, 'Gothic Sculpture: Studio and Workshop Practices', in P. Lindley (ed.), *Making Medieval Art* (Donington, 2003), 74ff.
58. Blunt, 69.
59. Morris, 211.
60. Bennett, 162. See the engraving in R. Gough, *Sepulchral Monuments in Great Britain* (London, 1786), I, Pl.LIII.
61. Bannister, *Tewkesbury*, 43.
62. *Ibid.*; Blunt, 69.
63. The claim in Verey, 366, that the effigy came from 'the same possibly Flemish school as that of Edward Despencer' is from I.M. Roper, *The Monumental Effigies of Gloucestershire and Bristol* (Gloucester, 1931), 536. For the date of the effigy, see E.S. Prior and A. Gardner, *An Account of Medieval Figure Sculpture in England* (Cambridge, 1912), 710.
64. BL MS Additional 29928 fol.65. C.A. Stothard, *The Monumental Effigies of Great Britain* (2nd edn., London, 1876), 134 and Pls 96 & 97.
65. *Dictionary of National Biography*, q.v.
66. They were buried in the eastern Lady Chapel, with their sister Cecily.
67. *Monasticon*, 62.
68. Cook, *Medieval Chantries*, 82, for the stone-cage type.
69. Stone, *Sculpture in Britain*, 182, states that 'the treatment of the effigy ... is conventional enough' implying that the kneeling figure above the chapel was the only effigy.
70. *Ibid.*, 262 n.21.
71. N.H. Nicolas, *Testamenta Vetusta* (London, 1826), I, 99.
72. Stone, 262, cites Edward's will from Nicolas's collection of abstracts. The next will after Lord Despenser's in *Testamenta Vetusta* is that of Mary Countess of Pembroke, dating from 1376. She explicitly orders that her body should be buried at Denny Abbey 'where my tomb is made'.
73. *Monasticon*, 62.
74. Nicolas, *Testamenta Vetusta*, 174-5.
75. *Monasticon*, 62: '*sepulta est infra chorum ... in sinistra viri sui sub lapide marmoreo*'.
76. Blunt, 71 n.1.
77. Angels kneeling on clouds (the heads are replacements) function as corbels to the multi-cusped arched and gabled doorways. Dingley, cccxliv, records the inscriptions painted on their scrolls: '*Hic deum adora*'.
78. See further ch.11. Harvey, *Perpendicular Style*, 222-3, does not include these pendants in his analysis of the first examples, perhaps because the pendants have been destroyed by the insertion of iron cross-bars to strengthen the chapel.
79. E.W. Tristram, *English Wall Painting of the Fourteenth Century* (London, 1955), 256. The figures are discussed and engraved in *Gent. Mag.*, 1849/2, 471-2. Despenser's devotion to the Trinity echoes that of the Black Prince who died in 1376 and whose tomb's tester at Canterbury Cathedral features the Trinity.
80. Paris, Bibl. Nat. MS lat. 765, Fitzwarin Psalter, fols.14-15. See L. Dennison, '"The Fitzwarin Psalter and its Allies": a Reappraisal', in W.M. Ormrod (ed.), *England in the Fourteenth Century* (Woodbridge, 1986), 42-66. L.F. Sandler, *Gothic Manuscripts 1285-1385* (London, 1986), cat. no.120.
81. Either was possible: at Canterbury Cathedral, the only two freestanding chantry chapels were those of Archbishop Thomas Arundel (d.1414) and Bishop John Buckingham (d.1399): the latter had a floor-level brass, the former a tomb-chest with a brass (Wilson, 'The Medieval Monuments', 475).
82. J. Carter, *Specimens of the Ancient Sculpture and Painting now remaining in this Kingdom* (London, 1887), pl.xxii; Bennett, 165. Gough, *Sepulchral Monuments*, I, Pl.LIII. J.P. Neale and J. Le Keux, *Views of the Most Interesting Collegiate and Parochial Churches in Great Britain* (London, 1824), pl.6, also shows the monument without the canopy.
83. Stone, *Sculpture in Britain*, 182-4. The 1937-8 conservation was by R.P. Howgrave-Graham and included the remodelling of the damaged nose. At the same time, the brown ochre was removed from the Founder's Chapel rebuses and the shields on the Warwick Chapel cleaned.
84. For the wider context see E. Howe, 'Divine Kingship and Dynastic Display: The Altar Wall Murals of St. Stephen's Chapel, Westminster', *Antiquaries Journal* 81 (2001), 274-5 and especially

in this context fig.10, of a similar date to the Trinity Chapel and its murals.

85. The apex of the gabled superstructure of Edmund Crouchback's monument in Westminster Abbey of *c*.1300 has two relief representations of Crouchback on horseback, as does the monument of Aymer de Valence of *c*.1325, slightly to its west.
86. It is possible that there was an early precedent for the depiction of a kneeling figure of the deceased, contemporary with the Crouchback tomb, at Tewkesbury itself. Bennett, 174, states that the effigies of Gilbert II de Clare 'formerly stood over one of the stalls, not far from his grave, in a pensive position, with an inscription in gold characters'.
87. *Monasticon*, 60.
88. Leland, IV, 138.
89. *Monasticon*, 60.
90. *Monasticon*, 60: '*Thomas Parkarus abbas octodecimus capellam erigi fecit ex lapide satis mirifice tabulatum, sub anno gratiae MCCCX CVII*'.
91. Blunt, 72. Parker continued to have high-level contact with the Despensers and in 1411, for instance, married Isabel Despenser to Richard Beauchamp, lord of Abergavenny.
92. This term is that of Cook, *Medieval Chantries*.
93. Leedy, *Fan Vaulting*, 207-8, for this vault. He does not suggest common authorship. The only real difference between them is the use of ogees on the panels of the conoids here.
94. The armour of Edward's kneeling figure is close to that of the Black Prince at Canterbury Cathedral but this cannot provide a secure date.
95. It is depicted in Dingley, cccxxxix, and given again on ccclviii, where the inscriptions on the angels' scrolls are also listed.
96. Bennett, 159. Abbot Alan (d.1202), formerly prior of Christ Church Canterbury, was Becket's biographer.
97. Lysons/Tombs, 150; but see also BL MS Additional 29928, fol.63.
98. See ch.1.
99. Leland, IV, 151.
100. See also the retrospective monuments at Gloucester Cathedral, where the effigy of Robert Curthose was made in the 13th century and set on a new base in the late middle ages and where Abbot Parker produced a monument for Osric, the Anglo-Saxon founder of the monastery, in the 16th century.
101. *Complete Peerage*, q.v. On petition in the same parliament, he obtained the reversal of the sentence of disinheritance and exile imposed on his ancestors Hugh I and Hugh the Younger, whereby any baronies that may be supposed to have been created by the writs of 1295 and 1314 became vested in him.
102. *Monasticon*, 62: '*apud Thekes. sepultus in medio chori sub lampade quae jugiter ardet ante corpus dominicum*'. The boss high above the altar has a hole for the chain of the pyx; that in front apparently still bears traces of the chain of the lamp which hung before it.
103. Blunt, 73.
104. *Monasticon*, 62.
105. For which, see W. Dugdale, *The Antiquities of Warwickshire* (2nd edn., London, 1730), I, 411.
106. *Complete Peerage*, q.v.
107. *Monasticon*, 63: '*Quae capella dedicata est ij die mensis Augusti anno Domini mccccxxxviij*'.
108. See further ch.6. Cook, *Medieval Chantries*, 172, claimed that the chapel was constructed within two years of her first husband's death.
109. I am grateful to Dr. Luxford for explaining his argument to me prior to publication.
110. See e.g. J. Goodall and L. Monckton, 'The chantry of Humphrey, Duke of Gloucester', in M. Henig and P. Lindley (eds.), *Alban and St. Alban's: Roman and Medieval Architecture, Art and Archaeology*, *BAA Trans* 24 (Leeds, 2001), 231-255.
111. See ch.11.
112. Those on the sanctuary side, and the canopies above them, were unfortunately restored under W.G. Bannister's supervision (Bannister, *Tewkesbury*, 78).
113. The pair of angels to the west on the north side are separately carved reliefs whereas those to the east have the base carved integrally and are part of the architectural block. They are wider than those to the east and have numerous minor differences of handling.
114. BL MS Additional 29928, fol.61; Bennett, 163-4; Gough, *Sepulchral Monuments*, II, 123-4. Neale & Le Keux, *Views*, 15-16.
115. From the south side exterior, west to east then down the south side interior, running east to west, then to the north side interior west to east, and finally on the north side exterior, east to west. The second transcription in J. Gough, *Description of the Beauchamp Chapel, adjoining to the Church of St. Mary at Warwick* (London, 1809), 24, is generally more accurate than that in Dugdale, *Warwickshire*, I, 413; but Gough inserted *omnipotens* which is not actually there. See also Carter's transcription in BL MS Additional 29928, fol.61.
116. Nash in *Vetusta Monumenta*, V, (London, 1835), 10, thought it was 'perhaps used as a confessional'.
117. The two niches here have the same painted decoration as is used on the back of the statue niches elsewhere on the chapel.
118. Bannister, *Tewkesbury*, 79; C.H. Bickerton Hudson, 'The Founders' Book of Tewkesbury Abbey', *TBGAS* 33 (1910), 65-66, suggested the kneeling figure of Isabel Despenser and the image of the Virgin and Child. Gough, *Short Guide* (1955), 22 thought that both niches and the similar opening on the north side were filled: 'perhaps the upper storey once contained kneeling figures of the Lady Isabel, of the Earl of Worcester and of her second husband, Richard Earl of Warwick'.
119. Dingley, cccxlii-iii; I owe this identification to Dr. Miriam Gill.
120. M. Aston, 'Death', in M. Horrox (ed.), *Fifteenth-Century Attitudes* (Cambridge, 1994), ch.12; E. Duffy, *The Stripping of the Altars* (Yale, 1992) ch.10, for Purgatory.
121. *Gent. Mag.*, XCIV p.ii (1824), 306-7. R.K. Morris with J. Luxford, 'Fragments from Tewkesbury Abbey', in S. Boldrick *et al.*, *Wonder: Painted Sculpture from Medieval England* (Leeds, 2002), 86, have independently come to similar conclusions. I am grateful to Laura Martin for her assistance with my work on this chapel's figure-sculpture in 1998. In 2003 Richard Morris and I placed sculptures back in their niches, and were able to demonstrate that the different sizes and shapes of the bases help fix where they belong (the lower bases are smaller).
122. Piece No.6 found in 1824 survives in the abbey collection, no.79/25N; the only one of the 1824 pieces still known to exist.
123. J.H. Blunt, manuscript notes, GRO P237 CW 4/30; I owe this reference to Richard Morris. The following are Blunt's identifications: '1. The base of an armed figure on which is the inscription in black letter "Rob Consull filius Regis" [I have corrected his transcription; 79/25A; no. 18 in the *Wonder* catalogue]; 2. A similar base inscribed "Willelmus Comes Glouc" [79/25B; no. 19 in the *Wonder* catalogue. This base does not have the scalloped form of the one above: the four lower bases of the chapel are smaller than the upper ones]; 3. The middle part of the figure of a knight whose surcoat bears the arms of Gilbert de Clare II, the Red Earl, Earl of Gloucester, as in the Isham Register [79/25J]; 4. A similar portion of a figure with the arms of Richard de Clare as in the Isham Register [79/25K]; 5. A similar portion of a figure in a mantle of the Garter, shewing that it is intended for Thomas Despenser, earl of Gloucester, as in the Isham Register [79/25L]; 6. A portion of a figure of Gilbert the last De Clare Earl of Gloucester, with an inverted torch in his hand signifying the extinction of male issue [79/25I]'.
124. Other fragments in the abbey collection are not listed here or in the earlier discovery.
125. Bickerton Hudson, 'Founders' Book', 65.
126. Nos.79/25Q (*Wonder*, fig.22) and 79/25R plus 79/25S. Thus three of the original 12 heads were extant in the 19th century, of which the one found in 1824 has no other record than *Gent. Mag.* of that year. It is not in the abbey collection.
127. See R. Deacon and P. Lindley, *Image and Idol* (London, 2002), 29-37.
128. See S. Badham, 'Status and Salvation: the design of medieval English brasses and incised slabs', *Transactions of the Monumental Brass Society* 15 (1996), 424ff; and A. McGee Morganstern, *Gothic Tombs of Kinship* (Pennsylvania, 2000).
129. P. Lindley, 'Absolutism and Regal Image in Ricardian Sculpture', in D. Gordon, L. Monnas and C. Elam (eds.), *The Regal Image of Richard II and the Wilton Diptych* (London, 1997), 60-83; Goodall and Monckton, 'The chantry of Duke Humphrey', 233-4.
130. The earl of Warwick's monument was constructed after Isabel's death, with a Purbeck marble tomb-chest unusually designed not by a master mason but by a sculptor or marbler; Wilson, 'The Medieval Monuments', 474 n.103. See also Lindley, *Gothic to Renaissance*, 68-9. It features gilt-bronze 'weepers', males to the south, females to the north, mainly Richard Beauchamp's progeny by his two

wives and their spouses. The most recent study of the tomb is in Morganstern, *Gothic Tombs*, 133-141.

131. F.J. Furnivall (ed.), *The Fifty Earliest English Wills in the court of probate, London* (London, 1882), 116-7. The contrast drawn between her donations of rich headdress and her effigy's hair cast backwards emphasize her symbolic renunciation of pride.
132. *Monasticon*, 63.
133. Bannister, *Tewkesbury*, 82.
134. *Monasticon*, 63.
135. The popularity of this type of effigy is discussed in detail by K. Cohen, *Metamorphosis of a Death Symbol: The Transi Tomb in the Late Middle Ages and the Renaissance* (Berkeley, 1973), 9; P.M. King, 'The Cadaver Tomb in England: Novel Manifestation of an Old Idea', *Church Monuments* 5 (1990), 26-38; and P. Binski, *Medieval Death: Ritual and Representation* (London, 1996), 139-152.
136. Wilson, 'The Medieval Monuments', 476-479.
137. Perhaps Thomas Porchalynhe, too, was foreign; it is unclear whether he was the artist or a member of her household.
138. Binski, *Death*, 142.
139. See also the funeral effigies, portraits of deceased monarchs, which were used as substitutes for their encoffined corpses in the funeral ceremonies: A. Harvey and R. Mortimer (eds.), *The Funeral Effigies of Westminster Abbey* (Woodbridge, 2003).
140. J.M. Cowper, *The Memorial Inscriptions of the Cathedral Church of Canterbury* (Canterbury, 1897), 137; the modern translation is Dr. C. Wilson's. On the north side it addresses those who walk down the aisle: 'Whosoever you are who will pass by, I ask for remembrance from you, you who will be like me, you who will afterwards die, horrible in everything - dust, worms, vile flesh'.
141. M. Gill, 'Preaching and Image in Later Medieval England', in C. Muessig (ed.) *Preacher, Sermon and Audience in the Middle Ages* (Leiden, 2002), 161.
142. A northern English Carthusian manuscript of the 15th century (BL MS Add 37049, fol.32v) also illustrates this *memento mori* function. The manuscript features an illustration, preceding a poem entitled 'A disputation betwyx the body and wormes'. The drawing shows a new tomb-monument with a painted effigy of a noblewoman 'wele a tyred in the moste newe gyse [well attired in the latest fashion]', raised to show, in the grave beneath, her corpse attacked by worms, beetles and other vermin.
143. Wilson, 'The Medieval Monuments', 478 and n.125. This is the Vulgate form of Job 19, 25-7.
144. Cowper, *Memorial Inscriptions*, 137; Wilson, 'The Medieval Monuments', 478 n.126.
145. Possibly because the countess was also represented in the upper section of her husband's chapel, in her finest attire.
146. J. Huizinga, *The Waning of the Middle Ages*, transl. F. Hopman 1924, (Harmondsworth, 1985), 134, argued that the late Middle Ages 'hardly assimilated more than a single element of the great complex of [earlier] ideas relating to death, namely, the sense of the perishable nature of all things'.
147. Binski, *Death*, 145.
148. To construe it as a form of metatomb, a subtle commentary on the pre-existing genres of tomb effigies at Tewkesbury, would be to misjudge the expressive power of the emphasis on physical death and decay which the cadaver effigy articulates. The belief system which underpins it (as it also underpins the other monuments)—the concern with Purgatory—was deeply held, as is shown by the monument's liturgical linkage to the pre-existing chantry for her first husband, which the countess greatly augmented.
149. Cf. King Edward IV's slab at Windsor.
150. For which see most recently, J. Goodall, *God's House at Ewelme* (Aldershot, 2001), 186.
151. I am indebted to Richard Morris for my knowledge of this stone.
152. Leland, IV, 160.
153. *Monasticon*, 64.
154. Rushforth, 'Burials', 131-148.
155. These included Sir Edmund Hampden, Sir Robert Whittingham and Sir John Lewknor beside the chapel of St. George; Sir William Vaux before an image or Our Lady of Pity; Henry Baron in front of the image of St. Clement; and Sir John Delves and his son besides St. John's chapel.
156. For discussion, see ch.10.
157. Atkyns, 722; Dyde, *The History and Antiquities of Tewkesbury* (London, 1790), 22.
158. Lysons/Tombs, 153.
159. BL MS Additional 29928, fol.58. See also Stothard, *Monumental Effigies*, pls.73 & 74; F. Were, 'Heraldry in Tewkesbury Abbey', *TBGAS* 26 (1903), 162.
160. Lysons/Tombs, 153.
161. See ch.3.
162. *Monasticon*, 64-5.
163. Modern views are based on a misunderstanding of the differences between burial vaults and the aisle vaults at Windsor.
164. See ch.4.
165. Gough, *Short Guide* (1955), 17; Verey, 367. Dingley's somewhat inac curate drawing shows a screen at the back: Dingley, cccxli; cf. Lysons, pl.LVII.
166. Blunt, 124; Bannister, *Tewkesbury*, 49.
167. The pendant and part of one of the sub-arches are missing in the plate in Neale and Le Keux, *Views*, pl.9 and were replaced in the 1828 restoration; Bennett, 168. Other minor restorations are also clearly visible. According to Roper, 'Monumental Effigies', 540, the canopy was copied for the throne in the House of Lords.
168. Gough, *Short Guide* (1955), 16.
169. It would otherwise have overhung the moulded base. Such a mistake demonstrates a separation between master mason and sculptor which is common in the Middle Ages.
170. G.McN. Rushforth, 'Tewkesbury Abbey. The Wakeman Cenotaph and the Starved Monk', *TBGAS* 47 (1925), 150-2; P. King, 'The Iconography of the 'Wakeman Cenotaph' in Tewkesbury Abbey', *TBGAS* 103 (1985), 141-8. See also P. King, 'The Wakeman Cenotaph and other British Vermin Tombs', *International Society for the Study of Church Monuments, Bulletin* 8 (1983), 172-3.
171. King, 'Iconography', 141.
172. *Ibid.*, 145-6.
173. *Ibid.*, 146.
174. e.g. Blunt, 124. Stone, *Sculpture in Britain*, 214, accepts the ascription to Wakeman.
175. There were many other 16th-century examples such as those to bishops Fox and Gardiner in Winchester Cathedral.
176. Rushforth, 'Wakeman Cenotaph', 151 n.3.
177. Cf. the 'picture of death' requested by Thomas Denny in 1527 at Cheshunt: 'As I am so shall ye be/ Now pray for me of y'r charity/ With a Paternoster and an Ave/ For the rest of the soul of Thomas Denny ...'; (Nicolas, *Testamenta Vetusta*, 629).
178. Cf. J. Wolff, *The Social Production of Art* (Basingstoke, 1993), 111.

Chapter 14 The Medieval Stained Glass

1. This chapter is a summary of ongoing research intended for publication in a forthcoming *Corpus Vitrearum Medii Aevi* volume.
2. For example, a record of heraldry made in the church on 23 April 1623, Bodleian Library, Ashmole MS 833, folio 383; Dingley, cccxlvi; Browne Willis, *A History of the Mitred, Parliamentary Abbeys and Conventual Cathedral Churches* (London 1718), Vol. I, 176, 178; J. Carter, 'Architectural and Monumental Drawings' vol. IV, 1788-89, London, BL Add MS 29,928, folios 77-84.
3. I am grateful to Dr. Richard Morris for notifying me about the few fragments excavated on the site.
4. The head is from a unique cartoon in a glazing scheme otherwise characterized by the reuse of a limited number of cartoons.
5. Litzenberger, 12.
6. *Ibid.*, 11. I am grateful to Richard Morris for information concerning the masonry of this window.
7. *Ibid.*, 25-7.
8. Massé, 16.
9. Bennett, 145.
10. Litzenberger, 113.
11. Ashmole MS, see note 1 above.
12. Dingley, cccxlvi.
13. *Monasticon*, 59; GRO P329/CW2/2 folio 9; Rudder, 746; Bigland, III, section 268.
14. GRO P329 CW2/41.
15. Bennett, 141, note. These heads were recorded in the pre-restoration photographs taken by the Kempe & Co. studio.
16. Photos derived from the Tower family archive (via Mr. Robin Feild), now in the National Monuments Record in Swindon.
17. Bennett, 152-3; Massé, 76, n.1.
18. G.McN. Rushforth, 'The glass in the quire clerestory of Tewkesbury Abbey' *TBGAS* 46 (1924), 289-324. I am grateful to Robin Feild for making available to me a copy of the text of Walter Tower's lecture to the Society of Antiquaries.

19. The east window of the Stapledon chantry at All Saints, North Moreton (Oxon.) and the east window of Gloucester Cathedral were both restored by Ward & Hughes with Winston's advice in 1861. Both preserve areas of stippled 19th-century glass replacing lost medieval areas.
20. Personal communication from the late Dennis King. I am grateful to Michael King for further assistance.
21. *Complete Peerage*, II, 36.
22. For a useful genealogical tabulation of the heraldry see Rushforth, 'Quire clerestory glass', 316ff.
23. *Complete Peerage*, II, 129-30.
24. *Complete Peerage*, IX, 376-7.
25. *Complete Peerage*, I, 346, IV 42-6.
26. *Complete Peerage*, IV, 269, 714-5.
27. *Complete Peerage*, XII pt. 2, 370-1.
28. *Complete Peerage*, VI, 346-8.
29. *Complete Peerage*, VII, 142-6.
30. *Complete Peerage*, I, 243.
31. *Complete Peerage*, II, 273.
32. N. Saul, *Knights and Esquires. The Gloucestershire Gentry in the 14th Century* (Oxford, 1981), 276.
33. In January 1329 Zouche abducted the widowed Eleanor and married her soon afterwards. In December of that year her lands were forfeit to the king, to be redeemed by an enormous fine of £50,000. *Complete Peerage*, XII, pt. 2, 959.
34. Rushforth, 'Quire clerestory glass', 320-1.
35. Bennett, 359-60.
36. The chronology is discussed in Michael Michael 'This little land of England is preferred before the great Kingdom of France: the quartering of the royal arms of Edward III' in D. Buckton and T.A. Heslop (eds.), *Studies in Medieval Art and Architecture presented to Peter Lasko* (Stroud, 1994), 113-26.
37. Ashmole MS, see note 1 above.
38. *Complete Peerage*, VII, 146-7.
39. *Complete Peerage*, III, 435, IX 598.
40. *Complete Peerage*, X, 388.
41. *Complete Peerage*, I, 373. A widow of child-bearing age was not normally allowed to marry within 12 months of the death of her first husband, in case she was *enceinte* at the time of his death.
42. *Complete Peerage*, IV, 273.
43. The relic had been purchased from Florenz V, Count of Holland. St Clair Baddeley, 'The Holy Blood of Hayles', *TBGAS* 23 (1900), 276-84. The royal abbey of Westminster, another building which influenced both Tewkesbury and Hailes, was also possessed of a relic of the Holy Blood, acquired by Henry III in the 1240s, M.E. Roberts, 'The relic of the Holy Blood and the iconography of the thirteenth-century north transept portal of Westminster Abbey' in W.M. Ormrod (ed.) *England in the Thirteenth Century* (Grantham, 1985), 129-42.
44. N.J. Morgan, *Early Gothic Manuscripts 1250-1285* (London, 1988), II, cat. 167, 167-7; L.F. Sandler, *Gothic Manuscripts 1285-1385* (London, 1986), II cat. 56, 64-6.
45. Morgan, *Gothic Manuscripts*, II, cat. 188, 195-200 and N. Reed Kline, *Maps of Medieval Thought* (Woodbridge, 2001) 65-70.
46. The Winchester and Chalgrove paintings are illustrated in Reed Kline, *Maps*, 71. I am grateful to David Park for bringing the Ickleton painting to my attention.
47. A. Henry (ed.) *The Mirour of Mans Saluacioune* (Aldershot, 1986), 197.
48. Dingley, ccclxvi.
49. G. Schiller, *The Iconography of Christian Art* (London, 1972), II, 186-9; E. Mâle, *The Gothic Image: Religious Art in France of the Thirteenth Century* (New York, Hagerston, San Francisco, London 1972), 369-75.
50. The evolution of the heraldic *Arma Christi* is charted in F.M. Lewis, 'Devotional Images and their Dissemination in English Manuscripts *c*.1350-1470', unpublished Ph.D. thesis, University of London 1989, 170-240.
51. A.B. Tonnochy, *A Catalogue of British Seal Dies*, (London, 1952), 176 and plate xviii.
52. William Grainger Ryan (ed.), *Jacobus de Voragine The Golden Legend* (Princeton, 1993), II, 201.
53. Eight figures are identifiable: Jeremiah, Joel, King Solomon and Daniel in NII, Aaron and King David in NIII, King Rehoboam in SII and Samuel in SIII.
54. There may have been as many as 88 figures. See M.H. Caviness, *The Windows of Christ Church Canterbury Cathedral, Corpus Vitrearum Medii Aevi* Great Britain II, (London, 1981), 7-10.
55. Leland V, 138.
56. The paintings were recorded by John Carter in 1782. For a discussion of tombs of kinship and an illustration of the Carter sketch see A. McGee Morganstern, *Gothic Tombs of Kinship* (University Park, PA, 2000), 71.
57. For Bristol and Gloucester see C. Winston, 'On the painted glass at Bristol, Wells, Gloucester and Exeter', *Memoirs Illustrative of the Art of Glass-Painting* (London, 1865), 160-74; for Southwark, A.V. Peatling, 'Ancient Stained and Painted Glass in the Churches of Surrey', *Surrey Archaeological Collections* 1930, 83-4; and for Warrington, E. Baines, *The History of the County Palatinate and Duchy of Lancaster* IV (London, 1891), 404
58. I am grateful to John A. Goodall for discussing this topic with me.
59. C.R. Dodwell, *Theophilus: the Various Arts* (London, 1961), 47-8; J. Vila-Grau, *El vitrall Gotica a Catalunya: Descoberta de la taula de viraller de Girona* (Barcelona, 1985).
60. It is now appreciated that the Lady Chapel at Bristol was only ready for furnishing in the later 1340s. The first recorded burial there was in 1351. See R.K. Morris, 'European prodigy or regional eccentric? The rebuilding of St Augustine's Abbey church, Bristol' in L. Keen (ed.) *'Almost the Richest City'. Bristol in the Middle Ages, BAA Trans* XIX (Leeds, 1997), 41-56. For Gloucester see J. Kerr, 'The east window of Gloucester Cathedral', *BAA Trans* VII (Leeds, 1985), 116-129.

Chapter 15 The Medieval Floor Tiles

1. H. Eginton, 'Kiln for Ancient Church Tiles found near Malvern', *Gent. Mag.*, CIII pt.ii (1833), 162.
2. J. Allies, *Antiquities and Folklore of Worcestershire*, (1856).
3. H. Hall, 'Notes on the tiles at Tewkesbury Abbey', *The Ancestor*, IX (1904), 46-64. I am grateful to Dr. J. Luxford for noting the existence of this article.
4. A. Kellock, 'Abbot Sebrok's pavement: a medieval tile floor in Gloucester Cathedral', *TBGAS* 107 (1989), 171-88.
5. J. Lewis, *The Medieval Tiles of Wales*, National Museums and Galleries of Wales (Cardiff, 1999).
6. A. Vince, 'The Medieval and Post-Medieval Ceramic Industry of the Malvern Region; the study of a ware and its distribution', in D.P.S. Peacock (ed.), *Pottery and Early Commerce* (London, 1977), 257-305.
7. L.J. Keen, 'The Medieval Decorated Tile Pavements at Worcester', in G. Popper (ed.), *Medieval Art and Architecture at Worcester Cathedral, BAA Trans* I (Leeds, 1978), 144-60.
8. The Founders' Book provides a completion date of 1423, see ch.6; but the styles of the chapel's architecture and associated sculpture fit better in the 1430s, see chs. 10, 13.
9. The tiles have been retained in the abbey collection.
10. See further ch.4.
11. As illustrated in Hall, 'Notes on the tiles', 58 (centre tiles); the vault tiles also include the arms of Somerville of Gloucestershire, as illustrated in *ibid.*, 55. I have not had the opportunity to inspect the pavement, and am grateful to Richard Morris for information and photographs.
12. I am grateful to Richard Morris for a photograph, but have not examined the tile. It has been deposited in the abbey collection, with other artefacts from Bruce Induni's restoration of the Despenser and de Bryan monuments.
13. Hall, 'Notes on the tiles'.
14. A. Vince and T. Wilmott, 'A Lost Tile Pavement at Tewkesbury Abbey and an Early Fourteenth-Century Tile Factory', *Antiquaries Journal* 71 (1991), 139.
15. For the abbey meadow excavation, see further ch.12.
16. A. Vince, 'The Medieval Floor Tiles', in R. Richardson & R. Shoesmith, (eds.) *A Definitive History of Dore Abbey* (Logaston Press, 1997), 77-84.
17. P.B. Chatwin, 'The Medieval Patterned Tiles of Warwickshire', *Trans. Birmingham Archaeol. Soc.* 60 (1936), 1-41.
18. J.B. Ward-Perkins, 'A Late Thirteenth-Century Tile Pavement at Cleeve Abbey', *Proc. Somerset Archaeol. Natur. Hist. Soc.*, 87 (1941), 39-55.
19. N. Griffiths and P. Robinson, 'A Re-examination of the Tile Designs from the Medieval Kiln at Nash Hill, Lacock', *Wiltshire Archaeol. Natur. Hist. Mag.*, 84 (1991), 61-70.
20. Hall, 'Notes on the tiles', 53, top.

21. Vince and Wilmott, 'A Lost Tile Pavement', 138-73.
22. A. Vince, 'Floor Tiles', in Hannan, 132-39.
23. Hall, 'Notes on the tiles', 64.
24. A. Vince, 'Medieval floor tiles', in C. Heighway and R. Bryant (eds.), *The Golden Minster: the Anglo-Saxon Minster and Medieval Priory of St. Oswald at Gloucester*, Council for British Archaeology Research Report 117 (York, 1999).
25. Hall, 'Notes on the tiles', 54, 57, 60.
26. E. Eames, 'The Canynges Pavement', *JBAA*, 14 (1951), 33-46.
27. Lewis, *The Medieval Tiles of Wales*, 58.
28. *Ibid.*, no.352.

Chapter 16 The Fabric from the Dissolution to the 20th Century

1. GDR 284, 54. Quoted in Hockaday 371.
2. Litzenberger, 133.
3. Bennett, 181 n.1.
4. *VCH Glos*, VIII, 161.
5. Bennett, 150.
6. *VCH Glos*, VIII, 156.
7. *Ibid.*, 163. For a detailed account of the theology of successive vicars and their relationships with their congregations, see Bennett, 185-194.
8. Litzenberger, 103.
9. *Ibid.*, 113.
10. Bennett, 306; Litzenberger, 127.
11. *Ibid.*, 129-130.
12. Massé, 45.
13. Tewkesburian, 284-298 quoting GRO P329/1 CW3/2. Numbers worshipping in the abbey seem always to have been a small proportion of the parish's population. In 1685 there were 85 borough freemen. The population was counted as 2866 in 1734; Jones, 142; *VCH Glos*, VIII, 120. In 1925 there were 489 Easter communicants and the parish population was 3,072; *TPM* no. 555 (March 1925), 34.
14. *VCH Glos*, VIII, 161.
15. Bennett, 151.
16. *VCH Glos*, VIII, 161.
17. Bennett, 150-51.
18. *VCH Glos*, VIII, 161; E.S. Smith, *Tewkesbury Abbey*, guidebook (Tewkesbury, 2nd rev. edn. 1934), 21.
19. GRO P329/1 CW2/2 f.96.
20. *Ibid.*, f.117.
21. Litzenberger, 6.
22. GRO P329/1 CW 2/3 f.51.
23. GRO P329/1 CW 2/2 f.67.
24. Bennett, 179.
25. GRO P329/1 CW 2/2 ff.75, 90, 94.
26. *Ibid.*, ff.63, 91.
27. *VCH Glos*, VIII, 161.
28. Litzenberger, 93.
29. GRO P329/1 CW2/1 343.
30. *Ibid.*, 472. The carved inscriptions in the head of the window have 'Francis Reeve / James Hill / Master Builders 1686'; see ch.21.
31. *Ibid.*, 376.
32. GRO P329/1 CW2/15; P329/1 CW2/2 f.308.
33. Bennett, 144; in Litzenberger, 97, a memorandum in the churchwardens' accounts for 1603-4 states: 'the leade rowfe over the chauncell was taken upp and newe builded', implying that this was when it was lowered.
34. Litzenberger, 78.
35. *Ibid.*, 91.
36. *Ibid.*, 92-3; this quantity of stone included the making of mullions, vases and stringcourses ('tables').
37. *Ibid.*, 92.
38. GRO P329/1 CW2/1 282-303 passim.
39. *Ibid.*, 475.
40. GRO P329/1 CW2/2 f.24. A brief was an appeal for public funds read out nationally in parish churches.
41. According to Bennett, 360-61, £1,470 was collected.
42. GRO P329/1 CW2/2 ff.187, 190, 203.
43. *Ibid.*, f.308; Bennett, 144.
44. Bennett, 153.
45. *Ibid.*, 113.
46. Litzenberger, 24-5.
47. *Ibid.*, 134-37 passim.
48. GRO P329/1 CW2/1 230-47 passim.
49. *Ibid.*, 282.
50. *Gent. Mag.* (December 1822), 495.
51. Litzenberger, 134.
52. GRO P329/1 CW2/1 50 provides the first of many annual references to the decoration.
53. Litzenberger, 126; GRO P329/1 CW2/1 486.
54. Litzenberger, 117. The two existing Gurney stoves in the north aisle probably date from the Scott restoration.
55. Lysons, 152.
56. *Ibid.*, 151-2.
57. *Ibid.*, 176.
58. *Gent. Mag.* (October 1826), 527.
59. GRO P329/1 CW2/3 f.51; probably the John Reid whose wall tablet is in St. John the Baptist's Chapel, see ch.17.
60. Bennett, 152-53, 362, records the details of the charges. For four consecutive years from 1825 a one shilling in the pound rate was levied on properties in the town; GRO P329/1 CW2/3 ff.72, 74, 76, 81.
61. GRO P329/1 CW2/3 f.81. Massé, 42, and Bennett, 153, records a lowering of the churchyard at this time.
62. *Gent. Mag.* (December 1822), 495; GRO P329/1 CW2/3 35.
63. R. Knight, *A Cursory Disquisition on the Conventual Church at Tewkesbury* (London, 1818), 53-54.
64. *Gent. Mag.* (October 1824), 306-7.
65. *Gent. Mag.* (December 1826), 628-30; Bennett, 165.
66. The only earlier reference to any attempt at conserving any of the medieval tombs can be found in Dingley, the late 17th-century antiquarian. Mr. Edward Alye (d.1616), three times bailiff of Tewkesbury, paid for the upkeep of the Guy de Bryan tomb from his own pocket; Dingley, cccxlv. It is Dingley also who gives the most direct evidence of the damage to the monuments during the Civil War; *ibid.*, cccxxxvii. Between February and April 1643 the town changed hands four times; *VCH Glos*, VIII, 117.
67. *The Builder* (5 September 1846), 424.
68. *Handbook* (6th edn., n.d. *c.*1892), 32.
69. J.L. Petit, *The Abbey Church of Tewkesbury* (Worcester, 1848), 49-50; for an appreciation of Petit's insights into the architectural history of the abbey, see E. Fernie, 'A Note on the Historiography of Tewkesbury Abbey', *BAA Trans* VII, 2-3.
70. V. Jansen, 'George Gilbert Scott and the Restoration at Chester Cathedral, 1819-1876', in A. Thacker (ed.), *Medieval Archaeology, Art and Architecture at Chester*, *BAA Trans* XXII (Leeds, 2000), 87.
71. See A. Jones, *Tewkesbury Abbey: Church or Ancient Monument?* (Tewkesbury, 1987), and C.F. Methuen, 'Restoration Past and Present 1875-1997', in *Tewkesbury Historical Soc. Bulletin* 8 (1999), 27-31.
72. *Tewkesbury Abbey: A Record of its Restoration and Re-opening in 1879*, GRO P329/1 CW4/10 n.p.
73. G.G. Scott, *The Restoration of the Abbey Church atTewkesbury* (1865), 8.
74. *Tewkesbury Abbey: Restoration and Re-opening*, GRO P329/1 CW4/10 n.p.
75. *The Abbey Church of Tewkesbury. A National Appeal for £6,770. Report of a public meeting at Lambeth Palace 28 March 1879*, passim. It was reported that £18,686 was spent on the restoration, excluding gifts; Kelly's *Directory of Gloucestershire* (1939), 344.
76. *Abbey Church. A National Appeal 1879* 15.
77. D. Welander, *The History, Art and Architecture of Gloucester Cathedral* (Gloucester, 1991), 471-3. For the medieval originals, see ch.15.
78. Massé, 76.
79. GRO P329 CW 4/30.
80. *Handbook* (1878), 29.
81. *Ibid.*, 30-31.
82. *Handbook* (6th edn., n.d. *c.*1892) 45; *TPM* no. 119 (November 1888), 4.
83. *Abbey Church. A National Appeal 1879*, 10.
84. F.B. Bradley Birt, *Tewkesbury: the Story of Abbey, Town and Neighbourhood* (Worcester, 1931), 231.
85. *Tewkesbury Abbey: Restoration and Re-opening*, GRO P329/1 CW4/10 n.p.
86. *Tewkesbury Abbey Restoration Fund* (n.d.), GCL 302.11; Bradley Birt, *Tewkesbury: the Story*, 219.
87. GRO P329/1 CW2/4; P329/1 CW3/6.
88. Quoted in Jones, 11.
89. Quoted in *GNQ* 7 (1896), 305.
90. Jones, 171; see also ch.8.
91. Massé, 34.

92. *Ibid*., 20.
93. Kelly's *Directory of Gloucestershire* (1939), 345.
94. *TPM* no. 536 (August 1923), 80.
95. *VCH Glos*, VIII, 158.
96. *Friends of Tewkesbury Abbey Appeal* (1935), 3, GCL R302.54.
97. *Ibid*., 16.
98. *Tewkesbury Appeal Fund Letter* (October 1938), GCL RR302.30.
99. L. Gough, *A Short Guide to the Abbey Church of St. Mary the Virgin at Tewkesbury* (5th edn., 1991), 14; see also ch.22.

Chapter 17 The Post-Reformation Monuments and the Churchyard

1. For an overview of the county's church monuments, late 16th- to mid-19th-century, see Verey and Brooks, 75-8.
2. R. Holland Martin, 'A plea for better consideration of the 17th- and 18th-century monuments in our churches', *TBGAS* 55 (1933), 45-53.
3. See further B. Kemp, *English Church Monumentds* (London, 1980), 75-77, 115-20.
4. Most recently in N. Llewellyn, *Funeral Monuments in Post-Reformation England* (Cambridge, 2000), ch.6.
5. See further Kemp, *Church Monuments*, 118.
6. Other examples include - Joseph Reeve (d.1651), Elizabeth Oldisworth (d.1684), Robert Eaton (d.1687).
7. Though it should be noted that as early as the 1630s, the master mason Nicholas Stone had introduced spiral columns to Cotswold craftsmen in his south porch of St. Mary-the-Virgin's church, Oxford.
8. Another example with Renaissance inspired pilasters is the monument to Maria Tayler (d.1762).
9. For the context to this revival, see N. Penny, *Church Monuments in Romantic England* (New Haven and London, 1977), ch.5.
10. He is buried in Bristol Cathedral.
11. For Victoria Woodhull Martin and the Abbey Lawn Trust, see further ch. 22, incumbency of Edward Pountney Gough.
12. J. Finch, *Church Monuments in Norfolk before 1850* (Oxford, 2000), 81.
13. C. Elrington, Preface to 1976 edn. of Bennett.
14. The circumstances of how he came to be buried in the abbey are unclear.
15. D. Eagle and H. Carnell (eds.), *The Oxford Literary Guide to Great Britain and Ireland* (Oxford, 1981), 254; also R. Hogan, 'Mrs. Craik', *Tewkes. Historical Soc. Bulletin* 2 (1993), 33-42.
16. For Thomas Collins' career, see Jones, 165-8; D. Willavoys, 'Thomas Collins', *Tewkes. Historical Soc. Bulletin* 7 (1998), 15-19, and 8 (1999), 46-9.
17. Kemp, *Church Monuments*, 71.
18. Penny, *Church Monuments*, ch.4.
19. *Handbook* (5th edn, n.d., *c*.1891), 35-6; also G. Strawford, *TPM* (August 1990).
20. N. Llewellyn, *The Art of Death: visual culture in the English death ritual* c.*1500*-c.*1800* (London, 1991), 136.
21. The work was done by Harrison Hill of Corby; Neil Birdsall, pers. comm. to Richard Morris, 2003.
22. Bennett, 369, records the ledger stone of Hankins (d.1782) and his wife (d.1805) 'in the Aisles surrounding the Chancel'; the wall tablet of 1837 was erected by his niece, as recorded on it.
23. Bennett, 364, 366, for Wynde and Alcock. *Ibid*., 363, records a tablet to Colonel John Wall (d.1808) on the south side of the high altar, and the inscription on the monument in question, to Robert Wall, records that 'he lies buried with his father John Wall in a vault near this spot'.
24. Holland-Martin, '17th- and 18th-century monuments', 49; Verey and Brooks, 76, 728. The components of the surrounds are imports, but it is worth considering whether the freestone busts of the deceased were carved locally.
25. R. Gunnis, *A Dictionary of British Sculptors 1660-1851* (London, new rev. edn., 1964), 365 (Thomas White), 430-1 (Richard Squire).
26. For Flaxman's career, see M. Whinney, *Sculpture in Britain: 1530 to 1830* (Harmondsworth, rev. edn. by John Physick, 1988), ch.23.
27. Presumably from the prolific family business of that name; see Verey and Brooks, 77.
28. *Ibid*., 728; Verey and Brooks also note monuments by Gardner of Tewkesbury in the vicinity: at Hasfield, 1820 (531), Staverton, 1818 (691) and Twyning, 1826 (782).
29. Arthur Price. pers.comm., Jan. 2003.
30. Anon., *Royal Academy Exhibitions 1905-1970*, vol.1 *A-D* (London, 1985), entry under 'Baker, P. Bryant'.
31. Richard Morris is very grateful to Mr. P. Webley, the abbey head verger, and Mr. G. Strawford, the honorary archivist, for considerable assistance in compiling this section. The former has conducted a survey of the churchyard memorials, and the latter is compiling a new survey of the ledger stones in the church.
32. See further Finch, *Church Monuments in Norfolk*, 79-80; Kemp, *Church Monuments*, 120.
33. Dingley, cccxlvii. See also W. Dyde, T*he History and Antiquities of Tewkesbury* (London, 3rd edn, 1803), 54, where the 'T H' is omitted from the drawing; Bennett, 367.
34. The full inscription reads in translation, 'Leger de Parr lies here: God on [*DYEVX DE*] his soul have mercy'. Nothing is known about the identity of Leger de Parr.
35. Bigland, III, 1284-6; also cited in C.T. Davis, *The Monumental Brasses of Gloucestershire* (London, 1899), 219.
36. The brass inscription plates are to Alice Jelfe (d.1606), wife of Thomas Jelfe (on the floor, near pier 2 of the nave south arcade); Elianor Freeman (d.1653, mural, north transept north wall); Amy, wife of John Wiatt (16[53], mural, bay 5 of the nave north aisle). Freeman and Wiatt are noted in Mill Stephenson, *A List of Monumental Brasses in the British Isles* (1926; repr. London, 1964), 155; Richard Morris is grateful to Gus Strawford for pointing out the Jelfe brass. The abbey also has empty stone matrices for the lost figural brasses of Maud de Burgh (d.*c*.1320) in the choir pavement, of Robert Fitzhamon (posthumous, late 14th-century) in the Founder's Chapel, and a pair of unknown kneeling figures externally on the nave north aisle wall (early 16th century, see further below); and until the Victorian repaving, the abbey possessed the matrix of the figural brass probably commemorating Prince Edward of Lancaster, son of King Henry VI, killed after the Battle of Tewkesbury (1471). For these lost brasses (except the external one, which is unrecorded), see variously Dingley, cccxlvii; Davis, *Gloucestershire Brasses*, 218-9; Massé, 79; Mill Stephenson, *Monumental Brasses*, 155.
37. One of the earliest is part of a simple limestone slab to John (d.1645), son of William Parker, in the ambulatory floor near the Wakeman Cenotaph. There are no 16th-century ledger slabs.
38. The last digit of Philip Godsall's date of death is now illegible, but the burial register records his interment on 20 April 1826; pers. comm., Pat Webley, March 2003. See ch.16 for burial vaults, especially in the chancel in the 18th century.
39. Bigland, III, section 268 on Tewkesbury; for the Hawlings, see further ch.4.
40. Bannister's lists are published in Tewkesburian, 300-48.
41. Richard Morris is grateful to Gus Strawford for this reference.
42. An Order in Council of 8 February 1855 directed the discontinuance of burials in the abbey church from 17 February 1855, and in the churchyard from 1 October 1856. A subsequent Order of 21 July 1855 allowed additional interments in specified graves and vaults in the churchyard, and a final Order of 29 December 1856 postponed the time for the discontinuation of general burials until 1 February 1857. Pers. comm., Pat Webley, March 2003.
43. The chest tomb of his father, William Banaster, and of William's family, still exists (albeit in a poor condition) towards the north-west corner of the churchyard, with the George's name recorded on it. Pat Webley notes that George should not have been permitted to be buried in the churchyard, because the Banaster vault is not specified in the Order of 21 July 1855 (see previous note) and he died after the final date for general burials; but probably the family made such a fuss that an exception was made.
44. See Jones and Grenville, 16.
45. *Ibid*. See also ch.1.
46. Cited in Bennett, 139.
47. Between bays 2 and 3. The brass consisted of two kneeling figures, with prayer scrolls rising to a depiction probably of the Trinity, showing similarities to the brass of the Denys family at Olveston (1505) and the mural brass of Sir Edmund Thame and wives at Fairford (1534), which has a Trinity; see Davis, *Gloucestershire Brasses*, 106-09 (Olveston), 144-6 (Fairford).
48. Bennett, 153-4.
49. *Ibid*., 154; the gates and trees are shown in the engraving in Dyde, *History and Antiquities* (3rd edn.), between 44-45.
50. This pair may have hung on the north porch originally; *VCH Glos*, VIII, 162.
51. *Ibid*., 162, suggesting a possible derivation from the churchyard cross mentioned in 1412.

52. The labels are on copper plates, probably about mid-20th century, near the ground; that for the 'Saxon altar' is missing. Richard Morris is grateful to Gus Strawford for noting their existence to him.
53. Bennett, 371; E.F. Potter, 'Some Notes on the Abbey Church of St. Mary the Virgin, Tewkesbury, for the use of the abbey guides' (29pp., unpublished, 1978), 21. The vertical stone has been removed from the socle in the slab.
54. Plate 59 in Godfrey's pioneering book on the subject, published by Batsford, London. The tomb is mid- 18th-century, with a scroll at each end, standing east of the path and towards the porch; its inscription has eroded away. For Cotswold churchyards, see H. Lees, *Hallowed Ground: the churchyards of Gloucestershire and the Cotswolds* (1993).
55. Richard Morris is grateful to Neil Birdsall for discussion of this point.
56. P. Honan, *Shakespeare: a Life* (Oxford, 1998), 400-2, 413 (family tree); Bennett, 373-4.
57. Richard Morris is grateful to Pat Webley for permission to reproduce these findings from his unpublished research.
58. For James Bennett's career, see C.R. Elrington's Introduction to Bennett (repr. 1976); also K. Ross, 'So kind a Friend and Benefactor', *Tewkes. Historical Soc. Bulletin* 2 (1993), 65-7, where his head stone is shown 'lop-sided'—since remedied.
59. Although the cremated remains of two members of the Vernon family were interred in the family tomb near the Abbey Halls in the 1970s; pers. comm., Pat Webley, March 2003.
60. For Samuel Healing, see Jones, 176-7; for Alfred Healing, see further ch.8.
61. Also the firm of Healing and Overbury was the architectural practice in charge of the abbey fabric between the 1930s and 1950s; see ch.21.
62. *Friends of Tewkesbury Abbey 7th Annual Report* (1940), 6-7;*VCH Glos*, VIII, 162.
63. Richard Morris is grateful to Pat Webley for help with this point.
64. For Gough's churchmanship, see ch.22.

Chapter 18 The Bells

1. *Ringing World*, 29 June 1934, 411.
2. For a critique of the tower and bibliographical references, see J.P. McAleer, 'The tradition of detached bell towers at cathedral and monastic churches in medieval England and Scotland (1066-1539)', *JBAA* 154 (2001) 64.
3. See Bennett, 129, 307.
4. McAleer, 'Detached bell towers', 54-83, for a full survey of examples.
5. Thanks to Ron Shoesmith for these parallels.
6. Bennett, 143.
7. The Turner watercolour painting is illustrated in Andrew Wilton, *The Life and Work of J.M.W. Turner* (London, 1979), 35.
8. Massé, 54.
9. GRO P329/1CW 2/1. These cover the years 1563-1703 and are quoted without further reference.
10. F. Sharpe, *The Church Bells of Herefordshire* (Brackley, 1976), 668.
11. GRO P329/IN 1/3.
12. Neither has William Ward been recorded as a founder.
13. For a discussion of Henry Farmer's work, see M. Bliss and F. Sharpe, *The Church Bells of Gloucestershire* (Sutton, 1986), 30.
14. On 15 November 1647 John Barnewood and Hester his wife took as an apprentice to bellfounding Richard Barnewood, son of Edmund, deceased. See *Gloucester Apprentice Registers 1595-1700*, BGAS Record Series No. 14.
15. Below this entry has been added in a different hand 'Who was ye Grand Rebel'.
16. In 1678 Richard Purdue and William Covey of the City of Bristol were employed to recast certain bells at St. Mary de Crypt, Gloucester, and the rehanging work was carried out by Abraham Rudhall. It is quite possible that the same combination was employed at Tewkesbury. See Conway-Jones, *The Ancient Society of Crypt Youths Gloucester* (undated, 1990?).
17. GRO P329/1CW 2/2. These accounts cover the years 1704-89.
18. This suggests that he was a bellhanger working with the Rudhall family, but his name is not otherwise known to me.
19. GRO P329/1CW 2/21. Abraham Rudhall III was a mercer.
20. GRO P329/1CW 2/28.
21. GRO P3291CW 2/3. These accounts cover the years 1789-48.
22. Bennett, 144.
23. The foundry seems to have been run by Edward Churchill and the following obituary appeared in the *Hereford Journal* of 23 August 1848: 'DEATHS. July 13, after a long and very severe affliction, aged 52, leaving a wife and six children to mourn their loss, Mr. Edward Churchill; upwards of thirty years bell-caster at the foundry of the late Mr. Rudhall, and of Messrs Mears, Mitre-street, Gloucester. The foundry at Gloucester was closed soon afterwards and the plant, including a primitive tuning machine that had been used since the 1790s, was transferred to the Whitechapel foundry in London.
24. Bliss and Sharpe, *Bells of Gloucestershire*, 610.
25. C. Pickford, *Bellframes. A practical guide to inspection and recording* (Bedford, 1993).
26. *Ringing World*, 19 July 1963, 486.
27. Extract from the *Cheltenham Journal*, quoted in Bliss and Sharpe, *Bells of Gloucestershire*, 610-11.
28. *Ringing World*, 29 June 1934, 411.
29. *Church Bells*, 10 April 1880, 307. In ringing parlance a peal is a length of at least 5,000 changes, taking about 3 hours to ring, depending on the weight of the bells.
30. *Church Bells*, 10 April 1880, 307. C.D.P. Davies is referred to as 'Esqre.'.
31. *Bell News*, 26 Nov. 1904, 445.
32. *Bell News*, 20 June 1914, 184.
33. These old bells have each lost their canons.
34. Taken from Bliss and Sharpe, *Bells of Gloucestershire*, 607-8, where the inscriptions are also given.
35. *Ringing World*, 4 December 1992, 1169.
36. Thanks to Malcolm Taylor for helpful suggestions.

Chapter 20 The Grove Organ

1. S. Bicknell, 'Carlton Cumberbatch Michell, a sketch', *British Institute of Organ Studies Journal* 23 (for 1999), 145.
2. *Musical Opinion*, 1885.
3. S. Bicknell, *History of the English Organ* (Cambridge, 1996), 290.
4. Bicknell, *British Institute of Organ Studies Journal* 23 (for 1999).

Chapter 21 Recent Archaeology and Architectural Works

1. Verey & Brooks, 713.
2. Sir Charles Peers is named as 'architect' with Thomas Overbury (father) on the plaque on the south-west crossing pier, commemorating the restoration of the tower in 1939; but in reality was probably a consultant. In the Festival and Appeal records, he is named as consultant to the Abbey Appeal, 1936-38.
3. A. Chatwin, pers. comm. to Richard Morris, June 1967, noted that 'the late W.I. Croome and my former partner, P.B. Chatwin, ... both had a special interest in this abbey'.
4. Though Thomas Overbury (father) had 'prepared a report upon the fabric of the church' in 1934; Thomas Overbury (son) of Healing and Overbury (Cheltenham), pers. comm. to Neil Birdsall, 29 Dec. 1977.
5. A brief unillustrated account was published in *Friends of Tewkesbury Abbey 7th Annual Report* (1940). The site was revisited in 2001, when the paving marking the outline of the chapel was laid; N. Appleton-Fox, 'Tewkesbury Abbey: a report on an archaeological watching brief', Marches Archaeology Series 202 (a report for the P.C.C., Sept. 2001), sections 6, 7.
6. The first appointment was for only two years, but thereafter has coincided with the abbey architect's quinquennial terms – 1993-97, 1998-2002. In 2003 the present incumbent is commencing his fourth term as archaeological consultant.
7. In 2003, the only other parish church in the diocese to retain an archaeological consultant is Cirencester.
8. Thomas Overbury (son), pers. comm. to Neil Birdsall, 29 Dec. 1977.
9. The late Professor Robert Baker and the late Mrs. Eve Baker, of the Eve Baker Trust, South Newington, Oxon.
10. See further, ch.9.
11. The consultant structural engineer was John Mason, a member of the Technical Panel of the Society for the Protection of Ancient Buildings.
12. The form of the roof suggests that it was a cheap solution devised probably in the 18th century to keep a low profile behind the classical parapets. The Department of the Environment offered grant aid (February 1979) in respect of work on the north porch roof and some other roofing repairs undertaken at this time.
13. The south transept gallery chapel (over the present Lady Chapel), 1994; the room over the sacristy and the chapels of St. John the Baptist and of St. Faith, all 1995; and the chapels of SS. Edmund and Dunstan and of St. Margaret, 1996.

14. Richard Stone *et al*, 'Tewkesbury Abbey: a report on a survey of part of the south transept apsidal chapel and the south side of the choir', Hereford Archaeology Series 223 (Sept. 1994); Richard K. Morriss and K. Hoverd, 'Tewkesbury Abbey: an analysis of the roofs of the ambulatory and ambulatory chapels', Hereford Archaeology Series 300 (Sept. 1997). These reports, for the P.C.C., have informed our text. Richard K. Morriss is an independent historic buildings consultant and not to be confused with his near namesake, the abbey's archaeological consultant.
15. The many fragments of Cotswold stone tile found on top of this vault and the other chapel vaults belonged to the first post-dissolution roof covering.
16. All the artefacts found during this work, and subsequent works mentioned in the text, are stored in the abbey collection.
17. The stone troughs may have been reused from an even older configuration of roofs.
18. A *terminus post quem* is 1821, when the roofs are depicted as existing in engravings of the exterior in *Vet. Mon.*, pls XXXIV, XXXV.
19. See Ruth Davis, 'Tewkesbury Abbey: report on the cleaning and conservation of the decorative polychrome on the nave vaulting and bosses', report to the P.C.C. (2000).
20. *Ibid.*, section 2.1; 'J D' may be J.D. Thomas Niblett, recorded at work on the vault in 1878. Also, '1879' is painted on the rere-arch of the north window in bay 4; R.K. Morris and D. Kendrick, 'Tewkesbury Abbey nave: cleaning and recording 1996',*Church Archaeology* 3 (1999), 20.
21. Davis, 'Cleaning and Conservation', sections 3.2, 5.1.
22. See further ch.9.
23. The précis of the discoveries here is drawn from Morris and Kendrick, 'Tewkesbury Abbey nave', 17-24; a briefer account is, Anon., *Roof Bosses in the Nave of Tewkesbury Abbey*, Friends of Tewkesbury Abbey booklet (Tewkesbury, n.d. *c.*2000).
24. For reference the bays are numbered 1 to 8, from east to west.
25. See ch.10 for the iconography of the bosses and illustrations.
26. See Massé, 70.
27. For the Milton organ restoration, see ch.19.
28. H.M. Colvin, *A Biographical Dictionary of British Architects 1600-1840* (New Haven and London, 3rd edn. 1995), 494. The identity of Francis Reeve is unknown, but he was presumably the other mason. Hill is known to have worked on several other jobs with a second mason, though of a different name (Francis Jones); see T. Mowl, '"The Wrong Things at the Wrong Time": 17th-century Gothic churches', in M. Hall (ed.), *Gothic Architecture and its Meanings 1550-1830* (Oxford, 2002), 91-2.
29. The arms of Charles Hancock, mayor, are at the bottom of the window, inside; those of the churchwardens are—William Jenings (top of the north main mullion, inside, painted), William Wilson (probably top of the south main mullion, inside, painted), Charles Wynde (top of the south main mullion, outside, carved). A full-sized bust of Wynde is on his monument in the nave south aisle; see ch.17.
30. See further ch.16. Stylistically the flame-like finials of the main pinnacles look to be pre-Victorian, either *c.*1720 or from further repairs in 1824-30 (that of the south-west turret has had to be renewed in 2002), and post-medieval details in a Romanesque style in the upper apertures of the turrets are similar to those at the west end of the nave north clerestory, which belong with the nave parapets replaced in the 1720s. The finials of the corner pinnacles are replacements apparently either from the late 19th century or from the first half of the 20th.
31. See further chs.1, 6.
32. 'Tewkesbury Abbey: a watching brief January 1996', Hereford Archaeology Series 267 (a report for the P.C.C., 1996), sections on The Soakaway and Conclusions.
33. Appleton-Fox, 'Watching brief' (Sept.2001), section 6.
34. Bennett, 158, noted the bones of a middle-aged person in a leaden coffin found in 1828 whilst digging around the east end of the church, and speculated that it might have been a burial removed from the eastern Lady Chapel.
35. 'An Archaeological Excavation at Tewkesbury Abbey', G.A.D.A.R.G. (report for the Abbey Lawn Trust, Sept. 1998). Richard Morris is grateful to Terry Scott-Moore for a copy of this report, which has informed our text.
36. Bennett, 152-3; E.F. Smith, *Tewkesbury Abbey*, guidebook (Tewkesbury, rev. edn 1931), 28, noted the canopy of Hugh III Despenser's tomb 'restored by a local mason' in 1828.
37. A handwritten notice carrying the name of R.P. Howgrave-Graham F.S.A., formerly displayed by the Trinity Chapel, noted about the figure of the kneeling knight—'The greater part had been severely scoured and covered with thick black paint; on the face were deposits of varnish, linseed oil and dirt and the nose was a misshapen repair in plaster ... No modern colour has been added [in 1937-8], the only replacement being the remodelled nose and the lost gilding ... The back of the effigy has lost less colour than the front. The dark colour below the mouth is the camail of chain armour though the loss of pigment at the sides gives it the appearance of a beard.' A photograph of the effigy's face, taken at the time, is in the Conway Library, Courtauld Institute of Art, London, labelled: ' Face only cleaned. Botched nose remains'.
38. Most of the work for the Bakers was carried out by Tony Leveson-Gower, Richard Lithgow and David Perry; Mark Perry, pers. comm. to Richard Morris, 3 Aug. 2003.
39. Prof. R. Baker, pers. comm. to Richard Morris, March-April 1982. The tiles taken up from the floor are stored in the abbey collection, as are various materials from the Bakers' other works at Tewkesbury. Very few of the tiles bore any patterns; pers. comm., Donald Smith, April 1982 (working for the Bakers).
40. Robert Baker, pers. comm. to Richard Morris, 11 Dec. 1983; the piscina stone was to be incorporated in the new floor of the chapel (1982).
41. *Ibid.*; he thought it was an oil on gesso technique, and compared it to examples in Orvieto (Italy).
42. *Ibid.*; no repainting was done, but the effigy was left in such a way that it was evident what had been done. The soot deposits from the Gurney stoves had eaten away paint surfaces right down to the stone. Obviously the Bakers thought the polychromy had been introduced by Gambier Parry in the late 19th century; but see also n.37 above.
43. The former notice on the Trinity Chapel (see n.37 above) also stated that in 1937-38: 'Similar disfigurement [presumably modern deposits of paint or varnish] was removed from the much-injured shields on the Beauchamp Chantry [Warwick Chapel] and a quantity of brown ochre which choked the detail was taken from the rebuses on the Founder's Chantry'.
44. The former north gate from the Warwick Chapel (its only gate before the new work) was moved to the Founder's Chapel and some brattishing added to it.
45. With regard to further research on the Bakers' works, their archive is in the care of the Perry Lithgow Partnership, conservators, of Kingham (Oxon.).
46. The settlement of the medieval openwork screen to the south choir aisle was also remedied as part of this scheme of works by Bruce Induni.
47. B. Induni, 'Tewkesbury Abbey, the deSpenser and deBrien tombs: report on the conservation work undertaken in 1992 to 1993', 1st draft [incomplete] to the abbey architect (n.d., *c.*1993); a complete final version of the report was never submitted.
48. For a short report of this work and that on the de Bryan tomb, see R.K. Morris, 'Tewkesbury Abbey', *Medieval Archaeology* 38 (1994), in 'Medieval Britain and Ireland in 1993', 211-12. In addition to the information given there about removing one panel of the Despenser tomb-chest in 1992-93, it should be noted that W.G. Bannister's *Guidebook* (1923 edn.) describes the opening and examination of the contents of the tomb-chest in the mid-1870s, when iron rings from his coffin were removed (now in the abbey collection).
49. The loose materials, together with the ferramenta removed from both tombs, were deposited in the abbey collection.
50. During the period, the abbey architect has also designed new altars for the chantry chapels (Trinity, Warwick and Founder's).
51. It was originally designed for Gloucester Cathedral.
52. The cupboards have removeable backs to permit inspection of these stones to monitor their condition.
53. A ceremonial rod carried before a church dignitary.
54. It had been spelt 'rememberance'.
55. See further ch.11, Medieval Carpentry and Timber Fittings.
56. The others are in the Trinity Chapel (designed 1982), in the screen in the north choir aisle, leading to the shop (designed 1983), and in the Warwick Chapel (*c.*1986). Keith Jameson of Winchcombe made those for the screen and the Warwick Chapel.
57. This palindrome was probably originally created by Leo, archbishop of Thessaloniki (*c.*795-870). Neil Birdsall is grateful to Hugh S.G. Knox for assistance with the source of the palindrome.

58. See C.F. Methven, 'The Story of Abbey Halls', *Tewkesbury Historical Society Bulletin 7* (1998), 37-43; and *id.*, 'Tewkesbury Abbey: Restorations Past and Present 1875-1997', *Tewkesbury Historical Society Bulletin 8* (1999), 31, for an account of the work. Also R. Shoesmith, 'Abbey Halls, Tewkesbury Abbey: archaeological recording and historical research', a report for the P.C.C., Hereford Archaeology Series 297 (Nov. 1996).
59. See further chs.13, 16.
60. Massé, 64-5, records the chapel as a museum by 1900. By 1906 the room over the sacristy was under consideration as the abbey museum, when a Mr. Potts undertook to plaster its walls for this purpose (TPM 1906); this room is noted as 'fitted up as the Abbey museum' in Smith, Tewkesbury Abbey, 46, and it still had glass cases in *c.*1980. Gifts to the museum (whether the chapel or the upper room) are noted, *inter alia*, in *TPM* 1906-1910.
61. Catalogue Nos 79/144 (tea-caddy), 79/157 and 79/158 (spear-head and horseshoe), 79/172-174 (truncheons). The spear-head is discussed in J.D. Blyth, 'The Battle of Tewkesbury', *TBGAS* 80 (1961), 118.
62. John Cherry (British Museum), pers. comm. to Richard Morris, 11 Oct. 1979, relaying the findings of Miss E. Carmichael, Dept. of Ethnography. The pot is Catalogue No. 79/29B.
63. A few stones too large for the store have been left in the public areas of the church. Richard Morris wishes to pay tribute to the many History of Art students and extramural students from Warwick and Birmingham universities respectively who assisted in this process; also to Bernard Beecher of Tewkesbury, the current on-site custodian of the collection.
64. *TR* (27 Sep.1879). These pieces are Nos 81/1, 81/2A, 81/2B.
65. *Handbook* (5th edn, n.d.), 75-80. These stones have been photographed but not yet catalogued.
66. R.K. Morris, 'William la Zouche monument', report to Mr. J. Yorke, Forthampton Court (21 April 2000). The stones include bosses from a Tudor rib-vault, not yet identified at the abbey.
67. I am grateful to Nick Joyce, architect and historic building consultant (Worcester), for drawing these examples to my attention. The stones at Gupshill Manor have been *in situ* for a considerable time, but the Tredington stones were discovered only in 2002.
68. A copy of the contract was bound into Frederick Moore's special large format edition of Blunt, opp. p.73, in the abbey's book collection formerly in the room over the sacristy, where it was seen by Richard Morris about 1980.
69. Some useful beginnings have been made recently with the short analysis by Diana Sutherland of the geology of the building stones from Holm Hill, in Hannan, 206-10; and the wider dissemination of Arthur Price's unrivalled knowledge of Cotswold stones in his brief 'Geology and Building Materials' introductions in D. Verey and A. Brooks, *Gloucestershire 1: the Cotswolds, Buildings of England Series* (3rd rev. edn, New Haven and London, 1999), 23-9, and in Verey and Brooks, *Gloucestershire 2*, 25-33. Richard Morris is very grateful to Arthur Price for information gleaned from him at a walk about around the abbey.
70. Bennett, 361, notes stone (type unspecified) brought from Bredons Norton for repairs to the church in 1720. Bredons Norton (Worcs.) is on the west side of Bredon Hill, with good access to the River Avon for transport, but the stone involved could be lias rather than limestone.
71. Mr. G. Dimes (Geological Museum), pers. comm. to the abbey's architect, 14 March 1980. The assessment is confirmed by a brief report from Arthur Price (April 1990), pers. comm. to Richard Morris, August 2003.
72. Litzenberger, 93.
73. Bennett, 153, for the paving; *ibid.*, 361, for the altarpiece.
74. *Ibid.*, 133, note, citing Leland.
75. For Lower Lias, see B.C. Worssam *et al*, *Geology of the Country around Tewkesbury*, British Geological Survey (London, 1989), 29, 42, Fig.7. Richard Morris is grateful to Arthur Price for advice on lias stone.
76. See further ch.9.
77. Tournai limestone (Belgium) has also been suggested recently as the material for the fragments of the ecclesiastical effigy of *c.*1200, Catalogue Nos 79/185, 81/1; Professor John Prentice, pers. comm. to Richard Morris, 9 June 2003.
78. I am grateful to Arthur Price for these provisional identifications; Doulting and Clipsham appear in John Hopkins' work of the 1970s in the cloister and on the tower pinnacles.
79. Malcolm Thurlby first suggested this possible provenance; the Catalogue No. is 79/181.
80. See G.L. Pearson, J.E. Prentice, A.W Pearson, 'Three English Stone Lecterns', *Antiquaries Journal* 82 (2002), 328-39; G. Zarnecki *et al*, *English Romanesque Art 1066-1200* (London, 1984), 200-03. Another possibility for a base-block of this design is that it came from a font stem, e.g. that at St. Petroc's, Bodmin (Cornwall).
81. See S. Boldrick *et al*, *Wonder: Painted Sculpture from Medieval England*, exhibition catalogue (Leeds, 2002), 86- 91. The P.C.C. is grateful to the William and Jane Morris Fund, Society of Antiquaries of London, for a grant in 1995-6 to enable a preliminary conservation report to be undertaken by David Perry of the Perry Lithgow Partnership.
82. For applications of dendrochronogy (tree-ring dating), see W.G. Simpson and C.D. Litton, 'Dendrochronogy in Cathedrals', in T. Tatton-Brown and J. Munby (eds.), *The Archaeology of Cathedrals* (Oxford 1996), 183-210.
83. The first that the archaeological consultant knew about the Abbey Meadow excavation was when he was kindly contacted by Dr. R.J. King of the John Moore Museum. More recently, the archaeological consultant was not informed in advance of the garden wall excavation (1998) on Lawn Trust land opposite the abbey's northern ambulatory chapels.
84. W. Rodwell, *English Heritage Book of Church Archaeology* (London, rev. edn. 1989), 14-15.
85. Litzenberger, ix. Richard Morris had drawn some template profiles of these mullions in 1967 for his postgraduate research, so fortuitously a record existed.

Tewkesbury Abbey in the 20th Century

1. *TPM*, September 1908, 64.
2. *Ibid.*, May 1911, 33.
3. *Ibid.*, May 1915, 51.
4. *Ibid.*, March 1918, 36.
5. *Ibid.*, September 1927.
6. *Ibid.*, July 1924, 90.
7. *Ibid.*, July 1924, 91.
8. *TR*, 10 May, 1930.
9. *Gloucester Journal*, 1 April 1933
10. *TR*, 1 April 1933.
11. *Ibid.*
12. *Church Times*, 11 September 1936, 267.
13. *TPM*, October 1938, 110.
14. *Ibid.*, November 1938, 117.
15. *Ibid.*, April 1939, 30.
16. *Ibid.*, January 1938, 5-6.
17. *Ibid.*, April 1939, 38.
18. *Ibid.*, October 1938, 107.
19. *Ibid.*, September 1941, 43.
20. *Ibid.*, June 1940, 158.
21. *Ibid.*, June 1942, 19.
22. *Ibid.*, January 1951.
23. *TR*, 20 December 1963.
24. *Friends of Tewkesbury Abbey Annual Report,* 1971, 9.
25. Dorothy L. Sayers, *The Zeal of Thy House*, (London, 1946), 110-11

Index

Many items have been grouped under the overarching headings of: Abbey, Tewkesbury (for general items); abbey church, architectural history and fittings; abbey church post-dissolution; abbey, monastic buildings; abbey monuments (with sub categories that include ledger slabs, wall monuments, and churchyard. There are also two categories of: abbots of Tewkesbury, one general and one for individually named abbots